The Collations

The Collations

Being a Collection of Twenty-Four Conferences
Divided into Three Parts

John Cassian, Abbot of Marseilles

Translated by
A Father of the Oxford Oratory

GRACEWING

First published in England in 2015
by
Gracewing
2 Southern Avenue
Leominster
Herefordshire HR6 0QF
United Kingdom
www.gracewing.co.uk

No part of this publication may be reproduced, stored in a retrieval system, or transmitted in any form or by any means, electronic, mechanical, photocopying, recording or otherwise, without the written permission of the publisher.

The right of Jerome Bertram be identified as the author of this work has been asserted in accordance with the Copyright, Designs and Patents Act 1988.

© 2015 Jerome Bertram

ISBN 978 085244 839 7

Typeset by Word and Page, Chester, UK

Cover design by Bernardita Peña Hurtado

CONTENTS

Introduction   vii

Part I

Preface   1

Collation I. Moyses I, On the Direction and Goal of a Monk   5

Collation II. Moyses II, On Direction   31

Collation III. Paphnutius, On the Three Renunciations   55

Collation IV. Daniel, On the Desires of the Flesh and of the Spirit   79

Collation V. Sarapion, On the Eight Deadly Sins   97

Collation VI. Theodore, On the Massacre of the Saints   121

Collation VII. Serenus I, On the Wandering Mind and on Wicked Spirits   141

Collation VIII. Serenus II, On the Principalities and Powers   169

Collation IX. Isaac I, On Prayer   193

Collation X. Isaac II, On Prayer   221

Part II

Preface   239

Collation XI. Chaeremon I, On Perfection   241

Collation XII. Chaeremon II, On Chastity   257

Collation XIII. Chaeremon III, On the Protection of God   279

Collation XIV. Nestor I, On Spiritual Science   307

Collation XV. Nestor II, On the Divine Gifts	329
Collation XVI. Joseph I, On Friendship	339
Collation XVII. Joseph II, On Vows	361

Part III

Preface	391
Collation XVIII. Piamun, On the Three Kinds of Monks	393
Collation XIX. John, On the Aims of a Monk or a Hermit	413
Collation XX. Pinufius, On the Purpose of Penance	429
Collation XXI. Theonas I, On the Celebration of Eastertide	443
Collation XXII. Theonas II, On the Illusions of the Night	475
Collation XXIII. Theonas III, On Being Sinless	493
Collation XXIV. Abraham, On Mortification	519

INTRODUCTION

THE TWENTY-FOUR CONFERENCES or *Collations* which were published by St John Cassian between 425 and 430 were likened by him to the twenty-four elders of the Apocalypse, who lay their crowns before the Lamb. Whatever glory they have, they attribute it all to the Word of God made flesh, who speaks through them, as He speaks through Cassian their editor, and indeed, if God wills, through their translator.

There were not, of course, actually twenty-four elders whose words contributed to the book, since several of them speak more than once. Nor does it appear that Cassian intended at the beginning to write twenty-four conferences: they appeared in three groups, and it seems that the first part, Conferences I to X, was originally intended to stand alone, culminating as it does in the two splendid conferences on prayer. In the introduction to the second part Cassian explains that the success of the first had encouraged him to set down seven more conferences, and that he had a further seven available if a third part was required.

This implies that the whole set of twenty-four conferences already existed at least in some form. The most natural explanation is that Cassian already possessed rough draughts or notes, and quite likely in Greek, which was his native tongue. It is usual, of course, to say that the Conferences are simply literary fictions, and that Cassian used this well-established form as a way of expressing his own teaching. If this is true, then apart from other considerations, Cassian must rank as one of Europe's earliest novelists, for he gives each of his elders a character and style of his own, and illuminates the Conferences with anecdotal material largely irrelevant to the subject at hand.

I wonder if I dare suggest that Cassian, while undoubtedly using an established literary form, does actually present to the world an account of real conversations held between himself, his friend Germanus, and the fifteen senior monks of the Egyptian deserts. The use of shorthand as a means of recording spoken discourse was well known in the fourth century, and the silence of Cassian while Germanus and the elders do all the talking might well be accounted for by his rapid note-taking, on wax tablets or papyrus. These shorthand notes could well have travelled with Cassian from Egypt to Constantinople, to Rome and at length to Gaul, and been available for him in his teaching and preaching long before he gave them final literary shape in Latin. That would explain how he is able to refer in advance to specific Conferences in the pages of the earlier work, the *Institutes*. It would also explain the inconsistencies of doctrine, and variations of emphasis, which characterise the contributions of the different Elders.

To what extent we have the opinions and words of the Fathers of the Desert, and to what extent we have Cassian's own thoughts, must remain unanswerable, just as we will never know how much survives of the teaching of Socrates and how much is Plato's own. The Platonic Dialogues are, of course, the literary model for Cassian's Conferences, and the interjections by Germanus are often no more than cues to stimulate further discourse like the "Yes indeed, Socrates" of a Protagoras or a Meno. However, on occasion Germanus expresses more than a token agreement, and he does feel free to disagree with an elder. That Cassian himself might disagree with the opinions of some of his elders, while retaining a deep respect for them, can be seen especially in three instances.

Three Areas of Disagreement

The first is made explicit by Cassian himself. Conference XVII is a discussion with Abba Joseph on the morality of breaking a promise. The two boys are troubled because they have promised to return to their monastery in Bethlehem, but they are convinced that they would gain much more spiritual profit if they broke that promise and remained in Egypt. Abba Joseph argues speciously that they can and should break their promise of obedience, and do what they feel to be best for themselves. Cassian records his words, but concludes the book by telling us simply how they ignored Joseph's teaching, went back to Bethlehem, and were rewarded for keeping their vow of obedience with permission to return permanently to Egypt. The whole Conference, therefore, including the narrative framework, serves to teach the proper virtue of monastic obedience, the virtue which Cassian stressed so much in Book IV of the *Institutes*. Joseph's casuistry was never accepted in the monastic tradition, which follows the invariable teaching that obedience to a lawful superior always takes precedence over our private judgment on what might be good for us.

A second area of disagreement is also hinted at in Cassian's own words, when he tells us the story of the insufferable Abba Theonas, who will talk at such length through Conferences XXI to XXIII. Theonas was a married layman, who was so impressed by a sermon from Abba John that he went home and told his wife that he was determined to leave her and become a monk. The practice of both parties in a marriage adopting monastic life was not uncommon, and indeed occurs still, but it has always been considered essential that the decision be mutual. In the case of Theonas the woman absolutely refused to become a nun, and told him in no uncertain terms that if she fell into sin as a result of his desertion, it would be his fault. Theonas ignored her, and Cassian adds an editorial comment to the effect that he takes no responsibility for the action, but simply records what happened. If, he says, you disapprove, don't blame the writer. He himself does not express disapproval, since other monks in Egypt whom he respects accepted Theonas and entrusted him with office, but we can read between the lines that Cassian, like all subsequent teachers, would not have allowed the sacrament of marriage to be so disdained.

The third area of disagreement is the most significant, since Cassian does not himself draw attention to the problem, and subsequent writers have blamed Cassian for teaching something erroneous. I refer to the vexed accusation of Semi-Pelagianism, which still may be raised by those who question Cassian's orthodoxy. The problem therefore needs to be met at greater length.

An Awful Warning against the Pernicious Heresy of Semi-Pelagianism

Perhaps the main reason for the eclipse of Cassian after the early seventeenth century was the accusation then levelled against him of Semi-Pelagianism. The actual word "Semi-Pelagianism" was first coined in the late sixteenth century, during the debates about grace which erupted at that time, and was used most notably by Jansen in his notorious work *Augustinus*. Only in the context of the Molinist and Jansenist crises was the word projected back a thousand years into the time of Cassian. (The Jansenists were also horrified by Chaeremon's insistence that God wills all to be saved, in XIII, 7; and Theonas' recommendation of frequent Communion in XXIII, 21.) There was indeed a debate about grace in his time, and it did rumble on for a century before being settled at the Council of Orange (529), but no one then ever thought of calling anyone a "semi-Pelagian".

What was at issue? The age-long controversies over grace hinge on the apparently irreconcilable principles expressed most concisely by St Paul: "with fear and trembling work out your salvation. For it is God who worketh in you, both to will and to accomplish, according to his good will" (Phil. 2:12–13). If the first verse is over-emphasised, we have the Pelagian Heresy full blown: the idea that we can work out our own salvation for ourselves. The extreme (which even Pelagius himself would have denied) is the concept of "muscular Christianity", a religion of works alone, which directs us to improve ourselves, take responsibility for our own destiny and earn our own places in heaven. Such a religion would, of course, make the Cross of Christ meaningless, indeed removes all point from the Incarnation itself. Christ merely becomes a "good example", no different essentially from any other admired leader. Cassian himself makes this point very well in his last book, *On the Incarnation*; the heresy was corrected at the Council of Carthage in 418, and has never seriously been revived.

On the other hand, if the second verse quoted from St Paul is stretched to extremes, we have the sheer stark horror of Predestination. If God does all the work, then those who are to be saved will be saved despite themselves, hurled into heaven by irresistable grace, and those to be damned are damned by God's will. It leaves us with the incredible image of a monstrous god who deliberately creates beings who have no possibility of avoiding eternal torment. Not surprisingly, the Church reserves her most vehement condemnation for this heresy: "not only do we not believe that some are predestined to evil by the divine power, but if there are any who wish to believe such an enormity, we with great abhorrence anathematise them".[1]

The truth, as always, is between the two perilous extremes. God takes the initiative in calling us to salvation. But we have the possibility of refusing. God encourages us, gives us the ability to improve our lives, gives us all the opportunities we need – but we are still free, to the very end of our lives, to refuse. Our free will, in effect, is only the freedom to damn ourselves; we cannot save ourselves, but God can, and is very willing to do so, if only we will let him.

The most recent authoritative statement of this point is in the *Catechism of the Catholic Church*, paragraphs 1,996–2,011. This clearly sets out the essential doctrine that God takes the initiative, and that all our work, all our merit, lies simply in freely co-operating with God's grace.

The controversy in the fifth century did not arise until after Cassian had already published his two most influential works, the *Institutes* and the *Collations*. They are not a response to any party in the controversy, but were cited by both sides during the subsequent debates. Only his *On the Incarnation* dates from during the controversy, and here Cassian explicitly repudiates the Pelagian heresy. How then did his name become involved in it?

What happened was that soon after the publication of the Second Book of *Collations* (426), St Augustine of Hippo was challenged by some African monks over his anti-Pelagian writings: they thought he had gone too far, and was opening the door to the denial of free will at all. Augustine's reply, *De Correptione et Gratia*, went even further, and was taken by many, especially in southern Gaul, as a contradiction of much of Cassian's teaching. It seemed that Augustine attributed too much to grace, left no place for the traditional monastic life and discipline, and denied any value at all to human choice or effort: in fact the spectre of Predestination was already in sight. Followers of Cassian challenged Augustine: followers of Augustine, notably Prosper of Aquitaine, in turn challenged Cassian. No one has ever raised any objection to the teaching of the *Institutes*, but Prosper did point out some inconsistencies in Collation XIII, which appears to suggest that human beings can take the first step towards God, in other words that grace does not always come first. This essentially, was the position eventually to be labelled "semi-Pelagianism", and it was corrected by the Council of Orange: "If anyone maintains that some are able to come to the grace of baptism through God's mercy, but others through their own free will – which, it is clear, is wounded in all those who are born from the transgression of the first man – he shows that he has departed from the orthodox faith."[2] The answer to the point in Conference XIII, xv, that Zacchaeus seems to have taken the first step towards salvation by climbing a tree to see Jesus, is quite obviously that Our Lord had taken the first step by coming to Jericho, quite apart from the prick of conscience which is normally the way in which the Holy Spirit first calls us to the dialogue of salvation.

Cassian himself would doubtless have agreed wholeheartedly with the Council of Orange, and in many places in his writings, notably the Fifth Collation, expresses impeccably what was to become the defined faith of the Church. The Thirteenth Collation stands alone in being sometimes inconsistent. We must remember that Cassian claims to be transmitting the teaching of different desert fathers of the previous century, and that we cannot expect

Introduction xiii

any Christian writer to anticipate the development of doctrine after his death. If St Cyril can escape blame for the Monophysite heresy, if St Thomas can be excused for denying the Immaculate Conception, and if St Augustine can be forgiven for opening the door to Luther, Calvin and Jansen, then our Cassian can surely not be held responsible for the comparatively uninfluential error of semi-Pelagianism. This is especially so if I am right in suspecting that Cassian really is giving us the actual opinions of the desert fathers: the centenarian Chaeremon, interviewed in about 390, could hardly be expected to have clarified his teaching on a point that was not to become controversial until forty years later. We have the benefit of being able to consult subsequent Church teaching: we can, and indeed must, correct the confused passages of the Thirteenth Collation with reference to the Catechism as a summary of all defined doctrine, but we really cannot blame Cassian himself, or allow the wrong conclusions which a few men once drew from a few passages to spoil our appreciation of the bulk of his teachings, which have inspired saints and sinners over the centuries.[3]

We should not allow minor controversies to deter us from seeking nourishment for our spiritual and moral life in the works of Cassian, as countless millions have done before us. But of all the topics which his garrulous old men discuss, none is so important, nor so illuminating, as that of prayer. That is why the two conferences of Abba Isaac on prayer, with which Cassian concluded the first selection to be published, are the ones to which we should most often return.

Flowers from the Desert

The first and most obvious point of Cassian's teaching on prayer is how difficult it is to pray, and how distractions can come crowding into the best of hermitages. A large proportion of the Collations hinge on this problem of distractions – how to clear the ground for prayer. No one was under any illusion that escaping into the desert meant an end to temptations. The tendencies to sin were brought with them, and could make themselves much more vehement away from the crowds. Some of the hermits were unable to cope with these temptations – St Jerome for instance was so plagued by the memories of girls he had known that he gave up the monastic life altogether and returned to the cities, where he ended his days as an academic surrounded by female research assistants. But the more sensible monks found themselves a spiritual director who could reassure them that such temptations are quite to be expected, and could advise them on how to go about dealing with them. The books on the Eight Deadly Sins in the *Institutes* give much advice which is still perfectly applicable today.

But distractions in prayer go beyond the obvious ones of temptations to sin. Distractions are thoughts of any type which come into the mind when we are trying to pray: they may be quite innocent thoughts in themselves, practicalities about the conduct of our daily life, or even questions about scripture and doctrine which don't happen to be the ones we are trying to concentrate on. Different Fathers come up with different suggestions on how to cope with this problem – and after all it is still the greatest problem in prayer today.

One very important point, made by Abba Serenus, is that distractions are only skin-deep. Cassian's friend Germanus had stated bluntly that he thought it is quite impossible to avoid distractions, and that obviously human nature is such that we cannot possibly keep our minds on any topic consistently. That, he says, is just the way we are made. No, replies Serenus, that's not the way we were intended to be; we are actually designed by God to be creatures of prayer, we should be able to gaze uninterruptedly at God: the problem is all the interference from below. But worry not, the devil can only make suggestions on the surface of the mind, he has no access to the real core of our being, where only God can penetrate.

This brings us to a vital point about prayer, that it happens on more than one level in the human person. Different writers have come up with different names for the various levels of conscious or unconscious soul – in modern jargon we have the Ego and the

Introduction

Id; St Paul talks about the Soul and the Spirit; others use words like Mind and Heart. Call it what you will – the fact remains that there are at least two main levels of thought, and prayer occupies them wholly. Or it should do. What happens during "distractions" in prayer is that the surface level (the "Conscious", the "Intellect", the "Thoughts", the "Mind") flits away somewhere after an enticing consideration, quite often indecent. Nevertheless the deeper level, the "Unconscious", the "Soul", the "Heart" or whatever, may still be intently occupied with God. In fact it is often precisely because the prayer is going on at this deeper level that the surface imagination has nothing to do, so it wanders off in search of amusement.

To put it crudely, God may often be listening to your prayer even when you are not. You may be conscious only of the irritating distractions, but the inner core of your soul can be filled with God's grace, and wonderful things may be going on down there which you will be unaware of. It is only the end result, an increase in your love of God and neighbour, that may give away what's been going on in the unconscious. If we think of that secret inner part of our being as the "heart", as the Bible calls it, then what happens in prayer is heart surgery – and we would all prefer that to be done under anaesthetic. God is operating on us, and he keeps us asleep during the operation. That means that "distractions" in prayer may be as irrelevant as whatever dreams you have while asleep on the operating table. It has the added advantage that if we really knew what marvellous things God is doing in our lives, we would be so overwhelmed that we would never get up off our knees.

Distractions, therefore, while they may well be due to the meddling of the devil, are not in the least bit dangerous unless we want them to be. Of course if we welcome the devil in, that is another matter, but all these involuntary distractions are in no way sinful, and can even be useful. Abba Serenus ends by reminding us that the devil finds it hard work tempting us, and that if we successfully resist him, he goes off in a state of exhausted dejection.

Abba Daniel comes up with another important point about distractions – that they can make an excellent examination of conscience. Although distractions are only on the surface of the mind, they often well up from a deeper level, and indicate that there are real roots of potential problems down there, which we shall have to deal with. For instance, if when we are trying to pray we find the mind is always coming back to the question of what's for dinner, endlessly planning shopping trips and menus, then we may well have a problem with gluttony. If we find that we are spending our time imagining what we would do if we were Pope, and how we would rearrange things in the church (when we can spare the time from being Emperor of the Universe or President of the European Union), then what we may be facing is a problem of vanity. If our prayer time is filled with memories of that person who has been behaving in a quite unforgivable way towards the people we love, then it may be anger that is our problem.

Whatever sins we are most liable to commit are the ones that show up in times of distraction. This is because during prayer we are relaxed and off guard, and so all the vermin crawl up out of the lower part of ourselves. We must observe them as they come up, and shoot them at once. Shooting them is very effectively done by regular and frequent confession.

We are often told that frequent confession is a modern development, and was unknown in the early Church. Cassian, along with many early Christian writers, would have been surprised to hear that: he emphasises over and over again the value of having a regular confessor, and being quite open and humble in telling him everything that is going on in our spiritual life. Examination of conscience is a vital part of the struggle against sin, and it is naturally followed by revealing to the confessor exactly what we have discovered down there. This gives the wise elder the chance to reassure us that all these difficulties in our spiritual life, all these temptations and failings, are perfectly normal, and can be dealt with in normal routine ways. We do not come up with original sins: the feelings, the emotions, the things we do and neglect to do, are all well known to the experienced confessor, and as often as not simple solutions can be applied.

Abba Moyses tells us an amusing story about bad or insensitive confessors: there was a Father who was so unsympathetic when

Introduction

a young man confessed thoughts of lust, that he sent the youth away in despair. A wiser Father, Abba Apollo, met the distressed youth and was so indignant that he prayed for the bitter old man to be made to experience the same temptations that the youth had confessed; as a result he was only just in time to catch him as he headed for the village to find a woman (Conference II, xiii). If we meet an insensitive or harsh father confessor, Cassian warns us, the problem is his, not ours: we should merely avoid going to him again and warn others against him.

To clear a space in our life for prayer we have to begin by becoming aware of the tendencies to sin in our lives, and deal with them as our confessors advise. We must recognise that distractions are only skin-deep and refuse to let them put us off trying to pray. Our prayer should be as far as possible without words and without ideas. Those brought up in a Jesuit tradition may be surprised to find that Cassian's advisers do not recommend using the imagination too much. Abba Isaac in particular warns us against trying to picture God, or even Our Lord, and fixing our imagination on an image. The danger is that we may come to believe that the imaginary picture is adequate to represent God, instead of being a token or pointer along the way. Many of the desert dwellers seem to have fallen into this trap, and thought that God really did have a human form. That may seem absurd to us, but it is still a real danger today: far too many people dismiss the notion of God altogether because they have been told to picture Him as an old man with a white beard. That is why the Church has always prohibited us making any picture of God the Father – the New Catechism renews the prohibition – because any such picture is a mere caricature. The white-bearded figure was Michelangelo's vision, not God's, and it has done incalculable harm to the Faith.

Instead, we are encouraged to try to keep the mind free of images. This will not be possible for very long, so the advice of Abba Isaac is to make short prayers, but frequently. He takes us through the *Our Father* as the ideal model prayer, but he also suggests using a short phrase of Scripture as our own particular favoured prayer for use on all occasions. His personal choice is the

Psalm verse, "O God come to my assistance; O Lord make haste to help me!" (Psalm 69: 1). Thus, when we wake up in the middle of a sermon and realise we have been thinking about tomorrow's supper, just say silently, "O God come to my assistance; O Lord make haste to help me!" and continue listening. If we are walking down the street and notice a distractingly pretty face, just murmur, "O God come to my assistance; O Lord make haste to help me!" and walk on, giving thanks to God for the beauty of creation. If we are struggling with an armful of washing, two shrieking babies and a barking dog, and then the telephone rings, simply gasp out, "O God come to my assistance; O Lord make haste to help me!" If everything is going beautifully and the setting sun is gilding the happy faces of your family as you relax in a perfectly tended garden, a grateful whisper of "O God come to my assistance; O Lord make haste to help me!" will not come amiss.

In other words the day – any day, the most busy and frantic of days – can be pinned to God by short but frequent prayers. Choose a phrase of the Scriptures, something from the Psalms, or from the Gospels, and make it your pet prayer for all occasions, and like arrows piercing heaven the repeated use of this prayer will attach your life to God.

For that after all is the end product, the purpose of prayer – attachment to God. Like all writers on prayer, Cassian's desert fathers can find little to say about the reality of prayer. They can tell us about the preparation, the difficulties, the benefits, but about prayer itself there is little to say. The old catechism told us that prayer is the lifting up of heart and mind to God, and that will do very well as a definition. It is the fulfilment of the first and the greatest commandment: "Thou shalt love the Lord thy God with all thy heart and all thy mind and all thy strength". That is what they went into the desert to do. Face to face with God, without any other consideration than to love Him, they learnt how much He loves us.

And the second commandment is like unto the first: "Thou shalt love thy neighbour as thyself". The test of whether we have got our prayer life right is whether we can love our neighbour. The most difficult of all tests is of course when we cannot get away from that neighbour: we learn most about love from the people nearest to us, in the family, at work, those we meet every day. That is why the desert fathers did their training in communities: as St Philip used to say, the greatest penance can be living in community. Once we have learned to love the people we have to live with, then we have something to offer the world.

Which is why Cassian's desert experience was brought back into the cities. In the thriving metropolis of Constantinople, teeming with commerce, sport and vice, St John Chrysostom was able to preach to his people using all the wisdom of the desert as he heard it from Germanus and Cassian, and could apply it in practical down-to-earth ways to the problems of his time.

The end product of all prayer can only be the love of God and of neighbour. All the different approaches to prayer must meet at that point. We do not pray for our own benefit, but of course prayer does benefit us enormously. Prayer is in fact our natural environment: as Abba Serenus pointed out, sin and distraction are unnatural intrusions into our lives. But as for what prayer in itself really is, we can only get hints and suggestions, for we are dealing with something beyond description. Abba Isaac goes so far as to say that prayer is something we can never be conscious of at all: if we know that we are praying, then we are not praying.

Perhaps the best definition of what really happens in prayer is the famous one which St John Vianney learnt from an old blacksmith sitting at the back of the church. When St John asked him why he was just sitting there looking at the crucifix without saying anything, he replied simply, *je l'avise, et il m'avise* – I look at Him, and He looks at me.[4]

Notes

[1] Council of Orange, 529, cited in Heinrich Denzinger and Adolf Schönmetzer (eds), *Enchiridion Symbolorum, Definitionum et Declarationum de Rebus Fidei et Morum* (Herder), Barcelona, Freiberg im Breisgau and Rome, 36th

edn, 1976 (henceforth D-S), 397; J. Neuner and J. Dupuis, *The Christian Faith*, Bangalore, 1982, p. 552.

[2] D-S 378; Neuner and Dupuis, p. 551.

[3] English versions of the important Conciliar texts are in Neuner and Dupuis, pp 544–53; though their editorial comment on p. 548 seriously misrepresents Cassian. For a detailed analysis of Semi-Pelagianism, see the *Dictionnaire de Théologie Catholique*, vol. XIV (1941), cols. 1796–1850; the author analyses Cassian's doctrine, and gives full references to all the sources.

[4] I began this translation, and was indeed half way through it, before the appearance of that of Fr Boniface Ramsey (New York, 1997). I don't think we need to think of the two versions as in any way competing – his is by far the more scholarly, and will give you all the relevant references for academic study of this important text; I am content to offer Cassian in a simple English form as spiritual reading for the masses. A reviewer of my version of the *Institutes* (Brockley, 1999) said I used "dynamic equivalence" – that's not fashionable in biblical or liturgical translation, but I make no apologies for using it (once I had discovered what he meant by it). I intended to make Cassian, as far as possible, speak modern English in order to help the modern reader learn to pray. He does quote the Douay Bible, rather than a modern version, but that is because the original usually follows the Vulgate, not the newly established Hebrew and Greek texts. The exception is when he quotes from Proverbs, using a different version closer to the Septuagint (LXX); here I have translated directly. In many other citations, Cassian's wording differs slightly from the Vulgate, and phrases are in a different order, doubtless because he is usually quoting from memory. The text I have translated is that edited by Michael Petschenig, in the Corpus Scriptorum Ecclesiasticorum Latinorum, vol. XIII, published in Vienna in 1886 (and reprinted in 2004), but with reference also to the more accessible Patrologia Latina (PL 49, 477–1328). Passages in the Patrologia omitted in CSEL are given in square brackets.

✣ THE FIRST PART ✣

*Containing the first ten conversations
with the Fathers who lived in the desert of Scete*

Preface

To Bishop Leontius and to Helladius

IN THE PREFACE TO MY FORMER WORK, that is to say in the twelve books which, with the Lord's help, treated of the training of a monk and the eight deadly sins, I made a commitment to our holy father Castor, which I have more or less paid off, as far as my poor abilities went. Those books can give evidence of whether his intention or my own was adequately fulfilled, and whether we were able to offer anything fit for your consideration or apt to the needs of all the holy brethren, in dealing with matters so deep and obscure that I think they have never before been described in writing. Now that the said Bishop Castor has deserted us and gone to Christ, I thought it should be to you, dearest Pope Leontius, and Helladius my holy brother, that I dedicate these next ten collations of the great Fathers, the hermits who lived in the desert of Scete – Castor himself had asked me to write them, for he was noted for his unparalleled zeal for holiness, and, in the fullness of his charity, unconscious of what a great burden he was laying on my weak shoulders!

One of you was associated with the man I have mentioned both in loving relationship and in the priestly dignity; nay more, in zeal for holy learning, and so he is right to request payment of the debt he has inherited; the other has modelled himself on the pious customs of the hermits, but not relying on his own ability, as some do, for he had already been prompted by the Holy Spirit to perceive the proper course to learn before he had learnt it. He is therefore eager to profit from the teachings of the hermits, rather than rely on his own imagination. This opens up for me a vast sea of work (and I thought I was safe in a quiet harbour!) for I must now attempt to set out in writing something of the customs and teaching of such great men. The frail dinghy of my intellect is going to be dashed about in the perils of the deep, for the life of a hermit is far above that of the monastery, and the contemplation of God in which those amazing men are ever wrapt is just as far above the present life which I follow in community. Your task therefore is to assist my labours with your prayers, otherwise these divine matters, which deserve at least an accurate description, even if not an eloquent one, will be put at risk, or else, landlubber as I am, I shall sink in the depths of such a subject.

Now to move on from the exterior visible conduct of a monk, which I discussed in my former work, to the invisible demeanour of the inner man. After the structure of the canonical Office, let us turn our attention to what St Paul describes as the ceaseless obligation of prayer. If you have read the previous work and earned the name of a Jacob, which means the "supplanter", by supplanting fleshly vice, now profit from the advice of the Fathers (not mine own), and progress in the sight of divine purity to attain the rank, so to speak, of an Israel and discover how to live on this summit of perfection. Let your prayers obtain for me both an accurate memory of what they told us, and a ready style to write it down, from Him who considered us worthy to visit those Fathers, to listen to them and live with them. Help me to recount what they told me in a holy and honest manner, to describe them as they expounded their own teaching, and (what is more important) to express it in our own language for your benefit.

What I want above all is that the reader be familiar with the previous volume as well as with these conferences, so that if he finds some matters difficult or impossible for his position and circumstances, or for the common custom and way of life, he may assess them not by the standard of his own ability, but according to the grandeur and sublimity of the speakers. Thus he will be able to imitate their zeal and their intention, once he has disentangled himself from the deadly way of life of this world, unrestrained by family obligations or secular business. Let him remember the sort of places the Fathers lived in, situated in the great wilderness far from the society of any other men; in the light of that realisation let him consider and assess what might seem impossible to the ignorant and uninformed who live an ordinary life. If anyone wants to arrive at a true opinion, and learn by experience whether this way of life is possible, let him first be eager to accept their advice in words and in action; then he will understand that what seems beyond human ability is not only possible but actually delightful. So now let us proceed to the conversations and instructions of the Fathers.

✣ THE FIRST COLLATION ✣
BEING THE FIRST OF ABBA MOYSES

On the Direction and Goal of a Monk

   I. Of the locality of Scete and the suggestion of Abba Moses.
  II. Of how Abba Moyses interrogated us on the means and the goal of monasticism.
 III. Our reply.
  IV. How Moyses examined us on our statement.
   V. The parable of one who competes in shooting at a target.
  VI. On those who renounce the world and aim at perfection but without charity.
 VII. On the quest for a tranquil heart.
VIII. On our principal task, which is the contemplation of divine matters, and the example of Mary and Martha.
  IX. A question, on why a man's good works do not endure.
   X. The reply, how it is not the reward but the activity that ceases.
  XI. On the perpetuity of charity.
 XII. A question, on how spiritual contemplation endures.
XIII. The reply, on directing the heart to God and of the kingdoms of God and of the devil.
 XIV. On the immortality of the Soul.
  XV. On the contemplation of God.

XVI. A question, about wandering thoughts.
XVII. The reply, on what the mind can do about its thoughts, and what it cannot.
XVIII. The soul compared to a watermill.
XIX. Of the three sources of our thoughts.
XX. How our thoughts are to be tested, shown under the simile of an honest moneychanger.
XXI. How Abba John was deceived.
XXII. Of the four types of assay.
XXIII. Of how a teacher is able to speak according to the merits of his audience.

I. The desert of Scete is the abode of some of the most respected monks, where all perfection is to be found. I was eager to consult Abba Moyses there, for he had the reputation of being the best scented flower in that bright garden, virtuous both in deed and in doctrine, and so I sought him out for instruction. With me was the holy father Germanus, who had been my comrade from our novitiate and first training in the spiritual combat, and continued to be so both in the community and in the desert, to the extent that everyone talked about there being but one mind and soul in two bodies, so close were we in companionship and ideals. Together we implored the holy Abba for instruction in progress, not without tears, for we were well aware of how strict he was, and how he would never agree to open the doors of perfection except for those who genuinely desired and begged him in real heartfelt contrition. Otherwise, were he to reveal those things which should only be uncovered to those who desire perfection, however necessary they be, to men who were not interested, or only slightly so, and would receive them unworthily or carelessly, he would surely fall under the suspicion of vain-glory, or of betraying what should be secret. However our prayers overcame him at last, and he began thus:

II. "Every art and every discipline," he said, "has its own *skopos*, that is to say its means, and its *telos* or goal. Anyone who diligently

I. On the Direction and Goal of a Monk

pursues that art keeps his eye on that goal, and for that purpose is willing and glad to undertake all effort, all dangers and expenses. A farmer for instance is not afraid either of the full heat of the sun or of frost and snow, but ploughs the soil tirelessly, and breaks up the hard clods of earth with regular harrowing, always keeping in mind the means, which is clearing the brambles, ridding the soil of all weeds, and working it over to reduce it to a fine earth for the seed to be evenly sown all over; and the goal which is to gain a rich harvest and a full crop. He knows there is no other way to achieve this, and that the result will be that he can be sure of his livelihood, and even increase his wealth. He is happy to empty his barns of grain and entrust it with his own labour to the empty furrows, unconcerned about the present expenditure in his confidence of a future crop.

Those who devote themselves to business enterprises are not afraid of risks at sea nor shy of any dangers, as long as the hope of profit encourages them towards their goal. Similarly those who aspire to military glory in this world, keep their eyes on the goals of honour and power, and care nothing for the expenses and dangers of a campaign. They are undaunted by the effort of present conflict in their longing for the prize of glory which they have set before themselves.

Our profession too has its own means and goal for the sake of which we undertake all endeavours, tirelessly and even gladly. Because of this we are not exhausted by the restraints of fasting, we are delighted with sleepless watching, we are not sated with continuous reading and pondering on Scripture, and are not deterred by our ceaseless labour, our poverty and deprivation of all property, nor by the terror of this enormous desert. Doubtless it was for the same purpose that you yourselves have abandoned your family ties, and set aside your homeland and so many worldly delights, for you have travelled so far to reach us poor country fools, who live in this ghastly wilderness. So tell me," he said, "what your intention is; and what is the purpose which has brought you to undertake all this so readily?"

III. He insisted on hearing our opinion on this question, so we answered, "We put up with all this for the sake of the Kingdom of Heaven".

IV. He replied, "Very well, you have given an apt answer on the goal; now before anything else you should investigate the *skopos* or direction to follow in order to attain that goal". We admitted our ignorance cheerfully, and he continued, "In every art or study there must be first of all a *skopos*, that is to say an inner direction or constant aim in mind, and unless you persist in adhering to that with all your might, you will never be able to enjoy the goal you desire. A farmer, as I mentioned, who has the goal of living at ease and in plenty on the produce of his fertile fields, follows the means or direction of cleansing his fields from all the brambles, and clearing away all useless weeds; by no other means can he hope to achieve the goal of tranquil prosperity than by his labour and foresight, which achieves what he intends as the result of his work.

A businessman likewise does not lose sight of his intention to accumulate goods, through which he may gain the wealth he longs for; it would be pointless to desire wealth without intending the means to gain it. Those who want the honour of some rank in this world, must first determine what duties and positions they will undertake, so that by following the proper course of their ambition, they can achieve the goal of the rank they covet.

Now, the goal of our way of life is certainly the Kingdom of God, but we must be at pains to discover what is the means. If we fail to discover this, our efforts will be in vain, since those who travel without a route only weary themselves in the journey without getting anywhere."

We were puzzled by this, so the old man continued: "The goal of our profession is the Kingdom of God, as we said, or the Kingdom of Heaven. Our direction, that is our means, is purity of heart, for without that it is impossible for anyone to reach that goal. If we set our sights in this direction, as if following a sure waymark, we will be safe on our path. If we let our attention wander a little from

I. On the Direction and Goal of a Monk

it, we should immediately turn it back to that direction, and bring it back again to its proper path. Our efforts must always return to this path, which will recall us if the mind should ever deviate even slightly from the route we have adopted.

V. "When those who are skilled at aiming weapons of war wish to display their skill in front of their earthly ruler, they compete in hurling their javelins or shooting their arrows at a tiny target painted to indicate different prizes; they are well aware that the prize they long for will only be theirs if they follow a straight course to the target. They will be sure to win if they are careful to aim in the direction they propose themselves, but if they lose sight of it they will have no way of knowing whether they have gone off the direct line of their target, or of how far off course their aim has wandered – that is if they have no point of reference to confirm that they are on the right lines or to correct them if they are wrong. Hence they will shoot wildly into empty space, with no way of judging where their mistake lies or where they went wrong, for those who have no guideline to tell them how far off course they have gone or how they may afterwards be corrected or brought back, can only be taught the proper skill by careful observation.

Now in the same manner the goal of our profession is eternal life, as St Paul tells us when he says, 'you have your fruit unto sanctification, and the end, life everlasting' (Rom. 6: 22). The means is purity of heart, which he rightly calls holiness, and the goal we have mentioned cannot be attained without it. You could paraphrase him thus: 'you take your aim by purity of heart, and your target is eternal life'. The same holy Apostle speaks elsewhere about this direction, and even gives it the specific name *skopos*, saying 'forgetting the things that are behind, and stretching forth myself to those that are before, I press towards the mark, to the prize of the supernal vocation of God' (Phil. 3: 13–14). It is clearer in the Greek, *kata skopon diōkō*, 'according to my direction I stretch forth'. It is as if he had said, 'With this direction I forget what lies behind me, that is the vices of my former life, and strive towards the heavenly prize, which is my goal'. For this reason we should use all our efforts to follow anything which can help us in this direction, namely purity of heart. Anything which draws us away from it should be shunned like a plague. This is the motive for everything we do and undergo. We abandon family, homeland, rank, wealth, worldly pleasure and all luxuries, precisely in order to preserve constant purity of heart. With this aim in mind our actions and thoughts are always properly directed to its acquisition. If we did not have the means continually before our eyes, our efforts would be utterly futile and inconsistent, vainly expended without any result, and we would also find that our thoughts wandered and were self-contradictory. If the mind had no direction to return to, which could absorb its chief endeavour, inevitably it would be distracted in varied ways, moment by moment, and external circumstances would be continuously pulling it back to the condition in which it had been before.

VI. "Now that is why it can happen that men who have renounced enormous wealth in this world, not just large sums in gold and silver but even great estates, may later on fly into a passion over a penknife, a pencil, a pen or a needle. Had they kept their hearts pure in contemplation, they would never have permitted themselves this passion over such trivial things, after abandoning great and valuable possessions, in order not to be disturbed by them. There are those who will guard a book so jealously that they will not let anyone else read it or even touch it, so that the very thing which gives advice on perseverance and charity becomes an occasion of deadly lack of perseverance. If you have given away all your possessions for the love of Christ, but retain your first attachment to a few trivialities to the extent that you are easily angered over them, you will be totally barren and fruitless, quite without the charity of an apostle. St Paul predicted this, saying, 'And if I should distribute all my goods to feed the poor, and if I should deliver my body to be burned, and have not charity, it profiteth me nothing' (I Cor. 13: 3). This makes it clear that perfection does not consist merely in poverty and the renunciation of all property,

I. On the Direction and Goal of a Monk

or in the rejection of rank, without the true possession of that charity the details of which the Apostle describes, and which consists essentially in purity of heart. For what does it mean to say 'charity envieth not, dealeth not perversely, is not puffed up, is not ambitious, seeketh not her own, is not provoked to anger, thinketh no evil', and so on (I Cor. 13: 4–5), except that we should offer to God a heart of perfect purity, and keep ourselves untouched by all anxieties?

VII. "Everything we do and everything we seek should be for this purpose. This is why we search out the desert, this is why we are seen to accept fasting, watching, manual labour, scanty clothing, reading and the other good works, namely so that we may be able to render our hearts free from sinful emotions and preserve them so, and ascend to the summit of charity by using these observances as steps. It can happen that some genuine necessity prevents us from performing our ascetic exercises, and we fall into gloom, anger and frustration for the sake of these exercises, although the very practices we had intended to perform were designed to prevent this. The profit we gain by fasting is not as great as the loss we suffer through anger, the profit from reading less than the damage incurred by the contempt of a brother. The secondary means, that is to say fasting, watching, psalmody and meditation on Scripture, are properly used by us for the sake of our principal means, namely purity of heart or charity, so we must not damage our chief virtue for the sake of these lesser ones. If that remains whole and entire within us, we shall suffer no loss if we are obliged to omit some of our secondary exercises. Similarly it will be fruitless to perform them all if we lack what we have identified as the principal aim for the sake of which we are doing everything else.

You do not acquire all the equipment for some craft and polish it up eagerly simply to own it without using it; the benefit to be expected from it does not lie simply in the mere possession of that equipment but in order to gain effectively the skill and the produce of that craft to which the equipment pertains.

Similarly perfection does not lie in fasting, watching, meditation on Scripture, poverty and the renunciation of all property, but these are tools to perfection. The goal of our discipline does not lie in those things, but through them we may come to that goal. The exercises would be performed in vain by someone who was contented with them as if they were the final good, and directed his heart exclusively to them rather than putting all his efforts into them for the sake of the goal to be achieved by practising them. He would possess indeed the equipment of our discipline but be ignorant of the goal for which alone it is effective. Anything at all which could disturb the purity of the mind or its tranquillity should be shunned as an evil, no matter how useful or necessary it seem. That is how we can discern how to avoid all tendencies to error and dissipation, and reach the goal we desire, following a sure path.

VIII. "Our main effort therefore must be to retain carefully that intention of heart without wavering, so that the mind is always intent on God and the things of God, and anything other than that, however important, is considered secondary, irrelevant or even dangerous. A parable of this state of mind can be found in the Gospels, beautifully demonstrated in Martha and Mary. Martha was busy at a holy and useful service, waiting on Our Lord Himself and His disciples, while Mary was only intent on spiritual learning, sitting at the feet of Jesus which she had kissed and anointed with ointment during her holy confession – she it was whom the Lord commended for she had chosen the better part which could not be taken away from her. For when Martha was hard at work, distracted by her loving care for the provisions, and saw that she alone was unequal to such a great service, she begged Our Lord for her sister's help, saying, 'hast thou no care that my sister hath left me alone to serve? Speak to her therefore, that she help me.' She was not calling her to do something disreputable, but to a praiseworthy service. But what does she hear from Our Lord? 'Martha, Martha, thou art careful and art troubled about many things. But one thing is necessary. Mary hath chosen the best

I. On the Direction and Goal of a Monk

part, which shall not be taken from her' (Luke 10: 40–2). You see that Our Lord places the chief good in simple sight, that is divine contemplation. We can therefore see that other virtues, no matter how necessary and useful we deem them, are to be placed in the second rank, for they are all subservient to this one. When Our Lord says 'thou art careful and art troubled about many things; but one thing is necessary', he places the supreme good not in actual good works, however praiseworthy and profitable, but in the contemplation of himself, which is simple and one. When he says few things are needed for perfect bliss, he means that our gaze is firstly fixed on the consideration of a few holy things. One who is already proficient in this contemplation progresses, with God's help, to the vision of what he calls the One, that is the vision of God alone. He passes beyond the deeds and wonderful service of the saints to feed on the beauty and wisdom of God alone. Mary, therefore, has 'chosen the best part, which shall not be taken from her'. We must observe this carefully – when he says 'Mary hath chosen the best part', he may well be silent about Martha, and certainly does not appear to rebuke her, but in praising the one he does imply that the other is inferior. And when he says, it 'shall not be taken away from her', he shows that the ministry of the other one can be taken away. Physical good works cannot really endure in a man, but he shows us that Mary's devotion can never be brought to an end."

IX. GERMANUS: "We are surprised at this – can we really say that our efforts at fasting, our diligent reading, our works of mercy, of justice and affectionate humanity will be taken away from us and will not endure as long as those who perform them? Especially when Our Lord promises a reward in the Kingdom of Heaven to those who do such things, when He says, 'Come, ye blessed of my Father, possess you the kingdom prepared for you from the foundation of the world. For I was hungry, and you gave me to eat; I was thirsty, and you gave me to drink', and so on (Matt. 25: 34–5). So how can these things, which bring those who perform them into the Kingdom of Heaven, be taken away?"

X. MOYSES: "I did not say that the reward of a good work will be taken away, for Our Lord also says, 'whosoever shall give to drink to one of these little ones a cup of cold water only in the name of a disciple, amen, I say to you, he shall not lose his reward' (Matt. 10:42). It is the activity itself that will be taken away, for it is necessary only to meet the bodily needs, the frailty of the flesh or the injustices of this world. Diligent reading and ascetic fasting are indeed useful to cleanse the heart and restrain the flesh, but only in this present age, as long as the 'flesh lusteth against the spirit' (Gal. 5:17). After all, we sometimes see these things laid aside even during this present life, when men are worn out by overwork, physical illness or old age, until human nature can no longer perform such works. How much more, then, will they cease in the age to come, when 'this corruptible must put on incorruption', this animal body which we have now 'shall rise a spiritual body' (I Cor. 15:53, 44), and the flesh shall begin to be such as no longer wars against the spirit! St Paul tells us clearly enough about this, 'for bodily exercise is profitable to little; but godliness' (and he must mean charity here) 'is profitable to all things, having promise of the life that now is and of that which is to come' (I Tim. 4:8). Clearly he shows us that those things which he says are of little profit will not go on being performed for all time, but it is only in this way that the height of perfection can be conferred on the one who works. 'Little' indeed can be taken two ways, either referring to the shortness of time, since physical work will not endure as long as a man's life either in this world or the next, or it may refer to the slightness of the benefit which physical labour gains, in as much as restraint of the body enables the first stages on our journey, not the true perfection of charity, which is what carries the promise of present and future life. We believe the performance of these works to be necessary precisely because without them we cannot rise to the heights of charity. And the works of compassion and mercy which you mention will be necessary in this world only as long as injustice and inequality reign, for even here such things would not be expected had there not been so many poor, needy and sick among us. It is through the wickedness of men that this state of affairs exists, in that they reserve to their own use things which the Creator of all destined for the use of all, indeed they hoard them without even having a use for them! Therefore as long as such injustice prevails in the world, works of mercy will be necessary, and profitable for those who perform them. They win us an eternal inheritance for our good intention and our compassionate will, but they themselves will come to an end in the world to come where equality will prevail. When inequality no longer exists (and these exercises are only needed because of that), everyone after all their manifold activities will progress to the love of God and the contemplation of the things of God in perpetual purity of heart. Those who have tried to devote themselves to improving their mind and knowledge while still in this world, show that they have already chosen to dedicate themselves with all their strength to such contemplation. Those on the other hand who devote themselves to works, as long as they live in this corruptible flesh, will endure after all corruption is put aside, and progress to what Our Lord and Saviour has promised when he said, 'Blessed are the clean of heart, for they shall see God' (Matt. 5:8).

XI. "Why are you surprised that these works which we have mentioned are to pass away, when the holy Apostle tells us how even the higher gifts of the Spirit will pass away, and states that charity alone will abide for ever? 'Whether prophecies, shall be made void, or tongues shall cease, or knowledge shall be destroyed.' But of charity he says, 'Charity never falleth away' (I Cor. 13:8). All the other gifts are granted for our use and our necessities, and for a limited time, so that once the need for them has passed they will undoubtedly cease at once. Charity is not limited to any time, for it not only works usefully in us in this present world, but it will also remain in the future when we have cast off the burden of physical needs, operating with greater effect and splendour, untainted by any defect but cleaving to God more closely and more intensely, perpetually incorruptible."

XII. GERMANUS: "But who is there, still living in the frailty of this flesh, who could be so continually dedicated to contemplation as to be unaware of a brother's arrival, of sick to be visited, of manual labour, or basic humanity to be shown to pilgrims and strangers? Who is there who is not restrained by the needs and care of the body? What sort of mind is strong enough to be totally wrapt in the invisible and incomprehensible God, and how? We long to learn."

XIII. MOYSES: "It is impossible for any man who dwells in this frail flesh to be completely attentive to God and, as you put it, totally wrapt in contemplation of Him. But we should be aware of the object on which the intention of our minds is to be fixed, and what should be the goal to which we must ever redirect our sight. When the mind attains this, it is glad, and when it is distracted it sighs in disappointment. It knows itself to have fallen away from the supreme good to the extent that it finds itself losing sight of this contemplation, so that it considers even a momentary distraction from the contemplation of Christ to be as bad as infidelity! When our attention wanders away from him, even for a moment, we have to turn back the eyes of our heart and apply our minds to him again straightaway. The whole matter rests in the inner part of the soul. Once the devil has been expelled, and the vices find no further dominion there, the kingdom of God will be established within us, as the Gospel says, 'The Kingdom of God cometh not with observation. Neither shall they say: Behold here, or behold there. For lo, the kingdom of God is within you' (Luke 17:20–1). Within us indeed can be nothing other than the knowledge of truth, or the lack of it, attachment to vice or to virtue – it must be either the devil or Christ for whom we prepare a kingdom in our hearts. St Paul describes the nature of this kingdom, saying, 'The kingdom of God is not meat and drink; but justice and peace and joy in the Holy Ghost' (Rom. 14:17). Thus, if the kingdom of God is within us, and that kingdom is justice and peace with rejoicing, it follows that those who abide in them are certainly in the kingdom of God. Contrariwise those who abide in strife, injustice and the sort of sadness that brings death, are already committed to the

I. On the Direction and Goal of a Monk

kingdom of the devil, to death and hell. By these signs we may distinguish the kingdom of God and of the devil.

In truth, if we direct the highest faculties of our minds towards the consideration of where heavenly virtues may be found, those that are truly in the kingdom of God, how can we imagine that situation other than as full and lasting gladness? What indeed is so appropriate or conducive to real bliss than deep peace and lasting joy? Now to reassure you that I am not talking simply from my own conjecture but am grounded on the certain authority of the Lord, hear how he explicitly describes the nature of that kingdom. 'For behold,' he says, 'I create new heavens and a new earth: and the former things shall not be in remembrance, and they shall not come upon the heart. But you shall be glad and rejoice for ever in these things which I create' (Isaiah 65: 17–18). And again, 'Joy and gladness shall be found therein, thanksgiving and the voice of praise, and there shall be month after month and sabbath after sabbath' (Isaiah 51: 3, 66: 23). Again, 'They shall obtain joy and gladness: and sorrow and mourning shall flee away' (Isaiah 35: 10). And if you want to know more clearly about the life of the saints in the heavenly city, hear what the Lord has to say about Jerusalem herself: 'I will make thy visitation peace, and thy overseers justice. Iniquity shall no more be heard in thy land, wasting nor destruction in thy borders: and salvation shall possess thy walls, and praise thy gates. Thou shalt no more have the sun for thy light by day, neither shall the brightness of the moon enlighten thee: but the Lord shall be unto thee for an everlasting light, and thy God for thy glory. Thy sun shall go down no more and thy moon shall not decrease. For the Lord shall be unto thee for an everlasting light: and the days of thy mourning shall be ended' (Isaiah 60: 17–20). St Paul too, when he promises that the kingdom of heaven is the fullness of joy, does not mean joy in vague or general terms, but is quite explicit about the joy which exists only in the Holy Spirit (Rom. 14: 17), though he is well aware of another sort of joy, a pernicious one, of which it is said 'The world shall rejoice' (John 16: 20), and 'Woe to you that now laugh; for you shall mourn and weep' (Luke 6: 25).

The kingdom of heaven can be understood in three ways. It can mean that heaven will reign, or that the saints will have dominion over others, as in 'Thou shalt have power over five cities, and thou over ten' (Luke 19:17, 19), or again as is said to the apostles, 'You also shall sit on twelve seats judging the twelve tribes of Israel' (Matt. 19:28). Alternatively, the heavens themselves can begin to be ruled by Christ, when all has been put beneath his feet and he begins to be God, All in All (cf. I. Cor. 15:28). Or finally that in heaven, we shall reign with the Lord.

XIV. "As long as we still exist in the body, each of us must be aware that we are eventually going to dwell in service to whichever destination we serve and partake in while still in this life. Let us be in no doubt that we will spend eternal life together with the one we have chosen to associate ourselves with and to serve now. Our Lord tells us this when he says, 'If any man minister to me, let him follow me; and where I am, there also shall my minister be' (John 12:26). Just as the kingdom of the devil is embraced by acquiescence in vice, so the kingdom of God is gained by the practice of virtue, and possessed in purity of heart and knowledge of the spirit. Where the kingdom of God is, be sure that there too is eternal life – where the kingdom of the devil lies, there assuredly lurk death and hell, and those who dwell there cannot so much as praise Our Lord, as the prophet tells us, saying, 'The dead shall not praise thee, O Lord: nor any of them that go down to hell' (that is, the pit of sin). 'But we,' he says, 'we that live' (not to sin, not to this world, but to God) 'we bless the Lord from this time now and for ever' (Psalm 113/114:17–18). 'For there is no one in death who is mindful of thee: and who shall confess to thee in hell?' (the pit of sin) (Psalm 6:6). The answer is, no one. Even if you profess yourselves a thousand times over to be a Christian or a monk, no one can acknowledge the Lord while he is sinning. No one who submits to what the Lord has condemned can be mindful of the Lord. Nor can one claim to be a servant of one whose commandments he scornfully repudiates.

This is the death in which the Apostle declares the luxurious

I. On the Direction and Goal of a Monk

widow to lie, saying, a widow 'who liveth in pleasures is dead while she is living' (I Tim. 5:6). And there are many who are dead while living in this body, and are unable to praise God since they lie in the pit; while in contrast there are many who may be physically dead but praise and bless God in the spirit, as in the texts, 'O ye spirits and souls of the just, bless the Lord' (Dan. 3:86), and 'Let every spirit praise the Lord!' (Psalm 150:6). In the Apocalypse the souls of the martyrs not only praise God but are also described as interceding (Apoc. 6:9–10). In the Gospel too, Our Lord speaks to the Sadducees, 'Have you not read that which was spoken by God, saying to you: I am the God of Abraham and the God of Isaac and the God of Jacob? He is not the God of the dead but of the living. All are alive in him' (Matt. 22:31–2). St Paul adds, 'therefore God is not ashamed to be called their God; for he hath prepared for them a city' (Heb. 11:16). The parable in the Gospel about the poor man Lazarus and the empurpled rich man (Luke 16:19 ff.) shows us that we are not idle after separation from the body, nor unconscious, for Lazarus found rest in a blissful abode, namely the bosom of Abraham, and the other was tormented in the unbearable heat of eternal fire. If we wish to comprehend what was said to the thief, 'This day thou shalt be with me in paradise' (Luke 23:43), what can it indicate other than that our former understanding survives in the soul, and that it also enjoys an appropriate destiny varying according to the merits of its actions? God would have never made this promise to him had it been true that the soul would be either deprived of perception or annihilated after separation from the body, for it was not his body that was to enter paradise with Christ, but his soul.

We must be careful to avoid – no, we must hold in total abhorrence – that vile heretical quibble which refuses to believe that Christ could have been found in paradise on the same day on which he descended into the pits, and so divides the saying, 'Amen I say to thee this day', and then they imagine a pause, 'thou shalt be with me in paradise'. As if that promise was not fulfilled at once after passing from this life, but can only be understood as to be fulfilled after the occurrence of the resurrection! They fail to understand what he revealed to the Jews, before his own resurrection, for they believed him to be bound by the constraints of human fleshly weakness, like themselves, 'No man' he says, 'hath ascended into heaven, but he that descended from heaven, the Son of Man who is in heaven' (John 3:13). It is clearly shown by these passages that the souls of the dead are not deprived of their perceptions, nor even of their affections, namely hope and sorrow, joy and fear, and they begin to some extent to have a foretaste of what is destined for them in the General Judgment. Contrary to the opinion of some sceptics, they are not dissolved into nothingness after passing from this life, but enjoy a fuller life, and apply themselves more fervently to the praises of God. Is it reasonable to set aside the evidence of Scripture and to make a superficial analysis of the nature of the soul according to our own limited intelligence? It seems to pass the bounds of stupidity, I might say lunacy, to entertain the idea that the more valuable part of man, that in which as St Paul tells us the image and likeness of God reside (cf. I Cor. 11:7; Col. 3:10), becomes senseless once this temporary burden of concealing flesh is laid aside, whereas it is that part which contains the whole strength of reason in itself, to the extent that it is capable of giving perception to the dumb and senseless matter of the flesh, just by inhabiting it? It is more logical, and more in accordance with the nature of reason itself, to suppose that once the mind has shuffled off the gross flesh which now hinders it, it can exercise its intellectual abilities even better, and far from losing them, find them more refined and acute.

St Paul recognises that what we have been saying is true, for he himself longed to depart from this flesh, so that liberated from it he could be more closely united with his Lord, saying, 'having a desire to be dissolved and to be with Christ, a thing by far the better' (Phil. 1:23). And, 'while we are in the body we are absent from the Lord', so that 'we are confident and have a good will to be absent rather from the body and to be present with the Lord. And therefore we labour, whether absent or present, to please him' (II Cor. 5:6–9). He refers to the existence of the soul in this present flesh as being 'absent' from the Lord and separated from

I. On the Direction and Goal of a Monk

Christ. Its separation and departure from the flesh he faithfully trusts to be entering the presence of Christ. More clearly, on the same point of the richness of the life of the soul, the Apostle continues, 'But you are come to mount Sion and to the city of the living God, the heavenly Jerusalem, and to the company of many thousands of angels, and to the church of the firstborn who are written in the heavens . . ., and to the spirits of the just made perfect' (Heb. 12: 22–3). In another place he refers to these spirits, 'We have had fathers of our flesh for instructors, and we reverenced them. Shall we not much more obey the Father of spirits and live?' (Heb. 12: 9).

XV. "The contemplation of God can be conceived in various ways. God may be acknowledged in wonder at His nature, beyond our understanding, though this wonder remains veiled while we hope for the promise to be fulfilled. He may also be perceived in the magnificence of his creation, or in recognition of his justice, or through the guidance of his daily providence. He may be contemplated when with an open mind we consider what he has done through his saints over the generations, or in fearful awe we admire the powerful authority with which he controls and directs all things, and the vastness of his knowledge and perception from which no secrets of the heart are hid; when we reflect that he counts and knows the sands of the sea and the number of its waves; when we contemplate in wonder that his knowledge extends to every drop of rain, the hours and the days of the centuries, all things past and yet to come; when we consider how inconceivable is his mercy and forbearance, tolerating the countless crimes committed in his sight minute by minute; when we perceive how he calls and chooses us in his loving grace, when we had no merits of our own before; when we are lost in admiration of the frequent occasions of salvation he offers to those to be adopted as his sons; how he ordained our birth so that from the cradle we could be taught about his grace and instructed in his laws, and how he himself overthrew our enemy needing nothing but our assent, and strengthened us for eternal happiness and rewards to come;

and finally, how in his wisdom he took on the Incarnation to save us, and distributed his wonderful Mysteries among all the nations. And there are countless other grounds for contemplation, which come to mind depending on the quality of our life and the purity of our hearts, by which God may be perceived in a pure sight, and may be retained. But no one will be able to retain this contemplation continually if any fleshly desires are still alive in him, for as the Lord says, 'thou canst not see my face: for man shall not see me and live' (Exod. 33: 20), that is to say no man with worldly and earthly passions."

XVI. GERMANUS: "But why is it that irrelevant thoughts creep into our minds against our will, or without our being aware, and lurk there secretly, so that it is really difficult to drive them out, let alone understand them and deal with them? Is it possible for the mind to become free of these thoughts, and never to be pestered by this sort of distraction?"

XVII. MOYSES: "It is impossible for the mind not to be distracted by thoughts, but with application it is possible either to entertain or to banish these thoughts. Although their origin is quite independent of us, we can choose whether to accept them. We can acknowledge that it is impossible for the mind not to be distracted, but that does not mean we have to be totally overwhelmed by these distractions, or by the spirits which are trying to influence us. Otherwise no human freewill could survive, nor would we have any chance of working to improve ourselves. We are able to a great extent to modify the nature of our thoughts, whether it be holy spiritual thoughts or material earthly ones that accumulate in the heart. Hence we recommend regular reading and meditation on Scripture, to give us the opportunity of remembering spiritual thoughts. For the same reason we sing the psalms, to assist us in developing real compunction. [Hence too we apply ourselves diligently to watching, fasting and prayer] so that the mind may be trained not to observe earthly things, but to reflect on heavenly ones. If we are careless and negligent of these matters, the mind

I. On the Direction and Goal of a Monk

is bound to settle into sordid vice, and turn rapidly towards the corruption of fleshly thoughts.

XVIII. "The operation of the mind can be aptly compared to a mill, the sort that is turned by the force of a head of water. As long as the pressure of water is maintained, the mill can never cease from its work, but the miller has the ability to decide whether it will grind wheat, barley or darnel. Whatever the person in charge of the work puts into the machine is what it will grind. In the same way throughout the course of this present life, a flow of temptations presses on the mind from all sides, and it is unable to be empty of turbulent thoughts. It is however able to make the effort of deciding which sort of thoughts it should prepare for itself or admit. For as we have seen, if we return frequently to meditation on Holy Scripture, and make our memory dwell on the recollection of spiritual matters, the desire of perfection and the hope of future bliss, the result will be the rising of spiritual thoughts, which will make the mind focus on the things we have been pondering. On the other hand, if we are overcome by idle carelessness, and fill our minds with empty tales of vice, or are entangled by worldly cares and unnecessary business, it follows that poison will be insinuated into the mind, springing up like some sort of darnel. As Our Lord and Saviour tells us, wherever the treasure of our works and intentions lies, there will our hearts be surely fixed (cf. Matt. 6: 21).

XIX. "This we must be aware of above all, that there are three sources of our thoughts, that is to say God, the devil and ourselves. They come from God, when in his kindness he visits us in the illumination of the Holy Spirit and leads us up to a higher state; or when we have been worsted through our failure to profit by grace, or by our idleness, and he corrects us with his saving compunction; or again when he opens the heavenly mysteries to us and turns our hearts towards nobler wishes and deeds. For instance, King Ahasuerus was prompted by the Lord to investigate the books of annals which recorded Mordechai's good deeds, so that he raised him to the greatest degree of honour and immediately repealed the wicked decree on the extermination of the Jews (Esther 6–7). Or again, when the prophet says, 'I will hear what the Lord God will speak in me' (Psalm 84/85: 9), and in another place, 'the angel that spoke in me said' (Zach. 1: 14). Similarly the Son of God promised that he would come with the Father and make his dwelling in us (cf. John 14: 23), and says, 'It is not you that speak, but the Spirit of your Father that speaketh in you' (Matt. 10: 20). The Chosen Vessel also says 'do you seek a proof of Christ that speaketh in me' (II Cor. 13: 3).

The sort of thoughts that arise from the devil are when he tries to pervert us through the pleasure of vice and his secret wiles, fraudulently offers evil for good in his subtle insinuations, and transforms himself into an angel of light (cf. II Cor. 11: 3). Or as the evangelist writes, 'and when supper was done (the devil having now put into the heart of Judas Iscariot, the son of Simon, to betray him)' (John 13: 2), and again, 'after the morsel Satan entered into him' (John 13: 27). Peter also spoke to Ananias, 'Why hath Satan tempted thy heart, that thou shouldst lie to the Holy Ghost?' (Acts 5: 3). What we read in the Gospel, we can find long before that in Ecclesiastes, 'If the spirit of him that hath power ascend upon thee, leave not thy place' (Qo. 10: 4). In the same way in the third book of Kingdoms an unclean spirit is represented as speaking to God against Achab, 'I will go forth and be a lying spirit in the mouth of all his prophets' (III Kings (I Kings) 22: 22).

Thoughts which arise from ourselves are when we recall naturally the things that we are doing, or have done or heard of. The saintly David says, 'I thought upon the days of old: and I had in my mind the eternal years. And I meditated in the night with my own heart: and I was exercised, and I swept my spirit' (Psalm 76/77: 6–7, LXX). Again, 'The Lord knoweth the thoughts of men, that they are vain' (Psalm 93/94: 11), and 'the thoughts of the just are judgments' (Prov. 12: 5). In the Gospel too, Our Lord says to the Pharisees, 'Why do think evil in your hearts?' (Matt. 9: 4).

XX. "Now we should be careful to scrutinise these three types of thought, and discriminate wisely between all the ideas which

I. On the Direction and Goal of a Monk

arise in our minds, first distinguishing their origins, causes and authors, so that we can know what value to lay on them, depending on the authority of the one who suggests them to us. Thus we shall be, as Our Lord commands, honest moneychangers. Their greatest skill and art is to test for pure gold (commonly called 22 caret) as opposed to ore which has been imperfectly refined in the fire, as well as bronze and base metal coinage which shines with a golden hue to imitate valuable metal. Their expert knowledge is not deceived, and they are quick to recognise coins issued by usurpers by their faces, as well as distinguishing coins with the images of real kings but illegally struck. Moreover they examine them carefully on the scales to see if any of the proper weight be lacking. The Gospel uses this example and simile to show that we too must do all these things in a spiritual way.

First of all, if any thought creeps into our hearts, or any theological opinion arises, we should scrutinise it closely to see if it has been refined by the divine heavenly fire of the Holy Spirit, or if it depends on surviving memories of Judaism, or originates from the pride of worldly philosophy which offers only a superficial piety. We shall be able to do this if we follow the Apostle's advice, 'believe not every spirit, but try the spirits if they be of God' (I John 4:1). That is how some have been deceived after their monastic profession, and swept away by the plausible speeches and opinions of certain philosophers. They begin by listening to things which appear to be consistent with devotion and religion, and shine as if with the glint of gold, but once they have been taken in by these superficial ideas, which are like forged brass coins, they become ever after empty and unhappy, either called back to the turmoil of this world or lured into the error and empty arrogance of heresy. We read in the book of Joshua of what Achan did, when he coveted the golden treasure in the Philistine camp and stole it, till he was struck by the curse and condemned to eternal death (cf. Josh. 7:21).

Secondly, we must be careful and observant, lest a depraved misinterpretation of the pure gold of Scripture deceive us through the sheer value of the metal. The subtle fiend attempted in this way to impose on Our Lord and Saviour as if he were a mere man, when he twisted what should be understood in general as referring to all the just, and attempted maliciously to apply it in particular to the One who needed no angel guardian, saying, 'He hath given his angels charge over thee: to keep thee in all thy ways. In their hands they shall bear thee up: lest thou ever dash thy foot against a stone' (Psalm 90/91: 11–12, Matt. 4: 6). In his sly pride he distorts the priceless words of Scripture and perverts them to their opposite sense, offering the image of an usurper under the pretext of deceitful gold, and tries to trick us with forgeries, suggesting that it would be a work of devotion to do something which had not issued from the legitimate mint of the fathers, and luring us to vice under cover of virtue; as when through immoderate and unsuitable fasting or excessive watching, overlong prayers and unsuitable reading, he deceives us and brings us to a bad end. Or again he can persuade us to embark on pious intercession and visiting, bringing us out of the spiritual enclosure of the monastery and from that secret cell of dear silence; he may suggest we become involved in the care and concerns of nuns and destitute women, and with these snares entangle a monk so irrevocably as to dissipate him in dangerous worries and occupations. Alternatively he can persuade him to desire a holy clerical preferment under the pretext of helping others, enticing him with spiritual profits, which would be a distraction from the humility of our profession and seclusion. All these things are contrary to our salvation and our profession, but screened by a veil of pious benevolence, they may easily ensnare the unwary and inexperienced. For they imitate the coins of a true king, in that they seem at first to be full of piety but they were not struck by legitimate moneyers, that is to say the approved Catholic fathers. They did not issue from the authentic public mint of their instruction, but were forged secretly by devilish guile, not without causing damage to the ignorant and inexperienced to whom they were passed. However useful or necessary they seem at first, if they afterwards begin to oppose the principles of our profession, and to bring down the whole body of our endeavour, it would be salutary to cut off and throw from us these limbs which cause us to fall, however necessary they be, even if they perform

I. On the Direction and Goal of a Monk

the work of right hand or foot. It is better to enter the kingdom of heaven lame but otherwise healthy, without the limb of one precept (namely active work and its result), rather than with the whole law to enter into some pitfall. By such dangerous practices we can be drawn away from our rule of life and the exercises we had undertaken, till we fall into such disarray that without taking future damage into account, all our past activities and their results are plunged into the burning fire of hell (cf. Matt. 18:8). Of this sort of delusion we find an elegant expression in Proverbs, 'There is a way that seemeth to a man right: and the ends thereof lead to the depths of hell' (Prov. 16:25, LXX). And again, 'The evil one causeth harm when he is fellow with the just' (Prov. 11:15, LXX), that is to say the devil deceives when he is disguised under the colour of sanctity. He indeed hates 'the voice of the instructor' (Prov. 11:22), that is the force for good which proceeds from the words and advice of the elders.

XXI. "I have heard that Abba John, who lives at Lycopolis, was recently deceived in this way. He had deferred partaking of any food for two days, and his body was weakened and emaciated, until the third day, when he was preparing his meal. The devil then came to him in the guise of a rough Ethiopian, and fell at his feet, saying, 'Be generous to me, for it was I who suggested this work to you.' The great man, who is perfect and sensible in his discernment, understood at once that under the pretext of self-control he had been practising unwisely, and had been duped by the sly fiend into prolonging his fast till he had burdened his body with a weakness that was not only unnecessary but positively harmful to the spirit. He had in fact been deceived by a forged coin; while he honoured the image of the true king on it, he had failed to discern whether it were legitimately struck.

The final test used by our worthy moneychanger is the examination of weight, as we have said. That will be carried out by us if we weigh to the exact scruple whatever has come into our mind to do, placing it on the scales of our hearts and bringing it to a perfect balance, to see whether it is full weight and common currency, and to test whether it be overweight in the fear of God, if it be just right, or if it be light because of human pride or some presumed novelty; whether vainglory has clipped some of its weight off, or pride has corroded it. In this way we put it to public assay, that is to the standard of the prophets and apostles, judging it by what they tell us, so that we may know whether it be whole and perfect and in accordance with them, or whether we should be careful to reject it as incomplete, spurious and not up to their standard or weight.

XXII. "Our assay must therefore be made in these four ways which we have described: firstly we must see if the material be real gold, or some deceitful alloy; secondly we must reject as spurious fakes any thoughts which make pretence of good works, bearing the image of the King illegally, and not legitimately struck; thirdly we must scrutinise our thoughts in the same way and repudiate those which, albeit of the purest Scriptural gold, bear the image not of the true King but of an usurper, because of their depraved heretical sense; and fourthly we must spurn any clipped coins, dangerously underweight, rejecting whatever does not come up to the standard of the elders, whenever corrosive vanity has eaten away the true weight and value. Let us not fall into the trap which Our Lord so earnestly warned us against, of losing the whole merit and reward of our labours. 'Lay not up to yourselves treasures on earth; where the rust and moth consume and where thieves break through and steal' (Matt. 6:19). If we do anything out of consideration for human respect, we must realise that it is what Our Lord calls treasure in earth, as if it were buried in the ground and covered with earth. It may be plundered by various demons, eaten away by corrosive vainglory, or devoured by the moths of pride, until it is of no value or use to the one who hid it. We must be careful to scrutinise every corner of our hearts, and examine diligently the tracks left by everyone who enters there, in case some beastly thought, some lion or dragon has passed through, and left its nasty footprints behind, which may provide them access, through our own negligent thoughts, into other areas of

I. On the Direction and Goal of a Monk

our inner hearts. Every hour and every minute we should plough the field of our hearts with the Gospel plough (that is to say the recollection of the Lord's cross) so that we may be able to root out and eliminate the nests of vile beasts and the lurking places of venomous worms."

XXIII. The old man noticed that we were amazed by this, and fired with unquenchable enthusiasm at his discourse. Impressed by our fervour he paused for a moment before adding, "My sons, you were so eager that you provoked me to speak at length, and inspired my discourse with a greater flame of enthusiasm in my response to your desire, so that I can clearly see that you have a real thirst for perfection. I would like to add a little about the excellence and grace of discretion, which takes the first place among other virtues, and to recommend its wonderful value to you with everyday examples as well as the teaching and opinions of the ancient fathers. For I remember many occasions when someone asked me, as you did, with signs of real distress, and although I was eager to give them some advice, I found myself unable, without any ideas, or words to express them. Thus I failed utterly to give them any consolation to go away with. You can see from this that it is only the Lord's grace that provides words for the speaker, according to the merits and desires of his audience.

Now since the remaining part of the night is far too short to explain all this, it would be better to spend it in bodily repose, for if we deny the flesh a moderate amount of sleep, we would break down altogether. We shall reserve the whole matter for a full discussion on some future day or night. It is appropriate for anyone who claims to know about discretion to begin by displaying their wisdom in this way, proving by patience whether they are or can be discreet and sensible. By cultivating the virtue which generates moderation, they can avoid falling into the contrary vice of indiscretion, otherwise their actual practice would undermine the force of the virtue they were talking about. Since discretion is such a good thing for us, we shall arrange to investigate it as far as the Lord gives us the opportunity; but its first requirement is not to exceed due measure and time in speaking about it, thus demonstrating the proper excellence of moderation which is the first of its characteristics to be discerned."

Thus the blessed Moyses brought his discourse to an end, and urged us to take a little sleep, although we were still alert and hanging on his words. He suggested that we lie down on the same mats we had been sitting on, and put *embrymia* under our heads to serve as pillows. (*Embrymia* are long flexible bundles of the thicker papyrus reeds. Bound together at intervals of eighteen inches, they can serve as a low seat, like a stool, for the brethren when they sit down for the Office. When placed under the heads of sleepers they provide a comfortable support for the head, and not too hard. They have proved extremely useful and appropriate for the monks' needs, being not only soft, but also easily and cheaply made, for the papyrus grows all along the banks of the Nile [and no one prevents all who want to use them from cutting them]. Moreover being of a very light material they are easily transported and moved when necessary.) At the old man's bidding, therefore, we finally settled ourselves to take some sleep, although repose was difficult as we were so excited and happy having heard his discourse, and were eagerly looking forward to the promised explanation.

✣

✧ THE SECOND COLLATION ✧
BEING THE SECOND OF ABBA MOYSES

On Discretion

    I. A preamble by Abba Moyses on the grace of discretion.
   II. The benefit that discretion alone confers on a monk, demonstrated in the teaching of Abba Antony.
  III. On how Saul and Achab were deluded through lack of due discretion.
  IV. What we find in Holy Scripture about the value of discretion.
    V. On the death of the elder named Hero.
  VI. Of how two brothers were ruined through inexperience in discretion.
 VII. Of another who was deluded through inexperience of discretion.
VIII. Of the delusion and ruin of a monk of Mesopotamia.
  IX. A question, on how true discretion may be acquired.
    X. The reply, on how to possess true discretion.
  XI. The teaching of Abba Sarapion, both on how thoughts wither away on confession, and on the danger of over confidence.
 XII. An admission of the shame which embarrasses us in revealing our thoughts to the elders.

XIII. The reply, on how embarrassment must be eliminated, and on the risks of being unsympathetic.
XIV. On the call of Samuel.
XV. On the call of the Apostle Paul.
XVI. On the need to seek discretion.
XVII. On immoderate fasting and watching.
XVIII. A question, on the proper degree of self-denial and eating.
XIX. Of the best way of receiving food daily.
XX. An objection, that permitting two buns would make asceticism too easy.
XXI. The reply, on how experience shows the wisdom of that ration.
XXII. What should be the usual measure of self-denial and of eating.
XXIII. How excess of seminal energy is restrained.
XXIV. Of the effort to eat consistently, and of the greed of Brother Benjamin.
XXV. A question, on how to keep to the same ration always.
XXVI. The reply, on not exceeding the ration of food.

I. After our early morning's rest, when the dawning sun finally shone upon us, we cheerfully renewed our requests for the promised discourse, and the blessed Moyses began accordingly: "Now I see you are awake, and so eager that I am afraid you have not taken advantage of the brief moment of rest which I intended to snatch from our spiritual conversation to refresh your bodies. I think that would have been advantageous to your physical wellbeing. Yet when I consider your enthusiasm, I have a greater anxiety to trouble me, for as I prepare to fulfil my promise, I realise I shall need to take great care in that preparation, because I see you so expectant and attentive; as the text says, 'When thou shalt sit to eat with a prince, consider diligently what is set before thy face, and partake of it, knowing that thou shouldst prepare the like' (Prov. 23:1–2, LXX).

II. On Discretion

Since we are to speak of the virtue of holy discretion, which we began to discuss last night and which brought our conversation to a close, I think it fitting to begin by examining what the Fathers said of its benefit. Once we know their opinion on the matter, and what those who came before us have said, we can look at many examples of mistakes and accidents which occurred to various men long ago as well as more recently, caused by their failing to follow discretion and falling into dire difficulties. After that I shall do my best to expound the usefulness and advantage of discretion. We can then proceed to learn more effectively how to cultivate and develop this virtue, aware of its value and grace. For it is no ordinary virtue, nor one that the average human intellect can easily understand, unless it be fortified by divine grace. Indeed we read that St Paul numbers it among the very highest gifts of the Holy Spirit: 'To one indeed, by the Spirit, is given the word of wisdom; and to another, the word of knowledge, according to the same Spirit; to another, faith in the same Spirit; to another, the grace of healing in one Spirit;' and a little further on, 'to another, the discerning of spirits'. And having run through the whole list of spiritual gifts, he adds, 'but in all these things, one and the same Spirit worketh, dividing to every one according as he will' (I Cor. 12:8–11).

You see that the gift of discretion is not merely natural, nor is it insignificant, for it is the greatest gift of God's grace. Unless a monk desire it with his whole heart, and possess a clear understanding, to discern the spirits that arise within him, he is bound to blunder about as in the darkest shades of night and fall not only when he is among dangerous pits and crags, but even on the most simple and straightforward paths.

II. "I remember that when I was young, and living in the Thebaïd where Saint Antony dwelt, one night the elders gathered to ask him about the grace of perfection. Their discussion went on from evening to dawn, and the whole night was occupied in this greatest of questions. They enquired at length about which was the virtue or practice that could best preserve a monk continuously free from the snares and deceits of the devil, or at least conduct him by an easy path and steady pace towards the heights of perfection. Each one put forward his opinion as he was minded to do. Some placed their trust in assiduous fasting and watching, because once the mind is rarefied by these and purity attained in heart and body, we are more easily united to God. Others stressed poverty and the renunciation of all property, which liberates the mind so that it can arrive more rapidly at God, freed from anything that might hinder it. Yet others considered that *anachoresis* was necessary, in other words isolation in a remote desert, where one could dwell and speak familiarly with God, clinging closer to him. Others again declared that it is charity that must be followed, meaning works of kindness, for the Lord in the Gospels promises the Kingdom of Heaven in particular for these, saying, 'Come, ye blessed of my Father, possess you the Kingdom prepared for you from the foundation of the world. For I was hungry, and you gave me to eat; I was thirsty and you gave me to drink', etc. (Matt. 25:34–5). After they had discussed how a reliable path to God could be constructed by these different virtues, and the greater part of the night had been taken up in the debate, the blessed Antony finally took a part.

'All these things which you have mentioned are indeed necessary, and profitable for those who thirst for God and long to reach him, but long experience of many events has shown that we cannot attribute the supreme grace to any of these. Time and time again I have seen men suddenly deceived and overthrown, although they had practised fasting and watching with diligence, withdrawn into marvellous solitude, undertaken to renounce all property to the extent that they would keep back not even so much as a day's livelihood or a single denarius, and performed works of mercy with wholehearted devotion. But after all this they were unable ever to bring the work they had begun to a fitting conclusion, and all their great fervour and admirable way of life came to a bad end. Now we can discover the principal path to God if only we analyse accurately what was the cause of their fall and delusion. They abounded in the practice of virtue, but discretion

II. On Discretion

alone was lacking, so that they were unable to persevere to the end. No other cause can be found for their fall except that they were insufficiently instructed by their elders, and unable to acquire the virtue of discretion. It is discretion which avoids extremes on either side and leads the monk to advance along the royal road, neither puffed up on the right by his own virtue, that is surpassing the reasonable degree of self-denial by foolishly presuming on his excessive zeal; nor deviating to vices on the left, through laxity in his obligations, that is allowing the opposite spirit to make him slack and tepid on the excuse of looking after his health. It is this discretion which the Gospel calls the eye and lamp of the body, in Our Saviour's words, "The light of thy body is thy eye. If thy eye be single, thy whole body shall be lightsome. But if thy eye be evil, thy whole body shall be darksome" (Matt. 6:22–3). Discerning all the thoughts of a man and his deeds, it examines all that is to be done and sheds light on it. If a man have the evil eye, meaning that it is bad in judgment and ignorant, deceived and deluded by overconfidence, it will make our whole body darkness. It darkens the mind totally, and all our actions are obscured by the blindness of vice and confusion. "If then the light that is in thee," he goes on, "be darkness; the darkness itself how great shall it be!" (Matt. 6:23). Let no one doubt that if our heart's judgment is erroneous, sunk in the darkness of ignorance, all our thoughts and works will become entangled in the greater darkness of sin once they have deviated from the guidance of discretion.

III. "'Saul was the first to be chosen by God as worthy to rule the people of Israel, but he did not possess this gift of discretion at all, and "his whole body being darksome", was eventually deprived of his kingdom. His light was turned to darkness and error, so that he was deceived into imagining that his own sacrifice would be more acceptable to God than obedience to the command of Samuel (I Kings (I Sam.) 15). Through an action which he had hoped would appease the divine majesty, he incurred nothing but blame. In the same way it was failure of discretion that misled Achab, King of Israel, after God had graciously granted him a splendid military victory; he thought his own compassion to be better than the execution of God's severe commandment, which in his own eyes he considered to be a cruel order. Softened by this thought he chose to temper his bloody triumph with mercy, but for this inappropriate mercy he incurred the inevitable sentence of death, as if his whole body too had become darksome (I Kings (I Sam.) 20).

IV. "'This discretion is not only the "light of the body" but is described by St Paul as the sun, when he says, "Let not the sun go down upon your anger" (Eph. 4:26). That this is the guiding principle of our life is shown in the text, "Those who have no guidance fall like leaves" (Prov. 11:14, LXX). It is appropriately called "counsel" without which as scripture tells us, we may not do anything at all. Not even the spiritual wine, which "may cheer the heart of man" (Psalm 103/104:15) may we imbibe without moderation, as in "Do all things with counsel, drink wine with counsel" (Prov. 31:3, LXX). And again, "As a city whose walls are ruined and do not encompass her, so is the man who doeth a thing without counsel" (Prov. 25:28, LXX). How perilous the lack of discretion is for a monk is demonstrated by the parable of a ruined city without enclosing walls. Here is where wisdom lies, here is understanding and sense, without which our interior castle cannot be built, our spiritual treasure cannot be amassed. As it is said, "By wisdom the house shall be built: and by prudence it shall be strengthened. By instruction the storerooms shall be filled with all precious and most beautiful wealth" (Prov. 24:3–4, LXX). This moreover I say is the strong meat which can only be digested by the healthy and strong, as in "Strong meat is for the perfect; for them who by custom have their senses exercised to the discerning of good and evil" (Heb. 5:14). It is shown to be so useful, nay necessary, for us that it is likened to the very Word of God and its virtues, as in the text, "For the Word of God is living and effectual and more piercing than any two-edged sword, and reaching unto the division of the soul and the spirit, of the joints also and the marrow; and is a discerner of

II. On Discretion

the thoughts and intents of the heart" (Heb. 4:12). From this we see clearly that no virtue can be acquired or preserved without the grace of discretion.'

Thus blessed Antony and all the others agreed in the opinion that it is discretion which leads a valiant monk on a sure path to God, and preserves from corruption the virtues that they had mentioned before. With discretion one can mount with little effort to the pinnacles of achievement; without it so many have failed to attain the height of perfection, despite their endless toil. It is discretion that begets all virtues, preserves them and governs them.

V. "Now to illustrate this decision, reached long ago by St Antony and the other Fathers, let us look at a modern example, as we had promised. You yourselves will remember, from the evidence of your own eyes, how a few days ago the elder called Hero was so deceived by the devil that he threw himself down from a high place into a deep pit, although he had lived in this desert for fifty years. We can all recall how he used to observe the rule of self-control with unusual strictness, and kept himself assiduously retired in solitude more than anyone else who lived here; after so much effort, by what argument or reason could our enemy deceive him into falling into such a serious error, to the distress of all who live in the desert? It was simply that he was lacking in the virtue of discretion, and chose to be governed by his own rule of life rather than to follow the advice and counsels of the brethren or the teaching of the elders. He was so strict in keeping always unbroken his custom of fasting, and so firmly enclosed in the privacy of his cell, that not even the solemnity of Easter Day could ever persuade him to join the common recreation of the brethren. All the brothers had assembled in the church that day, to keep the yearly festival, and only he thought himself unable to join them, fearful that they might think he had relaxed his rule of life if he accepted a share in a few vegetables. Deceived by this presumption, he welcomed the angel of Satan reverently as if he were an angel of light (I Cor. 11:14), and readily obeyed his command to throw himself headlong into a well so deep that you cannot see to the bottom; presumably he was confident in his angel's promise that he could not possibly come to any harm because of the merits of his virtuous efforts. Trusting in this, in order to prove his immunity indisputably by experiment, he threw himself into the well on an unlucky night, deluded that he would demonstrate his enormous merit by emerging unharmed. It took considerable effort for the brethren to haul him out, and he was already so weak with loss of blood, that he died two days later. Worse than that, he remained so stubborn in his delusion that not even the evidence of his own death could persuade him that he had been duped by the cunning of the fiend. As a result, the brethren, who were so shocked at his death, could only with difficulty persuade their priest, Abba Paphnutius, not to condemn him as a suicide, one unworthy of commemoration and the sacrifice for the dead, in their consideration of the great efforts he had made over so many years living in the desert.

VI. "What can I say about the two brothers who lived the other side of the Thebaïd desert, where Saint Antony once dwelt, and were so little guided by discretion that they ventured into the immense empty desert with the intention of eating nothing whatever except what the Lord himself would provide for them? They were wandering in the wilderness, and already weak with hunger, when they saw far off some Mazices (a tribe which is wilder and more ferocious than any other, inclined to bloodshed through sheer savagery, not like other men who are moved by desire of plunder). Contrary to their custom, these approached with the offer of bread. One of the brothers had sufficient discretion to see that this was as it were a gift from the Lord, and accepted it joyfully and with thanks. He acknowledged that the food was provided by God, and that God alone could bring it about that men who were ever eager for human blood should bestow the means of life on those who were already weak and fainting. The other, on the contrary, refused the food because it was being offered to him by a man, and so perished of starvation. Now although they had both made a bad beginning in their reprehensible resolution, one of them was assisted by discretion to acknowledge a better way than what he had rashly and foolishly undertaken; the other, stubborn in his foolish confidence, and virtually devoid of discretion, brought on himself the death which the Lord had wished to avert, refusing to believe that it was by divine inspiration that these wild savages had put aside their wonted ferocity and were offering not the sword but bread.

VII. "What also can I say of that other one (whose name I will not mention, for he is still alive) who welcomed the devil under the guise of an angel of light for so long that he was continually taken in by his revelations, and imagined him to be the herald of justice? As well as that, the demon provided him with light in his cell, night after night without any lamp. Eventually he was commanded by it to sacrifice to God his own son (who lived with him in the monastery), in order that by making such an offering he might appear no whit inferior in merit to Abraham. He was deluded by this argument to the extent that he would have carried out the unnatural murder straightaway, had not the boy noticed him sharpening a knife unusually, and looking for bonds to tie him up for immolation; he guessed the crime that was being planned, and took to his heels in terror.

VIII. "It would take too long to tell of how that monk of Mesopotamia was deluded; he displayed a self restraint which few in that province could equal, and practised it in the seclusion of his cell for many years, but eventually was deluded by the demon in dreams and revelations until, after so much virtuous effort, which surpassed all the other monks who lived in that place, he tragically lapsed back into Judaism and the mutilation of the flesh. For the devil, wishing to lure him on to docility in the future by accustoming him to visions, revealed to him what was perfectly true over a long period, so that he was accepted as a true prophet. Finally he showed him all the Christian people together with the leaders of our religion and faith, in other words the Apostles and Martyrs, overshadowed and darkened, deformed and defaced with every sort of stain, and in contrast the Jewish people together with Moses, the patriarchs and the prophets, exulting in great joy, shining with brilliant light. He persuaded him that if he wished to share in their merit and bliss he should be quick to accept circumcision. No one would ever have been so woefully deceived had he been diligent in pursuing the art of discretion. There are many more examples and stories which demonstrate how perilous it is to be lacking in the grace of discretion."

IX. GERMANUS: "You have adequately demonstrated by these recent examples as well as the ancient teaching that discretion is in a sense the fountain and root of all virtues, but we would love to know how we should acquire it, and how to distinguish whether it be truly from God, or false and devilish. According to that Gospel parable which you used before, bidding us be skilful moneychangers, when we see the image of the true King impressed on a coin, how may we recognise when it is not lawfully struck, and reject it as a fake (to use the vulgar word you introduced into yesterday's discourse)? How do we acquire that skill which you have demonstrated we need, to be spiritual moneychangers in the Gospel sense, in your ample and excellent speech? There would be no point in acknowledging the value and merit of discretion, if we remain ignorant of how to seek and find it."

X. MOYSES: "True discretion cannot be acquired, except through true humility. The first test of humility is this: if we subject to the direction of our elders not only all our actions but even our thoughts; no one should trust his own judgment, but should accept their decision in all matters, to learn from their teaching how to distinguish between good and bad. This principle will guide a young man in proceeding directly on the true path of discretion, and moreover will preserve him unscathed through all the deceits and snares of the enemy. No one can ever be deceived if he lives by the example of the elders rather than by his own whim, neither can the sly foe take advantage of his inexperience, if he knows not how to conceal in dangerous shame the thoughts that arise in his heart, but allows the mature judgment of the elders to decide whether he should admit them or reject them. An evil thought withers away as soon as it is made known, so that even before any discerning judgment can be pronounced, by the sheer virtue of confession, the evil worm is dragged out into the open, as if from a dark and secret lair, and once exposed and shamed, crawls away. For his vile suggestions remain within us only as long as they are concealed in our hearts. For a clearer understanding of the benefit of this teaching, I refer you to what Abba Sarapion did, and which he frequently recounted to his disciples for their instruction.

XI. "'When I was very young,' said Sarapion, 'and living with Abba Theonas, I was habitually troubled by an assault of the enemy in this manner: after I had eaten my noon meal with the old man, I used to conceal one bun every day in my clothing, and eat it in the evening without his knowledge. Although I was continually committing this theft through sheer self-indulgence, and the lack of discipline which concealed desire brings, as soon as my deceitful greed had been satisfied, I would come to my senses and be more distressed with guilt than the pleasure of eating it had been worth. I found that I was being compelled, day after day, to perform that dismal deed, forced to do it as if by Pharoah's slave-drivers, to make a change from bricks (cf. Exod. 5); how it grieved my heart! I was quite unable to rid myself of this terrible obsession, and too ashamed to admit my secret pilfering to the old man.

But God determined to free me from the yoke of slavery; one day some of the brethren came to Theonas's cell to seek for instruction, and after our meal was over a spiritual conversation began. In response to the questions they put, the old man spoke about the vice of greed and how hidden thoughts oppress us. He explained the nature of such thoughts, and how terribly powerful they are until they be revealed. I was struck with remorse at the truth of his teaching, and terrified by my accusing conscience, almost believing that Theonas spoke thus because the Lord had revealed my secret to him. At first I was roused to private grief, then as remorse grew in my heart I burst out into open sobs and tears, till I produced from my pocket, the witness and receiver of my theft, the bun which I had secreted to eat later as my naughty custom was, and placed it in the open. Lying on the ground, I confessed that I had been secretly eating every day and asked forgiveness. With freely flowing tears, I begged the Lord for absolution for my terrible obsession. Then Theonas said, "Courage, my boy, your confession has absolved you from your sin even without my saying anything. You have today triumphed over the foe which had defeated you, and your confession has frustrated him more than ever you suffered from him through your silence. Unless you or someone else had refuted him by speaking out, you would still be letting him dominate you. As Solomon said, 'because sentence is not speedily pronounced against the evil, the heart of the children of man will be filled that they may commit evils' (Qo. 8:11, LXX). That is why the foul fiend can no longer disturb you now you have made this admission, and the evil worm can no longer claim a lair within you, for your saving confession has pulled him out of the darkness of your heart into the open."

Theonas had hardly finished speaking when, lo, a flaming torch emerged from my clothing and so filled the cell with the stench of sulphur that we could hardly remain within it for the powerful reek. Theonas resumed his instruction: "Look," he said, "the Lord has made the truth of my words visibly manifest, for the source of temptation has been driven out of your heart through the confession which has saved you, as you have seen, and you can be sure that the enemy, now exposed, can find no further hold over you since he has been publicly expelled."

This then was the testimony of the elder Sarapion, 'The tyrannical hold which the devil had over me had been destroyed by the virtue of confession, and remained ever after secure, so that the enemy never again attempted to insinuate even the memory of that greed nor did I ever again feel myself tempted by the desire to pilfer.' We find that opinion beautifully expressed in Ecclesiastes: 'If a serpent bite without hissing, the snake charmer hath no

II. On Discretion

escape' (Qo. 10:11, LXX). In other words, if the serpent is silent its bite is much more dangerous, meaning when the suggestions and thoughts of the devil are not made clear by confession to the snakecharmer, being the spiritual director, who can heal the wound forthwith by verses of Scripture and has the skill to extract the serpent's venom from the heart. Without confession he is unable to aid the one who is in danger of perishing.

This is the means by which we can easily come to understand true discretion: follow in the footsteps of the elders, never presume to do anything new, or rely on your own judgment, but proceed in all matters according to their teaching and example of life. Instructed in this way, anyone can arrive at a perfect degree of discretion, and remain immune to all the snares of the enemy. There is no other vice by which the devil can so quickly seduce a monk and lure him to his death than by persuading him to ignore the teaching of his elders and to trust in his own judgment, his own opinion and ideas.

The various arts and skills that human knowledge has devised, though they have no purpose other than convenience in this temporal life, cannot be learnt except by being taught, however much we may touch them or see them. It would be absurd to imagine that this art alone needs no instructor, when it is invisible and obscure, and cannot be perceived except by a pure heart, especially as mistakes here cause not just temporary damage which can be easily repaired, but the loss of the soul and eternal death! It is not against a visible enemy that we strive day and night, but against the invisible and pitiless; it is a spiritual combat, not just against one or two foes but a countless throng, and the outcome is all the more dangerous as the enemy presses harder and the strife is hidden. That is why we must always follow the footsteps of the elders with the greatest care, and everything that arises in our hearts must be revealed to them without any shamefaced concealment."

XII. GERMANUS: "The main reason why we have been so embarrassed about revealing our evil thoughts, and were ashamed to expose them in saving confession, is that we have known someone who was believed to be a leader among the elders of Syria who, when one of his brother elders revealed his thoughts in simple confession, was so moved with indignation as to rebuke him severely. Thus it came about that we used to keep our thoughts to ourselves and were frightened to reveal them to the elders, thus unable to find a remedy to cure them."

XIII. MOYSES: "Just as not all young men are equally fervent in spirit or formed in discipline and good behaviour, so not all the elders either can be found to be equally perfect or trustworthy. The worthiness of an old man does not lie in his white hair, but in the efforts of his youth and the work he has done in the past. 'The things that thou hast not gathered in thy youth, how shalt thou find them in thy old age?' (Sir. 25: 5). 'For venerable old age is not that of long time, nor counted by the number of years: but the understanding of a man is grey hairs. And a spotless life is old age' (Wisdom 4: 8–9). Therefore we should not follow and imitate every old man whose hair is white and whose only recommendation is long life, nor should we receive his teaching and instruction, but we should listen only to those whom we can discover to have passed a praiseworthy life, and during their youth had followed not their own whims but the teaching they in turn received from those before them. For there are some, indeed alas the majority, who have grown old in the same idle tepidity in which they passed their youth, and claim authority not because of their maturity but simply their age. The Lord rebukes them clearly enough in the prophesy, 'Strangers have devoured his strength and he knew it not: yea, grey hairs also are spread about upon him and he is ignorant of it' (Hosea 7: 9). It is sheer longevity that has projected these men as a model for youth, not a holy life, nor any distinction in our profession worth imitating. It is their seniority which the subtle fiend puts forward as a snare for the young, who take their authority for granted. It is by their example, in his insinuous wiles, that he is quick to overthrow and delude even those who might have been led on to a perfect life by their teaching or that of others; by the teaching of these elders he deludes the young into dangerous laxity or deadly despair.

Now I will give you an example of this, but omitting the name of the person involved, so that I will not incur the same reproach as he did in revealing his brother's sin. I will briefly tell you of something that happened which can give you the warning you need. One of the young men, and not the least worthy of them, went to an elder (who is well known to us) for the sake of improvement, and confessed to him in all simplicity that he was troubled by lustful thoughts and the temptation to sexual sin. He trusted that the old man's prayers would bring him consolation, and that he would find a remedy for the weakness he suffered, but the other reviled him in bitter language, calling him a miserable wretch and unfit to be called a monk if he was tempted by such base lusts. By his reproaches he wounded him all the deeper, until he drove him out of his cell, depressed, discouraged and plunged into gloom. He was so dejected that he was no longer looking for a remedy against temptation but pondering on how he could fulfil his desires instead, when Abba Apollo happened by, one of the finest of the elders; he deduced from his gloomy countenance that he was silently reflecting on some distressing and powerful temptations, and asked him why he was so depressed. At first, when the old man urged him gently, the younger was unable to give any reply at all, but Apollo realised increasingly that it was no light matter that he wanted to conceal in such silent sorrow, for he was unable to keep his face from showing it, and so pressed him more urgently for the cause of his hidden grief. Thus urged, he admitted that he was heading for the village, because the other elder had deemed him unable to be a monk, and that he was incapable of controlling the urges of the flesh and finding any cure for them, so he was going to look for a wife, abandon the monastic life and return to the world. The elder Apollo consoled him gently, admitting that he himself was troubled with the same sort of temptations and emotions every day, so that there was no need for him to give up, nor to be surprised at these passionate urges, which are overcome simply by the mercy and grace of God, not by sheer effort. He persuaded him to defer his departure for one day, and to return to his cell, while he went at once to the monastery of the aforesaid elder.

When he reached him he flung out his arms and burst into tears as he prayed, 'O Lord, who alone art the loving judge and the secret doctor of the hidden things of men and of all human weakness, transfer the temptations of that youth to this old man, so that he may learn in his old age how to be compassionate to the weakness of the labourer, and to understand the frailty of youth.' He had hardly finished this heartfelt prayer when he saw a loathly savage standing outside his cell and hurling fiery darts towards him. The old man was deeply wounded by these, and dashed out of his cell, running hither and thither like a drunkard or a fool, rushing in and out. Eventually, unable to remain still within, he began to set out on the same path that the young man had taken. Abba Apollo realised that he had been driven mad by the assaults of the furies, and understood that his heart had been penetrated by the devil's fiery dart, which he had watched being hurled towards him; this was causing his mental confusion and the disturbance of his senses by its intolerable burning. He approached him and said, 'Where are you heading for? For what reason have you forgotten your age and dignity? Why are you running around like a disturbed adolescent?' The other was so confused by his guilty conscience and base passions, that he imagined that the thoughts of his heart were revealed, but he concealed his inner thoughts from Apollo, not daring to give any reply to his urgent enquiry.

'Go back to your cell,' said Apollo, 'and be aware in future that up to now the devil has either failed to notice you or considered you beneath his contempt, not worth reckoning among those whom he is daily provoked to tempt and torment because of their progress in learning. Only one of his darts has reached you, and after wasting so many years in your profession you were unable even for a single day to endure it, let alone repel it! The reason why Our Lord allowed you to be wounded like that is so that at last in old age you might learn to sympathise with the weakness of others, and your own experience might teach you

II. On Discretion

to understand the frailty of youth. In dealing with a young monk suffering from the devil's attentions, you not only failed to console him and care for him, but you so depressed him that he despaired altogether. All you did was surrender him into the enemy's hands, for him to be tragically destroyed. The enemy would surely not have attacked him so fiercely, as he has just now condescended to assault you, had he not been envious of his future progress, and observed great virtue in his soul, so that he was quick to attempt to pervert him with his fiery darts. He assuredly recognised him to be the stronger, for he considered him worth the effort of such a violent attack.

'So now learn to be sympathetic to those in difficulties, after this experience; never drive the weak to despair nor rebuke them with rough words, but build them up with mild and gentle consolation. As Solomon the wise says, "Deliver them that are led to death: and those that are drawn to death forbear not to redeem" (Prov. 24: 11, LXX). Follow Our Lord who did not break the bruised reed, nor extinguish the smoking flax (cf. Matt. 12: 20). Beg that grace of the Lord that you too may be able to sing truthfully and in very fact, "The Lord hath given me a learned tongue, that I should know how to uphold by word him that is weary" (Isaiah 50: 4). For no one can endure the assaults of the enemy, no one can extinguish or repress the fires of the flesh which burn with a natural heat, unless the grace of God come to the aid of our weakness, protect us and strengthen us. Now that we have finished this salutary lesson, by means of which Our Lord wished firstly to free this youth from his dangerous trials, and then to teach you to about the strength of temptation and the need for compassion, let us all pray together that the Lord will order the removal of that scourge which he had allowed to be laid upon you for your benefit. "The Lord woundeth and cureth: he striketh, and his hands shall heal" (Job 5: 18), and "The Lord humbleth and he exalteth, he killeth and maketh alive: he bringeth down to hell and bringeth back again" (I Kings (I Sam.) 2: 6–7). Let him quench the burning darts of the enemy which at my instigation he permitted to inflict you, in the gift of the dew of his Spirit.'

And so, at the prayer of that old man, the Lord took away again the temptation which he had allowed to be so suddenly inflicted. That story clearly shows us that we should never rebuke someone for the sins he has confessed, nor easily despise the grief of one who suffers. Therefore do not allow the inexperience or shallowness of one man, or of a very few, to deter you and prevent you following the way handed down by our predecessors, even if the enemy has taken advantage of their old age to deceive the young. Never conceal anything through embarrassment, but confess everything to the elders, so that you may receive from them a remedy for your wounds, and an example from their faithful way of life. We shall receive a similar reward and experience the same result, as long as we so not attempt to do anything presuming on our own judgment.

XIV. "So pleasing to God is this teaching that we can see it recommended even in Holy Scripture, where the practice can be found deliberately inculcated. For instance, the Lord chose the boy Samuel to be a judge, but he did not want even him to learn from divine revelation on his own – no, he was to run to his master, Eli, again and again (I Kings (I Sam. 3)). Although it was the Lord who was calling him to hear, He wanted him to learn from the teaching of an older man, even one who had sinned against God. He preferred that one whom He deemed most worthy of his vocation should still receive his instruction from an elder, in order to demonstrate the humility of the one called to the service of God, and give the example of obedience to lay before those younger than him.

XV. "Paul also, was called by Christ himself, who spoke to him, and could have immediately given him all instruction in the way of perfection at once, but instead he was directed to Ananias and bidden learn the way of truth from him, in the words, 'Arise, and go into the city; and there it shall be told thee what thou must do' (Acts 9:7). Christ sent even Paul to an older man, to be instructed by his teaching rather than His own, lest what would have been right to do for Paul might become for others an example of presumption. Otherwise everyone might persuade themselves that in like manner they too could be instructed by the teaching of God alone rather than being trained by those older than themselves. St Paul himself tells us how detestable is this self-confidence, not only in his epistles but by his own example, for he tells us that he went up to Jerusalem for the sole purpose of conferring with his fellow apostles and those senior to himself, in a private intimate conversation, about the Gospel teaching which he had been proclaiming to the nations in the power of signs and wonders accompanied by the grace of the Holy Spirit. 'I conferred to them the gospel,' he says, 'the gospel which I preach among the gentiles; lest perhaps I should run or had run in vain' (Gal. 2:2). So who could be so blind and arrogant as to entrust himself to his own judgment and discretion, when the Vessel of Election admits that he himself needed to confer with his fellow apostles? It is abundantly clear from this that the Lord does not show anyone the way of perfection if he despises the teaching and practice of the elders, when he has the opportunity of being instructed by them, and if he treats with contempt that principle which he should have most carefully observed, 'Ask thy father, and he will declare to thee: thy elders and they will tell thee' (Deut. 32:7).

XVI. "With all our might we should strive for the prize of discretion through the virtue of humility, which is what preserves us unscathed from excess on either side. The old proverb goes, 'ends meet', in other words, extremes come to the same thing. Extremes in fasting and in gluttony both lead to the same conclusion, and unreasonable hours of wakefulness have the same effect on a monk as the torpor of sluggish sleep. Excess of self-denial inevitably leads to being so weakened that one falls into the same state as one who is careless and lax. Thus we often observe that those who could not be deluded through gluttony, have been brought to ruin through too much fasting; collapsing through weakness they have fallen into the very vice they had been fighting. Unreasonable watching and vigils have ruined some whom sleep could not conquer. Hence in St Paul's words, we must follow a moderate path, 'by the armour of justice on the right hand and on the left' (II Cor. 6:7). Moderated by discretion we must pass between both extremes, so that we do not let ourselves be carried away from the path of self-denial we have been bequeathed, nor fall through dangerous laxity into the lusts of the palate and the flesh.

XVII. "I remember myself that I often lost my appetite for food, until after two or three days without meals, not even the thought of eating came into my mind. I also denied myself sleep (at the devil's prompting!) until for several days and nights I had to pray the Lord to grant a little repose to my eyes, for I realised that I was in greater danger through lack of sleep and food than if I had yielded to greed and sloth. Just as we must be careful to avoid sliding into dissolute vice through the passion of fleshly desire, not indulging ourselves in food before the set time, nor presuming to take more than our due, in the same way we must renew our strength with food and rest at the proper time, even if we do not feel like it. Both extremes arise from the side of our enemy, and excessive self-denial can be more dangerous than unrestrained repletion, for it is possible to progress from the latter to moderation as our conscience gives us salutary discretion, whereas from too much self-restraint there is no escape."

XVIII. GERMANUS: "But what is the proper degree of self-restraint, so that we can proceed unharmed between the two extremes, and keep in sight that steady middle path?"

XIX. MOYSES: "We have heard our predecessors debate this matter many times. They discussed the merits of different views on self-restraint, between those who supported themselves on pulses alone, or on boiled vegetables, or fruit, and they suggested to everyone a diet simply of bread, saying the ideal quantity is two buns, that is to say small loaves weighing just about a pound."

XX. GERMANUS: "We are glad to hear it, but would reply that we can hardly consider that to be self-denial, for we would be unable to eat quite as much as that."

II. On Discretion

XXI. MOYSES: "If you wish to experience how rigorous this rule is, just keep to that measure, without taking the extra dish of vegetables on Sundays and Saturdays, not even on the excuse of a visiting brother; for when the flesh is fattened on these it will not only be able to exist on a lesser amount on other days, but it can even do without food altogether with no difficulty as long as it is supported by the addition of the food it has already received. But one who contents himself always with the aforesaid measure will be unable to do this, nor to defer taking food until the following day. In fact I remember our elders (and I myself have experienced the same, as I recall) kept up this degree of austerity only with great effort and difficulty, and by confining themselves to that measure felt such a hunger that they found it very difficult to set this limit to their eating, and not without tears and sighs.

XXII. "This is the usual standard for self-denial: according to a man's ability, his health and age, each should allow himself as much food as is necessary to sustain the body, not as much as his appetite demands. Either extreme would cause him great damage, for anyone who fails to keep to this moderation would alternate between constricting his digestion with starvation, and distending it through overeating. On the one hand a mind weakened through lack of food loses the strength to pray and is driven to sleep through the feebleness of an emaciated body; on the other hand if it is bloated with overeating it will be unable to pour forth before God a prayer that is pure and aspiring. Nor is it possible to preserve chaste purity continuously if moderation is not observed, for even on the days when one appears to mortify the flesh with stricter self-restraint, a meal taken previously continues to supply the body with the fuel of fleshly desire.

XXIII. "That which has once been generated in the body through excess of food must emerge somehow, and it is emitted naturally, for the human body cannot tolerate retaining an overabundance of any type of energy, which would be toxic and dangerous. Hence it is right and reasonable to restrain our body by austerity. Although as long as we exist in the body we cannot escape the necessities of nature, at least we can reduce this sort of emission to occur only infrequently, ideally not more than three times or so in a year. Even if this happens without any provocation during sleep, the dream is a reliable index of the sexual desire within. That is why what we have described is the proper degree and measure of self-denial, and it is approved by the opinion of the fathers: a daily ration of food accompanied by a daily hunger. This will preserve both soul and body in a state of equilibrity, so that we neither faint for weakness through fasting, nor burden the mind with excess. The result of such frugality is that after vespers one does not feel as though one remembered having eaten.

XXIV. "This cannot be achieved without effort, which is why those who do not know perfect discretion prefer to extend their fast for two days, and to keep for tomorrow what they should have eaten today, so that when they do come to eat they may gratify their appetite. You must be aware of your fellow countryman Benjamin, who did this obstinately; he refused to accept his two buns a day and keep to the regular discipline of steady self-restraint, but opted always to keep a fast on alternate days, so that when he came to eat he could fill his stomach with a double ration. He indulged his appetite in consuming four buns and by this repletion made up for his fasting on the other days. No doubt you remember how all this ended, he being so stubborn and determined to follow his own whims rather than the teaching of the elders – he abandoned the desert and returned to the empty philosophy of this world and the trivialities of the age. His case demonstrates the truth of the elders' doctrine, and his fall shows us all that no one who trusts in his own opinion and follows his own judgment can ever reach the pinnacle of perfection, nor elude the perilous wiles of the devil."

XXV. GERMANUS: "How may we observe this ration without interruption? For sometimes brothers arrive in the afternoon, after the statutory fast has been broken, and it is necessary either to take something additional to the set ration while entertaining them, or to fail badly in that charity which we are commanded to display to all."

XXVI. MOYSES: "Both considerations must be observed with equal attention. We must keep strictly to the ration of food for the sake of purity and self-restraint, and we must at the same time display charity and respect to visiting brethren for the love of God. It would be absurd if we were to offer a meal to a brother, as if to Christ, without partaking of it with him, or to hold ourselves aloof from him while he eats. Now we can escape fault on either side if we observe this custom: of the two buns which we are allotted at noon as the canonical ration, one should be eaten, the other reserved until the evening for the sake of the eventuality that a brother may arrive so that we can eat it with him. Thus we would add nothing to our usual amount, and would not be at all put out by the arrival of a brother, which should be an occasion of joy to us. We can offer him charitable hospitality without dispensing ourselves from our strict fast. Then if no one has arrived, we can freely consume the second bun as part of our due canonical ration. It will be light enough not to burden the stomach in the evening, since the other bun has already been consumed at noon, whereas those who imagine they are keeping the fast more strictly and defer the whole meal until the evening often suffer indigestion. A recent heavy meal prevents us from feeling light and fresh during evening or night prayer, which is why it is preferable and beneficial to appoint noon as the time for the meal. If a monk has eaten then, he will not only feel light and empty during the night vigils, but once his food has been digested, will be fresh also for the evening prayer."

In this manner the saintly Moyses taught us and nourished us in two courses; in the present conversation he explained to us about the grace and virtue of discretion, and in the previous one he taught us the reason and direction of self-denial, and the goal of our profession. Thus he shed a clearer light on what we had been seeking in simple spiritual fervour and the love of God but with closed eyes, as it were. He made us see how far we had wandered away during that time from purity of heart and the right line towards our goal, for the practice of any visible art of this world can only be pursued through following the proper direction, and cannot reach its goal without a clear knowledge of it.

✧ THE THIRD COLLATION ✧
BEING THAT OF ABBA PAPHNUTIUS

On the Three Renunciations

    I. On the way of life of Abba Paphnutius.
    II. On the discourse of that elder, and our response.
    III. The theory of Abba Paphnutius about three types of vocation, and three renunciations.
    IV. The explanation of the three vocations.
    V. How the first type of vocation is of no avail to the idle, and the last no disadvantage to the strong.
    VI. Of the three renunciations.
    VII. How we may seek the perfection of each renunciation.
    VIII. Of the true wealth, in which lies the beauty of a soul, or its defilement.
    IX. Of the threefold nature of riches.
    X. That no one can be perfect if he has made only the first step in renunciation.
    XI. A question, on man's free will and the grace of God.
    XII. The reply, on how God's grace is dispensed without destroying free will.
    XIII. That the direction of our path comes from God.
    XIV. How it is through the light of the Lord's teaching that knowledge of the Law is conferred.
    XV. How the understanding by which we can recognise the commandments of God, and the good will to perform them are both gifts from the Lord.
    XVI. How faith itself is a gift from God.

XVII. How moderation and the endurance of temptation are granted to us by the Lord.
XVIII. How the Lord grants us to have a perpetual fear of God.
XIX. How it is from the Lord that the beginning of good will and its performance come.
XX. How nothing in this world can be done without God.
XXI. An objection, on the force of free will.
XXII. The reply, that our free will ever requires the help of the Lord.

I. In that choir of saints, who shone in the night of this world like brilliant stars, we observed Saint Paphnutius glittering with the light of knowledge like a star of the first magnitude. He was a priest of our congregation (that is to say the one situated in the desert of Scete) and lived there until old age. Although it was five miles away from the church, he never moved away from the cell which he began to inhabit as a novice to somewhere nearer; despite the weariness of his years he never grumbled about that long walk every Saturday and Sunday, nor was he content to return empty handed, but he carried back to his cell, on his shoulders, the pot of water which was to last him the whole week. Although he had passed his ninetieth birthday, he never allowed a younger monk to take that work on himself.

In his youth he had applied himself so diligently to the monastery school that after a short time there he was enriched equally in good obedience and in knowledge of all virtue. He mortified all his passions through the practice of humility and obedience, and thereby eliminated all vice, to grow in all the virtues inculcated by the profession of monasticism and the teaching of the earliest fathers. Even while he dwelt among a crowd of brothers, he had been athirst to be inseparably united to the Lord, and so, fired with the longing to progress further, he soon explored the furthermost desert so that he might be more easily united to his Lord, without any further human company to hinder him. Here

III. On the Three Renunciations

too he surpassed even the strength of the hermits, so great was his zeal, in his intense longing for the pure contemplation of the divine; he shunned all company and penetrated into even wilder and more remote desert places, where he lived for many years, so that even the hermits only saw him occasionally and with difficulty. It was believed that he enjoyed the daily company of angels, and in token of that privilege they conferred upon him the name of Wild Ox.

II. We were eager to learn from the teaching of that master, and so we arrived at his cell with our thoughts in a whirl, just as day was drawing to a close. After a short silence, he began to inquire about our intentions, and the reason why we had left our fatherland, had travelled across so many provinces for the love of the Lord, had endured want and the solitude of the desert and were so determined to imitate an austerity of life which those who were born and brought up in that state of poverty and need could scarcely endure. We answered that we had sought him out as a teacher and master, so that from such a great man we could drink in the perfect instruction which we knew, from what many had told us, lay within him. We did not want to be burdened with his praise, for there was nothing in us to merit that, nor did we need a discourse from him to inflate our conceit, for the enemy had often enough plagued us with that when we were in our own cells. Therefore we begged him to tell us something to strike us and humiliate us, not something which we could be proud or boastful about.

III. The holy Paphnutius began thus, "There are three types of vocation, and three renunciations which we know to be necessary for a monk in whichever type of calling he be. Now we must begin by looking carefully at the reason why we have said there are three types of vocation. If we claim that we have been called by the first type to dedicate ourselves to God, our behaviour should be in accordance with that dignity, for it would be of no use to have made a sublime start if we do not reach a conclusion to match our beginning. If on the other hand we know that we have been drawn out of this world by the very lowest type of vocation, the less worthy the beginning we have made to our religious life, the more effort we shall need to make if we are to bring ourselves zealously to a better conclusion. We should also take care to learn about the second subject, the threefold renunciation, for we shall never be able to reach perfection if we are ignorant of this, or if we make no effort to put into practice what we know.

IV. "I will explain each of these three types of vocation distinctly. The first is from God, the second through men, the third by necessity. A vocation comes from God when our heart is inspired, sometimes even when we are asleep, and we are roused to a longing for eternal life and salvation, urged by a truly perfect conscience to follow God, and to adhere to his commands. In the Holy Scriptures we read of the call of Abraham, at the voice of the Lord, to leave his native land, the affection of all his kin and his father's house. 'Go forth out of thy country,' said the Lord, 'and from thy kindred, and out of thy father's house' (Gen. 12:1). Saint Antony, as we know, was called in the same way, and received his vocation from God alone. He went into church and heard the Gospel where Our Lord says, 'He who hates not his father and mother and wife and children [and lands], yea and his own life also, he cannot be my disciple' (Luke 14:26), and, 'if thou wilt be perfect, go sell what thou hast and give to the poor and thou shalt have treasure in heaven. And come, follow me' (Matt. 19:21). He took this counsel of the Lord as if it was directed to himself in particular; with whole-hearted repentence he at once renounced all his property and followed Christ, without any human suggestion, encouragement or direction.

The second type of vocation is, as we said, through men, when we are fired with the desire of salvation through the example of certain holy men, or at the initiative of a teacher. In this case too we recognise that the call comes through the grace of God, although it is because of the teaching and virtues of these men that we surrender ourselves to the profession of this way of life. This too we can see in Sacred Scripture, when the children of Israel were liberated from captivity in Egypt through Moses (Exod. 14).

The third type of vocation is that which derives from necessity, when we have been entangled in the riches and pleasures of this world, and then trials suddenly come upon us. We may be threatened with death, or the loss of goods and reputation, or struck by the death of those we love, so that we are compelled to run to the Lord whom we had disdained to follow while things went well for us. We find many passages of Scripture about this involuntary vocation, such as when we read of the Lord handing the children of Israel over to their enemies because of their sins, and of how they turned back to the Lord again because of their cruel and savage treatment. 'The Lord raised them up,' it says, 'a saviour called Aod, the son of Gera, the son of Jemini, who used the left hand as well as the right.' And again, 'They cried to the Lord who raised them up a saviour, Othoniel the son of Cenez, the younger brother of Caleb' (Judges 3: 15, 9). The psalmist says the same sort of thing, 'When he slew them, then they sought him: and they returned, and came to him early in the morning. And they remembered that God was their helper; and the Most High God their Redeemer' (Psalm 77/78: 34–5). And again, 'They cried to the Lord in their affliction: and he delivered them out of their distresses' (Psalm 106/107: 19).

V. "Of these three types of vocation, albeit the first would seem to depend on the best principles, we do occasionally find perfect men, full of the fervour of the spirit, among those of the third type, although it seems to be so poor and unreliable. Comparable to those who had entered the Lord's service for the best of reasons, they pass the remainder of their lives in praiseworthy zeal. Likewise there are those who decline from the first rank into tepidity and they often come to a sad end. The former took no harm from the fact that they had been converted by necessity, rather than by an act of their own will, in as much as it was the goodness of the Lord that provided the occasion for their repentence; the latter gained no advantage from having more sublime reasons for their vocation, if they took no care during the rest of their lives to reach a fitting conclusion.

It was no disadvantage in the quest for perfect bliss that the Abba Moyses (the one who lived in the part of the desert that is called Calamus) fled to the monastery in fear of his life, being under a charge of manslaughter. He took such advantage of his forced conversion that he changed it into a willing one in his eager zeal, and so he attained the very pinnacle of perfection. There are others whom I will not name who have profited nothing from entering the Lord's service with a better will, for they afterwards became lazy and hardened in heart, fell into sinful sloth and plunged into the depths of hell. We can see this point clearly in the call of the Apostles – what benefit was the exalted rank of Apostle to Judas? He had willingly accepted the same dignity that Peter and the other apostles held, but having begun his vocation in such a splendid way he spoilt it through greed and the love of money, and brought it to a vile conclusion, breaking out in savage ingratitude, and betraying his own Lord. Or what disadvantage was it to Paul that he was suddenly blinded and called to the way of salvation as if he were unwilling, for he followed the Lord ever after in such fervour that he perfected his first compulsion through willing devotion, and brought his life, resplendent in such great virtues, to an incomparable conclusion? It all depends on the conclusion; that is how we can discern whether one who was at first consecrated in the best of intentions, has come to grief through negligence, or one who was drawn to the profession of monk through need, has made the most of it and come to perfection through the fear of God and through love.

VI. "Now we must treat of the renunciations, which the authority of the Fathers and Holy Scripture declare to be three in number, and each one of us must fulfil them all. The first is to renounce all material riches and worldly power. The second is to repudiate the former manners, vices and attachments of soul and body. The third is to withdraw our thoughts from all temporal and visible things, to consider only the things to come, and to desire only what is invisible. We read that the Lord called Abraham himself to perform all three renunciations at once, when he said to him, 'Go forth out of thy country, and from thy kindred, and out of thy father's house' (Gen. 12:1). First he says 'out of thy country', that is from power in this world and earthly wealth. Then 'from thy kindred', that is from the previous way of life, the customs and vices which cling to us from our birth and are as familiar as relations and family. Thirdly, 'out of thy father's house', that is from any memory of this world which may come before our eyes.

We hear God speaking to us through David about the two fathers, namely the one we are leaving behind and the one we should seek, in the psalm, 'Hearken, O daughter, and see, and incline thy ear: and forget thy people and thy father's house' (Psalm 44/45:11). The one who says 'hearken, O daughter' must be her true father, but he shows us that the one of whom he says she should forget both house and people was also truly a father to his daughter. This happens when we are, like Christ, purged from the attachments of this world, and as St Paul says, we 'look not at the things which are seen, but at the things which are not seen. For the things which are seen are temporal; but the things which are not seen are eternal' (II Cor. 4:18). As spiritually we come out of this temporary and visible home, we direct our eyes and thoughts into that home in which we are to dwell for ever. We shall achieve this if, while we are living in the flesh, we begin to serve the Lord not according to the flesh, making the words of St Paul our own, in very fact, 'Our conversation is in heaven' (Phil. 3:20).

These three renunciations match the three books of Solomon: Proverbs relates to the first renunciation, for by them we may cut off the desire of earthly things and the vices of this world; Ecclesiastes tells of the second renunciation, for in it everything we do under the sun is described under the heading of vanity; the Song of Songs speaks of the third, for there our thoughts transcend all visible things and in the contemplation of heaven are united to the Word of God.

VII. "It will not be of much use to us to have made the first renunciation in all enthusiasm and faith, if we do not pursue the second with the same care and zeal. Once we have attained this, we may proceed in turn to the third, for we can apply all our thoughts to the matters of heaven, leaving the home of our first father. By that I mean the one who was our father from our birth according to the old nature and our former way of life, when we were by nature 'children of wrath even as the rest' (Eph. 2:3). We remember that he had been our father, but we have now directed our whole thoughts towards heaven. It is of this paternity that it was said of Jerusalem, which had spurned God her true father, 'Thy father was an Amorrhite and thy mother a Cethite' (Ezech. 16:3), and in the Gospel, 'You are of your father the devil; and the desires of your father you will do' (John 8:44). When we dismiss him, we pass from visible things to the invisible, and can say with the Apostle, 'We know, if our earthly house of this habitation be dissolved, that we have a building of God, a house not made with hands, eternal in heaven' (II Cor. 5:1). And to continue what we quoted earlier, 'Our conversation is in heaven; from whence also we look for the Saviour, our Lord Jesus Christ, who will reform the body of our lowness, made like to the body of his glory' (Phil. 3:20–1). The Psalmist also says, 'I am a stranger on the earth, a sojourner as all my fathers were' (Psalm 38/39:4 and 118/119:19). We shall become like those of whom Our Lord says to his Father in the Gospel, 'They are not of the world, as I also am not of the world' (John 17:16). Again he speaks to the apostles, 'If you had been of the world, the world would love its own; but because you are not of the world, but I have chosen you out of the world, therefore the world hateth you' (John 15:19).

We shall be fit to attain the perfection of this third renunciation when our thoughts are no longer burdened by contact with gross flesh, but after assiduous self-denial have become free from all earthly affections. By prolonged meditation on the Holy Scriptures and spiritual considerations, they have turned towards the invisible, to the extent that they are no longer aware of being wrapped in frail flesh and located in the body, attentive now only to the nonmaterial things above. The mind is caught up into such a degree of abstraction that it is unaware of any physically audible sound, and unconcerned by the memories of men long past; it does not even notice with physical sight great obstacles and vast material objects. No one can understand the truth and purpose of this except one who has observed in his own experience what I have told you. The Lord calls his mental gaze away from all present matters, so that he considers them to be not just passing away but virtually past, and sees how they dissipate into nothingness like empty smoke. Like Enoch he walks with God, and is caught up from the ways and dealings of men so that he is not found among the trivialities of this age. We read in Genesis about Enoch, how this happened to him in the body: 'Enoch walked with God, and he was not found, because God had caught him up' (Gen. 5:24, LXX). St Paul also says, 'by faith Enoch was translated that he should not see death' (Heb. 11:5). Of that death, Our Lord speaks in the Gospel, 'every one that liveth and believeth in me shall not die for ever' (John 11:26).

We must therefore, if we would achieve true perfection, be quick to renounce our family, our fatherland, the riches of this world and its pleasures, eliminating these things from our hearts as well, and never allowing our desires to dwell on those things again. It is said of the men whom Moses led out, albeit they never returned physically, that their minds had gone back to Egypt, for they abandoned God who had brought them out with such signs and wonders, and worshipped the idols of Egypt which they had repudiated. As Scripture tells us, 'in their hearts they turned back into Egypt, saying to Aaron: Make us gods to go before us' (Acts 7:39–40). Let us not be condemned with those who tarried in the desert, and after eating the bread of heaven began to long to feed on all sorts of shameful things; let us not grumble as they grumbled, 'It was well with us in Egypt, when we sat over the fleshpots, the cucumbers come into our mind, and the melons, and the leeks, and the onions and the garlic' (Exod. 16:3, Num. 11:5, 18). What happened as a type long ago among that people, is now fulfilled daily among those of our order and vocation. Anyone who returns to his old interests after renouncing the world, and is called back by his previous desires is in effect crying out in his heart with them, 'It was well with us in Egypt'. I am afraid there are quite as many who do this as we read there were in the crowds of murmurers under Moses. Six hundred thousand armed men were counted leaving Egypt, and of these no more than two survived to enter the Promised Land.

We must therefore be quick to learn from those few rare examples of virtue, for just as in the type we have been discussing, so in the Gospel we find, 'Many are called, but few are chosen' (Matt. 22:14). Renunciation of material things will not be of any use to us, nor will the leaving of Egypt in geographical terms, unless we are able to achieve that renunciation of heart which is greater and more availing. Of the physical renunciation, St Paul speaks thus, 'If I should distribute all my goods to feed the poor, and if I should deliver my body to be burned, and have not charity, it profiteth me nothing' (I Cor. 13:3). The holy Apostle would not have said that had he not foreseen in the spirit that there would be those who had given all their possessions to feed the poor but were unable to reach the perfection of the Gospel and the high summit of charity, precisely because they retained their former vices and their unrestrained behaviour in their hearts, as pride or intolerance ruled them. Never taking pains to rid themselves of these, they failed to attain the Charity of God which never fails. Having fallen short at this second step of renunciation, they made still less progress towards the third, which is far superior.

Ponder more carefully over this: St Paul did not only say, 'If I should distribute goods', for it might appear that he was talking of one who has not even fulfilled the Gospel counsel entirely, but was keeping back something for himself, as do a number of the lukewarm; no, he says, 'If I should distribute all my goods to feed the poor', that is even if I have totally renounced the riches of this world. And to that renunciation he adds another greater one, 'And if I should deliver my body to be burned, and have not charity, it profiteth me nothing'. He is talking in effect about one who had distributed all his possessions to feed the poor, according to that counsel of the Gospel, which says, 'If thou wilt be perfect, go sell what thou hast and give to the poor and thou shalt have treasure in heaven. And come follow me' (Matt. 19:21). If I had renounced everything, reserving nothing for myself, and in addition to this had suffered martyrdom, the burning up of my flesh, yeilding up my body for Christ; yet had I been impatient, irritable, jealous or proud, or gratified when others suffer, or grasping of my own rights, or plotting evil, or failing to endure all events with patience and goodwill, then it would have been of no avail to have made that external renunciation and martyrdom while the interior was still caught up in ancient vices. Repudiating in the first fervour of conversion the basic goods of this world, which are in themselves neither good nor evil but neutral, I would have failed to take steps to eliminate the poisonous elements of a vicious heart, or to achieve that charity of Our Lord which 'is patient, is kind; envieth not, is not puffed up, is not ambitious, seeketh not her own, thinketh no evil, beareth all things, endureth all things' (I Cor. 13:4–7), and in short will never allow those who pursue it to fall into the clutches of sin.

VIII. "Now we must make every effort to ensure that our inner self rejects and repels the wealth of vice which it had accumulated during our former life, and which is truly our own, clinging tightly to body and soul. If we do not repudiate the vices and eliminate them while we are still in this body, they will not leave us in peace even after death. In the same way the virtues and charity herself which is their source, if we acquire them in this world, will render those who love them splendid and radiant after this life is over, just as vice defiles the thoughts with unsightly stains and transmits them into eternity thus disfigured. The beauty of a soul, or its defilement, depend on its virtues or its vices. The tint we take from them either makes the soul radiant and beautiful, fit to hear from the psalmist, 'The king shall greatly desire thy beauty' (Psalm 44/45:12), or renders it dark, foul and deformed, so that the soul admits the corruption of its own decay, saying, 'my sores are putrified and corrupted, because of my foolishness' (Psalm

37/38: 6). The Lord himself asks, 'Why is not the wound of the daughter of my people closed?' (Jerem. 8: 22). This is the wealth that truly belongs to us, which is attached to the soul and lives on, and which neither emperor nor enemy can confer on us nor take away. This is the wealth which not even death can take away from the soul. If we renounce this wealth, we may attain to perfection, if we cling to it we shall suffer death eternal.

IX. "Holy Scripture teaches us that there are three types of riches, namely good, evil and indifferent. Evil ones are those of which it is said, 'The rich have wanted, and have suffered hunger' (Psalm 33/34: 11), and 'Woe to you that are rich; for you have your consolation' (Luke 6: 24). It is rejecting this sort of riches that is the height of perfection. These are the poor whom Our Lord refers to in the Gospel, when he praises them saying, 'Blessed are the poor in spirit, for theirs is the kingdom of heaven' (Matt. 5: 3). And in the Psalm, 'This poor man cried and the Lord heard him' (Psalm 33/34: 7) and again, 'The poor and needy shall praise thy name' (Psalm 73/74: 21).

Good riches are those which are acquired through great virtue and merit, which as David says a just man is praised for possessing, 'The generation of the righteous shall be blessed, glory and wealth shall be in his house: and his justice remaineth for ever and ever' (Psalm 111/112: 2–3). And again, 'The ransom of a man's life are his riches' (Prov. 13: 8, LXX). In the Apocalypse we read of these riches that he who does not possess them is poor and bare. 'I will begin to vomit thee out of my mouth. Because thou sayest: I am rich and made wealthy and have need of nothing; and knowest not that thou art wretched and miserable and poor and blind and naked. I counsel thee to buy of me gold, fire-tried, that thou mayest be made rich and mayest be clothed in white garments; and that the shame of thy nakedness may not appear' (Apoc. 3: 16–18).

Indifferent riches are those which are capable of being either good or bad, depending on the intention and character of those who use them. St Paul says of these, 'Charge the rich of this world not to be highminded nor to trust in the uncertainty of riches, but

III. On the Three Renunciations

in the living God who giveth us abundantly all things to enjoy. To do good; to be rich in good works; to give easily, to communicate to others; to lay up in store for themselves a good foundation against the time to come, that they may hold on the true life' (I Tim. 6:17–19). But this is the wealth which that rich man in the Gospel horded up and never assisted the poor with it, from whose crumbs the poor Lazarus at his doors longed to fill himself – but the rich man was condemned to the unbearable fire of hell and eternal woe (cf. Luke 16:19–31).

X. "Once we have repudiated the visible wealth of this world, we shall have left behind not our own property but that of others, however much we might boast of how we had amassed it through our efforts or inherited it from our parents. But as I have said, nothing is our own save what we possess in the heart, what cleaves to the soul, what no one can possibly take from us. Christ speaks about these visible riches to those who cling to them as if they were their own, reluctant to share them with the needy, rebuking them as follows: 'If you have not been faithful in that which is another's, who will give you that which is your own?' (Luke 16:12). It is not only our daily experience that shows us that these riches belong to others, but Our Lord's words as well, naming them thus. Peter too spoke to the Lord about these vile visible riches, 'Behold, we have left all things and have followed thee; what therefore shall we have?' (Matt. 19:27). But indeed they left nothing more, surely, than some cheap nets, and those in need of repair. When he says 'all things' we must understand this to mean the renunciation of vice, which is truly a great thing, for we do not read that the apostles left behind any material property, any more than the Lord did, of sufficient value that He might promise them the grant of such a reward of glory. Yet they were worthy to hear him say, 'in the regeneration when the Son of Man shall sit on the seat of his majesty, you also shall sit on twelve seats judging the twelve tribes of Israel' (Matt. 19:28). Now if even those who have perfectly renounced earthly visible wealth are still not able by their own efforts to rise to the third and highest degree of renunciation, which so few achieve, what opinion of themselves should they have who have not even achieved the first and easiest step, but retain their previous base wealth along with their previous lack of faith, having nothing to boast of but the bare name of monk?

As we have said, the first renunciation is that of extraneous things, and of itself is insufficient to confer perfection unless one progress to the second, which is renouncing what really is our own. By this step we eliminate all vices, and so we may ascend the third step of renunciation on which we spurn not only all worldly affairs and all material human possessions, but also the whole range of attributes which are supposed to be so splendid, treating them as frivolities soon to pass away. Rising above all these in mind and heart, we may look, as the Apostle says, 'not at the things which are seen, but at the things which are not seen. For the things which are seen are temporal; but the things which are not seen are eternal' (II Cor. 4:18). Thus we may be fit to hear the great promise that was made to Abraham, 'Come into the land which I shall show thee' (Gen. 12:1).

It is clear enough from this that unless you perform the three renunciations we have described wholeheartedly, it is impossible to arrive at the fourth step, which is the grant of a reward and prize for making the renunciation, that is to say, being declared fit to enter the land of promise. That land is totally free from the seeds of thorns and briars of vice, for it is possessed in purity of heart, after all passions have been expelled from the body. It is not our own virtue or effort that reveals it, but the Lord himself promises that he will show it us: 'Come,' he says, 'into the land which I shall show thee.' This makes it clear that the our salvation begins and originates in the Lord's call, for he says, 'Come out of thy country', and also that the pinnacle of our perfect purity must be attributed to him, for he says, 'Come into the land which I shall show thee', that is, not a land which you can discover for yourself or find by your own cleverness, but one which I will show you though you are ignorant of it and not even looking for it. You can surely understand that it is at the Lord's invitation that we run on the way of salvation, led along it by His guidance and light, until we arrive at the perfection of all bliss."

XI. GERMANUS: "Where then is our free will? What of our works which are considered so praiseworthy, if God both initiates and concludes everything necessary for our perfection?"

XII. PAPHNUTIUS: "This would be a serious objection if any work or discipline were to involve no more than a beginning and an end, and there were no means in the middle. Now we know that God operates in different ways for our salvation, and our part is to take advantage of the means God has given us, or to fail to do so. God took the initiative in calling, 'Come out of thy country', and Abraham responded with obedience. Just as 'into the land' demanded the response of action, so 'which I shall show thee' shows that is the grace of God which both commands and promises. We must be clear that although we make every effort to practice the virtues, nevertheless we can never achieve perfection by our own application. Human endeavour and work is quite incapable of earning the reward of such bliss except in as much as that the Lord cooperates with us, and guides the heart to where it should be until we achieve it. We should pray moment by moment with King David, 'Perfect thou my goings in thy paths: that my footsteps be not moved' (Psalm 16/17: 5), and 'he set my feet upon a rock: and directed my steps' (Psalm 39: 3). Through ignorance of the good or subjection to passion our will tends rapidly towards sin, but the invisible guide of human thoughts is pleased to divert them towards virtue. One little verse of the Psalms shows us that clearly enough: 'being pushed I was overturned that I might fall', which describes the weakness of free will, 'but the Lord supported me' (Psalm 117/118: 13). Here too we see how the help of the Lord is ever granted, for when our free will is about to bring us down, and we seem to be tempted, the Lord puts forth his hand to hold us up and strengthen us. In another place, 'If I said: my foot is moved', that is to say tripped by my own free will, 'thy mercy, O Lord, assisted me' (Psalm 93/94: 18). Here too he links the Lord's help with his own wavering, admitting that it needed the mercy of God, not his own endeavour, to prevent his foot from slipping. Again, 'According to the multitude of my sorrows in my heart', arising indeed from my own free choice, 'thy comforts have given joy to my soul' (Psalm 93/94:19). These comforts have entered my heart through your inspiration, and implanted there the consideration of good things to come, the things which you have prepared for those who do good works in your name; they have taken away all grief from my heart, and brought the greatest joy instead. Again, 'Unless the Lord had been my helper: my soul had almost dwelt in hell' (Psalm 93/94:17), he admits that he would have been destined for the pit through the depravity of his free will, had he not been saved by the Lord's assistance. 'With the Lord', indeed, not by human choice, 'shall the steps of a man be directed.' And when the just man, through his own choice, 'falls, he shall not be bruised', why? 'for the Lord putteth his hand under him' (Psalm 36/37:23–4). This clearly declares that no man is righteous enough to earn his own salvation, unless in his loving kindness God were to give his hand to support him in his temptations and peril, otherwise he would fall headlong into destruction, tripped by the weakness of his freewill.

XIII. "The holy men of old never claimed that it was through their own efforts that they successfully followed their path towards the acquisition of virtue and its perfection, but they tell us that they begged the help of God, saying, 'Direct me in thy truth' (Psalm 24/25:5), and 'direct my way in thy sight' (Psalm 5:9). Another writer declares that he came to understand this, not just through faith but through experience, and observing the nature of things; 'I know, O Lord, that the way of a man is not his: neither is it in a man to walk and to direct his steps' (Jerem. 10:23). And the Lord himself says to Israel, 'I will hear him and I will make him flourish; from me is thy fruit found' (Hosea 14:9).

XIV. "Even the knowledge of the Law which they daily sought to acquire, comes not through diligent reading, but in the light of

III. On the Three Renunciations

God's teaching, for they say to him, 'Show, O Lord, thy ways to me, and teach me thy paths' (Psalm 24/25: 4). And 'Open thou my eyes: and I will consider the wondrous things of thy law' (Psalm 118/119: 18) and 'Teach me to do thy will, for thou art my God' (Psalm 142/143: 10) and again thou art 'he that teacheth man knowledge' (Psalm 93/94: 10).

XV. "King David begs the Lord to grant him the understanding by which he could recognise the commandments of God, despite knowing that they are written in the Book of the Law, for he says, 'I am thy servant; give me understanding that I may know thy testimonies' (Psalm 118/119: 125). Surely he already possessed understanding by nature, and could easily have discovered the commandments of God as they are described in the Law, but still he begs the Lord to help him understand them better, knowing that his natural abilities would be quite insufficient to do so without daily enlightenment by God; only thus could his mind be given the insight to understand the spiritual meaning of the Law, and clearly recognise his commandments.

The Chosen Vessel also clearly teaches what we have been saying, 'It is God who worketh in you, both to will and to accomplish, according to his good will' (Phil. 2: 13). [And again, 'Understand what I say; for the Lord will give thee in all things understanding' (II Tim. 2: 7).] Is it not obvious that he is saying that both our own good will and the ability to complete the work are instilled in us by the Lord? Here again, 'For unto you it is given for Christ, not only to believe in him, but also to suffer for him' (Phil. 1: 29). Here too he declares that from God come both the beginning of our conversion in faith and our endurance of suffering.

David also understood this and prayed that the Lord would give him this same grace, saying 'Command thy strength, O God: confirm what thou hast wrought in us' (Psalm 67/68: 29). He shows us that the first step towards salvation, granted him by the grace of God, would not suffice were it not brought to perfection through the same grace and continual assistance. Not our own free will, but 'The Lord looseth them that are fettered'; not our strength, but 'The Lord lifteth up them that are cast down'; not the effort we make in study but 'The Lord enlighteneth the blind'. (In the Greek it reads *kyrios sophoi typhlous*, 'the Lord maketh the blind wise'); not our precautions but 'The Lord keepeth the stranger'; not our courage but 'The Lord lifteth up (or supporteth) all that fall' (Psalms 145/146: 7–9, 144/145: 14).

We say these things, not to deny the value of our study, our work, and the efforts we make as if they were pointless and unnecessary, but so that we may recognise that without the help of God we cannot even attempt, let alone succeed by our works in attaining such a great prize of purity, were it not granted to us by the merciful help of the Lord. 'For the horse is prepared for the day of battle, but the Lord giveth assistance' (Prov. 21: 31, LXX), 'because no man shall prevail by his own strength' (I Kings (I Sam.), 2: 9, LXX) [and 'vain is the horse for safety' (Psalm 32/34: 17), so that 'He that glorieth may glory in the Lord' (I Cor. 1: 31)]. We should always sing, with King David, 'My strength and my praise are' – not my free will, but – 'the Lord, who is become my salvation' (Psalm 117/118: 14). This too the Teacher of the Nations knew well, and declares that he was made a fitting minister of the New Testament not by his own merits and works, but through the mercy of God: 'not that we are sufficient to think anything of ourselves, as of ourselves; but our sufficiency is from God'. (We could translate it less elegantly but more literally as 'Our suitability is from God'.) And he continues, 'who also hath made us fit ministers of the New Testament' (II Cor. 3: 5–6).

XVI. "The Apostles realised that everything necessary for salvation was granted them by the Lord, to the extent that they considered faith itself to have been his gift. They said 'Lord: increase our faith' (Luke 17: 5), for they were not so arrogant as to imagine that the fulness of faith came from their own choice, but knew it to be conferred on them by God. The Author of human salvation teaches us the same, showing how weak and fickle our faith is, quite inadequate without the help of the Lord to strengthen it; for he said to Peter, 'Simon, Simon, behold, Satan hath desired

III. On the Three Renunciations 73

to have you, that he may sift you as wheat, but I have prayed for thee, that thy faith fail not' (Luke 22:31–2). There was another who realised this in himself, and saw his faith as it were on the verge of final shipwreck in the waves of disbelief; for he begged Our Lord to support his faith: 'Lord, help my unbelief' (Mark 9:23). All the apostolic men of the Gospel were vividly aware that everything that is good stems from the help of the Lord, and admitted that their own faith was incapable of remaining firm through their own will and effort alone, for they asked the Lord to grant them faith and to strengthen it. If Peter himself needed the help of God lest he fail, who could be so arrogant or foolish as to imagine that he did not need the Lord's help daily to preserve his faith? Especially when Our Lord himself expressly states it in the Gospel; 'As the branch cannot bear fruit of itself, unless it abide in the vine, so neither can you, unless you abide in me', and again, 'Without me you can do nothing' (John 15:4–5). How stupid and blasphemous it is to attribute any good works to our own ability and not to the helping grace of God, is abundantly proved by the Lord's own teaching that no one can produce any good spiritual fruit without the inspiration and co-operation of God. 'Every best gift and every perfect gift is from above, coming down from the Father of lights' (James 1:17). And Zachariah also says, 'For what is the good thing? it is of him, and what is the beautiful thing? it is from him' (Zach. 9:17, LXX). St Paul is consistent in teaching this: 'What hast thou that thou hast not received? And if thou hast received, why dost thou glory, as if thou hadst not received it?' (I Cor. 4:7).

XVII. "St Paul also tells us that the great endurance by which we can resist temptation consists not in our own fortitude but in the mercy of God, and his guidance. 'Let no temptation take hold on you, but such as is human. And God is faithful, who will not suffer you to be tempted above that which you are able, but will make also with temptation issue, that you may be able to bear it' (I Cor. 10:13). The same Apostle teaches us that God adapts our minds and strengthens them for all good works, and performs in us the things which are pleasing to himself: 'And may the God of peace, who brought again from the dead the great pastor of the sheep, our Lord Jesus Christ, in the blood of the everlasting testament, fit you in all goodness, that you may do his will, doing in you that which is pleasing in his sight' (Heb. 13: 20–1). He writes to the Thessalonicans also, praying for the same outcome: 'Now our Lord Jesus Christ himself, and God and our Father who hath loved us and hath given us everlasting consolation and good hope in grace, exhort your hearts and confirm you in every good work and word' (II Thess. 2: 15–16).

XVIII. "That the very fear of God, which enables us to hold firm to him, is instilled in us by the Lord, is clearly shown by the prophet Jeremiah, speaking in the person of God: 'I will give them one heart and one way, that they may fear me all days: and that it may be well with them and with their children after them. And I will make an everlasting covenant with them and will not cease to do them good: and I will give my fear in their heart, that they may not revolt from me' (Jer. 32: 39–40). Ezechiel also says, 'I will give them one heart and will put a new spirit in their bowels: and I will take away the stony heart out of their flesh and will give them a heart of flesh: that they may walk in my commandments and keep my judgments and do them: and that they may be my people, and I may be their God' (Ezek. 11: 19–20).

XIX. "These texts show us clearly first that the beginning of the will to good is granted us by the inspiration of the Lord, when he calls us to the way of salvation, either directly, or through the preaching of some man, or by sheer necessity; secondly that the perfection of our virtue also stems from him in the same way. Our own part is this: to follow the teaching and help of God. It is how we do this, either diligently or not, that determines whether we merit either a reward or a fitting punishment. That depends on whether we have neglected his kind and providential plans for our happiness, or have taken pains to co-operate with them in loving obedience. This point is clearly set out in Deuteronomy: 'When the

III. On the Three Renunciations

Lord thy God shall have brought thee into the land, which thou art going in to possess, and shall have destroyed many nations before thee: the Hethite, and the Gergezite, and the Amorrhite, and the Chanaanite, and the Pherezite, and the Hevite, and the Jebusite: seven nations much more numerous than thou art, and stronger than thou: and shall have delivered them to thee: thou shalt utterly destroy them. Thou shalt make no league with them, nor make marriages with them' (Deut. 7:1–3).

Scripture tells us that it is through the grace of God that they were led into the land of promise, that many nations were destroyed before them, and that more numerous nations were delivered into their hands, nations stronger than the people of Israel. But we are told that it was up to Israel whether they would strike them to their destruction, or preserve them and spare them, whether they would strike a covenant with them, and intermarry with them or not. You can see clearly enough from this passage how much we should attribute to free will, how much to the dispensation and daily help of God. It is through God's grace that the opportunities for salvation are given, and events turn out favourable to our victory; whereas it is our part to follow up the benefits God has granted us, whether in eagerness or sloth.

You can see this point in the story of the healing of the blind men. The fact that Jesus passed before them was an act of divine grace and providence. That they called out, saying 'O Lord, thou Son of David, have mercy on us!' (Matt. 20:31) is the work of their faith and trust. That they received their sight was the gift of divine mercy. We can see how both the grace of God and the exercise of free will remain after the reception of a gift from the story of the ten lepers who were cured together (Luke 17:11 ff.). Of them only one used his free will to return and give thanks properly; the Lord enquired after the nine, and commended the one, showing that he continues to benefit even those who do not remember his goodness. This too is a gift, on his initiative, that he welcomes and praises the thankful one, and enquires after and chides the ungrateful.

XX. "We must believe with a firm faith that nothing at all can be done in this world without God. We have to admit that everything that happens is either at his will or with his permission; that is to say, good things are done at the will and with the help of God, bad things with his permission. When the divine protection is withdrawn from us because of our wickedness and hardness of heart, the devil or the vile passions of the flesh are allowed to dominate us. The Apostle teaches this clearly enough, saying, 'For this cause, God delivered them up to shameful affection, and again, 'as they liked not to have God in their knowledge, God delivered them up to a reprobate sense, to do those things which are not convenient' (Rom. 1: 26, 28). The Lord himself spoke through the prophet, 'My people heard not my voice: and Israel hearkened not to me. So I let them go according to the desires of their heart: they shall walk in their own inventions.'" (Psalm 80/81: 12–13).

XXI. GERMANUS: "Surely this same text undeniably proves free will, for it goes on, 'If my people had heard me', and, 'my people heard not my voice' (Psalm 80/81: 14, 12). When it says 'If they had heard me', it shows that it was in their power to accept or to refuse his judgment. So how is it that our salvation is not dependent on us, when he himself has given us the ability either to listen or not to listen?"

XXII. PAPHNUTIUS: "You have accurately analysed the words 'If they had heard me', but you have not taken account of who it is that is speaking, and who listens or does not listen, nor of the sequel, 'I should soon have humbled their enemies, and laid my hand on them that trouble them' (Psalm 80/81: 15). No one should distort what we have been saying about nothing being possible without the Lord, and try to misinterpret it as a defence of free will to the extent of wanting to remove from men the grace of God and his daily providence, by quoting, 'My people heard not my voice', and, 'If my people had heard me, if Israel had walked in my ways', etc. Consider that just as the people's disobedience proves the existence of free will, so God's daily care for them is proved, by his

III. On the Three Renunciations

calling to them and warning them. For when it says 'If my people had heard me', it is obvious that he had already been speaking to them, which the Lord did not only in the written law but also by his daily prompting, as is spoken through Isaiah: 'I have spread forth my hands all the day to an unbelieving people, that contradict me' (Isaiah 65:2, LXX). Both points can be demonstrated by the text that follows: 'If my people had heard me, if Israel had walked in my ways, I should soon have humbled their enemies, and laid my hand on them that trouble them' (Psalm 80/81: 14–15). Just as the disobedience of the people demonstrates the existence of free will, so the beginning and conclusion of that verse demonstrate the providence and assistance of God. It shows that he had been the first to speak, and would afterwards have brought down their enemies, had the people only listened to his word. We do not want to deny man's free will in what we have been saying, but to show how necessary for it is the daily help and grace of God."

Having instructed us in these words, Abba Paphnutius dismissed us from his cell before midnight; we were somewhat subdued, thinking soberly over what he had said. The chief benefit we had gained from his discourse was that although we had formerly been of the opinion that we could have reached the height of perfection merely through a complete renunciation of the first type, which we had been trying to carry out with all our might, now we began to understand that we had hardly begun to dream about what monasticism involves. Although we had been instructed by the monastery Fathers about the second type of renunciation, we had not even previously heard of such a thing as the third type of renunciation, in which lies all perfection, and which so far exceeds the two previous types.

✧ THE FOURTH COLLATION ✧
BEING THAT OF ABBA DANIEL

On the Desires of the Flesh and of the Spirit

    I. On the life of Abba Daniel.
   II. The question, of why a sudden change of mind may arise, from inexpressible joy to gloomiest depression.
  III. The reply, on the question proposed.
  IV. The two reasons for God's testing us in his wisdom.
   V. How our study and labour avails for nothing without God's help.
  VI. How beneficial it may be for us to be abandoned by the Lord for a while.
 VII. Of the benefit of that combat which St Paul describes, between the flesh and the spirit.
VIII. A question, why in this text St Paul adds will as a third factor after the opposed desires of flesh and spirit.
  IX. The reply, on how the intellect may ask correctly.
   X. That the word "flesh" does not have a single meaning.
  XI. What St Paul means by "flesh" in this passage, and what the desire of the flesh may be.
 XII. What our will is, and how it is poised between the desires of the flesh and of the spirit.
XIII. Of the value of the hesitation which arises from the battle of flesh and spirit.
XIV. On the irrevocable malice of the evil spirits.

XV. The advantage to us of the desires of the flesh being against the spirit.
XVI. Of the urges of the flesh, which will cause more serious falls if we are not humble.
XVII. Of the tepidity of eunuchs.
XVIII. A question, on the relationship between the carnal and the sensual man.
XIX. The reply, on the three types of soul.
XX. Of those who renounce the world without zeal.
XXI. Of those who renounce great things but are obsessed by little ones.

I. Among others who excelled in Christian wisdom, we met Abba Daniel. He was in every way the equal of any of the dwellers in Scete, but was also adorned with the special grace of humility. Saint Paphnutius, the priest of that part of the desert, promoted him to the office of deacon because of his purity and gentleness, despite his being younger than many of the others. The Saint was so pleased with his merits that he recognised him to be his equal in grace and virtuous life, and so was quick to raise him to the priesthood and his own rank. He was not content to leave him to serve in an inferior capacity, but wanted to provide a suitable successor for himself, expecting that he would survive him with the dignity of the priesthood. Daniel, however, not forgetting his former humility, never took upon himself the functions of the higher order when Paphnutius was present, but always performed the functions of a deacon as before while Paphnutius offered the spiritual sacrifice. In the event Saint Paphnutius was disappointed in his choice and hope of a successor, despite being such a great man that he often possessed the gift of foresight, for it was not long before Daniel, whom he had designated as a successor, went before him to God.

II. We asked this holy man Daniel how it can happen that sometimes we could be dwelling in our cells, with great attentiveness of heart, and filled with an inexpressible joy and inner delight, so

IV. On the Desires of the Flesh and of the Spirit

that not a word, not even a thought intruded, but prayer was pure and prompt, the thoughts full of spiritual benefits, aware that effective petitions easily winged their way to God even in sleep; and then suddenly for no apparent cause we would be filled with such anxiety and crushed under so unreasonable a gloom that we would feel our spirits dried up, and the very cell seemed unbearable, reading intolerable, prayer itself as wavering and indistinct as a drunkard, until neither by tears nor by mental effort could we bring our thoughts back to their former path. The more urgently we applied ourselves to God, the more violently our elusive thoughts were driven to wild imaginations, so drained of spiritual benefit that neither a longing for the kingdom of heaven, nor the fear of hell could stir our intentions out of this deadly torpor. Daniel replied as follows:

III. "The elders have told us that the dryness of mind which you have described can have three causes. It can arise either from our own negligence, or from the attacks of the devil, or from the Lord who tests us in his wisdom. If it is from our own negligence, it is because through our fault we have been careless and lazy in times past, feeding idly on evil thoughts, and making thorns and briars sprout on the soil of our minds, till they choke us, and we become quite sterile, bereft of all spiritual benefit or contemplation.

It may happen through the assault of the devil, for even if we have applied ourselves to good learning, the enemy is subtle enough to penetrate the mind so that we are drawn away from our best intentions either unknowingly or unwillingly.

IV. "If it is the Lord who is testing us in his wisdom, then there can be two reasons: the first is that we are briefly abandoned by him in order that we may become aware of the weakness of our minds, in real humility, and thus avoid being at all elated by the purity of heart which we had formerly possessed as a gift on his visitation. Tested by his abandoning us, we come to understand that our own tearful efforts are quite unable to recover that state of joyful purity, for our former attentiveness of heart was conferred on us by his mercy, not by our own efforts, and can now only be begged for through his grace and the light of his countenance.

The second reason for testing us is to demonstrate our perseverance, and the constancy of our desire, to prove our eagerness and urgency in begging the Holy Spirit to return to visit us whom he had deserted. Recognising how much effort it takes to recover that lost spiritual joy and glad purity, we may be the more careful to preserve it when we have found it, and to cherish it, for if you believe something to be easily recovered, you will take little care to preserve it.

V. "This shows us clearly how the grace and mercy of God are always at work in us to produce good results. If he desert us, our own studied labour will be useless, and no amount of mental strife will suffice to recover our former state without his aid. The text is fulfilled in us which says, 'it is not of him that willeth, nor of him that runneth, but of God that sheweth mercy' (Rom. 9:16). Grace however does not disdain to visit those who are negligent and dissolute, with a holy abundance of spiritual consolations such as those you have mentioned, for so it encourages the unworthy, awakens the slothful, and enlightens those oppressed by the darkness of ignorance. Mildly it prompts us and corrects us, penetrating into our hearts until we are persuaded by its insistence to rise out of our state of idle somnolence. Often enough when divine grace visits us we are overwhelmed by a sweet scent beyond the skill of any human perfumer, till our thoughts are so enchanted by delight that we are rapt into a spiritual maze, forgetting ourselves to be still clothed in flesh.

VI. "King David knew how beneficial it can be that God conceal himself, or I might even say desert us, for he refused to pray that we should never be deserted by God at all, knowing how little that would profit us, or anyone striving for perfection: he did however pray that this desertion should be modified, saying, 'O do not thou utterly forsake me' (Psalm 118/119:8). This is as much as to say, I know well that you customarily withdraw from your holy ones,

IV. On the Desires of the Flesh and of the Spirit

so as to test them. In no other way could they be tempted by the enemy were they not to some extent deserted by you; therefore I do not pray that you should never desert me, for that would do me no good at all. How else could I become aware of my weakness, so as to say, 'It is good for me that thou hast humbled me' (Psalm 118/119: 71), or how could I gain experience in fighting, which I would surely never do if the divine protection were always over me unceasingly? The devil would never dare to assault me as long as I am sustained by your defences, and repeat that resentful accusation against both me and you, and again cry out in slander of your champions, 'Doth Job fear God in vain? Hast thou not made a fence for him, and his house, and all his substance round about?' (Job 1: 9–10, LXX). Nay, rather I will pray that you do not forsake me utterly, or as the Greek says, *heōs sphodra*, to an extremity. It is as beneficial for me that you withdraw from me a little to prove my perseverance in longing, as it would be dangerous for you never to allow me to be deserted for the sake of my merits and of my sins. No human virtue can endure for long if it is tempted continuously without your aid, but it would swiftly fall to the power and influence of the enemy were you not aware of man's strength, and the umpire of his contests, 'who will not suffer us to be tempted above that which we are able; but will make also with temptation issue, that we may be able to bear it' (I Cor. 10: 13).

We find something similar in the Book of Judges, where it speaks mystically about the extermination of the spiritual enemies that threatened Israel, 'These are the nations which the Lord left, that by them he might instruct Israel . . ., that they might learn to fight with their enemies', and a little further on, 'The Lord left them, that he might try Israel by them, whether they would hear the commandments of the Lord, which he had commanded their fathers by the hand of Moses, or not' (Judges 3: 1–4). It was not that God grudged peace to the Israelites, or planned evil for them, but he preserved their enemies for their own benefit; thus through being always under pressure from the attacks of these foes they might never imagine they could do without the help of God, and through meditating on this always and through prayer they would be safe from complacency, and never lose the skill and practice of warfare. For it often happens that ease and prosperity overthrow those who could not be defeated by adversity.

VII. "St Paul also tells us the value of this conflict within ourselves, 'For the flesh lusteth against the spirit; and the spirit against the flesh. For these are contrary one to another; so that you do not the things that you would' (Gal. 5:17). Here you find a sort of civil war within our bodies, provoked by the loving providence of God. If something is found in all of us without any exception, what can we think but that it has become a natural attribute of human kind, since the fall of the first man? And if it is a congenital factor in all of us, may we not believe that it is in us through the will of the Lord, for our benefit and not for our harm? The reason for this warfare, that exists between the flesh and the spirit, is thus explained: 'so that you do not the things that you would.' Now if God has seen to it that we cannot be in control of ourselves, that in fact we cannot act as we should like to, it must be the case that it would be dangerous for ourselves if we were in control. The conflict is therefore beneficial, granted to us by God's providence, and it urges and drives us towards a better state. Without this conflict, peace would undoubtedly be dangerous for us."

VIII. GERMANUS: "We understand that point well enough, but in order really to understand what St Paul means, we would like something to be explained to us more clearly. It appears that three factors are mentioned here: the first is the conflict of flesh against spirit, the second the yearning of spirit against flesh, the third is our own will which is placed in between, when he says, 'you do not the things that you would.' On this point although, as I said, we have arrived at some understanding from what you have told us, still we would like to take the opportunity of this conversation to enquire into it more deeply."

IX. DANIEL: "It is a function of the intellect to discern the various points of a question, and the greatest sign of intelligence is to know

IV. On the Desires of the Flesh and of the Spirit   85

what you do not know. Thus it is said, 'Even a fool, if he asketh a question, shall be counted wise' (Prov. 17:28, LXX). Although the questioner is ignorant of the answer to the question he sets, yet his prudence in asking, and the fact that he knows that he does not know, is reputed to him for wisdom, in as much as he wisely acknowledges that there is something he does not know.

According to your division of the text there are three things which the Apostle names, the lust of the flesh against the spirit, that of the spirit against the flesh, and the cause or reason for their conflict against each other, namely that we be unable to do what we would. But there is a fourth factor which you have ignored – that we be able to do what we would rather not do. Now what we must do is to recognise the force of the first two, that is the desires of flesh and spirit, and then discern what our will is, which lies between the two; finally in the same way we can discern what is contrary to our will.

X. "The word 'flesh' in Holy Scripture can be understood in many different ways. Sometimes it means the whole man, who is made up of body and soul, as in 'The Word was made flesh' (John 1:14), and, 'All flesh shall see the salvation of God' (Luke 3:6). Sometimes it means sinful and carnal men, as in 'My spirit shall not remain in man for ever, because he is flesh' (Gen. 6:3). It can be used for sin itself, as in 'you are not in the flesh, but in the spirit' (Rom. 8:9), or, 'flesh and blood cannot possess the Kingdom of God', and the sequel, 'neither shall corruption possess incorruption' (I Cor. 15:50). Sometimes it means family and kin, as in 'Behold, we are thy bone and thy flesh' (II Kings (II Sam.), 5:1) and St Paul says 'I may provoke to emulation them who are my flesh and may save some of them' (Rom. 11:14).

We must therefore inquire which of these four meanings should be applied to 'flesh' here. Surely the sense in which it is said 'The Word was made flesh' and 'All flesh shall see the salvation of God', cannot be the right one, any more than that which applies in 'My spirit shall not remain in man for ever, because he is flesh', for 'flesh' is not simply used in this way to mean sinful man, in our text 'the flesh lusteth against the spirit; and the spirit against the flesh' (Gal. 5:17). He is not speaking about substances, but about accidents, for in one single man they struggle, evenly or unevenly, with every change of time and circumstance.

XI. "Now since by 'flesh' in this passage we do not mean man, that is the nature of mankind, but the will of the flesh and its base desires, in the same way by 'spirit' we do not mean any substance but the good spiritual desires of the soul. St Paul uses it in this meaning in an earlier passage where he says, 'I say then: Walk in the spirit; and you shall not fulfil the lusts of the flesh. For the flesh lusteth against the spirit; and the spirit against the flesh. For these are contrary one to another; so that you do not the things that you would' (Gal. 5:16–17). Since both lusts, namely of the flesh and of the spirit, exist in a single person, a civil war is waged within us every day, since the lust of the flesh which rushes headlong into vice, delights in the pleasures which bring immediate gratification. On the other hand the opposing lust of the spirit is so eager to be totally wrapped up in spiritual study, that it would like to do without even the necessary works of the flesh. It longs to be able to perform them in such a way that no anxiety burdens its frailty. The flesh rejoices in ease and pleasure, the spirit does not even acquiesce in the most natural of desires. The flesh longs to take its fill of sleep, to be full fed; the spirit is so eager for watching and fasting that it is reluctant to admit even as much sleep and food as is essential for life. The flesh wants to overflow with wealth of every kind; the spirit is content without even its daily subsistence of meagre bread. The flesh wants to be noticed, glistening in the baths, by a throng of daily admirers; the spirit is delighted with squalid rags and the inaccessible vastness of the wilderness, shunning the presence of all mankind. The flesh thrives on honour and praise from men, the spirit is glad when persecution and injury is brought upon it.

XII. "Now between these two desires, the will of the soul finds itself in a most difficult position midway; it does not sink into

IV. On the Desires of the Flesh and of the Spirit

the depths of vice, nor does it aspire to the heights of virtue. It is so easily swayed by carnal passion that it is unable to endure the suffering necessary to acquire what the spirit desires. It would like to obtain physical chastity, but without chastising the body, to acquire purity of heart without the effort of vigils, to abound in spiritual virtue while pampering the body, to possess the grace of patience without restricting its manner of life, to exercise the humility of Christ without surrendering worldly honours, to pursue simple piety along with advancement in this world, to serve Christ in the praise and favour of men, to proclaim the fullness of truth without offending anyone in the slightest. In short, it wants to secure future happiness without yielding up anything in the present.

Such a will can never bring us to true perfection, but leaves us perilously tepid, making us luke-warm like those whom the Lord chides in the Apocalypse: 'I know thy works, that thou art neither cold nor hot. I would thou wert cold or hot. But because thou art luke-warm, I will begin to vomit thee out of my mouth' (Apoc. 3:15–16). Only the rise of internal war can disturb this state of tepidity. If we become accustomed to this will of ours and consent to let ourselves relax into a state of ease, the stings of the flesh will arise at once, and pierce us with passion and vice, giving us no chance to remain in the state of purity we desire, but dragging us off to the cold path of luxury we shun, choked with thorns. On the other hand, if we are inflamed with the ardour of the spirit, try to quench the works of the flesh without taking any account of human frailty, and attempt to make ourselves over totally to unreasonable efforts in virtue, not without spiritual pride, then the weakness of the flesh intervenes, draws us back from that excessive and blameworthy spirit, and impedes us. In this way the opposing desires compete with each other in such a struggle, that the soul's will is unready either to surrender totally to fleshly desire or to expend itself in the struggle for virtue. To some extent it settles at a sound moderation, for the two competing sides prevent the soul from consenting to what is worse; like a spiritual balance poised over the body it regulates the limits of spirit and flesh, and prevents the mind from being elated with the spirit on the one hand, or submitting to the stings of carnal vice on the other.

While this battle rages every day within us, we shall find ourselves driven unwillingly but beneficially towards the fourth point, to the acquisition of purity of life, not in ease and relaxation, but through real effort and a contrite heart. Physical chastity we will attain after strict fasting, hunger and thirst and watching; control over the heart through reading, vigils, ceaseless prayer and solitary poverty; endurance of trials through practice. We will serve our Maker in the midst of abuse and rebuke; follow the truth under the hatred of this world, and even its enmity, if need be. While this struggle continues within us, we shall be drawn away from disgraceful sloth and inspired to the work we are unwilling to do, which is the pursuit of virtue. An ideal balance keeps us in the middle and moderates our tepid will, for the ardour of the spirit on one side, and the frigid lust of the flesh on the other, combine in a moderate warmth. The desire of the spirit does not let us be swept away by unrestrained vice, and the frailty of the flesh restrains the spirit from an unreasonable appetite for virtue. We are prevented from teeming with the maggots of every sort of vice, just as we are saved from the rise of pride, that worst of sins, which could pierce us with its deadly dart. It is the proper balance between these competing sides, that succeeds in showing us a safe and moderate path between either power, and teaches the soldier of Christ to march always on the Royal Road.

Thus it comes to pass that, when the will is luke-warm and feeble the mind rushes headlong towards the desires of the flesh, but is checked by the desire of the spirit from giving consent to these earthly pleasures; on the other hand if our spirit is so unreasonably fervent and elated as to aim at impossible and imprudent heights, our weak flesh draws it back to a fair assessment, till it transcends the sluggish will with suitable moderation, and enters on the path of perfection with a steady pace but some real effort. We find that the Lord did something similar in the story of the building of the Tower of Babel in the Book of Genesis, for the sudden confusion of tongues put a stop to the blasphemous attempt of

IV. On the Desires of the Flesh and of the Spirit

wicked men (Gen. 11). Understanding would have been dangerous, and would have continued to work against God, indeed against the real interests of those who tried to challenge his divine majesty, had not God in his providence divided their tongues against each other, and through the confusion of languages forced them to a better state. Those whom perilous agreement had spurred to their own destruction, were recalled to salvation by a good and useful misunderstanding; Through the agency of confusion, they began to understand human weakness, when in their evil accord they had been too proud to recognise it.

XIII. "The hesitation which is born in us as a result of this struggle between two sides, is very beneficial to us, and the delay caused by this confusion is useful, for the weight of the body often restrains us and recalls us from the excesses which we have, to our danger, mentally conceived, into a better state, either of subsequent penance, or of some improvement. Thus we are often corrected by the delay to our progress and the time of reflection this entails. In fact those who have no fleshly obstacle to delay them from fulfilling the desires of their hearts, that is to say the devils and the evil spirits, despite having fallen from the highest rank of the angels, are seen to be far worse than any man. For as for them it is immediately possible to fulfil their desires, their wicked designs are carried out in irrevocable evil without delay; their thoughts are quick to conceive, so their performance is swift and uncompromising in action. Their easy ability to carry out what they desire assists them so that no salutary period of reflection can moderate the evil they have plotted.

XIV. "A spiritual being, which is unfettered by any bond of flesh, can find no excuse for the depraved will that arises in itself, and therefore has no possibility of pardon for its malice. They are not racked by an outward fleshly urge towards sin, as we are, but inflamed by a pure will to evil, which is why their sin is without forgiveness, their fall without recovery. Because their fall was due to no earthly material temptation, they can find neither pardon nor opportunity for penance. You can easily understand from this not only that the conflict which arises within us between flesh and spirit is not dangerous, but on the contrary that it is positively beneficial.

XV. "The first advantage is that it shows up our desires and our negligence at once, and like a diligent tutor never allows us to deviate from the strict path of duty. Should we be led by over-confidence to an excessive degree of strictness, we are checked and rebuked by the scourges of passion, and brought back to a more suitably low level. Secondly, if we have been a long time without an emission of seed, in a period of pure unbroken chastity granted by the grace of God, to the extent that we imagine that we will never again be disturbed by the urges of the flesh, and as a result are secretly proud of ourselves as if we were immune to the corruption of the body, then a sudden emission will humiliate us and bring us down to earth, graphically reminding us that we are but men. In other types of sin, more serious ones and more dangerous, we run risks without thinking, and are less easily brought to repent of them, but in this case the conscience is easily humiliated, and by such an event is stung to remember the temptations we had forgotten. We recognise easily enough if we have been impure through natural urges, but fail to recognise the greater impurity of spiritual vice. Running quickly back to correct the former frailty, we are warned not to be over-confident in keeping purity, for we see that by a slight neglect of the Lord we had lost it. We cannot preserve this gift of purity except by the grace of God alone, and we learn from experience, that if we are determined to search always for integrity of heart, we must strive especially to obtain the virtue of humility.

XVI. "If we become proud of our physical purity, it will lead to all sorts of pernicious sins and crimes, which is why we would gain nothing whatever, no matter how chaste we be. We can see this in the case of the angelic powers we mentioned above, which suffered no temptation of the flesh, but simply out of pride of heart were

IV. On the Desires of the Flesh and of the Spirit

cast down from the heights of heaven into eternal ruin. We would become, therefore, luke-warm, thoroughly and without remedy, if we had nothing to remind us of the negligence that resides in our conscience or in our flesh, and we would be careless in our constant striving for perfect piety. We would have no way of measuring our austerity or our continence, were we not humiliated and brought to earth by these fleshly temptations, which make us watchful and eager in the struggle against spiritual vice.

XVII. "That is why we can observe that those who are physical eunuchs are very sluggish in temperament; being free from the needs of the flesh, they do not consider themselves obliged to strive for physical purity, or to be heartfelt in penance. This carelessness makes them slack, so that they do not really seek to gain perfection of heart or to rid themselves of spiritual vices, nor are they quick to do so. Although it is a physical condition that causes this, it affects the soul, which is a much more serious matter, and these are they who proceed from being cold to luke-warm, which the Lord declares to be the worse state."

XVIII. GERMANUS: "We must agree that the conflict between flesh and spirit is beneficial, as you have so well explained it to us, and we can believe it, having the matter as it were at our fingertips. But we would like to have this further question explained to us in the same way; what is the relationship between the carnal and the sensual man, and how can it happen that the sensual be worse than the carnal?"

XIX. DANIEL: "According to what we read in Scripture, there are three types of soul: the first carnal, the second sensual, the third spiritual. We meet this distinction in St Paul. He speaks of the fleshly soul thus, 'I gave you milk to drink, not meat; for you were not able as yet. But neither indeed are you now able; for you are yet carnal.' And he continues, 'For whereas there is among you envying and contention, are you not carnal?' (I Cor. 3:2–3). Of the animal soul he also speaks, 'The sensual man perceiveth not these things that are of the Spirit of God. For it is foolishness to him' (I Cor. 2:14). Of the spiritual soul he says, 'The spiritual man judgeth all things; and he himself is judged of no man (I Cor. 2:15). And again, 'You, who are spiritual, instruct such a one in the spirit of meekness' (Gal. 6:1).

Therefore, after we have renounced the world and ceased to be carnal, that is to say after we have begun to withdraw from worldly affairs, and to refrain from the open abuse of the flesh, we should be quick to make every effort to gain the status of spiritual souls. We must not flatter ourselves over the fact that we have renounced this world as far as the outer man is concerned, or given up the contamination of physical fornication, as if we had thereby attained the heights of perfection. That would only make us lazy about eliminating the other passions, so that we would hover midway without ever attaining the grade of spiritual. We might think that our perfection is adequately catered for by separating ourselves outwardly from the way of life of this world and its pleasures, or by becoming immune to the corruption of the flesh, but that would settle us into that tepid state which is condemned as the worst of all, so that we become fit for nothing but to be spewed out of the mouth of the Lord, as he says, 'I would thou wert hot or cold. But because thou art luke-warm, I will begin to vomit thee out of my mouth' (Apoc. 3:15–16).

It is appropriate that the Lord should say that those who had once been received into his bosom in charity but had become poisonously tepid should be vomited out with a spasm of the chest; for they might have offered him a nature truly saved, but had preferred to be expelled from his bosom; in this they were much worse than those who had never entered into the Lord's mouth, just as we detest what nausea compels us to eject. If something is cold, it is made warm simply by being taken into the mouth, and we find it nourishing and good to the taste; but if something has been once vomited forth because it is poisonously tepid, we find it repulsive to look at even from a distance, let alone approach it to our lips. That state is rightly considered the worse, since a carnal man, some pagan living in the world,

IV. On the Desires of the Flesh and of the Spirit

can more easily be converted and saved, to reach the height of perfection, than one who professes to be a monk but does not follow the way of perfection according to the discipline of the rule, but has fallen away from that fire of spiritual zeal which he once had. The worldling may be humiliated by his physical vices, and realise that he is impure, corrupted by the flesh; then he is struck with compunction and runs to the font of true purification and perfection, to repudiate the frigid state of unfaithfulness he had been in, and so he is fired with spiritual zeal and easily flies up to perfection. But, as I have said, one who has made a luke-warm beginning and abuses the very name of monk, without seizing hold of the way of perfection in the proper zealous humility, once infected with this wretched contagion, and thereby become slack, will never again know what it to be perfect, nor can learn from the instruction of others.

He says in his heart, as we hear the Lord saying, 'thou sayest: I am rich and made wealthy and have need of nothing,' and is fitly addressed by the words that follow, 'and knowest not that thou art wretched and miserable and poor and blind and naked' (Apoc. 3:17). He becomes worse than the worldling, for he does not realise that he is wretched, blind and bare, in need of correction and the instruction of others to be reformed. Because of this, he will not listen to any saving word of encouragement, failing to see that everyone considers him a disgrace to the name of monk, and even if they all think him a saint and honour him as a servant of God, he is bound to be condemned to a greater punishment in the future.

Why go on about a matter which experience shows us so clearly? It is common to see those who are cold and carnal, the worldlings and the pagans, arriving at spiritual zeal, but the tepid and the sensual, never. We see in the revelation how the Lord detests such men, and bids the spiritual men who are preachers to refrain from teaching or instructing them, not to waste the seed of the saving word on soil so barren and infertile, choked with noxious weeds. Spurning such, let them cultivate virgin soil, that is to say, let them put all their effort into proclaiming the saving Word to the pagans and the worldly, for it is said, 'Thus saith the

Lord to the men of Juda and Jerusalem: Break up anew your fallow ground, and sow not upon thorns' (Jerem. 4: 3).

XX. "It is shameful to admit that there are many who have made no alteration to their former way of life and their vices, but have merely changed their status and secular dress. They work to accumulate money, though they had none before, they never give up what they actually had. What is worse, they try to increase their wealth under the pretext that they ought to provide for their servants, or their brethren, or to save up to form a community which they arrogantly intend to found as if they were already abbots. Were they truly intent on the way of perfection they would on the contrary put their efforts into getting rid not only of their money but even of their former interests and all their concerns, placing themselves alone and bare under their superiors' orders, not taking control of others, nor even of themselves. But on the contrary what happens is that they are anxious to take command over their brethren, are never obedient to their superiors, and from this proud beginning those who long to teach others are never capable of learning themselves, or of performing what they teach. Hence inevitably they are blind leaders of the blind, as Our Lord said, and they fall into the pit together (Matt. 15:14).

Pride may well be one single vice, but it has two aspects; in one they feign a serious and grave demeanour, in the other they dissolve in giggles and laughter with unrestricted licence. In one mood they are pleased to keep quiet, in the other they resent being restrained by the rule of silence. They are not ashamed to talk at length, even on foolish and unsuitable things, for their real embarrassment is to appear less cultured than others. In one mood they arrogantly put themselves forward for ordination, in another they despise it, considering it beneath their former dignity or inappropriate for their high birth and virtuous life. Which of these moods is the worse I leave to each one to consider.

Disobedience has only one form, violating the commands of one's superior, whether through over-eagerness for work, or love of ease. It is equally perilous to subvert the rules of the monastery

IV. On the Desires of the Flesh and of the Spirit

for the sake of repose as for watchfulness. It is as bad to ignore the abbot's command in order to read as it would be in order to sleep. Despising a brother gives rise to just as much pride if it is for fasting as for feasting, except that vices which pretend to be virtues and put on the guise of spirituality are more dangerous and more difficult to cure than those which are openly displayed for the sake of carnal delight. The latter faults, being public and visible can be tackled head-on, and cured; the former, being wrapped in the cloak of virtue, remain unhealed, and cause those who are taken in by them to suffer more grievously and with greater peril.

XXI. "It often happens, absurdly, that men begin with a great zeal for renunciation; they abandon family, wealth and military rank, and take themselves off to a monastery, but we find they are so obsessed with things which they cannot do without, and are necessary even in this way of life, that they are defeated by them, however small and cheap they be, until the worry about them exceeds their concern for all their former wealth. It proves of little benefit to them that they have repudiated great fortune and property, for they have transferred to trivial little things that avarice, to end which they had made such a great renunciation. They can no longer exercise the vice of greed and avarice towards precious things, but it survives towards cheap objects, so that they have not eliminated their former desires but simply altered them. They are slaves to their excessive attachment to a rug, a basket, a bag, a book, [a mat] or something of the sort, however cheap, with the same possessiveness as before. They preserve and guard these things with quite as much care, and are not ashamed to quarrel with their brethren over them, or even, alas, take them to law. Labouring under the disease of ancient greed, they are not content to possess the few things which bodily necessity compels a monk to keep in accordance with the common allowance and amount, but display their avarice of heart in that they want their necessaries to be better quality than the others, or they go beyond the bounds of reason in looking after them, taking such great care to defend them from being taken by others, though they ought to be held in common with all the brethren. It is as if the danger of the vice of avarice lay in the quality of the metal, not in its own nature, and whereas it would be wrong to be in a passion over great matters, it is quite all right if the matters are trivial. Is it not rather that we cast away precious things in order to learn to despise base ones? What difference does it make if someone is inflamed with longing for great and splendid objects, or for commonplace ones? Rather he is more to blame if he has rejected great things only to be entangled in lesser ones. Renouncing the world in this manner will not achieve perfection of heart, for although the name of poverty is there, the lure of riches has not gone away."

✣ THE FIFTH COLLATION ✣
BEING THAT OF ABBA SARAPION

On the Eight Deadly Sins

    I. How we came to Abba Sarapion's cell, and asked him about the different vices and how they attack us.
   II. Abba Sarapion speaks on the Eight Deadly Sins.
  III. Of the two types of sin, and their fourfold action.
  IV. A summary of the passions of gluttony and fornication, and how to cure them.
   V. How Our Lord alone was tempted without sin.
  VI. The nature of the temptation which Our Lord suffered from the devil.
 VII. How sins of vainglory and pride are committed without the body being involved.
VIII. On the love of money, which is unnatural, and what difference there be between it and natural vices.
  IX. How melancholy and depression arise with no external cause, unlike the other vices.
   X. Of how six sins are in agreement, and two are in opposition to them.
  XI. Of the causes and natures of each sin.
 XII. How vainglory may be put to use.
XIII. On how the vices all attack in different ways.
XIV. Of how defence against the vices must be directed according to how they assail us.
 XV. How we can do nothing against sins without God's help, nor may we boast of our victory over them.

XVI. On the symbolism of the seven nations whose land Israel took, and why they are sometimes called seven and sometimes many.
XVII. A question, on how the seven nations are compared to eight sins.
XVIII. The reply, on how the number of eight nations is made up to match the eight sins.
XIX. Why the commandment was to leave the one nation, but to exterminate the other seven.
XX. How the nature of gluttony can be compared to an eagle.
XXI. An argument against the philosophers, that gluttony always remains.
XXII. Why God promised to Abraham that he would destroy ten nations before Israel.
XXIII. How beneficial for us it is to occupy the territory of the vices.
XXIV. How the lands from which the Canaanite tribes were expelled had been promised to the descendents of Shem.
XXV. Various texts on the meaning of the eight vices.
XXVI. Once we have defeated gluttony, we must turn our attention to obtaining the other virtues.
XXVII. How the order of contests is not the same as that of the sins.

I. Among those venerable old men one called Sarapion was so distinguished for the grace of discernment that I think his conversation well worth writing down. We requested him to say something about the attacks of vice, and to explain how they arise and what causes them, and so he began:

II. "There are eight deadly sins which plague the human race; specifically the first is gluttony or pampering the stomach, the second fornication, the third the love of money or avarice, the fourth anger, the fifth melancholy, the sixth depression, which is anxiety or listlessness, the seventh vainglory or conceit, the eighth arrogant pride.

III. "These sins fall into two types; they are either natural, like greed, or unnatural, like avarice. Their action is fourfold, for some cannot be committed without physical action, like gluttony and fornication, some are performed with no bodily involvement, like pride and conceit, some are caused by external events, like the love of money and anger, while others arise from interior emotions, like depression and melancholy.

IV. "We will speak of these as briefly as possible, illuminating them with texts from Scripture. Gluttony and fornication lie within us by nature, and often arise simply from the urges and motions of the flesh without the mind being involved. However they need an external object to satisfy them, and so are committed through the action of the body. 'But every man is tempted by his own concupiscence . . . . Then, when concupiscence hath conceived, it bringeth forth sin. But sin, when it is completed, begetteth death' (James 1:14–15). The first Adam could not have been deceived by gluttony had he not possessed something edible which he wrongly misused; the second Adam likewise was not tempted without some material enticement, for he was told 'If thou be the Son of God, command that these stones be made bread' (Matt. 4:3).

It is obvious that fornication is not committed without the body, for God speaks to Job about this spirit, 'His strength is in his loins, his power in the centre of his belly' (Job 40:11, LXX). For this reason these two sins in particular, which are committed through the agency of the body, need some special bodily remedy as well as spiritual healing in the soul. Mental resolution alone is insufficient to quench the pangs of these two vices, in the way in which it can deal with anger, melancholy and the other passions which we know we can combat with mental strife alone, without any bodily penance; no, in this case physical penance is necessary, performed by fasting, watching and hard work, with isolation in addition, for just as these vices arise always through the fault of both body and soul, so they cannot be overcome except through effort on both parts.

Granted that the Apostle deems all sins to be carnal, in as much as he includes enmity, wrath and heresy among the other works of the flesh (Gal. 5:19–21), nevertheless we divide them into two categories for the sake of curing them and understanding their nature more accurately. Some of them we call carnal, some spiritual. The carnal are those which pertain especially to carnal physical pleasures, which so delight and sate the body that it even disturbs the mind at repose, and drags it into consenting to pleasure against its will. St Paul speaks of this matter: 'In which also we all conversed in time past, in the desires of our flesh, fulfilling the will of the flesh and of our thoughts, and were by nature children of wrath, even as the rest' (Eph. 2:3). Those we call spiritual arise from the instinct of the soul alone, and do not cede anything to fleshly delight, but rather grieve the body severely, nourishing the sick soul with the food of a wretched pleasure. That is why these sins demand a medicine of heart alone, whereas the fleshly ones will not be cured except through the twofold remedy we have mentioned. Hence those who pursue purity are well advised to begin by withholding the actual objects of these carnal passions from themselves, the objects which can generate in the sick soul the occasion or the memory of those passions. A twofold disease needs a twofold remedy. Lest the lusts of the body break out into actual sin, distracting sights and objects should be kept well away; and lest the mind begin to brood over such matters, we should meditate more earnestly on Scripture, be watchful and careful, and isolated in a remote place. In the case of other sins, human company is no disadvantage, rather it is a great advantage to those who really want to be free from them, since such sins are greatly shamed by human respect; they are healed all the more quickly the more frequently they are openly challenged.

V. "Our Lord Jesus Christ, as the Apostle tells us, 'was tempted in all things like as we are, without sin' (Heb. 4:15), that is without

V. On the Eight Deadly Sins

being touched by passion, without feeling the pangs of carnal desire, whereas we inevitably are stung by them, however unaware or unwilling we may be. He himself indeed was not begotten or conceived in the usual human manner, for the Archangel announced the manner of His conception thus: 'The Holy Ghost shall come upon thee and the power of the Most High shall overshadow thee. And therefore also the Holy which shall be born of thee shall be called the Son of God' (Luke 1:35).

VI. "He himself, who possessed the image and likeness of God uncorrupted, had to be tempted by those passions by which Adam was tempted when he still remained in the unblemished image of God, that is to say gluttony, vainglory and pride, not by those passions which he embroiled himself in through his own fault after disobeying God's command and defacing his image and likeness. It was through gluttony that he dared to taste the forbidden fruit; vainglory made him listen to 'your eyes shall be opened' and pride to 'you shall be as gods, knowing good and evil' (Gen. 3:5). We read that it was to these three sins that Our Lord and Saviour was tempted: gluttony when the devil said to him, 'Command that these stones be made bread'; vainglory in, 'If thou be the Son of God, cast thyself down'; pride in, 'he showed him all the kingdoms of the world and the glory of them, and said to him: All these will I give thee, if falling down thou wilt adore me' (Matt. 4:3–9). By his example he taught us how we should overcome the tempter in the same sort of temptations which he suffered. That is why both the first man and Our Lord are named Adam (I Cor. 15:45). One was the first in ruin and death, the other the first in the resurrection and the life. Through one the whole human race was condemned, through the other the whole human race is liberated. The one was made of pure and undefiled earth, the other was born of the Virgin Mary. Thus it was fitting for Christ to endure the same temptations as Adam, but not necessary to exceed them, for he who had conquered gluttony could not be tempted by fornication which comes from the same root, proceeding from excess of food; the first Adam too would have escaped that sin, had he not been deceived by the devil's wiles into admitting the vice which is its mother.

That is why the Son of God is not said to have come in sinful flesh without qualification, but 'in the likeness of sinful flesh' (Rom. 8:3). He was in the flesh true enough, eating, drinking and sleeping, really feeling the piercing nails, but he did not suffer the sin which flesh incurred through its weakness in reality, but only by imputation. He did not suffer the burning pangs of fleshly desire, which our nature causes to attack us even against our will, but he participated in a semblance of that fallen nature. Since he truly consummated everything which we have to do, and carried all the infirmities of humankind, it appeared that he suffered from this passion too, in as much as he too seemed to bear the tendency to weakness and sin in his flesh because of the aforesaid infirmities. But the devil tempted him only in those vices with which he had ensnared the first Adam, for he imagined that if he found him to fail in these first temptations, he would have been brought down by the other sins as well, like any man. But since he did not fall in the first contest, he could not have been attacked in the second area of weakness which springs from the root of the first. The devil saw that he did not in any way admit the first element of sin, so it was vain for him to hope that he would reap any fruit where neither seed not root had been admitted.

Admittedly according to Luke, the last temptation is the one where he says 'If thou be the Son of God, cast thyself from hence' (Luke 4:9). This can be understood as relating to the vice of pride. The previous one in Luke's Gospel (which Matthew places third) when the devil promises him all the kingdoms of the world which he showed him in a moment of time, is understood of avarice. It is because after Christ's victory over gluttony, the devil did not bother to tempt him with fornication but passed on to avarice, knowing that to be the root of all evil. Conquered here too, he dared not try him with any of the vices which follow next (knowing well that they spring only from the seed of avarice) but proceeded to the last temptation of pride. He knew well that pride troubles those who are perfect and have conquered all other vices, and

V. On the Eight Deadly Sins

he remembered how pride it was, without the incitement of preceding sins, that caused himself, he who had been Lucifer, and many others, to be cast down from heaven. Thus it is well set forth according to the order which St Luke follows, as we have recounted it; the sly fiend attacked both the first Adam and the last with the same design and system of temptation. To the first Adam he said, 'your eyes shall be opened', to the second, 'he showed him all the kingdoms of the world and the glory of them'; to the former 'You shall be as gods', to the latter 'If thou be the Son of God' (Gen. 3:5 and Luke 4:9).

VII. "To continue the order of our exposition on how sins are committed through the other vices (since we found ourselves obliged to interrupt that order by our discussion on gluttony and the temptations of Christ), vainglory and pride are usually committed without the body being involved in any way. How could they require physical action, since they are not driven by passion but bring total ruin on the soul simply through the will, in its pursuit of praise and the winning of human respect? What physical effect did the ancient pride of Lucifer have? For he conceived that pride in mind and thought alone, as the Prophet said, 'Thou saidst in thy heart: I will ascend into heaven. I will exalt my throne above the stars of God.... I will ascend above the height of the clouds. I will be like the Most High' (Isaiah 14:13–14). He had no teacher in that pride, he committed that sin in thought alone, to his eternal ruin, no physical actions followed after he became a tyrant.

VIII. "Avarice and wrath arise in a similar manner, both being stirred up usually by outward occasions, although they are not of the same nature, for one is unnatural, the other arises within us through original sin. Often those who are already weak complain that they are plunged into these vices through some irritation or instinct, and are provoked by others into falling into wrath or avarice. It is clear that the love of money is unnatural, for we cannot find its origin to lie within us, nor is it stirred up by things which relate to the enjoyment of soul or body, or to the necessities of life. For surely there is nothing wanted for the necessities of our common nature except daily food and drink; all other possessions, no matter how carefully and lovingly they are hoarded, seem to be foreign to human need and of no use for sustaining life. As a result this vice, which is beyond nature, only troubles monks who are lukewarm and badly grounded. Natural passions do not cease from troubling even the best of monks, who live in the wilderness. To prove this point again, there are certain nations which we know to be altogether free from this vice of avarice, for they have never admitted such a weakness through custom or practice. We believe that the elder world, before the Deluge, was for a very long time ignorant of this mad desire. It can be demonstrated that it is easily eliminated when a sincere monk rids himself of all his property and undertakes the discipline of the monastery, without suffering even a single denarius to remain for himself. We could cite thousands of men as witnesses to this fact, men who quickly rid themselves of all their wealth and eradicated this vice to the extent that they never felt the slightest temptation again. Yet they could not become complacent, for they had to fight continually against gluttony, striving with great watchfulness of heart and physical self-restraint.

IX. "As we have already said, melancholy and depression usually arise without any external cause. They are frequently observed to cause great distress to those living alone in the desert away from the company of men, as anyone who lives in the wilderness and knows about a man's inner conflicts can witness to be true through his own experience.

X. "Now although the eight sins have different origins and varying effects, nevertheless the first six (that is to say gluttony, fornication, avarice, wrath, melancholy and depression) are linked together in a sort of chain of causality, the excess of each one in turn giving rise to the next one. From an excess of gluttony springs fornication, from fornication avarice, from avarice wrath, from wrath melancholy, and from melancholy depression, in a logical order. In the same way and in the same order we should combat these sins, and we should open the battle against each one from the previous one. If you want to destroy the damaging spread and overgrowth of some tree, it is easier if you first expose and then cut the roots on which it depends. A flood of polluted water is stemmed by searching out and blocking up the source and channels it comes from. Thus if you would defeat depression, you must conquer melancholy first; to dispel melancholy, first get rid of wrath; to extinguish wrath, first trample on avarice, to strip away avarice, suppress fornication; to undermine fornication, the sin of gluttony must be restrained.

The two remaining, that is conceit and arrogant pride, are linked to each other in the same sort of relationship as the six we have just mentioned, so that as the first grows it generates the second, for the excess of conceit brings forth the germ of pride. However they are quite different from the six former vices, and cannot be associated with them in the same way. They are not generated by occasion of them in any way, but on the contrary arise in a directly contrary manner. When one series is eradicated, the other blossoms more abundantly, when the latter is destroyed, the former multiplies and grows with greater vigour. That is why these two types of sin attack us in different ways; we fall into each one of the first six as a result of having fallen to the preceding one, but it is when we are victorious and especially after a signal triumph, that we are in greatest danger of the latter two. In each series, the more a preceding vice grows the more does the next one; when the preceding one diminishes, so does the next. Because of this, if we would exclude pride, we must first focus on conceit. If we have defeated the first sin, the next one will be abated, and once we have eliminated the previous vice, subsequent temptations wither away. The eight sins are linked to each other and connected in the way we have mentioned, but they are further divided into four pairs of associates; gluttony is especially linked to fornication, avarice to wrath, melancholy to depression and conceit to pride in a customary coupling.

XI. "Now we must speak in turn on the nature of each of these sins. Gluttony is divided into three types: the first is when it urges a monk to be eager to eat before the proper appointed time; the second when he is pleased to stuff his belly by devouring all sorts of food; the third when he longs for delicate and refined foods. These three will harm a monk seriously, unless he takes great care to rid himself of them all with equal zeal. Just as it is never legitimate to presume to break the fast before the statutory hour, in the same way we must avoid overeating, or the quest for extravagant and delicate foods. From these three germs derive the different sorts of dangerous sickness of the soul. From the first arises hatred of the monastery, thence repugnance, until finally it becomes impossible to endure remaining there, so that inevitably the monk departs, or even runs away suddenly. The second stirs up the fiery pangs of luxury and lust. The third wraps the clinging coils of avarice around the necks of its victims, never permitting a monk to practice the perfect poverty of Christ.

We can detect whether the germs of this vice be within us by observing what happens if we happen to be detained by one of brethren over a meal, whether we be content to accept the sort of food that is provided for us, or boldly demand something extra or of better quality. There are three reasons why that should never happen; firstly because a monk should turn his thoughts always to endurance and frugality, and as St Paul says, learn to be content with what he has (Phil. 4:11). He will never be capable of restraining the hidden and more violent passions of the body if he is offended at tasting something less pleasant, and unable to mortify the pleasure of taste even on one occasion. Secondly because it sometimes happens that the type of food we like is temporarily not available and we would embarrass the provider in his need or frugality, exposing the poverty, which he would rather only God should know about. Thirdly, it could happen that the sauce which we want added would be displeasing to others, and we would find ourselves upsetting many people for the sake of satisfying our own taste and desire. For these reasons we should always restrain this tendency in ourselves.

V. On the Eight Deadly Sins

There are also three types of fornication; the first is consummated by the joining of both sexes; the second is when no woman is involved – for this God's punishment of Onan the son of the patriarch Judah is recorded (Gen. 38:10). In Holy Scripture it is called 'uncleanness', and St Paul comments here, 'I say to the unmarried and to the widows; it is good for them if they so continue, even as I. But if they do not contain themselves, let them marry. For it is better to marry than to be burnt' (I Cor. 7:8–9). The third is in thought alone, of which Our Lord speaks in the Gospel, 'whosoever shall look on a woman to lust after her hath already committed adultery with her in his heart' (Matt. 5:28). The holy Apostle mentions all these three types together, and says they should be quelled, when he says, 'Mortify therefore your members which are upon the earth: fornication, uncleanness, lust' (Col. 3:5). Again, he mentions two of them in Ephesians, 'Fornication and all uncleanness, let it not so much as be named among you,' and he continues, 'Know you this and understand: that no fornicator or unclean or covetous person (which is a serving of idols) hath inheritance in the Kingdom of Christ and of God' (Eph. 5:3, 5). We must beware of all three with equal care, for a like sentence of exclusion from the Kingdom of Christ hangs over all.

Avarice has its three types: the first is when a monk does not allow himself to be stripped of his wealth and property; the second which persuades him to take back with greater greed property which he had once dispersed or given to the poor; the third which drives him to desire the acquisition of wealth which he had never possessed before.

Wrath too is of three types; the first which seethes within us (the Greeks call it *thymos*); the second which breaks out in words and actions (they call it *orge*), and the Apostle says, 'Lay you also all away: anger, indignation . . .' (Col. 3:8); the third is not spent in a moment like the preceding but is fostered for days or for years – they call that *menis*. All three are to be shunned by us and condemned.

Of melancholy there are but two types: one arises when wrath subsides or we have suffered injury or our desires are hindered and frustrated; the other proceeds from some unaccountable mental worry or anxiety.

Depression also has two types, one drives the sufferers to drowsiness, the other urges them to desert their cells and abscond.

Vainglory, though it be of many forms and complex, and can be divided into different varieties, does however have but two main types; in the first we are elated by carnal external circumstances, in the second we are inflamed by the empty glory because of our desire for hidden spiritual progress.

XII. "There is one occasion on which vainglory may be usefully cultivated by beginners, namely by those who are still troubled by fleshly vice. For example, if at a time when they are being tempted by the spirit of fornication, they think about either the dignity of the priestly state, or the opinion of everyone who believes them to be holy and pure, in this way they may quell the unclean urgings of desire by the consideration that they are base and beneath the dignity either of one's own estimation or of holy order; thus they can combat a greater evil with a lesser one. For it is better to be in some way taken with conceit than to fall into the fires of fornication, from which they cannot recover, or only with difficulty after a fall. One of the prophets aptly expresses this point, saying in the person of God, 'For my name's sake I will remove my wrath far off: and for my praise I will bridle thee, lest thou shouldst perish' (Isaiah 48:9). That is to say, as long as you are concerned with the flattery of vainglory, you will never fall to the depths of the pit and sink irrevocably through the commission of mortal sin.

We should not be surprised that this passion has such power that it can restrain someone from falling into the guilt of fornication, for it has been abundantly proved by many examples that someone whom it has once infected with its virus can become so stubborn as to be able to fast not just for two days but for three. Indeed we have heard several men living in this desert admit that when they lived in the monasteries of Syria they were able easily to endure five days without food, whereas now they are so hungry by the third hour that they can hardly bear to defer their daily meal until noon. On this point Abba Macarius spoke aptly; when someone complained that in the desert he was racked by hunger at the third hour, whereas in the monastery he had often gone without eating for whole weeks and not felt hungry, he replied, 'Here there is no witness to your fasting, who could nourish you and strengthen you with his praise; there the admiration of men and your own conceit kept you well fed.'

A parable of the point we made on how vainglory can drive out the vice of fornication is found nicely set out in Kings, when Nebuchadnesar the King of Assyria took captive the people of Israel who had already been defeated by Necho the King of Egypt, and transported them from the borders of Egypt to his own territory; he did not restore them to their former freedom in their native land but carried them off to his own country, taking them further off than when they were imprisoned in Egypt (IV Kings (II Sam.) 23–4). The parable may be aptly applied here, for whereas it may be better to be a slave to the sin of vainglory than to fornication, yet it is more difficult to escape from the domination of vainglory. The longer the journey the captives are taken, the more laborious the return to their native soil and ancestral liberty. Rightly is the prophet's rebuke earned, 'Why art thou grown old in a strange country?' (Bar. 3:11). One who is not rejuvenated from his earthly vices is properly said to be growing old in a foreign land.

Arrogant pride also has its two types; the first is carnal, but the second spiritual and more dangerous, for it particularly attacks those whom it finds well advanced in various virtues.

XIII. "All these eight sins attack the whole human race, but they do not affect everyone in the same way. In one man the spirit of fornication obtains the chief hold; in another, wrath rides roughshod; in a third conceit holds sway; in yet another pride sets up its stronghold. We are all attacked by all of them, but each of us struggles in our own manner and order.

XIV. "We must therefore join battle against these sins in this manner: each one should discern the sin which most assails him, and struggle against that one in particular. He should devote his whole mental energy and concern to watching it and attacking it, directing the darts of his daily fast against it, continually shooting at it with flights of arrows, of heartfelt sighs and groans. The effort of watching, and the meditations of his heart are directed against it; prayer to God is poured out ceaselessly with tears, earnestly beseeching him to quench its attacks.

No one can merit a victory over any vice until he comes to learn that it is impossible for him to win the victory through his own efforts. It is needful for him to persevere day and night with real earnestness, if he would be cleansed. And when he perceives that he has been freed from it, he should examine his conscience again with the same intention, to discern which of the remaining vices is now the most dangerous, so that he can direct all his spiritual armoury against that one. Once he has conquered the stronger passions in this way he will have an easy and swift victory over the others, for the mind is strengthened by its triumphs, and in assaulting the weaker foes gains a ready success in battle. This is what gladiators do, who compete before the Emperor of this world against all manner of beasts in the hope of a prize, in the type of spectacle called a *Pancarpon*. They look out for the stronger and more ferocious animals and make their first forays against them; once these have been slaughtered, they can easily make an end of the more frail and timid creatures. Once we have overcome the stronger passions, then we are ready for a crowning victory over the weaker ones in due turn, with no difficulty. While we are fighting chiefly against one vice, we should not worry that we are failing to keep an eye out for the darts of others as if we might be taken by surprise and wounded unexpectedly, for that never happens. It could not be that someone who is concerned to cleanse his heart and has armed his thoughts to strive against one particular vice, would not have a general detestation and similar vigilance against the others. How indeed could one ever deserve to triumph over the one passion which he wanted to be rid of, if he made himself unworthy of receiving the prize of victory through submission to other vices? But since the main concern of our hearts is to make a special effort against one sin in particular, we will pray more earnestly for that, begging with great zeal and attention for the ability to discern it more clearly and thus obtain a speedy victory. The Lawgiver himself teaches us that we should join battle in this order, but not trusting in our own strength, for he says, 'Thou shalt not fear them, because the Lord thy God is in the midst of thee, a God mighty and terrible. He will consume these nations in thy sight by little and little and by degrees. Thou wilt not be able to destroy them altogether: lest perhaps the beasts of the earth should increase upon thee. But the Lord thy God shall deliver them in thy sight: and shall slay them until they be utterly destroyed' (Deut. 7: 21–3).

XV. "In the same way he warns us not to boast of our victory over them, saying, 'After thou hast eaten and art filled, hast built goodly houses and dwelt in them. And shalt have herds of oxen and flocks of sheep, and plenty of gold and silver, and of all things: thy heart be lifted up, and thou remember not the Lord thy God, who brought thee out of the land of Egypt, out of the house of bondage, and was thy leader in the great and terrible wilderness' (Deut. 8: 12–15). Solomon also says, in Proverbs, 'When thy enemy shall fall, be not glad: and in his ruin let not thy heart rejoice, lest the Lord see and it displease him, and he turn away his wrath from him' (Prov. 24: 17–18). That is to say, if the Lord sees your pride he may cease to crush your enemies, and once he has deserted you you would begin to be oppressed once more by the passion which you had been dominating through God's grace. Otherwise the Prophet would not have prayed thus, 'O Lord, deliver not up to beasts the souls that confess to thee' (Psalm 73/74: 19), for he knew that there have been some who, because of their pride, had been given over to the vices which they had once overcome, to humiliate them. We should therefore know from our own experience as well as from many Scriptural texts, that we are incapable of overcoming such great foes by our own strength without the aid of God to support us; and every day we should attribute our victories to him.

The Lord warns us of this, again through Moses: 'Say not in thy heart, when the Lord thy God shall have destroyed them in thy sight: For my justice hath the Lord brought me in to possess this land, whereas these nations are destroyed for their wickedness. For it is not for thy justices, and the uprightness of thy heart that thou shalt go in to possess their lands, but because they have done wickedly, they are destroyed at thy coming in' (Deut. 9: 4–5). Could anything be more clearly spoken against the evil presumptuous idea that attributes all that we do to our own choice or effort? 'Say not in thy heart,' he says, 'when the Lord thy God shall have destroyed them in thy sight; For my justice hath the Lord brought me in to possess this land.' Isn't this written clearly to make those hear who have closed their mental eyes and ears? When the war against your carnal vices goes well, and you see yourself liberated from such filth and the ways of the world, never imagine this is due to your own strength and cleverness, being puffed up by the success of the struggle and your victory; never believe that you have won the victory yourself through your work and study, by your own free will, over the spirit of wickedness and the sins of the flesh. You would certainly have no chance of overcoming them without the help of the Lord to fortify you and protect you.

XVI. "These are the seven nations whose land the Lord promised to give to the children of Israel when they came out of Egypt. As St Paul says, we should interpret everything recorded that was done to them as a parable for our instruction (I Cor. 10: 6). So it says, 'When the Lord thy God shall have brought thee into the land, which thou art going in to possess, and shall have destroyed many nations before thee: the Hethite, and the Gergezite, and the Amorrhite, and the Chanaanite, and the Pherizite, and the Hevite, and the Jebusite: seven nations much more numerous than thou art, and stronger than thou: and the Lord thy God shall have delivered them to thee: thou shalt utterly destroy them' (Deut. 7: 1–2). The reason why they are called much more numerous is because there are more vices than virtues. Whereas only seven

V. On the Eight Deadly Sins

nations are listed, in the war against them they are mentioned without number, for it is said, 'And he shall have destroyed many nations before thee.' They were more numerous than Israel, being a people of fleshly passions which spring from this sevenfold root of vice. They teemed with murders, quarrels, heresies, thefts, slanders, blasphemies, greediness, drunkenness, calumnies, mockeries, foul speech, lies, perjury, stupidity, indecency, unrest, plundering, bitterness, contention, hatred, contempt, grumbling, provocation, despair and many other things, which it would be overlong to list. We may think them trivial, but we should listen to what St Paul says, and the opinion he gives of them, 'Neither do you murmur, as some of them murmured, and were destroyed by the destroyer,' and on provocation, 'Neither let us tempt Christ, as some of them tempted and perished by the serpents' (I Cor. 10: 9, 10). On calumny, 'Love not calumny, lest thou perish' (Prov. 20: 13, LXX), and on despair, 'who, despairing, have given themselves up to lasciviousness unto the working of all uncleanness, unto covetousness' (Eph. 4: 19). Contention is condemned like wrath, indignation and blasphemy, as we can clearly see from the same Apostle's words, 'Let all bitterness and anger and indignation and clamour and blasphemy be put away from you, with all malice' (Eph. 4: 31). There are many similar passages.

Although vices are much more numerous than virtues, once we have defeated the eight principal sins from which the others undoubtedly flow, all the rest are subdued and eradicated permanently with the elimination of the eight. For it is from gluttony that greediness and drunkenness derive, from fornication come foul language, indecency, stupidity and mockery. From love of money come lies, deceit, theft, perjury and the obsession with profit, slander, violence, cruelty and rapacity; from wrath come murder, contention and hatred. From melancholy come rancour, weakmindedness, bitterness, despair; from depression come sloth, laziness, importunity, unrest, vagrancy, mental and physical instability, verbosity and curiosity. From vainglory come strife, heresy, boasting and the quest for novelty; from pride come contempt, envy, disobedience, blasphemy, grumbling and calumny.

We can see from the very nature of their attacks that these plagues are stronger than us; for the desire of carnal delight and vice burns more fiercely within us than zeal for virtue, which is not gained except through great mortification of heart and body. Look with the eyes of the spirit at these innumerable hosts of foes, as the Apostle lists them, 'Our wrestling is not against flesh and blood, but against principalities and powers, against the rulers of the world of this darkness, against the spirits of wickedness in the high places' (Eph. 6:12). See also what the ninetieth psalm says of the just man, 'A thousand shall fall at thy side, and ten thousand at thy right hand' (Psalm 90/91:7), and you will easily discover that they are much greater in number and stronger than us. We indeed abide in the flesh and are earthly, while they have a spiritual and aery nature."

XVII. GERMANUS: "How is it therefore that there are eight sins which assail us, when Moses only numbers seven nations opposed to the people of Israel; and how can it be suitable for us to occupy the territory of sins?"

XVIII. SARAPION: "Everyone is absolutely agreed that there are eight deadly sins which attack a monk. They are prefigured by the pagan nations, even though not all of them are listed here, because in Deuteronomy Moses, or rather the Lord through him, is speaking after they had come out of Egypt and had already been liberated from the strong nation of the Egyptians. The parallel can be aptly applied to us, for we have escaped from the snares of this age, and can claim to be already free from greed, that is the indulgence of taste and stomach. Against the seven remaining nations we have a continuing struggle, but the first, being defeated, is no longer counted. Even so, Israel was not given its land to possess, but to leave it for ever and come out of it as the Lord commanded them. Hence our fasting needs to be reasonable, so that unreasonable self-denial does not weaken us and cause a physical illness which would make it necessary to return to the land of Egypt, that is to say, to revert to the former pleasures of the table which we cast off when we renounced the world. This fulfils the parable of those who had gone out into the desert of virtue, but again yearned for the flesh pots by which they sat in Egypt.

XIX. "The commandment was not that the nation in which the children of Israel had been born should be exterminated, only that they should leave their territory. In contrast, the other seven were to be wiped out completely, and for this reason: no matter how ardent the spirit be in which we have entered the desert of virtue, it is never possible to get away from the neighbourhood and domination of gluttony, and its daily occasion. The desire for food to eat remains always innate and natural to us, however eager we be to eliminate excessive appetite. What we cannot totally eliminate, we must avoid by self-denial. Of this it is said, 'make not provision for the flesh in its concupiscences' (Rom. 13:14). Since we retain the need for nourishment which we are commanded not to cut off totally but to fulfil without excessive desire, clearly we should not exterminate the nation of Egypt but be careful to separate ourselves from it, thinking not about excessive delicate banqueting, but as St Paul says, being content with our daily sustenance and clothing (I Tim. 6:8). In the Law this is expressed figuratively, 'Thou shalt not abhor the Egyptian, because thou wast a dweller in his land' (Deut. 23:7, LXX). We cannot deny the body its necessary victuals without harming it, which would be a sin on the soul, but the other seven emotions should be completely eradicated from our innermost souls, being harmful altogether. Of these it is said, 'Let all bitterness and anger and indignation and clamour and blasphemy be put away from you, with all malice' (Eph. 4:31), and a little later, 'Fornication and all uncleanness or covetousness, let it not so much as be named among you, or obscenity or foolish talking or scurrility' (Eph. 5:3–4). It is possible to pluck up the very roots of these vices, which are parasites on nature, but we can never eliminate the occasion of gluttony. However hard we try, we must always be what we were born to be. This is demonstrated not only by our own way of life, feeble though we be, but by that of all who are perfect; the pangs of other vices may have receded, we may have sought the desert in all earnestness and in total poverty, but still we cannot be rid of the need to prepare our daily meal, and to grow our food year by year.

XX. "An appropriate metaphor for this temptation, which affects every monk no matter how profoundly spiritual he may be, is the eagle. It flies up beyond the clouds to a great height, out of the sight of all mortal flesh, away from the surface of the earth, but then it stoops again to the lowest valleys and lands on the ground to tear at decaying bodies, driven by its need for nourishment. You can see clearly that the spirit can never be cut off from the desires of the stomach, as from other vices, or be quite free from them as in other cases; no, all it can do is to restrain and limit its excessive demands through strength of mind.

XXI. "One of the elders was disputing with some pagan philosophers about the nature of this vice. They took him, in his Christian simplicity, for a rustic that they could easily refute, but he put his case neatly using the following parable: 'My father left me beholden to many creditors; I paid most of them in full, and am free from all their importunity, but there is one that I cannot satisfy although I pay him every day.' They did not understand the point of the riddle, but begged him to explain it. 'I was by nature,' he said, 'enslaved by many vices, like pressing creditors, but the Lord inspired me to desire my freedom, and so I renounced the world and repudiated the entire fortune which I would have inherited from my father, which satisfied all those vices; from those I am completely free. But the pangs of hunger I have never been able to quench. Even though I reduce myself to the smallest and meanest ration, I do not escape its constant pressure. I have to meet its ceaseless demands, make endless repayments with great effort, and pay instalments towards a debt which is never satisfied.' The philosophers, who had despised him as an ignorant peasant, acknowledged that he had perfectly understood the first division of philosophy, that is to say, ethics.

V. On the Eight Deadly Sins

They were amazed that he, aided by no worldly education, had instinctively grasped what they had been unequal to, despite much thought and long study.

That is enough to say about gluttony in particular; we should return to the discussion which we had begun about how to deal with vices in general.

XXII. "When the Lord spoke to Abraham about things to come, he did not reckon the nations whose land he would grant to his posterity as seven, but ten, a point which had escaped you (Gen. 15:18–21). That number can be made up by adding idolatry and blasphemy, for before learning about God and receiving the grace of baptism, the pagans were enslaved to idolatry, the Jews to blasphemy, while they were dwelling in the metaphorical Egypt. One who renounces the world, and comes out of Egypt by the grace of God, with gluttony to some extent subdued, enters the desert of the spirit, already free from the assaults of three nations, and can take up the struggle against just those seven which Moses enumerates.

XXIII. "We are commanded to occupy the territory of these aggressive nations for our benefit, as we may understand thus. Each sin has its own location in the heart, and it will defend that part of the innermost soul for the extermination of Israel, which is to say the contemplation of great and holy matters, and it will oppose it ceaselessly. Virtues and vices, indeed, cannot co-exist, 'for what participation hath justice with injustice? Or what fellowship hath light with darkness?' (II Cor. 6:14). Yet once the vices have been overthrown by the people of Israel (that is the virtues which fight against them), the location which lust or fornication had occupied in our hearts is taken over by chastity; that held by anger is occupied by patience; the place where melancholy lurked to brood on death is possessed by a saving sorrow that is filled with joy; where depression laid waste becomes the abode of resoluteness; the site trampled by pride is exalted by humility. As each vice is driven out their locations, or emotions, are taken over by the contrary virtues. This is fittingly declared of the sons of Israel, being the souls that see God, for when they have driven all those passions out of the heart, we can see that they are recovering their own homeland, not occupying the possessions of others.

XXIV. "As ancient tradition teaches us, the lands of the Canaanites, into which the children of Israel were led, had originally been allocated to the sons of Shem when the world was partitioned, and the descendents of Ham had wickedly invaded them and taken them by force. Thus God's judgment is proved right in driving the Canaanites out of the foreign land which they had wrongly occupied, and restoring to Israel their ancient patrimony which had been allotted to their race when the world was divided up. This can be clearly recognised by us as a parable of our own condition. It was God's will that the possession of our hearts should belong by nature to the virtues, not to the vices. After the fall of Adam the virtues were driven from their homeland by insolent vices, represented by the Canaanite tribes, so that when they were restored by God's grace through our own care and effort, they can be seen to be recovering their own lands, not occupying those of others.

XXV. "The Gospel speaks of these eight vices in this manner: 'When an unclean spirit is gone out of a man, he walketh through dry places seeking rest and findeth none. Then he saith: I will return into my house from whence I came out. And coming he findeth it empty, swept and garnished. Then he goeth and taketh with him seven other spirits more wicked than himself; and they enter in and dwell there; and the last state of that man is made worse than the first' (Matt. 12: 43–5). Just as we read in one place of seven nations, not counting the Egyptians from whom Israel had already come out, so in the other text we hear of seven unclean spirits returning, not counting the one who we are told had left the man before. Solomon also describes the sevenfold root of sin in Proverbs: 'If your enemy calleth to you in a loud voice, trust him not, because there are seven mischiefs in his mind' (Prov. 26: 25, LXX). Therefore, if the spirit of gluttony has been overcome but begins to flatter you with a humble approach, begging you to relax your earlier zeal a little, and grant a little more than moderation and the official ration permit, do not revert to your subjection to greed, do not become careless in the face of attack because you have found yourself a little less troubled by the stings of the flesh, otherwise you will soon relapse into your former decadence and gluttonous ways. That is why the defeated spirit says, 'I will return into my house from whence I came out', and the spirits of the seven other sins will come in with it, which will cause you more pain than the one temptation which you had formerly overcome, for they will soon drag you down to much worse sins.

XXVI. "That is why we undertake fasting and self-denial, and must advance quickly after the defeat of gluttony; we should not let our hearts lie unoccupied by the virtues we need, but should quickly populate the innermost parts of the soul with them. Otherwise the spirit of desire might return and find us empty and unoccupied, whereupon it will not be content just to make its own entry alone, but will introduce into the soul with itself the sevenfold germ of vice, till our end is worse than our beginning. The soul that brags of having renounced this world but is enslaved by eight sins, will be worse and more unclean, liable to a greater suffering, than it was formerly in the world, before professing either the name or the life of a monk. The seven other spirits are called more evil than the one which had been expelled first, because the lure of hunger, that is greed, is not dangerous in itself, unless it gives entry to worse temptations, namely fornication, avarice, wrath, melancholy or pride, which are in themselves undoubtedly virulent and dangerous to the soul. There is no chance of attaining perfect purity if you think you can achieve it by this one exercise of physical fasting alone, unless you recognise that the purpose of this discipline is to humiliate the body with fasting in order to enter the lists against the other vices more easily, unhindered by the weight of indulged flesh.

XXVII. "We should be aware that not everyone follows the same order in these contests, for as we have said, we are not all attacked in the same way. Thus each one of us must open the battle against sin according to the type of attack we most suffer. One man may have to make his first assault against the third sin, another against the fourth or fifth, and so on, depending on which sin assaults us most. We must join battle according to whichever manner of attack we sustain. A successful and triumphal outcome in this way will enable us to arrive at purity of heart and the fullness of perfection."

Thus spoke Abba Sarapion to us on the nature of the eight deadly sins, explaining the types of sin which lurk in our hearts, the causes and effects of which we had not previously recognised properly or distinguished, although we suffer the effects of them every day; he spoke so clearly that we seemed to be looking them before our very eyes, as if in a glass.

✣ THE SIXTH COLLATION ✣
BEING THAT OF ABBA THEODORE

On the Massacre of the Saints

I. A description of the desert, and the problem of the massacre of the saints.
II. The reply of Abba Theodore to the question put.
III. Of three conditions in this world, the good, the bad and the indifferent.
IV. How no one can suffer evil from another against his will.
V. An objection, on how God can be said to create evils.
VI. The reply to the question put.
VII. A question, on whether it be a sin to put a just man to death, since the just man reaps such a reward from death.
VIII. The reply to the preceding question.
IX. The examples of Job tempted by the devil, and the Lord betrayed by Judas; and how for the just man both prosperity and adversity can lead to salvation.
X. Of the virtue of a perfect man, metaphorically called ambidextrous.
XI. Of the twofold nature of temptation, and the threefold purpose for which it occurs.
XII. How a just man must be like a seal, not one of wax but of onyx.
XIII. A question, whether the mind can persevere constantly in the same position.
XIV. The reply to the above question.

XV. The danger of leaving one's cell.
XVI. Of how changeable heavenly virtues are.
XVII. That no one falls suddenly into ruin.

I. There is in Palestine, near the town of Tekoa which gave birth to the prophet Amos (Amos 1: 1) a wide desert which stretches as far as Arabia and the Dead Sea. The River Jordan flows into it, and disappears, and the ashes of Sodom are strewn over a vast extent. For a long time there were monks living there in great holiness of life, but they were suddenly wiped out by rampaging Saracen brigands. Their bodies were held in great respect by the clergy of that region as well as by all the Arab people, and were laid up among the relics of martyrs. However a great crowd from two different towns met and quarrelled violently over them, till their rivalry over possession of these holy relics led to swords being drawn. In their devotion they contended over which might have the better claim to the burial of their relics; some based their claim on living near the place where they had dwelt, others were proud of being near their place of origin. We and our friends for our part were considerably disturbed by the problem of the death of these brethren, as were many who lived in those parts, and wondered why men of such merit and of such great virtues should be killed by brigands in this way. Why had the Lord allowed such a crime to be committed against his servants, surrendering men who were marvellous in every way into the hands of the wicked?

We took our question sadly to Saint Theodore, a man remarkable for his practical instruction. He was living in Cellae at the time, a place lying between Nitria and Scete, five miles from the monasteries in Nitria, and distant eighty dreary miles from the remoteness of Scete where we were then living. We poured out our complaint over the death of the men I have mentioned, surprised at God's tolerance in allowing men of such merit to die thus. They were so holy that they should have been able to preserve others from trials of this sort, not to mention saving themselves from the hands of the wicked – why then had God permitted such a crime to be perpetrated against his servants?

VI. On the Massacre of the Saints

II. The holy Theodore replied, "This is the sort of question that troubles those who possess but a little faith and knowledge, thinking that it is in the brief space of this life that the reward and prize lies for the saints, a reward which is not granted in this life but is stored up for the future. Otherwise, as St Paul says, we whose hope in Christ is not for this life only, 'are of all men most miserable' (I Cor. 15:19). We who have in this world received nothing of what we were promised would through our lack of faith lose even the world to come, so let us not be led astray by such errors. In ignorance of the truth we would be timid and fearful, a prey to tribulation; if we saw ourselves given up to such trials we might attribute to God either injustice, or lack of concern for humankind (which would be a wicked thought!) as if he did not shield holy men who live good lives from trials, nor repay good with good in this life, nor evil with evil – thinking thus we would deserve the sentence which the prophet Zephaniah pronounces on those 'that say in their hearts: The Lord will not do good, nor will he do evil' (Zeph. 1:12). Or perhaps we would find ourselves among those who abuse God with these complaints, 'Every one that doth evil is good in the sight of the Lord, and such please him: or surely, where is the God of judgment?' (Mal. 2:17). The blasphemy which follows would also ensue, 'He laboureth in vain that serveth God, and what profit is it that we have kept his ordinances and that we have walked sorrowful before the Lord of hosts? Wherefore now we call the proud people happy, for they that work wickedness are built up: and they have tempted God and are preserved' (Mal. 3:14–15). Now to escape the ignorance which is the root cause of this error, we should first know what is truly good, what is evil; we should hold on this matter the true teaching of Scripture, not the false one of the crowd, and avoid altogether the deceitful error of the unfaithful.

III. "There are three conditions in this world, the good, the bad and the indifferent. We must inform ourselves of what the good really is, what is evil and what indifferent, so that through this true knowledge our faith may remain unshaken, fortified in all its trials. We should not consider anything to be the supreme good for man other than virtue of soul, which leads us to God in real faith and makes us cling to that unchangeable good. On the other hand, nothing is to be called evil except sin alone, which cuts us off from the goodness of God and unites us to the evil one, the devil. In between are those things which can be turned towards either side depending on the choice and will of those who use them. Examples are wealth, power, honour, physical health and strength, good looks, life itself and death, poverty, ill-health, injury and such matters which, depending on the free choice of the individual, may be used for a good end or an evil one. Riches indeed are often used for good, as St Paul says, urging 'the rich of this world . . . to give easily, to communicate to others, to lay up in store for themselves a good foundation against the time to come, that they may lay hold on the true life' (I Tim. 6:17–19). In the Gospel, good is spoken of those who 'make unto you friends of the mammon of iniquity' (Luke 16:9). But riches are diverted towards evil if they are accumulated just to be hoarded or squandered, and not distributed for the needs of the poor. Power also, and honour, physical health and strength, are all indifferent and apt for either outcome, as we can easily see from the many saints of the Old Testament who were possessed of all these things, living in great wealth and esteem, and physical strength, but were acknowledged as most acceptable to God. Others who used them badly, and diverted them to evil ends, were justly punished and exterminated, as the books of Kings often recount.

That life itself and death are indifferent is shown by the birth of St John, or of Judas. The life of one was of such benefit to himself that others also rejoiced at his birth, for it says, 'And many shall rejoice in his nativity' (Luke 1:14), whereas of the other's life it is said, 'It were better for him if that man had not been born' (Matt. 26:24). Of the death of St John, as of any saint, it is written, 'Precious in the sight of the Lord is the death of his saints' (Psalm 115/116:15), whereas of the death of Judas and his like it is said, 'the death of the wicked is very evil' (Psalm 33/34:22). We can see from the happiness of Lazarus, the ulcerous beggar, how bodily

VI. On the Massacre of the Saints

illness may be an advantage; for Scripture does not suggest he had any merits other than enduring poverty and sickness with patience – and for this he deserved to win a place of bliss in the bosom of Abraham (Luke 16: 20–31). Poverty, oppression and suffering, which the whole world considers evil, can also be found beneficial, necessary indeed, given that holy men never try to escape them, and indeed through their eagerness for them and heroic endurance became friends of God in strength, to win the reward of eternal life; as St Paul says, 'for which cause I please myself in my infirmities, in reproaches, in necessities, in persecutions, in distresses, for Christ. For when I am weak, then am I powerful . . ., my power is made perfect in infirmity' (II Cor. 12: 9–10). For that reason, we must not imagine that those who are most renowned in this world for wealth, rank and power, have thereby attained the greatest good which lies only in virtue, but only something indifferent; if the just use them wisely and well they are beneficial and helpful (for they provide an opportunity for good works which bear fruit in eternal life), while if others use these means badly, they are dangerous and damaging, giving occasion to sin and death.

IV. "If we have clearly understood this definite and primary distinction, and recognise that nothing is good except virtue alone which comes from the fear of God and his love, nor anything evil except sin alone, which cuts us off from God, we may now enquire whether God has ever allowed any evil to be inflicted on his saints, either of himself or through others, and we shall find that this has certainly never happened. No one has ever been able to force the evil of sin on another who was unwilling and resisting, but only on one who accepted it through a weak spirit and corrupt will. In the case of the holy man Job, the devil afflicted him with every evil in his armoury in the attempt to force him to sin; he stripped him of all his property, caused him the dreadful grief of losing his seven sons, slain so unexpectedly, and proceeded to wound him terribly from the crown of his head to the soles of his feet, loading intolerable pain on him, but could not impose the stain of sin on him in any way; Job remained unmoved by all this and never agreed to a single blasphemous word."

V. GERMANUS: "But we frequently read in Scripture that God created evils, and inflicted them on mankind, as in 'There is none besides me. I am the Lord and there is none else. I form the light and create darkness, I make peace and create evil' (Isaiah 45:6–7). And again, 'Shall there be evil in a city, which the Lord hath not done?' (Amos 3:6)"

VI. THEODORE: "Often indeed Scripture does improperly refer to God's punishments as 'evils', not that they are evil in themselves, but because they are perceived as evil by those who receive them for their own benefit. When men speak of divine dispensation, they have to use human terms and emotions. In the same way a doctor may lovingly use surgery or cautery to cure those who are gangrenous with suppurating ulcers, but the patients call that evil. The spur and the bit are unpleasant to a recalcitrant horse. Every sort of discipline is unpleasant at the time for those under training, as the Apostle says, 'Now all chastisement for the present indeed seemeth not to bring with it joy but sorrow; but afterwards it will yield to them that are exercised by it the most peaceable fruit of justice.' and further back, 'For whom the Lord loveth, he chastiseth; and he scourgeth every son whom he receiveth. For what son is there whom the father doth not correct?' (Heb. 12:6–11). Thus 'evil' is sometimes used to mean 'affliction', as in, 'And God repented with regard to the evil which he had said he would do to them, and he did it not' (Jon. 3:10, LXX) and also, 'You, O Lord, are gracious and merciful, patient and rich in mercy, and ready to repent of the evils' (Joel 2:13, LXX). Evils, in this case, are the trials and punishments which he is compelled to bring upon us because of our sins. Another of the prophets well knew the value of such punishments for some whose salvation he did not grudge, for in their own own interests he prayed, 'Pile evils upon them, O Lord, pile evils on the haughty of the earth' (Isaiah 26:15, LXX), and the Lord replied 'Behold, I will bring in evils upon them' (Jer. 11:11).

VI. On the Massacre of the Saints

Sorrows, that is, and desolation, which will chasten them for the moment until they are made to return to me, hurrying back to the one they have despised in their prosperity. Hence we cannot really call these things 'evils', for they are beneficial to many, and bring to life the seeds of eternal joy.

Now to return to the question you asked, anything which could be reputed evil, that our enemies or anyone else brings upon us, should not be so reputed, but believed to be indifferent. They should be assessed, not as the one who inflicts them in his fury intends them, but as the one who sustains them does. So that when death is inflicted on a holy man, we should not consider it to be an evil, but something indifferent. For a sinner it would indeed be an evil, but for the just it is repose and freedom from evil. 'For the death of the just is repose, of a man whose way is hidden' (Job 3:23, LXX). The righteous man suffers no ill from death, for he endures nothing new; through his enemy's sin, he receives what was bound to come upon him by the common law of nature, and yet he wins assurance of eternal reward. He pays the debt of human death, which must be paid anyway by inflexible law, and his suffering bears abundant fruit, with the reward of a great prize."

VII. GERMANUS: "So if a just man suffers no wrong from being slain, but actually gains a reward, how can we call it a sin for one to put him to death, which does not harm him but benefits him?"

VIII. THEODORE: "We have been talking about the nature of good and evil and of what we called the indifferent, not about their effect on those who perform them. A wicked and sinful man should not go unpunished because his malice was unable to harm the just man. For the just man's endurance and strength benefits not the one who inflicted death or suffering, but himself who patiently endured what was done to him. The other is rightly punished for his savage cruelty, for his intention was to inflict evil, while the just man suffers no evil because he sustains the trials and afflictions with strong-minded patience. Thus he turns what was intended to be evil into a means towards a better state giving rise to eternal life in bliss.

IX. "Job returned no joy to the devil, who made him all the more illustrious by tempting him, but rather acquired great merit by enduring patiently. Judas gained no exemption from eternal pain because his treason had brought salvation to the human race. We should consider not the outcome of the deed but the intention of the performer. For this reason we should always keep this principle in mind, that no one can have evil inflicted upon him by another unless his own weakness and corrupt heart admit it. One verse of St Paul confirms this opinion: 'We know that to them that love God all things work together unto good' (Rom. 8:28). In saying, 'all things work together unto good', he includes not only prosperity of all kinds but even the things commonly considered adverse. The same Apostle in another passage describes how he has passed through them, saying, 'By the armour of justice on the right hand and on the left. By honour and dishonour; by evil report and good report; as deceivers and yet true; ... as sorrowful, yet always rejoicing; as needy, yet enriching many' (II Cor. 6:7–10). All the benefits that he says lie on the right hand are termed 'honour' or 'good report' by the holy Apostle, whereas things considered adverse he terms 'dishonour' or 'evil report', lying on the left hand, and it is these that form weapons of righteousness for the perfect man, if he endures them gladly when they come upon him. Fighting with these, and using as his weapons the very things which seem to oppose him, he plies them valiantly as bow, sword and shield to strengthen him against all who assail him. Thus he wins an outcome of endurance and virtue, earning an honourable triumph for steadfastness with the same deadly weapons with which his enemy had been attacking him. He is not proud in prosperity nor cast down by adversity, but proceeds on a smooth path, on the Royal Road. He is not deflected from his calm progress onto the right side by joy, nor to the left by any assaults of gloom or sadness. 'Much peace have they that love thy law: and to them there is no stumbling block' (Psalm 118/119:165), and it

VI. On the Massacre of the Saints

is said of those who are affected and changed by every event as it occurs, 'a fool is changed as the moon' (Sir. 27:12). When it is said of the perfect that 'to them that love God all things work together unto good' (Rom. 8:28), it is also said of the foolish and weak, 'All things go against a foolish man' (Prov. 14:7, LXX). He gains nothing from prosperity, he is not improved by adversity. Surely it belongs to the same virtue to endure grief with courage, and to be moderate in favourable circumstances; he who is overcome by either is unable to bear both. It is however easier to be tripped up by prosperity than by ill-fortune. Adversity can restrain and humiliate even those who resist, and with saving repentance can make them sin less or reform them, whereas prosperity inflates the thoughts with soothing but dangerous flattery, and brings to total ruin those who are confident of future bliss.

X. "There are some men in Holy Scripture called in parable *amphoterodexioi*, that is to say, ambidextrous – like Ehud in the Book of Judges, 'who used either hand as his right' (Jud. 6:7). We can imagine as a metaphor that we too possess this quality, if we are able to use correctly both prosperity on the right, and ill-fortune on the left, using them both as the right and turning whatever comes upon us into what the apostle calls 'armour of justice.' Thus we can see how on both sides, with both hands so to speak, our inner person may prosper. There has never been a saint who lacked the use of his left hand, for perfect virtue is found when he can use either as his right hand for a good purpose. To understand what we are saying more plainly, a holy man has a right hand which is spiritual success; he uses it when he is zealous and master of all his desires and passions; safe from any attack of the devil he can reject and eliminate all carnal vice with no trouble or difficulty. Raised above the earth he can look upon all present earthly things as so much smoke, or empty shadow; he can despise them, for they soon pass away, when he longs and yearns for the things to come in his mental exhilaration, and indeed sees them more clearly, feeding upon spiritual insights. He perceives the shining heavenly mysteries laid up for him, he pours out eager pure prayer to God, he is so fired with the spirit that his whole being is transfixed by the invisible things of eternity and he scarcely believes that he still exists in the flesh.

In the same manner he uses his left hand, when he is caught up in a whirlwind of temptation, inflamed with the burning desires of the flesh, inflamed with the passion of fierce anger, battered by the forces of pride and vainglory, crushed with the sadness that leads to death, assaulted and ensnared by the wiles of depression; when he loses all spiritual fervour and is sunk in listlessness and inexplicable grief; when he loses touch with holy aspirations and thoughts and even finds psalms, prayers, reading and the isolation of his cell abhorrent. In such case all the means to virtue seem unbearable and tedious – when a monk feels all this happening he should realise that he is being pressed from the left side. Now if when he is in the state we have described as being on the right he avoids being at all elated by vanity, and when he is attacked from the left he is firm in resisting, nothing will make him lose heart. Then he will in fact take up an armour of endurance from both sides, in his strife for virtue, and will be using either hand as his right. Victorious on both fronts he will gain the palm of victory over both conditions, both those to right and to left.

We read that holy Job achieved this, for he gained a crown on the right when he was the wealthy father of seven sons; in his riches he made a daily practice of offering a sacrifice of purification to the Lord for them, wanting to display them more to God than to himself, as worthy members of the family; his doors were open to every comer, he was the limb of the cripple and the eye of the blind; the shoulders of the weak were warmed with the fleeces of his flock, he was the father of the orphan and the husband of the widow, and not even in his thoughts did he take pleasure in the misfortune of his enemy (Job 29: 12–16). And then he gained a more glorious triumph with greater valour over his foes on the left side. When he was bereft of his seven sons in one moment, he was not crushed with bitter grief like a father, but rejoiced in the will of the Creator, as God's true servant. From being wealthy he was made poor, stripped of his riches, his health turned to sickness, his fame and reputation reduced to shame and disgrace, yet he retained his strength of mind unwavering. Bereft of all his property, of all his fortune, he lay on the dunghill; like a savage butcher of his own flesh he scraped off the effluvia with a potsherd and plunged his fingers into deep ulcers to pull out tangles of worms from every limb. Yet in all this he fell into no blasphemous despair, uttered no murmur against his Creator; nay he was in no way daunted by such a cumulation of bitter trials, but even tore the garment which alone of all his wealth survived to him to cover his body, and cast away the clothing which he might have salvaged from the fiend's assault, choosing to be naked beyond the bareness which the enemy had already inflicted on him. The hair too of his head, which alone remained of his former splendour, he cut off and hurled at his tormentor; shearing away what the savage foe had left him, he scorned him and reviled him with these heavenly words, 'If we have received good things at the hand of God, why should we not receive evil? Naked came I out of my mother's womb, and naked shall I return thither. The Lord gave, and the Lord hath taken away. As it hath pleased the Lord so is it done. Blessed be the name of the Lord' (Job 2:10, 1:21).

Joseph is another one we can call 'ambidextrous', for in his prosperity he was his father's favourite, more pious than his brothers, more pleasing to God; in adversity he was chaste, faithful to his master, acquiescent in his imprisonment, unmindful of wrongs, generous to his enemies, and towards his jealous brothers who had done their best to be his murderers he was not only loving but even munificent.

Such men and those like them are rightly called ambidextrous, for they use either hand as the right one, and passing through the trials the Apostle mentions they can say with him, 'by the armour of justice on the right hand and on the left, by honour and dishonour, by evil report and good report', and so on (II Cor. 6:7–8). Solomon also speaks of the right and the left in the person of the Bride in the Song of Songs, 'His left hand is under my head, and his right hand shall embrace me' (Song 2:6). He tells us that both are beneficial, but the left hand he puts beneath the head, because adverse circumstances should be subdued by the mighty heart. Their benefit to us lies in that for a time they exercise us and instruct us towards salvation, making us perfect and steadfast. The right hand of the Bridegroom embraces us for our comfort and to keep us safe for ever, drawing us to him and uniting us to him securely. We shall therefore be ambidextrous when we too are unchanged by abundance or lack of this world's goods; when prosperity cannot drive us to slacken into perilous decadence, nor adversity plunge us into despair and complaint; giving thanks to God alike in either case we shall reap the same reward in favourable and unfavourable times. The truly ambidextrous Teacher of the Gentiles tells us this of himself, when he says, 'I have learned, in whatsoever state I am, to be content therewith. I know both how to be brought low, and I know how to abound (everywhere and in all things I am instructed); both to be full and to be hungry; both to abound and to suffer need. I can do all things in him who strengtheneth me' (Phil. 4: 11–13).

XI. "Now although we have explained that there are two types of temptation – in prosperity, that is, and in adversity – we must know that there are three purposes for which everyone suffers temptation. In most cases it is to test them; in some to improve them, in a few as punishment for their sins. We read about the testing of holy Abraham and Job, and many other holy men who suffered great trials. In Deuteronomy we find what Moses said to the people: 'Thou shalt remember all the way through which the Lord thy God hath brought thee for forty years through the desert, to afflict thee and to prove thee: and that the things that were in thy heart might be made known, whether thou wouldst keep his commandments or no' (Deut. 8: 2). In the Psalms too, it says, 'I proved thee at the waters of contradiction' (Psalm 80/81: 8). To Job also is said, 'Dost thou think that I spoke to you other than that thou mayest be justified?' (Job 40: 3, LXX).

For their improvement, God suffers his righteous ones to be tempted in various ways, either for their light and trivial sins or to humiliate any elation because of their own purity. As he

VI. On the Massacre of the Saints

scrutinises every stain of thought, every hidden spot of tarnish (to use the prophet's word) he anneals it for a time so that he can send it on to its future testing as purified gold, permitting nothing to remain in them which the purgatorial fire of judgment may find after this life and afflict them for. 'Many are the afflictions of the just' as the Psalm says (Psalm 33/34:19), and, 'My son, neglect not the discipline of the Lord; neither be thou wearied whilst thou art rebuked by him. For whom the Lord loveth, he chastiseth; and he scourgeth every son whom he receiveth.... For what son is there whom the father doth not correct? But if ye be without chastisement, whereof all are made partakers, then are you bastards and not sons' (Heb. 12:5–8). And in the Apocalypse, 'Such as I love I rebuke and chastise' (Apoc. 3:19). In Jeremiah a prophecy is made of them under the figure of Jerusalem, in God's person, 'I will utterly consume all the nations among which I have scattered thee. But I will not utterly consume thee: but I will chastise thee in judgment, that thou mayest not seem to thyself innocent' (Jer. 30:11). David too prays for this saving correction, 'Prove me, O Lord, and try me: burn my reins and my heart' (Psalm 25:2), and Jeremiah again says, aware of the value of this testing, 'Correct me, O Lord, but yet with judgment: and not in thy fury' (Jer. 10:24). Isaiah too says, 'I will give thanks to thee, O Lord, for thou wast angry with me. Thy wrath is turned away: and thou hast comforted me' (Isaiah 12:1).

Temptations may be inflicted as punishment for sin, as when the Lord threatens that he will bring plagues on the people of Israel, 'I will send the teeth of beasts upon them, with the fury of creatures that trail upon the ground' (Deut. 32:23); 'in vain have I struck your children: they have not received correction' (Jer. 2:30). In the Psalms we read, 'Many are the scourges of the sinner' (Psalm 31/32:10), and in the Gospel, 'Behold, thou art made whole: sin no more lest some worse thing happen to thee' (John 5:14).

A fourth reason may be added, for we find on the authority of Scripture that some suffered sore trials simply in order that the glorious work of God might be made manifest in them; for instance in the Gospel, 'Neither hath this man sinned, nor his parents; but that the works of God should be made manifest in him' (John 9:3), and 'This sickness is not unto death, but for the glory of God, that the Son of God may be glorified by it' (John 11:4). There are other types of punishment too, for some who exceeded the bounds of evil were struck down immediately, like Dathan and Abiram, and Korah of whose condemnation we read (Num. 16), and especially those of whom the apostle says, 'For this cause, God delivered them up to shameful affections ... to a reprobate sense' (Rom. 1:26, 28), which must be considered the most grievous of afflictions. The psalmist says of them, 'They are not in the labour of men: neither shall they be scourged like other men' (Psalm 72/73:5). These are the ones who do not deserve to be saved when the Lord comes, nor to receive the medicine of temporal suffering, for they, 'despairing, have given themselves up to lasciviousness unto the working of all uncleanness, unto covetousness' (Eph. 4:19). In the stubbornness of their hearts and frequent commission of sin their guilt exceeded anything that could be purged in this brief life, or punished in this present world. The Word of God rebukes them through the prophet, 'I destroyed some of you, as God destroyed Sodom and Gomorrah; and you were as a firebrand plucked out of the burning; yet you returned not to me, saith the Lord' (Amos 4:11). Jeremiah also says, 'I have killed and destroyed my people, and yet they are not returned from their ways' (Jer. 15:7), and 'thou hast struck them, and they have not grieved: thou hast bruised them, and they have refused to receive correction. They have made their faces harder than the rock and they have refused to return' (Jer.5:3). The prophet saw that all the healing power of remedies in this world was wasted on them in vain, and gave up all hope of their salvation, declaring, 'The bellows have failed, the lead is consumed in the fire, the founder hath melted in vain: for their wicked deeds are not consumed. Call them reprobate silver, for the Lord hath rejected them' (Jer. 6:29–30). The Lord admits that he had vainly applied the purging fire to save those who were obstinate in their sins, under the image of Jerusalem, encrusted with the deep corrosion of her sins. Thus he complains, 'Set a

VI. On the Massacre of the Saints

brass jar empty upon burning coals, that it may be hot, and the brass thereof may be melted: and let the filth of it be melted in the midst thereof.... Great pains have been taken, and the great rust thereof is not gone out, not even by fire. Thy uncleanness is execrable: because I desired to cleanse thee, and thou art not cleansed from thy filthiness' (Ezek. 24:11–13).

Like a skilled doctor, when the Lord has tried every type of cure and seen that for this disease no possible kind of remedy will be of any avail to overcome such a cumulation of evil, he is forced to give up his merciful, if painful, treatment. He declares this, saying, 'and my indignation shall not rest in thee, and my jealousy shall depart from thee' (Ezek. 16:32). In other cases, when the heart has not been hardened by frequent sin, it is not necessary to use such severe and caustic (so to speak) fiery remedies, but a word of saving advice is sufficient to cure them; 'I will heal them as their tribulation hath been heard' (Hosea 7:12, LXX).

We are not unaware that there are other reasons for rebuking or chastising those who have grievously sinned; neither to expiate their guilt, nor to wipe away the punishment for their sins, but so that the living might be edified and impressed. This we can see in the cases of Jeroboam son of Nebat, or Baasha son of Achiah, cited against Ahab and Jezebel, who are rebuked by God thus: 'Behold, I will bring evil upon thee, and I will cut down thy posterity, and I will kill of Ahab him that mingeth against the wall, and him that is shut up, and the last in Israel. And I will make thy house like the house of Jeroboam the son of Nabat, and like the house of Baasa the son of Achias: for what thou hast done, to provoke me to anger, and for making Israel to sin. The dogs shall eat Jezebel in the field of Jezrahel. If Ahab die in the city, the dogs shall eat him: but if he die in the field, the birds of the air shall eat him' (III Kings (I Kings) 21:21–4). The great curse too that was spoken, saying, 'Thy dead body shall not be brought into the sepulchre of thy fathers' (III Kings (1 Kings), 13:22) was not because a momentary punishment would be sufficient to expiate the blasphemous thoughts of Jeroboam, who first set up the golden calves to make the people stray for ever more, and wickedly cut them off from the Lord; nor was it to wipe out their great and innumerable crimes; no, it was for the benefit of those who are careless of the life to come, or disbelieve it entirely, who are stirred only by the thought of temporal things, so that they might be put in fear by the punishments they did respect, and through hearing of this retribution come to realise that the divine majesty is not unconcerned about human deeds and their daily supervision. Through things which greatly frightened them, they might come to understand that God is the avenger of all wrongs. That is why we find some men punished with immediate death for minor faults, such as the fomenters of discontent whom we mentioned earlier, or the man who gathered wood on the Sabbath (Num. 15: 32), or Ananias and Sapphira who kept back a little of their property through lack of trust (Acts 5). The punishment was not proportionate to the sin, but since they had been found guilty of disobeying new commandments, they were needed to give an example to others of grief and fear, as they had been examples of sin. Thus anyone who attempted such crimes afterwards would be aware that he would be repaid in the judgment to come in the same degree that they suffered, even if punishment were deferred for the present.

We seem to have gone on too long talking about types of temptation and punishment, digressing from the subject we intended. The point we were making is that a perfect man remains ever constant in trials of either kind, and to that point we shall now return.

XII. "The mind of a just man should never be like wax, or any other malleable material, which easily takes the impress of a seal, but retains that shape and design only until it is remoulded with the impress of a different seal. It never preserves any shape of its own, but always changes and adopts the form impressed upon it. No, our minds should be like a seal-matrix of onyx, which preserves its shape invariable and stamps and moulds to its own image everything it encounters – it can never be remoulded by any impress."

VI. On the Massacre of the Saints

XIII. GERMANUS: "Is it possible for our minds to preserve a single position constantly, and to persevere in that intention always?"

XIV. THEODORE: "According to St Paul, you must either progress day by day, 'and be renewed in the spirit of thy mind' (Eph. 4: 23), and 'stretch forth myself to those things that are before' (Phil. 3: 13), or if you neglect to do this, you must decline and lapse back into a worse state. For that reason the mind cannot possibly remain in the same position; it is as if someone were trying to drive a boat against a raging torrent with oars; either by sheer strength of arm he will cleave the swirling stream and force his way upwards, or if his hands fall slack, he will be dashed down again by the flood. Hence it is a clear indicator of decadence if we realise we are making no progress. On the day that we become aware that we have made no advance, we must surely acknowledge that we have been driven backwards. As I said, the human mind cannot remain in one position; as long as we are in this body we cannot attain the pinnacle of saintly virtue which is to abide immovable. Something must always be added or lost; no creature has such a degree of perfection that it is not subject to the law of change. We find this in the book of holy Job: 'What is man that he should be without spot; and he that is born of a woman that he should appear just? Behold, among his saints none is unchangeable: and the heavens are not pure in his sight' (Job 15: 14–15). God alone can we call unchangeable, as the holy prophet was once compelled to acclaim, 'But thou art always the selfsame' (Psalm 101/102: 28); and he says of himself, 'I am the Lord, and I change not' (Mal. 3: 6). He alone is good by nature, he alone is always full, always perfect, to whom nothing could ever be added, from whom nothing taken away. We must therefore apply ourselves with unremitting zeal to the pursuit of virtue, and busy ourselves ever with its exercise, for if our efforts fail, we shall straightaway find ourselves in decline. I say again, it is impossible to remain in the same frame of mind, that is without gaining an increase of virtue or suffering its loss. Not to progress is to decline, and if we no longer desire to advance we will not escape the danger of falling back.

XV. "Now we must remain constantly within the cell. Every time you return and re-enter, it is as if you were beginning afresh to live there, all confused and disturbed by every occasion of going out. If we once lose the recollection we had acquired by living within the cell, it cannot be recovered except by great effort and strain. Thus one who returns to his cell is not so much thinking about the progress he had lost, and how he might have added to it had he not left his cell, but is glad if he only feels that he has recovered the state from which he has fallen. Just as time, once past and wasted, can never be recovered, so attainments once lost cannot be restored. No matter how determined the mind be hereafter, the only progress will be that of the new day, the only gain that of present time. The past, once lost, is gone for ever.

XVI. "Even heavenly powers are subject to change, as is proved by those of their number who have fallen through the fault of their own evil wills. Thus we must not imagine that those who persevere in the bliss for which they were created are unchangeable by nature, simply because they were not corrupted by the other side. To be of an immutable nature is quite another thing from remaining unchanged as a result of hard work and good intentions, through the grace of God, who is truly immutable. Anything we can acquire or preserve through attention, can be lost through inattention. Thus it is said, 'Praise not any man before death' (Sir. 11: 30), since as long as one is still in the competition, still in the arena so to speak, however accustomed to victory, however many medals he wins, he can never be quite free from anxiety, and the risk of an unexpected failure. That is why God alone is called unchangeable, he alone is good, for his goodness belongs to him by nature, not through effort, and he can never be anything but good. There is no virtue that a man can possess unchangeably, but if you would preserve it in its present condition, you must guard it with the same care and attention with which you acquired it [or, to speak more correctly, you must preserve it with the support of God's assisting grace].

VI. On the Massacre of the Saints

XVII. "We must not imagine that anyone who has fallen did so by a sudden collapse: he was either deceived by the rise of a wicked habit, or through long carelessness his strength of mind gradually declined, so that as his vices grew little by little, he fell into a wretched state. 'Pride goeth before contrition, and evil thought before a fall' (Prov. 16:18, LXX). Just as a house never collapses all of a sudden, unless the foundations were originally at fault, or the inhabitants are consistently lazy, so that tiny raindrops make their way in and gradually weaken the covering of the roof. Eventually after long neglect the roof gapes open and falls, letting full torrents of rain and hail pour in. 'By slothfulness a roof shall be brought down, and through the idleness of hands the house shall drop through' (Qo. 10:18, LXX). Solomon tells the same parable about the soul in other words, 'Rain in a winter's day shall drive a man from his house' (Prov. 27:15, LXX). He elegantly compares the idle mind with a neglected house and roof, for at first only the tiniest raindrops of passion penetrate the soul, but if they are ignored for being small and trivial, they rot the beams of virtue, till a storm of vices pours in. Thus on a wintry day, in other words when the devil attacks with temptations, the mind is driven out of the house of virtue, whereas if it had been watchful and diligent in preserving it, it could have reposed there as if in its own home."

We listened to this, and were filled with an infinite spiritual joy, so that our happiness of mind after this discourse was greater than the grief we had formerly felt over the massacre of the saints. Not only had we been instructed on the matter which worried us, but as a result of making our enquiry we had discovered things we had not even thought of asking about, in our poor ignorance.

✧ THE SEVENTH COLLATION ✧
BEING THE FIRST OF ABBA SERENUS

On the Wandering Mind and on Wicked Spirits

    I. On the chastity of Abba Serenus.
   II. On how the aforesaid elder questioned us about the state of our thoughts.
  III. What we answered about our wandering thoughts.
  IV. The Elder's discourse about the nature of the soul and its powers.
   V. On the perfection of the soul, under the parable of the centurian in the Gospel.
  VI. On persevering in the control of our thoughts.
 VII. A question, about the wandering mind, and the assaults by wicked spirits.
VIII. The reply, on how God assists us, and on the power of free will.
  IX. A question, on the connection between the soul and the devils.
   X. The reply, on the manner in which unclean spirits are linked to human minds.
  XI. An objection, whether unclean spirits can be inserted into the souls of those who they have possessed, or can be united to them.
 XII. The reply, on the manner in which unclean spirits dominate the possessed.
XIII. That a spirit cannot be penetrated by another spirit, but only by God who is incorporeal.
XIV. An objection, that it is believed that the demons can read human thoughts.

XV. The reply, on what power the demons have over human thoughts, and what they do not have.
XVI. A simile, to show how unclean spirits detect human thoughts.
XVII. That it is not the same demons that inculcate all human temptations.
XVIII. A question, on whether any order and regularity in tempting is observed among demons.
XIX. The reply, how the demons can agree on a pattern of temptation.
XX. That the powers which oppose us are not all equally strong; nor do they have the power of tempting us at their whim.
XXI. That it is not without effort on their part that demons fight with men.
XXII. That the devil does not have a choice over whether to harm us.
XXIII. On the reduced power of the devil.
XXIV. The method by which the devils effect an entry into the bodies of those they are to possess.
XXV. That it is more wretched to be a slave to vice than to the demons themselves.
XXVI. On the death of the prophet who was deceived, and on the illness of Abba Paul which was justified by the benefit he received from it.
XXVII. On the temptation of Abba Moyses.
XXVIII. That those who are handed over to unclean spirits should not be despised.
XXIX. An objection, why is it that those who are troubled by wicked spirits are barred from Holy Communion.
XXX. The reply to the question put.
XXXI. That those who are not deemed worthy to be tested in this way during their lifetime are the more unfortunate.

VII. On the Wandering Mind and on Wicked Spirits

XXXII. On the diverse aims and intentions of the spirits of the air.
XXXIII. A question, on the origin of the diversity among spiritual beings.
XXXIV. The reply to the question proposed is deferred.

I. Abba Serenus was a man of great holiness and self-discipline, who lived up to his name; we admired him very much more than the others, and would like to commend him to the attention of the studious. The only way to carry out this intention is to attempt to put his conversation into our little book. Apart from all the other virtues which, through the grace of God, were manifest in his actions and gestures, nay even displayed on his face, he did have the special grace of an infused gift of chastity, so that he was not in the least disturbed by natural urges, not even in sleep. I feel that I should begin by explaining how he reached this singular purity, aided by God's grace, since it may appear to be beyond the bounds of human nature.

II. He strove tirelessly to achieve internal chastity of mind and heart, through prayer night and day, fasting and vigils. When he saw that he had obtained the goal of his prayers, and that all the passion of fleshly lust was extinct in his heart, he was fired with such a great delight in purity that he set his sights on a higher target, in his love of chastity. With stricter fasting and more fervent prayer he aspired to attain in the outward man the same degree of self-control which God had granted to his inner person; so that he might not be troubled again even by that common natural arousal which occurs even to babies and infants. Having experienced the granting of one boon, which he knew full well was by God's grace, not his own effort, he was the more eager to attain this one as well, for he believed that it was much easier for God to quell these motions of the flesh, which can be eliminated by human artifice, drugs, medicines or even surgery, than to grant the spiritual purity which he already had, something beyond the possibility of human art or effort. As he persevered with the intention he had adopted, in heartfelt prayer and tears, an angel came to him in a vision of the night, and appeared to open his abdomen, extracted a burning tumour from his bowels and threw it away, returning his intestines to their places as before. "Lo," he said, "the sting of your flesh has been cut out; be aware that from this day forth you have obtained that lasting purity of body which you had faithfully requested." That is enough to record about the divine grace which was the special gift of this memorable man. I do not consider it necessary to say much about his other virtues, which he held in common with other great men, lest it should detract from the feature which was special to this man, the characteristic which belonged to him in particular.

It was during Lent that we asked to see him, inspired by a great longing for his conversation and teaching. He gently inquired of us what was the nature of our thoughts and our interior state, and what advantage our long dwelling in the desert had been in the quest for purity, and we addressed him with this lament:

III. "The passage of time, and our experience of contemplation in the desert, which you would have thought should have brought us to perfection in the inner man, has in fact gained us nothing; we have learnt only what we are incapable of being, we have not made ourselves what we want to be. We find that we have neither achieved firm and constant purity, as we had hoped, nor any great degree of endurance and knowledge, but we have simply become more confused and ashamed. We practice all our exercises diligently and perfectly every day, in order that we might progress from our timid beginnings to sure and lasting excellence, and so begin to understand what before we knew but vaguely or not at all. With a steady pace, so to speak, we hoped to advance in that discipline until we could achieve it without any further difficulty. But see – far from advancing like that, when I strove to carry out these exercises for the sake of purity, all I found I could achieve was the knowledge of what I was incapable of. With all that heartfelt contrition, all I felt was sorrow, for I was never

VII. On the Wandering Mind and on Wicked Spirits

without cause for grief, nor ever ceased to be what I should not. What then is the use of knowing what is best if we are unable to achieve what we know? For when we feel the aspirations of our hearts tending towards the contemplation which is our goal, our thoughts unconsciously turn away and slide back all the more eagerly into their former paths. Filled daily with distractions, the mind is always being swept away into innumerable dead ends. The improvement we wanted seems hopeless, and our discipline pointless, for our minds are dissipated moment by moment with unseemly distractions. As soon as we apply ourselves to the fear of God and the contemplation of the spirit, the thoughts flit away again before they can be properly concentrated. When we come to ourselves we realise that our minds have wandered far from their intended path, and we call them back to the meditation they had deserted, with the full intention of keeping them there and fixing them with sure bonds, but even as we try, our thoughts escape from the mind as slippery as an eel. For that reason, frustrated by such daily experience, and observing that we have failed to attain any strength of mind, we have been reduced in desperation to decide that these mental distractions are not our fault, but simply part of the natural human condition."

IV. SERENUS: "It is a dangerous thing to imagine that we can make any decision about the nature of anything before examining the matter closely and considering it accurately, or to conjecture anything about our own disabilities or offer an opinion about the value and nature either of the exercises themselves, or on the experience of other peoples. It is as if someone who did not know how to swim, but knew that water was unable to support the weight of his own body, presumed to decide from his limited experience that no one still clothed in solid flesh would ever be able to float on a liquid. We would consider a judgment more reliable if it came from one who ventured to state, on his own observation, that it is not only possible but easily done by others, proving it by sure reasoning and the evidence of his own eyes. 'The mind', it has been said, 'is ever wandering, wandering greatly'. The same sentiment is found in the Wisdom of Solomon, 'the earthly habitation presseth down the mind that museth upon many things' (Wisdom 9:15). By our very nature, our thoughts can never remain blank, but unless they are given some field of action, to occupy them properly, are bound to wander of their own accord. They flit about everywhere, until after long training and daily exercise (a task you describe as fruitless), they become accustomed to preparing suitable matter for consideration, around which a strong rampart of will is erected, with the determination to remain steadfast, until they are strong enough to resist the enemy's suggestions and distractions, and abide in the state and manner desired. We must not ascribe this wandering of the thoughts to our own true nature or to God who created us, for Scripture tells us truly, 'God made man right, and he hath entangled himself with evil imaginations' (Qo. 7:30, LXX). The nature of our thoughts depends on us. 'When a good thought approaches the wise, a prudent man will lay hold upon it' (Prov. 19:8, LXX). If there is any subject which our prudence and industry could lay hold of, then it is our own idleness and lack of discretion, not our nature, that is at fault if we do not grasp it. The Psalmist also agrees with this, when he says, 'Blessed is the man whose help is from thee: in his heart he hath disposed to ascend by steps' (Psalm 83/84:6). You see how it lies in our own power whether we advance, that is to say direct our thoughts to God, or decline, turning to earthly carnal things instead, as we determine in our hearts. Had it not lain within our power, would Our Lord have rebuked the Pharisees, saying, 'Why do you think evil in your hearts?' (Matt. 9:4). Or would he have given order, through the prophets, 'Take away the evil of your devices from my eyes' (Isaiah 1:16), and, 'How long shall hurtful thoughts abide in thee?' (Jer. 4:14). Nor would the Lord have threatened, through Isaiah, that our thoughts would be examined on the day of judgment as well as our deeds, for he says, 'I come that I may gather them together with all nations and tongues' (Isaiah 66:18). Let us not be found worthy of condemnation for our thoughts, or have to be on our defence in that fearful judgment day, as St Paul warns us, saying, 'their thoughts between themselves accusing or also defending one another, in the day when God shall judge the secrets of men, according to my Gospel' (Rom. 2: 15–16).

V. "An apt parable of this perfect state of mind may be found in the Centurian in the Gospels, where is described in metaphor that constant virtue which is not swept away by every passing thought but has the discretion either to admit the good or to dismiss the bad without difficulty: 'For I also am a man subject to authority, having under me soldiers; and I say to this, Go, and he goeth, and to another, Come, and he cometh, and to my servant, Do this, and he doeth it' (Matt. 8: 9). We too, if we strive manfully against distractions and combat our vices, will be able to subdue them to our will and command, quench the fleshly temptations that war against us, and subjugate to the command of reason that regiment of unruly thoughts. Under the saving banner of the Lord's Cross we will repulse throngs of hostile powers from our borders, and in recognition of such exploits will be promoted to the spiritual equivalent of centurian. In Exodus we find this ordained by Moses in parable: 'and appoint of them rulers of thousands, and of hundreds, and of fifties, and of tens' (Exod. 18: 21). Thus we too can be elevated to this high rank, and will be well capable of taking command; we will not be swept away by thoughts we do not want, but will be able to abide with the ones in which we take spiritual delight, and cleave to them. To evil considerations we can command, 'Go', and they will go, to good ones, 'Come', and they will come. To the servant – that is the body – we can command chaste behaviour, and it will obey with no contradiction, without stirring up pangs of lust against us, but demonstrating complete docility to the spirit.

The weapons this centurian bears, and the war for which he is equipped, are described by the Apostle, who says, 'For the weapons of our warfare are not carnal, but mighty to God' (II Cor. 10: 4); their quality then is 'not carnal' and weak, but of the spirit, and 'mighty to God'. He informs us next on the combats for which they are to be used, 'unto the pulling down of fortifications, destroying counsels, and every height that exalteth itself against the knowledge of God; and bringing into captivity every understanding unto the obedience of Christ; and having in readiness to revenge all disobedience, when your obedience shall be fulfilled' (II Cor. 10: 4–6). Although it will be necessary to go through this in detail, that must be left to another occasion. All I want to do now is to explain to you the types of our weapons, and their use, for if we wish to fight in the wars of the Lord, and to be enrolled among the Gospel centurians, we must gird ourselves with them valiantly. 'Take up', says St Paul, 'the shield of faith wherewith you may be able to extinguish all the fiery darts of the most wicked one' (Eph. 6: 16). Faith therefore is our shield, which can intercept the fiery darts of lust and quench them through fear of future judgment and trust in the kingdom of heaven. 'The breastplate of charity' (I Thess. 5: 8), is that which encloses and protects our vital organs, and receives the deadly thrusts of temptation, repels their impact, and prevents the devil's weapons from piercing our inner self. 'Charity beareth all things, believeth all things, endureth all things' (I Cor. 13: 7). Then, 'for a helmet, the hope of salvation' (I Thess. 5: 8). A helmet is the protection for the head, and our head is Christ. We must fortify that against all temptations, with the hope of future good as if with an impenetrable helm; in particular we must preserve that faith undamaged and whole. If we lose any other limb we may be crippled but we can still survive, but without a head no one has any chance of staying alive. 'And the sword of the spirit (which is the Word of God)' (Eph. 6: 17). 'For the Word is more piercing than any two-edged sword, and reaching unto the division of the soul and the spirit, of the joints also and the marrow; and is a discerner of the thoughts and intents of the heart' (Heb. 4: 12). That is to say, it divides and dissects whatever it finds in us of earth or the flesh. Anyone who is armed with these weapons is ever protected against hostile missiles, and will never be depopulated, carried off captive into enemy territory, chained in bonds of obsessive thoughts; nor will he hear the prophet saying, 'Why art thou grown old in a strange country?' (Bar. 3: 11). Like a victorious conqueror he will remain in the area of thought which he himself chooses.

Would you like to know about the strength and courage of our centurian, with which he wields the weapons we have been talking about, not carnal but mighty to God? Hear the King himself, summoning his strong men into his spiritual army, how he calls them beloved and tests them, 'Let the weak say: I am strong, the man who suffereth will be a fighter' (Joel 3:10, LXX). Do you see how the wars of the Lord are not fought without the weak and suffering? It is in that weakness that our Gospel centurian found strength, for he says confidently, 'when I am weak, then am I powerful,' and 'power is made perfect in infirmity' (II Cor. 12:9–10). One of the prophets also speaks of this weakness, 'And the weak man among you shall be as the house of David' (Zach. 12:8, LXX). The man who suffers will fight in this war, for his suffering is that of which it is said, 'patience is necessary for you; that doing the will of God, you may receive the promise' (Heb. 10:36).

VI. "We have learnt from our own experience how closely we must cling to God. It is not impossible, if we have mortified our pleasures and cut off the desires of this world, and we find confirmation of this in the testimony of those who speak faithfully for God: 'My soul hath stuck close to thee' (Psalm 62/63:9), and 'I have stuck to thy testimonies, O Lord' (Psalm 118/119:31). Also, 'It is good for me to adhere to my God' (Psalm 72/73:28), and 'He who is joined to the Lord is one spirit' (I Cor. 6:17). We should not be so wearied by the wandering of our thoughts as to relax our guard; for 'he that tilleth his ground shall be filled with bread: but he that followeth idleness shall be filled with poverty' (Prov. 28:19). Nor should we be deterred from attempting this self-control by dangerous despair, for 'in much work there shall be abundance; in every effort; but he who is idle and without pains shall be in want' (Prov. 14:23, LXX). And again, 'a man who is in sorrows laboureth for himself, and doeth violence to his own loss' (Prov. 16:26, LXX). Similarly, 'The kingdom of heaven suffereth violence, and the violent bear it away' (Matt. 11:12). There is no virtue that is acquired without effort, nor can anyone arrive without great contrition of heart at the calm state of mind you desire. 'For man is born to labour' (Job 5:7). One who would arrive at perfect manhood, 'unto the measure of the age of the fullness of Christ' (Eph. 4:13), must be always intent on his sublime purpose and work for it with great zeal. No one will arrive at that degree of maturity in the life to come otherwise than by preparing for it and being steeped in it during this present life. While still in this world he must anticipate it, bearing the title of a glorious member of Christ; in his own body he will possess the advance on that union by which he can be incorporated into Christ's Body, desiring one thing only, thirsting for one alone, bending his thoughts and not only his actions to one end; for in this present life he holds an advance instalment of what is promised for the life of the saints to come, namely that 'God may be All in All'" (I Cor. 15:28).

VII. GERMANUS: "Presumably our wandering thoughts could be constrained, were it not that there is such a great number of surrounding enemies that constantly drive them to where they would rather not go, or rather to where their own fickle nature would impel them. We had believed that it is impossible for this frail flesh to resist so many powerful and terrible foes, but we have been inspired to a new opinion by your almost heavenly discourse."

VIII. SERENUS: "No one who has any experience of the struggles of the inner man can doubt that our enemies press us hard. But we assert that they attack our progress only as instigators to evil, not as having power to compel. Otherwise none of us would ever be able to avoid sin, to the extent that our enemies wanted to instil it into our hearts, had they the power not only to suggest crimes but even to force them on us. Therefore just as they have the ability to tempt us, so we have the power to reject them and the freedom to agree with them. If we are afraid of the strength of their attacks, we should counteract them with the shielding assistance of God, of whom is said, 'Greater is he that is in you than he that is in the world' (I John 4:4). God's auxiliaries fight for us with much greater strength than the throng who combat us, for God does not just suggest good works but encourages and supports them, to the extent that he often entices us to our salvation without our will or knowledge. It follows that no one can be deceived by the devil unless he chooses to grant him the assent of his will. The Preacher puts this point clearly: 'for because sentence is not speedily pronounced against the evil, the heart of the children of man is filled, that they might do evil' (Qo. 8:11, LXX). We can see from this that everyone who sins does so because when evil thoughts arise he fails to block them at once. For it is said, 'resist the devil, and he will fly from you'" (James 4:7).

IX. GERMANUS: "Now may I enquire whether it is the case that the soul has such a close and unguarded association with the wicked spirits that they can be not so much joined as united with them; and that the devils can speak to the soul secretly, can insert and inspire it to whatever they want, can tempt it to their desires, and can read its thoughts and emotions clearly; so that there is such a union between them and the mind that it is quite unable to distinguish what originates from their insinuations from what proceeds from its own will, were it not for the grace of God."

X. SERENUS: "We should not be surprised if spirit can be joined to spirit, invisibly, or can exercise an unseen force for whatever it wants. They have a certain similarity of nature and affinity, just as men do. In fact a description of the nature of the soul can be appropriately applied to their nature as well. Nevertheless it remains quite impossible for these spirits to be inserted or united to the soul to the extent that one comprehends the other completely. God alone can be properly said to do that, whose nature alone is incorporeal and simple."

XI. GERMANUS: "This opinion seems to be contradictory to what we have observed in the case of possession, when the victims say things with the voices of unclean spirits and do things unconsciously. How can we say that the spirits are not united to their souls, when we see them become no more than their instruments, deprived of their true nature, and their gestures and emotions are transformed into those of the spirits, to the point that they speak with their voices, act with their gestures, follow their wills, not their own?"

XII. SERENUS: "What you have said about the possessed does not contradict what I said before, although they may well speak with the voice of unclean spirits, perform what they do not want to do, and be compelled to tell of what they do not know. I am convinced that this infestation of spirits can afflict them in more than one way. Some are so badly affected that they are unaware of what they are doing or saying, while others are conscious and can remember it later. We must not imagine that this happens by infusion of the unclean spirit to the extent that it reaches the very centre of the soul, and is almost united with it, so rapt into it that it can speak its own words and ideas through the mouth of the sufferer. We cannot believe that this is possible. It is reasonable to conclude that it does not happen through any weakness of soul, but through a defect of the body, inasmuch as the spirit invades the organs which are the seat of mental powers, and burdens than with an immense and unbearable weight; this then obscures the thought process with impenetrable darkness, which obstructs the senses. The same thing can be seen happening as a result of drunkenness, disease, excessive cold, and other external factors affecting the health. In the case of holy Job the devil was restrained by the Lord's command from molesting him thus, although he had been given power over his body, for God said, 'Behold, I give him over into thy hands; but yet save his mind' (Job 2:6, LXX). In other words, do not make him insane by damaging the seat of the mind, [intruding into his power of thought, and blighting the reason with which he will have to resist you]; do not overwhelm the understanding and wisdom which is his defence, or suffocate his innermost heart with your oppressive weight.

XIII. "Even though a spirit may quite easily insert itself into base solid matter (that is to say flesh), we must not imagine that it

VII. On the Wandering Mind and on Wicked Spirits

can be united to a soul, which is itself a spirit, to the extent of rendering it coextensive with its own nature. Only the Blessed Trinity can do that, penetrating the whole intellectual sphere; not only does it embrace and surround the soul, but the incorporeal actually enters the corporeal and is infused into it. We admit the existence of spiritual beings, angels, archangels and the other Powers, not to mention our own souls and the thin air around us, but we must not consider them to be incorporeal. In their own terms they do have real bodies, although much more subtle than ours. That they are bodies is shown by St Paul, who says, 'there are bodies celestial and bodies terrestrial,' and further on, 'It is sown a natural body: it will rise a spiritual body' (I Cor. 15: 40, 44). We can gather from this that there is nothing incorporeal except God alone, and that spiritual and intellectual natures can not be penetrated except by him alone, for he alone is the All, is everywhere and in all things. He sees and illuminates the thoughts of men, their internal emotions and the secrets of their hearts, and of him alone does the Apostle declare, 'The Word of God is living and effectual and more piercing than any two-edged sword: and reaching unto the division of the soul and the spirit, of the joints also and the marrow; and is a discerner of the thoughts and intents of the heart. Neither is there any creature invisible in his sight; but all things are naked and open to his eyes' (Heb. 4: 12–13). David also says, 'He who hath made the hearts of every one of them' (Psalm 32/33: 15), and 'He knoweth the secrets of the heart' (Psalm 43/44: 22). This Job says as well, 'thou only knowest the hearts of the children of men'" (II Chron. 6: 30).

XIV. GERMANUS: "According to your teaching, these spirits are not even able to see into our thoughts. But I think this is absurd; after all, Scripture says 'If the spirit of him that hath power ascend upon thee' (Qo. 10: 4), and 'the devil having now put into the heart of Judas Iscariot, son of Simon, to betray' the Lord (John 13: 2). How can we think that our thoughts are not open to them, when we are conscious that the greater part of the seedbed of such thoughts is prepared by their intrusive interference?"

XV. SERENUS: "There is no doubt that unclean spirits can discern the nature of our thoughts, but it is only by collecting information from our outward appearance, that is from the behaviour, words and interests to which they observe us most inclined. They are quite unable to reach our thoughts, which never escape from the inner mind. Even the thoughts which they themselves have insinuated, whether we accept them and to what extent, they can only perceive from a man's external actions and indications, not from the actual nature of the soul, the internal activity hidden in the very marrow of the mind, so to speak. For instance, if they have suggested gluttony, they can perceive that the pangs of greed have taken hold on a monk if they observe him glancing anxiously at the sun out of his window, or asking concernedly what time it is. If they have insinuated lust, they can tell if he has willingly received the wound of desire if they notice him physically aroused, or at least failing to recoil as he should from the suggestion of unclean pleasures; thus they know that the arrow of lust has pierced the centre of his soul. If it is melancholy, or anger or rage that they have suggested, they can detect whether these have entered the soul by outward actions and noticeable behaviour; for instance if they catch him quietly fuming, sighing with indignation, his face changing from pallor to red. Thus they can tell subtly who is subject to which vice, and can know for certain which of us is subject to whichever vice they have suggested, as they observe whether our bodily indications show consent to it, and behaviour is in accordance with it. We should not be surprised that these aery spirits can observe this, since we see it frequently done by perceptive men, who can detect a man's inner state from his posture, expression and other outward signs. Much more likely, therefore, that these spiritual beings can detect such things, for they are surely much more subtle and intelligent than us!

XVI. "It is like when burglars are exploring a house they wish to plunder, to investigate the owners' hidden wealth. In the depth of night they cautiously sprinkle grains of sand, in order to detect by the tone of the noise the falling sand makes whether there are

VII. On the Wandering Mind and on Wicked Spirits

hidden treasures which they cannot see; the sound they hear gives sure information on each material or metal. In the same way the spirits who are investigating the treasure of our hearts, sprinkle evil suggestions on them like sand, and watch the type of physical effect which results, so that they can tell what lurks in the inmost part of a man, as if by the tone which the secret treasury gives out.

XVII. "This too you should know, that not every demon instils every temptation, but particular spirits inculcate particular vices. Some favour uncleanness and obscenity, others blasphemy, others provoke their victims to anger or rage, others feed them on melancholy, others ruin them with vainglory or pride. Each one insinuates into human hearts the vice which it prefers itself. Nor do they inculcate their depravity into everyone to the same degree, but provoke their victims according to the weather, the place, and their aptitude."

XVIII. GERMANUS: "Must we then believe that they follow a set order and regularity in wickedness, so to speak? Do they have some structure to their tempting, and a calculated method of attack? But it is commonly agreed that only the good and respectable can have any method or regularity, as Scripture says, 'Seek for wisdom among scorners, and you will find it not' (Prov. 14:6, LXX), and 'Our enemies are without sense' (Deut. 32:31, LXX). We also find, 'There is no wisdom, there is no prudence, there is no counsel among the wicked'" (Prov. 21:30, LXX).

XIX. SERENUS: "It is quite true that there can never be any lasting agreement among the wicked about anything, nor can there be any real consistency even in the vices they most enjoy. As you have said, there can be no regularity or method in irregular matters. Occasionally, however, they have to come to a temporary agreement, depending on the needs of the task in hand and the profit to be gained from combining. We can detect this clearly in the case of our warfare against evil spirits, for they keep to certain times and fluctuations, and even haunt certain places in particular where they are known to be especially troublesome. They are obliged to plan their attack with differing temptations to certain vices at different times, as we can see clearly from the fact that no one can be swept away by vanity at the same time that he is afire with the desire of lust. Nor can anyone be puffed up with swelling spiritual pride if he is at the same time humiliated by physical greed. No one can dissolve into indecent laughter and mirth when he is being provoked to violent anger, or suffering the pangs of gloomy melancholy. Each spirit must assail the mind in turn, so that if it has to depart defeated, it can give place to another spirit which will attack more fiercely; if it withdraws after a victory then in the same way it passes the victim on for another to tempt.

XX. "We should not fail to recognise that they are not all equally fierce and enticing, and not all evils are of the same strength. Beginners and the weak only have to contend with the minor spirits, but if these fiends are overcome, more and more daunting bouts await the Christian champion. Depending on the strength and skill of the individual, the difficulty of the contest increases. Indeed none of the saints would be able to endure such great hostile assaults, or survive their onslaught at all, nor could they bear their savage cruelty were not Christ the merciful referee of the contest, the umpire of the ring – he matches the abilities of the contendents and restrains their attacks if they are beyond the limit, providing, with the temptation, a solution, so that we may be able to bear it (cf. I Cor. 10:13).

XXI. "Do not imagine that they engage in this struggle without effort on their part. They too feel anxiety and distress in the conflict, especially when they are matched against the stronger, that is to say holy men who are perfect. Otherwise there would be no conflict or struggle, and their deception of men would be straightforward and risk-free, so to speak. St Paul explains how matters are: 'Our conflict,' he says, 'is not against flesh and blood, but against Principalities and Powers, against the rulers of the world of this darkness, against the spirit of wickedness in the high

VII. On the Wandering Mind and on Wicked Spirits

places' (Eph. 6:12). He also says, 'I so fight, not as one beating the air' (I Cor. 9:26), and 'I have fought a good fight' (II Tim. 4:7). In saying fight, struggle, battle or combat, it is implied that there has to be sweat, labour and effort on both sides, and both parties would be equally glum and depressed by defeat, both equally elated in victory. If only one were fighting desperately while the other overcame easily and effortlessly, simply using his will and strength to crush the opponent, you would not call it a contest, a battle or a struggle, but simply an unjust and unreasonable tyranny. No, the devils themselves have to work hard at invading the human race; it is only with effort that they overcome and win the victory they desire over anyone, and they suffer the same embarrassment in defeat that we feel when defeated by them, as in the text, 'The head of them compassing me about: the labour of their lips shall overwhelm them' (Psalm 139/140:10). See also, 'His sorrow shall be turned on his own head' (Psalm 7:17), and 'let the snare which he knoweth not come upon him: and let the net which he hath hidden catch him: and into that very snare let them fall' (Psalm 34/35:8). That is to say, he will fall into the pit which he himself had dug to catch men.

They grieve no less than we do, and just as they hurt us, so they can be hurt; when overcome they depart in turmoil. There was one who was gifted with insight into the inner man, who daily observed their fall and confusion in this manner, and he saw too how they exulted over the fall and distress of others; he prayed to the Lord in his anxiety not to give them cause for such joy himself, 'Enlighten my eyes, that I never sleep in death: lest at any time my enemy say: I have prevailed against him. They that trouble me will rejoice when I am moved' (Psalm 12/13:4–5). Again he wrote, 'O Lord my God, let them not rejoice over me. Let them not say in their hearts: It is well, it is well, to our mind: neither let them say: We have swallowed him up.' and 'they gnashed upon me with their teeth. Lord, when wilt thou look upon me?' (Psalm 34/35:24–5, and 16–17). 'He lieth in wait in secret like a lion in his den. He lieth in ambush that he may catch the poor man' (Psalm 9/10:9), 'seeking their meat from God' (Psalm 103/104:21).

When they have exhausted all their efforts, and failed to achieve our deception, they are bound to be 'confounded' over their wasted toil, 'and ashamed together, that seek after my soul to take it away' (Psalm 39/40:15). 'Let them blush and be ashamed together, who rejoice at my evils' (Psalm 34/35:26). Jeremiah also says, 'Let them be confounded, and let not me be confounded: let them be afraid and let not me be afraid: bring upon them the day of affliction, and with a double destruction destroy them' (Jer. 17:18). Have no doubt that when we defeat them they are destroyed with a double destruction; firstly because while men are in pursuit of holiness, they who once possessed it have lost it, and have become the cause of human loss; secondly because they who are spiritual by nature have been defeated by earthly flesh. Any one of the saints can declaim with joy on seeing their ruin and his own triumph, 'I will pursue after my enemies, and overtake them: and I will not turn again till they are consumed. I will break them, and they shall not be able to stand: they shall fall under my feet' (Psalm 17/18:38–9). The same sacred writer prays for help against them, saying, 'Judge thou, O Lord, them that wrong me: overthrow them that fight against me. Take hold of arms and shield, and rise up to help me. Bring out the sword, and shut up the way against them that persecute me: say to my soul: I am thy salvation' (Psalm 34/35:1–3). When we have overthrown them, with all our passions subdued and quenched, we shall be fit to hear the sentence of blessing that follows, 'Thy hand shall be lifted up over thy enemies: and all thy enemies shall be cut off' (Micah 5:9).

When in our reading and chanting of sacred scripture we come across passages like all those above, we must understand them as directed against these spiritual evils which assail us day and night, otherwise we would fail to find in them anything to help us be mild and patient; indeed, we would be developing dangerous emotions which contradict the Gospel. We would find ourselves provoked not so much to pray for our enemies or love them, but actually to hate them with a perfect hate, to curse them, and pour out ceaseless prayers against them! It would be a wicked blasphemy to imagine that holy men who loved God could write in such a vein, for even though before the coming of Christ no actual law had been laid on them, they anticipated the last dispensation, transcending the commandments to prepare the way for the precepts of the Gospel, and to strive for the perfection of the apostles.

XXII. "The story of holy Job demonstrates clearly enough that the devil does not possess any power that could really hurt us, for the devil was granted no permission to tempt Job beyond what God allowed. In the Gospel the evil spirits themselves admit this, when they say, 'If thou cast out hence, send us into the herd of swine' (Matt. 8:31). How much less ability they have to choose to enter a human being created in the image of God you can see from the fact that they were powerless to enter unclean dumb animals without God's permission. Otherwise it would be quite impossible for anyone to abide in the desert; not just the young men whom we can observe living very piously in the wilderness, but even the perfect would fail, surrounded by such a legion of foul fiends, if they had the ability and the freedom to hurt us or assail us at their pleasure. We find this teaching confirmed by Our Saviour's words, when he spoke to Pilate in the humility of his human nature, 'Thou shouldst not have power against me, unless it were given thee from above' (John 19:11).

XXIII. "We know well, both from our own experience and from what the elders have told us, that the devils no longer have as much power as they once had, when hermits were first starting, and very few monks yet dwelt in the desert. In those days they were so fierce that very few people could tolerate living in the wilderness, only those who were well balanced and advanced in age. Even in the monasteries where eight or ten of them lived together, the attacks were so violent, the visible manifestations so common, that they would not dare all to sleep at the same time, but in turns some rested while others kept watch, devoting themselves to psalms, prayer and reading. When nature demanded sleep they woke the others to keep a similar watch over those who then went to rest. Now that we live in confident safety, not only we old ones who might appear to have been toughened by experience, but even the younger ones, we must draw one of two conclusions: either the glory of the Cross has so penetrated the desert and shone with such grace that the wickedness of the devil is restrained, or we are so careless that their attacks have become milder than before, because they disdain to attack us with the same intensity with which they used to rage against the valiant warriors of Christ. They could be doing us greater damage with sly temptations which we fail to notice. For we do see some of our brethren lapsing into such sloth that they need to be stimulated with stern rebukes; otherwise they would abandon their cells and turn to worse troubles, wandering about and becoming entangled in the more earthy vices, so to speak. Yet great profit can be expected from them if they will only persevere in staying put in the desert, however idle; the usual advice the elders give for their great edification is, 'Sit in your cells; eat and drink and sleep as much as you like, but just stay there continually.'

XXIV. "It is agreed that unclean spirits can only effect an entry into the bodies of those they are to possess if they have already taken possession of their minds and thoughts. Once they have stripped them of the fear of God and the awareness of Him, and of all spiritual considerations, they invade them confidently and conquer them easily, for they have been disarmed of all divine protection and guard; they take up residence in them as if in their own property.

XXV. "Indeed those who do not appear to be possessed by demons in a bodily manner may be far more grievously troubled because they have taken possession of their souls, that is to say they are entangled in vices and the devil's pleasures. The Apostle tells us, 'by whom a man is overcome, of the same also he is a slave' (II Pet. 2:19). The worst part of their suffering is that they are so enslaved that they do not even realise that they are being

VII. On the Wandering Mind and on Wicked Spirits 161

attacked or dominated in this way. But as for being bodily handed over to Satan or to great infirmities, we know of very holy men who suffered that for slight offences; it was through the mercy of God, so that not the slightest spot or stain might remain in them on the day of judgment, for every spot of dross on the heart (as the prophet, or rather God himself, puts it) is refined away in this present life, in order that they might be able to pass into eternity like purified gold or silver, needing no punishment in purgatory. 'I will clean purge away thy dross,' says the prophet, 'and I will take away all thy tin. After this thou shalt be called the city of the just, a faithful city' (Isaiah 1: 25–6). In another place, 'As gold and silver are tried in the furnace, so the Lord trieth the hearts' (Prov. 17: 3, LXX), and again, 'for gold and silver are tried in the fire, but acceptable men in the furnace of humiliation' (Sir. 2: 5). This too, 'whom the Lord loveth, he chastiseth; and he scourgeth every son whom he receiveth' (Heb. 12: 6).

XXVI. "We can see an example of this in the case of the prophet, the man of God, in the Third Book of Kings: he was killed suddenly by a lion because of one act of disobedience, and one that he committed through the machinations of another, not through his own choice or his own fault. Scripture says, 'the man of God was disobedient to the mouth of the Lord; and the Lord hath delivered him to the lion and he hath torn him, according to the Word of the Lord, which he spoke to him' (III Kings (I Kings) 13: 26). In this occurrence is shown firstly the atonement for present sin, and how wrong the unwary man was, and also the merits of righteousness, for the Lord handed his prophet over to punishment for a moment only. Thus he revealed his mercy, as well as the self-restraint of the predator, for that savage beast did not dare to eat any part of the body which had been given over to him.

Other examples of this sort of thing happened in our own time, and are well known, being the trials undergone by Abba Paul and Abba Moyses who lived in the area of the desert named Calamus. The first of these used to live in the desert near the city of Panephysis; this we remember only recently became a desert, after a flood of salt water, which was driven continually by the north wind, till the marshes grew and overflowed the adjacent land and the whole surface of the area was covered. The old villages were abandoned by all their inhabitants because of this, but they still stood up like islands. This is where Abba Paul came for the sake of purity of heart, in the silent peace of the desert, and let alone seeing a woman's face, he could not endure so much as to let his eyes rest on a woman's clothing. Once when he was on a journey to the cell of a certain elder, along with Archebius who was his disciple in the wilderness, a woman happened by; he was so offended at meeting her that he fled back to his hermitage without achieving the visit which had been his devout intention, running away as he would have done from neither lion nor frightful dragon. He paid no attention to Abba Archebius who was calling him back, and entreating him to continue on the journey they had begun, to visit the elder as they had intended. Now, granted that he did this through zeal for chaste purity, it was not wise or prudent, but exceeded the measure of reasonable self-discipline, for he did not just shun intimacy with women, which is indeed dangerous, but their very presence. He was straightaway afflicted with a stroke, so that his whole body was paralysed, and he was unable to move or use any of his limbs. Not only his hands and feet, but even his tongue was affected, so that he could not express himself, and his ears too had lost the power of hearing, so that all that remained of his humanity was an immovable and unfeeling body. In fact he was reduced to such a state that being cared for by men would have been quite inadequate to cope with his illness; he needed to be nursed by women. He was taken to a convent of holy nuns, and these women ministered to his needs, giving him food and drink, which he could only ask for with a nod, and coping with his bodily functions. Under this care he survived about four years until his life came to a close. He was so paralysed and unable to use any part of his body, that none of his limbs recovered their power of movement and feeling; but despite this he achieved such an abundance of grace that when the sick were anointed with the oil which had touched his corpse, not to say

VII. On the Wandering Mind and on Wicked Spirits

his body, they were immediately cured of all afflictions. Hence even the pagans came to admit that because of his illness it had become abundantly obvious that it was the loving providence of the Lord that had weakened his limbs, and the grace of healing had witnessed to his purity and declared his merits through the power of the Holy Spirit.

XXVII. "The second of those we have mentioned as living in this desert was Abba Moyses, a man indeed unique and beyond compare, but he was punished for a single utterance, when in disputing with Abba Macarius he spoke too harshly, asserting some opinion. He was given over immediately to a dire demon, which so filled him that he tried to eat human vomit. That this affliction was brought on him from the Lord to refine him, so that no trace of his sin would remain, can be seen from the fact that his cure was so rapid, and from the identity of the one who cured him, for it was Abba Macarius who straightaway applied himself to prayer, and the wicked spirit fled and vanished faster than I can say.

XXVIII. "From all this it should be clear that we should never despise or shun those whom we see undergoing different trials or given over to wicked spirits. Our faith must be firm about these two points: firstly that no-one at all is tempted by these spirits except with God's permission; secondly that whatever God brings upon us, whether it seem grievous at the time, or pleasant, is prescribed for us for our own benefit, as if by a doting parent or compassionate doctor. They are therefore given over for their correction, as if to schoolteachers, so that when they depart from this world they may pass to the new life already purified, or at least may have less to suffer, for as St Paul says, they are handed over to Satan for a time, 'for the destruction of the flesh, that the spirit may be saved in the day of Our Lord Jesus Christ'" (I Cor. 5:5).

XXIX. GERMANUS: "But then how is it that in our home province we see them not just despised and shunned by men, but actually permanently barred from Holy Communion; according to the Gospel text, 'give not that which is holy to dogs, neither cast ye your pearls before swine' (Matt. 7:6)? From what you were saying the humiliation of these trials should be understood as given for the sake of their purification, and for their benefit."

XXX. SERENUS: "If we hold to the opinion – nay, the belief – which I have expounded, that everything which happens is through the Lord, and if we trust that all things can be turned to the good of souls, we will assuredly refrain from despising them, and will even pray for them ceaselessly, as if for our own members, sympathising with them in heartfelt compassion and affection, for 'if one member suffer anything, all the members suffer with it' (I Cor. 12:26). We recognise that without them we ourselves cannot be complete, for they are our members, in the same way that we read on St Paul's authority that our ancestors were unable to reach the fulfilment of the promise without us; 'all these, being approved by the testimony of faith, received not the promise; God providing some better thing for us, that they should not be perfected without us' (Heb. 11:39–40). I have never heard any of our own elders forbid them to receive Holy Communion; on the contrary, they considered it should be given them every day, if possible. Nor is the sacrament being given to demons to eat, for the Gospel text which you quote out of context, 'give not that which is holy to dogs', does not apply to this case; no, we must believe it is for the healing and guarding of body and soul. When a man receives Holy Communion, any spirit that lurks hidden within his limbs flees away as if from a burning fire. That is the way we saw Abba Andronicus being cured recently, among others. The enemy pressed harder and harder on him whenever he saw that he was deprived of the heavenly remedy, and the longer he was away from the healing sacraments, the more fiercely and frequently he was assailed.

XXXI. "The ones who should really be considered wretched and pitiable are those who have defiled themselves with all sorts of

VII. On the Wandering Mind and on Wicked Spirits

sins and crimes, but show no external sign of being possessed by the devil, nor do they suffer any trials commensurate with their works, and receive no correcting discipline. They do not deserve a swift and prompt remedy in this world, for their 'hard and impenitent hearts' exceed all penalty in this life; they 'treasure up to themselves wrath, against the day of wrath and revelation of the just judgment of God' (Rom. 2:5), when 'their worm shall not die, and their fire shall not be quenched' (Isaiah 66:24). The prophet cries out against them, when he laments the sorrows of the saints, seeing them burdened by woes and tribulations, while sinners proceed through this world with no punishment to humble them, rejoicing indeed in abundance of riches, and great prosperity in everything they did. Fired with burning zeal and ardent in spirit, he says, 'My feet were almost moved, my steps had well-nigh slipped, because I had a zeal on occasion of the wicked, seeing the prosperity of sinners. For there is no regard to their death; nor is there strength in their stripes. They are not in the labour of men: neither shall they be scourged like other men' (Psalm 72/73:2–5). Be sure they will be punished in the future, along with the devil, for they were not good enough to be punished like other men as sons are corrected and trained. Jeremiah also complains to God about the prosperity of the wicked, although he admits that he has no doubts about the Lord's justice; 'Thou indeed O Lord art just, if I plead with thee.' He continues, asking about the reasons for this inequality, 'but yet I will speak what is just to thee: why doth the way of the wicked prosper? Why is it well with them that transgress and do wickedly? Thou hast planted them, and they have taken root: they prosper and bring forth fruit: thou art near in their mouth and far from their reins' (Jer. 12:1–2). The Lord laments their destruction, through the prophet, and sends physicians and doctors anxiously to their aid. He even calls them to lament in the same way, saying, 'Babylon is suddenly fallen and destroyed: howl for her, take balm for her pain, if so she may be healed' (Jer. 51:8). The angels, who are entrusted with looking after human salvation, reply in despondency – or perhaps the prophet is speaking for the apostles, spiritual directors and teachers, who see such hardness of heart and impenitence, and reply: 'We would have cured Babylon, but she is not healed: let us forsake her and let us go every man to his own land: because her judgment hath reached even to the heavens and is lifted up to the clouds' (Jer. 51: 9). Isaiah calls to Jerusalem about their incurable condition, speaking in the person of God: 'from the sole of her foot unto the top of the head, there is no soundness therein: wounds and bruises and swelling sores. They are not bound up, nor dressed nor fomented with oil' (Isaiah 1: 6).

XXXII. "Doubtless the unclean spirits have as many different purposes as do men. Some of them, the ones the people call Fauns, are manifested as wayward spirits and practical jokers, which infest certain places and roads. They are not interested in tormenting the passer-by whom they delight in deceiving, but are content with mockery and delusions, which are intended to weary them more than harm them. Others merely spend the night in giving men harmless dreams. But others are so filled with wrath and indignation that they do not baulk at tormenting with dire wounds the bodies of those they have possessed, and they even attack those passing far off, and rush on them in a fierce assault, like those described in the Gospel which were so frightful that no one dared pass that way (cf. Matt. 8: 28). It must be these and those like them who are so insatiable in their fury that they take delight in wars and murders.

There are others who infect the hearts of their victims with empty pride; these are the ones popularly called Bacuci. As a result they carry themselves unnaturally high, now applying themselves to certain actions and gestures, now apparently condescending to someone, affable and mild, behaving gently and moderately, in the imagination that they are famous and universally admired; now they demonstrate their respect for great men by bowing profoundly, now they fancy that others are respecting them, and they behave in every way like those who are really great, alternating haughtiness and condescension.

VII. On the Wandering Mind and on Wicked Spirits

Others there be which try to provoke men to lies, and even to blasphemy. We have some experience of this ourselves, for we once heard a demon openly admit that it was responsible for promulgating the evil of heresy through Arius and Eunomius. We read of something like this in the [fourth] Book of Kings, when the spirit admits 'I will go forth, and be a lying spirit in the mouth of all his prophets' (III Kings (I Kings) 22:22). St Paul refutes those who are deceived by them, saying, they 'give heed to spirits of error and doctrines of devils, speaking lies in hypocrisy' (I Tim. 4:1–2). The Gospel speaks of other types of demon, such as the deaf and dumb (Luke 11:14; Mark 9:16, 24). The prophet informs us that some spirits provoke impurity and lust: 'the spirit of fornication hath deceived them, and they have committed fornication against their God' (Hosea 4:12). In a similar way, Scripture speaks of nocturnal demons, daytime ones, and the noonday devil (Psalm 90/91:13). It would take too long to go through all the books of Scripture and examine them closely to enumerate the whole variety of demons: the prophet speaks of onocentaurs, hairy ones, sirens, the Lamia, hoopoes, ostriches, and urchins (Isaiah 13 and 34); the psalmist of the asp and the basilisk (Psalm 90/91:5–6); the Gospel of the lion and the dragon, and the scorpion (Luke 10:19), and St Paul tells of the Prince of this world, the Rulers of the present darkness, and the Spirits of Wickedness (Eph. 6:12; John 14:30). We must not imagine that these names were chosen casually or at random, for they relate to how these creatures are either comparatively harmless, or positively dangerous towards us, distinguishing the degree of rage or fierceness. In proportion to the measure of evil, or of the domination which various venomous creatures have over each other, these spirits are given metaphorical names according to the depth of their malice; for instance one which is distinguished for the violence of its raging and its ferocity, is named after the lion; another after the basilisk, because of the deadly virus which kills before you notice it, another, less malicious, is called an onocentaur, an urchin or ostrich."

XXXIII. GERMANUS: "We are in no doubt that the various orders mentioned by the Apostle refer to these beings, in that our combat is 'not against flesh and blood, but against principalities and powers, against the rulers of the world of this darkness, against the spirits of wickedness in the high places' (Eph. 6:12). But we would like to know how this variety among them arose, and how such different degrees of wickedness came to be. Were they created like that, so that they found themselves arranged in this order of malice, and serve in the ranks of wickedness?"

XXXIV. SERENUS: "Now the discussion of your questions has already robbed us of our whole night's rest; we did not even notice the approach of dawn but our conversation has been protracted without intermission until sunrise. Once we begin to look at the solution of the question you have posed it will lead us into a deep and wide ocean of further questions, which the short time remaining to us will not permit us to cross, so I really think it would be better to defer it until another night. Then I shall be delighted to speak to you at length about the question you have posed, and I too would benefit greatly from it. We would then have the opportunity to explore freely every inlet of your question, given a favourable breeze by the Holy Spirit. Now allow us to take a little rest and dispel the sleep which is creeping over our eyes, for day is breaking; then we shall go to church, as we should do on this Sunday morning, and after Mass we shall return here and with a redoubled enthusiasm discuss whatever the Lord gives us for our common instruction, according to your desire."

✧ THE EIGHTH COLLATION ✧
BEING THE SECOND OF ABBA SERENUS

On the Principalities and Powers

I. On the kindness of Abba Serenus.
II. We ask again about the variety of spiritual wickedness.
III. The reply, on the many types of instruction in Holy Scripture.
IV. On ambiguous passages in Holy Scripture.
V. That the question under consideration should be considered among those to be answered conditionally.
VI. That there is nothing which God creates evil.
VII. On how the Principalities and Powers began.
VIII. On the fall of the devil and his angels.
IX. An objection, that the fall of the devil had its origin in the deception of Eve.
X. The reply, on how the devil first fell.
XI. On the punishment of the deceiver, and of the ones deceived.
XII. On the crowding of devils, and the disturbance which they continually cause in the air.
XIII. How the warfare which these angels wage against mankind is also internecine to themselves.
XIV. How it came to pass that spirits of evil acquired the titles of Principalities and Powers.
XV. That there is good reason for the names Angels and Archangels to be given to spiritual virtues.

XVI. On the obedience which the demons give to their princes, revealed in a vision to one of the brethren.
XVII. How two angels are ever in attendance on each man.
XVIII. The story of the two sages, which demonstrates the variety of wickedness among evil spirits.
XIX. How the demons can make no progress against a man unless they first attack his mind.
XX. A question, about the apostate angels who are recorded in Genesis as having lain with the daughters of men.
XXI. The solution to the aforesaid problem.
XXII. An objection, how can the alliance of the race of Seth with the daughters of Cain be called profane before the Law forbade it?
XXIII. The reply, that from the very beginning men were subject to the judgment of natural law, and its penalty.
XXIV. That those who sinned before the Flood were justly punished.
XXV. How we must understand what the Gospel says about the devil, that he is a liar as is his father.

I. When we had completed the functions of the day, and the congregation had been dismissed from the church, we returned to the old man's cell, and were first entertained very generously. For instead of the ordinary fish sauce which he usually spread on his daily meal, with a dash of oil on top, he mixed up a measure of fine sauce and poured more oil than usual on it. (They all put a drop of oil onto their daily food, but not in order to taste much of its flavour, for they put on so little that it is hardly enough to make them able to swallow their food, let alone slip it down; no, they do this to quell their pride of heart and avoid any murmur of conceit which might so easily arise unawares if they fasted more strictly. You see, the more secret their self-denial is, performed before no human witnesses, the more subtle remains the temptation to pride

VIII. On the Principalities and Powers

in this secrecy.) After that he presented us with rubbed salt and three olives each, then he placed before us a dish of chick pease of the sort they call *trogalia*, of which we each took five peas, and also two damsons with a red fig each. It is considered impolite to take more than that number in this part of the desert. When we had finished our meal, we began to ask him again if he would answer our question as he had promised, and the old man replied, "Remind me of your problem, and we will begin to investigate it at once."

II. Germanus replied, "We were asking how the great variety of powers hostile to men arose, and why the differences. St Paul lists them thus, 'For our wrestling is not against flesh and blood, but against Principalities and Powers, against the rulers of the world of this darkness, against the spirits of wickedness in the high places' (Eph. 6:12). And elsewhere, 'Neither angels nor principalities nor powers, nor any other creature, shall be able to separate us from the love of God, which is in Christ Jesus our Lord' (Rom. 8:38–9). But whence do so many rival enemies arise against us? Must we believe that it was the Lord who created these forces, in order that they should war against humanity in these various ranks and files?"

III. SERENUS: "The author of Holy Scripture, who wished to instruct us about these things, wrote some things clearly and openly for the benefit of those of limited understanding, so that they would not be confused or misled by shadowy obscure passages, and moreover would need no training to read it, but could find instruction and advice in the literal sense of the text. But there are other passages which are so involved and obscured with difficulties, that a vast field of campaign opens before us for our discussion and consideration.

There are many obvious reasons why God has so ordained it. Firstly, it is so that a veil might be drawn over the spiritual comprehension of the divine Mysteries, otherwise everyone, faithful and profane alike, would have an equal understanding and knowledge, and there would be no distinction in virtue and discretion between the idle and the diligent. As it is, given that there is a great variety of levels of understanding among the faithful themselves, the shortcomings of the indifferent can be shown up, and the diligent commended for their eager attentiveness. That is why Scripture is aptly compared to a fair and fertile field; it produces many crops which can serve for human nourishment without any preparation on the fire, whereas others are either unpalatable or even poisonous to men unless they are softened and transformed over the flames until they lose their raw harshness. And then there are some which can be used in either way; when raw they are not unpleasant or tough, but when cooked over the fire they become more palatable. There are besides many other crops which only serve as food for cattle and dumb beasts, or are suitable for wild animals and birds, though useless for human food; in their natural raw state without any cooking they provide the nourishment that animals need.

This parable can be clearly manifested in the garden of Holy Scripture which is so fruitful. Here some passages shine with an open and obvious literal sense; they need no subtlety of interpretation, but by their simple meaning provide abundant nourishment for those who hear. Such are 'Hear, O Israel: the Lord our God is one Lord,' and 'Thou shall love the Lord thy God with thy whole heart, and with thy whole soul, and with thy whole strength' (Deut. 6: 4–5). Then there are passages which need to be expounded with an allegorical interpretation, softened by contact with a spiritual fire, otherwise they are useless as food to nourish the inner man, and even quite detrimental; from reading these more harm than good would follow. Such are passages like, 'Let your loins be girt and lamps burning' (Luke 12: 35), and 'He that hath not, let him sell his coat and buy a sword' (Luke 22: 36). Also, 'He that taketh not up his cross and followeth me, is not worthy of me' (Matt. 10: 38). There have been some enthusiastic monks, full of 'a zeal of God, but not according to knowledge' (Rom. 10: 2), who understood this literally, and made themselves wooden crosses which they carried around on their shoulders

VIII. On the Principalities and Powers

always. This provoked those who saw them to laughter rather than edification. And then there are passages which can be taken in either sense, that is both historical and allegorical; they can and should be found beneficial under both interpretations, furnishing vital nourishment for the soul. Examples are 'If one strike thee on thy right cheek, turn to him also the other' (Matt. 5:39), and 'When they shall persecute you in this city, flee into another' (Matt. 10:23). Also, 'If thou wilt be perfect, go, sell what thou hast and give to the poor and thou shalt have treasure in heaven. And come, follow me' (Matt. 19:21). Finally there are texts which serve to 'bring forth grass for cattle' (Psalm 103/104:14), and the fields of Scripture are full of such fodder, being the straightforward simple historical narrative. Simpler people, incapable of anything profound or sublime can be improved by these, made more capable of pursuing their daily life and work according to their state and condition – as it is written 'Men and beasts thou wilt preserve, O Lord' (Psalm 35/36:7).

IV. "When it comes to passages which can be easily explained, we may be consistent in our opinion and confident in declaring it. However, there are passages which the Holy Spirit inserted into Holy Scripture which are obscure, and require our prayer and study, for his intention is that we should compare different ideas and interpretations. We must then be cautious and slow in gathering opinions, since approval or agreement with them depends on the choice of the individual student. It often happens that different opinions are given on a single passage, and both of them can be reasonably accepted. Without any danger to the faith either may be believed, absolutely or conditionally – that is to say without complete acceptance or total rebuttal. Neither opinion should be dismissed, if both are found compatible with the faith. Examples are the question of whether Elijah came in the person of John the Baptist, or is to be expected before the last coming of Christ (Matt. 11:14), and about the Abomination of Desolation which has already stood in the Holy Place, meaning the statue of Jupiter which we read was set up in the Temple in Jerusalem, but which will stand again in the Church at the coming of the Anti-Christ (Dan. 9:27; II Macc. 6:2). Also all the passage of the Gospel which follows (Matt. 24:15 ff.), fulfilled already before the Fall of Jerusalem, but to be fulfilled again before the ending of this world. Neither interpretation eliminates the other, and the later one is not ruled out by the former.

V. "Now the question you asked has not been adequately or frequently considered by anyone, and there is no agreed solution; as a result our own opinion will probably seem uncertain to others. We must be moderate in asserting it, since the matter does not touch on our faith in the Trinity, and the question can be considered as one of the ambiguous ones, even though it will be answered with obvious Scriptural texts, not just an opinion based on mere conjecture and imagination.

VI. "We must be clear that there is no question of God creating anything which is evil by nature, for Scripture says, 'All the things that God had made were very good' (Gen. 1:31). It would be an insult to God, and contrary to Scripture, to suggest that He had created these beings as they are, or made them so, in their varying degrees of malice, always active in the deception and ruin of mankind. How could God be the creator and source of evil, how could he form beings wicked in will and nature, in such a way that they would remain forever in their wickedness, never able to change and adopt the will for good? But the reason which we accept for their variety is drawn from the Holy Scriptures through the teaching of the Fathers.

VII. "None of the faithful can be in any doubt that before God created this visible world, he made the spiritual Powers of heaven, which were to devote themselves ceaselessly to giving thanks and constant praise, in the knowledge that they had been formed out of nothing by a loving Creator solely to enjoy this happiness. We should not imagine that God only began his work of creation after this world had been formed, as if he were idle, with no providence

VIII. On the Principalities and Powers

or divine plan through all those uncounted ages before. How could we imagine him alone, with no object on which to exercise his good will, deprived of all occasion for his munificence? It would be unworthy and inappropriate to think so about his immense majesty, which is without end and beyond comprehension, for the Lord himself speaks of these Powers thus: 'When the stars were all made together, and all my angels praised me with a great voice' (Job 38:7, LXX). They were, therefore, present at the creation of the stars, before that beginning when we are told heaven and earth were made, and are clearly demonstrated to have been created in that they are described as praising the Creator in a great voice of wonder, when they witnessed all this visible creation proceeding out of nothing. There is no doubt at all that God created all the Powers and Virtues of heaven before the beginning in time which Moses declares, which refers to the age of this world according to the historical or Judaic sense – I mean the time-bound 'beginning' of Genesis, in contrast to our own use of the word 'beginning' referring to Christ the origin of all things, in whom the Father created them, as St John says, 'All things were made by him, and without him was made nothing' (John 1:3). No, it is before the 'beginning' mentioned in Genesis that all those heavenly powers and virtues were assuredly created. St Paul names all of them in order thus: 'For in Christ were all things created in heaven and on earth, visible and invisible, whether' Angels or Archangels, 'Thrones, or Dominations, or Principalities, or Powers. All things were created by him and in him' (Col. 1:16).

VIII. "We learn of the fall of certain of the Princes out of this great number from the lamentations of Ezechiel and Isaiah, where we recognise their moving grief over the Prince of Tyre, or that Lucifer who arose at the dawn. The Lord spoke thus to Ezechiel: 'Son of Man, take up a lamentation upon the king of Tyre: and say to him: Thus saith the Lord God: Thou wast the seal of resemblence, full of wisdom and perfect in beauty. Thou wast in the pleasures of the paradise of God: every precious stone was thy covering: the sardius, the topaz and the jasper, the chrysolite and the onyx and the beryl, the sapphire and the carbuncle and the emerald: gold the work of thy beauty: and thy pipes were prepared in the day thou wast created. Thou wast a cherub stretched out and protecting, and I set thee in the holy mountain of God; thou hast walked in the midst of the stones of fire. Thou wast perfect in thy ways from the day of thy creation, until iniquity was found in thee. By the multitude of thy merchandise, thy inner parts were filled with iniquity, and thou hast sinned: and I cast thee out from the mountain of God and destroyed thee, O covering cherub, out of the midst of the stones of fire. And thy heart was lifted up with thy beauty: thou hast lost thy wisdom in thy beauty. I have cast thee to the ground: I have set thee before the face of kings, that they might behold thee. Thou hast defiled thy sanctuaries by the multitude of thy iniquities and by the iniquity of thy traffic' (Ezek. 28:11–18). Isaiah also speaks of another, 'How art thou fallen from heaven, O Lucifer, who didst rise in the morning? How art thou fallen to the earth, that didst wound the nations? And thou saidst in thy heart: I will ascend into heaven, I will exalt my throne above the stars of God, I will sit in the mountain of the Covenant, in the sides of the north. I will ascend above the height of the clouds. I will be like the Most High' (Isaiah 14:12–14). Yet Scripture tells us that they were not the only ones to have fallen from that summit of bliss, for the dragon dragged down a third part of the stars in its fall (Apoc. 12:4). One of the apostles also tells us plainly, 'And the angels who kept not their principality but forsook their own habitation, he hath reserved under darkness in everlasting chains unto the judgment of the great day' (Jude 6). Then when we are told, 'But you like men shall die: and shall fall like one of the princes' (Psalm 81/82:7), it can only mean that many of the Principalities did fall. We can deduce from these texts that the variety and differences in rank which the hostile powers are said to possess, are parallel to the differences in the holy virtues of heaven. It may be because they still retain their former degrees and ranks in which they were created, or because as they fell from heaven they attained these degrees and titles of rank in inverse order, the degree of wickedness which each one

VIII. On the Principalities and Powers

developed in evil being parallel to the virtues which still remain in heaven."

IX. GERMANUS: "But we have always believed that the fall and perdition of the devil, when he was thrown down from his angelic rank, was caused by his jealousy, when he deceived Adam and Eve by his sly trickery."

X. SERENUS: "If you read Genesis you will see that his perdition and fall did not begin then, since it bestows the name of serpent on him before Adam and Eve were deceived, saying, 'The Serpent was wiser' (or, according to the Hebrew, 'more subtle') 'than any of the beasts of the earth which the Lord God had made' (Gen. 3:1, LXX). So you can see that he had lost his angelic holiness before the deception of the first man, given that he had earned that name of infamy, but was even distinguished below all creatures of the earth for evil craft. Scripture would never have used such a name for a good angel, or for one who had persevered in bliss, calling him 'the serpent, wiser than all the beasts of the earth'. Such a name could not possibly be applied to Gabriel or Michael, and would be inappropriate even for a good man. Clearly therefore the name serpent, and the comparison with the beasts of the earth, indicate not the dignity of an angel but the infamy of the fiend. Thus the reason for the jealousy and intrigue which led him to deceive mankind stems from his former ruin. He saw those who had been recently formed from the mud of the earth being invited to share in that glory, from which he could remember falling, he who had been one of the Princes. His first fall, when his pride led him to disaster and earned for him the name of serpent, was followed by a second fall through his jealousy. There did still remain something of his former uprightness in that he could have some conversation and some influence over men, but by the Lord's decree he was rightly thrown down to the depths. No longer could he perceive anything sublime or walk proudly as before, but must creep close to the ground, and crawling on his belly feed on the works of vice. Thus the secret foe was henceforth revealed, and an enmity between him and mankind established, a separation which is greatly to our benefit. Feared as an evil foe, he can no longer harm mankind with feigned friendship.

XI. "This story chiefly instructs us to avoid evil advice, for granted that the author of deceit was inflicted with an appropriate punishment and condemnation, he also who had been deceived did not escape punishment, although somewhat lighter that that inflicted on the originator of the deceit. We see this stated expressly: Adam, who was deceived, or rather as St Paul puts it, was 'not seduced' but an accomplice in deceit (I Tim. 2:14), was consigned to an expiatory punishment, merely condemned to labour in the sweat of his brow, the result of a curse not on him but on the earth, made sterile. It was the woman, who persuaded him to this sin, who was condemned to the multiplication of woes and pains with grief, being forever sentenced to the yoke of submission. The serpent, the first originator of evil, was laid under a curse for ever. We must therefore be most on our guard and wary of evil advice, for just as their author is punished, so those who are deceived escape neither guilt nor punishment.

XII. "Our atmosphere is overcrowded with spirits poised between heaven and earth, which are neither idle nor peaceful in their flight, so that it is a great benefit that divine Providence has veiled them and concealed them from human perception. Otherwise men would be utterly terrified and debilitated through terror of their presence, and horror at the appearance under which, if it were permitted them, they would present themselves, trying to alter themselves into forms intolerable for us to look upon with the eyes of the flesh. Unless indeed mankind were so vitiated by their example as to imitate them and so become daily more wicked like them! Thus an evil relationship would grow up between men and the unclean powers of the air, a perilous alliance indeed. Those sins which now are committed among mankind are concealed behind enclosing walls, or at a great distance, and with a certain amount of shame – but if men could see the evil spirits clearly they might be incited to greater depths of depravity, and there might not remain even a momentary interval of restraint from committing these crimes; whereas now we are often compelled against our will to pause from the sin which we had begun to desire, through physical tiredness, domestic work, or the concerns of daily life.

XIII. "We should not doubt that the warfare which they wage against mankind is also waged among themselves. For just as there is discord and enmity among certain nations, who welcome them in a slavish familiarity with evil, so among themselves such conflicts never cease. We find this clearly foreshadowed in the vision of the prophet Daniel, when the angel Gabriel speaks to him thus: 'Fear not, Daniel; for from the first day that thou didst set thy heart to understand, to afflict thyself in the sight of thy God, thy words have been heard: and I am come for thy words. But the Prince of the kingdom of the Persians resisted me one and twenty days: and behold Michael, one of the chief princes, came to help me, and I remained there by the King of the Persians. But I am come to teach thee what things shall befall thy people in the latter days' (Dan. 10:12–14). It should be clear that the Prince of the kingdom of the Persians is a hostile power which favours the Persian nation against the People of God. That power rejoices in obstructing the archangel's resolution of the problem for which the Prophet had besought the Lord, and in delaying the saving message which the archangel was to bring to Daniel, for the consolation of the people of God, of whom the Archangel Gabriel is protector. Gabriel admitted that because of the violence of the enemy's attack he had been unable to come to Daniel, had not Michael the Archangel come to his help. Assailing the Prince of the kingdom of the Persians, Michael joined battle with him and defended Gabriel from his attacks so that he was able to come and instruct the prophet, after twenty one days had passed. A little further on, he says, 'Dost thou know wherefore I am come to thee? And now I will return, to fight against the Prince of the Persians. When I went forth, there appeared the Prince of the Greeks coming. But

I will tell thee what is set down in the Scripture of truth: and none is my helper in all these things but Michael, your Prince' (Dan. 10: 20–1). And again, 'At that time shall Michael rise up, the great prince, who standeth for the children of thy people' (Dan. 12: 1). We also read of the Prince of the Greeks, mentioned in the same manner, as one who favoured the nation under his care, and was equally opposed to the people of Israel and the Persian nation. We can deduce from this that the wars and conflicts which the nations wage against each other are stirred up by the Powers opposing each other; they rejoice in the victories of their own nations, they lament their defeats, and for that reason there can never be agreement among them, for each one of them battles in constant jealousy on behalf of his own particular nation against the protectors of other nations.

XIV. "Now apart from the opinion which we have just expounded, we can also say that the reason why they are called Principalities and Powers is obviously that they dominate the different nations and protect them; alternatively that they exercise authority over minor spirits and demons, who themselves admit that they are legion, as in the Gospel (Luke 8: 30). They could not be called Dominations did they not have some area over which to exercise domination, neither Principalities and Powers had they not some subjects over whom to wield power. We find this stated clearly in the Gospel, when the Pharisees say blasphemously, 'He casteth out devils by Beelzebub, the Prince of devils' (Luke 11: 15). We also find them called 'Rulers of the world of this darkness' (Eph. 6: 12) and another one is called 'the Prince of this world' (John 14: 30). St Paul assures us that when all things are subjected to Christ, they will lose these ranks, saying, 'he shall have delivered up the kingdom to God and the Father; when he shall have brought to nought all principality and power and virtue' (I Cor. 15: 24). This can only happen when those over whom they had been exercising power, domination or principality, are liberated from their control.

XV. "There can be no doubt that names are also given to the good members of those ranks, and the titles appropriate to their duties, merits and dignity. Angels, that is 'messengers' are obviously so named from their duty of bearing messages, and Archangels because they preside over the angels themselves, as the meaning of the name shows. Dominations are those which dominate over others, Principalities have charges over which they are princes. Thrones are so called, because they remain close to God, as his servants and familiars, so that the divine majesty rests especially upon them as if on a throne, and weighs upon them, so to speak, in a closer manner.

XVI. "We can tell that the unclean spirits are controlled by powers more wicked than themselves, and obey them, from the evidence of Scripture, for we find in the Gospel that when the Pharisees denigrate Him, the Lord replies, 'If I cast out devils by Beelzebub, prince of devils . . .' (Luke 11:19). We can also deduce the same fact from famous visions and the experience of many of the saints. When one of our brethren was travelling in this part of the desert, and day drew to a close, he found a cave and sat down in it, wishing to celebrate his evening devotions there. While he was still chanting the usual psalms, the hour of midnight passed. He finished his office, and laid his tired body down to rest awhile, when suddenly he began to notice a countless throng of demons gathering from all sides, which crowded the air and formed a long procession, some following their prince, others preceding him. The prince himself was distinguished from the rest in size as well as fearful aspect; he entered, a throne was set in place, and he sat there on a raised tribunal, to examine the work of each one in detail. Those who could not claim to have successfully deceived their prey he ordered to be branded with infamy and driven from his sight as lazy and worthless, reproaching them in terrible rage for their fruitless waste of time and effort. Those on the other hand who declared that they had deceived their charges were greatly praised and to the exultation and favour of all were sent forth as doughty warriors with honours in the sight of all to be an example to them.

Among this throng, a certain vile fiend arrived gleefully as if to report a signal triumph. He named a well-known monk, and claimed that after a siege of fifteen years he had at last prevailed over him, and was that very night going to ruin him through the vice of fornication. He had not only instigated him to carnal sin with a certain consecrated virgin, but had even persuaded him to keep her for himself by a civil marriage. His tale was greeted with unbounded joy on behalf of all, and he was promoted by his prince with the highest praise, going out with a crown of great distinction. When dawn broke, and this whole throng of demons vanished from his sight, our brother was unconvinced by what the unclean spirit had claimed, and greatly angered that it had tried to deceive him with its customary cumulation of lies, and to impugn his brother with the accusation of such baseness. He remembered the Gospel warning that 'he stood not in the truth, because truth is in him. When he speaketh a lie, he speaketh of his own; for he is a liar, and his father' (John 8:44). He went to Pelusium, which he knew to be the dwelling of the one whom the unclean spirit claimed to have fallen. The brother was well known there, but when he enquired after him he discovered that on the very night when the vile fiend had reported his fall to its regiment and commander, he had left his former monastery, headed for the village, and fallen into a life of sin with the maiden who had been mentioned.

XVII. "Scripture informs us that every one of us is attended by two angels, a good one and an evil one. Of the good angels, Our Saviour says, 'Despise not one of these little ones; for I say to you that their angels in heaven always see the face of my Father who is in heaven' (Matt. 18:10). We also read, 'The angel of the Lord shall encamp about them that fear him: and shall deliver them' (Psalm 33/34:8). and in the Acts of the Apostles it is said of Peter that, 'It is his angel' (Acts 12:15). Of these two angels, the Book of the Shepherd gives a full explanation. If we think of the one which plagued holy Job, we can see clearly that it was the one which always assailed him, and had never prevailed in him to sin,

VIII. On the Principalities and Powers

which is why it had begged the Lord for power, because it had been defeated, not by Job's virtue but by the constant protection of the Lord. Of Judas also it is said, 'May the devil stand at his right hand' (Psalm 108/109: 6).

XVIII. "We have reliable information about the variety among demons even from the story of the two sages who used magical arts to investigate the extent of the inertia or of the vigour and savage wickedness that could be found among them. These were the ones who despised the holy Antony, thinking him an ignorant unread man; unable to do him any other harm, they did their best at least to drive him from his cell with their magic tricks and demonic wiles. They sent the vilest fiends against him, who were spurred to the attack by their own jealousy, for great crowds of men came daily to consult him, as a servant of God. But as he resisted them, now making the sign of the cross on his breast and brow, now kneeling in humble prayer, not even the worst of demons dared to come near him, but had to return unsuccessfully to the sages who sent them. They sent back others, more wicked still, which also returned empty, having wasted their evil powers and expended them to no effect. More powerful yet were the ones despatched against the conquering champion of Christ, but they were no more successful than the rest. The only result of so great an assault mounted with such magical art, was to provide ample proof of the enormous virtue that resides in the profession of Christianity. They had imagined that those savage strong shades were capable of drawing down the sun and the moon, had they been directed against them, but found them not only incapable of harming Antony, but not able even to drive him out of his monastery for a moment.

XIX. "The two sages, amazed at this, came to Abba Antony and confessed their great attack on him, and the reasons for their secret jealousy in attacking him; they begged that they might be made Christians straightaway. He asked them which day it was that they had made their attack, and admitted that on that day he had indeed been bothered with terribly distracting thoughts. Thus the blessed Antony proved the point I made yesterday during our conversation, and explained it; that the demons cannot possibly invade anyone's mind and body, and have no power to make any serious assault on anyone's soul, unless they have first stripped him of all thoughts of holiness and left him empty and bare of spiritual contemplation.

We must know, furthermore, that there are but two ways to subject unclean spirits to us: either they are made to submit to faithful holiness through the grace and power of God, or they can be conjured with pagan sacrifices and spells and fawn upon their masters like slaves. This is the theory the Pharisees followed, when they imagined that Our Lord and Saviour himself had gained control over the demons by these arts, when they said, 'He casteth out devils by Beelzebub, the Prince of devils' (Luke 11:15). They were accustomed to hear that their own magicians and warlocks had gained power over the demons subject to Beelzebub, as if they were his slaves, by invoking that name and offering the sacrifices which they knew Beelzebub delighted in.

XX. GERMANUS: "As God willed it, we heard recently in common a reading from Genesis, which gives us the opportunity to enquire about something we had long been wanting to know: what, we ask, are we to think of those apostate angels who are recorded as having lain with the daughters of men (Gen. 6:2)? Can this be literally true of any spiritual nature? There is also a text in the Gospel which you have just quoted about the devil, 'that he is a liar and his father' (John 8:44). We would also like to know who we are to understand his father to be."

XXI. SERENUS: "You have posed two important questions, which I shall endeavour to answer in the order you asked them. There can be no question of beings that are spiritual by nature being able to sleep with women carnally. If such a thing had once been literally possible, why does it not happen occasionally now, why do we not observe women bringing to birth through diabolical

VIII. On the Principalities and Powers

conception without any contact with a man or human seed? It is certain that the demons take delight in impure desires, which they would naturally prefer to satisfy in themselves, rather than force men to it, were it at all possible for them. The Preacher tells us that 'What is it that hath been? The same thing that is. What is it that hath been done? The same that shall be done. Nothing under the sun is new, neither is any man able to say: behold, this is new: for it hath already gone before in the ages that were before us' (Qo. 1: 9–10. LXX).

Now this is the solution to the problem. After the death of Abel the just, to avoid the whole human race having to stem from the impious fratricide, Seth was born in the place of his deceased brother. He succeeded not only to his brother's inheritance, but also to his virtues and devotion. His descendents followed their ancestor in righteousness, and remained ever aloof from acknowledging kinship and association with the race that descended from the sacrilegious Cain; the genealogy itself demonstrates this, where we read, 'Adam begot Seth, Seth begot Enos, Enos begot Cainan, Cainan begot Malaleel, Malaleel begot Jared, Jared begot Henoch, Henoch begot Mathusala, Mathusala begot Lamech, and Lamech begot Noe' (Gen. 5: 4–30). The genealogy of Cain is described quite distinctly: 'Cain begot Henoch, Henoch begot Irad, Irad begot Maviael, Maviael begot Mathusael, Mathusael begot Lamech, Lamech begot Jabel and Jubal' (Gen. 4: 17–21). The family which descended from the just man Seth married only within their own line and kin, and remained long-lived because of the holiness of Seth and Adam their ancestor. They were never tainted with the sacrilegious malice of the evil family which preserved the strain of wickedness as an inheritance from Cain their forefather. This segregation endured for generations, till the line of Seth, rising from a virtuous stock, came to be called angels of God, for the sake of their holiness, or, as some manuscripts have it, they were called sons of God. In contrast, Cain's family were called sons of men, because of their wickedness, and that of their ancestors, and their base conduct.

Although hitherto there had been a worthy and salutary

segregation between them, it happened that the sons of Seth (the ones called sons of God) noticed the daughters of the race of Cain, and were struck with longing for their beauty, taking them to themselves as wives. The women instilled their ancestral evil into their husbands, and rapidly corrupted their native holiness and ancestral simplicity. This is what the Psalm refers to, where it says, 'I have said: you are gods, and all of you the sons of the Most High. But you like men shall die: and shall fall like one of the princes' (Psalm 81/82: 6–7). They fell away from the knowledge of natural philosophy which they had inherited, that knowledge which the first Adam had evidently received and passed on reliably to his descendents, for he perceived from the beginning the nature of all creatures. He observed this world in its infancy, still soft, trembling and unformed, and he was filled with wisdom; the grace of prophecy besides was instilled into him by the Holy Spirit, so that he who dwelt in the yet unfinished world might give names to all the creatures. He perceived the fierceness of every beast, the venom of every serpent, as well as the properties of herbs and trees, and the qualities of stones; he anticipated the changes of times yet unknown, so that he could truly say, 'The Lord has given me the true knowledge of the things that are: to know the disposition of the whole world, and the virtues of the elements; the beginning, and the ending, and the midst of the times, the alterations of their courses, and the changes of seasons; the revolutions of the years, and the dispositions of the stars; the natures of living creatures, and rage of wild beasts, the force of winds, and reasonings of men, the diversities of plants, and the virtues of roots. And all such things as are hid and not foreseen I have learned' (Wisdom 7: 17–21, LXX).

This was the knowledge of all nature that the line of Seth had inherited from their forefather through successive generations, as long as it remained separate from the sacrilegious line; they perceived all things in holiness, for use in the worship of God and for the benefit of their common life. Yet when they mingled with the race of evil, they diverted their God-given wisdom to profane and evil studies, at the prompting of the devils, and boldly learnt curious arts of malice, charms and magical practices. Thus they taught their children to abandon the sacred rites in the Name of God, and to worship these earthy spirits, or fire, or the demons of the air. Although it does not really touch on the solution to your problem, I shall briefly run through the manner in which this knowledge of occult things was not destroyed in the Flood but survived to succeeding ages, since my explanation gives me an occasion to do so. According to ancient tradition, Ham the son of Noah, who had been tainted with these superstitious and blasphemous arts, realised that he would be unable to bring with him into the Ark any book to remind him about these matters, for he was to enter it in company with his father and his brothers, all holy and just men. Therefore he engraved his evil arts and wicked commentaries on plates of various metals which would not be corroded by the waters of the Flood, as well as on hard stones. Once the Flood had receded, he sought out what he had hidden, and passed on the seeds of sacrilege and lasting wickedness to his posterity.

In this way the popular opinion is confirmed which believes that it was angels who delivered to men the various arts and spells, for it was from those evil children of the sons of Seth and the daughters of Cain, as we have seen, who became mighty hunters, men of violence and passion, who were called the Giants for their physical size, their cruelty and malice. These were the first to raid borders and carry out robberies on men, choosing to live by plunder instead of being content to earn their living by work in the sweat of the brow. Their crimes increased to the point that the world could be cleansed by no other means than the Deluge. Thus, since the sons of Seth were seduced by lust to disobey the commandment which they had hitherto observed by natural instinct from the beginning of the world, it became necessary for the written law to restore it afterwards: 'Thou shalt not give thy daughter to his son, nor take his daughter for thy son, for she will turn away your hearts to abandon your God, and to follow their gods and serve them" (Deut. 7:3, cf. Exod. 34:16, III Kings (I Kings) 11:2).

XXII. GERMANUS: "It would be right to accuse them of the sin of lawbreaking, when they presumed to make these marriages, had the commandment you have quoted been given to them; but since no decree had yet prescribed the observance of this segregation, how can this racial mixing be called a sin for them, who had never been forbidden to do so? A law can only condemn things in the future, not the past."

XXIII. SERENUS: "When God created man, he gave him a complete knowledge of the law to be his by nature. Had mankind preserved this knowledge intact, as the Lord intended, it would have been quite unnecessary to give the other law which was later promulgated in written form. If the internal law had survived within us, the gift of an external law would have been superfluous. But since, as we have seen, natural law had become deeply corrupt as a result of the free practice of sin, the strict distinctions of the Mosaic law were granted to accuse, to examine, to punish, and also, as the very words of Scripture tell us, to assist. Thus fear of immediate punishment would prevent the benefit of natural conscience being extinguished, as the Prophet said, 'He gave us the law to assist us' (Isaiah 8:20, LXX). St Paul also describes the Law as being like a tutor given to children, to teach them and watch over them, so that they would not forget and fall away from the right conduct which had been instilled into them by nature (Gal. 3:24). All the saints observed the commandments of the law without reading any of it in writing, before the law was given, before the flood indeed, which proves that a knowledge of the whole law had been instilled into mankind from the beginning of creation. How otherwise would Abel have known, before the law commanded it, that he should offer a sacrifice to God from the firstfruits of his flocks and of their richness, were he not so taught by the natural law instinctive within him (Gen. 4:4)? Or how could Noah have distinguished between clean and unclean beasts, when this legal distinction had not yet been decreed, were he not informed by natural knowledge (Gen. 7:2)? Or again, how did Enoch learn to walk with God, when no one had taught him the enlightenment of the law (Gen. 5:22)? Where did Shem and Japheth read, 'Thou shalt not uncover the nakedness of thy father', when they walked in backwards to cover up their father's body (Gen. 9:23, Levit. 18:7)? Who warned Abraham to refuse the plunder of his enemies that he was offered, lest he earn vengeance for his pains? Or to give tithes to Melchisedek, as the Mosaic law prescribed (Gen. 14:20, 22)? What inspired Abraham and Lot to offer humane assistance to wanderers and pilgrims, and to wash their feet, when the glorious commandment of the Gospel had not yet been given (Gen. 18, 19, cf. John 13:34)? Where did holy Job learn such great faith, such chaste purity, such compassion, meekness, mercy and humanity, such as we hardly see fulfilled nowadays even by those who have the Gospels by heart? Do we ever read of any saint from before the Law who transgressed any commandment of the Law? Was there any of them who did not obey, 'Hear, O Israel, the Lord our God is one Lord' (Deut. 6:4)? Which of them failed to listen to 'Thou shall not make to thyself a graven thing, nor the likeness of any thing that is in heaven above, or in the earth beneath, nor of those things that are in the waters under the earth'? Was there anyone who failed to 'honour thy father and thy mother', or to keep the following commandments of the Decalogue, 'Thou shalt not kill, thou shalt not commit adultery, thou shalt not steal, thou shalt not bear false witness, you shall not covet your neighbour's wife' (Exod. 20:4–17)? Did they not also keep the greater commandments which the Gospel enjoins as well as the Law?

XXIV. "We can be sure that God created all things perfect in their origin, and that there was no need for anything to be added to his original dispensation, as if it had been ill-considered and incomplete; nor, if everything had remained in the state and manner in which it was created, would any further disposition be necessary. Hence we can agree that those who sinned before the Law, and even before the Flood, were justly condemned by God, for they disobeyed the natural law, and deserved punishment without excuse. And we should not fall into that disrespectful blasphemy in which those who are ignorant of this reasoning accuse the God of the Old Testament, undermine our faith and grumble over why our God should have chosen to allow so many centuries to pass without the Law and to have promulgated the Law only after thousands of years. They imagine that at the beginning of the world he had only an inadequate grasp of the situation, and afterwards realised how to do better; having learned from his mistakes, they say, he began to make better arrangements and to improve on his original dispensation with a better one. How contrary this idea is to God's full knowledge of all things to come! What a great blasphemy, what heretical madness to offer such opinions about him! The Preacher says, 'I have learned that all the works which God hath made in the beginning continue for ever: we cannot add anything, nor take away from those things' (Qo. 3:14, LXX). Therefore, 'The Law is not made for the just, but for the unjust and disobedient, for the ungodly and for sinners, for the wicked and defiled' (I Tim. 1:9). Those who found all the salutary discipline they needed in the instinctive natural law, needed no external law to be given them in writing to support the natural law. We can see clearly from this that there was no need for a law committed to writing to be given in the beginning, for as long as natural law remained undamaged and whole, it would be superfluous. Nor could the perfection of the Gospel be given them before they observed the law, for those who would not accept that they should avenge their injuries with an equal retribution, but react to a slight slap with fists and wounding weapons, seeking the lives of their aggressors for the loss of a single tooth, would not be capable of hearing, 'If one strike thee on thy right cheek, turn to him also the other.' Nor could you say to them, 'Love your enemies' (Matt. 5:39, 44), if the most that could be hoped for is that they would love their friends and keep away from their enemies, merely refraining from hating them and being too eager to oppress them or kill them.

XXV. "The other point you made about the devil, that 'he is a liar and his father' (John 8:44), where the Lord seems to be

VIII. On the Principalities and Powers

accusing both him and his father of being liars, is quite absurd if you take it that way. We have already observed that a spirit cannot generate a spirit, any more than a soul can procreate another soul. Obviously human generation can produce a physical body, but St Paul makes a clear distinction between the authorship of the two natures, that is the flesh and the soul. 'We have had fathers of our flesh for our instructors; and we reverenced them. Shall we not much more obey the Father of Spirits, and live?' (Heb. 12:9). Here is a clear enough difference: men are declared to be the fathers of our bodies, while God alone is consistently named as the father of our spirits. However even in the forming of our physical bodies men only assist, for God the creator of all is the one who really creates us. As David says, 'Thy hands have made me and formed me' (Psalm 118/119:73), and Job says, 'Hast thou not milked me as milk, and curdled me like cheese; thou hast clothed me with bones and sinews?' (Job 10:10–11, LXX). The Lord said also to Jeremiah, 'before I formed thee in the bowels of thy mother, I knew thee' (Jer. 1:5). The Preacher too, makes a clear and appropriate distinction between the characteristics and origins of both natures, investigating the first beginnings from which each one proceeds, and the final purpose to which each one tends. In making this distinction between soul and body, he explains, 'and the dust return to the earth as it had been, and the spirit return to God, who gave it' (Qo. 12:7, LXX). Could anything be more obvious: he tells us that the material of our bodies, which he calls 'dust', and which takes its origin from the seed of man, and is generated through his cooperation, being derived from the earth, returns again to the earth. The spirit, on the other hand, which is not procreated by the union of man and woman but is to be specifically attributed to God, returns as he says to its author. The same point is expressed by the breath of God which first made Adam a living being. With these texts we can firmly establish that no one can be called the father of spirits except God alone, who makes them at his will, out of nothing. Men can only be called the fathers of our bodies.

It follows that the devil, given that he was created as a good angel or spirit, has no father other than God who created him. When he became puffed up with pride and said in his heart, 'I will ascend above the height of the clouds. I will be like the Most High' (Isaiah 14:14), he became a liar, 'and he stood not in the truth', but bought forth deceit out of his own store of wickedness, being not only a liar but the very father of the lie itself (John 8:44). He promised divinity to man, saying 'you shall be as gods' (Gen. 3:5), not remaining in the truth, but being a murderer from the beginning, for he lured Adam into becoming mortal, and stirred up the death of Abel at his brother's hands.

But see, dawn is approaching to bring an end to our discussions which have entertained us for two nights. The frail bark of our conversation has been led across a deep sea of questions to find a safe harbour of quietness, in this remote place which is so pleasing. The more the wind of the Holy Spirit drove us across the deep, the wider the expanse that opened ever before our eyes, for as Solomon remarked, 'it is further from us that it was, it is a great depth. Who shall find it out?' (Qo. 7:25, LXX). Now let us pray the Lord to preserve within us a constant fear and love of him, which will never fail, so as to make us wise among men, and safe always from the weapons of the enemy. With these virtues to guide us, it is impossible to fall into the snares of death. There is this difference between the perfect and the imperfect: the perfect have charity established and matured, so to speak, holding firm and enduring to protect them, making it easy to persevere in holiness; in the imperfect on the other hand charity is but weakly based, and easily cools, which makes them more often and more rapidly entangled in the snares of sinners."

We listened to this, and were so inspired by his discourse that we left the old man's cell with our minds more alert than when we had arrived, thirsting for the satisfaction of his teaching.

✧ THE NINTH COLLATION ✧
BEING THE FIRST OF ABBA ISAAC

On Prayer

    I. Prelude to this conference.
   II. What Abba Isaac said on the nature of prayer.
  III. How to prepare for pure and sincere prayer.
  IV. On the fickleness of our thoughts, comparable to a feather or to down.
   V. On the causes of our minds being burdened.
  VI. On the vision which one of the elders had, on the lack of tranquillity of his brother.
 VII. A question, on whether it be more difficult to preserve holy thoughts than to acquire them.
VIII. The reply, on the varying nature of prayer.
  IX. On the four types of prayer.
   X. On the order in which the types of prayer appear.
  XI. On supplication.
 XII. On prayer.
XIII. On intercession.
XIV. On thanksgiving.
 XV. Whether all must use all four types of prayer together, or separately and on different occasions.
XVI. Which types of prayer we should aim at.
XVII. How Christ used all these four types of prayer.
XVIII. On the Lord's Prayer.
XIX. On the words, "Thy Kingdom come".
XX. On the words, "Thy Will be done".
XXI. On the Supersubstantial, or Daily Bread.

XXII. On the words, "Forgive us our trespasses" etc.
XXIII. On the words, "Lead us not into temptation".
XXIV. How we should not pray for anything other than what is contained in the model of the Lord's prayer.
XXV. On the nature of the most sublime prayer.
XXVI. Of the different causes of compunction.
XXVII. Of the varying nature of compunction.
XXVIII. A question, on why bursting into tears is beyond our control.
XXIX. The reply, on the different forms of contrition which give rise to tears.
XXX. That tears should not be forced when they do not arise spontaneously.
XXXI. What the Blessed Antony said about the state of prayer.
XXXII. How we may tell that our prayer is heard.
XXXIII. An objection, that such trust in being heard seems to apply only to saints.
XXXIV. The reply, on the various things which may cause our prayers to be heard.
XXXV. On how prayer should be made within the cell, and with closed doors.
XXXVI. On the value of short silent prayer.

I. In the second book of the *Institutes* I promised to write about constant prayer and ceaseless entreaty: the discourses of the elder which I am about to set forth, that is to say Abba Isaac, will fulfil that promise, God willing. Having done that I shall consider that I have satisfied the demands of Pope Castor of happy memory, as well as the requests of your holiness, Pope Leontius, and of yourself, dear brother Helladius. The original length which I had planned for this volume has been exceeded beyond my expectations, although I did attempt to confine my material into a brief form, and also passed over a great deal more in silence. So following my full account of various monastic subjects, which I had hoped to cover more succinctly, the blessed Isaac will conclude in the words that follow.

II. "The goal of every monk, and the aspiration of his heart, is to achieve full and uninterrupted constancy in prayer, unshaken in his mental tranquillity and perpetual purity, in so far as is granted to human weakness. To achieve that we untiringly perform all our physical labour and carry out our spiritual discipline wholeheartedly, for the two are inseparably linked to each other. Just as the accumulation of all the virtues helps towards perfection in prayer, in the same way these virtues cannot remain constant or survive intact unless they are all closely linked to our prayer. The constant prayer and deep tranquillity which we have spoken of cannot be acquired or perfected without the virtues, and the virtues themselves which lead to prayer cannot be attained without it. We cannot speak aright on the practice of prayer, nor in a short discourse can we penetrate its primary purpose which is achieved by the accumulation of all the virtues, unless we enumerate and explain in order each of the qualities that need to be either eliminated or acquired to attain to prayer. As in the Gospel parable, whatever is necessary to construct the lofty tower of the spirit must be calculated and carefully made ready. These materials will not be prepared properly, and will not admit the pinnacle of perfection to be set squarely upon them unless the whole series of vices have first been eliminated, the roots of passion torn up and killed off, and strong foundations of simple humility laid on the solid living ground of our hearts (so to speak), or on the rock which the Gospel mentions. On these foundations the tower of spiritual virtues can be constructed and will stand unshaken, raised up to the very heights of heaven, confident in its own strength. If it stands on such a base, it matters not what a downpour of passions falls upon it, nor what raging torrents of persecutions batter against it like rams, nor what fierce storms of hostile spirits assault it and press upon it, for it will not be threatened with ruin, nor will any threat disturb it.

III. "Now in order to make our prayer as fervent and pure as it should be, we must observe the following points. Firstly, we must eliminate all concern over things of the flesh. Then we should exclude not just involvement in business and litigation, but the very memory of them; we should in the same manner rid ourselves of gossip, frivolous or excessive conversation and ribaldry. Above all, the emotions of anger and melancholy must be stifled, and the poisonous roots of physical lust and greed for money quite torn up. In this way we shall have pulled out and cut off these vices and any like them, which are visible in the sight of men, and have made a start on improving ourselves with the type of purification that is completed in pure simplicity and innocence. After this we can lay the first solid foundation of profound humility, which will be strong enough to support a tower reaching to heaven, on top of which we can lay courses of spiritual virtue, preserving the soul from all kinds of enticing distractions, so that little by little our spiritual gaze is elevated to the contemplation of God. If our thoughts have been busy about anything before our prayer, the memory of it is bound to recur while we are praying. For this reason we should prepare ourselves before the time of prayer to be such as we should like to find ourselves while praying. The mind, during prayer, is affected by what has gone before, so that as we set ourselves to calm our thoughts, the memory of previous actions, words and feelings flits before our consciousness. It may make us angry if that is the emotion we felt before, or it may make us sad; it may recall ancient desires and long past complaints; it may remind us of some ludicrous saying or even (for shame) some happening which provokes us to frivolous giggling, or it may make us relive earlier conversations. So if there is anything which we would not want to intrude on our prayer, we should be quick to eliminate it from our secret thoughts before we pray. Thus we can fulfil the Apostle's bidding, 'pray without ceasing' (I Thess. 5:17), and 'In every place lifting up pure hands without anger and contention' (I Tim. 2:8). There is no other way of fulfilling this precept, than by purifying the mind of all stain of vice, and applying it to virtue and natural good things, till it feeds on nothing but the contemplation of Almighty God.

IV. "The mind can be appropriately compared to the lightest of feathers, like down, for if such a feather is not weighted or saturated by the contagion of some moisture from outside, the slightest breath of air will be enough to whisk it up into the sky, through its natural mobility. If it is sprinkled or soaked in moisture, it will be weighed down, never to be caught up in aery flight by its own mobility, and it is is instead forced onto the ground by the weight of the moisture within it. In the same way our own thoughts, if they are not weighed down by persistent vice or worldly concerns, or soaked in the poisonous moisture of lust, can be swept up into the heights by the gentlest breath of spiritual meditation, buoyed up by their natural purity, and deserting the lowly concerns of earth, are caught up into the invisible heavens. That is why Our Lord gives us such sound advice, 'Take heed to yourselves lest perhaps your hearts be overcharged with surfeiting and drunkenness and the cares of this life' (Luke 21:34). Thus if we wish our prayers to pierce the heavens, and the heavens above the heavens, we must take care to cleanse our thoughts from all earthly vices and the dregs of passion, and restore them to their natural simplicity, until our prayer rises straight to God, with no weight of sin to hold it back.

V. "We should note which are the matters which Our Lord specifies as burdening the mind. Not adultery, fornication, murder, blasphemy or theft, which all agree to be deadly sins and damnable – no, it is surfeiting and drunkenness and the cares of this life. No one living in the world would avoid these, or consider them wrong, and I am ashamed to say many who call themselves monks entangle themselves in these very things, thinking them harmless or even profitable. Now granted that these three things taken literally do indeed weigh down the soul, cut us off from God and press us down to earth, it is nevertheless easy to abstain from them, especially for us who live so far away, cut off from the business of this world, so that we have no occasion to entangle ourselves in material worries, drunkenness and surfeit. But there is another sort of surfeiting and drunkenness, no less dangerous; a spiritual sort, difficult to elude, as well as material cares and worries which may still trouble us frequently. This may happen even here living in the desert, despite our having given up all our property entirely and abstained from wine and all sorts of fine foods, for the Prophet says, 'Make yourselves sober, you who are drunken, though not with wine' (Joel 1:5, LXX). Another also says, 'Be astonished and wonder: waver and stagger: be drunk, and not with wine: stagger, and not with drunkenness' (Isaiah 29:9). It must follow therefore that what the prophet calls staggering and drunkenness can only be the 'wrath of dragons'. See from what stock the wine is produced: 'Their vines are of the vineyard of Sodom, and of the tendrils of Gomorrah.' Do you want to identify the fruit of this vine, the produce of these tendrils? 'Their grapes are grape of gall, and their clusters most bitter' (Deut. 32:32–3, LXX).

Now even though we are purged from all vices, and sobered from excess of all passion, though we abstain from drinking wine and indulging in fine food, our hearts will still be weighed down with a far more dangerous surfeiting and drunkenness. The fact that we can never be free from worldly worries, even though we are not concerned with this world's business at all, is clearly shown in the instructions of the elders, who define that anything more than what daily necessity requires, for life and essential bodily needs, counts as worldly care and worry. For example, if the needs of our bodies could be satisfied for a shilling, but we are eager to expend toil and effort in earning two or three shillings; if two tunics are sufficient for clothing, one for the day and one for the night, but we desire to be masters of three or four; if again one or two rooms suffice for a dwelling, but we take delight and pride in ample accommodation and build ourselves four or five rooms, and these beautifully decorated and larger than necessity requires – why then we shall be giving ourselves over to worldly delights in so far as we are able.

VI. "We have sure evidence which tells us that this does not happen without diabolical interference. It happened that one of the most experienced elders was passing the cell of one of the brethren, who suffered from the mental disturbance we have been describing. He put himself to much trouble every day, labouring

IX. On Prayer

on unnecessary buildings and decorations. The elder watched him from a distance, chiselling away at a hard stone with a heavy mallet, and noticed a barbarian standing beside him, placing his hands on his, and striking blows with the mallet together with him, urging him to this work with fiery brands. The elder watched for a long time, astonished at the malice of the devil, and how the brother had been so easily deceived. When the brother became excessively tired and desired to finish his work and rest, the fiend stirred him to take up the mallet again, urging him not to leave off the work he had begun, so that he was so encouraged by this pressure that he worked tirelessly without noticing the damage the work was doing to him. Finally the elder, moved by how he had been made the sport of such a malicious fiend, came up to the brother's cell and greeted him. 'What', he said, 'is this work you are doing, brother?' The other replied, 'We are working on this exceedingly hard rock, and are scarcely able to cut it at all.' The elder answered, 'You did well to say "we", for you were not alone when you were chiselling, but there was another with you whom you did not see, one who was not so much aiding you in the work but forcing you to do it.'

We can see from this that the virus of worldly entanglement may be present in our thoughts, however careful we be to abstain from business of the sort which we would be unable to pursue or complete even if we wanted to, even if we despise certain vices which would, if we committed them, make us infamous in the eyes of worldly men as well as spiritual; or even if we are strict and diligent in repudiating things which could be within our power and would be considered quite respectable. Matters which seem slight and trivial, which we see others of our profession do casually, still have the ability to disturb the mind just as much as those greater matters which could be expected to fill up the senses with worldly anxiety. Even when the burden of this world has been laid down, they do not permit a monk to aspire to God, on whom all his thoughts should be fixed; for the slightest separation from God, the supreme good, must be considered by a monk as tantamount to sudden death and a miserable end. But when the mind is grounded in such peace, free from all toils of fleshly passion, and the heart cleaves closely to God the one supreme good, then is fulfilled St Paul's command, 'pray without ceasing' (I Thess. 5:17), and 'In every place lifting up pure hands without anger and contention' (I Tim. 2:8). When what we may call the sense of the mind is absorbed in purity, and purged from earthly desires to take on the likeness of an angelic spirit, then prayer will be pure and sincere, whatever comes into the mind, whatever it considers, whatever it does."

VII. GERMANUS: "If only it were as simple and as easy always to preserve the seeds of spiritual contemplation as it is to acquire them! They can certainly be conceived in our hearts, either through repeating the Scriptures, or recalling our spiritual progress, or indeed through contemplating the heavenly sacraments, but no sooner are they conceived than they vanish, and flee away without our consent. Moreover, when the mind finds an alternative matter for meditation, and yet others creep in, the first ones that we had fastened on escape in rapid flight; there is no constancy in the mind, no stability in striving to hold onto holy thoughts, so that if we do happen to retain them we must acknowledge that it is by chance, no credit to ourselves. So how can we claim that it was our choice that gave rise to such thoughts, if we are incapable of persevering in them?

But we should not let a long digression on this question delay our consideration of the matter we had begun to discuss, the constant state of prayer; we must defer it to another occasion, for we are more eager to know about the nature of prayer, particularly since the Apostle urges us never to cease from it, saying 'pray without ceasing' (I Thess. 5:17). So we would like to be informed firstly about its nature, what sort of prayer we should utter ceaselessly, and then about how we may be able to retain that prayer and practice it without intermission. It is no small task for the heart to achieve this, as our own constant experience shows, as well as your holy profession, for you have defined the purpose of monasticism and its perfection as consisting in the work of prayer."

VIII. ISAAC: "I do not consider that it is possible to understand all the varieties of prayer without a really contrite heart and a pure soul, under the guidance of the Holy Spirit. There are as many varieties of prayer as there are moods and variations in any one soul, and indeed in all souls together. So we must acknowledge that, because of the grossness of our hearts, we are incapable of distinguishing every type of prayer, but we can at least attempt to outline them to the extent that our mediocre experience permits us to do. It is according to the degree of purity that each person achieves, and the nature or mood to which circumstances incline him, or to which his own striving brings him, that prayer varies from moment to moment, so that no one can possibly make a prayer that is consistently the same. You pray in one way when alert, another when weighed down by melancholy or desperation, another when cheered by spiritual success, another when depressed by accumulated assaults, in another when you ask forgiveness for your sins, another when you beg for an increase in grace or some virtue, or at any rate for the extinction of some vice; in another way when you are struck by the consideration of hell and fear of future judgment, another when inspired by the hope and desire of good things to come, in another when in need and peril, another in safety and peace; in another when enlightened by the administration of the heavenly sacraments, another when restricted by failure of virtue and dryness of perception.

IX. "Having said that about the nature of prayer, we now have the considerable task of explaining each type of prayer in turn, not to the degree that the vastness of the subject might demand, but to the extent that the limited time at our disposal allows, or indeed as much as our small intelligence can grasp, and our sluggish hearts conceive. St Paul distinguishes four types of prayer, saying, 'I desire, therefore, first of all, that supplications, prayers, intercessions and thanksgivings be made' (I Tim. 2:1). We can be sure that the Apostle did not make these distinctions without good reason. We should first investigate what he means by supplications, prayers, intercessions and thanksgivings, and then consider whether the one who prays should pray in all these four ways equally; that is to say whether all should be performed simultaneously in every act of prayer, or whether they should be offered one after another and separately, as if we should offer supplication at one moment, prayer at another, now intercession, now thanksgiving. Alternatively, should one person make supplication, another prayer, another intercession, and another render thanksgiving to God, according to their capacity and age, in the manner in which each one decides to apply himself?

X. "Now firstly we must treat of the qualities of the different types of prayer, and what to call them; distinguishing between prayer, supplication and intercession. Then we must consider whether to take them separately or all at once. In third place we must examine whether the order in which St Paul names them has any significance for the reader, or whether we should imagine that he made a simple enumeration indifferently – a view which I consider absurd. We can hardly imagine that the Holy Spirit spoke through the Apostle casually and without purpose! For that reason we shall consider each type of prayer in the order we have stated, as far as Our Lord enables us.

XI. "'I desire, therefore, first of all, that supplication be made . . .' (I Tim. 2:1). Supplication is beseeching or entreating for sins, in which each one of us is struck with compunction for sin either present or past, and begs forgiveness.

XII. "Prayers are the means by which we offer our promises to God; the Greek word is *eukhē*, or 'vow'. For where the Greek text says, 'I will render my prayers to the Lord', the Latin says, 'I will pay my vows to the Lord' (Psalm 115:4/116:14). Taking this literally, it means, 'I will pay my prayers to the Lord.' When we read in Ecclesiastes, 'If thou hast vowed anything to God, defer not to repay it' (Qo. 5:3), the Greek accordingly says, 'if you pray a prayer to the Lord, defer not to repay it.' This must be fulfilled by each of us. We make a prayer or vow, when we renounce this

IX. On Prayer

world and undertake to make ourselves dead to all worldly actions and conversations, ready to serve the Lord wholeheartedly. We make such a prayer, when we promise to disdain the glory of this age and spurn all earthly wealth, to cleave to Our Lord with our hearts contrite and our spirits humbled. We make a prayer when we undertake to preserve ourselves in the purest chastity of body and unshaken patience, or pledge ourselves to pluck out of our hearts the roots of wrath and of the sadness that works death; if we are careless and neglect to do that, and revert to our old ways, we shall have failed, and become guilty in our prayers or vows; of us it can be said, 'It is much better not to vow, than after a vow not to perform' (Qo. 5: 4, LXX). In the Greek it runs, 'It is better not to pray, than after a prayer not to perform.'

XIII. "In third place we have intercessions, which we make on behalf of others while we are in the fervour of the spirit. It may be for those dear to us, or for the peace of the whole world that we ask; and in the words of St Paul, we make entreaty 'for all men, for kings and for all that are in high station' (I Tim. 2:1–2).

XIV. "In the fourth place we find thanksgivings, when our thoughts are caught up in gratitude to the Lord, either for his past benefits, or for those of the moment, or considering what God has stored up in the future for those who live him. Our best prayers are often made in that frame of mind, when the spirit is stirred up in great joy to pour out thanks to God, beyond the power of words, when it perceives with unclouded sight the rewards laid up for the saints in time to come.

XV. "Now occasions often do arise for making profound prayer in all these four types. Repentance for sins gives birth to supplications, just as a pure conscience, in fidelity to what it offers and constancy in what it promises, produces prayers. Intercession arises from the fervour of charity, while thanksgiving is inspired by the remembrance of God's goodness and his great love towards us. Thus we can see how the most fervent prayers are frequently made, afire with love, so that it is established that all these types of prayer we have mentioned are useful, indeed necessary, for each of us. In one and the same person his varying emotions give rise to pure and devout prayer, now supplication, now prayer, now intercession, now thanksgiving. Nevertheless the first type belongs especially to beginners, who are still stung with remorse at the memory of their sins, the second to those who are making some spiritual progress and are desirous of virtue in sublimity of mind. The third is for those who have perfectly fulfilled their vows in their actions, and are inspired by their charity to intercede for others, mindful of their weakness. The fourth is for those who have already drawn the thorn of guilt from their hearts, and are in conscience free, perceiving with unclouded minds the great things the Lord has done and his mercy, either granted in the past, or bestowed at present, or prepared for the future, and are caught up in the fervour of their souls into that fiery prayer which human language can neither conceive or express.

Nevertheless it does sometimes happen that a mind which is proficient in that true pure state, and has begun to take root there, can conceive all the types of prayer simultaneously, flickering over them all like a consuming flame beyond comprehension, and pours out prayers to God beyond words, in the purity of its strength. It is the Holy Spirit himself who utters these prayers to God in groans too deep for words, and beyond our own understanding. In an instant of time the Spirit grasps so much, and expresses it in supplication without words, as at other times we cannot even call into our memory, let alone express in speech. In whatever state a man may be, he can on occasion utter pure and fervent prayer. Even one in the first lowly state of those who simply think of judgment to come, who is still in fear and dread of trial and punishment, may be so struck for a moment that he is filled with the enthusiastic spirit of full entreaty no less than one who in a pure heart considers the magnificence of God and recalls it, dissolving into joy and gladness unspeakable. According to Our Lord's words, he may begin to love more because he knows himself to have been forgiven more (Luke 7: 47).

XVI. "Nevertheless we should try to pray in accordance with the progress of our life and the growth of our virtues, using types of prayer which are based either on the consideration of the good in store for us, or on the fire of charity. Alternatively, speaking simply for beginners, we should use prayer suited to the acquisition of virtue and the extinction of all vice. There is no other way to attain those heights of prayer which we have mentioned, except by leading the mind step by step through these types of prayer in order.

XVII. "Our Lord himself deigned to give us an example to introduce these four types of prayer, so that in this matter too might be fulfilled what was said of him, 'the things which Jesus began to do and to teach' (Acts 1:1). He took on the model of supplication, when he said, 'My Father, if it be possible, let this chalice pass from me' (Matt. 26:39). Also in the Psalms it is said, in the person of Christ, 'Oh God, my God, look upon me; why hast thou forsaken me?' (Psalm 21/22:2) and other similar passages. Prayer is demonstrated in, 'I have glorified thee on the earth; I have finished the work which thou gavest me to do', and also, 'for them do I sanctify myself, that they also may be sanctified in truth' (John 17:4, 19). There is intercession, in saying, 'Father, I will that where I am, they also whom thou hast given me may be with me; that they may see my glory which thou hast given me' (John 17:24), and indeed, when he says, 'Father, forgive them, for they know not what they do' (Luke 23:34). There is thanksgiving when he says, 'I confess to thee, O Father, Lord of heaven and earth, because thou hast hid these things from the wise and prudent and hast revealed them to little ones. Yes, Father; for so hath it seemed good in thy sight' (Matt. 11:25–6), and also when he says, 'Father, I give thee thanks that thou hast heard me. And I knew that thou hearest me always' (John 11:41–2). Although these four types of prayer were uttered separately and at different times, in the manner we have already described, as Our Lord offered them distinctly, nevertheless he did demonstrate them all together, included in a perfect supplication, namely that which we find so copiously poured at the end of St John's Gospel (chapter 17). This text is over long to cite here, but the earnest student will be able to discover the truth of this by reading it himself. St Paul also, in the Epistle to the Philippians, arranges these four types of prayer in a slightly different order, but clearly shows us how they should sometimes be offered within the framework of a single supplication; for he says, 'In every thing, by prayer and supplication, with thanksgiving, let your petitions be made known to God' (Phil. 4:6). Here he wishes us to understand in particular that thanksgiving and intercession should be included in our prayer and supplication.

XVIII. "After these types of prayer follows a higher and more sublime state, which is formed in the contemplation of God and the fervour of charity. The mind is then caught up into love and intimately linked to God, as to our own father, and speaks to him in particular devotion. Our Lord gave us a formula of prayer to demonstrate how we should earnestly seek this state; for he said, 'Our Father' (Matt. 6:9–13). Thus we acknowledge the God and Lord of the universe to be our own Father, and claim that we have been brought from the condition of slaves into the state of adopted sonship. We continue, 'Who art in heaven', as we repudiate in abhorrence the way of life which we follow as wanderers in this world, one which separates us far from our Father, and we are spurred by eager desire towards that place where we acknowledge our Father to dwell. We admit nothing from this earth which can make us unworthy of our profession, or of the dignity of that adoption, which can deprive us, as if unfit for our own inheritance, and bring down upon us the terror of his severe justice.

When we have been promoted to that grade of sonship, we should display a devotion appropriate to good sons, turning our attention not to our own benefit but to the glory of our Father, for we say to him, 'Hallowed be thy name.' We bear witness that our longing and our joy are for the glory of our Father, following the example we are given, 'He that speaketh of himself seeketh his own glory; but he that seeketh the glory of him that sent him, he is true and there is no injustice in him' (John 7:18). The Vessel of Election was inspired by this thought when he said he would choose to be cut off from Christ if only a greater family could be acquired for him, and the whole people of Israel be saved, added to the glory of the Father. Cheerfully he chooses to die for Christ, knowing that no one can actually die for the sake of life (Rom. 9:3). Again he says, 'We rejoice that we are weak and you are strong' (II Cor. 13:9). We should not be surprised if St Paul chose to be cut off from Christ for the sake of Christ's glory and the conversion of his brethren, the salvation of his race, for the Prophet Micah also offered to become a liar, cut off from the inspiration of the Holy Spirit, if only the people of the Jewish nation could escape the disastrous captivity which his own prophecy foretold. 'Would God I were not a man that hath the spirit,' he says, 'and that I rather spoke a lie!' (Micah 2:11). We should not forget the prayer of Moses the Lawgiver, who was prepared to die along with his sinful brethren, saying, 'I beseech thee, Lord: this people hath sinned a heinous sin .... Either forgive them this trespass, or if thou do not, strike me out of the book that thou hast written' (Exod. 32:31–2). The phrase 'Hallowed be thy name' can also be properly understood thus: the holiness of God is our own perfection. So when we say to him, 'Hallowed be thy name', we are in effect saying, Make us, Father, to be such as can be fit both to understand what your holiness is, and to receive it, and indeed that our spiritual way of life may demonstrate your holiness. This is fulfilled in us when men 'see our good works, and glorify our Father who is in heaven' (Matt. 5:16).

XIX. "The second petition of this perfect prayer begs for the kingdom of our Father straightaway. This can mean that kingdom in which Christ reigns from day to day among the saints, when the empire of the devil has been driven out of our hearts, with the extinction of every foul vice, and God has begun to reign within us in the sweet savour of virtue; when fornication is vanquished by chastity, wrath defeated by mildness, pride trodden underfoot by humility, till Christ reigns in our thoughts. It can also surely mean when the appointed time has come and the promise made to all the perfect among the sons of God is fulfilled, when Christ says to them, 'Come, ye blessed of my Father, possess you the kingdom prepared for you from the foundation of the world' (Matt. 25: 34). When our gaze is fixed on that Day, and our desires look expectantly there, we say to him, 'Thy Kingdom come'. It is on the evidence of our own conscience that when Christ appears we will know that we ourselves will soon be ranked among his companions. No wrongdoer would ever dare to say that, or to wish for the Kingdom, for he would not want to see the Judge on his bench, knowing that in that presence he would receive no prize nor reward for merit, but punishment instead.

XX. "The third supplication of the sons of God is, 'Thy will be done on earth as it is in heaven.' There can be no greater petition than to long for earthly things to be made equal to those of heaven. To say 'thy will be done on earth as it is in heaven' means nothing less than that men should become like angels. Just as the angels perform the will of God in heaven, so men who are on earth should perform not their own will but his in all things. No one can be capable of saying this sincerely except the one who believes that God ordains all things for our benefit, whether they seem good to us or bad, and that he is more careful and more concerned for our salvation and happiness than we are for ourselves. It can also be understood as referring to the will of God for the salvation of all, as St Paul tells us, 'He will have all men to be saved and to come to the knowledge of the truth' (I Tim. 2: 4). The prophet Isaiah also says, speaking in the person of God the Father, 'all my will shall be done' (Isaiah 46: 10). So when we say, 'thy will be done on earth as it is in heaven,' we are in effect saying that those who are still on the earth should be saved through faith in you, Father, just as those in heaven are already.

XXI. "Next comes, 'Give us this day our *epiousion* bread', that is to say *super-substantial* (Matt. 6: 11). The other evangelist has 'daily bread' (Luke 11: 3). The first reading refers to the sublimity of this Bread, and the quality of its nature, being above all substance,

IX. On Prayer

sublime, magnificent and holy above all creation; the second refers to its appropriate use and the benefit it confers. When it says 'daily', it shows us that without that Bread there is no day when we are capable of living the spiritual life. When it says 'today', it shows us that we should receive that Bread every day, and that having received it yesterday is not enough, but that it should be administered to us today as well. That daily necessity reminds us that we should say this prayer at all times, for no day passes when we do not have need of receiving this nourishment, to strengthen the heart of our inner self. 'Today' can also be understood of this present life, that as long as we remain in this world, he may grant us this bread. We know well that those who deserve it will receive this bread in the age to come, but we ask you to grant it to us today, for unless we be fit to receive it in this life, we cannot partake of it in the next.

XXII. "'Forgive us our trespasses, as we forgive those who trespass against us.' How marvellous is the mercy of God! He has bestowed on us a form of prayer, and established a discipline for our conduct which is pleasing to him, tearing up the roots of wrath and gloom by means of the formula he has given us to fulfil his command of ceaseless prayer; but more than that, he has given those who pray an opportunity and opened for them a path to call down upon themselves a merciful and loving judgment from God. He has given us power, so to speak, to influence the judge's sentence on ourselves, forcing him to pardon our sins by our own example of forgiveness, for we say to him, 'forgive us as we forgive others.' Anyone can be confident in relying on this prayer in asking forgiveness for himself, if he has forgiven those who are in debt to him – not, I might add, those in debt to the Lord. There are of course some of us who, to show ourselves tolerant, connive at things which are committed in defiance of God, however gravely sinful – how wrong this is, especially when we are found merciless and implacable when it comes to exacting justice for the slightest offences against ourselves! Anyone who does not wholeheartedly forgive the brother who sins against him, is calling down on himself a condemnation, not pardon, when he says this prayer. By his own words he asks for a harsh judgment, saying, 'forgive me as I forgive others.' If he were treated as his own prayer demands, the only outcome would be that he would suffer implacable wrath and an irrevocable sentence, following his own example. If we would be judged mercifully, we too should be merciful towards those who have offended us. We will be repaid in the same manner as we repay those who have harmed us by any sort of malice. There are some who, taking fright at this, remain silent at this point while the whole congregation are singing this prayer in church; they are afraid of committing themselves, rather than excusing themselves, with these words, but they do not understand how futile it is to attempt to deceive the judge of all by this elusion, for he has wished to show us the manner in which he will judge his suppliants. It is his desire not to be found wrathful and inexorable towards us, so he has offered us a model for judgment, so that just as we would like to be judged by him, so we should judge our brothers when they sin against us; for there will be 'judgment without mercy to him that hath not done mercy' (James 2: 13).

XXIII. "There follows, 'And lead us not into temptation'. This raises considerable problems. If we are to pray that we may not be allowed to be tempted, then how can the virtue of endurance be found in us, for the text says, 'He that hath not been tried, hath not been proven' (Sir. 34: 11)? And again, 'Blessed is the man that endureth temptation' (James 1: 12). The meaning, therefore, of 'lead us not into temptation' is not that we should not be permitted to be tempted, but that we should not be allowed to be overcome when subject to temptation. Job was tempted, but not led into temptation. He offered no insolence to God, nor did he blaspheme and utter wicked words to conform to the will of the tempter to which he was being lured. Abraham was tempted, Joseph was tempted, but neither of them was led into temptation, for neither of them gave consent to the tempter.

Then comes, 'But deliver us from evil', that is to say, do not suffer us to be tempted by the devil beyond our strength, but with

IX. On Prayer

the temptation give us the 'issue that we may be able to bear it' (I Cor. 10:13).

XXIV. "You see now how a model form of prayer is offered to us by the very judge to whom that prayer is to be used. Here is no request for wealth, no thought of honour, no desire for power or strength, nor any mention of bodily or worldly livelihood. The creator of eternity does not will us to implore him for transitory things, nor for base and earthly matters. It would be a great insult to his magnificence and generosity if anyone were to omit his prayers for eternal benefits and prefer to demand something transitory and temporary. By such a base form of prayer he would be calling on himself the judge's wrath rather than his mercy.

XXV. "Now granted that this prayer appears to contain the fullness of all perfection, being established and decreed by the Lord's own authority, it serves to lead his servants on to a yet higher state of prayer, as we have mentioned, and brings them to a sublime and fiery prayer which is known and experienced by few, indeed is beyond description, to speak truly. It transcends all human reason, and is distinguished by being without the sound of any voice, any movement of speech, any use of words. The soul is illuminated by an influx of heavenly light, utters no narrow human sentiments but with all its senses together gushes out copiously as if from a fountain, and yearns for the Lord in a way beyond description. In a moment of time it pours forth so much, that when the soul returns to itself it cannot easily state or remember what has occurred. Our Lord himself gave us an example of this state of prayer, in the entreaty which we are told he poured forth silently when alone in the mountains, as well as when he was in an agony of prayer and drops of blood gushed forth, showing his unparalleled fervour (Luke 22:44).

XXVI. "No one is sufficiently experienced to be capable of giving a full account of all the varied occasions which can give rise to compunction, and the ways in which the soul is aroused and fired with the purest most fervent form of prayer. We will mention a few of them as examples, in so far as the Lord gives us light to remember them now. Sometimes it happens that a particular verse of a psalm gives us an occasion of fervent prayer while we are chanting; at other times the tuneful singing of one of the brethren inspires the mind to wake and be intent on prayer. It can happen that a distinguished and dignified cantor causes great fervour among those who attend, as can the preaching of a perfect man, and his spiritual instruction which often stirs up to fruitful devotion the feelings of those who had been supine. We have observed that the death of a brother, or someone dear to us causes us to be no less rapt into sincere compunction. On other occasions the memory of our own tepidity and negligence has brought us a saving fervour of spirit. As you can clearly see, there can be no shortage of suitable occasions for God's grace to wake our minds up from their tepid slumbers.

XXVII. "It is no less difficult to define the manner in which these profound stirrings of prayer are produced in the recesses of the soul. Often this saving compunction is the fruit of an indescribable joy and eagerness of spirit; it may break out into shouts under the impulse of a gladness too great to bear, so that for joy and exuberance of heart it may be heard in the next cell. On the other hand it sometimes happens that the soul is so rapt in silence, in the quiet secrets of its depths, that amazed by its sudden illumination all sound of voice is suppressed, and the astonished spirit either contains all its feelings within itself, or gives vent to them and pours out groans beyond words to express its desires to God. On other occasions the soul is so filled with compunction and grief that it cannot express itself otherwise than in abundant tears."

XXVIII. GERMANUS: "Even my limited experience knows that compunction can affect us like that sometimes. Often enough I have been in tears at the memory of my sins, and the Lord has visited me with such an indescribable joy that the very vastness of that gladness has convinced me not to despair of pardon. I can imagine no higher state, were it within our capacity to bring it on. Yet often I have been trying with all my might to arouse similar tears of compunction, calling to mind all my mistakes and sins, but have been unable to summon up any quantity of tears, for my eyes remained as dry and hard as flints, not a drop of moisture appearing in them. As a result, although I am overjoyed when I do burst into tears, I am more grieved when I am unable to produce them when I want."

XXIX. ISAAC: "A flood of tears does not always derive from the same emotion or virtue. Sometimes tears arrive, caused by the thorn of sin pricking our hearts, as it is said, 'I have laboured in my groaning, I every night I will wash my bed; I will water my couch with my tears' (Psalm 6:7). And again, 'Let tears run down like a torrent day and night: give thyself no rest, and let not the apple of thy eye cease' (Lam. 2:18). Another occasion for tears is the remembrance of eternal bliss and the longing for that brilliance to come, when unbearable joy and immense gladness burst forth in copious tears; the soul thirsts for God, the fountain of life, saying, 'When shall I come and appear before the face of God? My tears have been my bread day and night' (Psalm 41/42:3–4). He cries out with sobs and grief daily, saying, 'Woe is me, that my sojourning is prolonged, . . . my soul hath been long a sojourner' (Psalm 119/120:5, 6).

Tears may flow also without any consciousness of guilt, but come simply through fear of hell and the consideration of the terrible judgment; the prophet was struck with that terror when he prayed to God, 'Enter not into judgment with thy servant: for in thy sight no man living shall be justified' (Psalm 142/143:2). Yet another type of weeping is not for one's own conscience but for the hardness and sins of another, as when Samuel wept for Saul (I Kings (I Sam.) 15:35), and we read that Jeremiah wept for the fate of Jerusalem in the Old Testament just as Our Lord did in the Gospel, saying, 'Who will give water to my head and a fountain of tears to my eyes, and I will weep day and night for the slain of the daughter of my people' (Jer. 9:1). Similar too are those tears of which we sing in the hundred and first psalm, 'I did eat ashes like bread, and mingled my drink with weeping' (Psalm 101/102:10). These are not such tears as flow in the sixth psalm from the person of a penitent, but are caused by worry over the difficulties and constraints of this life, for the just suffer during this life on earth. This we can see not only from the text of the psalm but from the title too, for it is written in the person of that poor man of whom the Gospel says, 'Blessed are the poor in spirit; for theirs is the kingdom of heaven' (Matt. 5:3). The title reads, 'The prayer of the poor man, when he was anxious, and poured out his supplication before God' (Psalm 101, title).

XXX. "Such tears differ enormously from those forced from a hard heart and dry eyes, although we may not believe the latter to be quite fruitless, for they do derive from a good intention, in the case of those who have not yet arrived at perfect knowledge, nor been able to be cleansed and purified from their past or present sins. Those who have already progressed in virtue should never force a profusion of tears in this way, nor put on affected weeping as an external show, for even if tears do result in this way, they will never bring about the benefit of spontaneous tears. They are more likely to depress the spirits of the supplicant, distract him with the effort, drown him in human misery, and cast him down from that heavenly sublimity on which the mind of the one who prays should always be fixed in admiration. Once his attention has been thus distracted this affected weeping forces him to concentrate on nothing more than producing fruitless drops of tears.

XXXI. "To understand the nature of true prayer, let me offer you not my own opinion but that of Blessed Antony. We remember that he often spent long hours in prayer, and was frequently abstracted in mind, so that when the sun began to rise we would hear him saying, in his spiritual fervour, 'Why do you interrupt me, old Sun, rising so soon, and dragging me away from the real light?' His usual saying about the goal of heavenly prayer, of more than human wisdom, was, 'A monk is not perfect in prayer as long

IX. On Prayer

as he is conscious of the fact that he is praying.' While admiring his teaching, I am going to be so bold as to venture to add a little from my own mediocre store, and will give you some indications from my own experience about the nature of the prayer which the Lord hears.

XXXII. "If while we are praying, we allow no hesitation to interrupt us, no sort of doubt to depress our trust in our supplication, and if we feel that we have obtained what we have been asking for in our effusion of prayer, then we can be confident that our prayers have reached God and taken effect. A man is worthy to be heard and to receive, in the measure in which he believes that he is observed by God, or that God can be present. Our Lord's teaching cannot fail, 'all things, whatsoever ye ask when ye pray, believe that you shall receive, and they shall come unto you'" (Mark 11: 24).

XXXIII. GERMANUS: "We believe that such trust in being heard derives only from a pure conscience, so how can people like us, whose consciences are still stung with the thorns of sin, be able to possess it? We have no virtues to support us and give us grounds to presume our prayers are being heard."

XXXIV. ISAAC: "We can see from the evidence of the Gospels and the Old Testament that there are various factors which may lead to our prayers being heard, depending on the various states of different souls. You will find that Our Lord tells us that when two agree on anything it will result in being heard, for he says, 'If two of you shall consent upon earth, concerning anything whatsoever they shall ask, it shall be done to them by my Father who is in heaven' (Matt. 18: 19). You find it also in the fullness of faith, compared to a mustardseed: 'If you have faith,' he says, 'as a grain of mustardseed, you shall say to this mountain, Remove from hence hither, and it shall remove; and nothing shall be impossible to you' (Matt. 17: 19). You find it too in persistent prayer, which Our Lord calls importunity because we persevere in asking without tiring: 'Amen, amen, I say to you, although he will not rise and give him because he is his friend; yet, because of his importunity, he will rise and give him as many as he needeth' (Luke 11:8). You find it also as a result of almsgiving, 'Shut up alms in the heart of the poor: and it shall obtain help for thee against all evil' (Sir. 29:15). It is found in the emendation of life with works of mercy, as in, 'Loose the bands of wickedness, undo the bundles that oppress', and a little further, after the prophet rebukes fruitless and vain fasting, 'Then shalt thou call, and the Lord shall hear; thou shalt cry, and he shall say: Here I am' (Isaiah 58:6, 9). Often too abundance of suffering makes us heard, as in, 'in my trouble I cried to the Lord: and he heard me' (Psalm 119/120:1) and again, 'Thou shalt not molest a stranger, for if he cry to me I will hear him, because I am compassionate' (Exod. 22:21, 27).

You can see how many methods there of obtaining the grace of a hearing, so that no one should be downcast in conscience and despair of asking for what pertains to eternal salvation. Remembering our wretched state, let us suppose that we are completely destitute of all the virtues we have described, and cannot even find two to agree in a praiseworthy manner, nor have so much as a mustardseed's worth of faith, nor the works of charity which the prophet describes – are we not still capable of that importunity which will gain for us all we desire? For that alone, Our Lord promised that he would grant all our prayers. We must therefore insist on our prayers with no doubt or hesitation; fear not that we shall fail to obtain everything we ask of God with such persistence. Our Lord encourages us, for it is his will to grant us the eternal good things of heaven, to press upon him determinedly, for he neither despises nor refuses such importunity, nay, he invites it and praises it. He promises, lovingly, that he will grant whatever hopes we persevere in expressing, saying, 'Ask and it shall be given to you; seek and you shall find; knock and it shall be opened to you. For every one that asketh receiveth; and he that seeketh findeth; and to him that knocketh it shall be opened' (Luke 11:9–10). In another place, 'all things whatsoever you shall ask in prayer, believing, you shall receive – nothing shall be impossible to you' (Matt. 21:22, 17:19).

IX. On Prayer

Even if we are devoid of all the causes which we have listed as leading to our prayers being answered, let our stubborn insistence encourage us, for that is within the power of whoever chooses, without either merit or effort. However anyone one who doubts that his prayer will be heard, will surely not be heard. We can learn from the example of blessed Daniel how tirelessly we should entreat the Lord, for although he was heard from the first day that he began to pray, he only received the result of his prayer after twenty one days (Dan. 10:2 ff.). Have no doubt that we should not cease from the prayers we have begun even if we feel we are slow in gaining an answer. It may be that the grace of an answer is delayed through the Lord's providence; perhaps an angel has been despatched to bring us some gift of God, but on leaving the face of the Almighty has been delayed by an opposing demon, and will doubtless be unable to bring to us the benefit we desire if he finds that we have abandoned the prayer we had begun. That would surely have happened to the said prophet had he not persevered in continuing his prayer until the twenty-first day, with incomparable determination. Nothing should make us despair of continuing to trust, even when we feel no indication that our prayer has been answered, but we should rely on our Lord's promise when he said, 'all things whatsoever you shall ask in prayer, believing, you shall receive' (Matt. 21:22). It is also worth remembering the teaching of the holy apostle John, which gives a clear answer to this question, 'This is the confidence which we have towards God: that whatsoever we shall ask according to his will, he heareth us' (I John 5:14). He bids us trust, fully and without doubting, only about matters which accord with the Lord's will, rather than our own convenience or temporal comfort. We are instructed to include this in the Lord's Prayer, for we say, 'Thy will be done', meaning not our own.

If we also remember St Paul's teaching, that 'we know not what we should pray for' (Rom. 8:26), we will realise that we do sometimes ask for things contrary to our own salvation, so that it is good that our prayers are denied by Him who knows our needs more precisely and more truly than we do ourselves. This certainly happened to himself, the Teacher of the Gentiles, when he prayed that the angel of Satan be taken away from him, although it was in accordance with the Lord's will that it was permitted to chastise him for his own benefit. He says, 'For which thing, thrice I besought the Lord that it might depart from me. And he said to me: My grace is sufficient for thee; for power is made perfect in infirmity' (II Cor. 12: 8–9). Our Lord himself, in his humanity, gave us an example of how to pray as of everything else, for he said in his prayer, 'My Father, if it be possible, let this chalice pass from me. Nevertheless, not as I will but as thou wilt' (Matt. 26: 39). Yet in truth his own will did not differ from the will of his Father, for he came 'to save that which was lost . . . and to give his life a redemption for many' (Matt. 18: 11, 20: 28). He himself says of this, 'No one taketh my life away from me; but I lay it down of myself. And I have power to lay it down; and I have power to take it up again' (John 10: 18). The holy David in the thirty ninth Psalm sings in the person of Christ on the unity of will which he ever possessed with his Father, 'That I should do thy will, O my God, I have desired it' (Psalm 39/40: 9). We read of the Father that 'God so loved the world as to give his only begotten Son' (John 3: 16), and we find it said of the Son, that he 'gave himself for our sins' (Gal. 1: 4). Of the Father we are told, 'He that spared not even his own Son, but delivered him up for us all' (Rom. 8: 32), and of the Son it is said, 'He was offered because it was his own will' (Isaiah 53: 7). In all things the will of the Father and the will of the Son are described as one, so that we are told the working of that will did not differ even in the mystery of the Lord's resurrection. For the holy Apostle proclaims that his bodily resurrection was the work of the Father, saying 'God the Father, who raised him from the dead' (Gal. 1: 1),, and the Son likewise declares that he will raise up the temple of his body, saying, 'Destroy this temple; and in three days I will raise it up' (John 2: 19).

With these examples to guide us, from Our Lord himself, we must conclude all our own petitions with a similar prayer, adding these words to our entreaties, 'Nevertheless, not as I will but as thou wilt' (Matt. 26: 39). We have observed that he who is totally absorbed in making his petitions will even find himself forgetting to make the three genuflections which customarily conclude the worship when our brethren meet together.

XXXV. "Above all, we should be careful to follow the Gospel precept, that we are to go into our private room, and close the doors, and there pray to our Father (Matt. 6:6). This is how we fulfil it: we enter our private room when we clear our minds entirely from all disturbing thoughts and anxieties, offering our prayers to the Lord in secret intimacy. We close the door to pray, when we keep our lips still, and in total silence pray to the one who examines the heart more than the words. We pray in secret when our prayers are within the heart, directed to God alone, with an attentive mind, so that hostile powers have no possibility of discovering the nature of our petition. That is why we pray in total silence – not only to avoid distracting our brethren, whether with whispers or loud cries, and intruding on the senses of the others who are praying, but also it is so that our intentions can be concealed from our enemies, who are especially pressing at times of prayer. Thus we will fulfil that commandment, 'Keep the doors of thy mouth from her that sleepeth in thy bosom' (Micah 7:5).

XXXVI. "For the same reason we should pray frequently, but briefly, otherwise if we take too long the enemy can insinuate something into our thoughts. True sacrifice is the 'sacrifice to God, an afflicted spirit' (Psalm 50/51:19). Saving victim, a pure libation, is the 'sacrifice of justice' (Psalm 50/51:21), the 'sacrifice of praise' (Psalm 49/50:23); true succulent offerings are 'holocausts full of marrow' (Psalm 65/66:15), which are offered in a contrite and humble heart. If we demonstrate that disciplined attentiveness of spirit which we have described, we shall be able to sing rightly, 'Let my prayer be directed as incense in thy sight: the lifting up of my hands, as evening sacrifice' (Psalm 140/141:2).

Time is passing and the night is at hand, which reminds us to conclude with a fitting prayer. Granted that we seem to have spoken at length, as much as our weak nature can bear, yet we must admit that we have said very little in proportion to the immensity of this difficult subject."

We were dazzled by Isaac's holy discourse, but not satisfied. We celebrated the evening prayer together, and allowed our bodies a little repose, till at first dawn we returned to our discussion, begging for further instruction, and rejoicing as much in having found such a teacher as in our trust in what had been promised. Although we had been shown how important prayer is, our discussion had brought us to realise that we were still ignorant of the manner and ability to acquire and preserve a constant habit of prayer.

✣ THE TENTH COLLATION ✣
BEING THE SECOND OF ABBA ISAAC

On Prayer

   I. Preamble.
  II. On the manner in which they announce Easter in Egypt.
 III. Of Abba Sarapion and the Anthropomorphite heresy which he contracted through ignorance.
  IV. How we returned to Abba Isaac and asked him about the error into which the aforesaid elder had fallen.
   V. The reply, on the origin of the heresy described above.
  VI. The reasons why Christ Jesus appears to each of us either in a lowly form or a glorious one.
 VII. In what consists our goal and the perfection of bliss.
VIII. A question, on how to learn that perfection through which we can arrive at the ceaseless recollection of God.
  IX. The reply, on the value of an understanding gained by experience.
   X. How to establish ceaseless prayer.
  XI. On the perfection of prayer to which the aforesaid teaching leads.
 XII. A question, on how spiritual recollection can be preserved unchanged.
XIII. On how fleeting are thoughts.

XIV. The reply, how we may acquire constancy of heart and thought.

I. While I am writing about the sublime way of life of the hermits, with the help of God to make up for my unpolished style, the course of my narrative obliges me to make a digression, inserting something which may seem like a monstrous carbuncle on a fair face: Nevertheless even from this I am sure the less educated will gain useful instruction on the question of the image of Almighty God, of which we read in Genesis, especially since it touches on an important doctrine, ignorance of which leads to a great blasphemy and weakening of the Catholic faith.

II. In the territory of Egypt they preserve the following ancient custom after the feast of Epiphany. (Priests in that province keep that feast both for the Lord's Baptism and his birth according to the flesh, and celebrate the two mysteries on a single festival, not on two separate days as we do in Western provinces.) Letters are sent by the patriarch of Alexandria to all the churches in Egypt to announce the beginning of Lent and the date of Easter, not only to all the towns, but to every monastery as well. Now according to this custom, a few days after the conversation with Abba Isaac which I have just recounted, the solemn letters arrived from Theophilus, bishop of the said city. In these, apart from setting the date of Easter, he gave a long dissertation on the foolish heresy of the Anthropomorphists, and refuted it in a fulsome discourse. Nearly all the monks who lived up and down Egypt received this with great indignation, being simple but erroneous; in fact the majority of the elders decided that the prelate involved should be shunned by the whole brotherhood as being depraved in a very serious heresy. It seemed to them that he opposed the teaching of Holy Scripture, and denied that Almighty God possessed a human form, although Scripture clearly states that Adam was created in his image. The monks who lived in the desert of Scete, who excelled all those of Egypt in perfection and wisdom, so opposed the letters that, with the exception of Abba Paphnutius who was

X. On Prayer

the priest of our own community, none of the other priests who presided over the three other churches of that desert would permit them to be read or referred to in their communities.

III. Among those who were ensnared by this heresy was Sarapion, a man of long standing austerity and well advanced in every aspect of monastic life. His lack of understanding of the doctrine in question prejudiced him against all those who held the true faith, all the more because he excelled virtually all other monks in the length of time he had spent in virtuous life. Paphnutius the priest had failed, despite many entreaties, to recall him to the true faith, which seemed to him like an innovation, never previously conceived or taught by his predecessors. Now it happened that a deacon named Photinus, a man of great learning, arrived from Cappadocia with the intention of visiting the brethren who dwelt in that desert. Paphnutius welcomed him gladly, as coming to confirm the faith which was contained in the letters of Patriarch Theophilus. He introduced him to the assembly, to explain before all the brethren how the entire Catholic Church of the East interpreted that passage of Genesis, "Let us make Man to our image and likeness" (Gen. 1:26). He demonstrated that, as all the leaders of the Church taught, the image and likeness of God was to be understood spiritually, as a metaphor, not simply and literally, and proved this at length with many scriptural passages. He showed how impossible it was for the immense and inconceivable majesty of the invisible God to be restricted within a human shape and likeness, for his nature is incorporeal, incomposite and simple, beyond the scope of eye to see or mind to conceive. At last old Sarapion was so moved by that learned man's many strong arguments that he returned to the faith of Catholic tradition. Paphnutius was overjoyed at his agreement, as were we all, for the Lord had not allowed a man of such long-established virtue, who had erred simply through inexperience and rustic simplicity, to continue for ever to deviate from the straight path of faith. We rose and poured out prayers of gratitude together, but the old man was very confused in his prayer, realising that the anthropomorphic image of the Godhead, which he had been accustomed to put before himself in prayer, had been eliminated from his heart. He burst into tears, sobbing loudly and prostrated himself on the ground, crying out in his deep distress, "Ah me, they have taken my God from me, and I have no one to hold on to; I do not know whom to adore, whom to supplicate." We were greatly moved by this occurrence, and because our thoughts were also still full of what we had gained from the previous discourse, we returned to Abba Isaac, and gazing at him intently, began in these words:

IV. "Even before this new matter which has arisen, the memory of what we had absorbed from your previous discourse on the state of prayer had already induced us to set all else aside and to return to Your Beatitude, but the serious error of Abba Sarapion has increased our desire, for we consider that error to be the fruit of the wiles of wicked devils. When we consider how through ignorance of his fault he had lost the benefit of so much praiseworthy effort, spent for fifty years in this desert, and had even run the risk of eternal loss, we are thrown into no little dejection. We would like to know first of all how and why he fell into so serious an error, and after that we want to learn how to attain to that state of prayer about which you have told us so much and so impressively. Your admirable discourse has brought us to the point of astonished amazement, but not to an understanding of how to attain or preserve that level of prayer."

V. ISAAC: "We should not be surprised if an uneducated man, who has never studied the nature and attributes of God in depth, has been up till now stuck in simple errors and grown accustomed to an old mistake, nor that he could be deceived and obstinate, so to speak, in his ancient error, for it does not derive from a recent trick of the devil as you suppose, but from the ignorance of ancient paganism. Just as the pagans used mistakenly to worship demons in human form, so still they imagine they should adore the incomprehensible and indescribable majesty of the true God beneath the restriction of some image. They do not believe they can grasp him or remember him at all unless they have some mental image to put before themselves, to which they can appeal in their supplications, which they can preserve in the mind and keep ever before their gaze. It is to that error that the text is well aimed, 'They changed the glory of the incorruptible God into the likeness of a corruptible man' (Rom. 1: 23). Jeremiah also says, 'My people have changed their glory into an idol' (Jer. 2: 11). Although this error first developed in the minds of some in the way we have described, in the case of others who had never been tainted with pagan superstition, it arose under the pretext of the passage which says, 'Let us make man to our image and likeness' (Gen. 1: 26). Because of simplicity or lack of education it happened that the heresy we call Anthropomorphism grew up under cover of that detestable misinterpretation, which perversely contended that the vast but simple nature of divinity could be contained within our own shape and a human form. But anyone who is instructed in Catholic teaching would shun this as a pagan blasphemy, and thus be able to reach that pure state of prayer in which no image of the divine, no bodily shape (for shame!) is intruded, and indeed he will not admit even the memory of anything said or done, no image nor form of any type.

VI. "As I said in my former discourse, each one's mind during prayer is either elevated or formed according to the measure of his purity. To the degree in which he is detached from the consideration of earthly and material things, as the state of his purity allows, he will be able to envisage Jesus in his inmost thoughts either still in the lowliness of his flesh, or glorified as he comes in the splendour of his majesty. Those who were unable to envisage Jesus coming in his Kingdom, being still hampered by their old Judaic weakness, were unable to say with the apostle, 'if we have known Christ according to the flesh, now we know him so no longer' (II Cor. 5: 16). Only those are able to see his divinity with unclouded eyes who have risen above their ordinary terrestrial concerns and thoughts, and have withdrawn with him to a lonely high mountain. Free from the turmoil of all worldly thoughts and worries, purged from all stain of vice, and elevated by the finest faith and outstanding virtue, they are shown the splendour of his face and the image of his brightness, for they are fit to gaze upon him with the soul's sight undimmed. Jesus can indeed be seen by those who live in cities, forts and villages, who are engaged in ordinary life and works, but not with that clarity with which he appeared to those who were able to climb the aforesaid mountain of virtue with him, namely Peter, James and John. In the same way he appeared to Moses in the desert, so too he spoke with Elijah. Our Lord wished to strengthen us and leave us an example of perfect purity, even though he himself, being the unsullied fountain of all holiness, needed for himself no help, no advantage from withdrawing into a lonely place, in order to acquire purity. The fullness of his purity could not be assailed by the squalor of the crowds, nor could he, who cleansed all that was unclean and made them holy, be tainted by contact with men. Yet he withdrew alone into the mountains to pray (Matt. 14:23), teaching us by the example of his retreat that, if we wish to pray to God with the affections of our hearts pure and whole, we should likewise retreat from all the confusing disturbance of the crowd. Thus, while still living in this body, we can at last to some extent adapt ourselves to the likeness of that bliss which is promised to the saints in the world to come, 'that God may be all in all' (I Cor. 15:28).

VII. "Then will be perfectly fulfilled in us the prayer of Our Saviour, when he prayed for his disciples to his Father, saying, 'That the love wherewith thou hast loved me may be in them, and they in us,' and earlier, 'that they all may be one, as thou, Father, in me, and I in thee; that they also may be one in us' (John 17:26, 21). When the perfect love of God, with which 'he hath first loved us' (I John 4:10), enters into the intentions of our hearts, then will Our Lord's prayer be fulfilled, a prayer which we believe can never be in vain. This will come to pass when all love, all desire, all intention, all effort, all our thoughts, our

X. On Prayer

whole life, our conversation, and all that we hope for, is God; when that unity which exists between the Father and the Son, between the Son and the Father, is infused into our hearts and minds. Just as he loves us with that true, pure and unbreakable charity, so we too shall be united to him in charity everlasting and inseparable; joined to him to the extent that all our hope, our understanding, our utterance, is God. Then we shall arrive at the goal we have spoken about, the one Our Lord longs to be achieved in us, when he prayed, 'that they all may be one, as we also are one; I in them, and thou in me; that they may be made perfect in one.' and, 'Father, I will that where I am, they also whom thou hast given me may be with me' (John 17:22–4). This is the goal of the hermit, this should be all his intention, to be fit to wear the likeness of future bliss in his body, to taste the pledge of that heavenly life in glory while still in this flesh. This, I say, is the aim of all perfection, that the mind may be raised daily above all fleshly concerns to the things of the spirit, until it becomes totally accustomed and intent on single-minded prayer."

VIII. GERMANUS: "Now our astonishment is greater even than our admiration of your former discourse which brought us back here to you. Yet the more we are fired by your teaching to long for perfect bliss, the greater despondency we feel, for we know not the method of searching out the means to such sublimity, or the manner of its acquisition. Because of this, we must ask if you would be so good as to listen patiently while we explain the result of our reflections in our daily meditation while living in our cell, because we need to set it out in words, maybe at length. We are aware that your holiness is not usually offended by the foolishness of the weak, or by the fact that it is stated publicly so that mistakes can be corrected. Our opinion is that in dealing with any sort of skill or knowledge it is necessary to begin with the simple rudiments, starting with the easiest basics, and to grow little by little, nourished on this metaphorical milk, and learning how to rise step by step from the lowest point to the top. After one has entered by the simple beginnings, through the gates of the task in hand, so to speak, one can arrive at the innermost fastness of perfection and ascend its towers with little effort. How for example could small children read simple groups of syllables, had they not first carefully learnt their basic letters? How can they proceed to read fluently if they are not yet capable of putting together short descriptive words? And how could someone unskilled in grammar acquire any readiness in public speaking, or any depth of philosophy? In the same way I am sure that in this most important of all arts, the knowledge of how to cleave to God, there must be some rudiments in which we should first be grounded, and on which the high pinnacles of achievement can be constructed.

We suspect that the first steps are to begin by knowing what sort of meditation can hold or contemplate God. Next we must know how to preserve this state, whatever it is, without losing it – and that, surely, is the peak of perfection. We wish therefore that you would show us the method of meditation by which God can be conceived in the thoughts, and held there always; then we could keep this in mind, and whenever we felt we were drifting away from meditation, we would have the means to return to that state and recover it without any roundabout delay or difficult investigation. It can happen that we be distracted from spiritual concentration, and then return to ourselves as if waking from a deadly sleep; then we rouse ourselves, as it were, to search for the meditation which had been broken, so as to be able to recover that spiritual state, but find that we are restrained by the very effort of enquiry, so that before we rediscover it we are again distracted from our efforts, and the intention we had conceived in our hearts melts away before we can gain that spiritual insight. We are sure that this confusion happens to us because we have no particular object of consideration or consistent focus to which the wandering mind can be recalled after all its distractions and excursions, to enter a tranquil harbour after such a stormy crossing. The mind is so encumbered by this ignorance, and so unwieldy that it is tossed about everywhere, as unsteady as a drunkard, unable to hold on for any length of time to any spiritual insight which it may have happened to glimpse by chance rather than design. For

X. On Prayer

one thought leads on to another, as an introduction and opening which never finds an end or a conclusion."

IX. ISAAC: "The fact that your question is so detailed and acute shows that you are not far from the purity you seek. No one would even ask about these things, let alone investigate and scrutinise them, were he not brought to consider these profound questions by earnest and genuine mental effort and persistent concern. It is the sincere intention of a disciplined life, put into practice, that makes you seek the threshold and knock at the gates of that purity. I can see that you are not just standing outside the gates of that true prayer we have spoken of, but have felt, with the hands of real experience, its inner treasures, and already touched its very secrets; I do not think it will be very difficult for me, now that you are wandering within the interior castle, to conduct you to its very keep, as the Lord will guide us; nor can there be any real difficulty that will prevent you understanding what will be shown you there. The man who knows well what questions to ask is close to their solution, he who has begun to understand where his ignorance lies is very near to wisdom. I do not think, therefore, that I will be accused of lightly giving away secrets if I put before you now what I kept back when I was talking to you before about the perfection of prayer; since you are already dedicated to the pursuit of this quest, I think God in his grace would reveal it to you even without the help of any words of mine.

X. "Now, your apt comparison was with the elementary instruction of infants, who cannot grasp the first rudiments of their letters, or recognise their shapes, or write them with a confident hand, unless they have models to copy, carefully outlined on their wax tablets; in that way they can keep looking at them and get used to imitating them every day. Likewise we must give you a model of spirituality, one that you can keep constantly before your eyes till you learn how to repeat it constantly and beneficially. Once you are accustomed to it, you will progress to a deeper insight. Here therefore is a formula of prayer for you, a model as you requested;

any monk who uses this, and aims at sincere divine contemplation, may drive out every other kind of thought and meditate ceaselessly on God. This prayer can be maintained in no other way than by being free from all bodily concerns and anxieties. It was only a few of the surviving ancient fathers who passed this formula on to us, and only a few of the truly devout among us who practice it.

Now, in order to keep the remembrance of God ever before you, use this formula of prayer constantly: 'O God, come to my assistance, O Lord, make haste to help me' (Psalm 69/70: 2). This verse, out of the whole of Scripture, is deservedly selected for our use. It meets every emotion that can affect human nature, and can be suitably adapted to every state of life, every occurrence. It provides an appeal to God against all adversity, it provides the humility needed for a good confession, it provides a constant protection against worry and fear, the remembrance of one's weakness, confidence in one's being heard, certainty that our protector is present and stands by us always. For he who constantly calls on his protector is certain that he always present. It provides fervour of love and charity, vigilance against attack, wariness of foes; observing itself besieged by day and by night it admits that it is only by our defender that we can be rescued. This little verse is an unbreachable wall against all the siegeworks of the attacking fiend, an unbreakable breastplate, a sturdy shield. When it finds the soul sunk in depression and anxiety, dejected by melancholy and gloomy thoughts, it prevents it from despairing of salvation, by showing that the one invoked is a constant observer of our struggles and is never far from his suppliants. Again, when it finds us elated by our spiritual triumphs and rejoicing in heart, it warns us not to be too inflated, nor to be complacent about our prosperity, for it shows us that it cannot last without God's protection, begging him to come to our aid not just always but with haste. This verse, I tell you, will be found invaluable for any one of us in whatever state we be.

One who is always asking for help in all matters demonstrates that he needs God's help not only in hard and grievous things, but just as much in easy joyful ones, in the former case to rescue him,

X. On Prayer

in the latter to preserve him – in neither case does he imagine human weakness can survive without God's grace. Am I racked with pangs of hunger, longing for foods which are unknown in the desert? Does the smell of lordly banquets waft past me in the wilderness? Do I feel myself dragged unwillingly to yearn for them? I have only to say, 'O God, come to my assistance, O Lord, make haste to help me.' Am I urged to anticipate the fixed time for eating, do I find great and painful difficulty in keeping to my usual ration of reasonable nourishment? With a sigh I have but to utter, 'O God, come to my assistance, O Lord, make haste to help me.' Does weakness of digestion prevent me from fasting through the demands of the flesh? Does a dry and constricted stomach deter me? If I would be granted what I am aiming at, to quell the fires of physical lust without the need for stricter fasting, my prayer is still, 'O God, come to my assistance, O Lord, make haste to help me.' If I go to the refectory at the proper time, and recoil at the sight of the bread, unable to eat anything of what is necessary for nature, I must cry out earnestly, 'O God, come to my assistance, O Lord, make haste to help me.'

If I desire to attend to my reading to calm my thoughts, and a headache occurs to prevent me, or if after three hours I find that sleep brings my face down onto the sacred page; if I am forced to defer the time for repose, or to prolong it, or to anticipate it, if heavy slumber compels me to cut short the ritual of the office and its psalms, in like case I must declare, 'O God, come to my assistance, O Lord, make haste to help me.' If sleep is denied to my eyes, and I find myself exhausted for many nights by the demon of insomnia, deprived of all repose in nightly rest, I will pray with a yawn, 'O God, come to my assistance, O Lord, make haste to help me.' If I have gone to my rest and the stirrings of the flesh come suddenly upon me, trying to persuade me in sleep to consent to its temptations, lest enemy fire consume the sweet flowers of chastity I will exclaim, 'O God, come to my assistance, O Lord, make haste to help me.' Do I feel the urging of lust extinct, and the heat of desire cooling in my body? I will say devoutly, to preserve that virtue, or rather that grace of God for as long as possible or for ever, 'O God, come to my assistance, O Lord, make haste to help me.'

Am I troubled by the stirrings of wrath, of avarice, of melancholy? Am I driven to lose my wonted friendly temper? Lest I be swept away by my rising wrath into the bitterness of spite, I will pray with the greatest earnestness, 'O God, come to my assistance, O Lord, make haste to help me.' Am I puffed up by listlessness, conceit or pride, my thoughts flattered by the sly consideration that others are tepid in their duties? To overcome that wicked suggestion of the enemy I have but to pray with true contrition of heart, 'O God, come to my assistance, O Lord, make haste to help me.' If I have put off the swelling of pride and found the grace of humility and simplicity with the spirit of true compunction, lest 'the foot of pride come to me, and the hand of the sinner move me' (Psalm 35/36: 12), lest I fall further as a result of elation at my victory, I shall proclaim with all my strength, 'O God, come to my assistance, O Lord, make haste to help me.' If in the innumerable varied distractions of my mind, the wavering fervour of my heart, I am powerless to gather back my wandering thoughts, or to make my prayer without interruptions and phantasms of vain matters, the memory of old words and deeds; if I find myself so constrained by this barren dryness that I cannot feel I am bringing forth any spiritual fruit at all; if I would be fit to be freed from this mental squalor, from which neither tears nor sighs avail to deliver me, all I need do is to pray, 'O God, come to my assistance, O Lord, make haste to help me.'

Do I discover that I have found steadiness of soul, constancy in thought, joy in the heart, am I filled by the Holy Spirit with joy unbounded and elation of mind? Am I overwhelmed with the sense of the Spirit, and gifted suddenly by the Lord with a revelation of the holiest doctrines, understanding of matters formerly hidden from me? If I would remain any longer in that state I must cry out sincerely and frequently, 'O God, come to my assistance, O Lord, make haste to help me.' Am I compassed about by the terrors of the night, aroused by phantasms of unclean spirits? My one hope of safety and life stolen away from me by fearful dread? I fly

X. On Prayer

to the refuge of this saving verse, crying out wholeheartedly, 'O God, come to my assistance, O Lord, make haste to help me.' Am I again stayed by the Lord's consolation, revived by his presence and aware that I am set about by countless thousands of angels, till I am confident enough to seek out and challenge the ranks of those whom I feared more than death, whose very touch and neighbourhood filled me with horror of mind and body? If I would preserve that bold confidence through the grace of God, I must wholeheartedly intone, 'O God, come to my assistance, O Lord, make haste to help me.'

This verse of prayer should be your ceaseless burden in adversity to sustain you, as in prosperity to preserve you from pride. The remembrance of this verse should be constantly pondered in your heart. You should not cease to repeat it whether you are at work, in service, on a journey. Sleeping, eating, in all nature compels you to do, repeat this prayer. This longing in the heart, this formula to work your salvation, will not only keep you safe from all assault of the enemy, but even deliver you from all taint of earthly life, leading you to the sight of what is invisible and heavenly, and conduct you to that degree of prayer which is beyond words and found by few. Let sleep find you meditating on this verse, until you are so accustomed to its unconscious repetition that you murmur it even while asleep. Let it occur to you when you first wake, let it precede all other thoughts as you arise, let it bring you to your knees as you get out of bed, let it accompany you in all your work and activity, let it follow you throughout the day. As Moses commanded us (Deut. 6:7), ponder on this when you are 'sitting in thy house and walking on thy journey', when you sleep and while you are awake, write this on your threshold and on the doors of your lips, place this on the walls of your house and in the storerooms of your heart, let this rousing verse be yours as you kneel to pray, when you rise up again, when you proceed to all the business of your life, let this prayer be strong and constant.

XI. "Let your mind hold this formula always, till it becomes set in ceaseless repetition and fervent meditation, till it rejects and banishes all the abundant wealth of alternative thoughts, reduced to the poverty of this one verse, and so come easily to the fulfilment of that blessing in the Gospel which precedes all other blessings, 'Blessed are the poor in spirit; for theirs is the kingdom of heaven' (Matt. 5: 3). Once you have become really poor in this mode of poverty, you will fulfil what the prophet said, 'The poor and needy shall praise thy name' (Psalm 73/74: 21). Truly, what greater poverty could there be, what holier, than that of one who knows himself to have no protection, no strength, but must ask another's generous help every day; one who knows that his life and possessions are supported at each moment by God's aid and can truly call himself a beggar of the Lord, crying out to him daily, 'I am a beggar and poor, may God assist me' (Psalm 39/40: 18, LXX). Thus he ascends to the knowledge of God which takes many forms, with God's own light to guide him, and begins to penetrate the deeper mysteries of holiness, as the Prophet said, 'The high hills are a refuge for the harts, the rock for the irchins' (Psalm 103/104: 18). This can be appropriately applied to what we have been talking about, for anyone who remains simple and innocent, without harming or annoying anyone but satisfied in his lowliness as long as he is protected from predators, is metaphorically an irchin or hedgehog, and well shielded by the concealing rocks mentioned in the Gospel, namely the remembrance of the Lord's passion. Defended by the ceaseless repetition of the verse we have quoted, it can repel the attacks of the encircling foe. Of these spiritual hedgehogs, the book of Proverbs also speaks, 'and the hedgehog, a weak people which maketh its bed in the rock' (Prov. 30: 26, LXX). What could be weaker than a Christian, what more frail than a monk, who is not permitted any revenge to retaliate against injuries, not even a murmur, not the slightest silent grimace within?

One who progresses from this state, possessing the simplicity of innocence and strengthened by the virtue of discernment as well, becomes able to exterminate poisonous serpents, trampling Satan under his feet, and in his mental alertness is aptly compared to a hart. He browses on what the prophets and apostles call

X. On Prayer

mountains, that is to say the lofty and exalted sacraments; he feeds on this sublime food and receives into himself all the meaning of the psalms. He begins to chant them as it they were his own compositions, not those of the prophets, uttering them as his own personal prayer in the depths of his heartfelt compunction, and feels that they are directed specifically at himself, their meaning not exhausted by what happens to the prophet or in him, but daily fulfilled and completed in himself.

Then indeed the holy Scriptures are more clearly opened to us, their veins and their marrow laid bare, when we become able not just to discern their meaning but even to anticipate it, and the meaning of the words is disclosed merely by reading them, without commentary. When we have acquired the same devotion as the one who sings or composes the psalm, we run ahead of its meaning as if we were its authors, rather than following it. I mean, that we grasp the force of what is said before its expression, and somehow see everything that we do or that happens to us in daily events, in the light of our preceding meditation on the psalms. As we chant the psalms our thoughts run over everything that our own fault has brought upon us, everything our diligence has gained, all that God's providence has conferred, all that the enemy's interference has inflicted, whatever our slippery failing memory has deprived us of, whatever human frailty has caused, in whatever our thoughtless ignorance has deceived us. All these accidents we will find expressed in the Psalms, so that we find in them a fuller and better understanding of all matters, as if we saw them in the clearest glass. Thus as we learn from these matters, we experience them as actual, not just theoretical, not merely things remembered, but things intrinsic to our nature. We conceive them, in our inner emotions; we realise their meaning derives from our own experience, not just something we have read. Thus the soul rises steadily to reach that incorruptible prayer we were speaking of in the previous Conference, in so far as Our Lord sees fit to grant it to us. It is not concerned with an imaginary picture, not even a sound, no words are distinguished, but the fiery longing of the heart, in an abstraction of mind beyond description, is poured out with an eager and dauntless spirit. The soul transcends all sensual and visible things, and pours itself out towards God in groans and sighs too deep for words."

XII. GERMANUS: "You have explained to us openly and clearly the traditional spiritual discipline we were asking after, as well as its full perfection. What could there be more perfect, more sublime, than to embrace the remembrance of God in such an apt form of meditation, to escape all the restrictions of visible things with the aid of a single verse, to sum up the whole of prayer in a few words? But one thing remains which we would like you to explain, namely how we may be able constantly to maintain that same verse which you have given us as a formula, so that, just as the grace of God has set us free from the thoughts of this world, we may abide unmoved in those of heaven."

XIII. "You see, when we are pondering on any text out of the psalms, we find our thoughts unconsciously distracted, drawn unwillingly and unwittingly towards some other part of Scripture. Just when we begin to meditate on the first text, and have not yet exhausted its meaning, the memory of the other text springs up and drives out the previous matter of meditation. From this we are drawn on to yet another, as another consideration intrudes, so that the mind roams from psalm to psalm, from the text of the Gospel to the epistles of St Paul, next to some part of the prophets, and thence to one of the sacred histories, tossed about inconstantly throughout the whole Bible. We have no choice over what to reject, what to retain, nor how to complete any full and proper consideration. We become tasters and samplers of spiritual learning, not its true begetters or owners. The mind is fickle always, and wandering, distracted in different ways like a drunkard, even during divine service, and never completes any task satisfactorily. For example: during prayer we remember a psalm or some reading; while we sing, we are thinking about something different from what the text of that psalm says. When reading, we want to be active and remember past occupations – in this way we receive nothing in a disciplined order, we pass nothing over, we seem to be constrained as if by random influences, without the ability to retain anything pleasing, nor to abide in it. Our need above all, therefore, is to know how to perform these spiritual exercises properly, at least how to hold firmly onto that verse which you have taught us as a formula, so that the beginning and the end of our perception rests not in its own fickleness but in our will."

XIV. ISAAC: "I had thought that in the course of our discussion on this state of prayer I had answered that point adequately, but since you have asked, I will briefly repeat what I said about strengthening the heart. There are three things which make a wandering mind stable: vigils, meditation and prayer. If you are diligent and consistent in these, they will confer stability on the mind. There is no other way of acquiring that, unless we have first banished all anxiety and cares about this present life through untiring persistence in hard work – not for the sake of material profit but for the spiritual benefit of the monastery. Thus we may fulfil the Apostle's command, 'Pray without ceasing' (I Thess. 5:17). He who only prays during the time that he is on his knees, hardly prays at all. He who, while on his knees, is distracted by the wanderings of his thoughts, is never praying. For that reason, we should conduct ourselves before the time of prayer in the manner we would like to be found during prayer. During the period of prayer the mind is bound to be influenced by its previous activity, and the thoughts on which it dwelt before prayer are those which during prayer will either elevate us to heaven or plunge us down to earth."

We listened in amazement as Abba Isaac concluded his second conference on the nature of prayer. We were lost in admiration of his teaching on the repeated use of that verse in prayer which we have recounted, which he gave us to memorise as if we were beginners hearing it for the first time. We were eager to put it into practice, although we found on trial that what we had imagined to be so satisfactory and easy was in fact more difficult in reality than our previous practice, which had been to flit over the whole body of Scripture in far-ranging meditation, without anything to tie us down specifically. It is certainly true that no one is excluded from perfection of heart by lack of education, and simplicity is no obstacle to acquiring purity of mind and heart. That is abundantly available to everyone, if only they preserve a healthy and vigorous intention towards God, through constant meditation on this one verse of Scripture.

✣ THE SECOND PART ✣

Containing the next seven conversations with the Fathers who lived in the Thebaïd of Egypt

Preface

To Bishop Honoratus and to Eucherius

MANY HOLY MEN who were desirous of learning from your example have scarcely been able to emulate your perfect virtue, with which you shine like brilliant lights to illuminate this world, O holy brothers Honoratus and Eucherius, but you in turn have been fired with admiration of those sublime men from whom we received our first training in the eremitical life. To such an extent did they you inspire you that one of you, being superior of a vast monastery, chose to structure his congregation on the teaching of those Fathers, although they had already learnt so much from observing your own holiness; the other decided to visit Egypt to study the Fathers in the flesh from his own observation. Leaving this province of Gaul gripped in the rigours of winter, he decided to migrate like a chaste dove to those lands which are close to the sun of justice and famous for the mature fruits of virtue. The exercise of charity demands of me to take account of the desire of the first, and the efforts made by the second, so that I will not shun the peril of writing, and thereby can add to the authority among his disciples of the first, and spare the other the necessity of such a dangerous journey.

Your faith was so fervent that you were not satisfied with the twelve books on monastic training which I wrote to the best of my ability and dedicated to bishop Castor of happy memory, nor by the ten Collations of the Fathers who lived in the desert of Scete, which I published at the urging of the holy bishops Helladius and Leontius. Now, so that you may follow the order of our journey, I decided to dedicate to you seven Collations by the first three Fathers that we met dwelling in the other desert, written in the same manner. In this way perhaps matters dealing with perfection which were rather obscure or neglected in my previous works may be developed. If that is not enough to satisfy your holy desire of learning, there are seven other Collations which are to be sent to the holy brethren who live in the islands of the Stoechades [Hyères], and I think that will be enough to fulfil your ardent desires.

✢ THE ELEVENTH COLLATION ✢
BEING THE FIRST OF
ABBA CHAEREMON

On Perfection

I. A description of the town of Thennesus.
II. Of Bishop Archebius.
III. A description of the desert where Chaeremon, Nestor and Joseph lived.
IV. On Abba Chaeremon, and the excuses he made about the question we asked.
V. Our reply to his protestations.
VI. Abba Chaeremon's thesis, that vices are overcome in three ways.
VII. The steps by which one may rise to the heights of charity, and how to remain secure there.
VIII. How excellent are those who abandon vice for charity's sake.
IX. How charity does not only turn slaves into sons, but even confers the image and likeness of God.
X. That perfect charity prays for our enemies, and how to detect a soul that is not yet purified.
XI. A question, why he called the emotions of fear and hope imperfections.
XII. The reply, on the different grades of perfection.
XIII. Of the fear that is generated by great charity.
XIV. A question, on the attainment of chastity.
XV. The explanation requested is deferred.

I. We were living in a monastery in Syria, and had received our first instruction in the faith, with a certain amount more, but began to long for a greater grace of perfection; we therefore decided to make for Egypt. There we explored the most remote desert of the Thebaïd, visiting several of the saints whose reputation had spread through the world, with the aim of learning from them at least, if not of imitating them. After a long voyage, we reached a city in Egypt called Thennesus. The inhabitants live completely surrounded by the sea and salt lagoons, so that, there being no soil to cultivate, they live by commerce alone. Their wealth and their possessions all come by trade, indeed even the materials for constructing their houses has to be brought by ship from afar, for the ground does not supply them.

II. When we turned up there, God, in his providence for our desires, granted that Bishop Archebius, that distinguished holy man, should be present. He had been called from a community of hermits to become bishop of Panephysis, but preserved his lifelong intention of solitude to the extent that he relaxed nothing of his previous lowly way of life, and took no pride in the honour bestowed upon him. He did not consider himself called worthy to be called to that office, but lamented that he had been expelled from the monastic way of life as unfit for it, for despite thirty seven years spent in that life, he had never been able to arrive at the purity he professed. Being in the aforementioned Thennesus for the purpose of electing a bishop, he greeted us warmly and kindly, once he knew our purpose of making enquiries of the holy fathers in the further parts of Egypt.

"Come," he said, "and begin by visiting some old men who live not far from our monastery; their age is shown by their bent bodies, but their sanctity shines in their faces. Simply looking at them can teach the observer much, and you can learn from their example of holy life, more than from any words, about that way of life which I grieve to have lost, and having lost am unable to pass on. I think that by this means I can make up a little for my inadequacy, if I am able to provide an opportunity for you to

XI. On Perfection

acquire more easily that pearl of great price, as the Gospel puts it (Matt. 13:45), which I myself do not possess."

III. He took up staff and scrip, as all travelling monks do there, and came with us as our guide on our journey to his city of Panephysis. The countryside there, as well as the wide fertile tracts adjacent (which, we were told, once provided the food for a king's table), had been flooded by the sea, when it suddenly overflowed its shores after a earthquake. Virtually all the farms had been destroyed, and that rich land covered with a salty deposit, so that it literally happened in that region what we sing metaphorically in the psalm, "He hath turned rivers into a wilderness: and the sources of waters into dry ground: a fruitful land into barrenness: for the wickedness of them that dwell therein" (Psalm 106/107: 33–4). In that area many villages had been situated on raised mounds, but when the inhabitants fled, the flood left them like islands which were ideal for those holy men who were looking for solitude. Among these were three very aged hermits named Chaeremon, Nestor and Joseph.

IV. The holy Archebius chose to begin by introducing us to Chaeremon, since he lived nearest to the monastery, and he was of a greater age then the other two. He had passed his hundredth year with his mind alone still alert, for his back was so bent with age and long prayers that he was virtually reduced to infancy again, and had to walk on his hands and feet. We gazed with admiration both at his countenance, and at his gait, for indeed though his whole body was frail and all but dead, he had never lost the composure of his previous austerity. We asked him humbly for an instructive discourse, explaining that we had come to him because of our great desire for spiritual learning. He sighed deeply and replied, "How can I give you any instruction, when I am senile and frail, so that I have relaxed my former discipline, and am deprived of any confidence in speaking? How can I presume to teach you what I do not do myself, how can I instruct another to do what I realise I perform less and less fervently? That is why

I have not permitted any younger man to live with me up to my present age, lest my example cause him to lapse from his austerity. A teacher has no effective authority unless he can reinforce his teaching with his own performance in the sight of his audience."

V. We were very embarrassed by this, but answered him thus: "We must grant that we ought to find sufficient instruction in the very difficulty of this site and your solitary life here, which a strong young man could hardly tolerate. Even if you remain silent, they are enough to teach us and bring us to repentance. Nevertheless we do ask you to break your silence for a moment, and instil into us something to help us at least admire the virtue we see in you even if we cannot imitate it. You will have observed our own lukewarmness, which does not deserve an answer to our question, but perhaps the effort we have expended in such a long journey will do so, for we have come here from our novitiate in Bethlehem out of a desire to hear you teach, and a longing for our own spiritual progress."

VI. Then spoke the holy Chaeremon: "There are three things which restrain a man from giving in to vice, namely the fear of hell or of justice in this world, hope and desire for the Kingdom of Heaven, and a yearning for good in itself with a love of virtue. Fear, we are told, shuns the taint of evil, 'The fear of the Lord hateth evil' (Prov. 8:13). Hope repels the attacks of all vices, 'and none of those that trust in him shall offend' (Psalm 33/34:23). Love also is fearless of the ruin of sin, for 'Charity never falleth away' (I Cor. 13:8), and 'Charity covereth a multitude of sins' (I Peter 4:8). For this reason the holy Apostle sums up the whole of our salvation under these three virtues, 'Now there remain faith, hope and charity, these three' (I Cor. 13:13).

Faith it is which makes us shun the contagion of vice through fear of future judgment and punishment; hope which summons our thoughts away from the present and spurns all the pleasures of the flesh in the expectation of heavenly reward; charity fires us with the love of Christ and fruitful virtues in a fervent heart, so that

XI. On Perfection

we utterly abhor whatever is opposed to that. Although all three appear to tend to a single end, and encourage us to abstain from things unlawful, yet they greatly differ in excellence from each other. The first two belong especially to those who are aspiring to perfection but have not yet conceived a longing for virtue; the third pertains especially to God, and those who have taken to themselves the image and likeness of God. God alone it is who performs what is good out of sheer goodness, with no fear nor promise of reward to spur him; for as Solomon says, 'The Lord hath made things for himself' (Prov. 16: 4). It is his own pure goodness that causes him to bestow abundant benefits on worthy and unworthy alike, for no insult can discourage him, no crimes of men provoke him, but he remains for ever perfect in goodness and unchangeable in nature.

VII. "One who aspires to perfection must begin at the first step, that of fear, which we properly call servile fear, for it is said, 'When you shall have done all these things that are commanded you, say: We are unprofitable servants' (Luke 17: 10). Next he must progress, rising to the higher step of hope, compared now not to a slave but to a paid servant, for he expects payment in recompense. He is confident in the forgiveness of sins and unafraid of punishment, being conscious of his good works, and is seen to expect the reward God has offered; yet he is unable to achieve that filial affection which trusts in the father's loving indulgence and has no doubt that all the father has is his. The prodigal son, who had lost the title of son along with his father's property, did not dare to aspire to it again, for he said, 'I am not worthy to be called thy son; make me as one of thy hired servants' (Luke 15: 19). After those husks the swine had, with which he was unable to satisfy himself, that is to say the vile nourishment of vice, he came to his senses and was struck with saving compunction, beginning to detest the filth of the swine, and afraid of suffering real hunger. Then he was in the condition of a slave, but conceived the desire for the status of a paid servant, thinking of the reward, and saying, 'How many hired servants in my father's house abound with bread, and

I here perish with hunger! I will arise and will go to my father and say to him Father, I have sinned against heaven and before thee, I am not worthy to be called thy son; make me as one of thy hired servants' (Luke 15: 17–19).

The father leapt up to meet him at the sound of his humble contrition, and received him with greater affection than the son offered, for he was not content merely to grant his request for a lower status but passed straightaway over the first two degrees; he restored him to his former rank as son. We must be swift to ascend to that third grade, that of sons who believe that all their father has is theirs, through the unbreakable grace of charity; thus we may be fit to receive the image and likeness of our heavenly Father and in imitation of his true Son may declare, 'All things whatsoever the Father hath are mine' (John 16: 15). The holy Apostle also confesses this of us, saying, 'For all things are yours, whether it be Paul or Apollo or Cephas, or the world, or life, or death, or things present, or things to come. For all are yours' (I Cor. 3: 22). Our Saviour's teaching also calls us to that likeness, 'Be ye therefore perfect, as also your heavenly Father is perfect' (Matt. 5: 48). In the previous stages of love the emotion of goodness is sometimes interrupted, when some lukewarmness, or some joy, or some pleasure causes strength of mind to waver, and obscures either the present fear of hell or the desire of future reward. But also in those stages we may be able to make progress, for once we have begun to avoid vice out of fear of punishment or hope of reward, we may pass on to the state of true charity, for 'Fear is not in charity; but perfect charity casteth out fear, because fear hath pain. And he that feareth is not perfected in charity. Let us therefore love God; because God first hath loved us' (I John 4: 18–19). There is no other way for us to rise to true and perfect charity, than by our loving him for the sake of nothing other than love of him alone, just as he first loved us for no other reason than for the sake of our salvation. We must take pains to arise with a perfect mind from fear to hope, from hope to the charity of God, or the love of virtue itself. Thus, arrived at the love of the good in itself, we may steadfastly retain that which is good, in so far as human nature can.

VIII. "There is a great difference between one who quenches the fires of vice in himself out of fear of hell or hope for future reward, and one who recoils from evil and impurity out of love for the charity of God, possessing holy purity merely through love and longing for chastity. He looks no longer at the promise of future reward, but rejoices in the consciousness of goodness at hand; whatever he does is without thought of penalty, and delights only in virtue. In this degree of charity, he does not take the opportunity to sin because no human witness is present, nor does he fall into secret sins of thought, for he guards the longing for virtue itself deep within himself, and anything opposed to virtue he shuns with the greatest horror, far from letting it into his heart. It is one thing for someone to hate the contagion of vice and sin out of delight in present good, another thing to refrain from unlawful lusts with a view to future reward; one thing to dread immediate suffering, and yet another to be afraid of future punishment. Finally, it is a much greater thing to be unwilling to leave what is good for the sake of goodness itself, than to refuse consent to evil out of fear of evil. In the first case the good is freely chosen, in the latter it is constrained, forced as if unwilling, whether out of fear of pain or desire for reward. One who only refrains from the enticement of sin out of fear, would revert again to what he wanted once the object of fear were removed. Hence he will never obtain real stability in goodness, nor ever be at peace from temptation, since he will not possess any firm and lasting repose in chastity. For as long as battle rages, there is an inevitable risk of being wounded. One who is in the midst of battle, however experienced a warrior, fighting fiercely and giving frequent mortal wounds to his foes, will still be occasionally touched by the enemy's weapons. But one who has defeated the assaults of vice, and already enjoys the security of peace, progressing to the love of virtue in itself, will preserve that true state of goodness to which he already belongs totally, for he believes that nothing could be worse than any threat to his purity. Nothing, he considers, is more precious or valuable than present chastity, and his greatest grief would be any pernicious loss of virtue, any deadly contagion of vice. Such a man would not be made more respectable by human admiration, nor reduced by being alone, for he carries about with him always his conscience, the judge of his thoughts as well as of his deeds. He is always alert to the demands of conscience, knowing that he cannot elude it, deceive it or escape from it.

IX. "If anyone has been found worthy to possess that state, relying on the help of God and not his own efforts, he has begun to advance from the condition of a slave (in which fear resides) and the hope of mercenary gain (in which he seeks not so much the goodness of the giver as the reward he gives) to the state of adopted son. Here there is no fear, no desire, but true charity which never fails and lasts for ever. The Lord, in rebuking someone, shows us that fear and that charity, and how they belong to different states, 'The son honoureth the father; and the servant his master. If then I be a father, where is my honour? And if I be a master, where is my fear?' (Mal. 1:6). A slave is bound to fear, for he who 'knew the will of his lord and prepared not himself, and did not according to his will, shall be beaten with many stripes' (Luke 12:47). It is through charity that one arrives at the image and likeness of God, and delights in goodness for the sake of the good itself. He will possess a similar feeling of mild patience, and will not be angry at any sinner's failure, but will beg for their forgiveness in his sympathetic understanding of their weakness. He will remember his own long struggle against similar temptations, until he was delivered through the Lord's mercy, set free from the attacks of the flesh by God's protection, not his own efforts. Thus he has come to realise that it is mercy, not wrath, that should hang over the wayward, and will sing this verse to God in a heart full of peace: 'Thou hast broken my bonds: I will sacrifice to thee the sacrifice of praise' (Psalm 115/116:16–17), and 'Unless the Lord had been my helper: my soul had almost dwelt in hell' (Psalm 93/94:17). Once he is established in this humble frame of mind, he will be able to fulfil that command of perfection we find in the Gospel, 'Love your enemies; do good to them that hate you; and pray for them that persecute and

XI. On Perfection

calumniate you' (Matt. 5: 44). And so we will be able to achieve that reward which is promised, for we will not only be wearing the image and likeness of God, but shall actually be called sons of God. 'That you may be the children of your Father who is in heaven, who maketh his sun to rise upon the good and bad, and raineth upon the just and the unjust' (Matt. 5: 45).

Saint John avers that he has achieved that state, when he says, 'We may have confidence in the day of judgment; because as he is, we also are in this world' (I John 4: 17). How can weak and fickle human nature be like him as he is, except by extending charity with a loving heart towards good and evil, unjust and just alike, thus imitating God? If we do good for the sake of goodness, we shall arrive at the perfection of the adopted sons of God, of which the same holy apostle says, 'Whosoever is born of God committeth not sin; for his seed abideth in him. And he cannot sin, because he is born of God' (I John 3: 9). And further on, 'We know that whosoever is born of God sinneth not; but the generation of God preserveth him and the wicked one toucheth him not' (I John 5:18). We should not understand this as referring to every sort of sin, but only mortal sins. If anyone is unwilling to give up such sins and be rid of them, we are told by the same Apostle that we should not even pray for such a one: 'He that knoweth his brother to sin a sin which is not to death, let him ask, and life shall be given to him who sinneth not to death. There is a sin unto death; for that I say not that any man ask' (I John 5: 16). On the other hand, about those sins which he says are not mortal, even those who serve Christ faithfully cannot avoid committing them, no matter how carefully they guard themselves. He says of these, 'If we say that we have no sin, we deceive ourselves and the truth is not in us.' And again, 'If we say that we have not sinned, we make him a liar; and his word is not in us' (I John 1: 8, 10). It is impossible for anyone, even of the saints, not to err in these little matters, incurred in words or thoughts, through ignorance, forgetfulness, necessity, choice or inadvertence. Such things are not without blame and cannot be overlooked, although they are quite different from that sort of sin which is called mortal.

X. "Now when someone has achieved that state of goodness and the imitation of God which we have described, he will put on the long-suffering patience of Our Lord himself, and will pray for his persecutors as he did, saying, 'Father, forgive them, for they know not what they do' (Luke 23:34). A sure and certain proof that a soul is not yet cleansed from the dregs of sin is when it does not sympathise with other peoples' sins in loving compassion, but affects the inflexible rigour of a judge. How could anyone achieve perfection of heart if he does not have what St Paul tells us can perform the law in its fullness? 'Bear ye one another's burdens,' he says, 'and so you shall fulfil the law of Christ' (Gal. 6:2). Otherwise we would not possess the virtue of charity, which 'dealeth not perversely, is not puffed up, thinketh no evil, beareth all things, endureth all things' (I Cor. 13:4–7). 'The just is merciful even towards his beasts, but the bowels of the wicked are cruel' (Prov. 12:10, LXX). You can be sure that a monk is a slave to precisely those vices which he condemns in others with severe and inhuman rigour. 'A rigorous king runneth into mischief', and 'He that stoppeth his ears against the cry of the poor shall also cry himself and shall not be heard'" (Prov. 13:17; 21:13, LXX).

XI. GERMANUS: "You have spoken powerfully and splendidly about the perfect love of God, but we are surprised that while you extol charity with such praise, you have said that the fear of God and the hope of eternal reward are imperfections. The Psalmist seems to have had a very different opinion about them, for he says, 'Fear the Lord, all ye his saints: for there is no want to those who fear him' (Psalm 33/34:10). And elsewhere, considering the justice of God, he admits that he was concerned with the contemplation of our reward, 'I have inclined my heart to do thy justifications for ever, for the reward' (Psalm 118/119:112). The Apostle also says, 'By faith Moses, when he was grown up, denied himself to be the son of Pharaoh's daughter; rather choosing to be afflicted with the people of God than to have the pleasure of sin for a time; esteeming the approach of Christ greater riches than the treasure of the Egyptians. For he looked unto the reward' (Heb. 11:24–6).

XI. On Perfection

So how can we consider these motives to be imperfect when the holy David boasts that he has done the works of the Lord's righteousness for the sake of repayment, and we are told it was because the Lawgiver looked to a future reward that he spurned the royal dignity which was his by adoption, and preferred dire oppression to all the treasures of Egypt?"

XII. CHAEREMON: "Holy Scripture challenges our free will to different levels of perfection according to the status and capacity of each. It is not possible to offer a uniform crown of perfection to all, for not all have the same strength, the same willpower or fervour. Thus God's word established varying grades of perfection in these virtues in varying measures. This appears also from the variety of the beatitudes in the Gospel. The blessing for some is the kingdom of heaven, for others possession of the earth, others are blessed for they shall be comforted, others for they shall be filled. We can believe that there is an enormous difference between dwelling in the kingdom of heaven and the possession of the earth, such as it is, between the reception of consolation, and the full enjoyment of justice. A great difference too between those who have received mercy and those who will be found fit to enjoy the glorious vision of God. 'One is the glory of the sun, another the glory of the moon, and another the glory of the stars. For star differeth from star in glory. So also is the resurrection of the dead' (I Cor. 15: 41–2). Thus in one place holy Scripture praises and blesses those who fear God, saying 'Blessed are all they that fear the Lord' (Psalm 127/128: 1), and promises them full bliss for that, while in another place it can say, 'Fear is not in charity; but perfect charity casteth out fear, because fear hath pain. And he that feareth is not perfected in charity' (I John 4: 18).

Again, since it is a glorious thing to serve the Lord, it says, 'Serve ye the Lord with fear' (Psalm 2: 11), and 'It is a great thing that thou shouldst be called my servant' (Isaiah 49: 6, LXX), as well as, 'Blessed is that servant whom when his lord shall come he shall find so doing' (Matt. 24: 46). On the other hand he says to the apostles, 'I will not now call you servants; for the servant knoweth not what his lord doth. But I have called you friends; because all things, whatsoever I have heard of my Father, I have made known to you', and earlier, 'You are my friends, if you do all things that I command you' (John 15:13–15). Hence you can see that degrees of perfection do vary, and that the Lord calls us on from good to better, for one who finds a blessing through being established in the perfect fear of God, may proceed as it is written 'from virtue to virtue' (Psalm 83/84:8), from one perfection to another, in other words rising with an eager mind from fear to hope; and then he is called to the more blessed state yet, which is charity. A servant who is 'faithful and wise' (Matt. 24:45) will progress to association as a friend, and then to adoption as a son.

That is the way you must understand my teaching. It is not that I consider it of no importance to reflect on eternal punishment, or the blissful reward which is promised to the saints, but that however useful these be to introduce men to the first stages of blessedness, yet charity which contains the greater trust and everlasting joy, will bring them on from servile fear and mercenary hope to the love of God and adoption as sons, thus making the perfect yet more perfect. 'In my Father's house', says our Saviour, 'there are many mansions' (John 14:2). Though all the stars we can see are in the sky, there is an enormous difference between the brightness of the sun, the moon, the morning star and the other stars. That is why the holy Apostle describes charity as being the far superior way, greatly excelling not only fear and hope, but all the gifts of the Holy Spirit, however great and marvellous they be. When he has gone through the whole list of spiritual gifts, and wishes to explain the parts of virtue, he begins thus: 'And I show unto you yet a more excellent way. If I speak with the tongues of men, and of angels . . ., and if I should have prophecy and should know all mysteries and all knowledge, and if I should have all faith, so that I could remove mountains . . ., and if I should distribute all my goods to feed the poor, and if I should deliver my body to be burned, and have not charity, it profiteth me nothing' (I Cor. 12:31–13:3). There you see how nothing can be found that

XI. On Perfection

is more precious, more perfect, more enduring I may say, than charity. 'Prophecies shall be made void or tongues shall cease or knowledge shall be destroyed, but charity never falleth away' (I Cor. 13: 8). Without charity not only those splendid different gifts of the spirit, but even martyrdom itself loses its glory.

XIII. "Anyone who is established in this perfect charity, is bound to proceed to that more sublime type of fear, derived from charity, in a more excellent degree – this fear is generated not by the dread of punishment, nor the desire for reward, but out of the abundance of love. With this sort of fear a son reveres his kind father, a brother his brother, a friend his friend, a spouse his bride, in loving affection. The fear is not of blows or abuse, but of the smallest diminution of love. It is displayed in attentive care, not only in every action but in words as well, lest the fervour of that affection dwindle in the slightest. One of the prophets beautifully describes the splendour of this sort of fear, 'riches of salvation, wisdom and knowledge: the fear of the Lord is his treasure' (Isaiah 33: 6). He could not have described more clearly the worth and dignity of that fear, than by saying that only the fear of the Lord is sufficient to safeguard those riches of salvation, the true wisdom and knowledge of God. It is not sinners whom the prophet calls to that fear, but the saints, as the Psalmist says, 'Fear the Lord, all ye his saints: for there is no want to them that fear him' (Psalm 33/34: 10). He who reveres the Lord with this sort of fear, is sure not to lack any perfection. It is obviously of the fear of punishment that St John writes, 'And he that feareth is not perfected in charity, because fear hath pain' (I John 4: 18). There is an enormous difference between the fear to which nothing is lacking, which is the treasurehouse of wisdom and knowledge, and that imperfect fear which is called only the beginning of wisdom. The latter contains within itself pain, and is expelled from the hearts of the perfect as the fullness of charity supervenes. 'Fear is not in charity; but perfect charity casteth out fear' (I John 4: 18). Truly, if the very beginning of wisdom consists in fear, what will its perfection be unless in the perfect charity of Christ, which contains that fear of perfect love in itself, and is called no longer the beginning but the very treasurehouse of wisdom and knowledge?

There are therefore two types of fear: one is for beginners, that is those who are still under the yoke and terrified as slaves, of whom it is said, 'A servant honoureth his master' (Mal. 1:6), and in the Gospel, 'I will not now call you servants; for the servant knoweth not what his lord doth' (John 15:15). Also, 'the servant abideth not in the house for ever; but the son abideth for ever' (John 8:35). It enables us to progress from the dread of punishment to the fullest freedom of charity and the confidence of God's friends and sons. The holy Apostle Paul himself had progressed from that state of servile fear through the power of the love of the Lord; looking back on what was inferior, he declares that he had received the superior good from God, 'For God hath not given us the spirit of fear; but of power and of love and of sobriety' (II Tim. 1:7). Those who blossom into the perfect love of our heavenly Father, and have been adopted by God to become sons instead of slaves, are encouraged by his words, 'For you have not received the spirit of bondage again in fear; but you have received the spirit of adoption of sons, whereby we cry: Abba, Father!' (Rom. 8:15). When the prophet describes the sevenfold grace of the Holy Spirit, it is that type of fear he means, for he speaks surely of the Spirit which descended on the Man who is God, in the mystery of the Incarnation: 'And the spirit of the Lord shall rest upon him: the spirit of wisdom and understanding, the spirit of counsel and of fortitude, the spirit of knowledge and of goodness,' and he adds at the end, as if the most important, 'and he shall be filled with the spirit of the fear of the Lord' (Isaiah 11:2–3). Here we should first notice carefully that it does not say, 'and the spirit of the fear of the Lord shall rest upon him,' in the same way he speaks of the others, but 'he will be filled with the spirit of the fear of the Lord.' This spirit is so vast and abundant that if it takes possession of anyone it does not occupy only part of the mind, but the whole. And rightly so. It clings to him with a charity that never fails, and does not only fill him, but takes possession of him, inseparably and fully; neither earthly joy not the blandishments of desire can

XI. On Perfection

diminish it. This never occurs with the other type of fear, the one which is driven out. It is therefore the fear of perfection, with which the God-Man was filled, we are told, for he came not only to redeem the human race but to give us a model of perfection and an example of virtue. The true Son of God could never have had that servile fear of punishment, for he 'did no sin, neither was guile found in his mouth'" (I Pet. 2:22).

XIV. GERMANUS: "You have explained to us about the perfection of charity – now it is the purpose of chastity about which we would like to know something more. We are in no doubt that the sublime summit of charity, as you have been talking about it up to now, conducts us to the image and likeness of God, and cannot possibly exist without perfect chastity, but we would like to know whether it is possible to attain that virtue permanently so that no temptation to lust will ever trouble our thoughts, and we may be able to continue alive in this body free from carnal passion, never scorched by the fires of desire."

XV. CHAEREMON: "It brings us great happiness and a special merit both to learn diligently and to teach the affection by which we cling to the Lord. As the Psalmist expresses it, meditation on this fills all the days and nights of our life (Psalm 1:2). Continually ruminating on this heavenly sustenance will satisfy our thoughts which ever hunger and thirst for righteousness. But we must take some consideration for brother ass, the body, as our blessed Saviour has decreed, lest we fail in the way, 'for the spirit indeed is willing, but the flesh weak' (Matt. 26:41). We must now look after the body by taking a little refreshment, so that afterwards the mind will be strengthened and more alert to investigate carefully the matters you have enquired about."

✧ THE TWELFTH COLLATION ✧
BEING THE SECOND OF
ABBA CHAEREMON

On Chastity

- I. What Abba Chaeremon said about chastity.
- II. On the body of sin and its limbs.
- III. On the mortification of fornication and uncleanness.
- IV. How human effort is insufficient to acquire pure chastity.
- V. On the utility of the temptations which come upon us from the fires of desire.
- VI. How patience quenches the fire of fornication.
- VII. On the different degrees of chastity.
- VIII. That no one can treat of the nature of chastity and its effects without experience.
- IX. A question, on whether it is possible to be free from bodily arousal even while asleep.
- X. The reply, that physical arousal during sleep does not offend chastity.
- XI. The great difference between chastity and continence.
- XII. On the special marvels which God performs for his saints.
- XIII. How only those who have experienced it can appreciate the joys of chastity.
- XIV. A question, about the type of discipline and the length of time it takes to acquire chastity.

XV. The reply, on the time needed to recognise the need for chastity.

XVI. On the purpose and healing nature of chastity.

I. When we had finished our repast, which we found more a burden than a pleasure, being so famished for the food of doctrine, the old man acknowledged that we were eager for him to pay us the debt he promised, of a discourse.

"I am pleased", he said, "not only by your thoughts being so set on learning, but also by the subject of the question you put. Truly you have followed a logical progression in your request, for the fullness of heavenly charity leads inevitably to the great prize of perfect and lasting chastity, and the joy is as great in receiving the one prize as the other. Charity and chastity are so closely linked that one cannot be possessed without the other. Your question, therefore, was whether that fire of lust, which our bodies feel as if burning within them, can ever be totally extinguished, and we will explain that in our second discourse. We must begin by examining carefully what the holy Apostle meant when he said, 'Mortify your members which are upon the earth' (Col. 3:5). We should investigate what these members are which should be mortified, before going on to the following questions. St Paul is not urging us to cut off hands or feet, or even genitals, but he wishes us to cut off the body of sin, which certainly exists in the limbs, as quickly as possible, in our zeal for perfect holiness. He says elsewhere that the 'body of sin may be destroyed', and why we should destroy it he explains next, 'to the end that we may serve sin no longer' (Rom. 6:6). He cries out for freedom from it, when he says, 'Unhappy man that I am, who shall deliver me from the body of this death?' (Rom. 7:24).

II. "This 'body of sin' is shown to be made up of many vices, so that every sin in deed, in word or thought adds a portion to it, and its limbs are aptly said to be on the earth. Those who are in thrall to them can never say, 'our conversation is in heaven' (Phil. 3:20). The Apostle specifies the members of this body: 'Mortify therefore

XII. On Chastity

your members which are upon the earth: fornication, uncleanness, lust, evil concupiscence and covetousness, which is the service of idols' (Col. 3: 5). He places fornication in the first place, meaning intercourse with women. In the second place uncleanness, which is without any contact with women, whether asleep or awake, taking us unawares through carelessness in thought. We should note that the old Law prohibits uncleanness, since it deprives the unclean of partaking in the sacred sacrifices, and goes so far as to command they be expelled from the camp of the muster, lest contact with them pollute the holy thing: 'If any one that is defiled shall eat the flesh of the sacrifice of peace offerings, which is offered to the Lord, he shall perish from before the Lord' (Lev. 7: 20), and, 'Whatsoever a person toucheth who is unclean, he shall make it unclean' (Num. 19: 22). In Deuteronomy also it says, 'If there be among you any man, that is defiled in a dream by night, he shall go forth out of the camp. And shall not return, before he be washed with water in the evening: and after sunset he shall return into the camp' (Deut. 23: 10–11). The third limb of the body of sin he mentions is lust, which lurks in the innermost part of the soul and can burst into flame without the body even being involved. The word lust is surely derived from liberty and liking.

After these greater sins he descends to the minor ones, calling the fourth limb 'evil concupiscence', which can be applied not only to the aforementioned vice of impurity but in general to any sort of wrong inclination. It is a disease of a corrupt will. The Lord speaks of this in the Gospel: 'whosoever shall look on a woman to lust after her hath already committed adultery with her in his heart' (Matt. 5: 28). It is a greater matter to be restrained in this desire of the mind when indecent sights offer it such an occasion. This shows clearly that if we would be perfectly pure it is not enough to be chaste in bodily self-control, but integrity of mind is needed as well.

And after all these others the last limb of that body of sin he mentions is covetousness, doubtless to show us that our thoughts must not only refrain from desiring other peoples' goods but should also be sublimely disdainful of one's own. We read in the

Acts of the Apostles that the whole multitude did this, for it says, 'The multitude of believers had but one heart and one soul. Neither did any one say that ought of the things which he possessed was his own; but all things were common unto them. For as many as were owners of lands or houses sold them and brought the price of the things they sold, and laid it down before the feet of the apostles. And distribution was made to every one, according as he had need' (Acts 4:32, 34–5). Lest we think it was only a few who achieved this perfection, St Paul tells us that covetousness is servitude to idols, and rightly so, for anyone who does not provide the poor with their needs and clings onto his money with a pagan possessiveness, is setting at naught the commands of Christ and incurs the guilt of idolatry, for he prefers the love of earthly possessions above the charity of God.

III. "Now if we can see so many people casting away their possessions for the sake of Christ, not only getting rid of the money they possessed, but even cutting the desire for it out of their hearts, it follows that we must believe that the fire of fornication can be extinguished in the same way. St Paul would not have linked an impossible thing with a possible one, but knowing that both were possible he commands us to mortify them both equally. The holy Apostle was so confident that we would be able to expel fornication and uncleanness out of our limbs that he says we should not just mortify them but abstain from even mentioning them. 'Fornication and all uncleanness or covetousness, let it not so much as be named among you; or obscenity or foolish talking or scurrility, which is to no purpose' (Eph. 5:3–4). More than that, they are dangerous, and equally capable of driving us from the kingdom of God, as he teaches us, 'For know you this and understand: that no fornicator or unclean or covetous person (which is a serving of idols) hath inheritance in the kingdom of Christ and of God' (Eph. 5:5). Elsewhere he says, 'Do not err; neither fornicators nor idolaters neither adulterers; nor the effeminate nor liers with mankind nor thieves nor covetous nor drunkards nor railers nor extortioners shall possess the kingdom of God' (I Cor. 6:9–10).

XII. On Chastity

We should be in no doubt that it is possible to expel the poison of fornication and uncleanness from our bodies, just as in the same way we are commanded to eliminate avarice, foolish talk and scurrility, drunkenness and thieving, which are easy to get rid of.

IV. "We must nevertheless be aware that even if we submit to the whole discipline of self denial, in hunger and thirst, watching, hard work and ceaseless study, we are still incapable of achieving lasting pure chastity on the strength of these works; no, it is through the effort we put in that we come to acknowledge and learn from experience, the best of teachers, that integrity is a gift granted only by God's grace. The only reason why we have to continue tirelessly in our exercises, is to win the mercy of the Lord through these hardships, until through God's kindness we are ready to be set free from the urgings of the flesh and the domination of our prevailing vices. It is not that these works can give us confidence to gain, through their means, the perfect physical chastity we desire.

The degree in which one can be fired with a deep desire to acquire chastity is equal to the longing others may have for money, or their ambition for the highest honours, or the intolerable desire for a beautiful woman, a longing which they yearn to fulfil with impatient fervour. Thus we may be inflamed with an insatiable longing for lasting integrity, till we disdain dainty foods and shun necessary drink. Indeed we must recoil from the very sleep nature demands, in that it is the sly betrayer of purity, the jealous opponent of chastity, and take it with a wary and suspicious mind so that each of us must examine ourselves every morning; if we can congratulate ourselves on purity achieved we must acknowledge that it has been granted by the Lord's protection, not by our own care and vigilance. We must recognise that our bodies will retain that integrity only as long as the Lord grants us in his kindness. One who has achieved that constancy should never be so proud as to trust in his own virtue, nor be deluded and off guard because of a long period without any emission, for he must know that he will find himself stained with a copious flow as soon as he separates himself from God's protection even for a moment. If he would have his purity continue for ever he should go to his rest with sincere contrition, a humble heart and unremitting prayer.

V. "If you would like clear proof of what I have been saying, so that you may be convinced of my opinion, and learn how it is in fact beneficial to have this struggle against the flesh which we feel in our bodies, although it may seem dangerous and difficult for us, you only have to think of those who are physically eunuchs, how sluggish and feeble they are when it comes to the pursuit of virtue. Is this not because they believe they are in no danger of losing their chastity? Not that you should imagine I am saying that no eunuch can ever be found who is distinguished for perfect self-denial, but that they too must overcome their nature, if any of them is aiming wholeheartedly at the prize of perfection. Once such a man is fired with zeal and longing for perfection, he must accept hunger, thirst, watching, poverty, all physical labour, not merely with endurance but actually with joy. For a man 'laboureth for himself in sorrow, and doth violence to his own destruction' (Prov. 16: 26, LXX). Also, 'A soul that is hungry shall take even bitter for sweet' (Prov. 27: 7). There is no other way to cut off or tear up the yearnings for things of this world, except by substituting salutary desires for the dangerous ones which we would like to be rid of. A lively mind will not be able to exist without some emotion of desire, fear, joy or sorrow, but will need to convert them to a good end. Hence if we want to root out the fleshly desires which are in our hearts, we must plant spiritual intentions in their place, so that our thoughts may be occupied with them and thus have some object to think about constantly, in order to rid themselves of the taint of present temporary pleasures.

Once our thoughts have been brought to that condition, through our daily exercises, then we will have sufficient experience to appreciate the meaning of that verse of the psalms which we are all accustomed to sing, but which only a few have the wisdom to understand fully, 'I set the Lord always in my sight: for he is at my right hand, that I be not moved' (Psalm 15/16: 8). The only man who can really grasp the force and intention of

XII. On Chastity

that text is one who has arrived at that perfect purity of mind and body of which we spoke, but knows that it is by the Lord that he is kept safe, moment by moment, lest he fall again, and that his right hand, which is to say his good work, is fortified by God alone. The Lord always stands at the right hand of his saints, not on their left, for there is nothing left for them to do; sinners and the wicked do not see him at all, for they have nothing right for the Lord to support, nor can they say with the Psalmist, 'My eyes are ever towards the Lord: for he shall pluck my feet out of the snare' (Psalm 24/25:15). No one can say that with conviction unless he has learnt to consider all things in this world dangerous, unnecessary or at best inferior in comparison with the heights of virtue, and has concentrated his whole effort, labour and care on cultivating purity in his heart. The mind that is whitened by monastic discipline and polished as it progresses will arrive at perfect purity in both mind and body.

VI. "The more placid and patient your heart is, the more easily you will advance in physical purity; the longer you admit the emotion of anger, the more difficult it will be for you to attain chastity. Nor will you quench the fire in the flesh unless you first restrain the wandering mind. Our Saviour shows us this clearly in the beatitude he proclaimed, 'Blessed are the meek; for they shall possess the land' (Matt. 5:4). There is no other way for us to gain possession of our own land, I mean to reduce the rebellious territory of this body to our control, than by first establishing our thoughts in patient meekness. No one can win the civil war against his own insurgent flesh unless he is first armed with meekness: 'for the meek shall inherit the land', and 'shall dwell therein for evermore' (Psalm 36/37:11, 29). The same inspired writer in the following verses of that psalm explains how we may obtain possession of that land, 'Expect the Lord and keep his way: and he will exalt thee to inherit the land' (Psalm 36/37:34). It is clear that no one can advance to take secure possession of the land unless he has kept to the stony way of the Lord, and observed his precepts, through mild and unshakable patience, and thus has been lifted up from the mud of carnal passion by the hand of the same Lord. 'For the meek shall inherit the land,' and not merely shall they possess it but they 'shall delight in abundance of peace' (Psalm 36/37: 11).

No one in whose flesh the civil wars of lust are still raging will enjoy that peace with security. Otherwise one is bound to be besieged by the fierce hosts of the devil, wounded by the fiery arrows of desire, and driven from the possession of his own land, until the Lord makes 'wars to cease even to the end of the earth. He shall destroy the bow, and break the weapons: and the shield he shall burn in the fire' (Psalm 45/46: 10). This fire refers to the one which the Lord came to kindle on earth, and the bows and weapons which he will break up are those with which the wicked spirits fight day and night against us, piercing our hearts with the fiery arrows of desire. Hence when the Lord makes war to cease, and sets us free from all burning temptations, we may advance to such a state of purity that we can be rid of that turmoil which makes us loathe ourselves, that is to say the flesh that is being assailed, and come to reverence our own bodies as tabernacles of purity. 'For there shall no evil come to him, nor shall the scourge come near his dwelling' (Psalm 90/91: 10). He arrives at that virtue of scriptural patience, in that his meekness makes him not only inherit the earth but he actually 'shall delight in abundance of peace' (Psalm 36/37: 11). When there remains any anxiety about conflict, there cannot be abundance of peace. It does not say 'they shall delight in peace' but 'in abundance of peace.' This clearly shows us what an effective remedy for the heart patience is; as Solomon says, 'the mild man is the healer of the heart' (Prov. 14: 30, LXX). It is not only the seeds of wrath, melancholy, depression, vainglory and pride that it eradicates, but of lust as well as all the others. 'The prosperity of kings is in longsuffering,' as Solomon also says (Prov. 25: 15, LXX). For one who is ever mild and at peace is never inflamed by the emotion of anger, nor eaten up with the sadness of melancholy and depression, nor is he inflated in empty vanity, or swelled by the tumour of pride. Much peace have they that love the name of the Lord; and to them there is no stumbling

XII. On Chastity

block' (Psalm 118/119: 165). It is therefore rightly said, 'The patient man is better than the valiant: and he that ruleth his wrath, than he that taketh cities' (Prov. 16: 32, LXX).

For us to achieve this deep and lasting peace, we must struggle against many temptations. Over and over again we must recite this prayer, in tears and groans, 'I am become miserable, and am bowed down even to the end: I walked sorrowful all the day long. For my loins are filled with illusions: and there is no health in my flesh, because of thy wrath: there is no peace for my bones, because of my sins' (Psalm 37/38: 7–8, 4). We shall truly lament like this if after a long period of physical purity we have come to hope that we have escaped the urges of the flesh altogether, and then we feel our emotions stirred and the arrows of desire piercing us again, even if it is only in a deceitful dream that impurity once again steeps us in ill humour. If anyone has begun to congratulate himself on long-kept purity of thought and deed, and has come to believe that he cannot again lose that chastity, he is bound to become proud in himself and say, 'And in my abundance I said: I shall never be moved' (Psalm 29/30: 7). The Lord will withdraw his help, for his own benefit, and he will feel the weakening of that state of purity he was confident about, finding himself tempted by the return of the evil spirit; let him run at once to the giver of integrity, let him acknowledge his weakness and confess, saying, 'O Lord, in thy favour', not my own, 'thou gavest strength to my beauty. Thou turnedst away thy face from me: and I became troubled' (Psalm 29/30: 8). Job also said, 'If I be washed as it were with snow waters, and my hands shall shine ever so clean: yet thou shalt plunge me in filth; and my garments shall abhor me' (Job 9: 30–1). He who had defiled himself through his own fault could not speak thus to his Creator. One who has arrived at a state of perfect purity is bound to learn frequently from his own inconsistency how, strengthened by the grace of God with the purity he desires, he may become fit to say, 'With expectation I have waited for the Lord; and he was attentive to me. And he heard my prayers; and brought me out of the pit of misery and the mire of dregs. And he set my feet upon a rock: and directed my steps' (Psalm 39: 2–3).

VII. "There are many grades of chastity which lead up to unsullied purity. Our own ability is insufficient to distinguish them adequately or to describe them, but since the course of my conversation demands it, I will attempt to outline them as far as my limited experience allows. A more perfect explanation can be left to the perfect, and I will not anticipate the judgment of those who possess a greater chastity in more fervent zeal, for as far as their devotion excels mine, so far does their ability to discriminate. Now I will distinguish six steps on the ladder to the summit of chastity, which differ from each other in sublimity to a noticeable degree; I shall pass over the intermediate stages, many though they be, for they are too subtle for men to discern, for the mind to observe or the tongue to describe. It is by these that perfect chastity grows in a gradual daily progress, just as the growth of our physical bodies happens indistinguishably day by day, so that without realising it men develop a habit of perfection, and acquire both strength of mind and maturity in chastity.

The first step in modesty is when a monk escapes carnal temptation while awake. The second is when his thoughts cease to dwell on his desires. The third is when he is not even slightly moved to lust by seeing a woman. The fourth, when he does not experience any fleshly arousal while awake. The fifth is when he is reminded of human reproduction either through study or unavoidable reading, but not the slightest assent to sensual interest troubles his thoughts, but he can consider such matters with a placid and pure heart as being a simple process necessary to the continuance of the human race, and gives him no more cause for concern than if he were thinking about bricklaying or any other procedure. The sixth step in chastity is when he is not troubled with lustful visions of women even while asleep. Such annoyances are certainly free from sin, but they are an indication that lust does still lurk in the unconscious. Fantasies like these may arise from different causes. One is troubled while asleep by the considerations one is used to attend to while awake. Those who have never experienced sexual intercourse are affected in a different way from those who have been joined to a woman.

The latter are usually disturbed by straightforward dreams, less impure, and can be purified with simpler care and less effort. The former however are troubled by more depraved and explicit fantasies, until gradually, according to the measure of chastity each one aims at, their thoughts are lulled to rest in disgust at the very matters they were formerly eager for, and the Lord grants them what the prophet promised would be the reward of the strong, 'I will destroy the bow and the sword and war out of the land: and I will make you sleep secure' (Hosea 2:18). Thus a man may arrive at the purity of Saint Serenus and a few others like him. I have distinguished that from the preceding six steps in chastity, for it is rare for men to believe it feasible, let alone possess it. Since it was granted to Serenus by a special gift of divine mercy, it cannot be set forth as a pattern for general aspiration, namely that our thoughts can be trained in pure chastity to such an extent that the natural processes of the body are extinguished, and there is never any flow of seed. I should mention the opinion of some who have spoken about this physical emission, that it does not happen to sleepers because of the effect of fantasies in dreams, but rather that the accumulation of this fluid causes impure thoughts to arise in the mind. As a result they claim that at times when it does not accumulate, there is no emission, and fantasies diminish.

VIII. "Now to detect such things, and to find out whether they be possible or not, is certainly beyond the capacity of anyone who has not, through long experience and purity of heart, arrived at the limits of flesh and spirit, guided by the Word of the Lord. The holy Apostle says of this, 'For the word of God is living and effectual and more piercing than any two-edged sword and reaching unto the division of the soul and the spirit, of the joints also and the marrow; and is a discerner of the thoughts and intents of the heart' (Heb. 4:12). Like an inspector or an arbiter, one who is situated between those limits examines and discriminates between what is necessary to human nature, and is bound to happen, and what is acquired by habits of vice and youthful carelessness. He does not settle for the mistaken opinions of the crowd about natural effects, nor does he agree with the prejudiced opinion of those without experience, but he analyses the quality of purity with an accurate, free and just assessment based on what he himself has done. He is never taken in by the errors of those who babble about human psychology but are corrupted by frequent self-indulgence, far more than nature demands, through their own fault. Their habit is to attribute great force to nature, and to justify their depravity by this force, although it cannot be the cause; they attribute their lack of self-control to the needs of the body, or even to the Creator himself, blaming nature for what is their own responsibility. Proverbs speaks aptly of this, 'The folly of a man corrupteth his steps; and he fretteth in his mind against God' (Prov. 19:3, LXX).

If anyone is unwilling to believe what I am claiming, I do ask him not to differ from my opinion without examining it and practising the discipline of this way of life. If he observes the traditional self-denial even for a few months, he will be able to realise the truth of what I have been saying. It is foolish to hold forth about any skill or field of study without first carefully and earnestly learning everything that relates to its perfect acquisition. For example, if I were to assert that you can make something like honey out of wheat, or alternatively produce a fine oil from wheat just as you can from rape or flax seeds, and if someone who knew nothing of these matters heard me, would he not burst out laughing at me for saying something contrary to natural law, and being a blatant liar? And then if I were to produce countless witnesses who would affirm that they had seen it done, had tasted it, had done it themselves, and if I were to explain the method and process by which wheat can be transformed either into the richness of oil or the sweetness of honey, but he remained stubborn in his ignorance, refusing to believe that either sweetness or richness could be produced from such grain – would it not prove that he was unreasonable and obstinate, rather than making my assertion ridiculous, given that it is backed by many reliable witnesses, clear proofs, and to crown it all actual experience?

Therefore one who has reached that state of purity with

his whole heart, will have his thoughts completely clear from temptations to this vice, and his body will simply emit superfluous humours during sleep. He will be confident in knowing his own nature and condition, so that if, after a long period, he finds his body again stained without his knowledge or consent, he can assign this to physical necessity, and has certainly reached the state of being the same at night as he is during the day, the same in bed as at prayer, the same whether alone or surrounded by a crowd. In short, he will never see himself in private in such a way as would embarrass him before men, nor will the all-seeing eye of God see anything in him which he would wish concealed from the gaze of men. When he begins to rejoice in the glad light of chastity, he can say with the prophet, 'night shall be my light in my pleasures, but darkness shall not be dark to thee, and night shall be light as the day, the darkness thereof, and the light thereof are alike to thee' (Psalm 138/139: 11–12). The inspired writer also tells how he has obtained this condition which appears to be beyond human nature, saying, 'for thou hast possessed my reins' (Psalm 138/139: 13). That is to say, I have not earned this purity through my own efforts or strength, but because you have killed the fire of lust which was in my loins."

IX. GERMANUS: "We have discovered for ourselves to a certain extent that through the grace of God it is possible to possess permanent physical purity while awake, and we cannot deny that those who are watchful can avoid any fleshly arousal, through careful discipline and discretion. However we would like to know whether it is possible to escape such disturbance while asleep. There are two reasons why we think this is impracticable, and although we cannot mention them without blushing, yet we would like to ask your indulgence in listening to them, because the necessity of curing them requires it, even if they are described in a slightly indelicate way. The first is that when the mind's vigilance is relaxed during sleep, there is no way to take notice of the approach of such arousal. Secondly, when the bladder is filled with accumulated urine while we are asleep, it weighs ceaselessly upon us under the pressure of the fluid within, and stiffens our weak members; the same thing happens naturally to infants and eunuchs. It thus happens that even if no consent to the pleasure of lust troubles the mind, yet it is humiliated and confused by the actions of the body."

X. CHAEREMON: "It appears that you have not yet understood the force of true chastity, since you imagine that it can only be preserved among the wakeful with the help of discipline. Hence you think that those asleep cannot preserve their integrity because the mind's guard is down. Chastity does not consist in strict discipline as you imagine, but in delight in our own purity for its own sake. When there is still some element of lust resisting it, we do not call it chastity but continence. You can see in the case of those who have received a deep-seated love of chastity through God's grace, that lack of vigilance while they are asleep is no problem – vigilance alone is surely unreliable even while they are awake. A vice that is suppressed only with an effort will only grant a temporary truce to the struggle, and will not permit you to remain permanently in security, no matter how much effort you make, whereas a vice that has been conquered through deep-seated virtue leaves you confident with no fear of disturbance, and grants you real and lasting tranquillity. For this reason, as long as we feel tempted by the desires of the flesh, we must recognise that we have not yet reached the heights of chastity, but are still in a weak position of continence, tired by a struggle in which the outcome remains ever in doubt. When you wanted to prove that this sort of movement of the flesh cannot be avoided, you pointed out that even eunuchs who have had their testicles cut off still experience it, and so you must be aware that they have only lost the ability to procreate, not the fire in the flesh nor the emotion of lust. It is obvious that they too, if they want to aspire to the degree of chastity we are pursuing, should not grow slack in their practice of humility, contrition and the discipline of continence, and we should never imagine that chastity is gained by them with any less effort or determination.

XI. "Perfect chastity is therefore to be distinguished from the laborious strife after continence by its lasting tranquillity. The true completion of chastity is when temptations to carnal activity no longer attack us, but we can treat them with sheer disgust, and thus retain a deep and inviolable purity – that is nothing less than holiness. This happens when the flesh ceases to war against the spirit, but comes to be in agreement with the spirit's longing for virtue, when the two begin to cement a solid peace together, and as the Psalmist says, 'brethren dwell together in unity' (Psalm 132/133:1). Thus they inherit the promise of happiness offered by Our Lord, who said, 'If two of you shall consent upon earth concerning any thing whatsoever they shall ask, it shall be done to them by my Father who is in heaven' (Matt. 18:19). One who fulfils the prophetic type of Jacob, that is to say the Supplanter, through the acquisition of continence and the supplanting of vice, will have the nerve in his loins deadened, so as to ascend to the status of an Israel, his heart always under control. The blessed David, inspired by the Holy Spirit, made the same distinction and order, for he says first, 'In Judaea God is known,' that is to say in the soul which is still constrained by the confession of sin, for 'Judaea' means 'confession', whereas in Israel, which means in 'the one who sees God' (or as others interpret it, the 'strength of God'), the righteous one of God is not merely made known but 'his name is great'. David continues, calling us on to higher things, and wishing to show us the place where the Lord takes delight, 'and his place is in peace' (Psalm 75/76:2–3). That is, God is to be found not in strife and effort in opposition to vice, but in the peace of chastity and in a heart at constant rest. If anyone has been found fit to obtain this place of peace, by quenching carnal passions, he will progress on from that stage to the antitype of Zion, being made the image of God, where God will make his dwelling. The Lord does not dwell in the struggle for continence, but in the true image of virtue, where he does not so much weaken or curb the powers of the bow but breaks them for ever, the bow, that is, which launches against us the fiery arrows of desire. You can see from this how, just as the Lord finds his place in the peace of chastity rather than the struggle for continence, so his dwelling place is in the image and contemplation of virtue. That is why the gates of Zion are rightly preferred to all the tents of Jacob, for 'the Lord loveth the gates of Sion above all the tabernacles of Jacob' (Psalm 86/87:2).

You went on to assert that the arousal of the flesh is inevitable because the bladder is filled with accumulated urine, and stirs up the flaccid member; now those who really desire purity are not in the least hindered by such a motion, which arises through necessity, and only momentarily during sleep. Nevertheless, if such a motion occurs, the command of chastity will reduce it to peace again, and they will be settled without any immodesty or even the slightest thought of lust. But since the physical laws of nature concur with the discipline of the mind, we should be wary of excess even in drinking water, since it is the accumulation of liquid every day that influences the otherwise dry parts of the body. By restraint in this manner the motion of the flesh which you consider inevitable becomes rare, and the fire becomes weak, tepid or even cold so to speak, the flame transformed into a dew without any burning force. It is like that wonderful vision of Moses, for the bush which is our flesh is not consumed although bathed in harmless flame, or the case of those three young men who were surrounded by the fire of the furnace in Babylon, but by the dew of the Spirit there was not even a smell of burning about their hair or clothes. We may begin even in this body to experience what was promised by the prophet to the saints, 'When thou shalt walk in the fire, thou shalt not be burnt: and the flames shall not burn in thee' (Isaiah:43:2).

XII. "Great indeed and wonderful, beyond the conception of men save for those who have experienced them, are the benefits which the Lord confers in his generous love towards his faithful even while they are still living in this vessel of corruption. The psalmist cried out, exalted in his purity of mind, not only in his own name but in that of all who have arrived at this state of being, 'Wonderful are thy works, and my soul knoweth right well' (Psalm 138/139:14).

XII. On Chastity

If he were believed to be speaking about any other emotion or any other work of God, we would not think the prophet had said anything important or new, for there is no man who does not recognise how marvellous are the works of God simply from the splendour of creation. But the daily operation of God's grace in his saints, and the special gifts which he pours out in abundance, are not recognised except by one who has received them. As a private witness to God's beneficence, in the secrecy of his conscience, he is unable to expound them in words, nor to comprehend them in his feelings and conscious thought, once he has left that fiery rapture and returned to material and earthly considerations.

Who is there who would not stand amazed at the Lord's work when he discovers in himself that the ravenous demands of the stomach, and the dangerous delicacy of the palate, are so restrained that now he scarcely takes a rare morsel of common food, and that unwillingly? Who would not be rapt in admiration of God's work, when he discovers that the fire of lust, which he had always considered innate, and unquenchable, has been so cooled that he does not feel the slightest disturbance in the movements of the flesh? Who would not stand in awe of the Lord's power, when he sees men who were once harsh and ill-tempered, roused to fury at their dependants however mildly they obey them, now transformed to become so meek that they are unmoved by any insults, and receive them with great joy when they are offered? Who, in short, would not admire the work of God, and cry out sincerely, 'I have known that the Lord is great' (Psalm 134/135:5), when he sees either himself or someone else transformed, from greed to generosity, from excess to restraint, from pride to humility, from effete delicacy to rough simplicity, cheerfully accepting poverty and deprivation of temporal goods? Such are the truly wonderful works of God, which the mind of the Prophet and those like him recognises, in amazement at the sight of the miraculous. These are the marvels which he has done on the earth, which the same inspired writer brings before all nations for their admiration, saying, 'Come and behold ye the works of the Lord, what wonders he hath done upon earth: making wars to cease even to the end of the earth. He shall destroy the bow, and break the weapons: and the shield he shall burn in the fire' (Psalm 45/46: 9–10). What greater prodigy could there be, than to transform grasping tax-collectors into apostles in a moment, to change savage persecutors into mild preachers of the Gospel, to make them spread at the expense of their own blood the very faith which they had been persecuting? These are the works of God which the Son affirms he performs constantly with his Father, 'My Father worketh until now; and I work' (John 5:17). Of these works the holy David sings, in the spirit, 'Blessed be the Lord, the God of Israel, who alone doth wonderful things' (Psalm 71/72:18). Of these Amos also speaks, 'He doth all things, he transformeth all things, he changeth the shadow of death unto dawn' (Amos 5:8, LXX). This is the 'change of the right hand of the most High' (Psalm 76/77:11), of this saving work of God the psalmist beseeches the Lord, saying, 'Confirm, O God, what thou hast wrought in us' (Psalm 67/68:29). We shall pass over the secret hidden plans of God, which the thoughts of his saints contemplate constantly within themselves, and the heavenly outpouring of spiritual joy, which makes a despondent soul leap into unexpected joy in the unseen movements of his heart, and the unspeakable and unheard joyful consolation which on occasion may rouse those sunk in sullen stupor to fervent prayer as if summoning them from the deepest sleep – this, I tell you, is the joy of which St Paul writes, 'that eye hath not seen, nor ear heard, neither hath it entered into the heart of man'. The heart, that is, of a man who is sunk in earthly vice, and clings to human emotions, seeing nothing of these gifts of God. The same Apostle concludes by saying of himself and of those like him who had already risen above the ordinary way of life, 'but to us, God hath revealed them, by his Spirit' (I Cor. 2: 9–10).

XIII. "In all these matters, the more the mind advances in real purity, the more distinctly it sees God. It is more likely to increase

XII. On Chastity

its own inner admiration for God than to find ease of expression to talk about him. Just as he who has no experience of this great joy will be incapable of perceiving it, so those with experience will be unable to express it in words. It is as if someone tried to describe in words how sweet honey is to one who had never tasted anything sweet; the one who had never tasted it could not grasp what sweetness means by listening, just as the other would be incapable of putting into words that sweetness which he knows well by taste. His own knowledge of the taste of honey leaves him only in silent admiration within himself of the sweetness he has experienced. In the same way anyone who has been found fit to achieve that state of perfection we have been describing, will ponder in the silence of his thoughts over the things that the special grace of the Lord has done for him, and will be so struck with amazement at all this that he will cry out from the depths of his heart, 'Wonderful are thy works, and my soul knoweth right well' (Psalm 138/139:14). It is a miracle, this work of God, when a fleshly man, living in the flesh, is able to repudiate the demands of the flesh, and through varied events and accidents can keep the tenor of his mind firm and steady, while things of all sorts happen around him. It was on a foundation of this sort of virtue that there was once a certain elder in Alexandria, who was surrounded by a mob of pagans, hurling curses and vile insults at him, till one of them said in mockery, 'What miracle has this Christ whom you worship done?' And he answered, 'The fact that I am not disturbed or troubled by these insults, or any others you may throw at me.'"

XIV. GERMANUS: "We are so astonished at this degree of chastity which is neither human nor earthly but truly heavenly and angelical, that we are more afraid of giving up altogether than encouraged to aim for it. But we would ask you to give us a full explanation of the type of discipline needed, and the length of time required to attain it and perfect it, so that we may believe it possible to achieve, and be encouraged to try, having a period of time set for us. We consider that while we live in this body it is virtually impossible, unless we be shown a structure and a path which may lead us to it."

XV. CHAEREMON: "It would be rash to assign a definite period of time to achieve the chastity we have been discussing, since both men and their desires vary so much, for it is not easy to give a set time even to learning material crafts and visible skills. Each one will approach it either faster or slower depending on the intentions in his thoughts, and the nature of his character. However we can at least give a precise idea of the type of discipline and the length of time needed for grasping the actual possibility of such chastity.

If one refrains from all idle conversation, quenches the emotions of anger and anxiety, and material cares, is content with a daily ration of two buns, and does not drink water to excess, if he limits his time of sleep to three hours (some allow four), and if he believes that he will not gain anything through the merits of this discipline and self-restraint but only through the mercy of God (since all human effort is futile without faith of that sort), then in no more than six months he may come to believe that this sort of perfection is not impossible. It is indeed evidence that purity is near when he begins to cease hoping in his own efforts. If he really understands the meaning of this verse, 'Unless the Lord build the house, they labour in vain that build it' (Psalm 126/127: 1). It will follow that he will not be proud of the merits of his purity since he knows that it has been achieved by the mercy of the Lord rather than his own care, nor will he be harsh and strict towards others, knowing that human virtue achieves nothing without the aid of God's grace.

XVI. "For any one of us who has been striving against the spirit of fornication with his whole heart, it is already a great triumph if he does not put his hope for healing in his own merit. Such a realisation may seem simple and obvious, but it is as difficult for beginners to grasp as perfect chastity itself. For if it should happen that they are granted a small measure of purity, at once they are puffed up by a certain conceit which creeps into the secrecy of their consciences. They imagine they have achieved

XII. On Chastity

something by their efforts, so that it becomes necessary for them to be stripped of that divine protection, until they are oppressed by the temptations which only divine grace had restrained to the point that they learn from their own experience that the goal of purity can never be achieved by their own virtue and strength.

Now to bring our long drawn out discussion on the goal of true chastity to a brief conclusion, and to sum up everything which has been said fully in different places, this is the summit of chastity: that a waking monk is never overwhelmed by the passion of lust, and sleeping he is not deluded by fantasies. If while he is asleep he experiences a motion of the flesh simply because the unconscious mind is off guard, as it arises without any temptation to desire, it will die down without disturbing the body at all. What we have said about the goal of chastity, such as it is, we have learnt from experience, not from other mens' words. Maybe the idle and careless will consider it impossible, but I am sure that learned and spiritual men will recognise my teaching and approve of it. There is such a difference between one man and another, as much as the objects of their attentions differ, namely as far as heaven differs from earth, or Christ from Belial. As Our Lord and Saviour told us, 'If any man minister to me, let him follow me; and where I am, there also shall my minister be' (John 12:26). And again, 'Where thy treasure is, there is thy heart also'" (Matt. 6:21).

So much did the blessed Chaeremon tell us about perfect chastity, and he concluded his admirable teaching on holy purity in those words. We were amazed, but eager; though he persuaded us, since the greater part of the night had passed, not to be deprived of the sustenance of natural sleep by giving our limbs a little rest, lest our thoughts lose the fervour of their intentions through the weakness of our bodies.

✧ THE THIRTEENTH COLLATION ✧
BEING THE THIRD OF
ABBA CHAEREMON

On the Protection of God

I. Introduction.
II. The question, of why no virtuous merit is imputed to hard work.
III. The reply, that without God's aid not only perfect chastity but any type of good is unattainable.
IV. An objection, on how the pagans can be said to preserve chastity without God's grace.
V. The reply, on the imaginary chastity of the philosophers.
VI. Without God's grace we are unable to perform any effective action.
VII. On God's great plan, and his daily Providence.
VIII. On the grace of God and on free will.
IX. On the effectiveness of our good will, and that of the grace of God.
X. On the weakness of free will.
XI. Whether the grace of God follows our goodwill or precedes it.
XII. That good will is not always to be attributed to grace, nor always to man.
XIII. That human efforts cannot equal the grace of God.
XIV. That God tests the strength of human will by tribulations.

XV. On the many different graces of vocation.
XVI. On the grace of God, which surpasses the limits of human faith.
XVII. How inscrutable is God's plan.
XVIII. How the Fathers taught that free will is insufficient for salvation.

Admonition: This Collation has often been accused of unsound doctrine on the relationship between grace and free will. As a result Cassian has often, though unjustly, been called a "semi-Pelagian". In other places in the Collations and Institutes Cassian is impeccably orthodox in an area which was undefined in his time: if in the present Collation the teaching of the Father he is reporting is at times inconsistent, correction should be made with reference to the Catechism of the Catholic Church, nos. 1,987–2,016. The question at issue here is in fact more to refute the Calvinist or Jansenist denial of the value of human co-operation with divine grace.

I. We took our brief repose and gathered for the morning office, meeting the old man again. Germanus was troubled with a great scruple, because during our previous discussion, which had instilled in us a great desire for a height of purity hitherto unknown to us, the old man had demolished all merit in human effort by quoting a single text. He declared that man, no matter what effort he puts into the quest for good results, can never come to any good, unless he accepts it as a gift of divine grace rather than the result of his labour. We were puzzling over this issue when the holy Chaeremon came towards our cell, and heard us whispering together. He accordingly completed the office of psalms and prayers more quickly than usual, and asked us what was the matter.

II. GERMANUS: "It seems that we are excluded, so to speak, from believing it possible to attain that splendid degree of virtue which you described to us last night. Surely it is absurd that the reward of our labours, which is to say the perfection of chastity,

XIII. On the Protection of God

cannot specifically be imputed to the efforts applied, although it is achieved through our own exertions. It would seem stupid to say, for example, that when a farmer exerts himself diligently in cultivating the earth, the harvest is not to be imputed to his labour."

III. CHAEREMON: "The very example which you have proposed shows us even more clearly that hard work is useless without God's help. When a farmer has put all his effort into cultivating the land, he cannot attribute his successful harvest and rich yield to his own industry, since it often happens that he expends it in vain, when it is not followed by the right amount of rain and good weather. Often enough we see a ripe harvest, grown to full maturity, snatched from the labourer's hands, so that no profit for so much hard work returns to the labourer, since it was not granted by the Lord's bounty. Just as a lazy farmer, who fails to till the soil regularly with his plough, is not granted a fruitful harvest by divine grace, so too the diligent labourer by night gains nothing from his constant care unless God's mercy favours him. Man in his pride can vaunt of no equality nor partnership in God's grace, but strives to claim some participation in God's munificence in consideration of his own labour as the instigator of divine bounty. He boasts of how the outcome of a rich harvest relates to the merits of his labour, but let him consider and ponder carefully how the efforts which he expends in the hope of riches are not capable of producing any results unless the Lord protect and strengthen him generously in all the work of the countryside. How futile his intention and his strength are, unless God's grace grants him that abundance which may so often be denied through drought or flood.

Now since the strength of his oxen, and the health of his own body, and all the profit resulting from work and activity are granted by the Lord, we must pray that there does not happen what scripture describes, a heaven of brass and a ground of iron (Deut. 28:23), when 'that which the palmer-worm hath left the locust hath eaten: and that which the locust hath left the bruchus hath eaten: and that which the bruchus hath left the mildew hath destroyed' (Joel 1:4). Nor is it in such case alone that the hard working farmer needs God's help, but to avert unexpected disaster, for even if the field is fertile and rich with the desired crop, he may be defrauded in the vain hopes he had, and may even be cheated of the plentiful harvest which had already been reaped and gathered into barn and byre. It should be clear from this that God is the source of all good thoughts as well as deeds, since he first inspires us with the will to holiness, and then grants us the perseverance, the strength and opportunity to fulfil our good desires, 'Every best gift and every perfect gift is from above, coming down from the Father of lights' (James 1:17). He it is who begins what is good in us, he develops it, he brings it to a conclusion, as the Apostle says, 'And he that ministereth seed to the sower will both give you bread to eat and will multiply your seed and increase the growth of the fruits of your justice' (II Cor. 9:10). Our part is every day to follow in humility where the grace of God leads us, otherwise we shall rightly hear Jeremiah rebuke us as stiff-necked, resisting with uncircumcised ears, as Scripture says, 'Shall not he that falleth rise again? And he that is turned away, shall he not turn again? Why then is this people in Jerusalem turned away with a stubborn revolting? They have laid hold on lying and have refused to return'" (Jer. 8:4–5).

IV. GERMANUS: "This opinion appears to lie open to the objection that it tends to destroy free will, although we cannot easily refute its piety. For we see many pagans, who deserve no help from divine grace, outstanding for the virtues of abstemiousness, tolerance and even, surprisingly, chastity. If the choice of free will is restricted, how can we believe that God gives them these gifts, when they follow the wisdom of this world, in complete ignorance not just of grace but of the very existence of God. Can they be found in possession of the sublime perfection of chastity through their own efforts, as we have read or learnt through what others have told us?"

V. CHAEREMON: "I am delighted that you are so enthusiastic to

XIII. On the Protection of God

learn about the truth that you even make frivolous objections, so that in refuting them you may see how reasonable and profound the Catholic faith is! How could a clever man make such contradictory remarks? Yesterday you affirmed that pure heavenly chastity was beyond the grasp of mortals at all, even through the grace of God, and today you think the pagans can possess it through their own efforts! But since I am sure you only suggested that in order to find out the truth, listen to what we have to say.

Firstly, you should never imagine that the philosophers acquired the sort of purity of thought which we expect, when we are enjoined that not merely fornication but impurity of any kind should not be named among us. They had merely a portion, a fraction of chastity, that is to say enough physical self-restraint to keep them from sexual intercourse. But when it comes to internal purity of mind, or that perfect and lasting purity of body, they were unable even to imagine it, let alone achieve it. Take the most famous of them, Socrates – he was not ashamed to admit it, as his own admirers tell. For it happened that a face-reader looked at him and said he has *ommata paiderastou*, that is he looks like a queer. His disciples interrupted, and wanted to vindicate their master's reputation, but he quelled their indignation in a single sentence, 'Peace, boys; I am indeed, but I can control myself.' You can see, then, that it is not just on my word but on the evidence of the philosophers themselves that we find they needed great effort to restrain themselves from performing acts of impurity, that is to say indecency. The desire and the pleasure in that passion had not been removed from their hearts. We are shocked to hear what Diogenes said, for that philosopher of this world was not ashamed to utter as a memorable saying what among us would not be spoken or heard without shame. For he said to one who was to be punished for adultery, as they say, 'Do not buy with your death what is sold for nothing.' It is clear that they knew nothing of the strength of true chastity which we seek. Hence it is clear enough that our circumcision, which is in the spirit, cannot be possessed except as a gift from God, and is to be found only in those who serve God with whole hearted contrition.

VI. "It is possible to demonstrate in many matters – in all in fact – that men need the help of God. Human frailty can accomplish nothing of what is necessary to salvation on its own, that is to say without God's help, and this is nowhere more obvious than in the acquisition and preservation of chastity. To defer for a moment a discussion of how difficult it is to be perfect, let us examine briefly how to go about it. Who, I wonder, can be strong enough, howsoever fervent in spirit, to be able to survive on his own strength, without the support of human encouragement, in the deprivation of the desert, and the diet of dry bread, which is not so much a daily hunger as the difficulty of having to eat so much of it? Who could tolerate drinking nothing but water without the Lord to console him? Or to do without that sweet and delightful morning's sleep for tired eyes and to confine his hours of repose within the harsh rule of no more than four hours? Or that ceaseless attention to reading? Or the endless round of work, without the prospect of present gain to encourage him? Who could perform that without God's grace? We cannot even see the attraction of all these things without divine inspiration, and we can certainly not carry them out without God's help. To make this clear, we have the benefit of having tried this discipline, as well as many clear signs and arguments. Surely we can think of so many things that we were eager to achieve, with no lack of fully fervent desire and strong will, but frailty intervened and our intentions were frustrated. Our aims would all come to nothing, save when our Lord's mercy comes to our aid. So it happens that there are countless men who really want to apply themselves to the pursuit of virtue, but few indeed can be found who have been able to persevere and endure it. Even in matters where we have no particular weakness to hinder us, the general ability to carry out our desires is beyond our control. We cannot even guarantee that our solitude is undisturbed, our fasting regular, our reading attentive, our time itself at our disposal, for occasions may often arise which drag us away from our holy practices, unwillingly indeed, so that we need to beg Our Lord for sufficient space and time to carry them out. Our own ability is certainly not enough,

XIII. On the Protection of God

did the Lord not grant us the opportunity to perform even things within our powers. St Paul comments, 'For we would have come unto you, once and again, but Satan hath hindered us' (I Thess. 2:18). It happens often, in fact, that we realise it was for our benefit that we were called away from our spiritual exercises, and our intended programme was interrupted against our will, so that some concession might be given to our weak bodies, and we find ourselves thus preserved for the progress of our salvation, despite ourselves. St Paul likewise speaks of this providence of God: 'For which thing thrice I besought the Lord that it might depart from me, and he said to me: My grace is sufficient for thee; for power is made perfect in infirmity' (II Cor. 12:8–9). Again, 'For we know not what we should pray for as we ought' (Rom. 8:26).

VII. "It was never God's plan to create man in order that he should perish, but that he should live for ever, and this plan remains unshaken. When he observes in his kindness that a spark of good will appears in us, however small, or if he strikes such a spark from our hearts as if from a hard flint, he cherishes it and encourages it, strengthening it with his inspiration, 'who will have all men to be saved and to come to the knowledge of the truth' (I Tim. 2:4). 'Even so it is not the will of your Father who is in heaven that one of these little ones should perish' (Matt. 18:14). And again, 'Neither will God have a soul to perish, but recalleth; meaning that he that is cast off should not altogether perish' (II Kings (II Sam.) 14:14). God is truthful, and does not deceive, as he affirms with an oath, 'As I live, sayeth the Lord God, I desire not the death of the wicked, but that the wicked turn from his way and live' (Ezech. 33:11). It is not his will that one of the least of these should perish – how than can we imagine without blasphemy that he does not wish the salvation of all, but only wants a few to be saved out of the many? Those who do perish do so against God's will, as he himself proclaims daily against each of them: 'Turn ye, turn ye from your evil ways: and why will ye die, O house of Israel?' (Ezech. 33:11). And again, 'How often would I have gathered together thy children, as the hen doth gather her chickens under her wings, and thou wouldest not?' (Matt. 23:37). 'Why then is this people in Jerusalem turned away with a stubborn revolting? They have laid hold on lying and have refused to return' (Jer. 8:5). The grace of Christ comes daily to our aid, for while he 'will have all men to be saved and to come to the knowledge of the truth' (I Tim. 2:4), he calls together all without exception, saying, 'Come to me, all you that labour and are burdened; and I will refresh you' (Matt. 11:28). Now if he were only calling a few, and not all in general, it would follow that not all are burdened by either original or actual sin, and it would not be true what is said: 'For all have sinned and do need the glory of God' (Rom. 3:23), and death would not be believed to have 'passed upon all men' (Rom. 5:12). Since all who perish do so against the will of God, Scripture can say that death itself was never fashioned by God, 'For God made not death, neither hath he pleasure in the destruction of the living' (Wisd. 1:13). It happens therefore, that we often pray for things disadvantageous to ourselves, and our prayer is therefore heard late or never; often too the Lord, like a solicitous physician, confers upon us things for our benefit, though we might think them harmful, and be unwilling to receive them. He frequently restrains our dangerous intentions and our perilous attempts, and prevents their harmful effects; we hasten towards death but he calls us back to salvation, and without our realising it he snatches us from the very jaws of Hell.

VIII. "Through the Prophet Hosea the Word of God gives us an elegant parable about his care and providence over us, under the image of Jerusalem the harlot, who chases desperately after the cult of idols. 'I will go after my lovers,' she says, 'that give me my bread and my water, my wool and my flax, my oil and my drink.' And God in his compassion replies, in his care for her salvation, not for her desires: 'Wherefore behold I will hedge up thy way with thorns and I will stop it up with a wall: and she shall not find her paths. And she shall follow after her lovers and shall not overtake them: and she shall seek them and shall not find. And she

XIII. On the Protection of God

shall say: I will go and return to my first husband, because it was better with me then, than now' (Hosea 2:5–7). In another place he describes the contempt and insults with which we, rebels as we are, revile the one who invites us to repentance and salvation: 'And I said: thou shalt call me father and shalt not cease to walk after me. But as a woman that despiseth her lover, so hath the house of Israel despised me, saith the Lord' (Jer. 3:19–20). Jerusalem he aptly compares to an adulteress, deserting her husband; his love and his patient goodwill he compares to a husband deserted by his wife. The loving kindness of God is directed ever towards the human race, no insult can force him to abandon his concern for our salvation, or to turn aside from his primal plan for us, no matter how overwhelming our sins. No better comparison for such love could be imagined, than that of a husband who yearns for his wife with burning love: the more he feels himself neglected by her, the greater the concern for her that inspires him. God's protection is with us always, and cannot be withdrawn, so much does our Creator love his creation; he does not only accompany us but goes before us also in his loving care. The inspired writer spoke from his own knowledge, acclaiming the Lord thus: 'My God, his mercy shall prevent me' (Psalm 58:11). When he observes goodwill arising in us, he shines upon it straightaway and strengthens it, encouraging our salvation; he grants increase to what he himself has planted, and what he sees emerging from our effort. For he says, 'before they call, I will hear, as they are yet speaking, I will hear' (Isaiah 65:24) and 'At the voice of thy cry, as soon as he shall hear, he will answer thee' (Isaiah 30:19). Not only does he kindly inspire holy wishes, but he also provides us with opportunities for life, he shows to those who stray the chance of a good work, the direction of the way of salvation.

IX. "Human reason cannot easily discern how it is that the Lord gives to those who ask, provides for those who seek, opens for those who knock. Moreover, he is found by those who do not look for him, he appears before those who have not sought for him, he extends his hands all day long towards a people that does not believe in him, nay, that speaks against him. He calls those who resist him and are far off, he draws to salvation those who are reluctant, he withdraws from those who desire to sin the will to carry out that sin, he lovingly hinders those rushing into evil. But to those who open to him freely, he grants the heights of salvation for our free acceptance, as it is said, 'If you be willing and will hearken to me, you shall eat the good things of the land' (Isaiah 1:19). 'Not of him that willeth, nor of him that runneth, but of God that sheweth mercy' (Rom. 9:16). What then is the meaning of 'God, who will render to every man according to his works' (Rom. 2:6)? And 'For it is God who worketh in you, both to will and to accomplish, according to his good will' (Phil. 2:13)? And, 'not of yourselves, for it is the gift of God. Not of works, that no man may glory' (Eph. 2:8–9)? Again, we must consider why it was said, 'Draw nigh to God; and he will draw nigh to you' (James 4:8), and in another place, 'No man can come to me, except the Father, who hath sent me, draw him' (John 6:44), and, 'Make straight the path for thy feet: and establish all thy ways' (Prov. 4:26, LXX). When we pray, we repeat, 'Direct my way in thy sight,' and 'Perfect thou my goings in thy paths: that my footsteps be not moved' (Psalm 5:9; 16/17:5). It is the same point of which we are admonished, 'make to yourselves a new heart and a new spirit' (Ezek. 18:31), for we are given a promise concerning this, 'And I will give them a new heart, and will put a new spirit in their bowels: and I will take away the stony heart out of their flesh and will give them a heart of flesh: that they may walk in my commandments and keep my judgments' (Ezek. 11:19–20).

Think of the Lord's command, 'Wash thy heart from wickedness, O Jerusalem, that thou mayest be saved' (Jer. 4:14), for the inspired writer begs it of the Lord, saying, 'Create a clean heart in me, O God; thou shalt wash me, and I shall be made whiter than snow' (Psalm 50/51:12, 9). We read elsewhere, 'Shine upon yourselves the light of wisdom' (Hosea 10:12. LXX), and of God himself is it said, 'he that teacheth men knowledge' (Psalm 93/94:10), and 'the Lord enlighteneth the blind' (Psalm 145/146:8). Truly we pray, along with the Psalmist, 'Enlighten my eyes that I never sleep in death'

XIII. On the Protection of God

(Psalm 12/13: 4). Do you not see that in all these texts is set forth the grace of God as well as our own free will? Although man to a certain extent can of his own decision increase his appetite for virtue, always he needs to be assisted. A man cannot enjoy good health at his own will, nor be rid of disease at his own choice. What use would it be to desire the grace of good health, unless the Lord who gives us the use of life itself, were also to grant a robust constitution? To make it abundantly clear, even in the goodness of our nature which is dependent on the benevolence of the Creator, our good intentions often come to nothing; St Paul too is a witness that without the guidance of Our Lord such intentions can never arrive at the perfection of virtue, 'For to will is present with me; but to accomplish that which is good, I find not' (Rom. 7:18).

X. "Holy Scripture confirms the freedom of our will, saying, 'With all watchfulness keep thy heart' (Prov. 4:23), but St Paul demonstrates its frailty in, 'God ... keep your hearts and minds in Christ Jesus' (Phil. 4:7). David the psalmist tells of the strength of free will, saying, 'I have inclined my heart to do thy justifications' (Psalm 118/119:112), but at the same time he teaches us its weakness, praying, 'Incline my heart into thy testimonies and not to covetousness' (Psalm 118/119:36). Solomon prays, 'But may he incline our hearts to himself, that we may walk in all his ways, and keep his commandments, and his ceremonies, and all his judgments' (III Kings (I Kings) 8:58). The Psalmist tells us of the power of free-will, saying, 'Keep thy tongue from evil: and thy lips from speaking guile' (Psalm 33/34:14), but he declares its weakness in the prayer we offer, 'Set a watch, O Lord, before my mouth: and a door round about my lips' (Psalm 140/141: 3). The Lord speaks of the ability of our free-will, 'Loose thy bonds from off thy neck, O captive daughter of Sion' (Isaiah 52:2), but the psalmist tells of its frailty, saying, that the Lord 'executeth judgment for them that suffer wrong', and, 'thou hast broken my bonds: I will sacrifice to thee the sacrifice of praise' (Psalm 145/146:7; 115/116:16–17). In the Gospel we hear Our Lord calling us to come to him of our own free will: 'Come to me, all you that labour and are burdened; and I will refresh you' (Matt. 11:28). Yet Our Lord also warns of its weakness, in the words, 'No man can come to me, except the Father, who hath sent me, draw him' (John 6:44). St Paul speaks of free will, 'So run that you may obtain' (I Cor. 9:24), but John the Baptist bears witness to its frailty, saying, 'A man cannot receive anything, unless it be given him from heaven' (John 3:27). We are bidden preserve our selves carefully, in the words of the prophet, 'Take heed to your souls' (Jer. 17:21), but another prophet, speaking in the same spirit, says, 'Unless the Lord keep the city, he watcheth in vain that keepeth it' (Psalm 126/127:1). St Paul writes to the Philippians to declare the freedom of their choice: 'with fear and trembling work out your salvation', but he proceeds at once to point out its weakness, 'for it is God who worketh in you, both to will and to accomplish, according to his good will' (Phil. 2:12–13).

XI. "Since these texts are contrasting and confusing, there remains a great question to ponder, namely whether God has mercy on us because we have demonstrated a beginning through our own good will, or whether God has mercy on us and as a result our will begins to be good. There have been many on each side of this question; they have made many assertions, and have involved themselves in various contradictory errors. For if we claim that the beginning of good will is in our control, what are we to say of Saul the persecutor, or Matthew the publican? The one was steeped in blood, and cruelty towards the innocent; the other depended on forceful plunder of the public, both were called to salvation. But if we assert that the first beginnings of good will are always inspired by God, what shall we say of the faith of Zacchaeus, or the devotion of the thief on the cross? Through their own choice they did violence to the kingdom of heaven, and anticipated their particular calls. Yet if we attribute to our free will the completion of virtue and performance of God's commands, how can we pray, 'Confirm, O God, what thou hast wrought in us' (Psalm 67/68:29), or, 'yea, the work of our hands do thou direct' (Psalm 89/90:17)? We know that Balaam was brought in to curse Israel but we can see

XIII. On the Protection of God

that although he was willing to curse them, he was not permitted to do so. Abimelech was restrained, so that he might not sin against God by touching Rebecca. Joseph was rescued from his brothers' jealousy, so that the sons of Israel might go down into Egypt; while they were hindered from fratricide, there was prepared for them relief from the famine. Joseph himself, once recognised by his brothers, said as much: 'Be not afraid, and let it not seem to you a hard case that you sold me into these countries: for God sent me before you into Egypt for your preservation', and further on, 'the Lord sent me before, that you may be preserved upon the earth, and may have food to live. Not by your counsel was I sent hither, but by the will of God: who hath made me as it were a father to Pharaoh, and lord of his whole house, and governor in all the land of Egypt' (Gen. 45: 5, 7–8). After his father's death his brothers were afraid, but he took away from their fear, saying, 'Fear not. Can we resist the will of God? You thought evil against me: but God turned it into good, that he might exalt me, as at present you see, and might save many people' (Gen. 50: 19–20). The holy David declares that this happened according to God's dispensation, when he says in the 104th Psalm, 'And he called a famine upon the land: and he broke in pieces all the support of bread. He sent a man before them: Joseph, who was sold for a slave' (Psalm 104/105: 16–17).

These two, therefore, the grace of God and freedom of will seem to be opposed to each other, but in fact they do agree, and we should accept them both equally. For the sake of our devotion we must join them together, for if we deny either of them to men, we shall be found to have transgressed the bounds of the faith of the Church. When God sees us willing to tend towards the good, he runs to meet us, guides us, strengthens us. 'At the voice of thy cry, as soon as he shall hear, he will answer thee' (Isaiah 30: 19), 'and call upon me in the day of trouble: I will deliver thee, and thou shalt glorify me' (Psalm 49/50: 15). On the other hand, if he sees us unwilling or growing slack, he stirs up our hearts with his saving encouragement, so that the will to good is restored or created within us.

XII. "We cannot believe that God created man in such a manner that he never wills nor performs good. No free choice would otherwise be left to him, if he could only will or perform evil, but was not allowed to will or perform good on his own. How then could it be true, what the Lord said after after the fall of the first man, 'Behold, Adam is become as one of us, knowing good and evil' (Gen. 3:22)? We cannot imagine that he was formerly totally ignorant of good, otherwise we would have to think he had been created as an unreasoning and unfeeling beast – something quite absurd and totally foreign to the Catholic faith. Indeed, as Solomon the Wise says, 'God made man right', that is, able to enjoy the knowledge of good, 'and he hath entangled himself with an infinity of questions' (Qo. 7:30), in other words he has become knowledgable of good and evil. After the Fall, Adam conceived the knowledge of evil, which he had not possessed, and did not lose the knowledge of good which he had already received. St Paul also makes it clear that the human race did not lose the knowledge of good after the Fall, when he says, 'For when the Gentiles, who have not the law, do by nature those things that are of the law; these, having not the law, are a law to themselves. Who shew the work of the law written in their hearts, their conscience bearing witness to them; and their thoughts between themselves accusing or also defending one another, in the day when God shall judge the secrets of men' (Rom. 2:14–16). In this manner the Lord blames the blindness with which the Jews rebelliously opposed him, for that blindness is not innate but chosen, in the words of the Prophet: 'Hear, ye deaf, and, ye blind, behold that ye may see. Who is blind, but my servant? Or deaf, but he to whom I have sent my messengers?' (Isaiah 42:18–19). And if anyone should imagine that you could ascribe that blindness to nature rather than choice, he continues: 'Bring forth the people that are blind, and have eyes: that are deaf and have ears' (Isaiah 43:8). Similarly, 'who have eyes and see not, and ears and hear not' (Jer. 5:21). Our Lord also says in the Gospel, 'seeing they see not, and hearing they hear not, neither do they understand' (Matt. 13:13). Isaiah expands on

XIII. On the Protection of God

this: 'Hearing, hear and understand not: and see the vision and know it not. Blinded is the heart of this people, they have made their ears heavy, and shut their eyes: lest they see with their eyes and hear with their ears and understand with their heart and be converted, and I heal them' (Isaiah 6: 9–10, LXX).

In rebuking the Pharisee he shows that the possibility of good was in them, saying, 'And why, even of yourselves, do you not judge that which is just?' (Luke 12: 57). He would surely never have said that to them, did he not know that they were capable of discerning what is just by their own natural judgment. We must therefore be wary of attributing to the Lord alone all the merits of the saints, and ascribing nothing at all to human nature except what is evil and corrupt. This opinion is refuted by those words of Solomon the Wise, or rather of the Lord himself, in the prayer offered when the construction of the Temple was completed: 'And David my father would have built a house to the name of the Lord the God of Israel. And the Lord said to David my father: Whereas thou hast thought in thy heart to build a house to my name, thou hast done well in having this same thing in thy mind. Nevertheless thou shalt not build me a house to my name' (III Kings (I Kings) 8: 17–19). Now, this thought and design of King David's – was it good and to be attributed to God, or evil and to be attributed to man? For if it was a good thought coming from God, why did he who inspired it then deny its performance? But if it was an evil design, deriving from man, why is it praised by the Lord? It remains therefore that it must be believed good, and from man. In the same way we can judge our own daily thoughts. David is not the only one who can be credited with thinking good thoughts, and we cannot be denied by nature the potential ever to conceive or think about anything good. It is certain therefore that the Creator's loving concern inserted all the seeds of virtue into our minds according to our nature, but unless they are stimulated by the mercy of God, they are incapable of coming to perfect growth. As St Paul tells us, 'neither he that planteth is anything, nor he that watereth; but God that giveth the increase' (I Cor. 3: 7). That man does possess a certain degree of freedom of choice is made clear by the book of the Shepherd, which states that each of us is attended by two angels, one good and the other evil, and that it is at a man's own discretion which of them he shall follow. Free will remains therefore in man always, because he is able either to ignore or to embrace the grace of God. Otherwise the Apostle would not have given the command, 'with fear and trembling work out your salvation' (Phil. 2:12), for he knew that we were able either to cultivate grace or neglect it. But lest they imagine that no assistance from God's aid was needful for salvation, he continues, 'for it is God that worketh in you, both to will and to accomplish, according to his good will' (Phil. 2:13). For the same reason he counsels Timothy, 'Neglect not the grace that is in thee' (I Tim. 4:14), and likewise, 'for which cause I admonish thee that thou stir up the grace of God which is in thee' (II Tim. 1:6). Writing, too, to the Corinthians, he encourages them, warning them not to prove themselves unworthy of God's grace by failing in works, 'And we helping do exhort you that you receive not the grace of God in vain' (II Cor. 6:1).

It was doubtless because Simon Magus only received saving grace without effect that he received it in vain. He was not prepared to obey the commands of Saint Peter, who told him, 'Do penance therefore for this thy wickedness; and pray to God that perhaps this thought of thine may be forgiven thee. For I see thou art in the gall of bitterness and in the bonds of iniquity' (Acts 8:22–3). God's mercy goes before the will of man, for it is said, 'My God, his mercy shall prevent me' (Psalm 58/59:11). But on the other hand, our will precedes the Lord who checks it, and underpins it for our benefit, so that our intentions may be put to the test, for it is also said, 'In the morning my prayer shall prevent thee' (Psalm 87/88:14), and again, 'I prevented the dawning of the day, and cried: my eyes to thee have prevented the morning' (Psalm 118/119:147–8). He calls us and invites us, saying, 'All the day long have I spread my hands to a people that believeth not and contradicteth me' (Rom. 10:21). Yet he is invited by us, when we say, 'All the day I cried to thee, O Lord: I stretched out my hands to thee' (Psalm 87/88:10). He is waiting for us, as it says in the prophecy, 'Therefore the Lord

XIII. On the Protection of God

waiteth that he have mercy on you' (Isaiah 30:18), and we wait for him, as it is said, 'With expectation I have waited for the Lord; and he was attentive to me' (Psalm 39/40:2) and 'I looked for thy salvation, O Lord' (Psalm 118/119:166). He strengthens us, saying, 'And I have chastised them and strengthened their arms: and they have imagined evil against me' (Hosea 7:15), but he encourages us to strengthen ourselves, when he says, 'Strengthen ye the feeble hands, and confirm the weak knees' (Isaiah 35:3). Jesus cries out, saying, 'If any man thirst, let him come to me and drink' (John 7:37), but the Psalmist cries out to him, 'I have laboured with crying; my jaws have become hoarse: my eyes have failed, whilst I hope in my God' (Psalm 68/69:4). The Lord seeks, saying, 'I sought, and there was no man; I called, and he did not answer me' (Song 5:6, LXX), yet he is sought by the Bride, who laments in tears, 'In my bed by night I sought him whom my soul loveth: I sought him and found him not; I called him, and he answered me not' (Song 3:1, LXX).

XIII. "The grace of God always co-operates with our free choice for a good end, it assists, protects and defends it in all matters, to the extent that it sometimes demands or expects motions of good will of us; otherwise it might appear that his gifts were being bestowed on those asleep or sunk in idleness. God seeks opportunities, when man has risen from his sluggish torpor, so that his generous bounty may not seem pointless, and he may bestow it on the pretext of some request or effort; nevertheless the grace of God remains ever free, for he pours out such an abundance, such a glorious immortality, such gifts of lasting bliss, on the slightest little acts of will. We should not imagine that it was because of any pre-existent faith on the part of the crucified thief that he was given his promise, nor can we say that the blissful life of paradise was totally gratuitous. Neither can we say that the two great crimes of King David were absolved because of his penance, which consisted in but two words, 'I have sinned against the Lord', rather than through the mercy of God, as he was permitted to hear through the prophet Nathan, 'The Lord also hath taken away thy sin, Thou shalt not die' (II Kings (II Sam.) 12:13). He had added murder to adultery: that was his own free choice; he was rebuked by the prophet, that was the grace of God's mercy. But again, he confessed his sin in humility, which was a work of his own free will; and he was granted pardon for such great crimes in a brief moment, which was the gift of a merciful Lord.

Why speak about such a quick confession, such an unparalleled generosity of divine response, when we can look so easily at the example of St Paul? He looked to the great reward in the future, and made light of his many tribulations: 'For that which is at present momentary and light of our tribulation worketh for us above measure exceedingly an eternal weight of glory', beyond all computation (II Cor. 4:17). In another place he declares the same truth, saying, 'For I reckon that the sufferings of this time are not worthy to be compared with the glory to come that shall be revealed in us' (Rom. 8:18). Therefore no matter how much human weakness tries, it can never match the reward to come; its own efforts cannot evoke divine grace to the extent that grace does not remain free. Hence the Doctor of the Gentiles acknowledges that he had been granted the rank of apostle through God's grace, saying, 'by the grace of God, I am what I am', yet at the same time he claims to have responded to that divine grace, saying, 'and his grace in me hath not been void; but I have laboured', and obtained, 'more abundantly than all they. Yet not I, but the grace of God with me' (I Cor. 15:10). When he says, 'I have laboured', he indicates the efforts of his free choice. When he says, 'Yet not I, but the grace of God', he demonstrates the power of divine protection. When he says 'with me', he shows us that grace co-operated with him in his sweat and toil, not in careless idleness.

XIV. "We read that God's justice made the same provision for Job, that tested athlete, when the devil demanded his unparalleled temptation. Had he resisted the foe entirely by the protecting grace of God, and not through his own strength, depending merely on divine providence with no patient virtue of his own, he would have survived all those accumulated trials and woes which the relentless cruelty of the fiend had devised, but the devil would have simply repeated the accusation against him which he had uttered at first, 'Doth Job fear God in vain? Hast thou not made a fence for him, and his house, and all his substance round about? But withdraw thy hand', in other words allow him to contend with me by his own strength, 'and see if he blesseth thee not to thy face' (Job 1: 9–11). Since the lying foe did not dare to repeat this slanderous accusation once the conflict was over, he admits that he had been conquered by Job's strength, not God's. Admittedly God's grace was not totally withdrawn from him, for he allowed the tempter only so much power to tempt as he knew Job had the strength to resist, but he did not shield him from the devil's attack to the extent of leaving no place for human merit, only ensuring that the vile fiend did not touch his mind and make him mad, so that he could overbear him in an unequal onslaught while his senses were powerless.

The Gospel also gives us the example of the Centurian, to show that the Lord himself sometimes tries our faith, to make it stronger and more splendid. Our Lord knew that he would cure the boy by the power of his word alone, but offered him a visit in person, saying, 'I will come and heal him.' But the Centurian, surpassing this offer in his overwhelming faith, said to him, 'Lord, I am not worthy that thou shouldst enter under my roof; but only say the word, and my servant shall be healed.' Our Lord admired and praised him, placing him above all those in Israel who believed, saying, 'Amen, I say to you, I have not found so great faith in Israel' (Matt. 8: 7, 8, 10). Had he possessed only what Christ had given him, he would have deserved neither praise nor merit, [and the Lord would have said, 'I have not given such faith to Israel'].

This trial of faith we find made by God's justice even on the great Patriarch himself, for it is said, 'After these things, God tempted Abraham' (Gen. 22: 1). It was not the faith which the Lord himself had breathed into him that he wished to test in his justice, but that which he had been able to demonstrate out of his own free choice, when he was first called and enlightened by the Lord. Thus his steadfast faith is rightly commended, and after the grace of God had been momentarily withdrawn for his testing, it came again to his aid, when he was told, 'Lay not thy hand upon the boy, neither do thou any thing to him. Now I know that thou fearest God, and hast not spared thy only begotten son for my sake' (Gen. 22:12). The lawgiver in Deuteronomy gives a clear teaching on how some sorts of temptation can be for our advantage, so that we can win the merit of perseverance: 'If there rise in the midst of thee a prophet or one that saieth he hath dreamed a dream, and he foretell a sign and a wonder: And that come to pass which he spoke, and he say to thee: Let us go and follow strange gods, which thou knowest not, and let us serve them: thou shalt not hear the words of that prophet or dreamer. For the Lord your God trieth you, that it may appear whether you love him with all your heart, and with all your soul, or not' (Deut. 13:1–3).

What then? Since it was God who permitted this prophet or dreamer to arise, are we to believe that he intended to protect those whose faith he was testing, to the extent that he would leave their free will no scope for resisting the temptation through their own strength? What would be the point of testing them at all, since he knew how weak and fragile their nature, if they had no possibility of resisting the tempter by their own strength? God's justice would not permit them to be tempted unless he knew what strength of resistance there was in them, so that they might be judged either culpable or praiseworthy by a just assessment of the outcome. St Paul speaks on the same point: 'Wherefore he that thinketh himself to stand, let him take heed lest he fall. No temptation will take hold on you, but such as is human. And God is faithful, who will not suffer you to be tempted above that which you are able; but will make also with temptation issue, that you may be able to bear it' (I Cor. 10:12–13). Now when he says, 'He who stands, let him take heed lest he fall', he attributed this heed to free choice, knowing that with the aid of grace it is possible either to stand, through taking heed, or to fall through heedlessness. When on the other hand he continues, 'no temptation will take hold on you, but such as is human', he demonstrates the weakness and inconstancy of minds not yet fortified, incapable of resisting

XIII. On the Protection of God

the assault of besieging evil spirits, against whom he knew that he himself fought daily, as did those who were perfect. Of those he writes to the Ephesians: 'For our wrestling is not against flesh and blood, but against principalities and powers, against the rulers of the world of this darkness, against the spirits of wickedness in the high places' (Eph. 6:12). And when he adds, 'God is faithful, who will not suffer you to be tempted above that which you are able', he is not praying that the Lord will not permit them to be tempted, but that they be not tempted beyond what they can endure. On the one hand he indicates the free faculty of human choice, on the other he demonstrates the grace of the Lord who moderates the onslaught of temptation.

In all these texts, we are shown the manner in which divine grace constantly arouses human free will: it does not always defend it or protect it, nor does it make it contend against hostile spirits by its own efforts. Thus the conqueror is made aware of the grace of God, the defeated of his own frailty. Hence he must learn to place his hope not in his own strength but in God's help, and to fly constantly to God's protection. This is not my own opinion, but is supported by clear passages in Scripture, as we may see from this passage about Joshua: 'These are the nations which the Lord left, that by them he might try Israel, whether they will keep the way of the Lord, and might learn to fight with their enemies' (Judges 3:1–2 and 2:22). If we may make comparison between the unparalleled mercy of our Creator and a mere mortal, a comparison not of equal care but of similar compassion, a loving and careful nurse carries her baby in her bosom for a long time, then begins to teach him to walk, first allowing him to crawl, then to stand up, but supporting him with her right hand while he attempts alternate steps; if she sees him totter she catches him at once, if he staggers she steadies him, if he falls she picks him up; she may stop him from falling, or allow him to fall gently, but she does pick him up after every fall. Yet once she has brought him through to childhood, and the vigour of young adolescence, she lays burdens and responsibilities on him, not to oppress him but to exercise him, and she permits him to compete with his equals. How much more does our universal heavenly father know us, those whom he carries in the bosom of his grace, those whom he may exercise in virtue through the use of their free will in his sight; he helps us in our toil, hears us when we call, attends to us when we seek him, rescues us from danger even when we are unaware of it.

XV. "In all this we can see 'how incomprehensible are God's judgments, and how unsearchable his ways' (Rom. 11: 33), the ways by which he leads the human race to its salvation. We may demonstrate this by the example of vocations in the Gospel. He chose Andrew and Peter and the other apostles, who had no concern over preparing their own salvation, purely through his spontaneous grace. Zacchaeus, on the other hand, who trustingly intruded himself into the Lord's sight, making up for his own shortness of stature with the height of the sycamore, was not only accepted but even singled out for the grace of having the Lord to stay in his house. Paul he summoned, unwilling and resisting as he was. There was another whom he commanded to stay close to him always, without granting his request for a brief delay to bury his father. When Cornelius was faithful in constant prayer and almsgiving, he showed him the way of salvation as if to reward him, telling him through a visiting angel to seek out Peter and learn from him the saving message which would bring salvation to him and all his household. Thus God in his wisdom arranges the salvation of men in many ways, according to his kindness, granting the gift of grace to each according to his capacity. He preferred to confer the healing of mankind not in a uniform manner, according to his power and majesty, but according to the measure of faith found in each one, as he showed himself to each. The leper who believed that the will of Christ alone would suffice to heal him, was cured by the simple assent of that will, when he said, 'I will. Be thou made clean' (Matt. 8: 3). When someone else begged him to come and lay his hands to raise his dead daughter, he went into the house and did what the man asked in the manner he had expected. Yet another believed that perfect healing was to be found in the proclamation of his word alone, and said to him, 'but only say the

XIII. On the Protection of God

word, and my servant shall be healed' (Matt. 8:8), whereupon the Lord brought the languishing limbs back to strength by the simple word of command, saying, 'Go, and as thou hast believed so be it done to thee' (Matt. 8:13). Yet others hoped for healing through the touch of his garments, and he bestowed health generously on them. Some asked for healing in their sickness, and he granted it, while to others he granted healing without their asking. Some he encouraged to hope, asking, 'Wilt thou be made whole?' (John 5:6) while to others he brought aid beyond their hopes. Of some he asked their wishes, before satisfying them, saying, 'What will ye that I do to you?' (Matt. 20:32) while when others were unaware of the way to obtain what they desired, he showed it to them, saying, 'if thou believe, thou shalt see the glory of God' (John 11:40). For some he poured out healing grace in abundance, so that the evangelist records that he 'healed all their sick' (Matt. 14:14). Yet with others the unfathomable depths of Christ's mercies was stopped up, as it says, 'he could not do any miracles there ... because of their unbelief' (Mark 6:5–6). Thus we see that God's mercy is adapted to the capacities of human faith: to one he may say, 'According to your faith, be it done to you' (Matt. 9:29), to another, 'Go and as thou hast believed so be it done to thee' (Matt. 8:13), to another, 'Be it done to thee as thou wilt' (Matt. 15:28), and to a fourth, 'Thy faith hath made thee whole' (Mark 10:52).

XVI. "Now no one should imagine that I have told you all this in the attempt to prove that the whole matter of our salvation lies in the quality of our own faith. That is the opinion of some heretics, who attribute everything to free will and declare that God distributes his grace according to the merits of each person. No, we have made it abundantly clear that God's grace overflows, and surpasses the narrow limits of human lack of faith. We can see this in that story in the Gospel, where the ruler thought it would be easier to cure his sick son than to raise him from the dead, and urged Our Lord to come quickly, saying, 'Lord, come down before that my son die.' Christ did indeed rebuke his lack of faith, saying, 'Unless you see signs and wonders, you believe not', but he did not limit his grace to match the man's weakness. Nor was it by his physical presence that he dispelled the deadly fever, as the other had expected, but by the word alone of his power, for he said, 'Go thy way, thy son liveth' (John 4:48–50). We read of the same overflowing grace when Our Lord cured the paralytic man; he had asked only that his body be set free from the weakness that held it bound, but Our Lord first brought healing to his soul, saying, 'Be of good heart, son. Thy sins are forgiven thee.' After that, because the scribes did not believe that he could forgive men's sins, he restored with a word the man's limbs which had been struck with paralysis, so as to refute their lack of belief. 'Why do you think evil in your hearts? Which is easier, to say, Thy sins are forgiven thee; or to say, Arise, and walk? But that you may know that the Son of Man hath power on earth to forgive sins (then said he to the man sick of the palsy), Arise, take up thy bed and go into thy house' (Matt. 9:2–6). Similarly, in the case of the man who had been lying on the edge of the pool for thirty eight years, hoping for a cure from the disturbance of the waters, he gave him an exceeding gift of grace. Wishing to encourage him to be healed and saved, he asked him, 'Wilt thou be made whole?' He was only complaining of the lack of human assistance, as he said, 'Sir, I have no man, when the water is troubled, to put me into the pond', but Our Lord forgave his unbelief and his ignorance, and restored him to perfect health by his own mercy, not by the means he had expected, saying to him, 'Arise, take up thy bed and go into thy house' (John 5:6–8).

We should not be surprised that such things are told of Our Lord's power, given that divine grace worked similar things through his disciples. Peter and John were going into the temple, and the man lame from birth, who did not know how to walk at all, begged for alms: they bestowed on him not the base coin he had asked for, but the gift of walking, granting him the unlooked-for prize of health, when all he had hoped for was a meagre alms. Peter said to him, 'Silver and gold I have none; but what I have, I give thee. In the name of Jesus Christ of Nazareth, arise and walk' (Acts 3:6).

XVII. "Through the examples we have taken out of the Gospels, it is clear enough that God takes care of the salvation of human beings in innumerable different ways, inscrutably. Some are willing and eager, and he calls them on to greater fervour; some are reluctant and slow, and those he compels. Now he assists us to carry out the good designs he sees in us, now he instils the first movements of such holy desires, granting us either the very beginning of good works, or perseverance in them. Hence in our prayer we implore the Lord to be not only our protector and saviour, but also our helper and guide. He is protector and saviour in that he first calls us, and entices us to salvation though we be ignorant and unwilling. He is called helper and refuge in that while we are attempting to carry out good works he gives us a safe conduct and fortifies us. St Paul in consideration of the many ways in which God bestows his grace upon us, imagines himself afloat in an immeasurably deep sea of the love of God, crying out, 'O the depth of the riches of the wisdom and of the knowledge of God! How incomprehensible are his judgments, and how unsearchable his ways! For who hath known the mind of the Lord?' (Rom. 11: 33–4). Now anyone who imagined that such a vast and mighty deep could be measured by human thought, would be trying to bring to nothing the wonder which the great Teacher of the Nations expressed at God's wisdom. Anyone who thought himself able to grasp, or to describe, the fullness of God's plan for the salvation of the human race, would be clearly contradicting the teaching of St Paul, asserting that God's judgments were comprehensible, his ways actually searchable. The Lord himself refutes such an idea: 'For my thoughts are not your thoughts: nor my ways your ways, saith the Lord. For as the heavens are exalted above the earth, so are my ways exalted above your ways, and my thoughts above your thoughts' (Isaiah 55: 8–9). When the Lord wished to express his designs for us in terms of human affection, and to find a model in human nature to express his love for us, the love which he pours out ceaselessly upon us in his mercy, he could find none more apt than that of a mother's tender care. This example he used, for nothing more dear to human nature could be found: 'Can a woman forget her infant, so as not to have pity on the son of her womb?' And, not content with this example, he goes further yet, saying, 'And if she should forget, yet will I not forget thee' (Isaiah 49:15).

XVIII. "Thereby those who have measured, not by words alone but through real experience either the magnitude of grace or the limits of human free-will, can understand that, 'the race is not to the swift, nor the battle to the strong, nor bread to the wise, nor riches to the learned, nor favour to the skilful', but 'all these things, one and the same Spirit worketh, dividing to every one according as he will' (Qo. 9:11; I Cor. 12:11). It is therefore a matter of faith, as well as of common experience, that the God of the universe, the loving father and kind healer of all, works in all men without favouritism, as the Apostle puts it. Now he inspires the first movements towards salvation, and instils the fervour of good will into everyone; now he grants an outcome to their work and makes it result in virtue. Now he calls back those who may be unwilling or unaware from the brink of ruin; now he grants them occasions and opportunities to be saved, and restrains their headlong rout from an outcome in destruction. Some he receives who are willing and swift; others reluctant and resisting, forced into consenting to be good. In short, we are conceded mercy by God as long as we do not always resist him, and do not persevere in refusal. That is the work of heavenly grace, not our own merit and effort, as we learn from the Lord's own words: 'And there you shall remember your ways and all your wicked doings with which you have been defiled: and you shall be displeased with yourselves in your own sight for all your wicked deeds which you committed. And you shall know that I am the Lord, when I shall have done well by you for my own name's sake and not according to your evil ways, O house of Israel' (Ezek. 20:43–4).

This then is the teaching of all the Catholic fathers, who declare that perfection of heart is not found in empty discussion, but in true reality through God's gift. First he fires each of us to desire all that is good, but in such a manner that the free exercise of

XIII. On the Protection of God

choice remains. Next he gives divine grace to make it possible to exercise these virtues, though still in such a manner as not to exclude the possibility of choice. Thirdly, God grants that we may remain steadfast in the virtues we have acquired, but without our freedom feeling itself constrained. This is the way in which the God of all is believed to work all things for all men; he inspires, protects and confirms, but does not take away the freedom of will which he himself created. If there be any subtle human argument or conclusion which appears to contradict this teaching, it should be shunned, rather than risk weakening our faith. Faith is not won through thought, but it is through faith that we win our understanding, as it is written, 'If you will not believe, you shall not understand' (Isaiah 7: 9, LXX). It is God who works all things in us, and all things are ascribed to our free will, and this is beyond the full comprehension of the human mind."

With this nourishment did the blessed Chaeremon strengthen us, until we no longer felt any fatigue from our long journey.

✣ THE FOURTEENTH COLLATION ✣
BEING THE FIRST OF ABBA NESTOR

On Spiritual Science

    I. What Abba Nestor said about the science proper to religious men.
    II. On how to acquire knowledge of spiritual things.
    III. Practical perfection consists of two stages.
    IV. The active life can be practised in many professions and activities.
    V. On perseverance in the profession we have undertaken.
    VI. On the inconstancy of the weak.
    VII. An example of chastity, to show that not everything should be imitated by all.
    VIII. On spiritual science.
    IX. That we must begin with practical wisdom before proceeding to the spiritual.
    X. On the need to grasp the discipline of true wisdom.
    XI. On the many ways of interpreting Holy Scripture.
    XII. A question, on how to stop remembering secular poetry.
    XIII. The reply, on how to remove what covers our memory like a sort of lichen.
    XIV. That an impure soul can neither teach nor understand spiritual science.
    XV. An objection, that there are many sinners who do have wisdom, and holy men who do not.
    XVI. The reply, that the wicked cannot possess true wisdom.

XVII. To whom one should reveal one's degree of perfection.
XVIII. The reasons why spiritual teaching may be fruitless.
XIX. That there are many who receive the grace of saving instruction even though they be unworthy.

I. To fulfil our undertaking, and continue the course of our journey, we come now to the conversation with Abba Nestor, a man distinguished in many ways, and very learned. He understood that we had memorised certain passages of Holy Scripture, which we wanted explained, and addressed us in the following words:

"There are many types of knowledge in this world, with an enormous variety of different disciplines and arts. Many of them are in fact useless, or only valuable for things in this present life, but none of them is without its proper method and process of training, by which those who wish may acquire them. Now if those arts are taught by specific set methods, how much more so should be our discipline and profession of religion. By this we are led to the contemplation of secret things relating to invisible matters, to seek the reward not of an earthly quest but of eternal bliss, and so this too may be acquired by a specific set method. There are in fact two stages in acquiring this knowledge. The first is practical and down to earth, by which our behaviour is improved, and our vices eliminated. The second is theoretical, and consists in learning how to contemplate the things of God, and his most holy revelation.

II. "Anyone who desires to achieve the theoretical knowledge must first labour to obtain the practical knowledge in every virtue. This practical knowledge may be held without the theoretical, but the theoretical cannot possibly be grasped without the practical. These steps are arranged and set in order, so that a man who is truly humble may ascend to the top. If he takes these steps in the order we have described, he will be able to attain the heights, which he could never do if he tried to omit or fly over the first step. Vain would it be to aspire to see God, if we have not learned to shun vice: 'For the Holy Spirit of discipline will flee from the deceitful, and will not dwell in a body subject to sins' (Wisdom 1: 5, 4).

III. "This practical perfection also consists of two parts. The first stage is to recognise the nature of each vice, and how to cure it. The second is, in the same manner, to discern the succession of virtues, and train our minds in their perfection. Thus we may say they are no longer forced, only to be brought under our control by imperious violence, but we may find them pleasant and delightful, naturally good, and the narrow rugged path may be climbed with ease. Now how could anyone be capable of attaining the state of virtue which is the second step of practical wisdom, or the contemplation of the spiritual things of heaven which constitutes the upper step of theoretical wisdom, unless he first came to understand the nature of his vices, and made efforts to extirpate them? As a result we must say that it is impossible to ascend to a higher state until you have finished with the lower. Still less can you comprehend things beyond you if you have not already been able to discern what is within yourself. Be aware, then, that we have a twofold task over which to labour; we must both expel vice and cultivate virtue. This is not merely my own opinion; it is something I have learnt from the words of the only one who really understands the capability and character of his creation: 'Lo, I have set thee this day over the nations, and over kingdoms, to root up and to pull down, and to waste and to destroy, and to build and to plant' (Jer. 1:10). To eliminate evil tendencies, he names four necessary actions: rooting up and pulling down, wasting and destroying. In the acquisition of perfect virtue and the means to salvation, he names only building and planting. It is clear, therefore, that it is more difficult to root up and pull down the unruly passions of body and mind, than to build or plant spiritual virtues.

IV. "Having seen that practical virtue consists of two stages, we proceed to divide it with respect to many different professions and ways of life. Some apply themselves totally to the search for the solitary life and purity of heart, like Elijah and Elishah in the Old Testament, and Saint Antony in our own lifetime, and the others who followed him. We know that they came to a very close union with God in the silence of the desert. Others gave themselves entirely to the formation of their brethren and the ceaseless care of a monastery, like the late Abba John, who was superior of a large monastery in the nearby city of Thmuis. We remember how he used to edify many who were of the same quality, performing miracles like those of the apostles. Yet others were happy to serve a hospice and provide a welcome, like the patriarch Abraham and Lot who thus pleased the Lord long ago, and more recently Saint Macarius, a man of singular patience and tolerance, who ran a hospice in Alexandria, and can be considered no whit inferior to those who explored the secrets of the desert. Others again undertake the care of the sick, others practice intercession for the unfortunate and the oppressed; others teach catechism, others give alms to the poor; in their piety and devotion they can be ranked among the greatest of men.

V. "Now it is useful and appropriate that each one should put all his effort and care into bringing to perfection the way of life he has chosen, or the grace he has been given. While he should praise and admire the virtues of others, he must never depart from the profession he himself has undertaken. As St Paul tells us, the Church is one body, but it has many limbs, and we have different gifts according to the graces given to us. It may be 'prophecy, to be used according to the rule of faith; or ministry in ministering; or he that teacheth, in doctrine; he that exhorteth, in exhorting; he that giveth, with simplicity; he that ruleth, with carefulness; he that sheweth mercy, with cheerfulness' (Rom. 12:6–8). No one limb can be jealous of the work that another does, for the eyes cannot do the task of the hands, nor the nose that of the ears. For this reason not all are apostles, not all are prophets, not all teachers, not all have the grace of healing, not all speak with tongues, not all can interpret (cf. I Cor. 12:28).

XIV. On Spiritual Science

VI. "Some, who have not been fully grounded in the profession they have undertaken, when they hear of the progress others have made in various studies and virtues are so fired with admiration of them that they try to imitate the way they live, which inevitably means that human frailty finds all its efforts vain. It is impossible for one single person to be distinguished in all the virtues we have mentioned at once. Anyone who tries to cultivate them equally, will inevitably find that while pursuing them all, he fails to achieve any one of them completely. Such a varied application would lead to dissipation rather than improvement. There are many paths that lead to God, so each of us should persevere in the one he happens to have started, not changing his course, until he become perfect in his particular profession.

VII. "Any monk who was so unwise as to try to change to a different course, would incur not only the dissipation which we have mentioned, but even the risk of death, since often things which some people have done to their credit may furnish a bad example for others. Practices which turned out well for some, for others may be extremely dangerous. I can give you an example: it would be wrong for any one to try to imitate the virtue and conduct of the one whom Abba John used to describe to us for our admiration, though not for our imitation. A man came to visit that elder, wearing secular dress, and bringing him the first fruits of his harvest, and found someone with him in the clutches of a ferocious demon. The demon despised the commands and orders of Abba John, and admitted that it would never leave the body it was besieging at his command, but was so terrified at the arrival of the newcomer that it departed as soon as he named the Name with reverence. Abba John was no little impressed at this manifest miracle, and was all the more surprised given that the man was in secular dress, so he began to ask him about his life and manner of conduct. The other said he was a layman, and lawfully married to his wife. John, still pondering his great virtue and grace, asked in more detail about his way of life. He replied that he was a peasant, and earned his living every day with his hands, and that he could think of no good he had ever done, except that he never set out for his work in the fields of a morning, nor returned home in the evening, without going into church to give thanks to God for granting him his daily sustenance. Nor had he ever made use of his own produce, without first offering God the first-fruits and tithes. He had never led his cattle through another man's crops without first muzzling them, lest his neighbour suffer any loss through his carelessness. Abba John still did not consider these practices enough to deserve such an outstanding gift of grace as he had witnessed, so he asked in greater detail what it might be that had conferred on him such favour; the other, forced to respect this interrogation, answered that although he had wished to be professed as a monk, he had taken a wife under compulsion from his parents, and so had accepted her eleven years before, but he had preserved her virginity so that she lived with him as a sister, without anyone else knowing. When old Abba John heard this, he was so impressed that he spoke out in front of him, 'It is not surprising that a demon who despises me is unable to endure the presence of this man, since he was unable to daunt his ardour when he was young, and even now dares not assail his chastity!' But having said that, Abba John while expressing his admiration, also warned his monks that none of them should attempt to do the like, for he knew that often things which some people can do are very perilous to others who try to imitate them, and that what the Lord grants to a few as a special favour cannot become the normal custom for all.

VIII. "We should return to the subject we had begun, namely spiritual science. We have already seen that practical wisdom is applied to many professions and studies. Theoretical wisdom, on the other hand, is divided only into two, which are the interpretation of the past, and spiritual understanding. Thus Solomon, after recounting the many graces of the Church, adds, 'all her domestics are clothed with double garments' (Prov. 31: 21). The subdivisions of spiritual understanding are the *tropological*, the *allegorical* and the *anagogical*; of which Proverbs says, 'Behold, thou shalt describe those things to thee three manner of ways, in the broadness of thy heart' (Prov. 22:20, LXX).

The history of matters long past, and of visible things, can be taken literally, as we read in St Paul: 'For it is written that Abraham had two sons: the one by a bondwoman and the other by a free woman. But he who was of the bondwoman was born according to the flesh; but he of the free woman was by promise.' The words that follow give us an allegorical interpretation, since things which actually happened are described as prefiguring what was to happen on a different occasion. 'For these are the two testaments. The one from mount Sinai, engendering unto bondage, which is Agar. For Sinai is a mountain in Arabia, which hath affinity to that Jerusalem which now is, and is in bondage with her children.' Then the Apostle proceeds to speak anagogically, ascending from spiritual mysteries to certain higher and more sublime issues: 'But that Jerusalem which is above is free; which is our mother. For it is written: Rejoice thou barren, that bearest not; break forth and cry, thou that travailest not; for many are the children of the desolate, more than of her that hath a husband' (Gal. 4:22–7). The tropological explanation is the moral one, applied to improving our life and giving us practical instruction, as if we were to interpret the two covenants as the practical and theoretical wisdom, or perhaps if we took Jerusalem or Sion to mean the human soul, as in 'Praise the Lord, O Jerusalem: praise thy God O Sion' (Psalm 147:12). Thus if we wanted to combine the four methods in one example, the single city of Jerusalem can have four meanings: literally the city of the Jews; allegorically the Church of Christ; anagogically the heavenly City of God which is the mother of us all; tropologically the human soul, which is often rebuked or encouraged by the Lord under this name, Jerusalem.

St Paul says this about the four ways of interpretation: 'But now, brethren, if I come to you speaking with tongues, what shall I profit you, unless I speak to you either in revelation or in knowledge or in prophecy or in doctrine?' (I Cor. 14:6). 'Revelation' applies to allegory, in which a historical narrative is explained with a spiritual meaning, for example we might try to interpret the passage, 'Our fathers were all under the cloud; . . . and all in Moses were baptised, in the cloud and in the sea, and did all eat the same spiritual food, . . . and drank of the spiritual rock that followed them; and the rock was Christ' (I Cor. 10:1–4). Here the explanation contains the allegorical sense of prefiguring the Body and Blood of Christ which we receive daily. Then 'knowledge', which St Paul mentions next, is the tropological interpretation, by which we consider all things carefully with reference to our practical conduct, whether they be useful and honourable or no. Thus we are commanded to judge for ourselves, whether 'it become a woman to pray unto God uncovered' (I Cor. 11:13) for the passage contains a moral meaning, as we have seen. 'Prophecy', which the Apostle puts in third place, means the anagogical, by which our text is applied to the invisible world to come. For example: 'And we will not have you ignorant, brethren, concerning them that are asleep, that you be not sorrowful, even as others who have no hope. For if we believe that Jesus died and rose again; even so them who have slept through Jesus, will God bring with him. For this we say unto you in the word of the Lord, that we who are alive, who remain unto the coming of the Lord, shall not prevent them who have slept. For the Lord himself shall come down from heaven with commandment and with the voice of an archangel and with the trumpet of God; and the dead who are in Christ shall rise first' (I Thess. 4:12–15). This type of encouragement is based on the method of anagogy. Then 'doctrine' must mean the simple exposition of the narrative, with nothing concealed from the understanding, but taken literally, as for example: 'For I delivered unto you first of all, which I also received: how that Christ died for our sins, according to the scriptures; and that he was buried; and that he rose again the third day . . . and that he was seen by Cephas' (I Cor. 15:3–5). Also, 'God sent his Son, made of a woman, made under the law, that he might redeem them who were under the law' (Gal. 4:4–5) and 'Hear, O Israel: the Lord our God is one Lord' (Deut. 6:4).

IX. "Now if you want to attain to the light of spiritual wisdom, not for the sake of boasting about it, but to acquire the grace of

XIV. On Spiritual Science

improvement, you should first be fired with desire for that bliss of which it is said, 'Blessed are the clean of heart; for they shall see God' (Matt. 5:8). Then you can aspire to what the angel said to Daniel, 'But they that are learned shall shine as the brightness of the firmament: and they that instruct many to justice, as stars for all eternity' (Dan. 12:3). Another prophet also said, 'Light for yourselves the light of wisdom, while there is yet time' (Hosea 10:12, LXX). I perceive that you already love reading: hold onto that, and make every effort to grasp practical wisdom, that is to say ethical knowledge, as soon and as fully as you can. Without that it is impossible to grasp theoretical wisdom, as I have said. Only those who have been made perfect by their own actions, rather than the teaching of others, can achieve that, as a reward after such labour and such effort. It is not by meditating on the law that they acquire wisdom, but by working effectively, so that they may sing with the Psalmist, 'By thy commandments I have had understanding' (Psalm 118/119:104). When all passions have been steamed away, they may say truly, 'I will sing, and I will understand in the unspotted way' (Psalm 100/101:1–2). He who adheres to the unspotted way, and walks in purity of heart, can understand the words he sings. For this reason, if you would pitch a holy tent for spiritual wisdom in your hearts, purge yourselves from every spot of sin, cut yourselves off from the cares of this world. The soul which is entangled in worldly matters, even in the slightest, can never attain the gift of wisdom, can never become the mother of spiritual perception, nor persevere faithfully in sacred reading.

First of all you should take care (especially you, John Cassian, since I am relying on you in particular to remember this, because you are still young enough to do so) not to let your reading and study, or the efforts you have made so eagerly, come to nothing through vain glory; keep a strict silence about it! This indeed is the first step in practical wisdom ['all the labour of man is for his mouth' (Qo. 6:7)], that you should receive all the instruction of your elders and their opinions with an open heart but a closed mouth. Store it up carefully in your heart, and be more concerned to practice it than to preach it. Through talking arise perilous overconfidence and vanity; through silent practice ripen the fruits of spiritual wisdom. Do not presume to contribute to the discussions of the elders, except to ask questions when ignorance might be dangerous or it is really necessary to know. There are some who are so puffed up by vanity that they pretend to ask questions to which they know the answer perfectly well, in the hope of showing off their learning. No one is worthy to receive the gift of wisdom if he applies himself to reading merely in the hope of acquiring a reputation among men. Someone who gave in to such a temptation would inevitably become entangled in other vices, especially pride. He would thus be laid low in the practical study of ethics, and quite unable to attain the spiritual wisdom which proceeds from it. Be therefore ever 'swift to hear, but slow to speak' (James 1:19), lest there chance to you what Solomon observes, 'hast thou seen a man hasty to speak? Know that a fool has more hope than he' (Prov. 29:20, LXX). Do not take it on yourself to teach anyone something you have not performed yourself. Our Lord himself taught us to preserve that order of procedure, for it is said about him, 'the things which Jesus began to do and to teach' (Acts 1:1). Beware not to leap into teaching before practising, and finding yourself among those of whom Our Lord speaks in the Gospel, saying to his disciples, 'All things therefore whatsoever they shall say to you, observe and do; but according to their works do ye not. For they say, and do not. For they bind heavy and insupportable burdens and lay them on men's shoulders; but with a finger of their own they will not move them' (Matt. 23:3–4). For if he 'that shall break one of these least commandments and shall so teach men shall be called the least in the kingdom of heaven' (Matt. 5:19), anyone who presumes to teach while neglecting many greater matters is destined to be not even the least in the kingdom of heaven, but the greatest in the pains of hell. Be careful, therefore, not to be misled by the example of those who have acquired a certain fluency in discourse and debate, able to expound whatever they want elegantly and at length, and are therefore credited with spiritual wisdom by those who are incapable of discerning its true nature and force.

XIV. On Spiritual Science

It is one thing to have a glib tongue and dazzling eloquence, quite another to enter into the veins and the marrow of the teaching of heaven. To contemplate the hidden depths of the mysteries with a pure heart is something which human learning can never obtain, neither can worldly wisdom, but only purity of heart in the light of the Holy Spirit.

X. "If you wish to arrive at true knowledge of Scripture, you should take pains to begin by acquiring steadfast humility of heart, which will lead you not to the knowledge that puffs up, but to that which enlightens, in the perfection of charity. It is impossible for the gift of spiritual science to come to an unclean mind. Be very wary, then, lest your study and reading give birth not to the light of wisdom, or the perpetual glory which is promised to the enlightened, but rather to the causes of perdition, vanity and arrogance. Then you should strive in every way to drive away all earthly worries and thoughts, applying yourself earnestly – no, devotedly – to sacred reading, until by constant meditation your mind is changed and moulded into the likeness of that meditation. Make yourself an Ark of the Covenant, containing the two tablets of stone, that is lasting adherence to the twofold covenant, and the golden urn, which is a pure and sincere memory which will preserve for ever the manna hidden within it, which is spiritual discernment and the lasting heavenly sweetness of the bread of angels; there too is the rod of Aaron, which is the triumphant banner of our true high priest Jesus Christ, blooming ever with the flowers of immortal memory. This is the rod which was cut from the stem of Jesse, and after such a death revived more vigorous yet. All this is protected by the two Cherubim, who are the fullness of historical and spiritual science. For the name 'Cherubim' is interpreted as 'multitude of knowledge', which carefully guards the mercy seat of God, that is your mental repose, and shelters it from all attacks of spiritual evil. In this way your mind will be borne up not only into the ark of the sacred Covenant, but also into the priestly kingdom. Absorbed into spiritual wisdom in an unbreakable longing for purity, it will fulfil the commandment about the priest which Moses gave, 'neither shall he go out of the holy places, lest he defile the sanctuary of the Lord' (Lev. 21:12). The sanctuary, that is, of his own heart in which he has promised the Lord shall ever dwell, saying, 'I will dwell in them and walk among them' (II Cor. 6:16). We must therefore be diligent in committing Holy Scripture to memory, and recalling it ceaselessly. By this constant meditation two benefits are gained. The first is that while we are reading, and preparing our reading, the mind is occupied so that no evil thoughts can ensnare it; the second is that while we are memorising and frequently repeating something we are not able to understand it at the time, but we can see it much more clearly later on, especially if we ponder it during our nightly meditation, to keep us from all evil actions and fantasies. In this way while we are at rest and all but asleep, we come to understand the most obscure passages, which while awake we would hardly begin to comprehend.

XI. "Through this practice our mental alertness grows, and even the appearance of Scripture begins to seem new. As we progress, so does the attraction of this holy study. In proportion to each one's intelligence, Scripture appears different: to the worldly it appears to treat of worldly things, but to the spiritual of divine. For these latter, what formerly appeared to be wrapped in clouds of obscurity is a subtlety beyond their fathoming, a splendour beyond endurance. As an example to make what we have been trying to say clearer, one Old Testament text will suffice; through this we can see how all the commandments of God can be applied to every sort of person, according to the stature of each. It is written in the law, 'Thou shalt not commit fornication' (Exod. 20:14). For worldly men, still enslaved by unclean passions, this should be observed according to its literal sense, and this will save them. Those who have already lost the desire for such prurient impurity must interpret it spiritually, and abstain from all idolatrous worship, all pagan superstition and fortune-telling, all reckoning of omens and lucky days or seasons, and they should certainly be free from any use of words or names which might betray the integrity of our

XIV. On Spiritual Science

faith. This is the fornication with which Jerusalem was defiled, who 'hath gone of herself upon every high mountain and under every green tree and hath played the harlot there' (Jer. 3:6). Again the Lord rebukes her through the prophet: 'Let now the astrologers stand and save thee, they that gazed at the stars and counted the months, that from them they might tell the things that shall come to thee' (Isaiah 47:13). This is the fornication of which the Lord accuses them elsewhere: 'the spirit of fornication hath deceived them and they have committed fornication against their God' (Hosea 4:12).

Anyone who is free from these two types of fornication, has a third to shun, which is that contained in the Old Law, and the traditions of the Jews. Of these St Paul writes, 'you observe days and months and times, and years' (Gal. 4:10) and again, 'touch not; taste not; handle not' (Col. 2:21). This surely refers to the traditions attached to the law, and anyone who falls into them has been unfaithful to Christ, not deserving of the apostle's words, 'I have espoused you to one husband, that I may present you as a chaste virgin to Christ.' No, to him will be applied the words which St Paul writes next: 'but I fear lest, as the serpent seduced Eve by his subtlety, so your minds should be corrupted and fall from the simplicity that is in Christ' (II Cor. 11:2, 3). If you escape the uncleanness of that sort of fornication, there remains yet a fourth, which is committed by adulterous heretical doctrine. Of this the holy Apostle says, 'I know that after my departure ravening wolves will enter in among you, not sparing the flock. And of your own selves shall arise men speaking perverse things, to draw away disciples after them' (Acts 20:29–30). He who is capable of resisting that, should beware lest he fall into the sin of fornication in a sense more subtle yet, which consists in wandering thoughts. All thoughts that lead us away from God, idle ones as well as immoral, should by the perfect man be considered as vile as fornication."

XII. GERMANUS: "I am struck with inner compunction at these words, and deeply distressed when I consider that all you have told us so fluently has only caused me a greater depression than I can bear. Apart from those things which commonly restrict the mind, and I am sure also trouble the weak, a peculiar impediment to salvation has arisen out of the knowledge of literature which I seem to have irremediably acquired. All through my long studies, my tutors' insistence influenced me to the extent that my mind is as it were infected with poetry; even during times of prayer I keep remembering the trivial stories and warlike histories which were instilled in me from my earliest childhood schooling. The memory of some indelicate poem arises while I am singing psalms, or praying for pardon for my sins, or I seem to see struggling heroes before my eyes. My imagination then dwells on these fantasies, which prevent my thoughts from concentrating on the things of heaven, and I cannot drive them out despite constant prayer."

XIII. NESTOR: "This matter, which makes you despair of ever being purified, can be easily and quickly resolved, if you simply apply to the reading and meditation of Holy Scripture the same earnest diligence which you tell us you put into those secular studies. Your mind is bound to be taken up with those poems until it finds something else to occupy it of equal interest and complexity. Thus instead of those futile worldly matters, you can think of spiritual and divine ones. Once you have really conceived such a study, and given it nourishment, it can drive out the previous interest, and stifle it altogether. It is impossible for the human mind to be totally vacant, without any thoughts; so as long as it has no spiritual study to occupy it, it is bound to concern itself with its former learning. Until the mind has something to return to and ponder in its ceaseless motion, it will have to fall back into its childhood training, and will ever be revolving what it has so long become accustomed to think about. Now to strengthen your spiritual science on a lasting base, it is not enough merely to practice it for a moment, like those who know it through what others say rather than from experience, noticing it like a scent on the wind, so to speak. No – it must be rooted within your bowels, examined and tested in detail; you should guard it with all diligence, so that even if you hear mentioned in conversation some point you know well, you should not listen to it carelessly and casually because you know it already, but you should commend it to your heart with as much concern as it deserves, for the message of salvation must ceaselessly be received into our ears, and constantly poured from our lips. No matter how often we hear sacred matters discussed, our minds will never be sated and conceive distaste for them, if they thirst for true wisdom. We can listen to them every day, as if to news we had been longing for, and the more often we hear it the more eagerly we listen to it and repeat it. By this repetition our perception of this wisdom is strengthened, and we can go over it again and again without fatigue. It is a clear proof of a tepid and arrogant soul to receive the remedy of saving doctrine with boredom or carelessness, however much effort it takes to learn it. 'For the soul that is full shall tread upon the honeycomb: and a soul that is hungry shall take even bitter for sweet' (Prov. 27:7, LXX). Now if this teaching has been diligently learned, committed carefully to the memory, and sealed in silence, it can be decanted later on like a vintage wine which gladdens the heart of man, mature in reason, after aging in patience, poured from the bottle which is your heart with a fine bouquet. Like an ever-flowing fountain it will flow from the springs of experience down the channels of virtue, and gush ceaselessly from the deeps of your heart. There will come to pass in you what is said in Proverbs to one who had performed this: 'Drink water out of thy own cistern, and the stream of thy own wells. Let the waters of thy fountain overflow, and let thy waters flow in thy streets' (Prov. 5:15–16, LXX). As the prophet Isaiah said, 'thou shalt be like a watered garden and like a fountain of water whose waters shall not fail. And the places which have been desolate for ages shall be built in thee. Thou shalt raise up the foundations of generation and generation: and thou shalt be called the repairer of the fences, turning the paths into rest' (Isaiah 58:11–12). You will reap that blessing which the same prophet proclaims, 'And the Lord ... will not cause thy teacher to flee away from thee any more; and thy eyes shall see thy teacher. And thy ears shall hear the word of one admonishing thee behind thy back: This is the way; walk ye in it: and go not aside neither to the right hand, nor to the left' (Isaiah 30: 20–1). It will thus happen that not only your deliberate mental reflections, but even your wandering thoughts and distractions become a holy and ceaseless meditation on the teaching of God.

XIV. "As I have already told you, no one can either understand or teach this wisdom without experience of it. How could someone incapable of absorbing it be able to teach? If any such were to be so presumptuous as to try to teach, his words would reach no further than the ears of his audience; vain and ineffective, they would be unable to pierce to the heart, for he would be given away by his failure to perform, and his futile vanity. He would be speaking, not from the treasury of a good conscience, but from the empty boasting of his arrogance. An impure soul cannot possibly acquire spiritual science, no matter how hard it tries to study it. No one pours a rare ointment, a refined honey, a precious liqueur, into a foul and corroded vessel. A jar which has contained corrupted filth will more likely contaminate even the finest myrrh than take up any savour or value from it. Clean things are far more readily corrupted than corrupt things made clean. In the same way unless it is purged from all the foul contagion of vice, the vessel which is our heart will be unfit to receive the blessing of that ointment the Prophet mentions; 'Like the precious ointment on the head, that ran down upon the beard, the beard of Aaron, which ran down to the skirt of his garment' (Psalm 132/133: 2). Nor can it preserve untainted that spiritual science, that eloquence of the Scriptures, which are 'sweeter than honey and the honeycomb' (Psalm 18/19: 11). 'For what participation hath justice with injustice? Or what fellowship hath light with darkness? And what concord hath Christ with Belial?'" (II Cor. 6: 14–15).

XV. GERMANUS: "This definition does not seem to us to be glowing with truth at all, not even probable! Since all those who have never received the faith of Christ, and those who corrupt it

XIV. On Spiritual Science

with wicked false teachings, are clearly of unclean heart, how can it be that there are many Jews and heretics (not to mention Catholics caught up in various vices) who are well acquainted with the Scriptures, and boast of their great knowledge of spirituality. There are on the other hand a great many saints with hearts cleansed from every stain of sin, who are content with pure and simple faith, and are ignorant of the more profound secrets of mysticism. So how can you maintain this opinion which states that only those who are pure of heart can have spiritual science?"

XVI. NESTOR: "Unless you carefully examine every word of a suggested opinion, you cannot properly rule on the value of its conclusion. We have already said that men of this sort have nothing but an ability to argue with fine eloquence, but are quite unable to enter the veins of Scripture and the secrets of spiritual wisdom. True wisdom is not possessed by any except the true worshippers of God, and is not possessed by that people to whom it was said, 'Hear, O foolish people, and without understanding: who have eyes and see not, and ears and hear not' (Jer. 5:21). Likewise, 'Because thou hast rejected knowledge, I will reject thee, that thou shalt not do the office of priesthood to me' (Hosea 4:6). But since, in Christ 'are hid all the treasures of wisdom and knowledge' (Col. 2:3), how could one who despised Christ, or having once found him then blasphemed him with sacrilegious words, or one who had defiled the Catholic faith with unclean actions – how can we believe such persons have acquired true wisdom? 'For the Spirit of God will flee from the deceitful, and will not dwell in a body subject to sins' (Wisd. 1:5, 4).

There is no other way to reach spiritual wisdom except the one which is so aptly described by one of the Prophets: 'Sow for yourselves in justice, and reap the hope of life; light for yourselves the lamp of wisdom' (Hosea 10:12, LXX). We have to begin by sowing in justice, that is to say cultivating active perfection by works of justice. Then we must reap the hope of life, which is gathering the fruit of spiritual virtues, by driving out fleshly vice. In this way we can light for ourselves a lamp of wisdom. The Psalmist too perceived that we should follow that order, saying, 'Blessed are the undefiled in the way: who walk in the law of the Lord. Blessed are they that search his testimonies' (Psalm 118/119:1–2). Now he does not begin by saying 'blessed are they that search his testimonies', and add afterwards, 'blessed are the undefiled in the way': this clearly shows us that no one can properly proceed to search the testimonies of God, had he not already entered on the way of Christ, unstained in his practical way of life.

The ones you were talking about do not possess this wisdom, which the unclean cannot have, but a pseudo-wisdom, the falsely called knowledge of which St Paul says, 'O Timothy, keep that which is committed to thy trust, avoiding the profane novelties of words and oppositions of knowledge falsely so called' (I Tim. 6:20). (In Greek it runs, 'turning aside from unholy empty words, and the resistance of pseudo-wisdom.') Those therefore who seem to acquire a form of wisdom, and those who apply themselves diligently to teaching the sacred volumes and memorising the Scriptures, but do not abandon their earthly vices, are aptly described in Proverbs: 'Like a golden earring in the nostrils of a pig, such is beauty for a woman of evil life' (Prov. 11:22, LXX). What would be the point of someone pursuing the decorative aspect of heavenly eloquence, and the precious appearance of Scripture, if by clinging to vile works and emotions, he were to trample it underfoot like filthy mud, or defile it with the empty wallowings of his lusts? What is beautiful in the hands of those who use it well, will never serve to adorn those others, but will instead deface them with worse stains. 'Praise is not seemly in the mouth of a sinner' (Sir. 15:9), and the Psalmist comments, 'Why dost thou declare my justices, and take my covenant in thy mouth?' (Psalm 49/50:16). Such souls there are, which never possess the fear of the Lord with any constancy, and of whom it is said, 'the fear of the Lord is discipline and wisdom' (Prov. 15:33, LXX); they attempt to grasp the sense of Scripture by diligent study, but the Proverbs says enough about them: 'What does it avail a fool to have riches, seeing the senseless cannot buy wisdom?' (Prov. 17:16). True spiritual wisdom is so far removed from that worldly wisdom

XIV. On Spiritual Science

which is defiled by carnal vice, that we know to our amazement of several who are tongue-tied and virtually illiterate but who do possess it. You can prove this by the example of the apostles, and many other saints, who took no pleasure in the empty enjoyment of the leaves of books, but were weighty with the true fruits of spiritual science. Of these we read in the Acts of the Apostles, 'seeing the constancy of Peter and of John, understanding that they were illiterate and ignorant men, they wondered' (Acts 4:13).

Therefore, if you are concerned to attain that ineffable fragrance of wisdom, before you do anything else, strive to obtain pure chastity from the Lord. No one who is still dominated by carnal emotions, especially the vice of fornication, can possess spiritual wisdom. 'In the prudent heart resteth wisdom: and he that fears the Lord shall find wisdom with judgment' (Prov. 14:33, Sir. 32:20). St Paul also teaches us the order which we have described for finding spiritual wisdom, for when he wishes to weave a catalogue of all his virtues, as well as their proper order, to expound which one follows which, and which generates which, he eventually says: 'in watchings, in fastings, in chastity, in knowledge, in long-suffering, in sweetness, in the Holy Ghost, in charity unfeigned' (II Cor. 6:5–6). By listing these virtues he obviously wants to encourage us to progress from watching and fasting to chastity, from chastity to knowledge, from knowledge to long-suffering, from long-suffering to sweetness, from sweetness to the Holy Ghost, from the Holy Ghost to the prize of unfeigned charity. If you were to use this practice and follow this order to arrive at spiritual wisdom, you will surely have what we spoke of, teaching that is neither sterile nor inert, but lively and fruitful, the seed of the saving Word, which when you have once commended it to the ears of your audience, will be watered by the ample dew of the Holy Spirit, and as the prophet promised us, 'and rain shall be given to thy seed, wheresoever thou shalt sow in the land: and the bread of the corn of the land shall be most plentiful and fat' (Isaiah 30:23).

XVII. "Once you have learnt something, not so much through reading as by hard won experience, and you are old enough and mature enough to teach, you should be careful not to be swept away by love of reputation to tell it at random to men of unclean life. Otherwise you would incur the rebuke of Solomon the wise: 'Seek not after the wicked in the house of the just, neither be led astray by the fullness of the belly. Delicacies are not seemly for a fool; nor is there work for wisdom where sense is lacking' (Prov. 24:15; 19:10, 18:2, LXX). No, it is more likely to lead to foolishness, for 'a bad slave will not be corrected by words: because he understandeth what thou sayest, and will not answer' (Prov. 29:19, LXX) and 'speak not in the ears of fools: because they will despise the instruction of thy speech' (Prov. 23:9, LXX). Also, 'Give not that which is holy to dogs. Neither cast ye your pearls before swine; lest perhaps they trample them under their feet; and turning on you, they tear you' (Matt. 7:6). You should conceal the mysteries of spiritual understanding from men of this sort, and sing in truth, 'Thy words have I hidden in my heart: that I may not sin against thee' (Psalm 118/119:11). But perhaps you will ask to whom you should dispense the mysteries of the divine Scriptures: let the wise Solomon instruct you, 'Give strong drink to them that are sad: and wine to them that are grieved in mind: let them drink and forget their want, and remember their sorrow no more' (Prov. 31:6–7). That is, give the joy of spiritual wisdom to those who have repented their former actions and are therefore saddened and depressed; it is like the 'wine that may cheer the heart of man' (Psalm 103/104:15): pour it out generously, revive them with the fullness of the word of salvation, lest they be swamped by their sorrow and despair of life, 'lest perhaps such a one be swallowed up with overmuch sorrow' (II Cor. 2:7). Of those on the contrary who are set in their tepid negligence, with no heartfelt grief to stir them, it is said, 'he that loveth good cheer shall be in want' (Prov. 21:17, LXX). Take great care, therefore, to avoid being so deceived by vain-glory that you are unable to share in the praise which the prophet utters for him 'that hath not put out his money to usury' (Psalm 14/15:5). Anyone who dispenses the word of God for the sake of human respect, that word of which it is said, 'the words of the Lord are pure words: as silver tried by the fire, purged from the

XIV. On Spiritual Science

earth, refined seven times' (Psalm 11/12: 7), is putting his money out to usury, and far from gaining praise for this, will deserve to be punished. He has squandered his master's money, for the sake of temporal gain, rather than that the Lord might return and 'at his coming should have received his own with usury' (Matt. 25: 27).

XVIII. "There are two reasons why spiritual learning can be fruitless. Either the one who teaches is recommending what he has not experienced himself, and is trying to instruct his pupil with nothing but empty words, or a listener who is vicious and depraved is incapable in his stubborn heart of receiving the saving doctrine taught him by a holy man. Of such, the Prophet says, 'The heart of this people is blinded, their ears are heavy to hear, they have shut their eyes: lest they see with their eyes and hear with their ears and understand with their heart and be converted, and I heal them' (Isaiah 6: 10, LXX).

XIX. "It often happens in the bountiful generosity of our God, 'who will have all men to be saved and to come to the knowledge of the truth' (I Tim. 2: 4), that one who has failed to show himself worthy to preach the gospel through an irreproachable way of life, may still acquire the grace of spiritual wisdom for the sake of the salvation of many. That reminds me that I ought to explain to you in another conversation how it is that the Lord also grants the gift of healing for the driving out of demons, but let us keep that until the evening when we have finished our repast. It is easier for the heart to take in what is taught to it in stages, and without excessive fatigue of body."

✣ THE FIFTEENTH COLLATION ✣
BEING THE SECOND OF ABBA NESTOR

On the Divine Gifts

    I. Nestor explains how miracles may be divided into three different types.
    II. What one should admire in holy men.
    III. How Abba Macarius raised the dead.
    IV. Of the miracle which Abba Abraham worked on a woman's breasts.
    V. Of the healing of a lame man, which the same saint effected.
    VI. That a man's merits cannot be assessed by the miracles he works.
    VII. That the virtue of God's gifts consists not in working miracles but in humility.
    VIII. That it is a greater miracle to expel one's own vices than other men's devils.
    IX. How far integrity of life excels the working of miracles.
    X. The story of how to test perfect chastity.

I. After our evening prayers, we were eager for the discourse Nestor had promised us, and sat down on our papyrus rolls as usual. We remained in silence for a time, out of respect for the old man, but he overcame our shy reluctance to speak with these words:

  "The course of our previous discussion leads us naturally to talk about spiritual gifts, which the elders tell us can be divided into three types. The first occasion for the gift of healing is when the grace of miracles is granted to chosen saintly men, for the sake of their holiness. We all know how the Apostles and many other saints displayed signs and wonders through the Lord's authority, for he said to them, 'Heal the sick, raise the dead, cleanse the lepers, cast out devils. Freely have you received; freely give' (Matt. 10:8).

The second is when the power to cure proceeds even from unworthy sinners, either for the sake of building up the church, or because of the faith of those who had brought their sick along, or of the ones who hoped to be cured themselves. Our Saviour says of these, in the Gospel, 'Many will say to me in that day: Lord, Lord, have not we prophesied in thy name and cast out devils in thy name and done many miracles in thy name? And then will I profess unto them: I never knew you; depart from me, you that work iniquity' (Matt. 7:22–3). On the other hand, if faith be lacking to the sick or their carers, he does not grant the exercise of the power to cure even by those who have been granted the gift of healing. The evangelist Luke tells us that: 'And Jesus could not do any miracles there ... because of their unbelief' (Mark 6:5–6). And Our Lord also says, 'there were many lepers in Israel in the time of Eliseus the prophet; and none of them was cleansed but Naaman the Syrian' (Luke 4:27).

The third type of healing is when it is done by the connivance of demons, in order that a man who is bound by obvious sins may be believed to be a holy servant of God. People may be so impressed by his miracles, that they can be persuaded to imitate his vices as well. Thus the door is opened to scepticism, and real holiness may be brought into disrepute, and moreover the man who imagines he possesses the gift of healing can be so puffed up with conceit that he falls grievously. So it can happen that the demons call on the names of men whom they know are without any merits of holiness, or any spiritual fruit; they pretend to be scorched by their virtue, and to be driven out of the bodies of the possessed. Of this, Deuteronomy speaks: 'If there rise in the midst of thee a prophet or one that sayeth he hath dreamed a dream, and he foretell a sign and a wonder: And that come to pass which he spoke, and he say to thee: Let us go and follow strange gods,

XV. On the Divine Gifts

which thou knowest not, and let us serve them: Thou shalt not hear the words of that prophet or dreamer. For the Lord your God trieth you, that it may appear whether you love him with all your heart, and with all your soul, or not' (Deut. 13:1–3). In the Gospel also, 'For there shall arise false Christs and false prophets and shall shew great signs and wonders, insomuch as to deceive (if possible) even the elect' (Matt. 24:24).

II. "For this reason we should never be so simple as to admire those who affect to work miracles by their own virtues; no, we must enquire whether they have attained perfection, their vices eliminated, their lives amended. That state can only be granted by God's dispensation, in response to a man's own devotion, not because of the faith of another or any reason besides. That is the practical wisdom which St Paul calls by the name of charity; charity which the apostle tells us to prefer to all the tongues of men and angels, to the fullness of faith which even moves mountains, to all wisdom and prophecy and the exercise of any power, even to the final glory of martyrdom (cf. I Cor. 13). For when he has named all the different types of gift, and said, 'To one indeed, by the Spirit, is given the word of wisdom; and to another, the word of knowledge . . .; to another, faith . . .; to another, the grace of healing . . .; to another the working of miracles' (I Cor. 12:8–10), and so on, see how succinctly he speaks of charity and how it is preferable to all the gifts: 'And I show unto yet a more excellent way' (I Cor. 12:31). See how the height of perfection and bliss does not consist in working miracles, but in pure charity. Rightly indeed, for all those other things will come to naught and pass away, whereas charity endures for ever. That is why we never see our Fathers concerned about the working of miracles, and they are never willing to perform them, despite the grace of the Holy Spirit which they possessed, except when they are compelled by some extreme necessity.

III. "An example is Abba Macarius, who was the first to find a home in the desert of Scete: he is recorded to have raised the dead. There was a heretic, a follower of the errors of Eunomius, who was trying to subvert the true Catholic faith with his subtle arguments, and had seduced a large number of people. Some Catholics were deeply concerned by the damage this heresy was causing, and asked the Blessed Macarius to come and save the ignorant people of all Egypt from being wrecked by this false belief. The heretic attacked him with his syllogisms, and attempted to entangle him in his Aristotelian brambles, but Blessed Macarius brought his long speeches to an end with a brief Apostolic phrase, saying, 'The kingdom of God is not in speech but in power' (I Cor. 4:20). Let us go to the cemetery and call on the name of the Lord over the first grave we find. Then we shall prove our faith by our works, as the Scripture says (cf. James 2:14), and declare the doctrine of the true faith by that evidence. We can demonstrate what is obviously true through the power of a miracle rather than by fruitless argument, as he who cannot be deceived shall indicate to us.' The heretic was much embarrassed at these words, in front of the crowd which surrounded them, but pretended for the moment to agree to the proposition, promising to be present on the following day. Yet when that day came, and everyone came eagerly to the appointed place in expectation of seeing this thing happen, he was so panic-stricken in the consciousness of his own lack of faith that he immediately fled from Egypt altogether. The Blessed Macarius waited for him, with the whole crowd, until noon, until he realised that his conscience had forced him to depart, and so he gathered the people who had been deceived by him and went to the cemetery as arranged.

Now there exists a peculiar custom in Egypt, because of the flooding of the Nile. For a large portion of the year the whole of the country is covered with its waters, turning into something like a wide lake, and it is impossible to cross the country except in punts. As a result they deposit the bodies of the dead in raised buildings, sealing them in with scented clay, for the soil there is so continually saturated that it is impossible to bury bodies in it; if they tried to do so the rushing waters would force the bodies to the surface again.

XV. On the Divine Gifts

Blessed Macarius approached one of the most ancient bodies and spoke to it: 'O man, if that heretic, that son of perdition, had come with me, and I had called on the name of Christ my God in his presence, would you have risen again, in front of all these people who have been nearly perverted by his deceits? Tell me!' The dead man got up, and expressed his agreement. Abba Macarius asked him what sort of man he had been while alive, and in what period of history he had lived, and whether he knew the name of Christ at that time. He replied that he had lived under the earliest Pharaohs, and had never heard the name of Christ in his own time. Abba Macarius replied to him, 'Sleep again in peace, with the others of your rank, till Christ raise you again at the end of time.'

Now the power and grace which was in him might well have remained hidden always, had not the needs of the whole province at risk compelled him to work that miracle, in his great devotion to Christ and his unfeigned love. The fact that he did so stems not from any thirst for fame, but the love of Christ and the benefit of the whole people. Something similar, as we hear in the Book of Kings, was also done by the holy Elijah, when he called down fire from heaven on the offerings laid on his altar, in order to liberate the whole people, whose faith was at risk from the blandishments of the false prophets.

IV. "I should also recall to you Abba Abraham, who was known as the *Haplous*, meaning the simple one, because of his simplicity and innocence. He had come out of the desert during Eastertide to help with the harvest in Egypt, and was stopped by a woman, who begged of him with tears, showing him her baby who was emaciated and nearly dead because she had no milk. He gave her a cup of water to drink, making the sign of the cross over it, and as soon as she drank it her breasts which had been dried up swelled with a marvellous abundance of milk.

V. "The same saint came to a village where he was surrounded by a mocking crowd, who jeeringly showed him a man whose knee was so distorted that he had been unable to walk for many years, but had become well used to creeping along with his disability. 'Show us, Abba Abraham,' they said, 'whether you are a servant of God. Give this man back his former health, and we will believe there is something in the name of Christ whom you follow.' He did invoke the name of Christ immediately, and bent down to stretch the man's withered foot. As soon as he touched it, the bent and useless knee straightened out, till the man received the ability to walk, which he had virtually forgotten after such a long illness, and so he departed rejoicing.

VI. "Men of this calibre took no credit to themselves for the working of such miracles, since they confessed that they were performed through God's mercy, not their own merits. They quoted the words of the Apostles to deflect men's admiration for their miracles, 'Ye men, our brethren, why wonder ye at this? Or why look you upon us, as if by our strength or power we had made this man to walk?' (Acts 3:12). They did not think it worth commending anyone for the gifts or marvels they had received from God, but rather for the fruits of their own virtues, and for what they had achieved by diligence of thought and careful labour. For as we have already mentioned, men of unclean thoughts and dubious faith have often cast out devils in the name of the Lord, and performed great wonders. The apostles noticed these, and asked, 'Master, we saw a certain man casting out devils in thy name; and we forbade him, because he followeth not with us.' Christ did indeed reply for the time being, 'Forbid him not; for he that is not against you is for you' (Luke 9:49–50), but he told them that at the end of time men will say, 'Lord, Lord, have we not prophesied in thy name and cast out devils in thy name and done many miracles in thy name?' and he would answer them, 'I never knew you; depart from me, you that work iniquity' (Matt. 7:22–3). Even those to whom he does grant the honour of signs and wonders for the sake of their holiness, he warns not to be boastful about it, saying, 'But yet rejoice not in this, that spirits are subject unto you; but rejoice in this, that your names are written in heaven' (Luke 10:20).

XV. On the Divine Gifts

VII. "Christ, the author of all signs and all virtue, when he was calling disciples to learn from him, shows clearly what it is that those who are truly chosen to follow him must learn in particular; 'Come to me, ... and learn of me,' not how to drive out devils by heavenly power, not how to cleanse the lepers, nor how to enlighten the blind or raise the dead – for such things, even if I do work them through some of my servants, do not give human nature the right to claim the praise of God, and my agent who does them can earn no reward where all the credit belongs to God. No, you must 'learn of me, because I am meek and humble of heart' (Matt. 11: 28–9). This it is that everyone can learn, everyone can practice, but the working of signs and powers is not necessary or appropriate for all, and is not granted to all. Humility is therefore the mother of all virtues, the firm foundation of heaven's building, the true gift of our bountiful Saviour. Humility it is which works all the wonders that Christ performed, with no danger of conceit, for those who imitate their humble Lord not in his spectacular miracles, but in the strength of humble patience. He on the other hand who sets out to give orders to unclean spirits, or to confer the gift of health on the unwell, or demonstrate some miraculous sign to the crowds, remains quite alien to Christ however often he may call upon that name during his displays, for in his pride of heart he is not following the path of humility. When Our Lord returned to his Father he left us a sort of last will, saying to his disciples, 'A new commandment I give unto you: that you love one another as I have loved you', and he adds immediately afterwards, 'by this shall all men know that you are my disciples, if you have love one for another' (John 13: 34–5). He does not say it is because you perform similar signs and wonders, but if you have a fitting love for one another, something which only the meek and humble can have. Our predecessors used to say that monks could not be holy, nor free from vain glory, if they proclaimed themselves openly to be exorcists and publicised the grace which they had merited, or rather usurped, in vaunting ostentation – no, all such efforts would be in vain. 'He that trusteth to lies feedeth the winds: and the same runneth after birds that fly away' (Prov. 10:4). And doubtless there will happen what the Proverbs say, 'As clouds and wind, and a rain that followeth, so is the man that boasteth and doth not fulfil his promises' (Prov. 25:14). Therefore, if anyone performs such a thing in front of us, we take notice only of his character of life, not of the marvel of the miracle. We do not enquire whether the devils are subject to him, but whether he possesses the characteristics of charity as St Paul describes them.

VIII. "It is in fact a greater miracle to expel the seeds of vice from our own bodies, than to drive unclean spirits from those of others; a more splendid sign to restrain the first movements of rising anger by the strength of patience than to give orders to the princes of the air; a finer thing to eliminate the gnawing pangs of depression from our own hearts than to purge the sickness of others and soothe their fevered limbs. In every way it is a greater and more heavenly virtue that is displayed when we heal the sickness of our own souls, rather than that of the bodies of others. The healing of the soul is a finer thing to the same degree that the soul exceeds the body. Yet the more excellent and precious it be by nature, the worse and more terrible its fall.

IX. "Our Lord speaks of these cures to his holy apostles, 'rejoice not in this, that spirits are subject unto you' (Luke 10:20). It was not their own strength that had driven out devils, but the power of the Name they had invoked; for that reason they were warned to claim no credit or reward for what had been performed by the power and virtue of God alone, but to be glad only about their inner purity of life and thought, for which their names were fit to be written in heaven.

X. "To give you a demonstration of what I have been saying, both from the evidence of those who have gone before us, and from God's own testimony, I will tell you what the blessed Paphnutius discovered about the value of miracles and the grace of purity,

XV. On the Divine Gifts

and what he learnt from the message of an angel besides, giving you his own description of his own experience. He had been living for many years in a very strict manner, till he imagined that he was quite free from any temptation of the flesh, for he had found himself superior to all the devil's assaults, which he met openly for a long time. But when some holy men came to him, he started to prepare for them a bean soup (of the type they call *athera*) and burnt his hand on the stove as the fire flared up more than usual. He was grieved by this, and began to ponder deeply within himself. 'Why,' he thought, 'am I not at peace with the fire, though I am no longer troubled by the fiercer flames of the devil? When it comes to that dread day of trial, how can I escape hurt as I pass through the unquenchable flame which investigates the merits of each of us, if this brief little external fire does not spare me?'

While he was sadly meditating on these matters he fell suddenly asleep, and an angel of the Lord came to him and asked, 'Why are you so sad, Paphnutius, because this earthly fire has not yet made peace with you? Still in your body there remains the disturbance of fleshly desires, not yet totally purged away. As long as its roots remain within you, they will never allow this temporal fire to be reconciled with you, for you will certainly not find it harmless until it occurs as a sign and proof that you have you have totally eradicated all such irregular motions. Now go and find a beautiful naked virgin. Hold her tight, and if you find that your heart remains tranquil and unmoved, and your bodily desires are at rest, then the touch of this visible fire will be as gentle and harmless as it was for those three boys in Babylon.'

The old man was so struck by this revelation that he did not attempt the risky experiment which heaven had proposed, but examined his conscience, and considered whether his heart were pure, realising that his chastity was not equal to such a test. 'No wonder,' he thought, 'if when the unclean spirits had ceased to trouble me I still felt the fury of that burning fire which I had imagined to be inferior to those savage attacks of the devils. It is a greater virtue, a more sublime grace, to quench the internal lusts of the flesh, than to control the external attacks of evil demons with the sign of the Cross and the power of the Most High, or to drive them out of the bodies of the possessed by invoking the Holy Name.'"

Thus far Abba Nestor spoke to us about the true operation of divine gifts, and by his learned teaching set us on our way as we continued on to the cell of the elder Joseph, which was about six miles further on.

✣ THE SIXTEENTH COLLATION ✣
BEING THE FIRST OF ABBA JOSEPH

On Friendship

    I. The first question which Abba Joseph asked us.
   II. The elder's discourse on unreliable types of friendship.
  III. What makes friendship indissoluble.
  IV. A question, whether we ought to do something useful even if our brother is unwilling.
   V. The reply, that lasting friendship cannot exist except among the perfect.
  VI. The means to preserve friendship unbroken.
 VII. That nothing is to be preferred to charity, nothing ranked lower than anger.
VIII. How dissension arises among spiritual friends.
  IX. That the spiritual causes of discord should be eliminated.
   X. The best way to consider truth.
  XI. How anyone who trusts in his own judgment is bound to be deceived by the devil.
 XII. Why we should never despise our juniors in discussion.
XIII. That charity is not merely an attribute of God, but God himself.
XIV. On the stages of charity.
 XV. On those who increase their own ill temper, or their brother's, by trying to conceal it.
XVI. That if a brother have any grudge against us, our offerings will be rejected by the Lord.

XVII. On those who think we should be more patient with laymen than with monks.
XVIII. On those who pretend to be patient but provoke their brothers to anger by their silence.
XIX. On those who fast out of spite.
XX. On how some pretend to be patient in offering the other cheek to be struck.
XXI. A question, how can those who are obeying Christ's command fail to achieve evangelical perfection?
XXII. The reply, that Christ scrutinises the will, not merely the deed.
XXIII. That the one who submits to the will of another is the one who is strong and healthy.
XXIV. That it is the weak who inflict injury, and cannot sustain it.
XXV. A question, how can the one who does not always tolerate the weak be strong.
XXVI. The answer, that the weak one does not permit himself to be tolerated.
XXVII. How anger should be restrained.
XXVIII. That if a friendship is begun with a contract it cannot be stable.

I. The Blessed Joseph, whose teaching and advice I am about to recount, was one of the three whom I mentioned in the first Collation of this part. He came from a distinguished family and was one of the leading men of his city, a place in Egypt called Thmuis. He was therefore well educated in the Egyptian language as well as the Greek, and so he was able to speak to us, or anyone else ignorant of Egyptian, in his own fluent Greek, with no need for an interpreter such as the others had used. He heard that we were eager to be instructed by him, and began by asking us whether we were brothers by blood. We told him that we had no physical relationship, but were bonded together in a spiritual brotherhood, and had always been close associates, from the very beginning of our monastic life, both in our travels which we had undertaken

XVI. On Friendship

together for the sake of our spiritual training, and when we were students in the monastery. He began his discourse as follows:

II. "There are many types of friendship or association, which link people together in different sorts of affection. Some have been recommended to each other so that they begin by acquaintance and grow into friendship. In others a contract or agreement about mutual benefit provides the occasion for a bond of charity. Others have been brought together by a common business interest, military service, craft or study, which can make even the hardest hearts soften towards each other: thus even those who enjoy being bandits in forest or mountain, rejoicing in bloodshed, are loving and kind to their partners in crime. Then there is another type of friendship, bonded by the instinct of a common nature and ties of blood, so that men naturally prefer their kinsmen, spouses, parents, siblings and children to strangers. We can observe this not only among humans but among all sorts of birds and animals. They are prompted by natural instinct to cherish and defend their chicks or cubs, and will often place themselves in danger of death for their sake. Even in the case of those wild beasts, serpents and birds, which lurk quite apart from others because of their ferocity and venom, such as the basilisk, the rhinoceros and the gryphon (whose very sight is said to be dangerous to all others), even they live at peace with their own kind, linked by their birth and likeness. Yet all these types of friendship I have mentioned, common to good and bad alike, to wild beasts and serpents, can surely not endure for ever. Frequently friends are separated or sundered by distance; time brings forgetfulness; hard words or a clash of interests divides them. Just as their association stems from differing causes, profit or desire, family or necessity; so they can be separated for various different reasons.

III. "Among all those others, there is one type of friendship that is indissoluble, where the bond is not for the sake of mutual benefit, nor because of some great duty or profit, nor caused by some contract or natural necessity, but purely because of a similarity in virtue. This is the friendship which no accident can sever, which is not interrupted or destroyed by any distance of time or place, for not even death itself can break it. This is true affection, unbroken, which grows in the perfection and virtue of two friends. Once such a pact has been made, no variety of interests can disrupt it, neither can any contentious difference of opinion. Nevertheless, we know of many who had been established in such affection, but, despite being linked in a most public manner in the love of Christ, they were unable to preserve their friendship permanently and unbroken. Although they relied on the principal good of fellowship, they did not maintain what they had intended with equal devotion, and their affection was only temporary, kept in being by patience on one part, but without equality of virtue on both sides. No matter how generous and tolerant the one may be, the weakness of character of the other is bound to end the friendship. Even if the strong patiently endure the weakness of those who seek but feebly for holiness, the weak themselves cannot long endure it. The seeds of corruption are within them, which will not suffer them to remain at peace. They are just like those who are in bad physical health, and always blame their poor digestion and illness on the incompetence of cooks or servants. No matter how carefully they are tended, they still blame the healthy for their own sickness, without realising that the cause of their problems lies in their own poor constitution.

Truly faithful and inseparable friendship, then, can only exist by the association of those equal in virtue. 'God who maketh men of one manner to dwell in a house' (Psalm 67/68:7). Unbroken affection can only survive among those who have the same intention, the same will, the same desires and dislikes. If you two desire to keep your friendship intact, you must be at pains to drive out your faults, to mortify your own desires, and to be united in the firm intention to fulfil faithfully what the Psalmist sings of with joy, 'Behold how good and how pleasant it is for brethren to dwell together in unity' (Psalm 132/133:1). You should understand 'together' as a spiritual unity, not a place. There is no advantage in sharing a house, if you differ in conduct and intention, nor is there

XVI. On Friendship

any disadvantage in being widely separated if you are established in equality of virtue. In God's eyes it is dwelling in unity of manners, not of place, that joins brethren in common habitation. Peace can never be perfectly preserved, if there is a difference of intention."

IV. GERMANUS: "What happens if one person wants to do something which he thinks to be godly and leading to salvation, and the other does not agree? Should the first act against his brother's will, or refrain from acting out of respect for the other's opinion?"

V. JOSEPH: "That is why I said that full and perfect friendship cannot survive except between perfect men of equal virtue. They should have but one will and one intention, and rarely or never should they differ in opinion in any question pertaining to progress in the spiritual life. If they ever begin to become heated in argument, it becomes clear that they were never at one in the manner we have described. No one can be perfect from the start, but all must begin by laying the foundation of perfection; you have not asked me about the greatness of friendship, but how to attain it, so I think I ought to give you a brief outline and rule to guide your progress, so that you can more easily attain the goal of patience and peace.

VI. "The first foundation of true friendship is laid in the contempt of material things, and indifference to all property. It would be monstrously unjust if after we have renounced the world and all its empty trivialities, some paltry possession were to remain and take precedence over the precious love of a brother. The second is that each one should deny his own preferences, lest he imagine himself wise and prudent, and prefer to follow his own will rather than his brother's. The third is to be aware that all things, however useful or necessary they seem, are secondary to the charity and peace desired. The fourth is to be sure not to be angry, whether for good or bad reasons. The fifth is that each be as earnest in seeking to calm his brother's anger against himself, even if it be unreasonable, as if it were his own, knowing that the other's grief is just as dangerous to himself as if he were incensed against the other, and he must do all he can to clear it from his brother's thoughts. Finally, a sure route to eliminating all vices together is to be constantly aware that he is to depart from this world. This conviction will allow no gloom to remain in the heart, and will also quell the stirrings of all desires and all sins.

Anyone who relies on these foundations will be free from either suffering or inflicting the grief of anger and discord. But if they are lost, the moment one becomes jealous of affection, and begins to instil the poison of bitterness into the heart of his friend, inevitably love will begin to grow cold, in frequent quarrels, and the wounded hearts of the friends will be sundered. For if one enters upon the path in the direction I have described, how could he ever find himself able to disagree with his friend? If he radically excludes the first occasion of strife (and such occasions are usually provided by the most trivial and insignificant matters), and claims absolutely nothing for himself, he will be able to fulfil totally what we read in the Acts of the Apostles about the unity of the faithful: 'the multitude of believers had but one heart and one soul. Neither did anyone say that aught of the things which he possessed was his own; but all things were common unto them' (Acts 4: 32).

How then could it happen for any matter of dispute to arise, if is not the result of his own will, or that of his brother, when he imitates his Lord and creator? For the Lord, speaking in the human nature he had taken on, said, 'I came down from heaven, not to do my own will but the will of him that sent me' (John 6: 38). How could anyone cherish a spark of bitterness, who has decided to test all his understanding and feeling, not according to his own judgment or at his own choice, but at his brother's, whether he approves or disapproves what is proposed? Thus he fulfils the Gospel command in humility of heart; 'nevertheless not as I will but as thou wilt' (Matt. 26: 39). How could he possibly admit anything that would grieve his brother, if he consider nothing more precious than peace, and never loses sight of Our Lord's teaching? For Christ said, 'By this shall all men know that you are my disciples, if you have love one for another' (John 13:35). Thus he indicates how he wished his flock to be recognisable in this world, as if by a spiritual badge, a badge which would be visible to others, so to speak. No one could find any cause for tolerating either in himself or in others an abiding rancour or grief, if he had once accepted the principle that there can be no good reason for anger, which is always destructive and wrong. He would be as incapable of prayer if his brother were angered against him, as if he himself were angered against his brother, if he is always humble enough to recall the teaching which Our Lord and Saviour gave us, 'If therefore thou offer thy gift at the altar, and there thou remember that thy brother hath anything against thee; leave there thy offering before the altar and go first to be reconciled to thy brother; and then coming thou shalt offer thy gift' (Matt. 5:23–4). It will be of no advantage if you simply claim that you yourself are not angry, imagining that you are thereby fulfilling the commandments, 'Let not the sun go down upon your anger' (Eph. 4:26), and 'whosoever is angry with his brother shall be in danger of the judgment' (Matt. 5:22), while you are hardhearted and contemptuous of another man's grievance which it is in your power to soothe. You would be evading the sense of Our Lord's teaching by this quibble, for as he told you not to be angry against another, so he tells you not to despise the grievance of another. It makes no difference to God, who 'will have all men to be saved' (I Tim. 2:4), whether you are condemning yourself or another. The perdition of anyone whatever is equally tragic, equally a triumph for the devil, who wishes the destruction of all, whether it is you or your brother who is lost. How therefore could anyone preserve even the slightest rancour against his brother, if he knows himself to be daily, nay hourly, on the point of departing this world?

VII. "Just as nothing can take precedence over charity, so there is nothing which deserves a lower place than wrath and anger. It is better to sacrifice anything, no matter how important or necessary, rather than defile it by the vice of anger. No matter how hard it seems, everything must be accepted and borne for the sake of preserving love and peace unbroken. Nothing can be considered more dangerous than wrath and rancour; nothing more beneficial than charity.

VIII. "Any paltry earthly matter is enough for our enemy to use to separate brothers in quick anger, if they are carnal and weak. In the same manner he separates spiritual brothers over differences of opinion. Hence arise most of the bitter contentions which St Paul condemns. Hence too the malicious fiend is able to create divisions between unanimous brothers. For true it is what Solomon the Wise spoke, 'Hatred stirreth up strifes: and charity protecteth all who strive not' (Prov. 10:12, LXX).

IX. "Now in order to conserve lasting specific charity, there is no point in eliminating the first cause of discord, namely that which arises from passing earthly matters, and despising all things of flesh, granting all the brethren an equal share in all the necessities of life, unless we also remove the second cause in the same way, that which so often arises under the colour of spiritual opinion, and in every issue come to a humble agreement of will.

X. "I remember when I was young, and first aspired to live with a companion, it frequently happened that we each came to some opinion, in our study of morals and Holy Scripture, such that we believed nothing could be more reasonable or true. But when we began to meet and compare our views, one or other would criticise some opinion, as we considered together, as being false or wrong; eventually such opinions would be condemned by our common judgment as pernicious, although formerly they had been insinuated by the devil and shone so brightly in order to generate discord more easily. Only our elders' warning, which we had remembered like an oracle of God, held us back from quarrelling, for they had given us a rule to follow, that neither of us should trust his own judgment more than his brother's, unless he wanted to be deceived by the subtlety of the devil.

XI. "As St Paul told us, it often happens that 'Satan himself transformeth himself into an angel of light' (II Cor. 11:14), so that he can deceive us and obscure our thoughts with a dark cloud, disguised as the true light of wisdom. Unless we consider everything with a meek and humble heart, and subject it to the consideration of a most experienced brother or well approved elder, carefully following their advice whether to accept or reject it, we would certainly find ourselves honouring the angel of darkness in our thoughts as if he were an angel of light, and so we would fall into the greatest peril. No one who trusts in his own judgment can ever avoid this danger; no, he must become a lover of true humility, and follow it, till with a heart full of contrition he can fulfil the Apostle's earnest entreaty: 'If there be therefore any consolation in Christ, if any comfort of charity, if any society of the spirit, if any bowels of commiseration; fulfil ye my joy, that you be of one mind, having the same charity, being of one accord, agreeing in sentiment. Let nothing be done through contention, neither by vainglory; but in humility, let each esteem others better than themselves' (Phil. 2:1–3). Also, 'with honour preventing one another' (Rom. 12:10), so that each one attributes more wisdom and holiness to his friend, and believes that the peak of true discernment is found in the other's judgment rather than his own.

XII. "As it so often happens, whether through the wiles of the devil, or through human error (for there is no one alive who cannot be deceived like anyone else), even the most acute and learned may come to a false conclusion, while someone of less intelligence and little worth may perceive the truth more clearly. No one therefore should flatter himself, no matter how learned he be, that he need not consult anyone else. Even if in his brilliance he eludes the devil's deceits, he will not escape the more dangerous snares of conceit and pride. Who could claim to rely simply on his own judgment without serious risk, rather than doing as the Vessel of Election did, through whom Christ spoke, as he testifies himself? He tells us that he went down to Jerusalem only in order to confer on what he had been preaching to the nations through the revelation and at the guidance of the Lord, in a private conversation with his fellow apostles of the Gospel (Gal. 2:1–2). This shows us that by doing this unity and agreement are preserved, and there need be no fear of any of the devil's plots or his ensnaring illusions.

XIII. "The virtue of charity is so exalted that the blessed Apostle John called it not merely an attribute of God but God himself, for he says, 'God is charity; and he that abideth in charity abideth in God, and God in him' (I John 4:16). Charity, we must know, is so divine that we can clearly observe in ourselves what St Paul says, 'the charity of God is poured forth in our hearts, by the Holy Ghost who is given to us' (Rom. 5:5). This is as much as to say, God is poured forth in our hearts, by the Holy Spirit who dwells within us. And he it is who, when 'we know not what we should pray ... asketh for us with unspeakable groanings. And he that searcheth the hearts knoweth what the Spirit desireth; because he asketh for the saints according to God' (Rom 8:26–7).

XIV. "It is possible for all of us to display that charity which is called *agape*, of which the holy Apostle says, 'Therefore, whilst we have time, let us work good to all men, but especially to those who are of the household of the faith' (Gal. 6:10). Charity is to be shown to all without distinction, for Our Lord bids us offer it to our enemies too, for he says to us, 'Love your enemies' (Matt. 5:44). The love called *diathesis*, that is to say affection, on the other hand, should be offered to only a few, those linked to us by a common way of life and association in virtue. Affection too may appear in many different forms. Parents are loved in one way, spouses in another, brothers in another, and children in yet another. Even within these types of affection there is great variation, and parents will be found not to love their children all in the same manner. We can see this in the example of the Patriarch Jacob, who was the father of twelve sons, loving them all with paternal charity, but holding Joseph in greater affection, as Scripture clearly tells us, 'And his brethren, seeing

XVI. On Friendship

that he was loved by his father, more than all his sons, hated him' (Gen. 37:4). It is not that a just man, who was their father, did not really love the rest of his family, but that he loved this one with greater affection and more tenderness, for he was to be a type of the Lord. We read of the same thing applying to St John the Evangelist, of whom it is said, 'one of his disciples, whom Jesus loved' (John 13:23), even though he certainly held all the remaining eleven in special affection, for they had all been chosen in the same way. The same evangelist tells us as much: 'as I have loved you, that you also love one another' (John 13:34). And in another place he says, 'having loved his own who were in the world, he loved them unto the end' (John 13:1). This particular affection does not mean that his love for the other disciples was but cool, but that there was a greater overflowing of love towards this one, conferred on him by his virginal dignity and bodily purity. This is recorded as a special distinction, not implying hatred for the others, but a more abundant grace of boundless love. We read the same in the person of the Bride in the Canticles, when she says, 'set in order charity in me' (Cant. 2:4, LXX). True charity is set in order like this, holding no one in hatred, but loving some more, for the sake of their merits. Although charity loves all in general, she selects some for herself to embrace in special affection. Again, among those who are among the highest and greatest in her affection, she chooses some who abound in love above the others.

XV. "There are cases to the contrary – if only we had never heard of them! Some of the brethren are so obstinate and hard-hearted, that when they become aware that their feelings are aroused against a brother, or a brother's against themselves, they try to disguise the gloomy thoughts which have arisen through indignation at the mutual hostility. They withdraw therefore from the company of those whom they should have pacified with humble apology and soothing words, and simply begin to chant some verses of the psalms. They may think that in this way they can assuage their bitterness of heart, but really they are increasing it by the insult, though they could quench it at once if they were prepared to be more concerned and more humble, for early repentance can heal their hearts, and soften their brother's mind. By this sort of cowardice, which is really pride, they tend their rancour, nourishing the seed of strife rather than uprooting it. They forget Our Lord's teaching, when he said, 'whosoever is angry with his brother shall be in danger of the judgment', and 'if thou remember that thy brother hath anything against thee, leave there thy offering before the altar and go first to be reconciled with thy brother; and then coming thou shalt offer thy gift' (Matt. 5:22–4).

XVI. "God does not wish us to despise another's grief, to the extent that if our brother has anything against us, he will not accept our offering. He will not permit us to offer prayers, until we make swift satisfaction to remove the grievance from his soul, whether it be there for good cause or bad. For he does not say, 'if thy brother have a just cause against thee, leave there thy offering before the altar and go first to be reconciled with thy brother', but 'if thou remember that thy brother hath *anything* against thee.' Even if it be something trivial and insignificant which arouses your brother's indignation, and it suddenly occurs to your memory, you should realise that you should not offer the spiritual sacrifice of your prayers, until you have apologised adequately to dispel the grievance from your brother's heart, no matter how it arose. Now if the Gospel bids us placate the angry, when the grudge is over some small thing in the past, arising from some trivial matter, how wretched it would be if we arrogantly conceal and underestimate serious current offences, committed through our own fault! How could we be so inflated with devilish pride as to be ashamed to apologise, to deny that we have caused our brother's grief, to disdain obedience to Our Lord's commands in a rebellious spirit, pretending that we cannot possibly observe or fulfil them? If it so happens that we find ourselves judging his commands to be impossible or inappropriate, we shall be, as St James says, 'not a doer of the law, but a judge' (James 4:11).

XVII. "There is another tendency which should be deplored: it can happen that a brother becomes angered by what someone has said, and someone else tries to calm him and entreats him, telling him never to conceive or nurse a grievance against a brother, according to the scripture, 'whosoever is angry with his brother shall be in danger of the judgment' (Matt. 5:22), and 'Let not the sun go down upon your anger' (Eph. 4:26). But the brother then retorts, 'If some pagan, or layman, had done this, it would be reasonable to tolerate it. But who could tolerate a brother who wrongs me like this knowingly, or utters such rude abuse?' That is as much as to say that patience should be displayed only to unbelievers and sinners, and not to everyone equally, or that anger may only be considered wrong if it is against a pagan, but it is right to be angry against a brother! Does not a mind excited by wrath do just as much damage to itself whomsoever it is directed against? What a display of obstinacy, what a disgrace, for someone to be so stupid and insensitive as not to realise what his own words imply! For it does not say, 'whosoever is angry with a stranger shall be in danger of the judgment', which according to their interpretation would make an exception for those who are our companions in faith and way of life: no, the Gospel clearly says, 'whosoever is angry with *his brother* shall be in danger of the judgment.' Granted that in strict truth we should consider every man to be our brother, nevertheless in this place the word 'brother' refers more specifically to one who shares our faith and way of life, than to a foreigner.

XVIII. "It can also happen that we may imagine we are being patient because we disdain to reply to an insult, but we still undermine our angry brother by our bitter silence, our disdainful bearing and gesture, so that we provoke him to more indignation by our silence that we could have done by violent words. Yet we consider we are not at all guilty in God's eyes because we have actually said nothing which could bring us before men's attention or disapproval! As if it was only in actual words that sin can be committed before God, rather than the intention behind them, as if guilt lay only in deeds, not in the will and desire to sin, or that in the Judgment God will not scrutinise what a man intended to do, but only his completed actions! It is not only by an actual quarrel that you can hurt someone, but by the intention of hurting him as well. That is why our Judge will truly assess not how a dispute arose, but by whose fault it arose. It is the effect of sin that is to be examined, not the order in which it is committed. What difference does it make whether someone kills his brother with a sword, or causes his death by some guile, when in either case he dies as a result of the same person's action or scheming? If you see a blind man tottering on the brink of a pit, and are able to warn him but disdain to do so, is that any better than pushing him in with your own hand? Is it a sin to strangle someone with your own hands, and not a sin to leave a noose to ensnare him, or to refrain from removing one if it were in your power?

In effect, there is no advantage in keeping silent, if our silence means that we wish to express by it what we would consider wrong to do in action. By our bearing and gesture we can cause greater wrath to arise in the one whom we should be placating, and we may seek to gain praise at the expense of his falling into sin. Is it not a far greater fault to wish for credit at a brother's fall? Silence of this sort is equally damaging to both, for it increases the grievance in the thoughts of the one, without letting it diminish in the other. The Prophet spoke a clear enough warning against this, 'Woe to him who giveth drink to his friend and presenteth his gall and maketh him drunk, that he may behold his nakedness! Thou art filled with shame instead of glory' (Hab. 2: 15–16). Another prophet says something similar, 'For every brother will utterly supplant, and every friend will walk deceitfully. And a man shall mock his brother and they will not speak the truth: for they have bent their tongue, as a bow, for lies and not for truth' (Jer. 9: 4–5, 3). Feigned patience can be more provoking than an angry word, and sullen silence creates more offence than violent speech. Subtle disdain from one who despises us is less tolerable than an enemy's blows. The psalmist speaks aptly of this, 'His words are smoother than oil; and the same are darts' (Psalm 54/55: 22). Also, 'the words of a talebearer are as it were simple, but they reach to the innermost parts of the belly' (Prov. 26:22). For some, this text can be well applied, 'with his mouth one speaketh peace with his friend, and secretly he lieth in wait for him' (Jer. 9:8), whereas the one who is being deceitful is in fact the one more deceived. For 'a man that speaketh to his friend with flattering and dissembling words spreadeth a net for his feet', and 'he that diggeth a pit shall fall into it' (Prov. 29:5, 26:27). When a great crowd came to arrest Our Lord with swords and clubs, there was no one more cruel in the assault on the author of our being than the one who was the first to greet him with a gesture of pretended honour, giving him the kiss of feigned charity. 'Judas,' said Our Lord, 'dost thou betray the Son of man with a kiss?' (Luke 22:48). Can your bitterness and hatred really be concealed under this gesture which should express true and dear affection? The psalmist adds force to this complaint in a strongly worded passage: 'for if my enemy had reviled me, I would verily have borne with it. And if he that hated me had spoken great things against me, I would perhaps have hidden myself from him. But thou a man of one mind: my guide, and my familiar: Who didst take sweet meats together with me: in the house of God we walked with consent' (Psalm 54/55:13–15).

XIX. "There is another type of sinful grief which I would not consider worth mentioning were it not that I know of several monks who are affected by it. When they are aggrieved or angered they stubbornly refuse to eat at all, to the extent, I am sorry to say, that monks, who while they are in good temper may claim that they cannot defer their meal as late as midday, even less to mid-afternoon, yet once they are glutted with sorrow or anger, are able to feed on their indignation enough to make up for their lack of food. This is obviously a sin bordering on sacrilege, for fasting is something which should be offered to God alone, to humble our hearts and purge our vices, and they endure it out of devilish pride. It is as bad as offering prayers and sacrifices to demons rather than God, and they would earn the rebuke of Moses, who said, 'they sacrificed to devils and not to God: to gods whom they knew not' (Deut. 32:17).

XX. "Yet another type of misbehaviour we have observed among certain brothers is that they pretend to be patient, but think nothing of stirring up discord, as long as it is not caused by what their opponent actually says. If it happens that someone lightly brushes against them, they offer some other part of their body to be struck, as if they were fulfilling that counsel of perfection which bids us, 'if one strike thee on thy right cheek, turn to him also the other' (Matt. 5:39). They are obviously unaware of the real meaning of that text, if they imagine that by their petulance they are practising evangelical patience. This vice must be rooted out; so that not only is retaliation and stored grievance forbidden, but we are commanded to appease the anger of the one who strikes us by tolerating even a second injury."

XXI. GERMANUS: "But why do you blame someone who carries out the Gospel command like that? He does not retaliate, and shows himself ready to endure a second injury."

XXII. JOSEPH: "I have just told you, that it is not just the action we perform, but the state of our mind and our intention that is to be considered. Now if you look closely at the thoughts and purpose of someone who is performing some action, you will observe that the virtue of mild patience cannot exist where there is the contrary spirit of impatient anger. Our Lord and Saviour teaches us that the profundity of the virtue of meek patience lies not merely in what we say, but in what we conceal in the secret depths of our hearts, and for this reason gives us this precept of evangelical perfection, 'if one strike thee on thy right cheek, turn to him also the other.' We should understand the 'other right cheek', which can only mean the face of the inner man, so to speak. If we really desire to extirpate every trace of anger from the depths of the soul, we should tolerate the blow directed at the right cheek of the outer person, and offer the right cheek of the inner man to be struck, through humble acquiescence. Thus the inner man shares in the suffering of the outer, supporting and underpinning the body which sustains the injury, so that the inner man is not even silently disturbed by the attack on the outer. Now you can understand how far those men are from evangelical perfection, which teaches us to remain patient not just in speech but in the interior of a placid heart. If our patience is assailed, we should preserve it in such a way that we keep ourselves from any angry disturbance, and also by accepting the wrong they do us, we can make the ones who are enraged against us become calm, till their wrath is sated, and their fury overcome by our mild behaviour. In this way we can fulfil St Paul's command, 'Be not overcome by evil, but overcome evil by good' (Rom. 22:21).

We may be sure that this cannot be achieved by those who utter words of mild humility in such a tone that they fail to placate the wrath enkindled against them, but actually make it rage more fiercely, both in their own emotions and in their brother's. Even if they are somehow able to remain calm, they will never reap any fruit of righteousness if they are arrogating the reputation of patience for themselves at the other's expense. This is quite foreign to the Apostle's definition of charity, which 'seeketh not her own' (I Cor. 13:5), but seeks instead what is the other's. Charity, I mean, does not seek the property of others, to profit by another's loss, nor does it hope to acquire something by despoiling the other.

XXIII. "In general we should be aware that he who subjects his will to another is more strong minded than he who is obstinate in defending his own ideas and opinions. If he tolerates and accepts his neighbour he plays the part of the strong and healthy; he who does not is like the weak and failing; he is the one who needs to be tended and cherished, excused even from necessary duties for the sake of rest and recovery. Let him not imagine he is losing any degree of perfection, if he agrees to relax any of his usual discipline, but on the contrary he should realise that by being patient and tolerant he is gaining much more. As St Paul says, 'you that are stronger ought to bear the infirmities of the weak' (Rom. 15:1), and 'bear ye one another's burdens; and so ye shall fulfil the law of Christ' (Gal. 6:2). The weak cannot support the weak; nor can sickness be supported and cured by one who suffers from the same sickness. It is the one who does not experience disease who can heal that disease. For it is rightly said, 'Physician, heal thyself' (Luke 4:23).

XXIV. "Be aware that the nature of this spiritual sickness is always such that men are quick and ready to offer insult and provoke discord, but are themselves quite unable to endure the slightest hint of injury. They display their violent vices, riding over others with careless abandon, but themselves incapable of tolerating the smallest things. As the elders have taught us, lasting and permanent charity cannot survive except among men of similar virtue and intention. Otherwise it is bound to be lost sooner or later, no matter how careful one party is to preserve it."

XXV. GERMANUS: "How then can the patience of a perfect man be praiseworthy, if he will not be able always to tolerate the weak?"

XXVI. JOSEPH: "I did not say that it is the virtue and patience of the stronger party which will be overcome, but the vile valour of the weaker. The latter feeds on the support he receives from the healthy one, but ever tends to make things worse, creating reasons why he should no longer be endured. Through comparing the obvious patience of his neighbour with his own poor impatience, he prefers to walk away rather than go on being supported by the other's generosity. So my advice for those who wish to preserve their friend's affection unbroken is above all that a monk should be careful on receiving the first slight, to keep not just his lips but his innermost thoughts quiet. If he feels in the least bit disturbed, he should keep absolutely silent about it, and be sure to follow what the Psalmist says: 'I was troubled and I spoke not' (Psalm 76/77:5), and, 'I said: I will take heed to my ways: that I sin not with my tongue. I have set a guard to my mouth, when the sinner stood before me. I was dumb, and was humbled, and kept silence from good things' (Psalm 38/39:2–3). He should not consider the present situation, and utter what his rising anger suggests immediately and what he is provoked to say, but he should call to mind the love that has existed before, consider how to restore peace and concord, and even while he is most frustrated, should think about that peace as something sure to be renewed. Thus he can keep himself for the delight of future reconciliation, without thinking of the bitterness of present discord, and will always give such an answer that once charity is restored he will have nothing for which to blame himself, or to be accused by the other. In this way he will fulfil the prophet's advice, 'when thou art angry, thou wilt remember mercy' (Hab. 3:2).

XXVII. "We should restrain all our emotions of anger, and govern them with prudence and discretion; otherwise we would be carried away by violent rage and stand condemned by that saying of Solomon, 'a fool uttereth all his wrath, a wise man dispenseth it in parts' (Prov. 29:11, LXX). That is, a fool is fired by his anger to avenge himself; a wise man lets his anger out little by little, moderating it with careful thought, and so gets rid of it. It is the same as what the Apostle said, 'not revenging yourselves, my dearly beloved; but give place unto wrath' (Rom. 12:19). Do not let your anger force you to be vengeful, but give anger its place, that is do not let your hearts be so furled with the reefs of weak minded impatience, that they are unable to cope with a storm of passion should it arise; no, spread your hearts wide, open the wings of charity to receive the gusts of anger against you, for charity 'beareth all things, endureth all things' (I Cor. 13:7). Your minds should be so broadened with tolerance and patience that there is room in them for healthy consideration, space for the black fumes of anger to spread and disperse themselves. Or you could interpret St Paul as saying, let us give a place to anger by receiving another's passion with a humble and peaceful heart, offering ourselves, as it were, as deserving of any insult, and bowing to the rage of our opponent.

In any case, if you turn St Paul's counsel of perfection to mean that it is those who walk away from the angry man that are 'giving place unto wrath', I think they are not removing the cause of strife, but actually increasing it. If our neighbour's wrath is not calmed at once by humble apology, walking away from him will provoke him, not appease him. Solomon says something similar: 'be not quickly angry: for anger resteth in the bosom of a fool' (Qo. 7:10), and, 'run not hastily in a quarrel; lest afterwards you repent of it' (Prov. 25:8, LXX). Not that in blaming hasty discord and strife, he is recommending they be delayed! We should take the following text in the same way: 'a fool immediately sheweth his anger: but he that dissembleth injuries is wise' (Prov. 12:16). He does not mean that the wise ought to conceal the shameful emotion of anger as if he approved of delayed wrath but only blamed it when it is hasty: no, it means that if anger happen to be unavoidable, through human weakness, we should hide it so that by wisely concealing it at first, it can be eradicated hereafter. For it is of the very nature of anger that when delayed it dwindles and dies away, but entered quickly it grows more and more fierce. Our hearts should therefore be widened and deepened, not restricted by narrow weak-mindedness, so that the storm of wrath can fill them completely. If our hearts are too narrow we would be unable to receive the broad commandment of God, as the Psalmist puts it, 'I have run the way of thy commandments, when thou didst enlarge my heart' (Psalm 118/119:32). Long patience is true wisdom, as we hear in many evident passages of Scripture: 'He that is patient is governed with much wisdom: but he that is impatient exalteth his folly' (Prov. 14:29). Scripture therefore commends him who asked the gift of wisdom from the Lord; 'and God gave to Solomon wisdom and understanding exceeding much, and largeness of heart as the sand that is on the sea-shore' (III Kings (I Kings) 4:29).

XXVIII. "One thing that has been proved by much experience is that those who enter into a friendship by beginning with a contract, can never hope to preserve unbroken concord. This may be because they have tried to make an association not out of a desire to be perfect, or at the bidding of apostolic charity, but out of earthly affection, trying to preserve it by compulsion and binding pledges; alternatively the sly fiend, to make them ministers of his mysteries, is provoked to sunder the bonds of friendship

XVI. On Friendship

more quickly. Certainly the most prudent teachers agree that true concord and indivisible union cannot exist except among men of improved character, with the same strengths and intentions."

This is what the saintly Joseph told us in his spiritual discourse on friendship, inspiring us to guard our lasting love for each other more ardently.

✣ THE SEVENTEENTH COLLATION ✣
BEING THE SECOND OF ABBA JOSEPH

On Vows

    I. On how we lay awake.
   II. Abba Germanus is concerned, remembering the vow we had made.
  III. What I thought of this.
  IV. Abba Joseph's question on the origin of our anxiety, and our reply.
   V. Abba Germanus explains why we might want to remain in Egypt and not return to Syria.
  VI. Abba Joseph asks whether we would gain a greater perfection in Egypt than in Syria.
 VII. The reply, on the different types of training in the two provinces.
VIII. How perfect men should never make an absolute commitment, but they may rescind their decisions without sin.
  IX. That it may be better to dispense with obligations than to fulfil them.
   X. Our question, on the anxiety we feel over the vow we made in our Syrian monastery.
  XI. The reply, that we should consider the intention, not the effect of our actions.
 XII. That a good outcome does not justify a malicious intention, nor does a bad outcome vitiate a good one.
XIII. Our reply, on the reason for having been obliged to pledge ourselves.

XIV. The elder explains that a course of action may be changed without blame, as long as its good purpose is achieved.
XV. A question, is it a sin if our weak conscience gives us occasion to lie?
XVI. The reply, that the truth of Scripture should not be compromised for the sake of weak consciences.
XVII. That the saints can use a lie without risk, like hellebore.
XVIII. An objection, that only those who lived under the Old Law could use deception with impunity.
XIX. The reply, that the licence to equivocate, which is not granted even in the Old Testament, has been used by many without guilt.
XX. That the Apostles themselves thought lying could sometimes be pardonable and the truth dangerous.
XXI. Whether we ought to reveal secret abstemiousness when people ask, and not lie, and whether we should accept what we have once refused.
XXII. An objection, that while it is right to conceal abstemiousness, we should not accept what we had once refused.
XXIII. The reply, that obstinacy in such a resolve is unreasonable.
XXIV. How Abba Piamun preferred to conceal his abstinence.
XXV. Scriptural examples of resolutions that were changed.
XXVI. That holy men cannot be stubborn and hard.
XXVII. A question, whether the text "I have sworn and am determined" contradicts the above opinion.
XXVIII. The reply, on the occasions when a resolve must be kept unbroken, and when it should be withdrawn if necessary.
XXIX. How secrets should be told to others.
XXX. No vows should be made on matters pertaining to the common life.

XVII. On Vows

MONITUM

Cassian's Jansenist critics have always concentrated on the 13th Collation with its ill-defined teaching on the relationship of grace and freewill, but this 17th Collation seems to be the more dubious. Abba Joseph's teaching on the permissibility of a lie does indeed contain much truth, but comes perilously close to suggesting that we may always lie our way out of a difficulty, and may compromise on the faith in order to save our lives. He also seems to be suggesting that our own assessment of what would be good for us may take preference over the clear duty of obedience owed to a superior. Needless to say the consensus of spiritual authority is against Joseph here. It is interesting that Cassian himself was obviously uneasy about what Joseph was telling him, and did eventually do the right thing, returning to his monastery as he had promised. The fact that his superiors in the event granted him permission to return to Egypt goes to prove that one can never go wrong by observing obedience.

I. When the previous conference had ended, and the stillness of the night ensued, Abba Joseph led us quietly to a separate cell to rest. However we were so enthralled by his words, burning in our hearts, that we were sleepless all night. We came out of the cell and walked about a hundred paces away, to sit in a more secluded spot, which gave us the chance of talking intimately together during the night. We sat down, and Abba Germanus began to sigh deeply.

II. "What are we to do?" he said. "What a quandary we find ourselves in, how unfortunate our circumstances! On the one hand the wise instruction of these saints is teaching us effectively what would be most useful for advancement in the spiritual life, but on the other hand the vow we have made to our superiors prevents us from choosing the better part. We have the opportunity of gaining from the example of so many great men, to perfect our lives, but our bounden promise demands that we return at once to our own monastery. And if we do go back there, we will never again be given a chance to travel here. Yet if we stay here and fulfil the longings we have, what are we to do about the promise we remember making to our superiors to return home as quickly as possible, when they gave us permission to make a rapid visit to the saints and hermits of this province?"

Troubled by this, we were unable to decide what we ought to do best for our salvation, and could only grieve at the harsh constraint laid upon us. We regretted our naivety and bashfulness which had so hampered us that we were unable to resist, even against our own best intentions, the entreaties of those who were trying to keep us back, till we were permitted to come here only under promise of swift return. In effect we lamented the fact that we had suffered from that type of shame of which it is said, "There is a shame which causes sin" (Prov. 26:11a, LXX).

III. I answered him, "Debating the subject will cause us a multitude of woes; let us take our problem to the old man and ask him, then whatever he decides we can take as an answer from God in heaven, and it will put an end to all our uncertainty. We need have no hesitation over what the Lord tells us through the lips of this elder, both because of his worth, and our confidence in him. By God's grace believers can often gather useful advice from the unworthy, and unbelievers from the worthy, as the Lord grants it for the sake of the speaker's merits or the listeners' faith." Abba Germanus readily agreed to what I said, as if it had been not my own opinion but a divine inspiration. We waited a little until the elder arrived, and it was time for the night vigil; we greeted him as usual, and celebrated the correct number of psalms and prayers. Then we sat down as before on the same papyrus bundles on which we had composed ourselves to sleep.

IV. The venerable Joseph looked at us, downcast as we were, and deducing that there was some good reason for this, asked us in the words of Joseph the patriarch, "Why are your countenances sad today?" (Gen. 40:7). We answered, "We are not like those servants of Pharaoh in prison, who dreamed a dream and lacked an interpreter – no, we have spent a sleepless night, and there is nothing to relieve the burden of our worry unless the Lord do so through the means of your wisdom." He, who shared the merits as well as the name of the patriarch, replied, "Is not the cure for human anxiety ever in the Lord? Tell me now; for God in his mercy is well able to grant you healing through my advice, as you already believe."

V. Germanus answered him, "We had thought that when we had seen your beatitude we would be returning to our monastery, not just nourished in spirit but quite replete. What we had received from your teaching we would imitate on our return, however inadequately. This we were obliged to promise our superiors, out of our love for them, imagining that we would be able to some extent to follow your sublime life and teaching in that monastery. Whereas we had thought that that this would bring us the fullness of joy, we are on the contrary plunged into intolerable grief, when we consider that what we know to be of benefit to us cannot be obtained that way. We are pressed on both sides. If we decide to honour the promise which we made at love's urging, in front of all the brethren in the cave where Our Lord shone forth from the virgin's womb, the Lord who is our witness, why then we would incur the greatest risk to our spiritual life. But on the other hand if we forget our promise and remain in this region, prepared to delay our obligations for the sake of our own perfection, we fear the dangerous consequences of a lie, of a promise not fulfilled. Nor can we console ourselves with the idea that we could make a swift return, redeem our pledge, and come back quickly to this place. We might indeed honour the promise we had made by a return journey, however disappointed, despite the fact that even a slight delay in the quest for virtue and spiritual perfection is very dangerous, were it not that we know full well that we would be bound not by charity alone but by the obedience owed to our superiors, so that we could not possibly be given permission to come back here ever again."

VI. After a pause, the saintly Joseph replied, "Are you sure that you can gain a greater spiritual benefit in this place?"

VII. GERMANUS: "True, we owe much gratitude to the teaching of those who taught us from our childhood to strive after great things, who gave us a taste for the good, and instilled a noble thirst for perfection into our hearts. But if you will trust our judgment, we find no comparison between that and the teaching we find here, not to mention your own way of life inimitable in its purity, which we believe was granted you by the merits of the very place itself as well as your strict method and intentions. To imitate your magnificent state of perfection, we are quite sure that the teaching we have received so briefly would not suffice, unless we add to it a long stay, so that over a lengthy period we may be instructed daily to dispel our slowness of heart."

VIII. JOSEPH: "It is obviously a good and holy thing, and in no way contrary to our profession, to perform scrupulously what we have promised. That is why a monk should never make rash vows; he may find himself compelled to perform what he has so foolishly promised, or have to break his word, changing his mind after consideration of a more appropriate action. But our purpose here is not to speak of a healthy state but to cure an unhealthy one, not to say what you should have done in the first place, but how to escape from this dangerous prospect of shipwreck, and we shall need careful counsel. When we are bound by no constraint, and held by no conditions, and there is a choice of advantages, the one of greater advantage should be chosen. When there is an opposition of disadvantages, in comparing the damage you should prefer the course that is less evil. Now from what you have told me, that rash promise has brought you to the point that either course will cause you great damage. You should therefore make your choice of that course which will cause you less disadvantage, or which can more easily be atoned for by making satisfaction. If you believe that remaining here will bring you a greater spiritual gain than you could acquire from the way of life in your monastery, and that you could not keep your promise without risking the loss of inestimable benefits, then it would be better to incur the guilt of untruthfulness and failing to keep your promise, for once you have taken that decision you will never need to repeat it, and it will not of itself lead to further sin: that would be better than to take the course which, as you tell me, would inflict on you a constant and unending disadvantage, through a tepid way of life. A rash resolution may be changed with little sin, or even with some praise, if the change is to a better course, and it should be counted not as a sin of inconstancy, but as the correction of an error, if you are rectifying a sinful resolve. All this can be abundantly proved by examples in Scripture, showing how dangerous it has so often been to adhere to one's resolutions, and what an advantage it can be for our salvation to abandon them.

IX. "That is most clearly proved by the examples of St Peter, and of Herod. The former abandoned the rash resolve he had come to, when he said, with an oath, 'thou shalt never wash my feet' (John 13: 8). He thereby merited an eternal fellowship with Christ and all the saints, from which blessed grace he would surely have been barred had he remained stubbornly by his word. [Judas it was who held true to his promise, and was condemned to death eternal, yet had he chosen to abandon his commitment rather than fulfil it, he would doubtless have been spared that fate. We see this in those two boys in the parable, who were told off to work in the vineyard, for one resisted his father's command, the other readily agreed (cf. Matt. 25: 28–31). Yet the latter gained nothing by his humble ready assent, since he failed to carry out his father's orders in practice, the other suffered nothing from his rejection of the command, since he changed his mind from what he had said, and performed what his father had intended, the work in question. He was to blame for his resolution, but praised for changing his resolve for the better. Consider too the example of the tyrant] Herod, who kept faith with his rash oath, and became guilty of the cruel death of the Lord's Forerunner. Through foolish fear of perjury, he plunged himself into damnation and the pains of death eternal (cf. Matt. 14).

[In the first place we should make good resolutions; but if we have failed in that, then in the second place we should change them for the better, and offer a helping hand to our intentions when they are down, so to speak. When our first plans are unsound, prudence bids us make better provision and change them. If our intentions falter in what we had first resolved, then our second thoughts will rescue them.] In all matters we should consider the goal, and plan our approach accordingly. Then, if we find, in the light of better advice, that we were heading the wrong way, the proper course is to abandon the erroneous intention and come to a better resolve, rather than to entangle ourselves in yet greater sin by clinging obstinately to our first resolution."

X. GERMANUS: "As far as our own desire goes, and our undertaking in the hope of spiritual profit, we would choose to stay close to you and learn from you. If we return to our monastery, we shall fall away from that sublime instruction, and moreover suffer great disadvantage from the mediocrity of the way of life there. Yet the Gospel command deters us: 'let your speech be, Yea, Yea: No, No. And that which is over and above these is of evil' (Matt. 5:37). We fear that nothing can justify transgressing such a command, and that what began so badly cannot come out well in the end."

XI. JOSEPH: "In all matters, as I have said, we should consider not the outcome of the work, but the intention of the worker; we should examine not what a man does, but what he wishes to do. We shall often find that men are rightly blamed for actions which afterwards turn out well, and on the other hand some can be given all credit for actions which are deplorable. It will be of no advantage, to one who acted with the worst intention, if his actions turn out to be beneficial, for he did not wish for the good outcome but intended one quite opposite. Nor will another be blamed for having started something in the wrong way, if his actions were neither in despite of God nor with the intention of sin, but he was simply bound by necessity to endure the initial wrong for the sake of his holy purpose.

XII. "To illustrate this with examples from holy Scripture, what result could ever happen of greater benefit and profit for the world than the saving death of the Lord? Yet it was of no advantage to the traitor, but a great disaster for him by whose hand the task was done. As it is said explicitly, 'it were better for him if that man had not been born' (Matt. 26:24). His actions were repaid not according to the real result, but according to the result he intended, or imagined he was going to effect. Again, can there be anything more vile than deceit and lies, even when committed against a stranger, let alone a member of one's own family, a father indeed? Yet the patriarch Jacob incurred neither condemnation nor blame, but actually gained the blessing of a perpetual inheritance (cf. Gen. 27). Rightly so, for Jacob did not desire the blessing reserved for the first-born through the lure of present gain, but through faith in perpetual sanctification, whereas Judas betrayed to his death the Redeemer of us all through the sin of avarice, not any desire for the salvation of man. For each of them the reward of their actions was allotted according to the purpose they had in mind and what they wanted to do, for Jacob had not intended to commit fraud, nor had Judas intended to save us. The reward each one received was just according to the principal goal in mind, not according to the good or evil that emerged despite their intentions. Hence the just Judge deemed Jacob to be blameless, even praiseworthy, for perpetrating that lie, since in no other way could he have acquired the blessing of the first-born. It cannot be called a sin to desire to receive a blessing. Had there been any other way to receive the grace of that blessing, the patriarch would have been truly an enemy to his brother, and deceitful and undutiful towards his father, if he had still chosen to follow this path which caused his brother loss and grief. You see, in God's eyes it is not the effect of an action, but the intention of the mind that counts.

Now having said all that, let us return to the question you have put, which was the reason for all I have said. I would like you first to tell me what was the purpose for which you committed yourselves to that vow."

XIII. GERMANUS: "The first reason, as I said, was that we were reluctant to grieve our superiors and to be disobedient to their orders. The second was, that we thought, in our naivety, that if we found anything good or wonderful in what we saw and heard among you, we would be able to put it into practice when we returned to our monastery."

XIV. JOSEPH: "I have already said that it is the purpose in mind that either commends a man or condemns him, as in the text, 'their thoughts between themselves accusing or also defending one another, in the day when God shall judge the secrets of men' (Rom. 2:15–16). Also, 'I know their works and their thoughts; I come that I may gather them together with all nations and tongues' (Isaiah 66:18). Now it seems you bound yourselves by this pledge out of a desire for perfection, in the belief that you could attain it by a course that, on mature judgment, you now realise is incapable of taking you to those heights. It makes no difference if it appears that things turn out other than planned, as long as you do not change your original intention, just as if a workman changes his tools it does not mean he is abandoning the work, if a traveller chooses a more direct and easy route he is not being lazy.

In this case also, to change a course that seems unwise should not be considered a failure of purpose. Anything done out of the love of God and devotion to the faith, 'having promise of the life that now is and of that which is to come' (I Tim. 4:8), is not only blameless but even greatly praiseworthy, however hard and unpromising it may have been in the beginning. There is no blame in withdrawing a rash promise, if whatever happens you preserve the *skopos*, that is the proposed goal of holiness. We do all things for the sake of offering a pure heart to God. If it is in this region that you can best achieve that, you need not fear changing the promise you were obliged to make, as long as that perfection of purity which was the aim of your promise, can be quickly attained according to the will of the Lord.

[This change cannot be called a lie, but rather a prudent and salutary correction of a foolish plan. To help untie this knotty

XVII. On Vows

problem, I will take an example from physiology: nature herself changes her course in us according to the majestic plan of God. We are transformed from infancy to childhood, from childhood to youth, from youth to age; our Creator designs us in this manner, and this changing with age involves no deceit. In the same way our inner person is developed through different ages, from the soft training we began with, progressing to the more severe, until those who had been infants arrive at that old age of the senses, 'unto a perfect man, unto the measure of the age of the fullness of Christ' (Eph. 4:13). Do not we consider this the attainment of perfection, not a deceitful inconsistency? In the same way the elementary laws of the Old Testament, which God's lawgiver proclaimed, were changed into the perfect beatitude of the Gospel. We do not understand this to mean that the old commandments were changed, but that they were fulfilled and perfected in the high and heavenly law. We consider that the inspired revelation was not abolished, but sublimated, not changed but perfected. As Our Lord said, 'Do not think that I am come to destroy the law or the prophets. I am not come to destroy, but to fulfil' (Matt. 5:17). What went before is not made obsolete, but the imperfect is brought to perfection.]"

XV. GERMANUS: "What you have said is very wise and reasonable, and according to it the scruple about our promise is not difficult to remove, were we not strongly deterred by the fact that it would seem to give weak consciences an opportunity for lying, if they once knew that there was any way that a sworn vow could be dissolved. Especially as the inspired writers are so vehement in his denunciation of such behaviour, 'thou wilt destroy all that speak a lie', and, 'the mouth that belieth killeth the soul'" (Psalm 5:7; Wisd. 1:11).

XVI. JOSEPH: "There are plenty of opportunities and excuses for damnation for those who are going to perish, or rather those who want to perish. Nor should we reject the evidence of scripture, and try to cut out of the text passages which might inspire depraved heresies, or confirm the Jews in their refusal to believe, or wound the pride of worldly wisdom. All such passages should be believed with devotion, held without hesitation, and interpreted according to the rule of faith. Therefore we should not allow the weak faith of others to make us deny the *economies*, that is the subterfuges which Scripture tells us the prophets and saints made use of. In the belief that we were making concessions to the weakness of others, we would find ourselves guilty of sacrilege, not merely of lying. But as I have said, we must admit the literal truth of what was done, and find an explanation in accordance with piety. In any case, those who are bent on sin will not be denied their excuse to lie if we attempt to contradict the texts we are about to give, and those we have given, or at any rate to clear them with laborious allegorical interpretations. How could the authority of these passages harm those who were already corrupted enough by their own will?

XVII. "Now we should consider deceit, and use it, as if it were something like hellebore. That is a medicine if it is taken in imminent danger of death, but deadly poison if it is taken when there is no such danger. In this way we read that holy men of whom God greatly approved used deceit to advantage. They incurred no guilt by so doing, but actually grew in righteousness. And if deceit brought them such a reputation, would not telling the truth have earned them condemnation? An example is Rahab: Scripture tells us of no virtues in her, but actually of an immoral life, but because she lied in order to conceal the spies and not betray them, she earned the lasting blessing of being incorporated into the people of God. Had she preferred to tell the truth, or to safeguard her fellow citizens, she and all her household would certainly not have escaped the fate that impended, nor would Rahab have been mentioned by the evangelists who wrote of the Lord's ancestry, and inserted in the list of patriarchs found worthy of bringing forth the Saviour of us all, in the succession of her line (Josh 2; cf. Matt. 1:5).

On the other hand Delilah, concerned for her fellow-citizens' advantage, betrayed the truth which she had discovered, and as a

XVII. On Vows

result suffered the pain of eternal loss, leaving behind her only the memory of her treachery. If disclosing the truth is likely to cause serious damage, then we may take refuge in deceit, as long as we feel the salutary reproach of a humble conscience. But when there is no excuse of extreme need, deceit should be carefully avoided as something deadly. Just as I said about a draught of hellebore, it is only healthy if it is taken at a time of crisis, and incurable mortal illness, but if it is consumed when the body is sound and in good health, its powerful poison instantly takes hold of the vital energies.

This we see clearly in the case of Rahab of Jericho and the patriarch Jacob: she could not have escaped death by any other means than this, nor could he have received the first-born's blessing. God does not only judge and assess our actual words and actions, but examines our intentions and purposes as well. If he sees that something has been done or pledged for the sake of eternal salvation, in the light of divine contemplation, no matter how harsh or unjust it may appear to men, God observes the secret devotion of the heart, and judges not the sound of the words but the intention of the will. It is the goal of the action, the aim of the performer, that must be considered, so that as we have seen some were able to be justified by a lie, and others by speaking the truth incurred the penalty of eternal death. With this in mind, the patriarch Jacob was not afraid to imitate his brother's hairy hide by wrapping himself in skins, and was praiseworthy in agreeing to his mother when she suggested this deceit. It appeared that by this means he could acquire a greater boon of blessing and justification than by observing the truth. He did not doubt that the blame for the deceit would be swept away in the torrent of his father's blessing, blown swiftly away like a mist before the breath of the Holy Spirit, and that the reward of virtue would be more richly poured out on him because of this pretence than it could be by ingenuous truth."

XVIII. GERMANUS: "It is not surprising that in the Old Testament such equivocation could be used, and several holy men told lies without blame, since we can see that much greater licence was permitted because of the roughness of the age. We are not shocked when the holy David, in his flight from Saul, met Achimelech the priest who asked him, 'why art thou alone, and no man with thee?' and replied, 'the king hath commanded me a business, and said: Let no man know the thing for which thou art sent by me . . ., and I have appointed my servants to such and such a place.' Then he said, 'hast thou here at hand a spear, or a sword? For I brought not my own sword, nor my own weapons with me, for the king's business required haste' (I Kings (I Sam.) 21: 1–2, 8). Or in this case, David came to Achish the king of Gath, and pretended to be raving mad, 'and he changed his countenance before them, and slipt down between their hands. And he stumbled against the doors of the gate; and his spittle ran down his beard' (I Kings (I Sam.) 21: 13). But in those days they were permitted to enjoy whole flocks of wives and concubines, and no sin was imputed to them for that; they frequently drew the blood of their enemies, with their own hands, and that was considered praiseworthy, not merely blameless. Now however, in the light of the Gospel we see that these things are quite forbidden, and cannot be done without great sin and sacrilege. In the same way we do not believe that anyone can use deceit, no matter under what pretext, without compromise, or blame. As Our Lord says, 'let your speech be: Yea, Yea: No, No. And that which is over and above these is of evil' (Matt. 5: 37). St Paul also agrees, saying, 'lie not one to another'" (Col. 3: 9).

XIX. JOSEPH: "That ancient liberty of having a multitude of wives and concubines, was rightly abrogated by the perfection of the Gospels, as being unnecessary now that the times have run their course, and the multiplication of the human race has been completed. For up to the time of the coming of Christ it was fitting that the primordial blessing should remain in force, which is, 'increase and multiply, and fill the earth' (Gen. 1: 28). It was proper too that from the root of that human fecundity, which prevailed in the synagogue in the conditions of the time, there

XVII. On Vows

should grow the buds of angelic virginity, and the scented fruits of continence ripen in the Church.

But even at that time deceit was forbidden, as the whole text of the Old Testament shows us clearly: 'thou wilt destroy all that speak a lie' (Psalm 5:7), and 'the bread of lying is sweet to a man: but afterwards his mouth shall be filled with gravel' (Prov. 20:17). Moses himself says, 'thou shalt fly lying' (Exod. 23:7). However a lie can, as we have said, be employed when there is great need, or some salutary outcome, because of which it should not be condemned. In the instance you mentioned of King David, when he fled from Saul's unjust persecution to Achimelech the priest, it was not for the sake of some gain, or with the intention of harming anyone, but only to preserve himself from that wrongful pursuit that he used deceitful words; indeed he refused to stain his hands with the blood of his enemy the king, even though God often put him into his power, saying, 'The Lord be merciful unto me, that I may do no such thing to my master the Lord's anointed, as to lay my hand upon him, because he is the Lord's anointed' (I Kings (I Sam.) 24:7). Therefore we cannot deny the lawfulness of the actions of holy men, which we read about in the Old Testament, for they did them either through God's will, or as a figure of the holy sacraments, or for the salvation of others; nor need we ourselves avoid deceit under pressure of necessity, since we see that even the apostles agreed to it when it was demanded in the consideration of some real benefit.

We shall leave that point for a moment, until we have dealt with the examples we find in the Old Testament; after that we can better look at how holy and righteous men can agree about this sort of equivocation, in the new covenant as well as the old. Now what shall we say of Chusai, who rightly deceived Absalom out of concern for David's safety? Scripture tells us that God approved of him, when he pretended to be loyal to Absalom, while deceiving him and plotting against him, to destroy the credit of his advisors: 'and by the will of the Lord the profitable counsel of Achitophel was defeated, that the Lord might bring evil upon Absalom' (II Kings (II Sam.) 17:14). There could be no blame for one who acted with a righteous intent, making a devout decision for the just cause, planning a pious deception for the safety and victory of the one whose devotion pleased God. Or what shall we say about that woman, who received the messengers sent by the same Chusai to David, and hid them in a well, spreading a sheet over its mouth, and pretending to dry sodden barley on it. 'They passed on in haste,' she said, 'after they had tasted a little water' (II Kings (II Sam.) 17: 20), and by this deception she secured them from the hands of their pursuers.

Now what would you have done, I ask, if a similar situation had arisen, now, when you live under the Gospel: would you have chosen to conceal them, telling a similar lie in the same manner, 'they passed on after they had tasted a little water', and so fulfil the precept, 'deliver them that are led to death: and forbear not to redeem those that are being put to death' (Prov. 24:11, LXX)? Or would you prefer to tell the truth and betray the hidden men to their pursuers? What of St Paul's words, 'let no man seek his own, but that which is another's', 'charity seeketh not her own', but 'those that are other mens', and 'as I also . . . not seeking that which is profitable to myself but to many; that they may be saved' (I Cor. 10: 24, 13: 5, 10: 33; Phil. 2: 4)? If we seek only for what is our own, and are obstinate in seeking what is profitable for ourselves, then it would be necessary for us to speak the truth even in these desperate situations, and so we would become responsible for the death of others. But if we put the safety of others before our own advancement, we shall fulfil the Apostle's command, and will certainly find it necessary to lie. Thus we cannot possess the true core of charity, nor take concern for the good of others as St Paul urges us, unless we relax slightly what would be appropriate for our own advancement in perfection, and choose to defer to the needs of others with real charity. In this way we can like St Paul become weak for the weak, so as to gain the weak (cf. I Cor. 9: 22).

XX. "It was by the inspiration of such examples that the holy apostle James, and all the leaders of the early Church, encouraged the apostle Paul to go through a pretence, taking account of the

XVII. On Vows

feelings of the weak. They urged him to be purified according to the precepts of the Law, to shave his head and to offer sacrifice, considering that the present wrong of that hypocrisy was of no account considering the gain which would be achieved by his continuing to preach (Acts 21). The Apostle Paul, by strict scrupulosity in this matter, could not have gained any merit proportionate to the loss to the whole world which his early death would have been. Had he not been preserved for the proclamation of the Gospel, by this beneficial hypocrisy, the world would surely have suffered that loss. Therefore we can agree to a deceit, which is necessary and pardonable, at whatever loss to ourselves, when the admission of the truth threatens a greater evil, and the merit to ourselves of confessing the truth cannot outweigh the damage it would cause. The same holy Apostle tells us elsewhere that he always observed this moderation, for he says, 'I became to the Jews, a Jew, that I might gain the Jews; to them that are under the law, as if I were under the law (whereas myself was not under the law), that I might gain them that were under the law; to them that were without the law, as if I were without the law (whereas I was not without the law of God, but was in the law of Christ), that I might gain them that were without the law. To the weak I became weak, that I might gain the weak. I became all things to all men, that I might save all' (I Cor. 9:20–3). This clearly means that he always adapted himself to the weakness and capacity of those he was instructing, and relaxed somewhat of the rigour of perfection. He did not keep to what might seem the strict requirement, but chose instead what was needed to benefit the weak.

Examining this text more closely, let us look at the Apostle's claim to virtue point by point. You may ask how he shows himself to have changed, to become all things to all men. How did he become a Jew to the Jews? Obviously when, despite holding to the opinion which he had proclaimed to the Galatians, 'behold, I, Paul, tell you, that if you be circumcised, Christ shall profit you nothing' (Gal. 5:2), he circumcised Timothy, thus adopting the appearance of continuing Judaism. And when did he make himself as if he were under the law, for those who were under the law? Clearly when

James, and the other elders of the Church were afraid of being attacked by a throng of believing Jews, or Christians with Jewish customs, who had found faith in Christ but still held to the ritual of the Old Law; they made this suggestion, in that situation, urging Paul, 'thou seest, brother, how many thousands there are among the Jews that have believed; and they are all zealous for the law. Now they have heard of thee that thou teachest those Jews, who are among the Gentiles, to depart from Moses; saying that they ought not to circumcise their children.' They continued, 'do therefore this that we say to thee. We have four men, who have a vow on them. Take these and sanctify thyself with them; and bestow on them, that they may shave their heads. And all will know that the things which they have heard of thee are false; but that thou thyself also walkest keeping the law' (Acts 21: 20–1, 23–4). Thus for the salvation of those who were under the law, he trampled upon his own principles for a moment. Although he had said, 'I, through the law, am dead to the law, that I may live to God' (Gal. 2: 19), he was made to shave his head, and be purified according to the law, and offer sacrifice in the Temple according to the rite of Moses.

Do you ask where he became as if he were without the law, for the salvation of those who were quite ignorant of the Law of the Lord? See the opening of his sermon to the pagan people of Athens, where scepticism reigned: 'for passing by and seeing your idols, I found an altar also, on which was written: To the Unknown God.' He began his discourse with their own cult, as if he were himself without the law, and takes the opportunity of that pagan inscription to introduce the faith of Christ, saying, 'what therefore you worship, without knowing it, that I preach to you' (Acts 17: 23). And a little further on, as if he were quite ignorant of the divine law, he chooses to quote a verse of pagan poetry instead of the teaching of Moses or Christ, 'as some also of your own poets said: For we are also his offspring.' Once he had assailed them with his own evidence, which was beyond dispute, he confirmed the truth by quoting the false, saying, 'being, therefore, the offspring of God, we must not suppose the divinity to be like unto gold or silver or stone, the graving of art and device of man' (Acts 17: 28–9).

XVII. On Vows

He made himself weak for the weak, when he permitted those who were unable to be continent to return together again, not by precept but by concession (cf. I Cor. 7:5). Or when he gave the Corinthians 'milk to drink, not meat', stating that he was 'with them in weakness and in fear and in much trembling' (I Cor. 3:2, 2:3). He made himself all things to all men, that he might save all, when he said, 'let not him that eateth despise him that eateth not; and he that eateth not, let him not judge him that eateth' (Rom. 14:3), and, 'he that giveth his virgin in marriage doth well; and he that giveth her not doth better' (I Cor. 7:38), and again, 'who is weak, and I am not weak? Who is scandalised, and I am not on fire?' (II Cor. 11:29). He expanded on his advice to the Corinthians in this way, 'be without offence to the Jews and to the Gentiles and to the church of God. As I also in all things please not men, not seeking that which is profitable to myself but to many, that they may be saved' (I Cor. 10:32–3).

It would surely have been beneficial to himself had he not circumcised Timothy, not shaved his head, not undergone the Jewish purification, not gone barefoot to offer the offerings of the law, but he did all these out of concern for the salvation of others, for he sought not what was useful for himself but for the many. Although this was done through the contemplation of God, yet it was not without an element of deceit. He who, through the law of Christ was dead to the Law, that he might live to God (cf. Gal. 2:19), and who had come to despise the justice of the law in which he had lived without complaint, considering it but as dung, that he might gain Christ (cf. Phil. 3:6–8), could not be sincere in offering what the Law required. We cannot believe that he who said, 'if I build up again the things which I have destroyed, I make myself a prevaricator' (Gal. 2:18), has fallen under his own condemnation.

Now since the action performed is not as significant as the intention of the performer, we can find contrary examples where the truth was harmful, a lie would have been beneficial. King Saul complained to his court of David's flight, and said, 'will the son of Jesse give every one of you fields and vineyards, and make you all tribunes, and centurions: that all of you have conspired against me, and there is no one to inform me?' and Doeg the Edomite gave away no more than the truth, when he said, 'I saw the son of Jesse, in Nobe, with Achimelech the son of Achitob the priest. And he consulted the Lord for him, and gave him victuals, and gave him the sword of Goliath the Philistine' (I Kings (I Sam.) 22: 7–8, 9–10). For that truth-telling he deserved to be rooted out of the land of the living, as the Psalmist says of him, 'therefore will God destroy thee for ever. He will pluck thee out, and remove thee from thy dwelling place: and thy root out of the land of the living' (Psalm 51/52: 7). The land, indeed, from which Doeg is to be rooted out for ever because he told the truth, is the same land in which the whore Rahab was established because she told a lie (cf. Josh. 6). Likewise we recall how Samson was foully betrayed by his wicked wife telling the truth, which had long been concealed by deceit; the truth which he foolishly revealed brought destruction upon him, for he had neglected to observe the prophet's counsel, 'keep the doors of thy mouth from her that sleepeth in thy bosom' (Mic. 7: 5).

XXI. "Here is an example of a problem which often, almost daily, occurs to us, which we can never avoid, no matter how careful we be, but whether we like it or not we have to confront. What, I ask, should we do, if when we have determined to postpone our meal, a brother arrives in the evening and asks whether we have eaten? Should we conceal our fasting, and hide our virtuous abstinence, or should we tell the truth about it? We might hide it, to fulfil Our Lord's command, 'that thou appear not to men to fast, but to thy Father who is in secret', and 'let not thy left hand know what thy right hand doth' (Matt. 6: 18, 3). But then we would be lying. Or we could reveal our virtuous self-restraint, and be hit by the Gospel teaching, 'Amen, I say to you, they have received their reward' (Matt. 6: 2). And then, what if someone firmly declines a drink offered by his brother, and vows never to accept it, whereas the other in gladness for his arrival was begging him to take it? Should he eventually give in to the brother who has fallen flat on the ground before him, and is sure that he cannot fulfil his

XVII. On Vows

longing for charity except by giving this service, or should he remain stubbornly true to his word?"

XXII. GERMANUS: "I don't think there is any doubt in your first example: it is better to conceal our abstinence than to display it to enquirers. In cases like this we too admit that deceit is inevitable. In the second case there is no necessity to lie, firstly because we can refuse the service our brother offers us without binding ourselves with a vow; and then because if we have once refused, we can stand by our decision."

XXIII. JOSEPH: "I am sure that such is the teaching in the monasteries where you received your first training in the religious life, where the superiors are accustomed to place their own wishes before the relief of the brethren, and stubbornly adhere to what they have once determined to do. Among us, on the other hand, our elders whose faith is attested by miracles of apostolic virtue, and who act always by judgment, and the discernment of spirits, rather than inflexible determination, are of the opinion that a much greater reward is to be reaped by those who make concessions to the weakness of others, than those who cling to their own resolutions. They consider that there is more virtue in concealing their abstemiousness by a necessary and humble deceit, as they call it, than in revealing it by a conceited declaration of the truth.

XXIV. "Abba Piamun, after twenty five years, took without hesitation some grapes and wine which a brother offered him, choosing to consume what he was given, although it was not his custom, rather than to publicise his abstinence which no one had known about. We should take into consideration what I remember to have been the consistent practice of our elders – they concealed their own miracles and their own actions, under the pretence of being those of others, if it were necessary to mention them in instructing the juniors. What can we call this but straight deception? If only we ourselves had something fit to tell the juniors and encourage their faith! If we did, we would certainly not hesitate to follow that example of concealment. It is better to deceive, by covering up in this way, than either to keep inappropriately silent about something that could be edifying to a listener, or to tell it truthfully about ourselves and brag about it on our conceit. St Paul, the Teacher of the Gentiles, gives is a clear example of this in his own case, for he preferred to speak of his great revelations under the cover of another person: 'I know a man in Christ . . . (whether in the body or out of the body, I know not: God knoweth), such a one caught up to the third heaven. And I know such a man . . . that he was caught up into paradise and heard secret words which it is not granted to man to utter' (II Cor. 12: 2–4).

XXV. "We cannot cover the whole subject in a short space, for who would be able to describe how virtually all of the patriarchs, and innumerable holy men have embraced an inheritance of deceit, so to speak? Some did so to save their lives, others out of desire for a blessing, others out of pity, others to keep some secret hidden, others out of zeal for God, others in order to investigate the truth. But though we cannot enumerate them all, we may not totally pass them over. The saintly Joseph was compelled by his piety to accuse his brothers falsely, and he swore by the health of Pharoah, saying, 'You are spies. You are come to view the weaker parts of the land', and then, 'send one of you to fetch your brother: and you shall be in prison, till what you have said be proved, whether it be true or false: or else by the health of Pharoah you are spies' (Gen. 42: 9, 16). Had he not terrified them by this merciful deception, he would never have been able to see his father and brother, nor to feed them in their distress, nor to cleanse the conscience of his brethren from the guilt of having sold him. The blame for having caused his brothers fear, through a lie, was not as great as the praise he deserves for using this feigned danger to bring his enemies and betrayers to penance and salvation. When they were in distress through this weighty deception, they were broken by the consciousness of their own real crime in the past, not of his false accusation, for they said, 'we deserve to suffer these things, because we have sinned against our brother, seeing

XVII. On Vows

the anguish of his soul, when he besought us and we would not hear. Therefore is this affliction come upon us' (Gen. 42:21). This confession brought them forgiveness from the brother against whom they had so cruelly sinned, and we may believe that through their saving humility their sin was quite wiped out.

And what of Solomon? He received a gift of wisdom from God, but in his first judgment used it only to utter a lie. In order to extract the truth, which a woman's deceit had concealed, he himself used a well-thought out deceit, saying, 'Bring me a sword, . . . divide the living child in two, and give half to the one, and half to the other' (III Kings (I Kings) 3:24–5). This pretended cruelty stirred the compassion of the true mother, but was accepted by the one who was not its mother: so he, judging the truth in his wisdom, pronounced a sentence which no one could fail to see was inspired by God. 'Give the living child to this woman, and let it not be killed; for she is the mother thereof' (III Kings (I Kings) 3:27).

We need not, and cannot give all the examples we can find, either reassuring or startling, of other cases where Scripture teaches us how holy men, and angels, and even Almighty God himself changed resolutions they had once made. That holy man David had made a resolution, with an oath, saying, 'May God do so and so, and add more to the foes of David, if I leave of all that belong to Nabal till the morning any that mingeth against the wall' (I Kings (I Sam.) 25:22). Yet when Nabal's wife Abigail pleaded and entreated for him, he withdrew his threat, relented his purpose, and chose to be considered inconsistent rather than to keep faith with his oath and perform it in cruelty. 'As the Lord liveth . . . if thou hadst not quickly come to meet me, there had not been left to Nabal by the morning light any that mingeth against the wall' (I Kings (I Sam.) 25:34). We should never consider imitating David's rash and hasty oath, taken in turmoil with his mind enraged, but we can find a model in his second thoughts and in his mercy.

Paul, the Chosen Vessel, wrote to the Corinthians, promising them that he would certainly return, saying, 'Now, I will come to you, when I shall have passed through Macedonia. For I shall pass through Macedonia. And with you I shall abide, or even spend the winter; that you may bring me on my way whithersoever I shall go. For I will not see you now by the way; for I trust that I shall abide with you some time' (I Cor. 16:5–7). He repeats this promise in his second epistle, saying: 'and in this confidence I had a mind to come to you before, that you might have a second grace; and to pass by you into Macedonia; and again from Macedonia to come to you, and by you to be brought on my way towards Judea' (II Cor. 1:15–16). But on wiser consideration, he admits openly that he is not going to carry out his promise, 'whereas then I was thus minded, did I use lightness? Or the things that I purpose, do I purpose according to the flesh, that there should be with me, IT IS, and IT IS NOT?' (II Cor. 1:17). He goes on to explain the reason why he decided to contradict his avowed purpose, rather than confer a grave burden on his disciples by coming to them, and to confirm this with an oath, saying, 'I call God to witness upon my soul, that, to spare you, I came not any more to Corinth; I determined this with myself, not to come to you again in sorrow' (II Cor. 1:23, 2:1).

When the angels refused to enter Lot's house in Sodom, they said to him, 'No, but we will abide in the street'. He begged them and persuaded them to change their minds, as Scripture tells us, 'he pressed them very much to turn in unto him' (Gen. 19:2–3). Now if they had known that they were going to turn in unto him, in refusing his invitation their excuse was deceitful; if they really meant to excuse themselves, then they are proved clearly to have changed their minds. Since we believe the Holy Spirit inspired the sacred volumes for no other purpose than for us to learn by their example, we can see that we need not cling stubbornly to our intended purposes, but can subject them to our free will. We may preserve our judgment free from any constraint of law, to be ready to follow whatever wise counsel may suggest, and without delay or refusal change unhesitatingly to what mature deliberation finds more useful.

To proceed to a more sublime example, when King Ezechias was on his bed, suffering from a severe illness, the prophet Isaiah spoke to him, in God's name, saying, 'Thus saith the Lord: Take order with thy house, for thou shalt die, and not live. And Ezechias turned his face to the wall and prayed to the Lord, and said: I beseech thee, O Lord, remember how I have walked before thee in truth, and with a perfect heart, and have done that which is good in thy sight. And Ezechias wept with great weeping.' Then it was said to Isaiah, 'Go and say to Ezechias, King of Judah: Thus saith the Lord the God of David thy father: I have heard thy prayer, and I have seen thy tears: behold, I will add to thy days fifteen years. And I will deliver thee and this city out of the hand of the king of the Assyrians, and I will protect it, for my own sake, and for David my servant's sake' (Isaiah 38:1–6, cf. IV Kings (II Kings) 20:1–6). How clear this is as evidence that in his mercy and loving concern the Lord prefers to change his word, adding fifteen years to the life of his suppliant onto the determined time of death, rather than to be found inexorable in his unchanging decree!

In a similar way God's rebuke to the Ninivites was, 'Yet three days, and Ninive shall be destroyed' (Jon. 3:4, LXX). His imminent threatening sentence was quickly appeased by their fasting and repentance, in ready affection he turned to the path of mercy. You could say that the Lord foresaw their conversion, and threatened the destruction of the city for the purpose of instigating their repentance and salvation: it would follow that those who are in charge of the brethren may threaten those who need correction with a punishment more harsh than they really intend to inflict, without being charged with deceit. Or you could say that God revoked his severe decree in consideration of their repentance, as is said through the prophet Ezechiel, 'if I shall say to the wicked: Thou shalt surely die: and he do penance for his sin and do judgment and justice, . . . he shall surely live and shall not die' (Ezek. 33:14–15). By that example we can learn that we should not be obstinate in standing by our resolutions, but be merciful in modifying any threat that we have been obliged to make. You should not think that this was an exceptional case for the Ninivites, since through the prophet Jeremiah he declares that he will act in this way in general, for anyone, and promises that when necessary he will not hesitate to change his decrees according to our deserts;

'I will suddenly speak against a nation and against a kingdom, to root out and to pull down and to destroy it. If that nation against which I have spoken shall repent of their evil, I also will repent of the evil that I have thought to do to them. And I will suddenly speak of a nation and of a kingdom, to build up and plant it. If it shall do evil in my sight, that it obey not my voice, I will repent of the good that I have spoken to do unto it' (Jer. 18:7–10). He says also against Ezechias, 'leave not out one word, if so be they will hearken and be converted every one from his evil way; that I may repent me of the evil that I think to do unto them of the wickedness of their doings' (Jer. 26:2–3). These texts prove that we should not be stubborn in adhering to our resolutions, but modify them with reasonable discernment, that a better course should always be preferred and chosen, and that we should not hesitate in changing to a course which is assessed as being more beneficial.

[Chapter XXVI in PL] What we may learn above all, from God's inestimable judgments, is that because he foresees the end result before anything is begun, he arranges everything in order and according to common sense and human needs, judging everything by what men actually do, rather than what they might do, or what he foresees in his inexpressible wisdom; thus he either rejects a man or calls him, either bestowing his grace upon him every day or withdrawing it. We can see this in the case of the election of Saul: God could not be unaware of his tragic end, but he chose him out of thousands of Israelites and anointed him as king, rewarding the merits of his life at the time, not taking account his sinful treachery in the future. But when he was afterwards rejected, God speaks as if he regretted his election, and complains in human terms and emotions, saying, 'It repenteth me that I have made Saul king: for he hath forsaken me, and hath not executed my commandments.' And we are told later, 'Samuel mourned for Saul, because the Lord repented that he had made him king over Israel' (I Kings (I Sam.) 15:11, 35). Through the prophet Ezechiel the Lord proclaims that he has ever operated in this way, and will treat all men like this at all times, 'Yea, if I shall say to the just that he shall surely live, and

XVII. On Vows

he, trusting in his justice, commit iniquity: all his justices shall be forgotten and in his iniquity, which he hath committed, in the same shall he die. And if I shall say to the wicked: Thou shalt surely die: and he do penance for his sin and do judgment and justice. And if that wicked man restore the pledge and render what he hath robbed and walk in the commandments of life and do no unjust thing: he shall surely live and shall not die. None of his sins, which he hath committed, shall be imputed to him' (Ezek. 33:13–16).

In the case of the people whom the Lord had adopted out of all the nations, when he had turned away his face of mercy because of their sudden apostasy, Moses pleaded for them, crying, 'Lord, I beseech thee: this people hath sinned a heinous sin, and they have made to themselves gods of gold. Either forgive them this trespass, or if thou do not, strike me out of the book that thou hast written. And the Lord answered him: He that hath sinned against me, him will I strike out of my book' (Exod. 32:31–2). When David complained of Judas and those who persecuted Christ, in the spirit of prophecy, he said, 'let them be blotted out of the book of the living', and since their crime was so great that they did not merit penance and salvation, he continued, 'and with the just let them not be written' (Psalm 68/69:29). The force of that prophetic curse was fulfilled in Judas, for when he had committed his treacherous sin, he went out and hanged himself. Thus, after his name had been blotted out, he could not return to penance and again deserve to be written in heaven with the just. Let there be no doubt that the name of Judas was really written in the book of the living, at the time when Christ gave him the rank of an apostle, and he too heard, with the others, 'rejoice not in this, that spirits are subject unto you; but rejoice in this, that your names are written in heaven' (Luke 10:20). He was corrupted by sinful greed for money, and was cast down from the register of heaven to the earth. Of him and those like him the prophet aptly spoke: 'O Lord, all that forsake thee shall be confounded: they that depart from thee shall be written in the earth: because they have forsaken the Lord, the vein of living waters' (Jer. 17:13). And another says, 'They shall not be in the counsel of my people, nor shall they be written in the writing of the house of Israel: neither shall they enter into the land of Israel' (Ezek. 13: 9).

XXVI. "We should not pass over in silence the precept that even if we have bound ourselves with a vow, under the influence of anger or some other emotion (and this is something no monk should do), we should still weigh up the merits of both sides of the question with an open mind, and compare whatever it is we have promised to do with whatever we are made to adopt instead. We should change without delay to the course which is judged to be the better, after our superiors have examined the case. It is better to break our word than to suffer the loss of something more devout and beneficial. We have no remembrance of the wise and approved fathers ever being stubborn and inflexible in such resolutions, but they were softened by good reasons like wax in the sun, and adopted the better course without hesitation when wiser counsel prevailed. Those whom we do recall clinging obstinately to their promises were always found to be unreasonable and lacking in due discretion."

XXVII. GERMANUS: "It appears from your argument, which you have fully elaborated, that a monk should make no vow, lest he appear either to be untrustworthy or stubborn. But then what are we to make of the passage in the Psalms, 'I have sworn, and am determined to keep the judgments of thy justice' (Psalm 118/119: 106)? What can swearing and determination mean except to keep inflexibly to what you have resolved?"

XXVIII. JOSEPH: "We are not talking about the great commandments, without which we cannot be saved at all, but about matters which we can dispense or observe without risk to our souls. Such matters, I mean, as continuous strict fasting, or perpetual abstinence from wine or oil, keeping entirely within the cell, attending constantly to reading or meditation – these things may be practised as we please without risk to our monastic profession and purpose, or they can be omitted without blame when it is necessary. But as for the keeping of the great commandments, we should stand firm to them, accepting even death if needful, and of these it is said, without compromise, 'I have sworn, and am determined'. The same applies to the preservation of charity, for the sake of which all else is to be set aside, rather than injure that good, peaceful and perfect virtue. We should pledge ourselves in the same way to the observance of chastity, and do the like for the faith, for decency and justice. All these things are to be kept with unwavering constancy, and the slightest deviation from them is accursed. But of the bodily exercises, which are said to be useful for the moment, we have already established that if we discover a more certain route to devotion, which suggests we should change them, then we are bound to them by no law, but may omit them and freely change to the better course. There is no danger in abandoning these bodily exercises for a while: but to abandon the great commandments even for a moment is perilous.

XXIX. "We should take the same care that if by chance a word fall from your lips which you had wished to be kept secret, the listener should not be troubled by an order of silence: it will be more likely to stay hidden if you pass it over casually and simply, since your brother will not be tormented by the temptation to divulge it if he thinks the matter is trivial, mentioned only in passing, and obviously unimportant since he heard it without being given any order to keep it quiet. If you make him swear an oath to keep the matter confidential, you can be sure he will soon let it slip. This is because the devil's attack will be all the greater upon him in order to grieve you and wrong you, and to make him an oath-breaker as soon as possible.

XXX. "A monk therefore should never take a vow over matters which only pertain to physical exercises, lest he provoke the enemy to assail him in these things which he observes as if bound by law, and is thus the more quickly compelled to abandon them. We are all established in the freedom of grace, and if we invent a law for ourselves, we are binding ourselves into slavery. Thus, if we find ourselves obliged to do something, which in other circumstances might have been quite lawful or even praiseworthy and deserving of thanks, we appear instead to be disobedient, sinfully untrustworthy. 'For where there is no law, neither is there transgression'" (Rom. 4: 15).

And so we decided to remain in Egypt, encouraged by the saintly Joseph's learned advice, as if by an oracle of God. However since we were still concerned about our promise, after seven years had passed we were pleased to fulfil our pledge. We returned to our monastery for just long enough to find courage to ask permission to return to the desert. We first paid due respect to our superiors, and then restored our former affectionate relationship with those who had not considered our frequent letters sufficient to maintain the bond of charity. Finally, once the uncomfortable scruple over our promise had been quite removed, with the friendly blessing of our superiors, we returned to the remote wilderness of Scete.

And so, most holy brethren, we have expounded the wisdom and teaching of those famous Fathers, as far as our ignorance was capable. Our clumsy writing may have confused the matter rather than explained it, but I hope that our rough style will not detract from the credit of such distinguished men. Our judge will consider it better for us to attempt an exposition of this splendid teaching, however clumsily, rather than keep silent altogether, since if the reader considers the sublime message, his understanding will not be affected by our untutored style, for we were more concerned to be useful than to be praised. [Not that I was unaware that to describe the sayings of the saints is perilous, and unlikely to gain me credit, but I put my foot into the snare very carefully, as they say, and did not shrink from letting myself risk rebuke in the vague hope of being useful to others.] I warn everyone who may happen to lay hands on this book, that they should be aware that anything they like is what the Fathers said, anything they dislike was my own, [but they all must find the life and teaching of the saints delightful].

❖

✢ THE THIRD PART ✢

Containing the last seven conversations with the Fathers who lived in the more remote parts of Egypt

Preface

To Jovinian, Minervius, Leontius and Theodore

After I had finished, with the grace of Christ, the ten Collations of the Fathers, which I composed at the request of the holy bishops Helladius and Leontius, I then dedicated seven more to that holy bishop, Honoratus by name, honoured for his merits, and to that devout servant of Christ Eucherius. Now I have set out to deliver as many more to you, my holy brothers Jovinian, Minervius, Leontius and Theodore. The last of whom it was who established holy religious discipline in these Gallic provinces by teaching the ancient paths of virtue; the rest of you have encouraged some monks to pursue their vocation in monasteries, and through your instructions have even urged others to the perfection of eremitical life. These collations of the greatest Fathers were designed for that purpose, and are suitable and moderate in all things for either vocation, which you have caused to flourish among so many monks both in our western lands and on the islands. Thus not only those who still remain under praiseworthy obedience in a community, but also those who have withdrawn a little way from your monasteries and practise the discipline of hermits, will find much instruction, suitable for different places and the measure of each one's capacity. Your efforts up till now have made it possible for them to be ready to receive the teaching and advice of the elders, since they are already prepared and accustomed to such exercises. With the volumes of the Collations they may welcome the authors of those Collations into their own cells; they may speak with them every day, in questions and answers. Thus they may follow that vocation, which is hard and virtually unknown in these parts; in all its perils they rely, not on their own initiative but on the many examples they have been given, and many warnings of sad detours. Thus they may learn to embrace the discipline of hermit life under their instructions, for those Fathers were trained by ancient traditions and their own long experience.

✧ THE EIGHTEENTH COLLATION ✧
BEING THAT OF ABBA PIAMUN

On the Three Kinds of Monks;
[and a Fourth recently arisen].

I. How we came to Diolcus, and were received by Abba Piamun.
II. What Abba Piamun said on how novices should be trained by the example of their elders.
III. That juniors should not dispute their elders' advice.
IV. Of the three kinds of monks which are in Egypt.
V. The founders of the cenobitic vocation.
VI. On the origin and order of anchorites.
VII. On the origin and way of life of the Sarabites.
VIII. On a fourth kind of monk.
IX. A question, on the difference between a cenobium and a monastery.
X. The reply.
XI. On true humility, and how Abba Serapion once detected someone's false humility.
XII. A question, on how true patience may be acquired.
XIII. The reply.
XIV. On the example of patience shown by a certain woman.
XV. On the example of patience given by Abba Paphnutius.
XVI. On the perfection of patience.

I. After we had met and spoken with those three elders, whose Collations we have already written up at the urging of our holy brother Eucherius, we were all the more eager to visit the more remote parts of Egypt, where a larger number of more perfect saints then resided. We came therefore to a village called Diolcus, near one of the seven mouths of the River Nile, not that our route took us there, but because we wanted to meet the holy men who live there. We had heard that there were many celebrated monasteries, founded by the earliest Fathers, and so like greedy merchants lured on by the hope of greater profit, we undertook the risk of a journey of discovery. After a long journey we arrived, and our gaze travelled over so many peaks of virtue, until as we looked around our eyes fell on Abba Piamun: he was the eldest of all the hermits living there, and was their priest, shining like a lofty beacon. Like that city in the Gospel which is set on a mountain-top, he was immediately conspicuous in our regard. The virtues and miracles which he displayed while we were present, through the grace of God giving testimony to his merits, are better omitted, to keep within our declared purpose, and the limits of this volume. For we did promise to write about the training and wisdom of the saints, as far as we could remember them, not about the miracles of God, intending to offer the reader the instructions necessary for him to perfect his life, not just a useless and vain tale of wonders which would be no help in dealing with vice.

The holy Piamun entertained us in kindly fashion, and we were most grateful to be so received. He realised we were not from that locality, and asked us with real concern, why we had come to Egypt, and from where. We told him we had come from a monastery in Syria in the search for perfection, and so he began as follows:

II. "Any man who desires to become skilled in any art, my sons, must give himself time to study the discipline he chooses, with great care and attention. He must follow the advice and training given by masters who are qualified in that art or skill; otherwise if he neglects to observe their patience and practice, he will have no hope of becoming like them, but will wish in vain. We

XVIII. On the Three Kinds of Monks

have heard of several people who came to these parts from your homeland, merely to travel around and observe the monasteries of our brethren, not prepared to accept the rules and discipline for the sake of which they came here, or to retire into their cells and attempt to put into practice what they had seen or heard of. They retained the customs and practices in which they had been trained, so that many considered they had changed their abode out of the need to escape poverty, not for the sake of making progress. In fact they proved unable to acquire any advancement, and because of their fixed minds could not even endure to remain for long in this region. This is because they had not changed their style of fasting, or their pattern of psalmody, not even their habitual clothing: what then can we imagine they wanted in this region except a livelihood?

III. "Now in your case, if you have been drawn to imitate our vocation for the sake of God, as we believe you have, you should put aside all the customs you have been trained to, and follow in all humility whatever you see the elders doing or teaching. You should not be disturbed or diverted from your purpose of imitating them, if you do not for the moment see the point of any thing or action, for if you think the best of everything, in simplicity, and are more concerned to copy whatever you see the elders teach or do, rather than to dispute it, you will find after putting it into practice that a full understanding of it all will follow. Anyone who begins to learn by arguing will never penetrate the truth of the matter, for the enemy will see that he trusts his own judgment more than the elders', and can easily drive him to the point that he will imagine those very things which are most helpful and salutary to be unnecessary or wrong. The sly fiend deceives him to the extent that in his over confidence he is obstinate in sticking to his own decisions, and convinces himself that the only path to holiness is the one he deems right and just, stubborn in his error.

IV. "Therefore you should begin by learning the origins of our way of life, how it began and where. Once you know the worth of its first founders you will be able to pursue more easily the study of the skill you have chosen, and become more eager to practice it.

There are in Egypt three kinds of monks. Two are excellent, the third lax and by all means to be avoided. The first kind is that of cenobites, who live together in community, and are governed by the judgment of one superior. Most of the monks living in all parts of Egypt are of this kind. The second is that of anchorites, who have first been trained in community, and become perfect in their actual way of life, before choosing seclusion in the wilderness. We ourselves hope to be counted as belonging to this group. The third is the detestable race of Sarabites.

We will speak of each of these in turn. Of these three kinds of monks you should first learn their founders, as I said. By doing so you may conceive a distaste for following a way of life that you should avoid, or a longing for the one you should follow, for each path must lead the follower to its own conclusion, the one that its founder and originator reached.

V. "The vocation of the cenobite dates from the time when the Apostles preached. The whole multitude of believers in Jerusalem were of this kind, as is written in the Acts of the Apostles: 'The multitude of believers had but one heart and one soul. Neither did anyone say that aught of the things which he possessed was his own; but all things were common unto them. Their possessions and goods they sold and divided them to all, according as every one had need. Neither was there anyone needy among them. For as many as were owners of lands or houses sold them and brought the price of the things they sold, and laid it down before the feet of the apostles. And distribution was made to every one, according as he had need' (Acts 4:32, 2:45, 4:34–5). Such, I tell you, was the entire Church, as now only a few can be found living in monasteries. After the death of the Apostles the multitude of believers began to cool, especially those who had come into the faith of Christ from different pagan nations, for the Apostles had asked nothing more of them than to 'abstain from things sacrificed to idols and from blood and from things strangled

XVIII. On the Three Kinds of Monks   397

and from fornication' (Acts 15:29), since they were so new to the faith and long accustomed to pagan ways. This laxity, which was conceded to the pagan converts because their faith was so weak at first, began gradually to contaminate the perfection even of the Church established in Jerusalem. As the number of beggars grew daily, and the number of new arrivals, the fervour of that first faith grew cold. Not only those who followed the faith of Christ, but even the princes of the Church fell away from their strict observance. There were many who thought that what was conceded to the pagans because of their weakness could be lawful for themselves as well, and thought they would come to no harm if they observed the faith and followed the way of Christ in full possession of their property.

Those who still retained the fervour of the Apostles preserved the memory of that early perfection, and moved away from the cities and from the company of those who imagined that a negligent and lax behaviour was lawful for themselves and for the Church of Christ. They settled in rural or remote places, and began to practice privately, and individually, what they remembered the Apostles had taught to the whole body of the Church. Thus there grew up a discipline among those disciples who had withdrawn from the common decadence. As time passed, they were separated from the common mass of believers, in that they abstained from marriage, and kept away from their families and the business of the world, and so they were called monks or *monazontes*, because of the monotony of their solitary life. It followed that because they dwelt together they came to be called *cenobites*, and their huts and residences *cenobia*. This was the only original form of monasticism, and takes precedence in grace as well as age. For many years it remained unchallenged and unchanged until the time of Abba Paul and Abba Antony. We can still see traces of this surviving in the stricter cenobia.

VI. "From the number of these perfect monks, and so to speak from their fertile root, sprang the flowers and fruit of the holy hermits or *anchorites*. I have just mentioned those we consider the originators of this way of life, namely Saint Paul and Saint Antony. They sought out the lonely desert, not out of cowardice, like some, or through sinful instability, but out of a longing for a higher profession, and the contemplation of God. Admittedly the first one, St Paul, is said to have first entered the desert out of necessity, to elude the suspicions of his family in time of persecution. Thus from the monastic life we have described, arose another way of perfection, whose devotees are called *anchorites*, that is those dwelling apart. They were not content with the victory they had won among men, trampling the devil's hidden snares underfoot, but they desired to confront the demons in open warfare and in a more obvious struggle. They were not afraid to penetrate the vast wilderness, in imitation of St John the Baptist, who spent his whole life in the desert. Elijah too, and Elishah, and those whom the Apostle commemorates, 'wandered about in sheepskins, in goatskins, being in want, distressed, afflicted; of whom the world was not worthy; wandering in deserts, in mountains and in dens and in caves of the earth' (Heb. 11:37–8). The Lord speaks figuratively of them to Job: 'Who hath sent out the wild ass free, and who hath loosed his bonds? To whom I gave a house in the wilderness, and his dwellings in the barren land. He scorneth the multitude of the city, he heareth not the cry of the tax-collector. He looketh round about the mountains of his pasture, and seeketh for every green thing' (Job 39:5–8, LXX). In the Psalms also, 'Let them say so that have been redeemed by the Lord: whom he hath redeemed from the hand of the enemy: . . . they wandered in the wilderness, in a place without water: they found not the way of a city for their habitation. They were hungry and thirsty: their soul fainted in them. And they cried to the Lord in their tribulation: and he delivered them out of their distresses' (Psalm 106/107:2, 4–6). Jeremiah described them too: 'It is good for a man, when he hath borne the yoke from his youth. He shall sit solitary and hold his peace, because he hath taken it up upon himself' (Lam. 3:27–8). These are the men who join in the lament and toil of the Psalmist: 'I am become like a pelican in the wilderness: I have

XVIII. On the Three Kinds of Monks

watched, and am become as a sparrow all alone on the housetop' (Psalm 101/102: 7–8).

VII. "While the Christian faith rejoiced in these two kinds of monks, even that order began to deteriorate, till there emerged that detestable breed of faithless monks, or rather there sprang up again that noxious weed which had flourished in the early church under Ananias and Sapphira till it was cut down ruthlessly by the Apostle Peter. It was considered vile and execrable by all monks, and never attempted by anyone, as long as the fear of that severe sentence remained fixed in the memory of the faithful. The blessed Apostle did not permit the aforementioned originators of that new wickedness to be healed through penance or any satisfaction, but cut down the poisonous stock and killed it at once. However, after long neglect and time's oblivion had sufficed for many to clear from their memory the example of the punishment of Ananias and Sapphira and the Apostle's severity, there arose the breed of Sarabites. These withdrew from the communities of cenobites, and looked after their own individual needs (which is why they are aptly called Sarabites in the Egyptian tongue),. They derived from the ranks of those we have described, but preferred to imitate evangelical perfection rather than truly seek it, stimulated by the prestige and praise of those who placed Christ's perfect poverty above all the riches of the world. With feeble minds they affected great virtue, compelled by their needs to adopt this profession, eager to acquire the name of monk without imitating a monk's discipline. They made no effort to adopt the training of a monastery, to subject themselves to the will of a superior, or to learn from their traditions how to overcome their own desires. They undertook no wise and prudent rule, no lawful learning, but made a renunciation only for public display, in the sight of men. Some remained in their own homes, using the privilege of the name of monk to pursue their ordinary occupations; others built themselves cells and called them hermitages, sitting in them by their own right and liberty, without submitting to the precepts of the gospel at all, which bids them take no concern for their daily living, no distractions about domestic affairs. Only those who have freed themselves from all worldly possessions and subjected themselves to the superiors of a monastery, till they cannot call themselves masters even of themselves, can truly observe those precepts without faithless hesitation. The Sarabites, on the other hand, disdain the restrictions of the monastery, and live by twos or threes in cells, not content to be governed by the loving rule of an abbot, but taking great pains to ensure they are free from the yoke of any superior, able to do their own wishes, free to travel anywhere or go out wheresoever they please, free to do whatever they want.

They may be more busy at their daily work than those who dwell in monasteries, toiling at it day and night, but they do not have the same faith or intention, for they do this, not that they may surrender the produce of their labour to the bursar, but to acquire money and hoard it up. See what a difference there is between them! True monks think nothing of the morrow, but offer to God the acceptable fruits of their labours; the Sarabites, lacking trust, are deeply concerned not just for the morrow but for years to come; do they think God is a liar, or without resources, that he should be unable to deliver the promised daily bread and clothing enough, or should not wish to? Monks devote their prayer intentions to attaining true poverty, bare freedom from all possessions; the others to amassing wealth and affluence. Monks compete in their labour to exceed the statutory work of the day, so that there may be more than the monastery needs, and the abbot may be able to distribute it to the prisons, hostels, hospitals and the poor. Sarabites labour so that whatever is over from their daily feasting may give them yet more abundant delight, or be stored up to satisfy their love of money. Even if we grant that this superfluity, which should not have been accumulated, can be distributed to a better end than I have implied, they still do not aspire to the merits of the virtue of poverty. For monks who bring in a great revenue for the monastery, but renounce it for themselves daily, remain in such humble obedience that they are deprived of the use of their own inherited goods, as well as those

XVIII. On the Three Kinds of Monks

their own labour has acquired, and are able therefore to renew every day their first fervent renunciation, depriving themselves of the fruits of their daily work. The Sarabites, on the other hand, are so elated when they make some donation to the poor that they fall into sin every day. Monks are crucified every day and become living martyrs, never giving in to their own will, in their patient observance, in which they remain faithful to the profession they had once embraced; Sarabites, by the weakness of their will, are plunged alive into hell.

The two kinds of real monks are competing in almost equal numbers in our province. In other regions, where I have had to travel for the needs of the Catholic Church, I have found that third kind, the Sarabites, in abundance, and almost alone. In the time of Lucius, the bishop of the Arian heretics, when Valens was on the throne, I brought alms to the brethren who had been banished from Egypt and the Thebaïd to the mines of Pontus and Armenia, because they remained firm in their Catholic faith, and it was then, in those parts, that we found a very few monasteries in some cities, whereas the name of anchorite had never even been heard.

VIII. "There is, to be sure, another, a fourth kind of monk, which we have seen arise recently. They pride themselves in the appearance of anchorites, and in the first flush of enthusiasm appeared to seek perfection in a monastery for a little while, but grew tepid rapidly. They were too proud to return to their previous way of life, and their sins, but were not prepared to bear the yoke of patient humility any longer; they were scornful of obeying a superior's command, but made for separate dwellings with the intention of sitting there alone, molested by no one, and making men consider them meek and humble. This way of life, or rather of laxity, once it has taken hold, never permits them to proceed towards perfection. Their vices, far from being cut off, actually grow stronger and worse, for there is no one to challenge them. Vice grows like a deadly virus, the more it is undetected the greater and more incurable the disease it causes, like a serpent deep within the patient. Out of respect for his lonely cell, no one dares to check the vices of such a solitary, and he himself would rather ignore them than be cured of them. Virtue, you see, only appears when vices are defeated, not concealed."

IX. GERMANUS: "Is there any difference between a cenobium and a monastery, or do both names refer to the same thing?"

X. PIAMUN: "It is true that some do use the word 'monastery' indifferently for 'cenobium', but there is a difference. 'Monastery' refers to a place of retreat, simply the place or habitation of monks; 'cenobium' relates to the quality and discipline of their way of life. The dwelling of a single monk can be called a monastery, but it cannot be called a cenobium unless there is a united common life among several inhabitants. In practice even the places where gangs of Sarabites lurk can be called a monastery.

XI. "Now since I can see that you have grasped the principles of the best kind of monasticism, namely that after training in a worthy cenobium you aspire to the lofty discipline of an anchorite, you must with all your hearts pursue the virtue of humble patience, which I am sure you learnt in your homeland. Do not put on a pretence of humility in words alone, or affected and unnecessary bodily prostrations during the office.

That sort of feigned humility was once elegantly mocked by Abba Serapion. Someone came to him, displaying the greatest abjection in costume and language, and Serapion begged him to spare him a prayer, as the custom is. The other would by no means accede to this request, declaring that he was so steeped in vice as not to deserve even to breathe the same air. He refused to sit on the roll of rushes, but sat on the ground instead. Nor would he allow Serapion to wash his feet, but after they had eaten together and custom allowed a conversation, Serapion began to rebuke him, gently and kindly, saying that a strong young man like that should not be an idle vagabond, wandering around everywhere with no purpose, but should reside in a cell and support himself by his own work rather than the generosity of others, as is the rule of the elders. Even the apostle Paul did this, though he was entitled to support for preaching the Gospel; he chose to work day and night, so as to provide with his hands a daily sustenance for himself as well as for those who helped him and were unable to work. The other was so grieved and pained by this that he was unable to keep his face from revealing the bitterness concealed in his heart. Serapion said to him, 'My son, before this you were accusing yourself of all sorts of crimes, fearlessly incurring an evil reputation by confessing such atrocious sins. Now, how has it happened that my simple advice, which was not prompted by any rancour, but an affectionate desire for your good, has so disturbed and angered you, that you cannot conceal it by your looks or behind a calm countenance? Could it be that when you were abasing yourself, you were expecting us to say, 'The just man is first accuser of himself at the beginning of his speech' (Prov. 18:17, LXX)? True lowliness of heart is to be kept not by affected humility in posture or word, but in your innermost thoughts. Such lowliness is displayed, and humility really proved, not when someone boasts of sins which no one believes in, but when he is unconcerned when other people sin rudely against him, and endures unprovoked insults with gentle peace of heart."

XII. GERMANUS: "We would like to know how to acquire and maintain such tranquillity that we may be able to preserve calmness of heart as easily as we can close the gates of our lips to keep silence, and to restrain the freedom to speak. For often, even though the tongue be restrained, the heart has lost its inner state of repose. That is why we thought that desirable placidity can only be found by one in a remote cell, dwelling alone."

XIII. PIAMUN: "True patience and tranquillity can only be acquired and maintained with deep humility of heart. If it springs from such a source, it will not need the help of solitary life in a remote cell. It requires no endowment with any external object, for it is based on inner humility, its mother and guardian. Thus if we are troubled by any passion, we can be sure that the foundations of humility are not laid firm within us, and that our structure will collapse in ruins at the shock of even a light gale. Patience is not praised or admired if it only preserves its intended placidity as long as no hostile blow assails it; it is glorious and distinguished if it stands unmoved while being battered by storms of temptation. For it is all the stronger in the very fronts on which the enemy believed it weak and vulnerable, most acute where it was thought to be blunt. As everyone knows, the word 'patience' derives from 'passion' and 'endurance', so that it is agreed no one can be called patient unless he endures without anger whatever attacks are brought against him. Solomon rightly praises him thus, 'The patient man is better than the valiant: and he that ruleth his spirit, than he that taketh a city' (Prov. 16:32, LXX). Also, 'He that is patient is great in much wisdom, but he that is impatient exalteth his folly' (Prov. 14:29, LXX).

Now when someone has been aggravated by some injury, and is aflame with wrath, we do not think that this really happened because the violence of the insult offered, for we can see that it is evidence of a hidden weakness. It is like Our Saviour's parable: he speaks of two houses, one founded upon a rock, the other on sand, and on both of them rain, floods and storms fell alike; the one founded on solid rock suffered no damage from that violent assault, whereas the one built on a shifting base of sand collapsed at once. It is clear from this that it did not fall simply because it was battered by storm and rain, but because it was foolishly founded on sand. The difference between a saint and a sinner is not that they are not tempted in the same way, but that one is not daunted despite a serious assault, the other gives in to a slight temptation. As I said, a just man would not be praised for his fortitude if he survived without being tested, since a victory cannot take place without engaging the foe. 'Blessed is the man that endureth temptation; for, when he hath been proved, he shall receive the crown of life which God hath promised to them that love him' (James 1:12). St Paul also tells us that virtue 'is made perfect in infirmity' (II Cor. 12:9) not in ease and leisure. 'For behold, I have made thee this day a fortified city and a pillar of iron and a wall of brass, over all the land, to the kings of Juda, to the princes thereof and to the priests and to the people of the land. And they shall fight against thee and shall not prevail: for I am with thee, saith the Lord, to deliver thee' (Jer. 1: 18–19).

XIV. "I would like to give you a couple of examples of this sort of patience. One is a certain religious woman, who pursued the virtue of patience so eagerly that so far from avoiding trials, she went to the extent of devising for herself occasions of grief, although she never let herself be overcome by these frequent troubles. She lived in Alexandria, and came from a distinguished family, serving the Lord devoutly in the house her parents left her. She went to bishop Athanasius, of sainted memory, and asked him to provide her with a widow to care for, who was being looked after at church expense. To give the actual words of her request, she said, 'Give me a sister to care for.' The prelate was pleased with the woman's request, and saw that she really desired to do a work of mercy. He asked for a widow to be chosen who was distinguished above all the others for respectable conduct and sobriety, so that the generosity of the donor would not be daunted by the greed of the recipient, and in her desire to profit by meeting her needs she might not suffer loss to her faith through offence at the other's bad conduct. The holy woman brought the widow to her home, and looked after her carefully, discovering how gentle and modest she was, and finding herself continually loaded with thanks for her kindness. A few days later she came back to St Athanasius. 'I did ask,' she said, 'for you to arrange for me to be given someone to care for, and to serve in her difficulties.' He still did not understand the woman's intention and desire, and thought that her request had merely been neglected through his provost's laziness. He asked, with some indignation, why the delay had occurred, and soon found that a widow, more respectable than most, had been sent to her. Accordingly he gave secret orders that the most wicked of all of them should be sent to her, who exceeded all the others in bad temper, arguments, drunkenness and garrulity. It was much easier to find this one – and she began to give her a home, serving her with as much or more care as she had the previous widow. All she received in the way of thanks for her attentions was foul abuse, continual trouble from her complaints and reproaches, slander and grumbling with muttered curses; thus her request to the bishop had brought her not repose, but a cross with dishonour, and her way of life was changed not from labour to leisure, but from leisure to labour. When these frequent arguments had reached the point that the vile woman could not be restrained even by laying hands on her, the other redoubled her attentive service, learning not so much how to overcome the ranting widow by restraint, but to overcome herself by humble subjection. Bruised by many assaults, she smoothed the harridan's rage with meekness and kindness. Being fully strengthened by these exercises, and having acquired the perfect virtue of patience which she had desired, she returned to bishop Athanasius, and thanked him for his discerning choice and the benefit she had received from the exercise. As she had hoped, he had finally given her a mistress to teach her patience, so that she was daily strengthened by those frequent complaints, as if by an athlete's ointment, till she had achieved a perfectly patient soul. 'At last', she said, 'you have given me someone to relieve, for that one you sent me before gave me more relief, by her honour and gratitude.'

That is quite enough to say about women, since talking of them is not just edifying, but embarrassing to us who are quite unable to remain in patience without hiding ourselves away in underground cells like wild animals.

XV. "The other example is that of Abba Paphnutius. He persevered constantly and diligently in the remote part of that desert of Scete, so famous and talked about, and he is a priest there now. The other anchorites there call him 'Wild Ox', because he always prefers to live alone as if it were his natural inclination. Even in youth he was so virtuous and graceful that the most distinguished men of the age admired him for his seriousness and unshaken constancy. They considered him the equal in merit and virtue of his superiors, despite being much younger than them, and decided he should

XVIII. *On the Three Kinds of Monks* 407

be enrolled among the elders. Then that jealousy, which once aroused his brothers against the Patriarch Joseph, inflamed one of Paphnutius' brothers with a gnawing bitterness. He wanted to spoil his good reputation with some excrescence or stain, and thought up an evil plot, finding his opportunity when Paphnutius had gone to church on a Sunday and was thus absent from his cell. The other crept in quietly and hid his own book among the woven mats which Paphnutius used to weave out of palm fronds. Confident in his cunning scheme, he too went to church as if his conscience was clear and pure.

Once the usual ceremony was over, he raised a complaint in front of all the brethren before Saint Isidore, who was the priest in that part of the desert before our own Paphnutius, claiming that his book had been stolen out of his cell. This complaint disturbed everyone, particularly the priest, since they had no suspicion or policy on such matters, and everyone was amazed at such an unheard of crime. No one in that part of the desert could remember anything like this before, nor has such a thing happened since. The accuser who had reported the deed urged that everyone should be kept in the church until some were chosen and sent to examine the cells of each brother in turn. The priest laid this charge on three of the elders, and they searched all the cells until they finally found the book hidden in Paphnutius' cell among the palm-mats or *siras* as they call them, just where the schemer had hidden them. The searchers brought it straightaway to the church and showed it to everyone, and Paphnutius, despite being really clear in his own conscience, offered himself for punishment as if he were admitting his guilt. He humbly begged to take the place of a penitent, considering in his bashful modesty that if he tried to argue himself out of the accusation he would only incur the reputation of a liar as well, since no one suspected anything other than what appeared to have been discovered.

He left the church, not cast down in mind but confident in God's judgment, and prostrated himself humbly before everyone, with profuse tears and prayers, and triple fasting. For about two weeks he subjected himself in bodily and spiritual penance, and on Saturday and Sunday mornings came back to the church, not to receive Holy Communion, but to prostrate himself on the church threshold and beg pardon. He who witnesses and scrutinises all hidden things did not suffer him either to punish himself more, or to be despised by others, for he made use of the devil who had been the instigator of the crime to reveal what that wicked brother had done, that thief of his own property, that detractor of another's reputation, in front of no human witness. He was seized by a dire demon, and revealed every sin he had committed in secret: the culprit betrayed his own crimes and deceit. He was severely troubled by that unclean spirit for a long time, and was unable to find deliverance even through the prayers of the saints who lived around him, though they could give orders to the demons through the power of their God-given gifts. Not even the special grace granted to the priest Isidore could drive out that cruel tormentor, although the Lord had given him such virtue that any one who was possessed and brought to him was cured no sooner than he crossed his threshold. No, Christ reserved the honour for young Paphnutius, so that the villain would be healed at the prayers of the one he had injured, and so be compelled to declare the fame of the one whom he had hoped, in his enmity, to strip of his reputation; thus he received pardon for his sin, and relief from his present suffering.

So it was that Paphnutius, while still young, showed promise of his future distinction, and in his early years sketched the outline of the perfection he was to increase in his maturity. If we would arrive at the summit of his virtue, we too should lay such a first foundation.

XVI. "There are two reasons why I had to tell you this story. Firstly, that we may consider the steadfast patience of this man, and that we might display a greater measure of patient tranquillity, given that we are tempted by the enemy to a much lesser extent than he experienced; secondly that we should be quite clear that it is impossible to be secure from stormy temptations and the devil's wiles, if we attribute our patience and all our security to being enclosed in a cell, living in the desert, associating with the saints, or anything else external to ourselves, rather than in the strength of our inner selves. Unless our thoughts are strengthened by the protecting power of the one who said, 'the kingdom of God is within you' (Luke 17: 21), it is vain to imagine that we can repel the assaults of our aerial foes with the help of the men we live with, to evade them by our choice of seclusion, to ward them off by the protection of a building. Saint Paphnutius possessed all these advantages, but the tempter managed to find a way of access to him; the walls he lived within, the loneliness of the desert and the merits of such a community of saints could not defend him from that wicked spirit. The holy servant of God did not put his hopes in these externals, but in the one who judges all hidden things, and was able to remain unshaken by that scheming assault. On the other hand, did not the one whose jealousy prompted him to such a crime enjoy the benefit of solitude, the protection of a remote dwelling place, the fellowship of the saintly priest Abba Isidore and the other holy men? Yet when the storming devil found him to be based on sand, he did not just batter his dwelling but overthrew it completely. Let us not search for peace in externals, let us not imagine that another man's patience can make up for our own lack of it. Just as the 'kingdom of God is within us', so also 'a man's enemies shall be they of his own household' (Matt. 10: 36). I have no enemy greater than my own sensuality, most intimately of my own household. For that reason, if we take proper care, we can hardly be harmed at all by our own internal foes. When those of our own household are not opposed to us, then the kingdom of God is possessed in a tranquil heart. If you consider the question carefully, I cannot be harmed by any man, however malignant, unless I am fighting against myself in a heart lacking peace. If I do suffer harm, it is not the fault of the attacker, but of my own impatience. Solid good food is beneficial when you are well, but dangerous if you are ill; it cannot harm the eater unless his own sickness gives it power to harm him. If any similar temptation were to arise among the brothers, let us not give the worldly an excuse for blasphemy and reviling, but remain firm on the path of tranquillity. We should not be surprised if concealed among the saints we find some who are perverse and blameworthy, for as long as we are being flailed and ground in the threshing floor of this world, there is bound to be some chaff, bound for eternal fire, mixed in among the grain. If there was a Satan among the angels, a Judas among the Apostles, a Nicolas, originator of vile heresy, among the chosen deacons, we can hardly be surprised if wicked men are found concealed among the saints. (Admittedly some claim that Nicolas the heretic is not the same as the one the apostles chose for the diaconate, but in any case he cannot be denied to have been counted as a disciple, and in those days it is clear that they were all as perfect as few can now be found in monasteries.) My object is not to tell you about the lapse of that brother, who fell into such a state in the desert, nor of his horrible sin which he afterwards expiated through his great and tearful penance, but to place before us the example of Saint Paphnutius. Let us not suffer from the scheming of the one whose pretended religion actually worsened his previous sin of envy, but let us follow the humility of Paphnutius with all our strength, which was not something which the desert produced in him at once, but something which he had acquired in the world, and brought to growth and perfection in the wilderness.

[Chapter XVII begins here in PL] Now you should know that the vice of envy is more difficult to heal than any other vice. Once it has infected someone with its virus, I can almost say it is incurable. This is the venom of which the prophet speaks in parable, 'For behold, I will send among you serpents, basilisks, against which there is no charm; and they shall bite you' (Jer. 8:17). The prophet is right to compare the pangs of envy to the deadly venomous bite of a basilisk, for it was envy through which the first originator and prince of all evil first fell, and continues to fall. For he destroyed himself before the one he envied; before he poured out the virus of death on mankind, he had ruined himself. 'By the envy of the devil, death came into the world, and they follow him that are of his side' (Wisd. 2:24–5). And just as there is no healing in penance for him who was first corrupted by this vile cancer, no poultice to bring relief, so too those who have surrendered themselves to be eaten up by envy, cannot be helped by any charm of holiness. They do not suffer through the fault of others, but through their prosperity, ashamed to reveal the truth of the matter, they look outside themselves for some other irrelevant cause for their distress. Since they are altogether false, a cure is not to be looked for, as long as the deadly virus, to which they will not admit, lurks deep within them. The Sage speaks wisely of this in another text, 'If a serpent bite not in silence, there is no abundance for the charmer' (Qo. 10:11, LXX). These are the silent bites for which alone the sage has no medicine. The vice is so untreatable, that it is exasperated by mildness, inflated by courtesy, irritated by generosity. As Solomon also says, 'Envy hath no mercy' (Prov. 27:4, LXX). The more another person tries to be humble and obedient, or steadfastly patient, or generous with his praise, the more the envious man is roused to greater envy, for he has no desire but the ruin and death of the other. No meek subjection on the part of their innocent brother could soothe the envy of the eleven patriarchs, as Scripture tells us: 'And his brethren, seeing that he was loved by his father, hated him, and could not speak peaceably to him' (Gen. 37:4). Nothing their brother could say, as he flattered them and humbled himself before them, could sate their jealousy; in their longing for his death they were only just satisfied by selling him. It is agreed that jealousy is the worst and most difficult to cure of all vices, for it is inflamed by the very remedies which extinguish the others. For instance, one who is grieved by a loss inflicted on him, will be appeased by generous compensation; one pained by an insult will be pleased with humble apology. But what can you do about someone who is more offended the more he sees your humble gentleness? His anger has not been caused by avarice, which can be satisfied by paying him, nor by receiving an injury or desiring revenge, which could be soothed by flattery, but simply by irritation at the prosperity of another. No one would be prepared to lose his goodness, give up his prosperity, and plunge himself into calamity in order to please the one jealous of him!

For this reason, we must beg the help of God, to whom nothing is impossible, to prevent this one bite of the basilisk from ruining everything in us which is alive and invigorated by the life-giving breath of the Holy Spirit. Other poisonous serpents, namely the sins and frailties of the flesh, are quickly committed and as easily absolved, weak creatures that we are. Scars may remain of the wounds they inflict, which may well disfigure our earthly bodies, but if a skilful snakecharmer, a singer of divine canticles, applies the antidote, the medicine of saving words, these scars cannot cause any inflammation leading to eternal death. Jealousy, however, like the venom of a basilisk, destroys the life of religion and faith before any physical wound is felt. It is a blasphemy against God himself, not against man, when someone hates nothing in his brother save the reward of his goodness, and blames no one except the judgments of God. This is the 'root of bitterness springing up' (Heb. 12:15) which climbs to the point that it opposes its own creator, who confers good things on men. Do not be confused because God threatened to send serpents and basilisks to bite those who had offended him by their sins: God can never be blamed for causing jealousy, but it is just and fitting to God's dignity that, while he grants good things to the humble, and denies them to the proud and outcast, those whom the Apostle says deserve to be 'delivered up to a reprobate sense' (Rom. 1:28) are stricken and consumed by envy as if it had been sent by God. As Scripture says, 'They have provoked me to jealousy with that which was no god, and I will provoke them to envy with that which is no people'" (Deut. 32:21, LXX).

With this discourse the holy Piamun encouraged our desire to progress from our first schooling in the monastery to the higher degree of anchorite. For it was from his teaching that we first gathered the rudiments of the solitary life, which we afterwards learnt in greater depth in Scete.

✧ THE NINETEENTH COLLATION ✧
BEING THAT OF ABBA JOHN

On the Aims of a Monk or a Hermit

    I. On the monastery of Abba Paul, and the patience of a certain brother.
    II. On the humility of Abba John, and our questioning of him.
    III. The reply of Abba John on why he had left the desert.
    IV. On how the aforesaid elder practised virtue as a hermit.
    V. On the advantages of the desert.
    VI. On the benefit of a monastery.
    VII. A question, about the fruits of solitude or community life.
    VIII. The reply to the question put.
    IX. On true and consummate perfection.
    X. On those who seek the desert before becoming perfect.
    XI. A question, on the healing of those who leave their monasteries too soon.
    XII. The reply, on how a solitary may discern his own vices.
    XIII. A question, on how one who has entered the desert without purging his vices may be healed.
    XIV. The reply, on their healing.
    XV. A question, on whether chastity should be tested in the same way as other virtues.

XVI. The reply, on the indications by which we may recognise it.

I. A few days later, urged by our desire for greater learning, we returned eagerly to the monastery of Abba Paul. There are normally more than two hundred brothers living there, but in honour of the festival which was being celebrated at that time, there was in addition a vast throng of monks gathered from other monasteries. What they were commemorating was the anniversary of the death of the abbot who had formerly governed the monastery. We have mentioned that community in order to tell you briefly about the patience of a certain brother, which was displayed in his unshakable good temper in the presence of the whole gathering. Although the intention of this book is something other, namely to record the teaching of Abba John, who had left the desert to submit himself in great humility to that monastery, I do not think it wrong to pass on to the studious something of great benefit in the acquisition of virtue, without wasting words.

The throng of monks were settled, in separate groups of a dozen or so, in a vast open-air court. One of the brothers brought in the tray he was carrying a little late, and the aforementioned Abba Paul, who was busily engaged with the crowd of serving brothers, noticed this and stretched out his hand to give him a slap, in the sight of everyone, so that the sound was audible even to those who sat facing away from him, or some way off. [He did this, in order to demonstrate to them all how patient the young monk was, and all the observers were much edified by such an example of modesty. How wise the elder was in doing this is proved by the outcome, for] The youth was so remarkably tolerant that he accepted it mildly, no word fell from his lips, nor could the slightest muttering of silently moving lips be seen; indeed his placid and modest countenance was not put out of colour in the slightest. This occurrence did not only surprise us, who had only just arrived from our Syrian monastery to observe the display of this virtuous patience in such a clear example, but impressed all the others who were not unaccustomed to such behaviour, so that the greatest

XIX. On the Aims of a Monk or a Hermit   415

among them were much edified by what happened. Not only was the young monk not disturbed by that paternal correction, but he did not even blush with embarrassment at being shown up before such a great crowd of onlookers.

II. In this monastery, then, we found a very aged man called John. I do not think I should pass over his words in silence, nor his humility, which exceeded that of all the other holy men, for he practised humility, the mother of all virtues, the solid foundation of the whole spiritual edifice, to such a degree as was unknown in our own earlier training. It is not surprising that we are unable to rise to that degree of excellence, we who are so far from being able to persevere into old age under monastic discipline, that we are hardly capable of enduring the yoke of obedience for as much as two years before flying off in search of a perilous liberty; for that short time we may have subjected ourselves to our novicemaster's will, but through our own free choice, not as the rule of obedience requires. We may appear to be learning the fruits of patient endurance, but that is only in expectation of the time when we will have greater freedom.

 Accordingly, when we found that old man in Abba Paul's monastery, we were immediately struck by his age, and the grace he had received, and with our eyes on the ground we began to ask him if he would tell us for what reason he had left the freedom of the desert, and that sublime vocation in which he had the reputation of exceeding all the others who followed it, preferring instead to accept the discipline of a monastery. He replied that he was unfit for the austerity of a hermit, and such a degree of sublime perfection, and had returned to novitiate training to see if he could at least fulfil those obligations and become fit for that vocation. Our protest at this humble reply overcame him so that he eventually began to speak to us.

III. "I do not by any means deny the value of the discipline of a hermit, though my leaving it may have surprised you; indeed I value it and embrace it with all my heart. I have spent thirty years in a monastic community, and am glad to have spent another twenty years as a hermit, and I have never been accused of being dilatory among those who pursued that life even imperfectly. However the purity which I had tasted there began to be corrupted by worry over material things, so that it seemed advisable to return to the monastery, in order to achieve quicker results from a more ordinary undertaking, and escape the danger of pride through attempting the more sublime profession. It is better to be observant in a lesser commitment than unobservant in a greater one. Because of this, if I say anything too loftily or freely, please do not attribute this to the vice of pride, but to my concern for your education, since you are so eager in your request that I do not think I can conceal any of the truth from you. Consider me motivated by charity more than conceit! I think I can be of some benefit to you if I set aside humility for a little and tell you simply the whole truth of what my purpose has been. I am sure that you will not accuse me of vainglory if I speak freely, nor will my conscience accuse me of lying or concealing the truth.

IV. "If anyone ever could be so contented with the lonely desert as to forget human company altogether, and say with Jeremiah, 'I have not desired the day of man, thou knowest' (Jer. 17:16), I too can claim, with the grace of the Lord, to have followed that path, or at least to have attempted it. By the Lord's loving mercy, I can remember that I was frequently enraptured to the point that I forgot that I was constrained by the burden of bodily weakness, my thoughts so detached from all external perception, and remote from all material concerns whatever, so that neither my eyes nor my ears performed their usual function. My mind was so filled with the contemplation of God, and spiritual considerations, that I often forgot in the evening whether I had taken any food, and was unsure the next day whether I had broken my fast the day before. For this reason, I used every Sabbath to set aside seven days' rations, that is to say seven buns of equal size, in my *prokherion* (which is a hand-held haversack), so that if I forgot to eat I would know about it. This habit made it possible to prevent my forgetfulness in another

XIX. On the Aims of a Monk or a Hermit

matter, since when the week was over, and the day of celebration came round again, the number of buns consumed would inform me of the date, and in my solitude I would not miss the festivity of the holy day, and the solemn assembly. But if my abstraction, as I have mentioned, made me confused about the day of the week, the allotted amount of daily work would tell me how many days had passed, and alert me to my mistake. I will pass over the other virtues of the desert in silence, for we are discussing the aims of the eremitical or monastic life, not numbers and quantities of virtues, but I will tell you briefly why I decided to abandon the desert, which is what you asked me about. The fruits of the solitary life, which I have mentioned, I will run over very briefly, for they should be considered secondary to the more sublime virtues.

V. "As long as there were very few hermits living in the desert, we had great freedom, and it was pleasant for us, in the vast open spaces, where we were often enraptured into heavenly ecstasy alone in the great wilderness. There was then no great crowd of visiting monks with needs to be cared for, to bother us with many cares and distractions. I was able to pursue the secrets of the desert in peace, living in a way that can be compared to that of the blessed angels, with ceaseless longing and wholehearted fervour. However a greater number of monks began to look for homes in that part of the desert, and the freedom of the open wilderness became restricted, which caused the fire of divine contemplation to grow cold, and burdened my thoughts with innumerable earthly and material concerns. I decided to pursue what had been my original purpose in adopting that way of life, rather than to grow sluggish in that sublime profession through having to supply earthly necessities. If I have lost that freedom, and those spiritual raptures, I have also got rid of endless worries about the morrow, and can console myself by keeping the commandment in the Gospel (cf. Matt. 6: 34). What I have lost in the way of sublime contemplation, I have gained through subjecting myself to obedience. It is a wretched thing for someone to undertake the pursuit of any skill or art, and be unable to reach its perfection at all.

VI. "For this reason I will tell you shortly what great advantages I enjoy in my present way of life. You may judge, when you have heard what I have to say, whether the advantages of the solitary life outweigh those here, and will be able to discern whether I chose to be bound by the restraints of this monastery out of distaste or out of appreciation for the purity of the desert. In my present way of life there is no requirement of daily labour, no anxiety over selling or buying, no unavoidable worry about an annual living, no concern over bodily things to be prepared not only for one's own use but that of a crowd of visitors, above all there is no danger of taking pride in the praise of men, which is more dangerous in God's sight than all these other things, and can often nullify every effort the hermit makes. I will pass over the movements of spiritual elation and the perils of vainglory which threaten a hermit's profession, and return to the problem common to them all, that is the general anxiety over making a living. This anxiety makes them exceed the measure, not just of the old dispensation, when monks were quite unaccustomed to the use of oil – no, they are not content even with the laxity of our own times. Formerly a whole years' supply of food could be ensured with a single gallon of oil, and a single bushel of beans for the benefit of visitors, but our modern needs are hardly met by two or three times that amount of food. This evil laxity has grown so dominant over some hermits that they are not content, as in former days, to mix a single drop of oil in their mixture of vinegar and brine, as our predecessors did, who followed the desert tradition with greater abstinence than we do, and used that drop of oil only to inculcate the grace of repelling vainglory; no, our moderns will break open an Egyptian cheese for their delectation, and pour over it more oil than necessary! In this way they use up two different foods for the enjoyment of a single taste, although each has its distinct flavour, which might have regaled those monks very satisfactorily on two different occasions. To such an extent has this luxury, this possession of material goods, increased, that I am ashamed to say hermits are beginning to keep quilts in their cells, under pretext of kindness and hospitality. I should not mention those gatherings of the brethren, which would astonish anyone who is really devoted to spiritual contemplation, with the undertaking and relinquishing of dignities, the visiting each other, conferring on various matters and endlessly arguing over what to do. Even at times when such interruptions seem to have ceased, the anticipation of these things is enough to disturb the thoughts even of those who are continually bent on being distracted. Thus it happens that the freedom of a hermit is so entangled in these concerns that it never rises to achieve that indescribable fervour of heart but loses the fruit of the eremitical vocation. Now I myself may well have lost one form of freedom, since I live in community and among crowds, yet I am not without peace of mind and tranquillity of heart, for I am free from all distractions. Unless the dwellers in the desert have that sort of freedom, they may well perform the work of a hermit, but will be denied its fruit, for it cannot be gained except in a heart at peace. If, having settled in a monastery, I have found any diminution of purity of heart, I can be content with consoling myself on the words of the Gospel, which is assuredly no less a thing than all those fruits of the desert, namely that I should think nothing of the morrow. Being subject to my abbot to the end, I can try to imitate him of whom it was said, 'He humbled himself, becoming obedient unto death' (Phil. 2: 8), and may become worthy to say these humble words, 'I came . . . not to do my own will but the will of him that sent me'" (John 6: 38).

VII. GERMANUS: "Since it is clear you have really taken on the obligations of both vocations, rather than just touching the rudiments as so many have done, we are eager to ask you what is the aim of a monk's life, and what of a hermit. No one can be in any doubt that no one could speak as accurately or fully about these matters, as one who had long and authoritative experience of both vocations in their perfection. You are qualified to teach us the truth about their merits and their goal."

VIII. JOHN: "I would try to convince you that it is quite impossible for one and the same man to be perfectly proficient in both vocations, except that there are a few examples to the contrary. If it is a great thing to find anyone perfected in either vocation, how much more difficult it must be to achieve perfection in both! In fact I am sure that it is all but impossible for humankind. And if such a thing were to occur, it could not be readily formulated as a general rule. Common principles can only be put forth about things which are within the capacity of many or all, not about the rarest situations which can occur to very few men. Something that is achieved only very occasionally, and by a very few, which exceeds the potential of common virtue, is to be kept out of any general instruction, being a gift granted beyond the bounds of human frailty. It can be mentioned as a wonder, but not as an example.

For that reason, I will briefly tell you what you ask, in so far as my mediocrity is capable of it. The aim of a monk is to mortify and crucify all his desires, and as the saving Gospel of perfection tells us, to take no care for the morrow (cf. Matt. 6:34). No one, to be sure, can achieve that perfection except in a monastery. The prophet Isaiah describes such a man, blesses him and praises him, 'If thou turn away thy foot from the sabbath, from doing thy own will in my holy day ... and glorify him, while thou dost not thy own ways and thy own will is not found, to speak a word: then shalt thou be delighted in the Lord, and I will lift thee up above the high places of the earth and will feed thee with the inheritance of Jacob, thy father. For the mouth of the Lord hath spoken it' (Isaiah 58:13–14). The perfection of a hermit is to clear his thoughts of all worldly concerns, and to unite them to Christ as far as human frailty permits. The prophet Jeremiah speaks of such a man, saying, 'It is good for a man, when he hath borne the yoke from his youth. He shall sit solitary and hold his peace: because he hath taken it up upon himself' (Lam. 3:27–8). The psalmist also says, 'I am become like to a pelican of the wilderness .... I have watched, and am become as a sparrow all alone on the housetop' (Psalm 101/102:7–8). Now unless each monk arrives at that goal which we have indicated for one of the two vocations, it will be in vain that he will have pursued either monastic discipline, or eremitical. In neither case will he have gained the greatness of his profession.

IX. "All this is but a fraction, not the whole of perfection in its completeness, but only a part. Real perfection is a rare gift of God, granted to very few. The one who is truly perfect, not in part alone, is the one who can tolerate with equal calmness either the austerity of the lonely desert, or the failings of his brethren in the monastery. In either vocation it is difficult to find anyone totally perfect; the hermit cannot find true detachment, which is spurning material things and doing without them, neither can the cenobite achieve the total purity he intends, even though we do know that Abba Moses and Paphnutius and the two Macarii did possess both virtues to the full. They were perfect in both vocations, residing further apart than other desert dwellers, feeding on the secrecy of solitude without ceasing, with all their heart; they never sought human company, but tolerated frequent visitors with all their faults. Indeed uncounted brethren flocked to them, out of curiosity, or the desire for improvement, and they remained patient and tolerant without wavering under so great a disturbance. One could believe they had taught and practised all their lives nothing but the common tasks of service for all comers, so that it was a matter of general dispute in which vocation their effort was most expended, namely whether it was in the purity of their eremitical life that their greatness of soul was more marvellously displayed, or in their service of the public.

X. "It does happen to some that they become so accustomed to the perpetual silence of the wilderness, that they are terrified of human contact, and if some brother chance to visit and draw them away from their secret solitude to the slightest extent, they are seething with inner anguish, and display clear indications of mental weakness. This happens particularly to those who have not been properly trained in a monastery, and have taken themselves off to the solitary life before their former vices had been quite purged away. They are ever imperfect and frail in one condition as in the other, and are driven whichever way the winds of emotion send them. Just as they are seething with impatience when brothers interrupt them or associate with them, in the same way while they sit in the desert they are unable to bear the enormous silence which is what they had been looking for. The reason is that they are ignorant of the real purpose for which they should desire and seek solitude, but imagine that the peak of virtue in their profession is to decline the fellowship of their brethren, and shun with detestation the company of men."

XI. GERMANUS: "How then can any remedy help us, and others like us? We are frail and wretched, for we have been imperfectly trained in monastic discipline, and had begun to yearn for a solitary life before driving out all our vices; how may we attain stability in an untroubled heart, and unshaken constancy in patience? Too soon have we abandoned our cenobitic way of life, the very schools and training grounds of this exercise, where our first beginnings should have come to fulfilment and been perfected! If we begin to live alone now, how could we acquire perfect tolerance and patience, how can conscience, which scrutinises our inner thoughts, discover whether these virtues be within us or not? May it not happen that being separated from human company, and without provocation from human irritation, we may be deceived into a false estimation of ourselves, believing that we possess unshakable mental tranquillity?"

XII. JOHN: "Those who truly seek healing will not be disappointed in finding a cure at the hands of the true doctor of souls; this is especially so in the case of those who do not despair nor carelessly neglect their weaknesses, or conceal their dangerous wounds or arrogantly refuse the medicine of penance; with a humble and careful mind they flee to the heavenly physician for the ills which they have contracted unavoidably through ignorance, error or necessity. We must be aware that, if we have withdrawn to the wilderness or a hidden place with our vices still unhealed, their effects alone will be restrained, our affection for them will remain alive. There still lurks within us the root of all those sins that have not been eradicated; indeed it writhes there, and these are the signs by which we may discern that it is alive in us: for example, if while

XIX. On the Aims of a Monk or a Hermit

we are living in solitude, we are waiting for the arrival of a brother, and there is a brief delay, so that our minds teem with anxiety, it shows us that the germ of impatience is alive within us. If we are expecting the arrival of a brother, and something makes him delay a little, and we accuse him of lateness in silent indignation, our thoughts disturbed by our unreasonable expectations, this clearly demonstrates that the vices of anger and melancholy are resident within us. Then if a brother wants to borrow a book to read, or something else to use, and the request annoys us, or we refuse and send him away, we should be in no doubt that we are entangled in the snares of avarice and love of money. If a sudden thought reminds us of some woman, or it happens as a result of our spiritual reading, and we find ourselves somewhat excited by that, we should be aware that the fire of fornication is not yet extinct in our bodies. Then again, if we start comparing our austerity and self-denial with that of others, and our thoughts are even the slightest bit elated, we can be certain that we are infected with the disease of pride. Now when we discover these indications of vice in our hearts, we must recognise clearly that we have only rid ourselves of the effects of sin, not our affection for it. If we were to mingle with human company again, these passions would immediately emerge from their lairs within our senses, and show themselves, not born for the first time when they erupt, but made public for the first time after lying long hid. Thus even the hermit may discern the roots of each vice fixed within himself by sure indications, he who strives to demonstrate his inviolate purity, not before the eyes of men, but in the sight of the one from whom no secrets of the heart can be concealed."

XIII. GERMANUS: "We understand very clearly what you have said about discerning the indications of weakness, and how we may be able to detect our failings and observe the vices which are hidden within us. We can comprehend it all from our daily experience, and what has long been happening in our own thoughts, just as you have said. What remains is to show us how to cure these diseases, now that you have so lucidly described their causes and diagnosis. There is no doubt that one who truly understands the original causes of a sickness, with conscience as witness, will be able to speak most accurately about its cure. Since Your Beatitude has taught us how to uncover our secret weaknesses, we are emboldened to hope for some sort of cure, for the clear diagnosis of a disease promises hope of healing. However, since you have said that healing has to begin in a community, and it is impossible to be cured in the desert if one has not been treated by the medicine of a monastery first, we are again cast into gloomy despair, for since we have left our monastery while still imperfect, we shall never find perfection in the desert."

XIV. JOHN: "Those who are anxious to be cured of their weaknesses will surely not want for healing, so we must look for a remedy in the same manner in which we found the symptoms of each vice. As we have said, hermits do not escape from the vices inherent in human company, therefore we cannot deny that the pursuit of virtue and the means of healing are available for those cut off from all such human society. When someone discovers, by the indications we have demonstrated before, that he is under attack from the emotions of anger or impatience, he should always exercise himself in the contrary virtues, suggesting to himself many sorts of insult or contempt as if they were inflicted on him by others, and accustoming his mind to accept with perfect humility any manner of assault that wickedness could impose. He should confront himself often with harsh and intolerable things, and ponder on them in great meekness and with the appropriate lowliness of heart. Let him consider all the sufferings of the saints, and of Our Lord himself, deeming himself to be worthy of any sort of vituperation or punishment, preparing to endure any degree of pain.

If it should happen that he be summoned to a gathering of the brethren (which seldom or never happens to the strictest desert dwellers), and he finds his thoughts offended in the secrecy of his conscience, even over trivial matters, then like a severe censor of secret emotion, he should rebuke himself promptly with those

XIX. On the Aims of a Monk or a Hermit   425

aggressive insults which he had exercised himself to tolerate by his daily meditation. Let him address himself with this strict criticism: 'Are you the same fellow who presumed to think himself capable of overcoming all woes with constancy, exercising yourself in the training ground of the desert? Did you suggest for yourself the worst stinging rebukes, and intolerable suffering? Did you imagine yourself strong enough to take them, and to be unshaken by any storm? How has that unconquered patience of yours been uprooted by such a mild verbal assault? How has so slight a breeze shaken that house of yours which you imagined to be so well constructed on solid rock? Where is that futile self-confidence which made you long for was in peacetime? "I am ready and am not troubled" (Psalm 118/119: 60), you said, or, "Prove me, O Lord, and try me: burn my reins and my heart" (Psalm 25/26: 2), and, "Prove me, O God, and know my heart: examine me and know my paths. And see if there be in me the way of iniquity: and lead me in the eternal way" (Psalm 138/139: 23–4). How has the mere shadow of an enemy daunted your whole array of battle?'

With such considerations he should reproach himself, never allowing his mental disturbance to go unchecked, but correcting his flesh with more severe fasting and watching, and punishing his fickle fault with the strong penalties of continence. By the flame of this exercise he may refine away in the desert what he should have purged while living in the monastery. To obtain a patience that is stable and enduring, with unwavering constancy he should remember the fact that by God's law we are permitted never to avenge ourselves, nor even to think of so doing, and we should therefore not be stirred to wrath by any sort of inconvenience or irritation. What greater injury could be inflicted on a soul than for it to be suddenly blinded by emotion and deprived of the radiance of the true and eternal light, prevented from contemplating the one who is 'meek and humble of heart' (Matt. 11: 29)? What woe could be worse than to lose the ability to distinguish righteousness, the principles and practice of discerning the good, and to commit sins calmly and consciously, sins which could hardly be considered pardonable in one distracted and out of his senses? Anyone who considers these miseries, and others like them, will easily bring himself to rise above all insults, and whatever injury or pain even the most savage foe may direct against him. He will judge nothing to be worse than wrath, nothing more precious than peace of mind and perpetual purity of heart. He will renounce not merely material things, but even those benefits which seem to be spiritual, if they can be gained in no other way than by the sacrifice of this peace of mind."

XV. GERMANUS: "These lesser wounds, namely wrath, melancholy and impatience, can be healed by meditating on adversity, as you have shown us, but we would like some instruction on what sort of healing is effective against the spirit of fornication. Can the fire of lust be quenched in the same way, by thinking about a yet greater degree of temptation? We think it would be directly contrary to chastity actually to increase the allurements of desire in us, even if the mind only glances at them in passing."

XVI. JOHN: "Even if you had said nothing, that question would have followed from what I said. Your acute observance has anticipated me, and I can see that you have effectively grasped the point, since your perceptiveness has gone further than my instruction. The obscurity of any question can be dispelled without difficulty, once you have anticipated the solution which is to follow, and taken the first step. In the case of the vices we have mentioned above, their cure is far from being hindered, and is actually greatly assisted by human company. The more public the evidence of one's impatience, the more painful the remorse it brings on the sinner, the quicker health will be conferred to the patient. Therefore those who live in the desert, and can have no irritation or stimulus from other people, need to take steps to arouse those temptations, so that as we struggle against them, in great mental effort, a cure may readily be found. However against the spirit of fornication there is a different situation, for it has a different cause. Just as we keep ourselves away from physical actions and contact with bodies, so we must totally eliminate the thoughts of such things from our

XIX. On the Aims of a Monk or a Hermit 427

minds. It is quite dangerous enough for even the faintest memory of this emotion to enter minds that are still weak and susceptible, for sometimes the mere thought of female saints or the reading of sacred scripture can stimulate them dangerously. For this reason our elders usually make discreet omissions when reading this sort of thing in front of novices. Those who are perfect and have achieved a great degree of chastity will certainly not be without temptations to try them, so that true integrity of heart may be examined before the incorruptible tribunal of conscience. For a truly holy man, this passion too may be tested in the way we have described above, namely that one who knows that the roots of this vice have really been plucked out, may choose to explore the grace of chastity by occasionally admitting some imagination to test it. However those who are less secure and perfect should by no means conduct this experiment, for it will be more dangerous than healthy to allow their thoughts to dwell on any contact with a woman, any seductive or lascivious caress. [How could such a test help men of this nature, in this area where the experiment itself is what we shun, the sin is the very thinking of it?] One who is firmly founded in virtue, who gives no mental assent to any thoughts of indecent behaviour, and does not experience any physical arousal, has proof of real purity. Practising purity rigorously in this way, not only will he preserve incorrupt in his thoughts the chastity he desires, but if it should happen, [as it sometimes does,] that he is obliged to come into contact with a woman's body [for some reason, he will be quite without any feeling of passion] and will recoil from it."

Abba John became aware that it was the ninth hour, and time for our meal, and so he brought his discourse to a conclusion here.

✣ THE TWENTIETH COLLATION ✣
BEING THAT OF ABBA PINUFIUS

On the Purpose of Penance and
How to Tell if Satisfaction has been Made

I. Of the humility of Abba Pinufius, and his efforts to conceal himself.
II. Of our arrival before him.
III. A question, on the purpose of penance and how to tell if satisfaction has been made.
IV. The reply, on the humility of our question.
V. On the manner of penance, and the evidence that we have been pardoned.
VI. A question, whether we should call to mind our sins for the sake of compunction of heart.
VII. The reply, to what extent we should remember past deeds.
VIII. Of the different forms of fruitful penance.
IX. The value for the perfect of forgetfulness of sin.
X. That we should refrain from remembering shameful sins.
XI. How to tell if we are forgiven, and how past crimes can be wiped out.
XII. Matters for which penance should be finite, and those for which it can have no end.

I. As I am about to tell what Abba Pinufius, that famous and distinguished man, had to say on the purpose of penance, I think the most important part of my material would be lost if I were to allow my concern for the reader's endurance to make me pass over in silence the praiseworthy humility of Pinufius. I did tell the story briefly in the Fourth Book of the Institutes, the one entitled "Of the Training of the Monks", but many who have not heard of that book may chance to read this one (*Institutes*, Book IV, chapters 30–1). All the authority of what is said is weakened if the merits of the speaker are concealed.

Pinufius was Abbot and Priest, ruling a large monastery not far from Panephysis in Egypt, as I recounted before. His admirable reputation for virtue and miracles so spread throughout the whole of that province, that he began to think he had already received the reward of his labours, through the praise of men. He feared that vain popularity would be his undoing, and deprive him of the reward of eternal bliss, so he fled his monastery secretly, and went to the remote and hidden monastery of Tabennae. He did not seek the privacy of the desert, nor the safety of the solitary life, for even the imperfect may desire that, unable to bear the burden of obedience in a community and relying on arrogant presumption, but he chose to subject himself to the discipline of a famous monastery. He dressed himself in secular clothes, lest his habit give away who he was, and lay at the doors weeping for many days, as their custom is. He cast himself on his knees before them all, and endured their long disdain, as they investigated his intentions, for they thought he was not sincere in seeking that life of holiness but in his old age was motivated by lack of food.

At last he obtained admission, and was deputed to assist a young brother in cultivating the garden. He obeyed everything his master told him, and won admiration for the holy humility with which he did all that the work he had been given demanded; he even laboured secretly in the night to carry out certain necessary tasks which the others shunned with distaste, so that when dawn came the whole congregation were amazed, wondering who had done such a useful work.

When he had passed about three years there, happy in the labour of humble obedience he had wished for, it happened that a certain brother who knew him arrived from the part of Egypt which he had left. He hesitated for a long time before recognising him, put off by his lowly garments and toil, but after convincing himself he fell prostrate at Pinufius' feet. The other brethren were at first astounded, but on the revelation of the name, which was famous even there for outstanding holiness, they were struck with shame and regret that they had delegated a man of such merit, and a priest, to that humble work. He was taken back to his monastery, weeping copiously, but surrounded by a company of brethren praising him. He blamed the accident of his detection on the devil's envy, as something that grieved him, and remained there only a brief time before again feeling the burden of the respect he was given for his position of authority. He took ship in secret, and crossed to Palestine, a province of Syria, where he was received into the monastery in which we were living, to live as if beginning again as a novice. The abbot asked him to live in our cell: and even there the merits of his virtue could not long lie hidden. He was detected again in the same manner, and summoned back to his monastery with great honour and praise, compelled at last to be what he was.

II. Not long afterwards we also came to Egypt, driven by our desire for holy instruction, and we sought him out with great love and affection. He received us very gracefully and humbly, as his own former cell-mates, and honoured us by accommodating us in his own cell which he had built on the further side of a garden. While we were there he gave an strict and sublime instruction in the assembly of all the brethren about the calling of a monk, when a certain brother was making his profession under the rule of the monastery: I gave a resumé of this, as best I could, in the Fourth Book of the Institutes (chapters 32–43). We thought those heights of self-denial quite incomprehensible and amazing, so that we imagined that we were too inadequate ever to aspire to them. Despondent and downcast, our very expressions revealing our sorrowful thoughts, we returned to the blessed old man with anxious hearts. He asked us at once why we were so gloomy, and Abba Germanus replied thus, with a sigh:

III. GERMANUS: "The sermon you preached taught us what we never knew, things both magnificent and sublime; it opened to us the hard road of perfect renunciation, and dispersed the mist which covered our eyes to reveal the hidden peak of heaven – but we were all the more depressed and discouraged for all that. We measured that immensity against our own poor strength, comparing the lowliness of our ignorance with the infinite height of virtue you showed us, and realised that we are too sinful to attempt to progress that far, indeed likely to fall away from the state we are already in. Crushed by the weight of our despondency, we are bound to fall from bad to worse. There is only one way to protect us, and to give us healing for our wounds: if you teach us something of the purpose of penance, and especially the way we can tell if it true satisfaction has been made. If we were sure that our past sins were absolved, we might be encouraged to attempt the heights of perfection you have described."

IV. PINUFIUS: "I am pleased indeed with the abundant fruit of your humility, which I observed with interest when I lived in the same cell as you, and I am especially glad that you have listened with such appreciation to the instructions I gave, least of all Christians as I am, even if it was only for the sake of its style. If I be not mistaken, you will follow my instructions as sincerely as I spoke them. Indeed from what I remember of your application to work, what I said is hardly equal to it, but you conceal the merits of your virtue as if what you practice every day leaves no mark on you. But since you have told me that the school of sanctity is unknown to you, as if you were still novices, and I praise you greatly for that, I will try to explain briefly what you have asked me so earnestly. I shall need to give you instructions which are beyond my own capability, on the strength of our old friendship. Many people have said much, in writing as well as in speech, about the prayer of penance and its value, and they have demonstrated how beneficial it is, how effective, how gracious. Penance is as it were laying siege to God, whom our past sins have offended, who threatens punishment justly for such great crimes; it forces him

XX. On the Purpose of Penance

against his will (if I may use such an expression) to restrain his avenging arm. But I am sure you know all this, both through your instinct for the divine, and your tireless study of Holy Scripture, and the first growth of your monastic profession sprang from that. You were not asking me so perceptively about what penance is, but about its purpose and the way you can tell whether satisfaction has been made, which others have omitted to say.

V. "For that reason I will attempt to satisfy your desire for instruction as briefly and succinctly as possible. The full and perfect purpose of penance is to never to admit again any of the sins which we have repented, and for which our conscience rebuked us. The test of satisfaction and pardon is whether we have expelled all affection for sin from our hearts. We should all be aware that we are not yet absolved from our former sins, if while we devote ourselves to expiation and remorse, the sins we have committed and others like them come before the mind's eye, and our inner thoughts dwell upon them, merely in memory, let alone taking pleasure in them. He who recognises that he has been absolved of his sins, and has received pardon for his past offences, may nevertheless feel the allurement of those vices in his heart, and dwell on them in imagination. The most perceptive witness to our penance and judge of our forgiveness resides in our conscience, which detects our absolution from sin while we are still alive in this body, before the day of reckoning, the day of judgment. Conscience it is that reveals whether we have made final satisfaction and received the grace of forgiveness. To repeat what I have said more forcefully, when all longing for present self-indulgence, and all passion is expelled from our hearts, then we can believe that the stains of past vice have been wiped away."

VI. GERMANUS: "We would like to acquire that holy compunction, which saves us in humility. Of this is it said in the person of the penitent, 'I have acknowledged my sin to thee: and my injustice I have not concealed. I said: I will confess against myself my injustice to the Lord' (Psalm 31/32:5). Thus we might merit to say the words that follow, 'and thou hast forgiven the wickedness of my sin' (Psalm 31/32:5b), and so prostrate ourselves in prayer as to elicit tears of repentance, through which we can be found worthy to gain pardon for our sins. As it is said, 'every night I will wash my bed: I will water my couch with my tears' (Psalm 6:7). Yet how can we do all this, if we drive out the memory of our sins from our hearts? After all we are commanded to remember them, for the Lord said, 'I will not remember thy sins, but thou keep them in remembrance' (Isaiah 43:25–6, LXX). That is why my practice is deliberately to try to apply my mind to the memory of my sins, whether I am working or praying. Thus I may be be more effectively humbled and brought to true contrition of heart, daring to say with the Psalmist, 'See my abjection and my labour: and forgive me all my sins'" (Psalm 24/25:18).

VII. PINUFIUS: "The question you asked before was not about the nature of penance but about its purpose and how we may know that we are forgiven: I think we have given an appropriate answer to that one. What you have said about calling sins to mind is useful enough, necessary for those still doing penance, so that they may cry out with much beating of breasts, 'For I know my iniquity, and my sin is always before me' (Psalm 50/51:5), and, 'I will think for my sin' (Psalm 37/38:19). As long as we are doing penance, and are still troubled by the memory of evil deeds, the fire of our conscience can only be cooled by the tears which spring from confession of guilt. But once we are established in humility of heart and contrition, persevering in effort and remorse, the memory of sin will be lulled, the thorns of conscience withdrawn from our tender souls by God's grace; then we can be sure we have reached the goal of forgiveness, and earned our pardon, purged from all stain of sin. There is no other route to this forgetfulness except by eliminating all vice, and all our former desires, in truly perfect purity of heart. Certainly those who neglect to purge themselves of vice, through idleness or indifference, can never attain that forgetfulness; no, only one who perseveres in repentance and tears of grief can wash away the stain of his previous offences, able to cry out to God in

XX. On the Purpose of Penance

the strength of an active will, 'I have acknowledged my sin to thee: and my injustice I have not concealed' (Psalm 31/32:5), and, 'My tears have been my bread day and night' (Psalm 41/42:4). Thus may he proceed to hear, 'Let thy voice cease from weeping and thy eyes from tears, for there is a reward for thy work, saith the Lord' (Jer. 31:16). These words also are addressed to him by the Lord, 'I have blotted out thy iniquities as a cloud and thy sins as a mist' (Isaiah 44:22), and, 'I am he that blot out out thy iniquities for my own sake: and I will not remember thy sins' (Isaiah 43:25). Thus can any man be freed from the 'ropes of his own sins', by which 'each one is fast bound' (Prov. 5:22, LXX), and sing to the Lord with thanksgiving, 'Thou hast broken my bonds: I will sacrifice to thee the sacrifice of praise' (Psalm 115/116:16–17).

VIII. "As well as the universal grace of baptism, and the precious gift of martyrdom which by blood achieves cleansing, there are many fruitful penances by which we may attain the forgiveness of sins. Eternal salvation is not promised only to the simple name of penance, of which the holy Apostle Peter said, 'Be penitent, therefore, and be converted, that your sins may be blotted out' (Acts 3:19), and both John the Baptist and the Lord himself said, 'Do penance; for the kingdom of heaven is at hand' (Matt. 3:2, cf. 4:17). Charity also can remove the burden of sin, 'for charity covereth a multitude of sins' (I Peter 4:8). Almsgiving likewise bears fruit in the healing of our own wounds, for 'water quencheth a flaming fire: and alms resisteth sins' (Sir. 3:33). Copious tears also may wash away sins, for 'every night I will wash my bed: I will water my couch with my tears' (Psalm 6:7). The psalm continues, to show that this weeping is not fruitless, 'Depart from me, all ye workers of iniquity: for the Lord hath heard the voice of my weeping' (Psalm 6:9). Confession of sins is another means to wipe them away, for 'I said: I will confess against myself my injustice to the Lord, and thou hast forgiven the wickedness of my sin' (Psalm 31/32:5), and, 'tell first thy iniquities, that thou mayest justify thyself' (Isaiah 43:26, LXX). Then by afflicting our hearts and our bodies, we may obtain remission of the sins we have confessed, in like manner, for 'see my abjection and my labour: and forgive me all my sins' (Psalm 24/25:18). Most of all, sins are forgiven through improvement of life, 'Take away the evil of your devices from my eyes. Cease to do perversely. Learn to do well. Seek judgment. Relieve the oppressed. Judge for the fatherless. Defend the widow. And then come and accuse me, saith the Lord. If your sins be as scarlet, they shall be made as white as snow: and if they be red as crimson, they shall be white as wool' (Isaiah 1:16–18).

Sometimes pardon for sin is obtained through the intercession of the saints, 'He that knoweth his brother to sin a sin which is not to death, let him ask, and life shall be given to him who sinneth not to death' (I John 5:16). Again, 'Is any man sick among you? Let him bring in the priests of the church and let them pray over him, anointing him with oil in the name of the Lord. And the prayer of faith shall save the sick man. And the Lord shall raise him up; and if he be in sins, they shall be forgiven him' (James 5:14–15). Often too the stain of sin is purged away by works of mercy and faith, as in, 'By mercy and faith sins are purged away' (Prov. 15:27b). Or it may be through the conversion and salvation of those who have been saved through our preaching and admonition, for 'he who causeth a sinner to be converted from the error of his way shall save his soul from death and shall cover a multitude of sins' (James 5:20). Or again if we are forgiving and merciful, we may receive the forgiveness of our own sins, 'For if you will forgive men their offences, your heavenly Father will forgive you also your offences' (Matt. 6:14).

Thus you can see how many gateways to mercy our loving Saviour has opened for us, so that no one who desires to be saved need be crushed by despair, seeing so many openings to life before him. If you say that you cannot purge your sins through fasting because of physical weakness, and are unable to quote the psalm, 'My knees are weakened through fasting: and my flesh is changed for oil' (Psalm 108/109:24), or, 'I did eat ashes like bread, and mingled my drink with weeping' (Psalm 101/102:10), why then, redeem your sins with generous almsgiving. Have you nothing to give to the poor? But no one is excluded from the necessity of almsgiving through poverty or lack of funds, since the two mites given by the widow were preferred to the munificence of the rich, and the Lord promises a reward for a cup of cold water – even so, you can be cleansed of sin by emending your life instead. Then if you are incapable of extinguishing all vice by practising perfect virtue, substitute compassionate concern for the wellbeing of others. If you complain that you are unfit for this ministry also, you can cover up your sins with loving charity. If you are so depraved that you cannot summon the strength for that, you must humbly beg the prayers and intercession of the saints to cure you of your sins. Finally, who could be incapable of saying humbly, 'I have acknowledged my sin to thee: and my injustice I have not concealed'? Through confessing like that he may be confident in continuing, 'and thou hast forgiven the wickedness of my sin' (Psalm 31/32: 5). If you are ashamed to give yourself away in front of men, do not cease to make confession in earnest prayer before him from whom nothing can be hidden, saying, 'I know my iniquity: and my sin is always before me. To thee only have I sinned, and have done evil before thee' (Psalm 50/51: 5–6). God it is who is ready to cure without shaming us publicly, to grant remission for sin without reproof. After this easy and swift assistance, God in his compassion has given us yet another and even easier path, leaving us with the freedom to choose our own forgiveness, claiming pardon for our sins by our intention in saying, 'forgive us our debts as we also forgive our debtors' (Matt. 6: 12).

Therefore, if anyone desires to gain the forgiveness of his sins, he should apply himself to these means, and never be so stubborn and hardhearted as to prevent the fountain of mercy from providing a saving remedy. Even if we perform all the things I have listed, they would be insufficient to expiate our sins, unless the Lord in his goodness and mercy washes them away. When he observes that we are humbly offering him the duty of our service and devotion, he adds his own unbounded generosity to our feeble efforts, saying, 'I am, I am he that blot out thy iniquities for my own sake: and I will not remember thy sins' (Isaiah 43: 25). When anyone has reached this state we have been describing, he will respond to the grace of forgiveness with regular fasting and mortification of heart, for 'without shedding of blood there is no remission' (Heb. 9:22). True it is that 'flesh and blood cannot possess the kingdom of God' (I Cor. 15:50). If anyone should keep back the sword of the Spirit (which is the Word of God) from this shedding of blood, he will surely incur the curse of the Prophet Jeremiah, who said, 'cursed be he that withholdeth his sword from blood' (Jer. 48:10). This sword it is which sheds the poisoned blood that supplies the matter of sin, that probes and cuts away whatever tumours of worldly flesh it finds in our bodies, which makes those who are dead to sin alive in God, flourishing in spiritual virtue. It stimulates tears, not now over the memory of crimes past, but in the hope of joys to come, no longer thinking of evils that are done with, but good things in the future, no more tears for grief over sin, but tears of joy in eternal gladness, 'forgetting the things that are behind', meaning carnal vice, we 'stretch forth to those that are before' (Phil. 3:13), which are the gifts and virtues of the Spirit.

IX. "You mentioned a while ago the deliberate calling to mind of past sins – now this we should by no means do. On the contrary, if such a memory forces its way in, it must be expelled at once. It will drag the thoughts away from the contemplation of purity, especially for those who live in solitude, and entangle them in the defilement of this world, choking them with the stench of sin. If you do recall sins that you have committed for the prince of this age, whether through ignorance or desire, even if no pleasure insinuates itself into these thoughts, the mere touch of that former corruption is bound to infect the mind with its stench, and drive away the sweet savour of sanctity, the scent of spiritual virtue. Therefore, when the recollection of past sin assaults the mind, we should spring away from it, just as a respectable and decent man does if he is solicited by a brazen wanton in public, whether by words or embrace. If he is not quick to extricate himself from her arms, and allows her even a moment of indecent speech, he will not escape the accusation of guilt and the contempt of passers by, no matter how much he repudiates any consent to impure desire. In the same way we too should be quick to disassociate ourselves from any evil intention, if we are taken unawares by the recollection of evil thoughts. Thus we may fulfil the words of Solomon, 'stand afar, do not delay in her place, neither cast thine eye upon her' (Prov. 9:18a, LXX). Otherwise the angels passing by, seeing us entangled in vile and immodest thoughts, will be unable to say of us, 'The blessing of the Lord be upon you: [we have blessed you in the name of the Lord]' (Psalm 128/129:8). It is impossible for the imagination to dwell on good thoughts, if the depths of our hearts are steeped in vile and earthly concerns. True it is what Solomon says, 'Thy eyes shall behold strange women: and thy mouth shall utter perverse things. And thou shalt be as one sleeping in the midst of the sea, and as a pilot in a great tempest. And thou shalt say, They have beaten me, but I was not sensible of pain: they drew me, and I felt not' (Prov. 23:33–5, LXX). When we have left behind all evil thoughts, and all worldly considerations, our intentions should be raised always to the heavens, as Our Saviour instructed us, for he said, 'where I am, there also shall my minister be' (John 12:26). It can often happen that one who is inexperienced may ponder over his own or others' faults in order to regret them, but is then ensnared by the slender bonds of lascivious desire; what he began under pretext of piety, he ends with sin and impurity. 'There are ways that seem to men right, and the ends thereof lead to the depths of hell' (Prov. 16:25, LXX).

X. "For this reason we should take pains to rouse ourselves to worthy compunction, through the desire of virtue and a longing for the kingdom of heaven, rather than through the evil memory of our sins. If you insist on standing over a drain and trying to stir up its effluent, you are bound to be choked with its pestilential stench.

XI. "As I have said so often, we can be confident that we have made satisfaction for our sins, once the actual desires and emotions which made us commit them have been eliminated from our hearts. No one may be sure that he has achieved this until he has wholeheartedly cut off all the occasions and excuses through which he fell into those sins. For example, if he has fallen into fornication or adultery through keeping company with dangerous women, he must be determined to avoid meeting them. If he is provoked to excess through too much food and wine, he must take prudent steps to restrain such immoderate consumption. Again, if it is through the desire and love of money that he has fallen into perjury, theft, homicide or blasphemy, he must sever himself from the alluring matter he so desires. If it is to the vice of anger that his pride drives him, let him eliminate the spark of arrogance through genuine humility. In this way, to extinguish all sin, we must first begin by removing the occasions and causes of each one. Then by curing them in this manner, we shall surely arrive at forgetfulness of our past offences.

XII. "What I have said about forgetfulness only applies to grave sins, those condemned also by the Law of Moses. They can be brought to an end through penance, as the desire and affection for them is cut off and eliminated by a worthy way of life. On the other hand we shall never lack for penance over the trivial sins into which the just man falls seven times daily, as it is written (cf. Prov. 24:16) and from which he rises. Through ignorance, or forgetfulness, through thought, word and inadvertence, out of necessity or physical weakness, or through improper dreams, we fail frequently every day whether willingly or not. For such sins David implored the Lord for purification and grace, saying, 'Who can understand sins? From my secret ones cleanse me, O Lord: and from those of others spare thy servant' (Psalm 18/19:13–14). St Paul also says, 'For the good which I will, I do not; but the evil which I will not, that I do' (Rom. 7:19). Further on he exclaims about this matter again, 'Unhappy man that I am, who shall deliver me from the body of this death?' (Rom. 7:24). It is so easy to fall in this way, so inevitable by our very nature, that we cannot totally avoid such sins no matter how circumspect and cautious we be. Of these the disciple whom Jesus loves tells us with authority, 'If we say that we have no sin, we deceive ourselves and his word is

XX. On the Purpose of Penance

not in us' (I John 1: 8, 10). For this reason one who aspires to reach the pinnacle of perfection will not achieve it simply by completing the purpose of penance, in other words by restraining himself from serious sin; no, he must exert himself constantly in a tireless pursuit of those virtues which will bring him the certainty of having made satisfaction. It will not be enough merely to abstain from vile crimes which the Lord detests, unless we also possess the delightful savour of virtue in which the Lord rejoices, in purity of heart, and in the perfection of apostolic charity."

This was all that Abba Pinufius had to say on the way we can know whether we are forgiven, and on the purpose of penance. He did in fact earnestly invite us to decide to stay, and live in his monastery, but we were called away by the reports we had heard of the desert of Scete, and so he sent us on our way, being unable to retain us.

✣ THE TWENTY-FIRST COLLATION ✣
BEING THE FIRST OF
ABBA THEONAS

On the Celebration of Eastertide

    I. How Theonas came to Abba John.
   II. The discourse of Abba John to Theonas and the others who came with him.
  III. On tithes and the offering of first-fruits.
  IV. How Abraham, David and other holy men surpassed the commandments of the Law.
   V. How those who live in the grace of the Gospel should surpass the commands of the Law.
  VI. How the grace of the Gospel, while it offers the kingdom of heaven to the perfect, also supports the weak with understanding.
 VII. How it is within our power to choose whether to live in the grace of the Gospel, or in fear of the Law.
VIII. How Theonas exhorted his wife to renounce the world too.
  IX. How, since his wife refused, he left her for the monastery.
   X. Cassian explains why he recounts this, lest he seem to recommend breaking the bonds of marriage.
  XI. The question, why in Egypt they do not fast during the whole of Eastertide, nor do they kneel to pray.
 XII. The reply, on how some things are good, some bad, some neutral.

- XIII. What sort of good fasting is.
- XIV. That fasting is not good in itself.
- XV. That things which are good in themselves should not be done for the sake of things less good.
- XVI. How something good in itself is distinguished from other good things.
- XVII. On the purpose and value of fasting.
- XVIII. That it is not always suitable to fast.
- XIX. A question, why fasting is relaxed for a whole fifty days.
- XX. The reply.
- XXI. A question, whether relaxing the strict fast impedes physical chastity.
- XXII. The reply, on preserving the habit of continence.
- XXIII. On the time and measure of eating.
- XXIV. A question, on the varying observance of Lent.
- XXV. The reply to that question, showing that the Lenten fast is a tithe of the year.
- XXVI. How we should offer our first-fruits to the Lord.
- XXVII. The reason why some observe a different number of days in Lent.
- XXVIII. Why it is called 'Forty days', when we fast for only thirty six days.
- XXIX. That those who are perfect surpass the legislation of Lent.
- XXX. On the original reason for Lent.
- XXXI. A question, how can we understand St Paul's words, that sin does not have dominion over us.
- XXXII. The reply, on the difference between the requirements of the law and of grace.
- XXXIII. That the precepts of the Gospel are lighter than the Law.
- XXXIV. How a man may be shown to be under grace.
- XXXV. A question, why sometimes we are worse plagued by fleshly thoughts when we are fasting more strictly.

XXI. On the Celebration of Eastertide 445

XXXVI. The reply, that this question should be kept for a future conference.

I. Before I begin to recount the conference we held with that great man Abba Theonas, I think I should briefly give you an account of his first conversion, because the merit and grace of the man can thus be best revealed to the reader.

When he was still young Theonas was committed to a marriage at the desire and command of his parents. They were devout, and concerned for his purity, but being afraid that he would fall as he entered the dangerous age, they thought it better to apply the remedy of lawful marriage to the adolescent turbulence they foresaw. He had lived with his wife for the space of five years, before he came to Abba John, who had at that time been chosen to be in charge of the monastic dispensary, in consideration of his holiness. No one is promoted to this office from his own choice or ambition, but only the one whom the whole community of elders consider to excel all others in merit, through seniority in age and the evidence of his faith and virtue. The young Theonas, then, came to the blessed Abba John out of his earnest devotion, bringing offerings along with other householders who used to compete with each other in contributing the tithes or first-fruits of their property to the famous old man. Abba John saw them approaching him with their many offerings, and was anxious to give them some reward in exchange for their devotion; he began therefore, in the Apostle's words (cf. I Cor. 9:11), to sow in the spirit what he had reaped in material gifts, and addressed them with these words of advice:

II. "I am delighted, my dear sons, to see your devoted generosity, grateful to receive the offerings which you have brought and entrusted to me to dispense; you have been faithful in contributing your tithes and first-fruits for the benefit of the poor, offering them like a sacrifice, a pleasing odour before the Lord. Be sure that there will be an abundant blessing on all these gifts you have offered, and on the whole of your property from which you have made this sacrifice to the Lord; be sure too that you will receive plenty of good things in this world also, because you have followed God's commandments. 'Honour the Lord with thy just labours, and give him of the fruits of thy righteousness: and thy barns shall be filled with abundance of wheat, and thy presses shall run over with wine' (Prov. 3: 9–10, LXX). Faithfully observing this pious practice, you can be confident that you have fulfilled the requirement of the ancient law, even though those who lived under it could not observe it, but ran inevitably into sin, for they were incapable of fulfilling the law and attaining the summit of perfection.

III. "According to the commandments of the Lord, tithes were to be given for the use of the Levites, offerings and first-fruits for that of the priests (cf. Num. 18: 26; 5: 9–10). The rule on first-fruits was that one fiftieth of fruit or animal produce should be dedicated to the service of the Temple or the priests. Those who were less fervent, and less faithful, reduced this; the more pious increased it, so that some offered a sixtieth part, others a fortieth of their produce. Those who are justified, for whom the Law was not given, prove themselves not to be under the law by not only fulfilling its requirements but actually exceeding them, and their piety is greater than the obligations of the law, for they add of their own free will to the obligation which was commanded.

IV. "In this manner we read that Abraham surpassed the commandments of the law, which was still in the future; when he had overcome the four kings, he refused absolutely to touch the spoils of the Sodomites, even though they were due to him as the conqueror, and their own king humbly offered him the booty he himself had brought back. Abraham called the Name of God to witness, saying, 'I lift up my hand to the Lord God the most high, the creator of heaven and earth, that of the very woof thread unto the shoe latchet, I will not take of any things that are thine' (Gen. 14: 22–3, LXX). David too can be seen to have surpassed the commandments of the Law, for though Moses commanded him to take vengeance on his enemies, he did not only refrain from this but even embraced his persecutors with love, and prayed devoutly to God for them, he wept bitterly over them and punished those who killed them. Elijah also and Jeremiah are shown to be not subject to the law, for although they could have enjoyed marriage without blame, they preferred to remain celibate. Elishah as well, and the others of his company, surpassed the commands of Moses as the Apostle says of them, 'they wandered about in sheepskins, in goatskins, being in want, distressed, afflicted; of whom the world was not worthy; wandering in deserts, in mountains and in dens and caves of the earth' (Heb. 11: 37–8).

What can I say about the sons of Jonadab, the son of Rechab? We read that when the prophet Jeremiah was told by the Lord to offer them wine, they replied, 'We will not drink wine, because Jonadab, the son of Rechab, our father, commanded us, saying: You shall drink no wine, neither you nor your children, for ever: neither shall ye build houses, nor sow seed, nor plant vineyards, nor have any: but you shall dwell in tents all your days' (Jer. 35: 6–7). For this reason they were worthy to hear the same prophet say of them, 'Thus saith the Lord of hosts, the God of Israel: there shall not be wanting a man of the race of Jonadab the son of Rechab, standing before me for ever' (Jer. 35: 19). All of these were not content merely to offer tithes of their possessions, but spurning profit, offered themselves and their own souls to God: and there is no exchange that a man can make for that, as the Lord tells us in the Gospel, 'what exchange shall a man give for his soul?' (Matt. 16: 26).

V. "We should therefore be aware of the obligations laid upon us, not by a legal requirement but by the consistent teaching of the Gospel: 'If thou wilt be perfect, go sell what thou hast and give to the poor and thou shalt have treasure in heaven. And come follow me' (Matt. 19: 21). If we offer tithes of our property to God we are still to some extent bound by the law, and have not yet risen up to the pinnacle of the Gospel, for once we have attained that, it will repay us not only with benefits in this present life, but with a reward to come. The old Law did not offer its followers the prize of the Kingdom of Heaven, but consolation in this life, saying, 'if a man do these things, he shall live in them' (Lev. 18:5). The Lord on the other hand said to his apostles and disciples, 'Blessed are the poor in spirit; for theirs is the kingdom of heaven', and, 'every one that hath left house or brethren or sisters or father or mother or wife or children or lands, for my name's sake, shall receive an hundredfold and shall possess life everlasting' (Matt. 5:3, 19:29). This is just, for it is more praiseworthy to abstain from what is lawful than from what is unlawful, in that out of devotion we refrain from using something which had been permitted to us because of our weakness. Now if those who offer the tithes of their produce faithfully are still observing the Lord's ancient commandments, but have not yet risen to the heights of the gospel, you can easily see how much further from those heights are those who do not even do that. How could those who disdain to observe the easy requirements of the Law ever have a share in the grace of the Gospel? Even the imperious voice of the Lawgiver testifies to this easiness, when he utters a curse against those who do not fulfil the law: 'Cursed is every one that abideth not in all things which are written in the book of the law to do them' (Gal. 3:10). But in the Gospel it is said of the excellent and sublime precepts, 'He that can take, let him take it' (Matt. 19:12). In the Old Law the strongly worded compulsion of the lawgiver betrays the inadequacy of the law, for he says, 'I call this day heaven and earth to witness, that if you do not observe the commands of the Lord your God, you shall perish out of the land' (Deut. 4:26). In the Gospel the splendour of the precepts is shown by the fact that he exhorts us rather than orders us: 'If thou wilt be perfect,' do this or that. Moses lays on those who refuse a burden that cannot be avoided; St Paul offers advice to those who are willing and hasten towards perfection. It is not a general requirement, nor something which the canons require of everyone, if I may use the expression; this is something too great and sublime for all to be able to apprehend, it is a counsel by which all are invited to receive grace. Thus those who are great can be justly crowned with the virtue of perfection, those who are small and incapable of filling up 'the measure of the age of the fullness of Christ' (Eph. 4:13) may well lose sight of the splendour of the great, as if they were shielded from the stars, but are also protected from the darkness of the curse which lies upon the law; they are not afflicted with disaster in this world, nor are they condemned to eternal punishment. Christ does not compel anyone to achieve the very summit of virtue by an obligatory command; he invites us to use our own free choice, and inspires us with saving advice and the desire for perfection. For where there is a precept, there is obligation; [where there is obligation there is difficulty, where there is difficulty there is negligence; where there is negligence there is sin, and where there is sin] there is consequently punishment. Those on the other hand who observe what the severe ancient law compels, merely avoid the penalty threatened in that law, rather than earning themselves a reward or prize.

VI. "In this manner while the words of the Gospel encourage the strong to sublime excellence, they do not suffer the weak to fall into the depths. To the perfect they grant a full blessing, while to the frail they bestow pardon. The old Law, on the other hand, treats those who follow its commands in a sort of intermediate way, keeping them as far from condemnation as it does from the perfection of glory. You can see what a wretched and base condition this is even from the circumstances of this present life, where it would be considered a poor thing for someone to expend so much effort merely to avoid appearing guilty among decent people, rather than to attain wealth and honour and glory.

VII. "It is therefore now within our own power to choose whether to live under the grace of the Gospel or in fear of the Law. You must take one side or other, depending on your actions. If you surpass the law, the grace of Christ will receive you; or else the law will keep hold of you, still bound to itself, still failures and in debt. One who is guilty of offending the law will never be able to acquire the perfection of the Gospel; even if he does make the empty claim of being a Christian, free through the grace of the Lord. We can adjudge someone to be still bound by the Law not only if he fails to complete what the Law requires, but also if he is content to observe no more than the Law, never bearing fruit worthy of his vocation and the grace of Christ. It is not the Gospel that says, 'thou shalt not delay to pay thy tithes and thy first-fruits to the Lord thy God' (Exod. 22:29); no, it says, 'go sell what thou hast and give to the poor and thou shalt have treasure in heaven. And come follow me' (Matt. 19:21). When the disciple asked Our Lord about the splendour of perfection, he was not granted even a brief hour to bury his father; not even human charity was to be placed before the love of God."

VIII. The blessed Theonas heard these words, and was fired with an irresistible longing for the perfection of the Gospel, as the seed of the word germinated in his heart, buried in the deep and well-tilled furrows of his breast. He was greatly humbled and struck by the fact that the old man had declared him not merely to have failed in the Gospel's requirements, but scarcely even to have carried out the commandments of the Law itself. He had indeed been accustomed to bring the tithes of his produce to the dispensary every year, but was grieved to realise he had not even heard of first-fruits. Yet even if he performed that duty as well, the elder's teaching showed that he was still far from the perfection of the Gospel, as he humbly admitted. He went home sorrowfully, filled with the sort of sadness that works repentance for true salvation. Sure now of his own resolution and determination, he was concerned for his wife's salvation, and applied all his anxious efforts to inspire her with a similar desire to the one that had taken hold of him, which was that they should both serve God in holiness and chastity. Day and night he admonished her, with tears, saying that they should not delay their conversion to a better life, for it was vain to imagine that their youth would preserve them from the risk of unexpected death, which falls upon infants, children and youths as often as on the old.

IX. His hardhearted wife refused to agree to his persistent entreaties, and alleged that in the flower of her youth she could

XXI. On the Celebration of Eastertide

not abstain from the consolation of marriage, and that if she fell into sin as a result of being deserted by him, it would be his fault for having broken the conjugal bonds. He on the other hand asserted that human nature was in so frail and uncertain a condition that it was perilous to remain entangled in carnal desires and actions any longer. He also added that no one could be excused for excluding himself from a good thing which he had discovered was worthy to attain, and that it was a greater evil to reject a known good than to fail to love one unknown. Moreover he would be subject to the accusation of inconsistency, if he preferred base earthly things to the great and heavenly gifts he had found. He told her that the splendour of perfection was appropriate to every age and sex, and that every member of the Church was called to ascend the summits of virtue, as St Paul says, "so run that you may obtain" (I Cor. 9:24). The ready and the swift should not wait for the slow and reluctant, for it is better for the lazy to be encouraged by the swift than for the swift to be held back by the lazy. In short he declared that he was determined to renounce this age, to die to the world in order to live with God. If he could not obtain the bliss he desired of entering Christ's service with his companion, he would rather be saved at the expense of one limb, entering the kingdom of heaven as it were lame, rather than to be condemned whole and complete (cf. Matt. 5:30).

He continued, "If Moses allowed them to dismiss their wives, because of their hardness of heart, why would Christ not permit this out of a desire for chastity? Particularly when the Lord links with a wife the other affectionate relationships, namely father, mother and children: not only the old Law but the Lord himself bids us show them all respect, but for the sake of his name and the quest for perfection he tells us not merely to repudiate them but actually to hate them. 'And everyone that hath left house or brethren or sisters or father or mother or wife or children or lands, for my name's sake, shall receive an hundredfold and shall possess life everlasting' (Matt. 19:29). He permits nothing to stand in the way of the perfection he preaches, to the extent of dissolving the bond with father or mother, though as St Paul tells us that is the first commandment bearing a promise: 'Honour thy father and thy mother, which is the first commandment with a promise; that it may be well with thee, and thou mayest be long lived upon earth' (Eph. 6: 2–3). Yet for the love of himself he bids us renounce them! Therefore, just as the Gospel teaching condemns those who break the bonds of marriage, unless the sin of adultery has already done so, in the same way is promised an hundredfold reward to those who reject the yoke of marriage for the love of Christ and the desire of chastity. For this reason, if you will at last be persuaded to accept the better part for me, namely that we might serve the Lord together and so escape the pains of hell, I will not refuse you conjugal affection, and indeed will love you with even greater intensity. I acknowledge you, I respect you, as the helpmate granted to me by the Lord's will, and in no way refuse to cling to you in an unbroken bond of charity; I will not separate myself from what the Lord joined to me by the law of my natural condition, as long as you yourself will be what the Creator wished you to be. But if you prefer to be not my helpmate but my deceiver, giving me not assistance but adversity, and if you imagine that this is what the sacrament of matrimony was intended for, to cheat you of the salvation which is offered, and to draw me too away from the discipleship of Our Saviour, then I will manfully follow the teaching of Abba John, indeed that of Christ himself, and no fleshly affection will be able to keep me away from the good of my spirit. For Christ said, 'If any man come to me, and hate not his father and mother and wife and children and brethren and sisters, yea and his own life also, he cannot be my disciple'" (Luke 14: 26).

Despite these and similar words, he failed to change the woman's mind, and she remained stubborn in her obstinacy. "If, then", said blessed Theonas, "I cannot rescue you from death, at least you will not separate me from Christ. It is safer for me to be divorced from a human being than from God." As the grace of God inspired him, he straightaway put his resolution into practice, not letting the fervour of his desire cool through any delay. He stripped himself of all earthly property and entered a monastery.

XXI. On the Celebration of Eastertide

There he quickly came to shine with such splendid holiness and humility, that when the time came for John of holy memory to leave this world for the Lord, and Saint Elias had also died, a man no less than his predecessor, Theonas was elected by common assent as the third to succeed him in the work of the dispensary.

X. Now no one should imagine that I have told you all this to encourage divorce. Marriage is in no way condemned by us, and we really believe the teaching of the Apostle who said, "Marriage honourable in all, and the bed undefiled" (Heb. 13: 4). No, we are only recounting faithfully to the reader the first conversion by which this great man was called to God. I ask the reader's good will, whether he approves or disapproves of the story, not to accuse me, the writer, for telling the truth, but to keep his praise or blame for the one who actually did what I have described. I have not been giving my own opinion on this matter, but simply describing a historical event; I claim no praise from those who approve of what he did, I expect no rebuke from those who disapprove. Let each one, as I said, keep to his own opinion: I only counsel you that you be careful, in your criticism, never to imagine your own judgment to be equal to or better than God's, for signs of apostolic virtue were evident in Theonas. Not to mention the reaction of so many of the fathers, who were far from blaming him for what he did, that they showed their approval by electing him to the ministry in the dispensary in preference to many other excellent men. I cannot believe that so many spiritual men, inspired by God, were mistaken, and as I said, their admiration was confirmed by many miracles.

XI. Now it is time to proceed with the discourse I promised you. Abba Theonas visited us in our cell during the fifty days of Eastertide, and we celebrated vespers together. Then sitting on the floor we began to interrogate him why they so carefully kept the observance of never kneeling down to pray during Eastertide, and never prolonging their fast till the ninth hour. We asked him this with interest, because we had never seen this practice observed in Syrian monasteries.

XII. Abba Theonas began to speak in reply to this: "It is a good thing for us to follow the authority of the Fathers, and the custom of those who have gone before us during such a long period down to our own age, even if we do not understand the reason. Therefore we should observe with reverence and care what antiquity has handed down. But since you would like to know the origin and reason for these customs, let me tell you what we have heard from our elders about them. Before citing the authority of sacred Scripture, I would like to say a little about the very nature of fasting, if I may, so that the authority of Scripture may confirm what I have said. God in his wisdom designated a proper time for everything, for all things favourable and for those considered to be adverse or grievous, in the book of Ecclesiastes: 'All things have their season: and there is a time for all things under heaven. A time to be born, and a time to die. A time to plant, and a time to pluck up that which is planted. A time to kill, and a time to heal. A time to destroy, and a time to build. A time to weep, and a time to laugh. A time to mourn, and a time to dance. A time to scatter stones, and a time to gather up stones. A time to embrace, and a time to be far from embraces. A time to get, and a time to lose. A time to keep, and a time to cast away. A time to rend and a time to sew. A time to keep silence, and a time to speak. A time of love, and a time of hatred. A time of war, and a time of peace.' And a little further on, 'And then shall be the time of every thing and of every deed' (Qo. 3:1–8, 17). None of these things is declared to be good for ever, except in so far as each of them is performed in its right time and in the right way. Things which are right, if they are done now, have to give place; if they are continued in wrongly or at the wrong time, they are shown to be useless or dangerous. This does not of course apply to things which are in themselves good or bad, and which can never give place to their contrary, such as justice, prudence, fortitude, temperance and the other virtues, and correspondingly the vices which are not capable of changing to their opposite, or mutating at all. It is the things which can sometimes give place to their opposite, and be found either good or bad depending on the way they are used,

XXI. On the Celebration of Eastertide

that are not considered either beneficial or harmful absolutely, in themselves, but only as the person doing them intends, and the time allows.

XIII. "For this reason we can now inquire about the nature of fasting, whether it is a good in itself, like justice, prudence, fortitude and temperance, which as we said cannot give place to their opposite. Or is it something neutral, which may sometimes be beneficial to practice, sometimes blameless to omit? If it be wrong sometimes to practise it, it may be praiseworthy sometimes to refrain from it. If we consider fasting to be among those first virtues, and rank abstaining from food as one of the principal goods, then it would be seriously sinful to take food, for anything opposed to a principal good must by definition be a principal evil. Yet the authority of Holy Scripture does not permit that, for if we fast in the belief that it would be sinful for us to partake of food, we shall gain no benefit from our fasting, and even find ourselves guilty of serious sin and sacrilege. As St Paul tells us, it is wrong: 'to abstain from meats, which God hath created to be received with thanksgiving by the faithful and by them that have known the truth. For every creature of God is good, and nothing to be rejected that is received with thanksgiving' (I Tim. 4:3–4). Moreover, 'to him that esteemeth anything to be unclean, to him it is unclean' (Rom. 14:14). We never read that anyone was condemned simply for taking food, but only if there was something associated with it, or some consequence which deserved condemnation.

XIV. "Therefore it is clear that fasting should be considered neutral, for as we may be justified in practising it, so we are not condemned for leaving it off, though we may be blamed for disobeying a command rather than for the actual eating. But for something good in itself, no time should be exempt, for no one is permitted to live without it, and its omission is bound to lead to negligence and evil. Nor can any occasion be granted for something evil in itself, for it is always harmful, and never fails to do damage whenever it is committed, never capable of changing to something praiseworthy. Things which do have proper times and methods, and can make us holy by practising them, though their omission is no sin, are clearly to be called neutral; for example marriage, agriculture, wealth, living alone, keeping watch, spiritual reading, meditation, and fasting itself which is our main subject.

None of these things is commanded by divine law, or the authority of Holy Scripture, to be observed on all occasions, nor to be practised in such a way that it would be wrong ever to interrupt it. Anything that is definitely ordered brings death if it is not fulfilled; but whatever is encouraged rather than commanded is beneficial if you do it, but blameless if you do not. For that reason all these things, or at any rate some of them, were commanded by our predecessors to be done prudently and wisely, depending on the reason, the place, the manner and the time. Any of them, done appropriately, are good and useful, if done inappropriately are wrong and harmful. For example, if a brother arrived in whom you ought to welcome Christ with kindness, and refresh him generously, and you preferred to keep a severe fast, would you not incur the charge of churlishness, rather than a reputation for piety? If someone was weak and physically frail, and needed food to recover his strength, but refused to relax the rigorous rule of fasting, would he not be considered a ruthless self-murderer, not someone concerned for his own salvation? In the same manner if there were a feast day that should be celebrated with a suitable meal and the usual abstinence necessarily relaxed, and someone wanted to keep to the strict observance of fasting without intermission, he would not be considered religious but ill-mannered and unreasonable. This will be found contrary to those who seek for human praise through their fasting, gaining a reputation for sanctity by the display of pallor, for the words of the Gospel declare that they have received their reward in the present life. They are like those whose fasting the Lord detests, speaking through the prophet who begins by saying in their behalf, 'Why have we fasted, and thou hast not regarded? Have we humbled our souls, and thou hast not taken notice?' He gives the reason at once why these men do not deserve to be heard: 'Behold, in the day of your fast your own will is found: and you exact of all your debtors. Behold you fast for debates and strife, and strike with the fist wickedly. Do not fast as you have done until this day, to make your cry to be heard on high. Is this such a fast as I have chosen: for a man to afflict his soul for a day? Is this it: to wind his head about like a circle and to spread sackcloth and ashes? Wilt thou call this a fast and a day acceptable to the Lord?' (Isaiah 58: 3–4). He continues to teach us how fasting and self-denial may be acceptable, telling us clearly that fasting alone is of no benefit, unless it have the following motives: 'Is not this rather the fast that I have chosen? Loose the bands of wickedness, undo the bundles that oppress. Let them that are broken go free: and break asunder every burden. Deal thy bread to the hungry and bring the needy and the harbourless into thy house: when thou shalt see one naked, cover him and despise not thy own flesh. Then shall thy light break forth as the morning, and thy health shall speedily arise, and thy justice shall go before thy face, and the glory of the Lord shall gather thee up. Then shalt thou call, and the Lord shall hear; thou shalt cry, and he shall say: Here I am' (Isaiah 58: 6–8). So you see how the Lord never defines fasting as good by nature, because it is good and pleasing to God not in itself but only through its results. Conversely, other accompanying motives can make it not just futile but actually hateful, as the Lord says, 'When they fast I will not hear their prayers' (Jer. 14: 12).

XV. "Mercy, patience and charity, and the command to practice the virtues we have mentioned in which exists a principal good, are not practised for the sake of fasting, but fasting is for them. I mean that the virtues which are truly good are gained by fasting, not that the exercise of such virtues leads up to fasting. The purpose of afflicting the flesh, the purpose of practising abstinence, is that we may attain charity, in which is the everlasting good, unchanging and true at all times. Skill in medicine, or goldsmithery, or any other art of this world is not exercised for the sake of the tools of the trade; the instruments are made for the art. They are useful to those who know how to use them, and unnecessary for those without that knowledge. Those who rely on them to perform their work find them invaluable, whereas those who are ignorant of their purpose but are simply happy to possess them, gain no benefit at all, if they think their only purpose is just to be kept, not to be put to use. The greater good is that for the sake of which neutral things are made; the highest good of all is that which is done for its own sake alone, and for no other cause.

XVI. "This is how to distinguish the things which we have described as neutral from others: we should enquire whether they are good in themselves rather than for something else, whether they are necessary in themselves and not for some other end, whether they are always unchangeably good and always retain that quality, never able to change to their contrary, whether their loss or cessation does not necessarily produce great evil; and furthermore, if whatever is contrary to them is evil by nature, and incapable of ever changing to become good. None of these ways to define the nature of something good in itself can be applied to fasting. It is not good of itself, nor is it in itself necessary, but it is practised for the sake of acquiring purity of heart and body, to quell the pangs of the flesh and reconcile the mind at peace with its Maker. It is not unchangeably good at all times, for we are not harmed by sometimes leaving it off, and if it is practised inappropriately it can be dangerous for the soul. Nor is its contrary evil in itself, that is taking natural pleasure in food; unless that is immoderate or luxurious, or leads to some other vice, it cannot be called evil, for 'Not that which goeth into the mouth defileth a man; but what cometh out of the mouth, this defileth a man' (Matt. 15:11). If something is good in itself, it is a fault and a sinful imperfection to perform it for some other end and not for itself. Everything is to be done for the sake of what is good in itself, and it is desirable for the sake of itself alone.

XVII. "Once we have grasped this definition of what fasting is, we should practice it with all our strength, as long as we are aware that it is suitable for us only if we keep to the right time, manner and

XXI. On the Celebration of Eastertide

degree. We should not consider it the goal of our hopes, but use it to arrive at purity of heart and apostolic charity. It follows that fasting, to which special times are allotted for practice or omission, as well as set measure and method, cannot be good in itself, but is something neutral. Other things, which are commanded us as being good, or forbidden as evil, with the authority of precept, suffer no exception of time when forbidden things may be done, mandated things omitted. There is no limit set to justice, patience, sobriety, modesty or charity; nor is there ever licence for injustice, impatience, wrath, immodesty, envy or pride.

XVIII. "Having said this about fasting, we should add the authorities from Holy Scripture, to prove that it is neither right nor possible to fast without intermission. In the Gospels, when the Pharisees and the disciples of John the Baptist are fasting, the apostles did not fast, being friends and companions of their heavenly Bridegroom. The disciples of John thought they possessed the whole truth about fasting, being followers of the great preacher of penance, who offered himself as an example to all the people, and did not only reject the varied types of food which men commonly use but even abstained entirely from common bread; they complained to the Lord, saying, 'Why do we and the Pharisees fast often, but thy disciples do not fast?' To which the Lord's reply shows us that it is not fitting or necessary to fast at all times, and gives us licence to eat at a time of festival or when charity demands: 'Can the children of the bridegroom mourn as long as the bridegroom is with them? But the days will come when the bridegroom shall be taken away from them, and then they shall fast' (Matt. 9:14–15). He spoke these words before the resurrection of his body, but they look forward to the time before Pentecost when the Lord ate with his disciples for forty days, and the joy of his continual presence prevented them from fasting."

XIX. GERMANUS: "But why do we relax our rigorous abstinence and eat for all fifty days, when Christ remained with his disciples after the resurrection for only forty days?"

XX. THEONAS: "Your question is appropriate, and deserves a full and truthful reply. After Our Saviour's ascension, which happened on the fortieth day after his resurrection, the apostles returned from the Mount of Olives where he had allowed them to see him returning to the Father, as we read in the Acts of the Apostles. They came to Jerusalem and waited the coming of the Holy Spirit for ten days, and when these had passed they welcomed him with joy on the fiftieth day: thus the number of days in the festal season is completed (cf. Acts 1:12 ff.). We can see a figure of this number of festival days foreshadowed in the Old Testament, when the priests are commanded to offer the firstfruits of bread to the Lord after seven weeks of days (Deut. 16:9). This offering to the Lord was fulfilled faithfully in the preaching of the Apostles, the sermon they gave to the people that day. The true firstfruits of bread, offered at the beginning of the new teaching, consecrated the first Christian people to the Lord from the Jews, for five thousand men were nourished with that bread (cf. Acts 2). Therefore these ten days too are to be celebrated with as much solemnity and joy as the previous forty. The tradition of this festal season has been passed down to us through the successors of the apostles as something to celebrate in the same manner. Therefore on these days we do not bend the knee in prayer, for kneeling is a sign of penitence and sorrow. All the way through the season we keep the same customs as on Sundays, when our predecessors taught us neither to fast nor to bend the knee, out of respect for Our Lord's Resurrection."

XXI. GERMANUS: "Can it not happen that the flesh is affected by this unaccustomed laxity during such a long festival, and may allow the germ of vice, once cut down, to sprout again? For the mind, burdened with meals taken more often than usual, may slacken its strict control over the servile body, and especially in youth our subjected limbs may be quick to rebel, if we take our usual food in greater quantity, or more freely take unusual meals?"

XXII. THEONAS: "If we think carefully about everything we do, and consult our own conscience, not anyone else's judgment, about purity of heart, we can be certain that this interval of festivity will never be an obstacle to proper self-control. As long as we measure out our indulgence and our continence on accurate scales, so to speak, the pure mind will avoid excess on either side. True discretion can judge whether too much delicacy is weighing down the spirit, or too severe an abstinence is depressing the other scale, namely the body, and thus we correct them by pressing down or raising up whichever side appears to be too light or too heavy. Our Lord wishes us to do nothing in his worship or honour without due moderation, for 'the king's honour loveth judgment' (Psalm 98/99: 4). For this reason Solomon the Wise warns us not to fall on either side through unbalanced judgment, saying: 'Honour God with thy just labours, and give him of the fruits of thy justice' (Prov. 3: 9, LXX). There is an incorruptible judge dwelling in our conscience, who alone is not deceived about the state of our purity, even though all others may be in error. Even if the heart is circumspect and alert, taking all precautions and great care, our judgment can still be wrong, whether we be inflamed with desire for unreasonable self-denial, or taken by a longing for excessive indulgence, if we weigh our strength with biassed scales. We may place our purity of soul in one pan, and our physical strength in the other, weighing them by the true judgment of conscience, and letting our interest in neither side unbalance us into tilting the scale out of balance towards excessive strictness or over-indulgence. Otherwise it would be said to us, if we exceeded in laxity or abstinence, 'If thou offerest well, but dost not divide well, thou hast sinned' (Gen. 4: 7, LXX). If we imagine we are making a proper sacrifice to the Lord, offering victims of fasting which we rashly extort from ourselves by violent convulsions of the digestion, he 'who loveth mercy and judgment' (Psalm 32/33: 5), will rebuke us, saying, 'I am the Lord that love judgment and hate robbery in a holocaust' (Isaiah 61: 8). Those on the other hand who presume to take their offering, that is the first-fruits of their work and activity, for their own use and to nourish their flesh, giving the leftovers to the Lord and the smallest of portions to him, are condemned by God's word as fraudulent labourers: 'Cursed be he that doth the work of the Lord deceitfully' (Jer. 48:10). Rightly does the Lord rebuke the one who deceives himself by such an unbalanced judgment: 'But vain are the sons of men, the sons of men are liars in the balances, that they may deceive' (Psalm 61/62:10). This is why St Paul warns us, to preserve a reasonable moderation and not to run to either extreme through excess, speaking of 'your reasonable service' (Rom. 12:1). Moses also condemns such excess, when he decrees, 'Let the balance be just and the weights equal, the bushel just and the sextary equal' (Lev. 19:36). Solomon also gives the same advice: 'Weights great or small, diverse measures, both are abominable before the Lord, and he who does so will be known in his inclinations' (Prov. 20:10–11, LXX). We should take care, not only in the manner already mentioned, but in this as well, not to have unequal weights in our hearts, nor twofold measures in the barns of our conscience. In this way we shall not presume to be so lax as to make for ourselves an indulgence to modify our strict rule, while we overwhelm those to whom we preach the word of the Lord with stricter commands and heavier burdens that we ourselves can carry. If we do that, are we not parcelling out and gathering the produce and fruits of the Lord's precepts with a twofold weight and measure? If we distribute them to ourselves in one way, and to our brothers in another, the Lord will justly rebuke us for having false scales and double standards, as Solomon teaches us, 'Diverse weights are an abomination for the Lord: a deceitful balance is not good in his sight' (Prov. 20:23, LXX). Surely we incur the guilt of using deceitful weights and double standards if we make a show before the brethren of a stricter way of life than we actually practise in the privacy of our cells. Out of thirst for human praise, we would be affecting to seem more abstinent and more holy in the sight of men, rather than in that of God. This is a plague to be shunned, nay to be abhorred! But we have wandered a long way from the question we were discussing, so let us return from our digression.

XXIII. "During the season under discussion we should keep festival in such a way that our relaxation is more beneficial than

XXI. On the Celebration of Eastertide 463

harmful to body and soul. The joy of the festival will not make our savage enemy lessen the demands of the flesh, nor will he respect the season and become gentle. On festival days we follow established custom, and in no way do we diminish our healthy pattern of abstinence, but we do extend our indulgent relaxation to the point that we receive the food which would have been taken at the ninth hour a little earlier, that is to say at the sixth hour during the time of festival. The usual amount and quality of food is not changed, lest the purity of body and integrity of mind which had been so carefully cherished during Lent, be lost through the relaxation of Easter. It would be of no use to us to win through fasting what we then rapidly lose through thoughtless over-eating, especially since we know that our enemy is so versatile that he would make a special assault on our purity at a time when he knows that the celebration of a feast had made us less careful about it. We should therefore be most careful never to let our mental energy be dissipated by easy mitigation, otherwise, I repeat, the chaste purity which we had gained so laboriously in Lent would be lost in the carefree repose of Eastertide. Therefore we never permit anything to be added to the quality or measure of our food, but we abstain on feastdays from those foods which we shun on fast days in order to preserve our purity intact. Otherwise the joy of the feast would be turned to sorrow if it woke in us the deadly struggle against our fleshly passions. That would deprive us of the greater festivity of the mind, rejoicing in happy integrity, and after a momentary pleasure of body we would begin to lament in long penitence that chastity of heart we had lost. We must beware not to incur the prophet's just rebuke, 'O Juda, keep thy festivals and pay thy vows' (Nahum 1:15). If the occurrence of a festival does not alter our constant self-denial, we shall be able to enjoy a spiritual holiday, for we cease from our manual labour, and 'there shall be month after month and sabbath after sabbath'" (Isaiah 66:23).

XXIV. GERMANUS: "What is the reason why Lent is kept here for six weeks, while in other regions it seems that they have added a seventh week, doubtless out of greater zeal for religion – yet neither number adds up to forty days, once you subtract Saturdays and Sundays. Thirty six days is all we can reckon out of the weeks we keep."

XXV. THEONAS: "Now some people in their simple piety would not bother about such a question, but since you have acutely observed what others might consider not worth asking about, and you want to find out the whole truth about our practice and liturgy, listen to the obvious answer to your question, so that you may be reassured that what our predecessors left us was not unreasonable. By the Law of Moses the general command was given to all the people, 'Thou shalt not delay to pay thy tithes and thy first-fruits' to the Lord thy God (Ex. 22:29). Now if we are commanded to tithe all our property and its produce, it is far more necessary to offer tithes of our very way of life, our behaviour and our work. This is manifestly fulfilled by our calculation of Lent. Of the total number of days which are comprised by the year coming full circle, the tenth part is thirty six and a half days. In seven weeks, if you subtract Sundays and Saturdays, thirty six days remain assigned to fasting. Then if you add the Easter Saturday vigil, when the fast is prolonged until cockcrow as Sunday dawns, we have not only the number of thirty six days but we can even include the tithe of the five days left over, if you add in the duration of the night, so that nothing will be missing from the full sum required.

XXVI. "What can I add about the first-fruits which should be offered daily by all who serve Christ faithfully? When men first awake from sleep, and rise eagerly as they revive from slumber, before they conceive in their hearts the emotion of any sense, or admit any memory or anxiety over domestic matters, they should consecrate their very first thoughts as a holocaust to God. Is not this the payment of the first-fruits of their produce, through Jesus Christ the high priest, giving thanks for the benefit of this life and the daily rehearsal of the resurrection? They rise from sleep and offer the sacrifice of their joy to God, calling on him with the first movement of their tongues, to celebrate the praises

XXI. On the Celebration of Eastertide

of his name; opening their sealed lips by singing hymns to him, they are making a sacrifice to God from the works of their lips. To him they bring the first offerings of their hands, their first steps; when leaving their cells they stand and pray, before using their limbs for any purpose of their own. Before doing anything of benefit to themselves, they direct their steps to the honour of God, and halt them for his praise. They offer the first-fruits of all their actions, by lifting up their hands, bending their knees and prostrating their whole bodies. How else can we fulfil what we sing of in the Psalms, 'I prevented the dawning of the day, and cried ... My eyes to thee have prevented the morning: that I might meditate on thy words', or 'In the morning my prayer shall prevent thee' (Psalm 118/119: 147–8; 87/88: 14)? When after quiet sleep we are called back to the light, as if from the darkness and counterfeit of death, as I said, we do not presume to make use of our bodily and mental powers for our own needs first. The morning which the psalmist speaks of 'preventing' means none other than the dawn which we should anticipate. Otherwise the enemy would plunder our finest first-fruits by plucking them himself, making us put ourselves first, or our business, or our cares over the earthly things we need to survive – these are the sly suggestions of the enemy by which he tries to delude us with foolish fantasies while we are still lying down and half drowsy, to confuse and ensnare us once we are aroused. That is why we should take all precautions, if we would actively fulfil the meaning of the verses I have quoted, to keep careful watch over the first thoughts that occur to us in the morning, so that our envious foe may not contaminate them by his quick activity, which would make the Lord reject our offering as something vile and base. If the enemy be not prevented by our watchfulness he will never give up his evil practice of anticipating us, and will not cease to frustrate us with his daily deceits. Therefore if we want to offer God the pleasing and acceptable first-fruits of our thoughts, we must take no ordinary care, especially in the early morning, to keep all our physical senses unimpaired and unsullied, as a sacred holocaust for the Lord. This type of devotion is practised even by many who live in the world, for they rise before the light of dawn, and never get involved in the domestic necessities of this life before hastening to church to consecrate the first-fruits of all their works and actions in the sight of God.

XXVII. "Your other question was on why in some provinces Lent is kept for six weeks, in others seven: it has the same reason, for the same proportion of fasting is observed in both reckonings of weeks. Those who have established an observance of six weeks are those who think they should fast on Saturdays. By keeping six days fast each week, in six weeks they complete the same number of thirty six days. As I have said, there is the same reason and the same proportion of fasting even though the counting of weeks makes it seem to differ.

XXVIII. "However since human carelessness has forgotten the reason for this custom, namely offering to God the tithe of thirty six and a half days out of the year, it has acquired the name of *Quadragesima*, 'Forty Days'. It may be that the name derives from the fact that Moses, Elijah and Our Lord Jesus Christ himself are recorded to have fasted forty days (cf. Exod. 34: 28; III Kings (I Kings) 19: 8; Matt. 4: 2). A parable of this too is the forty years during which Israel sojourned in the wilderness (cf. Deut. 29: 5), and the forty stages through which they passed, which are not inappropriately applied as types of our practice. It is also possible that this tithing took the name of *Quadragesima* from the customary taxes: there is a public tax which is commonly called *Quadragesima*, for that is the proportion allotted to the Emperor's use, just as the King of all the ages demands a tax from us for the gift of our life, and that can aptly be called a *Quadragesima*.

Although it is irrelevant to your question, since I am talking about Lent, I think I should not pass over the fact that our elders have often told us that the enemy has a long-standing custom of attacking the whole tribe of monks on those days in particular. In particular, monks are strongly tempted to abandon their cells, for just as in the type the Egyptians oppressed the children of Israel

XXI. On the Celebration of Eastertide

with violent injustice, so in the antitype the Egyptians attempt, with hard and dirty labour, to discourage the true Israel, namely the body of monks, from leaving the land of Egypt for that quiet which is dear to God, and migrating to the wilderness for our salvation. Thus Pharaoh rages against us, saying, 'They are idle, and therefore they cry, saying: Let us go and sacrifice to the Lord our God. Let them be oppressed, with works, and let them be busied in their labours, that they may not regard vain words' (Exod. 5: 8–9. LXX). Indeed the wicked, in their vanity, ascribe to great vanity the holy sacrifice of God, which is not offered except in the desert of a free heart, for 'to sinners, devotion is an abomination' (Sir. 1: 26).

XXIX. "He who is righteous and perfect is not confined by the legislation of Lent, nor content with the mild requirements of the canons, which the authorities of the Church have laid down for those who are entangled in secular joys and concerns all year long. They are bound by this legal necessity to be free for the Lord at least on those days, and to dedicate to the Lord a tithe of what might be called the fruits of the total days of their life which they would otherwise devour totally. The just, on the other hand, for whom 'the law is not made' (I Tim. 1: 9), and who do not dedicate a mere tenth part to spiritual works, but the whole length of their lives, are free from the legal requirement of tithing; they can therefore have the courage to relax the fixed fast with no special dispensation, if a true and holy need arises to make them. The small proportion of a tenth is not thereby diminished for them, for they have offered themselves to the Lord with all they have. He who has offered nothing to God of his own choice could not do such a thing without seriously defaulting, for he is compelled by inflexible law to pay his tithes. You can see from this that a servant of the law can never be perfect, one who merely avoids what is forbidden and performs what is commanded; those only are truly perfect who do not make use of what the law allows them. Thus although it is truly said of the Law of Moses that 'the law brought nothing to perfection' (Heb. 7: 19), yet we read of many perfect men in the Old Testament, for they surpassed the commandments of the Law to live under the perfection of the Gospel, knowing that 'the law is not made for the just man but for the unjust and disobedient, for the ungodly and for sinners, for the wicked and defiled' (I Tim. 1: 9).

XXX. "You should know that this way of observing Lent did not apply as long as the Church remained inviolate in her primitive perfection. They were not then bound by the demands of our discipline, or compelled by any legal sanction to keep within the stern bounds of fasting, for they passed the whole course of the year in a consistent fast. It was only when they declined from the zeal of the Apostles, that the multitude of believers began to rely on their own wealth; no longer did they divide it for everyone's benefit as the Apostles had instituted, but each one looked after his own interests, not only retaining but even trying to increase their wealth, for they were not content with following the example of Ananias and Sapphira. Then the bishops together decided that men who were bound by secular obligations, and virtually ignorant of continence or compunction, so to speak, should be called back to holiness by canonical regulations on fasting. They compelled them to offer tithes, which would benefit those of weak faith, and in no way prejudice the perfect, for those who were established in the grace of the Gospel surpassed the law by their own free devotion. Thus they could come to that blissful state which St Paul mentions, 'sin shall not have dominion over you; for you are not under the law but under grace' (Rom. 6: 14). Truly sin can have no domination over one who dwells faithfully in the freedom of grace."

XXXI. GERMANUS: "What the Apostle says cannot be false, when he promises freedom from anxiety not to monks alone but to all Christians in general, but it does seem rather obscure to us. He tells us that all those who believe in the Gospel are free from the yoke and exempt from the domination of sin – how then is it that the domination of sin still rules over all the baptised, as Our

Lord teaches us when he said, 'whosoever committeth sin is the servant of sin'" (John 8: 34).

XXXII. THEONAS: "Your question raises a real difficulty, and although I know the inexperienced cannot explain or understand it, yet I will try to explain it to you as well as I can, and give you a brief outline. If only you are clever enough to follow up my teaching with action! Things that are learnt from experience, not from instruction, cannot be explained by one who has no experience, nor can they be grasped or remembered except by one who has been trained and grounded in the same discipline.

I think therefore that we should begin by asking what is the purpose or intention of the law, and what is the discipline of grace and its perfection. From these considerations we can begin to understand the domination of sin, and how to eliminate it. The law, for example, expressly commends the marriage bond, saying, 'Blessed is he who hath seed in Sion, and a household in Jerusalem', and 'cursed be the sterile that hath not borne' (Isaiah 31: 9, LXX, and unknown source). Grace, on the other hand, invites us to perfect and incorrupt purity, and to holy chaste virginity, saying, 'Blessed are the barren that have not borne, and the paps that have not given suck', and 'If any man hate not his father and mother and wife, . . . he cannot be my disciple' (Luke 23: 29, 14: 26). The Apostle also says, 'It remaineth that they also who have wives be as if they had none' (I Cor. 7: 29). The Law says, 'Thou shalt not delay to pay thy tithes and thy first-fruits' (Exod. 22: 29). Grace answers, 'If thou wilt be perfect, go sell what thou hast and give to the poor' (Matt. 19: 21). The Law does not prohibit revenge in retaliation for abuse or injury, saying, 'Eye for eye, tooth for tooth' (Exod. 21: 24). Grace wishes us to demonstrate our patience by tolerance of any injury or blows heaped upon us, and commands us to be prepared to endure twice the burden: 'if one strike thee on the right cheek, turn to him also the other. And, if a man will contend with thee in judgment and take away thy coat, let go thy cloak also unto him' (Matt. 5: 39–40). Law bids us hate our enemies, grace tells us to love them, and bids us always pray for them to God (cf. Matt. 5: 44).

XXXIII. "Therefore, anyone who has managed to ascend the heights of evangelical perfection will be raised at once above all law, through the merits of his great virtue; he will think little of all the commandments given through Moses, knowing himself to be under the grace of Our Saviour alone, and that it is only through his help that he had arrived at so sublime a state. Sin does not dominate over him, because all affection for any other thing is excluded by 'the charity of God which is poured forth in our hearts, by the Holy Ghost, who is given to us' (Rom. 5: 5). He cannot long for anything forbidden, nor shun anything commanded. His whole intention and desire is always directed to the love of God, and he is so far from being captivated by the lure of evil that he does not even take advantage of what is permitted him. The law safeguards the rights of marriage; while it restrains unbridled dissipation, it permits a man to have one wife only. Nevertheless the pangs of carnal desire cannot be dulled: it is difficult to confine a fire which is given fuel, however cautiously, so as to keep it within fixed limits, and not to break out and burn whatever it touches. If fuel is constantly brought before it, even if it is not allowed to burn beyond limits, it is still going to burn, however restricted. The desire itself is blameworthy, those who become accustomed to conjugal rights will be eager for adulterous passion. Those on the other hand in whom Our Saviour's grace has enkindled the holy love of purity, burn up all the thorns of fleshly desire in the fire of the Lord's charity, so that not the slightest spark of vice can threaten the coolness of integrity. The servants of the law are encouraged to what is illicit by using what is licit; those who share in grace reject what is lawful and thus are ignorant of what is not. As sin lives even in the love of spouses, so it does in those who are content with merely paying their tithes and first-fruits. One who is slow or negligent in paying cannot avoid sin, whether in the quality, the amount, or the daily distribution. He who is commanded to serve the poor unceasingly with his own

XXI. On the Celebration of Eastertide

possessions, no matter how faithfully or zealously he does it, is still unlikely not to fall frequently into the snares of sin. Those however who have not rejected the counsels of the Lord but have made over all their property to the poor, have taken up their cross and followed the dispenser of heavenly grace – these cannot be dominated by sin. When a man dispenses property that has already been consecrated to Christ, and lovingly gives money away as if it were not his own, then he cannot be worried by mistrustful anxiety over preserving his livelihood, gloomy hesitation cannot dampen the joy of almsgiving. What he has once offered to God he can dispense to others, with no consideration of his own needs, or fear of restricting his means. He is certain, once he has arrived at that poverty he desires, that he will be fed by God more surely than the birds of the sky.

In contrast, one who retains his worldly wealth, and is only constrained by the old law to give away part of his property, paying his tithes and first-fruits, may well dampen down the fire of his sins with the dew of almsgiving, but no matter how generously he distributes his money, he will be unable to free himself totally from the domination of sin, unless by the grace of Our Lord he manages to shed even the desire of possessing property. One who exacts eye for eye and tooth for tooth, as the Law commands, cannot escape familiarity with the relentless empire of sin, just as if he chooses to retain hatred for his enemy. If he desires to avenge his injuries in retaliation, and nurses bitter hatred for his enemies, he is bound to be ever aflame with wild anger and rage. He however who lives under the light of Gospel grace overcomes the evil one, not by resisting but by accepting the blow on his right cheek and even by readily offering the other as well; when one would go to law with him over his tunic, he offers him his cloak as well. When he loves his enemies and prays for those who persecute him, he has shaken off the yoke of sin and burst its bonds (cf. Matt. 5). He lives not under the law, for that does not destroy the seeds of sin, as the blessed Apostle rightly says of it, 'there is indeed a setting aside of the former commandment, because of the weakness and unprofitableness thereof; for the law brought nothing to perfection' (Heb. 7:18–19). The Lord also speaks through the prophet, 'I gave them statutes that were not good, and judgments in which they shall not live' (Ezek. 20:25). No, he lives now under grace, which does not merely cut off the branches of evil, but tears up the very roots of evil desires.

XXXIV. "Anyone who is eager to learn the doctrine of evangelical perfection is constituted under grace; no longer is he oppressed by the domination of sin. This is being under grace: to fulfil the commands of grace. Anyone who does not wish to be subjected to the full perfection of the Gospel must know that, baptised he may be, monk he may be, but he is not under grace; he is still bound by the constraints of the law, and burdened by the weight of sin. It is the intention of Christ, who welcomes all who have received the grace of adoption, not to destroy but to build, not to annul the commandments of Moses but to fulfil them. There are many who are ignorant of this, and neglect the splendid counsels and exhortations of Christ, becoming careless in relying on their presumed liberty, till they not only fail to achieve the precepts of Christ, which seem too hard for them, but even despise as outdated the commandments of the Mosaic law, given to then when they were but beginners. In their wrong-headed freedom, they speak the words St Paul condemns, 'we shall sin, because we are not under the law, but under grace' (Rom. 6:15). They are not truly under grace, for they have never risen to the height of Our Lord's teaching; neither are they under the law, for they do not even accept those little commandments of the law, but oppressed by the rule of sin in two ways they imagine they have received the grace of Christ, only in order to make themselves strangers to him by the misuse of their freedom, and fall into that state which the apostle Peter warns us against: 'as free, and not as making liberty a cloak for malice' (I Pet. 2:16). St Paul also says, 'you, brethren, have been called unto liberty.' That is, you are loosed from the domination of sin, but only so that you 'make not liberty an occasion to the flesh' (Gal. 5:13), imagining that the abolition of legal restraints means licence to sin. Our liberty exists only where

XXI. On the Celebration of Eastertide

the Lord makes his dwelling, as St Paul also shows us, 'The Lord is Spirit. And, where the Spirit of the Lord is, there is liberty' (II Cor. 3: 17). I am not sure whether I can really explain what the holy apostle means here, in the way which those who have experience of it could, but one thing I do know is that it is open to everyone, even without an explanation, if they follow the practical or active discipline perfectly. They will not need to strive to understand by argument what they have already learned through practice."

XXXV. GERMANUS: "You have revealed to us an obscure matter which I think few know about. But we would like you to add this too for our advancement, namely to explain to us carefully why it happens that when we are strictly fasting and exhausted by it, the stirrings of the body assail us even more fiercely. Often when we wake from sleep we find that we have suffered the stain of bodily weakness, and we are so dejected that we do not have the confidence to get up and pray with a clear conscience."

XXXVI. THEONAS: "Your earnest desire to follow the way of perfection seriously and perfectly, rather than just casually, encourages me to continue tirelessly with this instruction. Your question is not about external chastity or visible circumcision, but about what is concealed, for you know that true perfection does not consist in external physical continence, since even the pagans may possess this through necessity or out of hypocrisy. No, it is that invisible purity which proceeds from your heart's desire which the holy Apostle preaches to us: 'For it is not he is a Jew, that is so outwardly; nor is that circumcision which is outward in the flesh. But he is a Jew that is one inwardly and the circumcision is that of the heart, in the spirit, not in the letter; whose praise is not of men, but of God' (Rom. 2: 28–9), who alone searches the secrets of the heart.

However, because the short space of the night which is all that remains is insufficient to satisfy your wishes, not long enough for an explanation of this very obscure point, I think it would be better to defer it for a while. Moreover it is a matter that should be discussed by us and opened to your minds without your thoughts being at all hampered by disturbing distractions. It should be investigated for the sake of a pure conscience, but cannot be taught or explained except by one who has experience of the gift of integrity; it is not a matter of argument and empty words, but one revealed by the inner faith of conscience, the greater force of truth. Knowledge and teaching on this point of improvement cannot be passed on except by an expert, nor received except by one who really longs for virtue and is eager in his desire for it; one who hopes to attain virtue, not merely to evoke it in empty speeches, but to strive for it with all his soul, not caring for futile verbosity, but yearning for purity of heart."

✧ THE TWENTY-SECOND COLLATION ✧
BEING THE SECOND OF
ABBA THEONAS

On the Illusions of the Night

    I. Of our return to Abba Theonas, and his encouragement.
   II. The proposed question is repeated, why greater abstinence may be followed by a greater struggle against the flesh.
  III. Three reasons why physical pollution may occur.
  IV. A question, whether one who is defiled by a fantasy of the night may go to Holy Communion.
   V. The reply, which are the occasions when this occurrence during sleep is reprehensible.
  VI. That sometimes bodily defilement is caused by the wiles of the enemy.
 VII. That no one may ever consider himself worthy of the Lord's Communion.
VIII. An objection, that if no one is without sin, then everyone must be excluded from Communion.
  IX. The reply, that there may be many holy men, but no one without sin except Christ.
   X. That the Son of God alone overcame the tempter without being wounded by sin.
  XI. That Christ alone came in the likeness of sinful flesh.
 XII. That all other holy and just men were not in the likeness of sin but its reality.

XIII. That the sins of the saints are not so serious as to take away the merits of their sanctity.

XIV. How we should understand St Paul's words, "I do not do the good that I want to do".

XV. An objection, that the Apostle must be understood to say this on behalf of sinners.

XVI. The proposed question is deferred.

I. After about seven days, when Pentecost was past, we came back in the early evening, that is after vespers had been sung, to the cell of Saint Theonas, eager in expectation of the promised discourse. The old man addressed us, alert, with a joyful countenance, and spoke to us very amiably:

"I am surprised that you were able to wait all these seven days for the answer to the question you posed me, so eager were you for knowledge. All that time has elapsed, and you did not ask me for payment of my debt to you. It is right, therefore, since you were kind enough to grant me such a long respite, that I should make no further delay in paying what I owe you. This is a pleasant sort of debt, which actually increases in value as it is paid. Not only does it enrich the one who receives it, but it also leaves the payer no less well off. He who dispenses spiritual goods wins a twofold profit. There is gain for the one who listens, in the progress he will make, and there is great gain also for him who delivers the discourse, for while instructing the listener, he is also encouraging himself in the desire for perfection. Your ardour is to my profit; your anxiety is my shame. I myself have been lazy in thinking about the matter, and would not have considered the question you asked at all, had you not woken me up from my drowsiness, in your fervent expectation, to ponder again on spiritual matters. So, let us put your question again, if you please, the one we decided to defer answering because of pressure of time.

II. "This, I believe, is what you asked: why it can happen that when we fast less strictly, we are less bothered by carnal temptations, whereas sometimes when we abstain more severely, and our

XXII. On the Illusions of the Night

bodies are weak and tired, we are particularly oppressed by these temptations, so that, as you admitted yourselves, we find on waking that we are moistened by the outflow of natural humours.

III. "Those who have gone before us have told us that there are three reasons for this defilement, which may break out at regular intervals but is always untimely in occurrence. It may be provoked by too much eating; it may slip in through carelessness in thought; it may be caused by the wiles of the enemy. In the first case it is the vice of gluttony, of eating too much, which generates an excess of the moist humour. When at a time of stricter fasting our chastity is stained, it is because of too much eating in the past, not, as you thought, our present hunger. If through bloated gluttony an excess has built up within the body, it will have to emerge, either voluntarily or involuntarily, no matter how emaciated the body be through fasting. For that reason we should keep away not only from delicate gormandising, but even from simple foods with the same degree of self-restraint. Nay, even an excess of bread and water should be avoided, so that the purity of body we have attained may last longer in us and become an image of true spiritual chastity. Admittedly we have to confess that there are some who, without any great mental effort, are very rarely polluted like this, either through being physically well tempered, or through age, and they may not even be troubled by these emissions at all. But it is one sort of merit to attain peace easily and without effort, another to deserve a triumph through glorious virtue. Such a man's strength, which vanquishes all vice, is fitly called miraculous, whereas one who is kept safe in idleness by goodness which he cannot avoid is more to be pitied than praised.

The second reason for these impure emissions is if the mind is ignorant of spiritual exercises, and unformed in the training of the inner man. This leads one to become used to continual inertia, and so sluggish that he fails to guard against the first entry of vile thoughts, slow to desire that high purity of heart, in the belief that the whole summit of perfect chastity consists merely in the external chastening of the body. It can happen, as a result of this careless error, that a multitude of shameless wandering thoughts constantly invades the mind, and the seeds of former vices may all remain within us. As long as these lurk inside us, no matter how strictly we chastise the body with fasting, they will always trouble our sleep with impure fantasies. Hence, before the normal interval, there is an emission of impure humour not out of natural necessity but through the deceit of an evil spirit. Although this cannot be totally controlled by weakening the body as much as by mental alertness and strength, at least by the helping grace of God, it may be reduced to no more than an occasional event. That is why to begin with the wandering senses should be controlled, so that the mind does not become used to these extravagances, and thus while asleep be drawn into worse excesses.

The third reason is when, after the practice of regular careful discipline, we long to acquire lasting chastity, through contrition in heart and body, but although we take great care over body and soul alike, our deceitful foe assails us with malice. He attempts to shake our confidence in our conscience, and to humiliate us as if we were guilty, and therefore on those days when we are especially anxious to be pleasing in God's sight, he stains us with the simple emission of fluid, without any pleasure in the flesh, or mental consent, or any deceitful fantasy. This is to deter us from receiving Holy Communion.

In some cases, when beginners have not yet weakened their bodies by long and strict fasting, this devilish deceit is intended to overthrow all their efforts for he knows them to be trying to fast more strictly. Hence, when they discover that a stricter bodily fast does not help at all in gaining purity, but even makes them more often polluted, they may come to reject as an enemy the practice of self-denial which is the true mistress of integrity and nursemaid of purity. We should therefore be aware that the purpose of purging ourselves from each vice in turn is not merely because the temptations to each of them occupy our thoughts, but because they are not content to dominate us without the company of others; they bring in the dreadful companionship of all the other vices, and occupy the conquered mind with a large

XXII. On the Illusions of the Night

company of oppressors. That is why we must defeat gluttony, not just for its own sake, lest burdensome over-eating corrupt us, nor merely because it may inflame us with carnal concupiscence, but lest it make us slaves of wrath, anger, depression and all the other passions. For if we are given our food and drink too little, too carelessly or too late, and we are oppressed by the domination of gluttony, we will be aroused by the stings of anger. Similarly, we cannot be enervated by voluptuous tastes without the vice of avarice, whose accumulated excesses provide the opportunity for luxury to revel. Avarice, therefore, vain-glory and pride, and the whole crowd of vices are linked into a fellowship, and every single vice, once it even begins to grow within us, will gradually introduce the others."

IV. GERMANUS: "We think it was by God's providence that this subject has been broached, so that we now have an opportunity to discuss what we could never have learnt if shame prevented us from asking with confidence. We are therefore encouraged by the course of your explanation to be bold enough to inquire: if we find ourselves defiled by a phantasm of the night at the time when we should be approaching the Blessed Sacrament, should we receive that sacred share of the food of salvation, or should we abstain?"

V. THEONAS: "We should take all the care we possibly can to preserve our chastity immaculate, especially at the time when we intend to assist at the holy altar. All precautions should be used to ensure that the bodily purity which we had preserved hitherto should not be lost during the night when we are preparing for communion at the sacred banquet. However our foul foe may try to deter us from being healed with that heavenly remedy, by deceiving our sleepy thoughts, though without any guilty pleasure, or deliberate consent to contaminate us. If in such a case we suffer an emission without our taking pleasure in it, either through natural necessity, or by the devil's design, intended to prevent our sanctification, why then we can and indeed must proceed with confidence to the grace of the saving banquet. But if it is through our own fault that this has occurred, we should examine our consciences, and take warning from the Apostle's words, 'whosoever shall eat this bread, or drink the chalice of the Lord unworthily, shall be guilty of the body and of the blood of the Lord. But let a man prove himself; and so let him eat of that bread and drink of the chalice. For he that eateth and drinketh unworthily, eateth and drinketh judgment to himself, not discerning the body of the Lord.' That is to say, he must distinguish that heavenly banquet from ordinary common food, and believe it to be such that it is not permitted to receive, except for one pure in mind and body. St Paul continues, 'therefore are there many infirm and weak among you; and many sleep.' We should understand the infirmity and the deaths to be spiritual, which he says arise particularly from that cause. Many, who presume to receive Our Lord improperly, become weak in faith, infirm in mind, entangled in constricting emotions, and fall into the sleep of sin, from which deathly slumber they never arise to saving watchfulness. He continues, 'But if we would judge ourselves, we should not be judged' (I Cor. 11:27–31), meaning that we should judge ourselves to be not worthy of receiving the sacraments, whenever we have been wounded by sin, and take care to approach them worthily by emending our lives in penance. Thus we will escape being chastised as unworthy by the Lord's dreadful punishments of spiritual infirmity, and can hasten back to the healing of our wounds, struck with remorse, lest we be held not good enough to be punished in the short space of this life, but be condemned in the life to come with the sinners of this world. We find this denunciation clearly in Leviticus: 'All that are clean shall eat of the flesh; if a soul shall eat of the flesh of the sacrifice of peace-offerings, which is offered to the Lord, and there shall be uncleanness in that soul, he shall perish before the Lord' (Lev. 7:19–20, LXX). In Deuteronomy likewise the unclean is segregated from the spiritual camp in allegory: 'If there be among you any man, that is defiled in a dream by night, he shall go forth out of the camp. And shall not return, before he be washed with water in the evening: and after sunset he shall return into the camp' (Deut. 23:10–11).

XXII. On the Illusions of the Night

VI. "Now I will show you more clearly that this sort of defilement can originate with the enemy: I once knew a brother who deservedly possessed his body and mind in chastity, with great watchfulness and humility, and was never troubled by illusions in the night, but he was defiled in his sleep with an impure emission whenever he was preparing himself to receive Our Lord in Communion. For a long time he abstained from the Blessed Sacrament in fear, but at length he brought the question to the elders, confident that he would receive a cure for his grief and affliction from their healing advice. The learned physicians investigated the first cause for that trouble, which is usually that one has consumed too much food, and they found that this did not apply to the brother I mentioned, and that his affliction never arose from the vice of over-eating. They came to this conclusion because the brother did not make any exception to his strict fasting on solemn feasts, when the pollution occurred. They then turned their investigation to the second cause of this affliction, asking whether it was the fault of his thoughts, which oppressed his body with impure illusions, after it was weakened by fasting. Even the most particular men may become somewhat elated at their physical purity, and be defiled because of the vice of pride, in that they imagine they had achieved by their own strength that bodily chastity which is God's greatest gift. They asked him whether he thought his own efforts sufficient to gain that virtue to the extent that he needed no help from God, and he repudiated the wicked suggestion with indignation, affirming humbly that he could not have kept his body pure on other days either, had he not been helped in every way by God's grace. They proceeded at once therefore to the third cause, deciding that it was the hidden work of the devil. Having proved that it was the fault neither of his soul nor body, they advised him to take part in the sacred banquet with full confidence. Otherwise, if he remained aloof, he would be so restricted by the subtle snares of our malicious foe that he would be unable ever to participate in the sanctifying Body of Christ and so be deprived for ever of the saving medicine through this deception. Once he had done that, the whole diabolical plot was revealed, for as soon as he was protected by the strength of the Lord's body, the usual delusions he had suffered came to an end. This made plain the enemy's wiles, and revealed how wise was the opinion of the elders, who taught that these impure emissions were not caused by any fault of body or the soul, but by the malicious deceptions of our enemy. Therefore, to rid ourselves of deceitful dreams which cause impure emissions, either permanently, or at least for some months (which is the more usual and humbler goal), we should begin with faith, trusting that we can receive the gift of purity from God's special grace, and then restrain excess in food and drink. It can only be superfluity of food and drink that generates these humours, which once formed have to emerge, so that the law of nature makes them flow whenever any illusion of pleasure gives them opportunity. If we refrain from over-eating, these impure humours will not be generated so much, so that both their emission and nightly illusions will trouble us more rarely or less intensely. Not only are emissions caused by imagination, but imagination may feed on excessive emissions.

If we want to be free from these distracting fantasies, we should strive with all our might. Firstly, to overcome the emotion of fornication, as St Paul bids us, 'Let not sin therefore reign in your mortal body, so as to obey the lusts thereof.' Secondly, to quell the unruly movements of the body and put them to sleep, 'neither yield ye your members as instruments of iniquity unto sin.' Thirdly, mortify the inner man so as to be in every way free from the temptations of lust, 'but present yourselves to God as those that are alive from the dead;' and progressing thus to achieve permanent peace within our bodies, 'your members as instruments' no longer of lust but 'of justice unto God.' Once we are thus founded in chastity, 'sin shall not have dominion over us' (Rom. 6:12–14). Now we are not under the Law, which commends the rights of lawful marriage, and thus preserves and fosters in us the potential which may break out into unlawful fornication, but we are under grace, which teaches incorruptible virginity, and restrains even the simplest harmless movement of the body, and pleasure even in lawful union. In this way the impure humours

XXII. On the Illusions of the Night

will be so dried up that we can become the noble and praiseworthy eunuchs, of which Isaiah prophesied, and deserve the blessing which he promised them: 'For thus saith the Lord to the eunuchs: They that shall keep my sabbaths and shall choose the things that please me and shall hold fast my covenant, I will give to them, in my house and within my walls, a place and a name better than sons and daughters. I will give them an everlasting name which shall never perish' (Isaiah 56: 4–5). Who are these sons and daughters, to whom these eunuchs are so preferred that they are said to have a better place and name, unless they are the holy men of the Old Testament who lived in the marriage bond, and by observing the commandments rightly attained the adoption of the sons of God? What is that name which is promised to them as something outstanding, equivalent to the greatest of rewards? Is it not that we can be called by the name of Christ? He speaks through the prophet in another place about that name: 'And I have called my servants by another name; in which he that is blessed upon the earth shall be blessed in God, Amen; and he that sweareth in the earth shall swear by God, Amen.' And again, 'And thou shalt be called by a new name which the mouth of the Lord shall name' (Isaiah 65: 15–16; 62: 2). Those who enjoy the great and singular blessing of purity in heart and body may surely sing the canticle which no other of the saints may sing, but only those who follow the Lamb wherever he goes: 'These are they who were not defiled with women: for they are virgins' (Apoc. 14: 4). Now if we wish to attain that exalted glory of those virgins, we must cultivate purity of mind and spirit with all our might, lest we fall into the company of the foolish virgins. Their virginity was of no use to them, since they had merely preserved themselves free from carnal corruption, virgins indeed, but dubbed foolish because in their vessels the oil of inner purity had run out, so that the clear splendour of their bodily virginity was obscured. Even outward chastity needs to be nourished with the fuel of inner purity, and that must be stimulated to preserve incorruption for ever. That is why those foolish virgins were not fit to enter the glorious chamber of the bridegroom along with the wise, for they had not kept their whole spirit and soul and body blameless for the day of Our Lord Jesus Christ. Those are the true and incorrupt virgins of Christ, those are the ones called worthy and distinguished eunuchs, who are not afraid, but do not wish to fornicate; not those who restrain their lusts, but those who have overcome every little mental temptation, the slightest urge of desire, those who have so refined that bodily sense, that I may say they experience no disturbance at its movements, nor even the very least temptation.

VII. "Nevertheless we should fortify our hearts with the guard of humility, keeping ever in mind this principle, that we can never possibly achieve such purity of mind, even if by God's grace we do all I have described, but must still believe ourselves unworthy of the communion of that sacred body. Firstly, because the heavenly manna is of such majesty that, as long as he is wrapped in this flesh, no one may eat of it relying on his own merits, but only on the free generosity of the Lord. Secondly, because no one can be so wary during his struggle in this world that he does not receive wounds from sin, however rare or slight. It is impossible not to sin through ignorance or carelessness [or vanity], through unwariness, in thought, or by necessity, through forgetfulness or while asleep. Even if it should happen that anyone could attain such a pinnacle of virtue that he could say without boasting what St Paul says, 'to me it is a very small thing to be judged by you or by man's day. But neither do I judge my own self. For I am not conscious to myself of anything' (I Cor. 4: 3–4), still he should know that he cannot be without sin. The same Teacher rightly adds, 'yet am I not hereby justified', not meaning that I will straightaway possess true glory if I believe myself to be just, nor that because my conscience does not strike me with remorse for any sin, I am therefore not marked with any stain of sin. There are many things which escape my conscience, but although they may be unknown and hidden from me, they are clearly known to God. He therefore continues, 'but he that judgeth me is the Lord' (I Cor. 4: 4). He alone, from whom the secrets of hearts are not hidden, can make a true judgment about me."

XXII. On the Illusions of the Night

VIII. GERMANUS: "You said before that only the saints may participate in the heavenly Sacraments, and now you tell us that it is impossible for a man to be completely free from sin. But if no one is free from evil, then no one is a saint, and it follows that a man lacking in sanctity may not participate in Christ's sacraments, and should not hope for the kingdom of heaven, which is promised by the Lord to saints alone."

IX. THEONAS: "We cannot deny that many are able to be holy and just, but there is a great difference between being holy and being immaculate. It is one thing for someone to be holy, that is consecrated to divine worship, and this adjective is commonly applied not only to men but also to places, the vessels and basins of the temple, as Scripture tells us. It is quite another thing to be without sin, which belongs only to the majesty of our one Lord, Jesus Christ. Of him the Apostle says 'who did no sin' (I Pet. 2:22), as something special and unique to him. If we too could pass our whole lives quite unstained by sin, St Peter's praise of Our Lord would have been common and ordinary enough, rather than something incomparable and divine. The Apostle also writes to the Hebrews: 'For we have not a high priest who cannot have compassion on our infirmities; but one tempted in all things like as we are, without sin' (Heb. 4:15). If we on our lowly earth could have this in common with our divine High Priest that we too could be tempted without committing any sin, why did the Apostle describe his merits as something unique and unparalleled, quite different from those of us men? It is by this one exception that he is distinguished from all of us, in that we are not tempted without sin, but he is tempted without sin. What man is there so strong and warlike that he is not vulnerable to his enemy's weapons? Who is there clad in flesh so impenetrable that he can mingle with the perils of battle at no risk? He alone it is, 'beautiful above the sons of men' (Psalm 44/45:3), who took on the condition of human death, with all the weakness of the flesh, who was never stained by contact with any evil.

X. "He was 'tempted in all things like as we are', first by the vice of gluttony, as the sly serpent tried to deceive him through hunger for food, in the same way that he had formerly seduced Adam: 'If thou be the Son of God, command that these stones be made bread' (Matt. 4: 3). From this temptation he contracted no sin, for although he undoubtedly had the power, he rejected the offer of food from the author of deceit, saying, 'Not in bread alone doth man live, but in every word that proceedeth from the mouth of God' (Matt. 4: 4). Then he was tempted to vainglory, according to our likeness, when he was told, 'If thou be the Son of God, cast thyself down' (Matt. 4: 6). He was not taken in by the sly suggestion of the devil, and refuted his vain tormentor with proof from Scripture, saying, 'Thou shalt not tempt the Lord thy God' (Matt. 4: 7). He was then tempted with the swelling of pride, as we might be, when the devil promised him all the kingdoms of the world and the glory of them, but he laughed at the tempter and repulsed his wickedness, answering him thus: 'Begone, Satan! For it is written: The Lord thy God shalt thou adore, and him only shalt thou serve' (Matt. 4: 10).

By these texts we are taught to resist the deceitful suggestions of our enemy with the authority of Scripture in the same way. Christ was again tempted to pride according to our likeness, when the same author of snares tried to confer on him the kingdom by means of men, since he had already rejected it when offered by the devil directly; again he laughed at the tempter's wiles, and committed no sin. 'Jesus therefore, when he knew that they would come to take him by force and make him king, fled again into the mountain, himself alone' (John 6: 15). He was tested again, in the way that we are, when he was beaten with scourges, struck by hands, defiled with insults and spittle, and carried his cross to the final torment; but he uttered no complaint, nor did his suffering drive him to the slightest burst of anger, but while hanging on the cross he prayed in his mercy, 'Father, forgive them, for they know not what they do' (Luke 23: 34).

XI. "Now if we too could preserve our flesh unstained by any sin, how should we understand St Paul when he tells us that

XXII. On the Illusions of the Night

Christ came in the likeness of sinful flesh? He informs us of this as something unique, said of him who alone is without sin: 'God, sending his own Son in the likeness of sinful flesh' (Rom. 8:3). We believe he took on the true and entire nature of human flesh, but with that assumed only the likeness of sin, not sin itself. The word 'likeness' does not relate to the reality of his flesh, as certain perverse heretics maintained, but to the likeness of sin. His flesh was real indeed, but without sin, only similar to sinful flesh. The one pertains to the reality of human nature, the other to our vicious behaviour.

He had the likeness of sinful flesh when he enquired about food as if he were ignorant and anxious, 'How many loaves have you?' (Mark 6:38). But just as his flesh was never subject to sin, neither was his mind to ignorance, which is why the evangelist tells us at once, 'And he said this to try him; for he himself knew what he would do' (John 6:6). He had flesh like unto sinful flesh when he asked for a drink from the Samaritan woman as if he was thirsty: but he was not debased by sin, for the woman in turn was inspired to ask for living water, and he would not allow her to thirst for it, but created in her a fountain of water leaping up into eternal life (cf. John 4). He showed his true fleshly nature when he slept in the boat, but he would not suffer the rowers to be deceived by this likeness of sin, for 'rising up he commanded the winds and the sea; and there came a great calm' (Matt. 8:26). He appeared to be subject to sin like everyone else when it was said of him. 'This man, if he were a prophet, would know surely who and what manner of woman this is that toucheth him, that she is a sinner' (Luke 7:39). But there was no mistake in reality, for he refuted the blasphemous thoughts of the Pharisee by forgiving the woman's sins at once. He was thought to bear flesh as sinful as that of others when, like a man faced with the prospect of death and struck with fear of approaching pain, he prayed, 'My Father, if it be possible, let this chalice pass from me', and, 'My soul is sorrowful even unto death' (Matt. 26:39, 38). But that sadness was innocent of any stain of sin, for the author of life could not fear death. He said indeed, 'No man taketh my life away from me;

but I lay it down of myself. And I have power to lay it down; and I have power to take it up again' (John 10:18).

XII. "Here is the great difference which distinguishes that Man who was born of the Virgin from all those generated by the conjunction of both sexes: we all carry in our flesh not the likeness of sin but its reality; he took on not the reality but the likeness of sin in true flesh. Even though the Pharisees should have remembered what the Prophet Isaiah said of him, that 'he hath done no iniquity, neither was there deceit in his mouth' (Isaiah 53:9), they were still deceived by his likeness to sinful flesh, so that they said, 'Behold a man that is a glutton and a wine-drinker, a friend of publicans and sinners' (Matt. 11:19). When he enlightened the blind man they said of him, 'Give glory to God. We know that this man is a sinner' (John 9:24). To Pilate they said, 'If he were not a malefactor, we would not have delivered him up to thee' (John 18:30). If anyone dared to claim that he is without sin, that arrogant blasphemous claim to equality would only serve to prove the truth of how singular and unique was the state of Christ. It follows that he too would have to say he had the likeness of sinful flesh, and no sin in reality.

XIII. "Scripture tells us clearly enough that holy and just men are not immune from sin, in the text, 'a just man shall fall seven times and shall rise again' (Prov. 24:16). What does 'fall' mean other than sin? Yet although the just man fall seven times, he is still called just, and the lapses of human frailty do not affect his righteousness: there is a great difference between the falls of a just man and of a sinner. It is one thing to commit a mortal sin, another to be caught out by a thought which is not free from sin; or to commit an offence through ignorance or forgetfulness, or through too careless and glib a tongue; to hesitate for a moment about some point of theology, or to be troubled by some subtle temptation to vanity, or through natural necessity to fall somewhat short of perfection. These are the seven types of lapse into which a holy man may well fall, but he does not thereby cease to be

XXII. On the Illusions of the Night

justified. Light and trivial they seem to be, but they do nevertheless prevent him from being without sin. He has material to do penance everyday, to ask pardon in sincerity, and to pray without ceasing for his own sins, saying, 'Forgive us our debts' (Matt. 6:12).

We could give many obvious examples of how the saints sinned, yet did not depart from righteousness: certainly Peter, the most blessed prince of the apostles, must be considered a saint, particularly on the occasion when the Lord said to him, 'Blessed art thou, Simon Bar-Jona; because flesh and blood hath not revealed it to thee, but my Father who is in heaven. And I will give to thee the keys of the kingdom of heaven. And whatsoever thou shalt bind upon earth, it shall be bound also in heaven; and whatsoever thou shalt loose on earth, it shall be loosed also in heaven' (Matt. 16:17, 19). What praise could be greater than this Our Lord gives him? What authority more sublime and blessed? Yet a moment later he spoke in ignorance of the mystery of the Passion, without realising the benefit it would be to the human race, and said, 'Lord, be it far from thee, this shall not be unto thee.' He deserved the rebuke, 'Go behind me, Satan; thou art a scandal unto me, because thou savourest not the things that are of God, but the things that are of men' (Matt. 16:22–3). Surely when the Lord of Justice rebuked him with these words we cannot believe either that he had never fallen, or that he had failed to remain in holiness and justice. Must we not admit that he suffered a fall, publicly, on the occasion when he was brought to deny his Lord three times, through fear of imminent persecution? But immediately he was struck with remorse and washed away the stain of his sin in bitter tears, so that he did not lose the merits of his holiness and justice. It is of him, and of saints like him, that we should understand the words of David, 'With the Lord shall the steps of a man be directed: and he shall like well his way. When he shall fall he shall not be bruised: for the Lord putteth his hand under him' (Psalm 36/37:23–4). Now the one whose steps the Lord directs must be called a just man. Yet of him it is said, 'When he shall fall he shall not be bruised', and this fall can only mean that he falls into some sin. 'He shall not be bruised', means that he will not long suffer the effects of sin, but though he appears to slip for a moment, he is lifted up by the help of God which he begs for, and by rising up so quickly, retains his state of righteousness. Even if he commits some momentary sin out of the weakness of the flesh, he will be upheld and restored by the Lord's hand. He does not cease to be holy after his fall, as long as he recognises that he cannot be justified by trusting in his own works, and believes that he will be set free from the constrictions of sin by the grace of God alone. Thus he will not cease to cry out with St Paul, 'Unhappy man that I am, who shall deliver me from the body of this death? The grace of God, by Jesus Christ, our Lord' (Rom. 7:24–5).

XIV. "When the Apostle Paul came to realise that no man can penetrate the inconceivable abyss of purity, for he is constantly drawn away by burning temptations, he began by saying, as one long tossed about in the depths, 'For the good which I will, I do not; but the evil which I will not, that I do. Now if I do that which I will not, it is no more I that do it; but sin that dwelleth in me. For I am delighted with the law of God, according to the inward man; but I see another law in my members, fighting against the law of my mind and captivating me in the law of sin that is in my members' (Rom. 7:19–20. 22–3). Considering all the frailty of his own nature, and terrified at the immensity of those depths, he flees to the safe harbour of God's help; oppressed by the difficulties of his voyage through life he despairs of his own natural weakness, and pleads with the one for whom nothing is impossible, for salvation from shipwreck. With a groan of anguish he cries out, 'Unhappy man that I am, who shall deliver me from the body of this death?' And then at once he found, in the loving mercy of God, that pardon which he had despaired of finding in his own weak nature, and he continued in confidence, 'The grace of God, by Jesus Christ, our Lord'" (Rom. 7:24–5).

XV. GERMANUS: "There are many who say we should understand the Apostle here as speaking not in his own person, but in that of a sinner. I mean sinners of the sort who would like to abstain from

XXII. On the Illusions of the Night

bodily vices and pleasures, but are trapped by past sins, enslaved by the lure of fleshly passion, and unable to control themselves. Crushed by their long habit of sin as if imprisoned by a cruel tyrant, they are unable to breathe the free air of purity. How could we properly say that of the saintly Apostle, whom we can be sure had reached the summit of perfection? How could he say, 'For the good which I will, I do not; but the evil which I will not, that I do'? Could he add, 'Now if I do that which I will not, it is no more I that do it; but sin that dwelleth in me', and continue, 'I am delighted with the law of God, according to the inward man; but I see another law in my members, fighting against the law of my mind and captivating me in the law of sin that is in my members' (Rom. 7:19, 22–3)? How could this be appropriate for the person of an Apostle? Was there ever any good which he was unable to do? Or what evil was there which he committed, unwillingly and unhappily, under the compulsion of his nature? To what law of sin could the Vessel of Election be made captive, he through whom Christ our Lord used to speak? It was he who declared that all who are disobedient, and 'every height that exalteth itself against the knowledge of God' (II Cor. 10:5), are brought into captivity, but of himself he confidently proclaimed, 'I have fought a good fight; I have finished my course; I have kept the faith. As to the rest, there is laid up for me a crown of justice which the Lord the just judge will render to me in that day'" (II Tim. 4:7–8).

XVI. THEONAS: "I was just about to enter the safe harbour of silence, and here you are trying to call me back to the vast deep of your profound questioning! But while we have an opportunity of a secure ground, and have completed such a long voyage of a conference, let us cast anchor for a moment in quietness. On another day, if no storm arise to prevent us, we shall see if the wind of the spirit is favourable and can spread our sails in discussion."

✣ THE TWENTY-THIRD COLLATION ✣ BEING THE THIRD OF ABBA THEONAS

On Being Sinless

    I. The Abba Theonas comments on the words of St Paul, "The good which I will, I do not".
   II. That the Apostle performed many good things.
  III. What is the true good, which the Apostle confesses he is unable to perfect.
  IV. Human goodness and justice are not good in comparison with the goodness and justice of God.
    V. No one can attend totally to the supreme good.
  VI. That those who imagine they are safe from all sin are like the partially sighted.
 VII. That those who claim that a man may be sinless are committing a twofold error.
VIII. Few are aware of what sin is.
  IX. How carefully a monk should keep God in mind.
    X. Those who are aiming at perfection are truly humble, and aware of their constant need of God's grace.
  XI. The explanation of the text, "I am delighted with the law of God, according to the inward man".
 XII. And of, "we know that the law is spiritual."
XIII. And of, "I know that there dwelleth not in me, that is to say, in my flesh, that which is good".

XIV. An objection, that the words, "the good which I will, I do not", apply neither to the unfaithful, nor to the saints.
XV. The reply to the proposed objection.
XVI. What the "body of sin" is.
XVII. That the saints have all truthfully confessed themselves to be unclean and sinful.
XVIII. Even the just and the holy are not without sin.
XIX. That even during the time of prayer, sin can hardly be avoided.
XX. From whom we can learn both freedom from sin and perfect virtue.
XXI. That even though we confess ourselves not to be sinless, we should not therefore separate ourselves from the Communion of the Lord.

I. When day returned, we pressed the old man eagerly to plumb the depths of the question raised by St Paul, and so he began:

"You are trying to demonstrate that the Apostle Paul was not speaking in his own person but in that of a sinner, when he said: 'The good which I will, I do not; but the evil which I will not, that I do. Now, if I do that which I will not, it is no more I that do it; but sin that dwelleth in me', and again, 'For I am delighted with the law of God, according to the inward man; but I see another law in my members, fighting against the law of my mind and captivating me in the law of sin that is in my members' (Rom. 7: 19–20, 22–3). Contrary to your opinion, these words demonstrably cannot possibly apply to the person of a sinner, but can only be properly said of those who are perfect, apt to the purity of those who imitate the merits of the apostles. How, for instance, could these words be said in the person of a sinner, 'The good which I will, I do not; but the evil which I will not, that I do.' Nor even could these apply, 'Now, if I do that which I will not, it is no more I that do it; but sin that dwelleth in me.' For what sinner is ever unwilling to debase himself in adultery or fornication? Who lays snares for his neighbour without wanting to? Who is forced by circumstances

XXIII. On Being Sinless

beyond his control to oppress someone with false accusations, to deceive him with fraud, to covet the goods of others, to shed their blood? No, scripture tells us that 'the race of man is diligently prone to evil from his youth' (Gen. 8:21, LXX). Those who are aflame with the desire of vice actually want to fulfil their desires; they are eagerly alert to any opportunity of committing sin, and are even afraid that they will not be able to satisfy their lusts. They boast of their shame and the extent of their crimes, as St Paul accuses them (cf. Phil. 3:19); they accumulate praise out of their own disorder. The Prophet Jeremiah also says of them that they are not unwilling, and that they do not perpetrate their vile sins with hearts and bodies at peace; he assures us they expend great efforts to commit sins, so that they are exhausted by achieving them, and they are not deterred from the desire of deadly sin even by the greatest difficulties and obstacles. 'They have laboured to commit iniquity' (Jer. 9:5).

How too can these words be said by sinners, 'I, myself, with the mind, serve the law of God; but with the flesh, the law of sin' (Rom. 7:25), for sinners clearly do not serve God with either mind or flesh? How can those who sin in the body be serving God with the mind, when the flesh finds the tinder for its sins in the heart? He who created both body and spirit tells us that the fountain and origin of sin lies in the heart: 'From the heart come forth evil thoughts, murders, fornications, thefts, false testimonies', and so on (Matt. 15:19). This is enough to prove that we cannot possibly apply these texts to sinners, for they do not hate sin, no, they positively enjoy it. They do not serve God either with mind or flesh, since their minds sin before their bodies, and sins of mind and thought come before the fulfilment of their desires in the flesh.

II. "It remains for us to deduce the full sense of the text from the speaker's intimate thoughts: what does St Paul mean by 'good', and what in contrast does he pronounces 'evil'? We must inquire into this according to his actual intention, not according to the bare significance of his words. We can explain his meaning according to its dignity, and examine its merits. We shall be able to understand the teaching which God inspired men to give, according to their own intention and will, only if we consider the condition and merits of those who taught. We must adopt the same intention, not in words alone but in action, for that is surely the intention according to which the whole idea was conceived, and passed on as teaching.

Therefore we shall inquire carefully as to what is that good in itself which St Paul was unable to achieve although he wanted to. We are aware of many good things which we cannot deny were possessed by nature, or acquired by grace in the blessed Apostle, and all those of similar merit. His chastity is a good thing, his continence is praiseworthy, his prudence admirable, his humanity generous, his sobriety watchful, his temperance is modest, his mercy is loving; in his holiness he was justified; all these things were undoubtedly present in St Paul and his companions in full measure, so that in teaching the faith they could rely on the authority of their virtue more than mere words. Were they not ever exhausted by their deep concern for all the Churches and their anxious watchfulness? What a great good is compassion, how perfect, when they were aflame for those who were caused to fall, were weak among those who were weak! (cf. II Cor. 11:29). And since the Apostle was endowed with such great gifts, we shall be unable to understand what 'good' it was that he lacked in perfection, unless we take on the intention with which he himself spoke. All those virtues, which we mentioned as his, shine indeed like precious gems, but if we compare them to that pearl beyond price for which the merchant in the Gospel sought, till he sold all that he possessed in his longing to buy it, then the merits of those others seem pale and contemptible. They could all be lost without regret, and innumerable goods be sold in order to enrich the merchant with the possession of that one only good.

III. "So what is that one good, which is placed above all those great goods without number, so that all else must be set aside in order to possess it alone? Is it not that better part which Mary chose, leaving aside her duties as kindly hostess, for that which

XXIII. On Being Sinless

was more splendid and longer lasting? Our Lord says of her, 'Martha, Martha, thou art careful and art troubled about many things; but few things are necessary, indeed only one. Mary hath chosen the better part which shall not be taken away from her' (Luke 10: 41–2). That thing, one and alone, is contemplation, the vision of God; for the sake of that all merits of righteousness are set aside, all our study of virtue deferred. All those good things which as we have said shone brilliantly in the Apostle Paul are good and useful indeed, truly great and excellent; but just as the metal called tin, which is reckoned as having some beauty and grace, is worthless in comparison with silver, and the value of silver pales in comparison with that of gold, gold too is despised in comparison with gemstones, but such jewels, no matter how splendid and how many, are surpassed by the one pearl without price – in the same way all the merits of holiness, good and useful as they are for the moment, and able to win the reward of eternity, are reckoned paltry, fit to be sold off, so to speak, in comparison with the merits of divine contemplation.

To confirm that judgment with the authority of Scripture, does not the text tell us in general, of all that God has created, 'all the things that God had made, and they were very good' (Gen. 1: 31, LXX)? And again, 'All the works of the Lord are exceeding good in their time' (Sir. 39: 21). Now these present things which are not simply called 'good' but are given the adjective 'very', are things which are useful for our life in this world, either for healing the body, or suitable for some benefit which we do not know about. We can see also that they are undoubtedly very good in as much as 'the invisible things of God from the creation of the world are clearly seen, being understood by the things that are made, his eternal power also and divinity' (Rom. 1: 20). As part of the great structured fabric of the creation of the world, and all things that are within it, they enable us to contemplate the Creator. But none of these things could be called good in comparison with the age to come, where there will be no alteration of goodness, no decay of true bliss to fear. The blessedness of that age is described thus: 'And the light of the moon shall be as the light of the sun, and the light of the sun shall be sevenfold, as the light of seven days' (Isaiah 30: 26). The great things of this world, then, and the marvels we can see, appear to be mere vanity once we compare them with what we have been promised in the future. As David says: 'all of them shall grow old like a garment, and as a vesture thou shalt change them, and they shall be changed. But thou art always the selfsame: and thy years shall not fail' (Psalm 101/102: 27–8). Nothing is stable in itself, nothing immutable, nothing good but God alone, and all creation that would obtain the bliss of unchanging eternity must do so only through participation in the grace of the Creator, and not through its own nature. We creatures cannot claim any merit for the goodness granted us by our Creator.

IV. "To give you more abundant evidence to prove this doctrine, do we not read in the Gospel that many things are called good, such as a good tree, a good treasure, a good man, a good slave? 'A good tree cannot bring forth evil fruit', 'a good man out of a good treasure bringeth forth good things', 'well done, good and faithful servant' (Matt. 7: 18; 12: 35; 25: 21). In themselves there can be no doubt that all these things are good. But if we look at the goodness of God, we will call none of them good, for Our Lord says, 'None is good but God alone' (Luke 18: 19). By that standard even the apostles are called evil, although by the nature of their calling they exceeded the human race in goodness in many ways. The Lord spoke to them, saying, 'If you then being evil know how to give good gifts to your children; how much more will your Father who is in heaven give good things to them that ask him?' (Matth: 7: 11). If our goodness is turned to evil by comparison with the goodness of God, in the same way our justice, compared with the justice of God, is compared to a stained rag, as the prophet Isaiah says, 'all our justices as a napkin that is soiled' (Isaiah 64: 6). Or, to give a better example, the commandments of the law were lifegiving, and we are told they were 'ordained by angels in the hand of a mediator' (Gal. 3: 19). They were 'holy, and the commandment holy and just and good' (Rom. 7: 12), as the same Apostle teaches us, but if we compare them to the perfection

XXIII. On Being Sinless

of the Gospel, they are not good at all, for the divinely inspired prophet tells us, 'I gave them statutes that were not good, and judgments in which they shall not live' (Ezech. 20: 25). The Apostle also assures us that the glory of the Law was outshone by the light of the New Testament, so that beside the brilliance of the gospel it does not shine at all, when he says, 'for even that which was glorious in this part was not glorified by reason of the glory that excelleth' (II Cor. 3: 10). The same comparison can be found in Holy Scripture in the opposite sense, namely in the merits which make compensation for sinners, so that those who are much less wicked can be considered righteous in comparison with the worse: 'Thou hast justified thy sister Sodom; what was the iniquity of Sodom thy sister?' and 'the rebellious Israel hath justified her soul, in comparison of the treacherous Juda' (cf. Ezech. 16: 52, 49; Jer. 3: 11). In the same way the merits of all the virtues which we have discussed already are good and precious in themselves, but are overshadowed by the brilliant light of contemplation. There have been many saints whose works were good, but because they were occupied with earthly matters they were held back and kept from the contemplation of the supreme Good itself.

V. "If someone is in the process of 'delivering the poor from the hand of them that are stronger than he, the needy and the poor from them that strip him' (Psalm 34/35: 10), while 'breaking the jaws of the wicked man and taking away his prey from out of his teeth' (Job 29: 17), could he have the tranquillity of mind to consider the glory of God's majesty, while actually engaged in his work of intercession? Or if one were giving alms to the poor, and welcoming crowds of refugees with human kindness, could he at the same time be gazing at the vastness of eternal bliss, while expending his thoughts on his care for his brethren? While he is burdened with the cares and sorrows of this present world, could he contemplate his future state with his heart free from earthly concerns? That is why the holy David says the one thing good for a man is to adhere closely to God, for he says, 'It is good for me to adhere to my God, to put my hope in the Lord

God' (Psalm 72/73:28). The Preacher too says none of the just can do this without faltering, saying, 'for there is no just man upon earth, that doth good, and sinneth not' (Qo. 7:21). Surely there has never been anyone, no matter how great among the holy and just, who could be imagined to possess that highest good, while still bound by the restrictions of this body. That would mean never departing from the contemplation of God; never taking his thoughts off the supreme good even for the briefest moment to think about earthly matters, never taking any thought for food, or clothing, or any other physical thing; never being concerned over welcoming the brethren, changing abode, building a cell; never wanting any property with which to help other people, nor anxious if he had nothing at all: but Our Lord warns us against all these things, for he said, 'Be not solicitous for your life, what you shall eat, nor for your body, what you shall put on' (Matt. 6:25). Even the Apostle Paul himself, who surpassed all other saints in the number of sufferings he endured, was not, we may be sure, able to be perfectly recollected at all times, for he himself tells the disciples, in the Acts of the Apostles, 'You yourselves know. For such things as were needful for me and them that are with me, these hands have furnished' (Acts 20:34). To the Thessalonicans also he writes, telling them that 'in labour and toil we worked night and day' (II Thess. 3:8). Although this won him a great reward in merits, his thoughts must inevitably have been diverted away from the contemplation of heaven to some extent by the attention he gave to his earthly work, holy and sublime though his mind was. He knew that he was to be rewarded with such great and real benefits, while considering the good of contemplation on the other hand; thus he had to balance the profit of his great labours on one side against the bliss of divine contemplation on the other. He pondered long over the options before him, the great happiness he enjoyed as a reward for his work, and the longing for inseparable union with Christ which beckoned him towards the dissolution of the flesh; he was perplexed and cried out, 'what I shall choose I know not. But I am straitened between two; having a desire to be dissolved and to be with Christ, a thing

XXIII. On Being Sinless

by far the better; but to abide still in the flesh is needful for you' (Phil. 1: 22–4).

[Chapter VI begins here in PL] Although he thus preferred the greater good, in many ways, to all the results of his preaching, yet he yielded to the consideration of charity, without which no one is worthy of the Lord. For the sake of those whom he was feeding like a nurse, with milk from the bosom of the Gospel, he did not refuse to be separated from Christ, at whatever cost to himself, for the benefit of others. His loving virtue was such that it drove him to the extent of choosing, if it were possible, to incur the ultimate evil of damnation, if it might save his brethren. 'For I wished myself to be an anathema from Christ, for my brethren; who are my kinsmen according to the flesh; who are Israelites' (Rom. 9: 3–4). That is to say, he was prepared to suffer not only temporal pains but even those of eternity, if it could mean that all men might enjoy the fellowship of Christ. For certainly the salvation of all the others would be of greater benefit to Christ, and so to myself, than my own.

[Chapter VII in PL] The Apostle longed to be dissolved from his body, in order that he might perfectly acquire the greatest good, which is the enjoyment of the vision of God, and close union with Christ; for that body is so frail, and so impeded by the necessities of its weakness, that it inevitably draws him away from union with Christ. It is impossible for a mind distracted by so many cares, impeded by such varied scathing sorrows, to be always in the enjoyment of the vision of God. Can the saints study so attentively, or be so intent on their purpose, that the enemy cannot sometimes take them unawares? Can you search out the secret places of the desert and cut yourself off from all human contact, to the extent that no idle thoughts can ever trouble you, no sight of anything material, no earthly occupation can distract you from the contemplation of God, which is alone true and good? Who could ever be so fervent in spirit that he is never distracted for a moment by seductive thoughts while he is trying to pray, and never lets his mind fall suddenly from heaven to earth? Not to mention other occasions of the wandering mind, which of us, at the very moment when he raises his thoughts to the heights in prayer to God, does not fall into a sort of abstraction, and so sin unwillingly in the very action through which he had hoped for forgiveness of sins? Who can be so alert and watchful that while he is singing psalms to God his mind never wanders from the meaning of Scripture? Who can be so close to God, so attentive, that he can pride himself on having carried out even for a single day that command of St Paul's that we should 'pray without ceasing' (I Thess. 5:17)? Now in truth those who are entangled in the baser sins may consider such things to be trivial and quite free from sin, but for those who know about perfect goodness even the slightest matters are very serious.

VI. "Imagine a large house, furnished with many utensils, vessels and chests; one person enters, with good eyesight and acutely observant, accompanied by another whose eyes are obscured by glaucoma. The one whose sight is impeded from seeing everything will think there is nothing there except cupboards, beds, benches, cots, things which he can detect by feeling them with his hands rather than seeing them; in contrast the one with clear eyesight, who can detect hidden things, will say there are many little things there, far too many to be counted; indeed if all these little things were gathered into one heap they would be so many as to equal the bulk of the few things which the other had merely felt, or might even surpass it. In the same way the saints, those who can see, who have tried to be perfect, can observe acutely in themselves things which our own clouded mental vision would not perceive. They condemn themselves bitterly, to the extent that although to our own superficial observation they are shining with the splendour of a pure conscience, untainted by the slightest sin, to themselves they seem to be spotted with many stains, should some vain and foolish thought creep into the forefront of their mind, or even if the memory of the next psalm to be recited distract their attention to prayer during the moment of silent adoration.

They would say that if we were entreating a powerful man for some material advantage, let alone life and liberty, we would devote our whole mind and demeanour to him; we would hang upon his consent with eager trepidation, ever afraid that a careless or inappropriate word might hinder the mercy of our judge. If we were in court, before any tribunal of earthly judges, and our adversary was seated opposite us, in the middle of his case for the prosecution, and we happened to cough, or sneeze, laugh or yawn or fall asleep – our jealous opponent would be quick to stir the judge to severity, and to our great peril. How much more so, then, when we are suppliant before him who knows all things hidden, in imminent danger of eternal death? Especially if, while we are seeking the mercy of that judge in earnest prayer, our cunning adversary is putting the case for the prosecution! It is not wrong to consider that it is no mere trivial offence but a serious sin of impiety to offer our prayers to the Lord while withdrawing from his sight as if he could neither see nor hear, in pursuit of some vain and foolish thought. Those however who hide the eyes of their hearts behind a thick veil of sin, and as Our Saviour says, 'seeing they see not and hearing they hear not, neither do they understand' (Matt. 13:13), are hardly aware of the great and deadly sins in the secrets of their hearts. No hidden thoughts occur to them, no secret emotions of desire can pierce their mind with sly and subtle urgings, nor can they perceive, with their clouded senses, how their souls are bound captive. They wander constantly among shameless thoughts, ignorant of how to grieve that they are drawn away from that contemplation which alone is of value; they do not regret what they do not have, since they let their minds sprawl over any thoughts that occur to them, and have no intention of keeping God firmly in mind, nor of desiring him above all things.

VII. "This is the cause of that error into which we may fall, when we are quite unaware of what the virtue of *anamartēsia* (which means sinlessness) is, but imagine that we can contract no fault at all from idle thoughts and pleasant mental dallying. Dulled by our stupidity, and blinded as it were, we notice nothing in ourselves except serious sins, and think we only need to avoid things which are punishable by the civil law; if we find ourselves innocent of such crimes, even for a moment, we imagine at once that we are totally free from sin. We may be distinguished from those who can see, in that we do not notice the many little faults which accumulate within us; we are not struck with salutary remorse if an unhealthy gloom descends on our thoughts, we are not grieved at the subtle prompting of vain-glory, nor do we sorrow for the lateness or tepidity of our prayer, or consider it a fault if while we are singing psalms or praying anything occurs to us other than the prayer or psalm itself. It does not embarrass us to admit carelessly into our hearts for a moment many things which we would blush to say or do before others, although we know they are open to the scrutiny of God, nor do we wash away the guilt of unseemly dreams by genuine sorrow. It does not grieve us if during our acts of charity, whether looking after the needs of our brethren or distributing alms to the poor, our cheerful generosity is clouded by restraining selfishness; nor do we imagine we suffer any loss if we lose our grasp of the remembrance of God to think about matters earthly and physical. The words of Solomon are aptly fulfilled in us: 'They have beaten me, but I was not sensible of pain: they drew me, and I knew it not' (Prov. 23:35, LXX).

VIII. "We can contrast those who rest the whole of their desire, their happiness and their blessing in the simple contemplation of holy and spiritual things; if they are distracted against their will even for a moment by an onrush of thoughts, they correct it with immediate penance as if it were a sort of sacrilege. They are upset that they have allowed some vile creature, to which their thoughts have been drawn, to take the place of their Creator, and consider it virtually a blasphemy. They may well turn their mind's eye back with all speed to the consideration of the glory of God, but they do not condone the darkness of earthly thoughts even for a moment, and deplore whatever has drawn their attention away from that true light. The blessed Apostle John wanted us all to have this attitude of mind: 'My sons, love not the world, nor the things which are in the world. If any man love the world,

XXIII. *On Being Sinless*

the charity of God is not in him. For all that is in the world is the concupiscence of the flesh and the concupiscence of the eyes and the pride of life, which is not of the Father but is of the world. And the world passeth away and the concupiscence thereof: but he that doth the will of God abideth for ever' (I John 2:15–17). The saints disdain all the concerns of this world, but it is impossible for them not to be momentarily distracted by the thought of them. There is no man, save Our Lord and Saviour, who can control the naturally wandering mind and remain fixed on the contemplation of God, never to sin through being lured away by the attraction of any earthly matter. Scripture tells us, 'the stars are not pure, in his sight' (Job 25:5), and, 'in his saints he does not confide, and he finds depravity among his angels', or, in the better translation, 'Behold, among his saints none is unchangeable: and the heavens are not pure in his sight' (Job 15:15).

IX. "I may aptly compare the saints, who are ever mindful of God, with those performers knows as tight-rope walkers, in that they have to proceed as if poised on a line stretched out and high up. Tight-rope walkers have to entrust their life and safety entirely to the narrow rope, well aware of the risk they run of dreadful death, if they lose their footing after the slightest stumble, or veer from the straight course. With amazing skill they pick their way across empty space, but if they do not keep on the narrow path before their steps with careful concentration their immediate and evident death is caused by the earth itself, which is the natural base of all things, and a solid strong foundation; not that the nature of the earth has changed, but because they fall upon it by the gravity of their own bodies. In the same way, the tireless goodness of God and his unchanging nature causes no harm to anyone, but if we fall from the heights and plunge into the depths, we will bring about our own death, indeed the very falling causes the death of the one who falls. 'Woe to them', he says, 'for they have departed from me: they shall be wasted because they have transgressed against me' (Hosea 7:13). And again, 'woe to them, when I shall depart from them' (Hosea 9:12). 'Thy own wickedness shall reprove thee, and thy apostasy shall rebuke thee. Know thou, and see that it is an evil and a bitter thing for thee, to have left the Lord thy God' (Jer. 2:19). 'He is fast bound with the ropes of his own sins' (Prov. 5:22). The Lord directs this reproach directly against such men, 'Behold, all you that kindle a fire, encompassed with flames, walk in the light of your fire and in the flames which you have kindled' (Isaiah 50:11) and, 'He who kindles malice shall perish from it' (Prov. 19:9, LXX).

X. "Now the saints are well aware that the weight of earthly thoughts is a constant burden for them; they fall away from contemplation, and are thus betrayed into the law of sin and death against their will or even their knowledge. To pass over other matters, they are drawn away from the vision of God even by works which, as I have explained already, are good and worthy but still material. They have therefore something to repent earnestly before God, something to humble them and warn them, so that they can call themselves sinners in sincerity, not as a form of words. They genuinely ask the Lord for pardon and grace for all their daily falls, since they are overcome by human frailty. Without ceasing they pour out tears in true penance. They appear to themselves to be entangled in temptations which vex them continuously with grief, to the very end of their lives, and they cannot even offer their entreaties without fear of distraction. They know that the burden of the flesh prevents them from reaching the goal they desire through human effort, and therefore they cannot attain that primal and sublime good which is their hearts' yearning. Taken captive by this world away from the vision of God, they appeal to his grace, 'that justifieth the ungodly' (Rom. 4:5), calling out with St Paul, 'Unhappy man that I am, who shall deliver me from the body of this death? The grace of God, by Jesus Christ our Lord' (Rom. 7:24–5). They know that they cannot reach the good they desire, and that they fall constantly into that evil which they do not desire, and actually hate, namely wandering thoughts and anxiety over physical things.

XXIII. On Being Sinless

XI. "Those who 'are delighted with the law of God, according to the inward man' (Rom 7:22), are those who pass beyond the visible universe and ever strive towards union with God. Yet they 'see another law in their members' (Rom. 7:23), intrinsic to the nature of man, which is 'fighting against the law of their mind', and takes the senses captive under the violent law of sin, compelling a man to leave the greatest good and to submit to earthly thoughts. Such thoughts may well seem necessary and useful to the body, arising as they do from the service of something necessary for religion, but in comparison with that good which delights the gaze of all the saints, they appear to be evil and to be shunned. For such thoughts distracted even the saints away from the joy of perfect bliss, for a short while. Truly this is a 'law of sin', brought upon the human race by the sin of its first father, through the fault of the one on whom the just judge passed this sentence: 'cursed is the earth in thy work; thorns and thistles shall it bring forth to thee; in the sweat of thy face shalt thou eat bread' (Gen. 3:17–19). This law, I tell you, is intrinsic to every mortal body, and fights against the law of the mind, keeping it away from the sight of God. The earth that was accursed in our work, began to generate the thorns and thistles of thoughts, since we have the knowledge of good and evil. These thorns pierce our budding virtues, so that we are unable to eat that Bread 'which cometh down from heaven' (John 6:33), and 'strengthens man's heart' (Psalm 103/104:15), except in the sweat of our brow. Every human being without exception is subject to this common law. There is no one, however holy, who can receive that Bread without the sweat of his brow and anxiety of heart, while ordinary bread we can see being eaten by plenty of rich people without sweat at all.

XII. "St Paul tells us that the law in question is a spiritual one, for he says, 'we know that the law is spiritual. But I am carnal, sold under sin' (Rom. 7:14). It is a spiritual law which makes us eat, in the sweat of our brow, that true Bread which comes down from heaven; but the being sold under sin makes us carnal.

What does this mean, and whose is the sin? Surely it is Adam who sinned, and in what I might call a damnable contract sold us into slavery and deceit. He was persuaded by the serpent to subject all his descendents to the yoke of perpetual slavery, seduced by the unlawful reception of that food. It is normal, among those who buy and sell, that one who wants to subject himself in service to another demands some price from his employer to compensate for the loss of his own liberty and his commitment to perpetual servitude. This, we can see, was clearly the case between Adam and the serpent. He received from the serpent a bite from the forbidden tree as the price of his freedom, and losing his natural liberty chose to give himself over to perpetual servitude to the one from whom he received the deadly price of the forbidden fruit. Bound by that contract, he subjected the whole of his offspring to perpetual bondage under the one whose slave he made himself. For does not a married slave beget only slaves?

What follows? Did the deceitful sly purchaser gain rights of ownership from our true legitimate Lord? No indeed. That one deceitful action could not enable him to gain possession of all God's property, nor could the true master lose ownership of that property, because he held the purchaser himself under the bond of servitude, fugitive and rebel though he was. But since the Creator had endowed all his rational creatures with free will, he would not restore to their pristine liberty, against their own will, those who had sold themselves unlawfully, through the sin of devouring concupiscence. Anything contrary to goodness and equity is abhorrent to the Author of justice and devotion. It would be evil if he were to withdraw the gift of freedom he had once granted us, unjust if he were to use his power to oppress and restrict free men from pursuing the privilege of the liberty they had been given. He reserved the salvation of mankind for an age to come, so that the destined fullness of time might be completed in due course. Adam's posterity had to wait long in the condition they found themselves in, until they could be liberated from the bonds of original sin, and the grace of God, their original master, could restore that state of primal liberty at the cost of his own blood. The Lord could indeed have saved them even then, but he would not, for justice could not tolerate breaking off the punishment that had been decreed.

Do you want to know why you were betrayed? Your Redeemer himself tells us plainly through the Prophet Isaiah, 'What is this bill of the divorce of your mother, with which I have put her away? Or who is my creditor, to whom I sold you? Behold, you are sold for your iniquities: and for your wicked deeds have I put your mother away' (Isaiah 50:1). Do you really want to know why he was unwilling to redeem you by the power of his strength, when you were subjected to the yoke of sin? Hear what he adds to the text I have quoted, how he rebukes those same slaves of sin for having caused their sale through their own free will: 'Is my hand shortened and become little, that I cannot redeem? Or is there no strength in me to deliver?' (Isaiah 50:2). The same prophet tells us what the obstacle was that prevented God's powerful mercy from operating: 'Behold, the hand of the Lord is not shortened that it cannot save: neither is his ear heavy that it cannot hear. But your iniquities have divided between you and your God: and your sins have hid his face from you that he should not hear' (Isaiah 59:1–2).

XIII. "Since that primal curse of God has made us carnal, and condemned us to thorns and thistles, and our first father sold us by an unjust contract, so that we are unable to perform the good we want to do, we are cut off from the remembrance of God on high, and find ourselves compelled to think about matters of human frailty. We may be burning with love for purity, but our natural instincts, which we cannot ignore, frequently force us against our will. We 'know that there dwelleth not in us that which is good' (Rom. 7:18), namely lasting deep peace in the vision of God and purity, which we have spoken of. There has happened to us a doleful divorce, for we wish in our minds to serve the law of God, and never want to remove our gaze from the divine brightness, and yet we are compassed about with the darkness of the flesh, and forced to turn away from what we know to be good, by the law of sin. Specifically, we fall away from sublime thoughts to the anxious considerations of this world; we are condemned to this by the law of sin, which is the righteous sentence of God, pronounced on the first sinner. Hence the holy Apostle admits openly that he, together with every saint, is bound by an inevitable compulsion to this sin, but on the other hand he confidently proclaims that no one is in danger of damnation for this, saying, 'There is now therefore no condemnation to them that are in Christ Jesus, . . . for the law of the spirit of life, in Christ Jesus, hath delivered me from the law of sin and of death' (Rom. 8:1–2). The regular grace of Christ, in effect, absolves all his saints from this law of sin and death (into which they are compelled to fall grievously, even against their will) when they pray the Lord for the remission of their sins. You can see, then, that the holy Apostle Paul spoke these words, not in the person of sinners, but of those who are truly holy and perfect: 'the good which I will, I do not; but the evil which I will not, that I do.' And also, 'I see another law in my members, fighting against the law of my mind and captivating me in the law of sin that is in my members'" (Rom. 7:19, 23).

XIV. GERMANUS: "Our opinion is that this text does not apply to the persons either of those who are involved in mortal sin, or of the Apostle and those who measure up to his standard, but we consider that it properly applies to those who have found the grace of God and the knowledge of the truth, but are still trying to free themselves from carnal vices. A long-established habit forcefully dominates their bodies, like a law of nature, and they are compelled by their accustomed passions. A habit of frequent sin becomes almost a law of nature, intrinsic to the weakness of our mortal bodies; it can affect a soul that is not yet schooled in the full knowledge of virtue, but whose chastity is still raw and tender, so to speak, and thus can force sin on them, subjecting them to the ancient domination of death, under the yoke of sin. It does not permit them to acquire the good of purity which they desire, but instead compels them to commit sins which they detest."

XV. THEONAS: "Your opinion is not satisfactory. You began by stating that the text cannot be applied to those who are really sinners,

XXIII. On Being Sinless

so it cannot be the case either that it refers to those who are striving to rid themselves of carnal vices. You have already distinguished them from the sinners, and must therefore count them, to some extent, among the faithful and holy. What sort of sins do you think they can commit, then, if they can be set free by the daily grace of Christ from the sins they commit after baptism? What do you imagine the Apostle means by the body of death, when he says, 'Who shall deliver me from the body of this death? The grace of God, by Jesus Christ our Lord' (Rom. 7: 24–5)? Surely that is clear enough, and you must admit the truth that he is not speaking of those mortal sins which earn the reward of eternal death, namely murder, fornication, adultery, drunkenness, theft and robbery. It must be the body of sin we have already discussed which is relieved every day by the grace of Christ. One who has been baptised and knows God, but falls into that body of death, must know that he is not going to be cleansed by the daily grace of Christ, that is the easy remission which Our Lord gives constantly for our mistakes, when we pray to him moment by moment; no, he must be purged by daily remorse and sorrow, grieving in our penance, or else be condemned in the age to come to the pains of eternal fire. St Paul tells us this as well: 'Do not err: neither fornicators not idolaters nor adulterers; nor the effeminate nor liers with mankind nor thieves nor covetous nor drunkards nor railers nor extortioners shall possess the kingdom of God' (I Cor. 6: 9–10).

What then is this law, warring in our members, which fights against the law of our minds, and drags us struggling away as captives to the law of sin and death? What makes us serve that law in our flesh, while still permitting us to serve the law of God in our minds? I do not think that he can mean the law of serious sin, or be talking about the deadly vices I have listed, for one who does those cannot serve the law of God in his mind, since it would be necessary for him to turn his heart away from God before committing any of them in the flesh. What does serving the law of sin mean, if not to carry out what sin commands? What is the nature of sin, to which a man of such perfect holiness can feel himself subject, while being confident that he will be set free by the grace of Christ? For he says, 'Unhappy man that I am, who shall deliver me from the body of this death? The grace of God, by Jesus Christ our Lord' (Rom. 7:24–5)? What law of sin do you imagine dwells in our members, which can draw us away from the law of God, making us not so much offenders as unhappy captives to that law of sin? We are not condemned to eternal punishment, but sigh over the interruption to our joyous bliss, seeking a helper to bring us back to happiness; we can cry out with St Paul, 'Unhappy man that I am, who shall deliver me from the body of this death?' To be taken captive by the law of sin means remaining in a state of committing sin. What is the good in itself, which the saints are unable to attain, except that which, as we have said before, makes all other things in comparison seem not to be good at all? We know of many things in this world that are good, such as modesty, continence, sobriety, humility, justice, compassion, temperance and devotion; but these are not equal to that supreme good. They can be practised not only by apostles but by ordinary people, and indeed if they do not practice them they will be punished either with eternal fire, or with a great deal of penance, as I have said – they are not set free by the daily grace of Christ.

It follows, then, that this text of St Paul can be appropriately applied only to the saints, who fall every day under the law of sin that we have described – not under a law of mortal sin. They are assured of their salvation, and do not plunge into vice, but as I have said many times, they fall away from the contemplation of God to thoughts of wretched corporeal things, deprived of the enjoyment of that true happiness. If they found themselves compelled to commit real sins every day by the law within their bodies, they would not be mourning lost happiness but lost innocence. The Apostle Paul would not call himself an 'unhappy man' but an 'impure man' or a 'criminal man'; he would not be wanting absolution from 'the body of this death', namely mortal life, but from vices and sins of the flesh. But he knew himself to be bound by the condition of frail humanity, in that he was distracted towards earthly cares and concerns, which are the subject of the 'law of sin and death'. He bewailed this 'law of sin' to which he was unwillingly subjected, and fled at once to Christ, saved by his redeeming grace which is ever present. That law of sin by nature generates the thorns and thistles of distracting thoughts and material worry, even in the soil of the Apostle's care-worn breast, but the law of grace soon uproots them. 'For the law of the spirit of life, in Christ Jesus, hath delivered me from the law of sin and death' (Rom. 8:2).

XVI. "The 'body of death' which we cannot avoid is that into which even the perfect, who have tasted 'that the Lord is sweet' (Psalm 33/34:9), must fall daily. They feel, as the prophet puts it, how 'it is an evil and a bitter thing for thee, to have left the Lord thy God' (Jer. 2:19). The 'body of death' it is that distracts them from heavenly contemplation to earthly things; when they are singing psalms or kneeling in prayer, it makes them think about human bodies, or stories, or business, or useless activities. It is because of the 'body of death' that, when they are eager to imitate the angels in holiness, and to cling closely to the Lord, they are unable to find the perfection of that good, because the body of death intervenes; they do the evil which they would not, meaning that their imagination wanders off to matters irrelevant to progress in perfect virtue. Finally, to prove conclusively that the holy Apostle was talking about holy and perfect men like himself, he specifically indicates and names himself, 'I myself' who speak these words, am telling you about the workings of my own conscience, not that of others. The Apostle commonly uses this form of speech when he wants to designate himself in particular: 'I, Paul, myself beseech you, by the mildness and modesty of Christ' (II Cor. 10:1), or 'but that I myself was not burthensome to you . . . . I did not burthen you' (II Cor. 12:13, 16). Or again, 'Behold, I, Paul, tell you, that if you be circumcised, Christ shall profit you nothing' (Gal. 5:2). And to the Romans, 'I wished myself to be an anathema from Christ, for my brethren' (Rom. 9:3). It is reasonable, therefore, to take him literally when he specifically says, 'therefore I myself', meaning the one you know to be an apostle of Christ, and whom you venerate so deeply, I whom you think so perfect and sublime, and through whom Christ speaks, 'I myself, with the mind serve the law of God, but with the flesh the law of sin' (Rom. 7:25). I admit it, I am from time to time distracted from heavenly thoughts to earthly ones through the condition of my human nature, my contemplation is brought down to concerns over ordinary matters, so that I know, moment by moment, that I am captivated by the law of sin. However much I long to be constant and unmoving before the law of God, I know that I cannot possibly escape the power that restricts me, except by flying always to the grace of Our Saviour.

XVII. "For this reason all the saints are struck with remorse every day, because of the frailty of their nature. When they consider their wandering thoughts and examine the inner secrecy of their consciences, they have to cry out in entreaty, 'Enter not into judgment with thy servant: for in thy sight no man living shall be justified' (Psalm 142/143:2). This too, 'Who can boast that his heart is clean, who can confide that he is pure from sin?' (Prov. 20:9, LXX) and again, 'For there is no just man upon earth, that doth good, and sinneth not' (Qo. 7:21). Also, 'Who can understand sins?' (Psalm 18/19:13). They know well that the righteousness of man is imperfect and always unworthy of the mercy of God, to the extent that even the prophet Isaiah, whose sins and iniquity were purged by the burning fire of the Word sent from the altar of God, he who saw God in such a wonderful way, who had gazed upon the great Seraphim, and heard the revelation of the secrets of heaven – even he cried out, 'Woe is me, because I am a man of unclean lips, and I dwell in the midst of a people that hath unclean lips' (Isaiah 6:5). I imagine that even then he would have been unaware of the uncleanness of his lips, had he not been found worthy to see what true perfect purity is, through the contemplation of God. In the light of that vision he realised at once his own uncleanness, which he knew not before. When he says, 'Woe is me, because I am a man of unclean lips', he confesses the uncleanness of his own lips, not those of the people, but what follows is obvious, 'and I dwell in the

XXIII. On Being Sinless

midst of a people that hath unclean lips.' In his prayer he admits the uncleanness of sinners as comprising virtually everybody, embracing in his common prayer not only the depraved but even the just, for he says, 'Behold, thou art angry, and we have sinned: in them we have been always, and we shall be saved. And we are all become as one unclean: and all our justices as a napkin that is soiled' (Isaiah 64:5–6). The prophet's teaching is clear enough, surely, relating not to one justice alone but to all our justices; he looks around at everything which men consider loathsome and unclean, and chooses to compare our justice with a soiled napkin, the nastiest and least clean thing he can find in human experience.

Your prickly objection is therefore quite clearly opposed to reality. You said just now that if no one is without sin, then no one is a saint, and if no one is a saint, then no one shall be saved. The crux of this question can be resolved by the prophet's words, 'behold, thou art angry, and we have sinned.' This means that you turn away from our haughty hearts and are negligence, and you have stripped us of your aid so that a whirlwind of sin has swept us away. It is as if someone were to say to the bright sun, 'look, you have set, and dark night has overcome us at once.' Yet when this man says the saints have sinned, and not sinned once but lived constantly in a state of sin, he does not despair of salvation at all, for he continues, 'in them we have been always, and we shall be saved.' This text, 'behold, thou art angry, and we have sinned', I can compare with St Paul's, 'Unhappy man that I am, who shall deliver me from the body of this death?' The following words, 'in them we have been always, and we shall be saved', agrees with the Apostle's conclusion, 'The grace of God, by Jesus Christ our Lord.' In the same way the prophet's earlier words, 'Woe is me, because I am a man of unclean lips, and I dwell in the midst of a people that hath unclean lips', seem to agree with the text I have quoted, 'Unhappy man that I am, who shall deliver me from the body of this death?' The prophet's next words, 'And one of the seraphim flew to me: and in his hand was a live coal (or stone), which he had taken with the tongs off the altar. And he touched my mouth, and said: Behold, this hath touched thy lips, and thy iniquities shall be taken away, and thy sin shall be cleansed' (Isaiah 6: 6–7); this comes to the same effect as St Paul's exclamation, 'The grace of God, by Jesus Christ our Lord!' You can see, therefore, that all the saints admit, with truth, that they are sinners, speaking in their own person, not in that of the people, but they do not thereby despair of their salvation, but are confident that the fullness of justification, which they know they cannot achieve in the frailty of human nature, is theirs through the grace and mercy of Our Lord.

XVIII. "The authority of Our Saviour also shows us that no one, however holy, can be free from debt to sin in this life. He gave his disciples a perfect formula of prayer, and among the other sublime and sacred sentiments therein, given only to the saints and those made perfect, and unsuited to the wicked and faithless; he bade them pray: 'forgive us our debts, as we also forgive our debtors' (Matt. 6:12). If this is the true prayer of the saints, as we must surely believe, who could be so bold and perverse, so inflated with devilish pride, as to declare himself free from sin? Does he think himself greater than the apostles? Does he accuse Our Saviour of speaking in ignorance or to no effect, in that he did not know that there would be some who were free from debt, or was pointlessly teaching them to recite a prayer of which he knew they would have no need? Yet every holy man recites this prayer daily: they follow the bidding of their King, in saying 'forgive us our debts'. If they are speaking the truth, why then no one is free from guilt; if they are not speaking the truth, then it is equally true that they are not free from sin, for they would be lying. That is why the wise Preacher, observing all the actions and concerns of mankind, declares without making any exception, 'there is no just man upon earth, that doth good and sinneth not' (Qo. 7: 21). That is to say, no one has ever been found upon earth, nor ever will be, so holy, so diligent, so attentive, that he is capable of cleaving so closely to the true and only good, that he does not find himself distracted and drawn away from it every day. While such a one cannot be declared immune from sin, it cannot be denied either that he is righteous.

XIX. "As a result, if anyone were to attribute *anamartēsia*, that is sinlessness, to human nature, he would be contradicting no mere theory but the sure evidence of his conscience and our own. He may pronounce himself to be without sin if he feels that he is never distracted from the greatest good, or if on examining his conscience (to say no more) he finds that he has celebrated just one Mass without the slightest distraction in word, action or thought – then let him declare that he is without sin! We, however, must admit that the teeming mind of man is not capable of excluding all idle and flitting thoughts, and must therefore confess in truth that we are not without sin. No matter how careful you may be to guard your thoughts, you will never preserve them to the extent that your soul desires, for our mortal condition prevents that. The more the human mind advances, and approaches the real purity of contemplation, the more it realises its unworthiness, as if in the mirror of that purity. It is bound to happen that as the soul reaches out towards the beatific vision, and looks forward in longing to greater things than it has now, it will always disdain its present state as unworthy and vile.

Clear sight yearns to see even further; the more blameless our life the more we find to reproach ourselves with. Improved behaviour causes us more tears and sorrow, as we strive to attain the virtues. No one can be satisfied with the level at which he finds himself: the more purified his thoughts, the more unclean he sees himself, finding more occasion for humility than for elation. The more diligently he strives for perfection, the more he realises he has still to attain. Even that special apostle, whom Jesus loved, and who reclined on his breast, tells us, as if giving us the Lord's own teaching, 'If we say that we have no sin, we deceive ourselves and the truth is not in us' (I John 1: 8). If, then, we declare that we are without sin, we will not have the Truth, who is Christ, within us. What have we achieved except to prove from our own lips that we are not just sinners but infidels and villains?

XX. "If we would truly examine our hearts, to see if *anamartēsia*, the property of sinlessness, is possible for human nature, who could be a better model to study than those who have 'crucified their flesh with the vices and concupiscences', to whom truly the 'world is crucified' (Gal. 5:24, 6:14)? They have plucked up the roots of all sins from their hearts, and made every effort to exclude the very memory and thought of sin, and yet every day they faithfully confess that they are not free from the stain of sin for as much as one hour.

XXI. "Not that we should deprive ourselves from the Communion of the Lord on the grounds that we are sinners – no, we should be more and more eager for Communion to heal the soul and purify the spirit. Indeed we should have the faith and humility to acknowledge ourselves to be unworthy of receiving such graces, and therefore have all the more need of a remedy for our defects. Otherwise we would be unable to receive Communion worthily even once a year, as is the custom in some monasteries where they are in such awe of the sacred dignity and power of the heavenly sacraments that they imagine only the saintly and immaculate ought to receive them, instead of realising that it is by receiving them that we become holy and pure. In fact they are committing a great sin of pride while appearing to avoid it, for they are deeming themselves actually worthy to receive Communion on the few occasions when they do so! It is much better to receive every Sunday, for the healing of our faults, admitting and confessing with real humility that we can never possibly approach the sacred mysteries on our own merits, rather than to be puffed up in the vain imagination that after a year we can make ourselves fit to receive. Therefore, to understand this teaching, and remember it fruitfully, let us beseech the Lord more earnestly, that in his mercy he will help us to apply ourselves to these matters, which unlike the other arts of mankind are not learnt in theory beforehand, but are realised by action and passing experience. This learning must be examined and refined by regularly conferring with spiritual men, as much as it is studied and practised in daily experience; otherwise it will wither through neglect or perish through forgetfulness."

☦ THE TWENTY-FOURTH COLLATION ☦
BEING THAT OF ABBA ABRAHAM

On Mortification

I. How we revealed the secrets of our hearts to Abba Abraham.
II. How the old man uncovered our mistakes.
III. What sort of places hermits should look for.
IV. What sort of work should be chosen by hermits.
V. How wandering about in the body distresses the anxious heart more than it relieves it.
VI. How a monk should guard his thoughts, shown by an example.
VII. A question, why it is considered an obstacle for us to live near our parents, while it is not an obstacle for the natives of Egypt.
VIII. The reply, that not everything is expedient for everyone.
IX. That those who can imitate the mortification of Abba Apollo need not fear the proximity of their parents.
X. A question, whether it is a disadvantage for a monk for his needs to be supplied by his parents.
XI. The reply, drawn from the teaching of the Blessed Antony.
XII. On the value of work, and the dangers of idleness.
XIII. A parable on the barber's wages, told to help us detect the deceits of the devil.
XIV. A question, where does this error of thought come from?

XV. The reply, on the three motions of the soul.
XVI. That it is the *rationale* which is the most corrupt part of the soul.
XVII. That the weakest part of the soul is the first to succumb to the devil's temptations.
XVIII. A question, whether the desire for more remote solitude that calls us back to our homeland is a good thing.
XIX. The reply, that it is a deceit of the devil to promise us repose in a more remote wilderness.
XX. How beneficial it may be to relax our observance when a brother visits.
XXI. How St John the Evangelist is recounted to have demonstrated the value of relaxation.
XXII. A question, how should we understand the words of the Gospel, "My yoke is sweet, and my burden light"?
XXIII. The reply, explaining the meaning.
XXIV. Why the yoke of the Lord may appear to be bitter and his burden heavy.
XXV. What benefits temptations confer on us.
XXVI. How those who make the full renunciation are promised an hundredfold in this life.

I. This is the twenty-fourth of our Collations, given by Abba Abraham, which we can offer you with Christ's help. Thus we conclude our account of the teaching and instruction of all the elders, and fulfil your requests, corresponding to the mystic number of twenty-four elders who we are told in the Apocalypse offer their crowns to the Lamb (Apoc. 4: 4). We think we are thus acquitted of all the debts which we have promised to pay you! If these twenty-four elders of ours were crowned with any glory because of the merits of their teaching, they will bow their heads and offer their crowns to the Lamb who was slain for the salvation of the world; he it was who deigned to grant them such excellent wisdom, and to give us the ability to express their profundity, however poorly, for the honour of his name. The credit for such grace must be paid back to the creator of all good things, and the more it is paid the more is still due.

For this reason we brought before Abraham the thoughts that troubled us, confessing anxiously how we were becoming more and more enamoured of returning to our native land and seeing our parents again. What chiefly gave rise to this desire was the memory of how our parents were so endowed with devotion and piety, that we were confident they would in no way oppose our intentions. We had carefully worked out how we might gain great benefit from their care, and would no longer be burdened with earthly worries, or any difficulty in pursuing the life we wanted, for they would be glad to cover the expenses of all our needs. As well as this, we were gratifying our thoughts with the hope of vain delights, imagining that we might reap a rich harvest in the conversion of many who would be inspired by our example and teaching to follow the path of salvation. Moreover we were constantly picturing to ourselves the actual locality where our families held their possessions, the beauty of the countryside, the vast extent of pleasant territory; we thought that those remote woods would be delightful for monastic life, and would also provide us with what we needed to survive.

We told the elder all this, revealing to him simply what was in our consciences, and assured him with many tears that we could not bear this temptation unless the grace of God came to our aid through his healing words. He remained silent for a long time, and finally sighed deeply before replying thus:

II. "These frail thoughts of yours reveal that you have not yet renounced the desires of this world, nor have you mortified your former longings. Your wandering desires proclaim how unstable are your hearts; you are accepting your exile and the loss of your parents only by your bodily presence here, though you should embrace it with your whole mind. All these memories would have been buried and banished from your hearts if you had grasped the reason for your act of renunciation, the main purpose of the solitary life we lead. I can see that you are suffering from that disease of sluggishness which is described in Proverbs, 'the sluggard is all in his desires', and 'desires kill the slothful' (Prov. 13: 4, LXX; 21: 25). All the earthly advantages which you have cited could be ours, if we thought they would help our purpose or that these pleasant joys could bear any fruit for us to compare with what we gain from this barren situation and bodily penance. We are not so destitute of parental love as to be without people who are glad to provide for us out of their own property, did we not remember Our Saviour's words which cut us off from anything which could flatter the flesh, for he said, 'If any man leave not (or "hate not") his father and mother and children and brethren, . . . he cannot be my disciple' (Luke 14: 26). Even though we are entirely cut off from the assistance of our families, we are certainly not without the possibility of help from the powerful of this world, who would provide very generously for all our necessities, joyfully and with thanks to us. We could be supported by their benevolence, and be quite without anxiety over our daily living, were it not for the severe warning we receive from the prophet, 'Cursed be the man that putteth his hope in man', and 'put not your trust in princes' (Jer. 17: 5, LXX; Psalm 145/146: 2).

We could, for example, have built our cells on the very banks of the Nile, so as to have water at our doorsteps, and not have to carry it on our backs for four miles, but St Paul warns us to be tireless in undertaking such labour, encouraging us with his words, 'everyone shall receive his own reward, according to his own labour' (I Cor. 3: 8). And we are quite aware that in our own country there are pleasant spots, with plenty of fruit-trees and fertile gardens to provide for our needs with the minimum of physical effort, were we not afraid of hearing ourselves condemned with the rebuke which was addressed to the rich man in the Gospel, 'thou didst receive good things in thy lifetime' (Luke 16: 25). Because we have despised these things and rejected them along with all the pleasures of this world, we are delighted with our desert, and prefer our fearful solitary dwellings in the wilderness to any other sort of pleasure. We would not choose the richest of gardens above

XXIV. On Mortification

our barren sands, for we are in pursuit not of temporal physical gain but the eternal reward of the spirit. It does not mean much if a monk makes his renunciation only once, and gives up whatever he owned at the time of his first vocation, unless he persists in that renunciation every day. As long as this life lasts we must say, with the prophet, 'I have not desired the day of man, thou knowest' (Jer. 17:16). The Lord also says in the Gospels, 'If any man will come after me, let him deny himself and take up his cross daily and follow me' (Luke 9:23).

III. "For this reason, a man who is anxious to watch over his inner purity should look for a place which will not be so fertile and productive as to encourage his thoughts to consider large-scale agriculture, and will not discourage him from remaining fixed in his cell. It should not compel him to do his work out of doors, so that his thoughts are blown about by the fresh air, and his whole mental energy dissipated along with the refined intention of his vocation. However careful and alert one may be, no one can watch over these thoughts or observe them except by enclosing himself, both body and mind, within the walls of a cell. Like a skilled angler, he should gaze into the clear depths of his heart to search out his livelihood, as the apostles did. Without moving he can watch the swimming shoals of thoughts to catch them; looking carefully into the depths, as if from a high rock, he can distinguish the ones a man could usefully reel in for himself, while being wise and discerning enough to ignore and reject those fishes which are poisonous or useless.

IV. "Anyone who remains constantly watchful will be able truly to fulfil the prophecy of Habacuc, who tells us clearly, 'I will stand upon my watch and ascend upon the rock: and I will watch, to see what will be said in me and what I may answer to him that reproveth me' (Hab. 2:1, LXX). How difficult this is, and how laborious, can be seen in the experience of those who used to live in the desert of Calamus or Porphyrion. Those parts are more remote and more distant from inhabited cities than the desert of Scete, for you would have to travel into the wilderness for at least seven or eight stages before reaching those lonely cells. Nevertheless, since the area is suitable for agriculture, they did not remain within their enclosure at all. As a result, when they came to live in these barren regions where we live, or in Scete, they were so troubled by disturbing thoughts and worries that they were unable to endure the silence of enclosure in their cells, as if they were novices, quite unaccustomed to the practice of solitude at all. Consequently, as soon as they came out of their homes, they were as distracted as any beginner. They had not learnt, through careful attention and firm purpose, how to quell a man's inner motions or to ride the storms of thoughts, for they had been used to outdoor labour every day, and wandering about, as distracted in mind as in body, under the open sky. Indeed their thoughts flew around, and their attention wandered just to the extent that their bodies moved around outside. Thus they became aware of the manifold vanity of the mind, and were unable to restrain its teeming thoughts; unable to bear contrition of heart, they imagined that constant silence would be intolerable for them. Although they had never found that rural work had tired them, they succumbed to idleness, and become wearied in the long days of quietness.

V. "We should not be surprised to hear that a monk, who lives in his cell as if within the strictest enclosure, and broods over his thoughts, can be suffocated by a mass of anxieties, and that when the man himself goes out they will burst out of their prison and rush about everywhere at once, like untethered horses. As they bolt from their stables he does receive a little relief, but it is only for a moment, for when a man has returned physically to his cell, the whole throng of thoughts will come back to their home, and the very fact that he is accustomed to letting them go will arouse in him yet more serious distractions. Those who cannot or will not yet resist their urges and desires, and become anxious within their cells because melancholy struggles against them more violently than usual, will stir up this problem against themselves worse than

XXIV. On Mortification

ever, if they allow themselves a more frequent permission to go out, relaxing their strict rule, even though they think that would be a remedy. It is like when people imagine they can quench a fever raging within them by drinking ice-cold water; we know that the temperature will be raised by that rather than lowered, and the disease will become much worse, even though there has been some momentary relief.

VI. "For this reason a monk should have his intention fixed on one thing only, and all his thoughts should begin and continue with this aim, which is to be constantly attentive to the contemplation of God. It is like someone who wants to crown his building with a dome: he must carefully draw a circle round the exact centre, and follow the proper procedure to construct the wall around it in a perfect circle. Anyone who tried to build a dome without fixing the centre point, no matter how careful or clever he be, could not possibly keep the circle regular without deviating. The irregularity will detract from the beauty of a perfectly rounded building, and can be seen at a glance, unless he constantly refers to the true centre, and follows the guidelines in regulating the interior and exterior construction of his work, till he completes his great task in the right way at the precise apex. Like that, our minds must be fixed immoveably, keeping the love of the Lord as their centre, all the time that we are constructing our great work; using the compasses of charity, so to speak, we must moderate and regulate all our thoughts, so that, with St Paul as our architect, the structure of our spiritual life will be built up in the proper way; otherwise it will not possess that beauty of the temple which the blessed David wanted to show the Lord in his heart: 'I have loved, O Lord,' he said, 'the beauty of thy house: and the place where thy glory dwelleth' (Psalm 25/26:8). No, without that centre we can build only an ugly building, a dwelling unworthy of the Holy Spirit, always on the point of falling; it will not be made glorious by the indwelling of that blessed guest, but will collapse into ruin and desolation."

VII. GERMANUS: "It is useful and appropriate for you to tell us the type of work that can be done within the cell. Its advantages are well known to us, through the example of your beatitude, in the imitation of the virtues of the apostles, as well as through the evidence of our own experience. However it is unclear why we should take such pains to avoid living close to our parents, which you do not avoid yourselves. You are advanced in the way of perfection, and blameless, but we observe that you live in your own homeland, and some of you even close to your home villages. Why should something that is harmless for you be considered dangerous for us?"

VIII. ABRAHAM: "We sometimes find that evil may come from good. If someone tried to act in a way that had brought the fruit of eternal life to others, but had not the same intention and aim, or was not their equal in strength, he would find it a snare and a delusion, and reap death from it. For instance the boy David, despite his strong hands, would have been no match for the warrior giant in combat, had he been clad in the heavy manly armour of Saul. In later life he laid low throngs of foes innumerable with such weapons, but had he used them at first they would have undoubtedly destroyed him. It was with wise discernment that he chose a type of weapon suitable to his age, and went out against his terrible foe, armed not with breastplate and shield, as he saw others wearing, but with the sling with which he knew how to fight. For this reason each one of us must consider carefully the measure of his strength, and take on the discipline suited to that. All forms of discipline are useful, but they are not all appropriate for all men. Living as a hermit is a good thing, but we do not therefore think it suitable for everyone. Many would find it not only useless but actually dangerous. In the same way, although we admit that the communal way of life in the care of the brethren is holy and praiseworthy, we do not therefore think everyone should follow it. The entertainment of guests is a richly fruitful work, but not all can exercise it without losing their patience. Therefore we must consider the differences between the way of life in your home

XXIV. On Mortification

country and in ours, and then carefully examine a man's strength and his vices and virtues, weighing each one on the appropriate scale. It can happen that a man of one nation may find something difficult or impossible, whereas others are so used to it that they take it naturally. Peoples who live at the opposite extremes of the earth can endure excessive cold or heat with no clothing on their bodies, which others who are unaccustomed to such climates could not tolerate, no matter how strong they are. In the same way it is in this province that you have been attempting to overcome your native character in many ways, striving with mind and body. You should consider carefully whether, in those regions which I am told are cooler, and hampered by the chill of infidelity, you would be able to bear such exposure. We have been accustomed to our holy way of life for a long time and have become strong by nature to endure; if you think you are our equal in constancy and virtue, you too will not need to avoid the proximity of your parents and brethren.

IX. "Now in order that you may have a good standard by which to measure your strength accurately, I will tell you a little story about a certain old man named Abba Apollo. After that, if on careful examination of your hearts you find yourselves in no way inferior to him in virtue and purpose, you may go and live in your homeland near your parents, without boasting or any danger to your intended profession. Then you can be confident over the degree of humility which you gained by choosing to live in this province, to which your travels have brought you; that humility cannot be disturbed by the proximity of those you love, nor the charm of your habitation.

The elder I mentioned was approached one stormy night by his brother, who begged him to leave the monastery for a while to rescue an ox which was stuck fast in a marsh. The brother asked him, with tears, for help, since he alone was unable to pull it out, but Abba Apollo replied to his persistent shouts, 'Why did you not ask our younger brother, whom you passed before you came to me?' The other thought that he must have forgotten that his brother was dead and buried, and that his mind had failed as a result of his excessive strictness and solitude; he answered, 'How can I call him out of his grave, when he has been dead for fifteen years?' To which Abba Apollo replied, 'And are you not aware that I also have been dead to this world these twenty years? I cannot leave the grave of this cell to bring you any assistance in matters pertaining to this world. Christ would not suffer me to relax the mortification I have undertaken even for a moment to pull out your ox, since he did not allow someone even the briefest delay to go and bury his father – a work which would be much quicker, more respectable and devout.'

Now search the secret places of your hearts, and consider whether you too could preserve such a strict control over yourselves with regard to your families. If you find that you have the same degree of mental mortification as Abba Apollo, then you may be sure that the neighbourhood of your parents and brothers will not be dangerous for you in the future. Then you can truly believe that you are dead to them, even when you live near them, and you will not allow them to be concerned over your needs, nor will you become lax through attending to them."

X. GERMANUS: "You have certainly not left us in any doubt on this matter. We are convinced that if we lived near our parents we would not be able to continue with this austere way of life, and going barefoot all the time; nor would we be able to provide for our livelihood through our own labour as we do here, where we are compelled to carry water on our shoulders for three miles. Both we and they would be too ashamed to allow us to do such things in their presence. However, would it hinder our vocation at all if they were to provide for all our needs, so that we could be free from concern about making a living and could give ourselves to reading and prayer? Without the labours that now distract us, we could be much more attentive to our spiritual studies."

XI. ABRAHAM: "I will answer you not with my own opinion, but with the teaching that Saint Antony gave when he rebuked an idle brother who was suffering from the same torpor as yourselves. This will cut the knot of your problem. For, as I have said, this brother came to St Antony and said that he found the life of a hermit in no way desirable, for he declared it was more virtuous to practice the way of perfection among men than in the desert. Saint Antony asked him where he lived, and he replied that he lived near his parents, and through their support was free from any concern or worry over daily work, so that he was proud to say he could give himself totally to reading and prayer with no distractions. The blessed Antony replied, 'Tell me, my son, whether you would feel any grief if they suffered any loss or distress, or if you would be similarly glad if they were prosperous.' The other admitted that he would do both these things. The elder continued, 'Know, therefore, that in the age to come you will share the lot of those with whom you associate in prosperity or adversity, in joy or grief.'

Nor was St Antony content with this saying, but entered a wider field of debate, saying, 'This way of life and tepid state of yours will not only cause you the loss I have mentioned, even if you are unaware of it, telling yourself that saying from Proverbs, "they have beaten me, but I was not sensible of pain: they drew me, and I felt not" (Prov. 23: 35). Or I may quote what the prophet said, "Strangers have devoured his strength and he knew it not" (Hosea 7: 9). No – it is not only that every day your thoughts are affected by changing circumstances, and constantly dragged down to the earth, but you are also defrauded of the produce of your hands, the just reward of your own labour. Since you are supported by your parents you are not able to prepare your daily food with your own hands, as St Paul teaches us. When he gave his last instructions to the elders of the church in Ephesus, he told them that even while he was occupied with his labours in preaching the Gospel, he was able to provide for himself as well as for those who were unable to provide for their own needs, saying, "you yourselves know, for such things as were needful for me and them that are with me, these hands have furnished" (Acts 20: 34). He tells us in another place that he did this to leave us a pattern for our benefit: "for we were not disorderly among you. Neither did we eat any man's bread for nothing; but in labour and toil we worked night and day, lest we should be chargeable to any of you. Not as if we had not power; but that we might give ourselves a pattern unto you, to imitate us'" (II Thess. 3:7–9).

XII. "We too could have been assisted by our parents, but we prefer our present poverty to all their riches, and would rather prepare our daily food through our own efforts than rely on the assured generosity of our families. We set aside that leisurely meditation on Scripture, which you commend, as well as that unprofitable reading, in favour of hard work and austerity. Doubtless we would have done otherwise with a glad heart if St Paul had suggested it would be useful, either in word or by example, or the teaching of the elders had laid it down as a salutary practice. But you should be aware that you will come by as much harm through idleness as the monk we have just mentioned, if, while you are in sound bodily condition, you allow yourselves to be supported by another's generosity in a way that is only right for the disabled. Indeed the whole human race seem to expect to batten on the charity of others, save only for the tribe of monks who live by their daily manual labour as the Apostle taught them. It is not only those who pride themselves in living on their family fortune, their servants' toil, or the rents of their lands, but even the kings of this world who are supported on charity. What our predecessors taught us is that whatever we accept for our daily needs which is not produced or paid for by our own work, should be counted as charity, and as St Paul said, when he forbade the idle to depend on the contributions of others, 'if any man will not work, neither let him eat' (II Thess. 3:10). Saint Antony gave that monk the teaching I have quoted, and he also taught us by his authoritative example to avoid the dangerous affection of our parents, and of anyone who would provide for our needs out of charity, and moreover to avoid the gratification of a pleasant dwelling place. To all the wealth of the world we should prefer these barren sands, dry as they are, these scorched areas of salt-pans, for they are of their nature free from the control of any man. Let us shun the company of men for the

XXIV. On Mortification

sake of the pathless waste, and even if the soil is naturally fertile let it not induce us to cultivate it on a large scale, for thus the mind would be distracted from its principal purpose, and become useless for the pursuit of holiness.

XIII. "Since you imagine that you can be supported by others, and are eager to revisit your homeland in the hope of greater profit, let me tell you a parable of Abba Macarius, which is both amusing and apt. He told it to someone who was troubled by the same desires, using the story as an appropriate medicine. 'There was in a certain city,' he began, 'a skilful barber, who would cut anyone's hair for threepence. He earned these meagre wages on his work, and out of that sum he bought each day what he needed to live; moreover after meeting his physical needs he could put into his purse a hundred pence every day. But although he was making this profit without fail, he came to hear of a city far away where people paid the barber a shilling each. When he heard this he exclaimed, "How long have I been content with this paltry wage, making threepence for my pains, when I could go there and accumulate riches on the lordly wage of a shilling!"

'Accordingly, he gathered up the tools of his trade, and at the expense of everything he had saved over a long period, made his way at great inconvenience to that prosperous city. On the day he arrived there he received a price for his work from everyone, as much as he had expected, and by the evening he found he had accumulated a large store of shillings. Joyfully he headed for the market, to buy what he needed for his supper. But when he began to buy at their exorbitant prices, he had to pay out all the shillings he had amassed for his bare subsistence, and did not bring home so much as a penny in profit. When he realised that his takings every day were being consumed like this, so that not only did he made no profit, but he was hardly able to meet the expenses of his daily needs, he came to himself and said, "I will return to my own city, and there earn my meagre wages again, which were enough to fulfil all my material needs and every day leave me enough over to save for the support of my old age. A small sum it may have appeared to be, but if I add to it regularly it will be not inconsiderable. Those pence brought me greater profit than the imaginary gain of all these shillings, which leave me nothing left over to save, and hardly support my daily needs.'"

Thus it is more profitable for us to gather the scanty produce of this wilderness with unceasing perseverance, where there are no material cares, no worldly distractions, no inflation of pride or vanity to corrupt us, no worries to threaten us over our daily needs. 'Better is a little to the just than the great riches of the wicked' (Psalm 36/37:16). Better, that is, than to pursue the greater reward, which we might acquire through the profitable conversion of many, but would be dissipated in the needs of making our way in the world, and the effort of our daily expenses. As Solomon tells us, 'Better is a handful with rest, than both hands full with labour, and vexation of mind' (Qo. 4:6). Such are the fantasies and the losses which are bound to occur to those weak souls who, while still in doubt over their own salvation, feel the need for mastery and the instruction of others; they are urged by the devil's wiles to undertake the conversion and government of others, but even if they could gain anything from this work of conversion, they would lose whatever they had gained through their impatience and their lack of formation. What the prophet Haggai said would be thus fulfilled, 'He that hath earned wages, put them into a bag with holes' (Hag. 1:6). Truly one is putting his wages in a bag with holes if he loses whatever he thought he had acquired by the conversion of others through his own intemperate heart and the daily distraction of his mind. Thus it happens that those who think they can instruct others, and thus win themselves a richer reward, are deprived of the benefit of their own advancement. 'Some are as it were rich, when they have nothing, and others are as it were poor, when they have great riches. Better is the poor man that provideth for himself than he that is glorious and wanteth bread'" (Prov. 13:7, 12:9, LXX).

XIV. GERMANUS: "The parable you have told us has made us realise how mistaken we were, as we listened to you, but we would

XXIV. On Mortification

also like to know what is the cause of our mistake, and its cure. Tell us how could it happen that we were so deceived. Certainly no one can supply a remedy for any sort of ill health unless he can understand the actual cause of the disease."

XV. ABRAHAM: "There is only one fount and origin of all vices, but passions and corruptions have different names depending on the nature of the part or organ, so to speak, of the soul that is infected. We can show you this by the parallel of physical diseases. Although they all have one cause, they are distinguished into different diseases according to the nature of the organ affected. For instance when the power of an evil humour invades the citadel of the body, namely the head, it generates headache; when it is the ears or eyes that are attacked, it develops earache or glaucoma. When it spreads to the joints and hands, it is called arthritis or rheumatism, when it flows down to the feet it is called gout. All these names are distinctions of one and the same evil humour, depending on the parts affected. Now to pass from visible things to invisible, we can be sure in the same way that the action of every vice lies in the parts or what I might call organs of the soul. The philosophers tell us that the soul has three principles of action, and the corruption must therefore affect either the *logikon*, which is the rational part, or the *thymikon*, which is the dynamic, or the *epithymetikon*, which is the libido. When the force of an evil passion attacks one of these principles, the vice acquires its name from the principle affected. If the plague infects the rational part, it will generate vanity, pride, envy, arrogance, presumption, contention and heresy. If it strikes the dynamic principle it will beget wrath, impatience, depression, melancholy, weakmindedness and cruelty. If it is the libido that is corrupted, it will produce gluttony, fornication, the love of money, avarice and vile earthly desires.

XVI. "Now if you want to know the fount and origin of your error, be sure that it is the rational part of your heart and soul that is corrupted, for that is where the vices of presumption and vanity originate. Therefore it is this part of the soul which needs to be cured first, by right discernment and the virtue of humility. It is a fault of the rational which makes you imagine you have already arrived at the pinnacle of perfection and are even capable of teaching others, thinking yourselves ideally suited to be instructors. As you have yourselves admitted, you became vainly elated and fundamentally unstable to no purpose. You will have no difficulty in cutting out this vice if you are grounded in truly humble discretion, and learn in your contrition how laborious and difficult it is for any of us to save our own souls. You must become inwardly aware that you are far from being capable of such presumptuous instruction, and must admit that you really need the help of a teacher.

XVII. "Since, as we have said, the rational is the most wounded organ or part of your soul, you must apply the remedy of true humility to it. You must realise that it is weaker than the other powers of the soul, and is therefore bound to be the first to succumb to the infection of the devil. It is the same in human bodies: certain diseases attack them, either through accident or through some corruption of the air, and the weakest parts are the first to be affected and damaged by these influences; yet although the disease is particularly sited in those parts, the same infection later spreads to the healthy parts of the body as well. In the same way when the pestilential wind of vice blows into the soul of each one of us, we should be particularly cautious about the passion which affects the weakest and most tender part, which is unable to resist the assault of our mighty foe. The point at which we run the greatest risk of being conquered is where a sleepy sentry is easily betrayed into opening the gate.

This is why Baalam was confident that he could ensnare the people of God, when he advised that the perilous trap should be laid for the children of Israel in that area where he knew them to be weakest. He was certain that if sufficient women were offered them they would fall straightaway into the vice of fornication, for he knew that it was the libido part of their souls that was most

XXIV. On Mortification

corrupt (cf. Num. 31: 16). We are all tempted to varying forms of malevolence, by the spirits of wickedness, which lay subtle snares for us in those areas of the soul which they know to be weak. For example, when they see that the rational part of the soul is corrupted, they try to deceive us in the way in which Scripture tells us the Syrians deceived king Ahab. They said, 'behold, we have heard that the kings of the house of Israel are merciful. So let us put sackcloth on our loins, and ropes on our heads, and go out to the king of Israel, and say: Thy servant Benadad saith: I beseech thee let me have my life' (III Kings (I Kings) 20: 31–2). Ahab was moved by this, not in real piety but out of a vain desire to be thought merciful, and said, 'If he be yet alive he is my brother' (III Kings (I Kings) 20: 32). Following this example, the tempters achieve the deception of ourselves too, in that rational part of the soul, and thus we commit offences against God in the very area where we had thought we would win a reward and reap the prize of piety. We must expect to hear the same rebuke as Ahab: 'Because thou hast let go out of thy hand a man worthy of death, thy life shall be for his life, and thy people for his people' (III Kings (I Kings) 20: 42). It is like when the evil spirit said, 'I will go forth and be a lying spirit in the mouth of all his prophets' (III Kings (I Kings) 22: 22). This was to be through the rational part of the soul, which it knew to be open to its deadly assault, so that it plotted to lay its lethal trap there. [In the same way our subtle enemy used the rational part of the soul to instigate Herod to the slaughter of so many infants, knowing that he was most corrupted in that part.] The same spirit thought it could attack Our Lord in that way, when it tempted him in all three powers of the soul, for it had found that in this way every human being could be entrapped, but it achieved nothing by its varied efforts. It attacked the libido in saying to him, 'command that these stones be made bread' (Matt. 4: 3); the dynamic part when it tried to make him desire power over this present age and the kingdoms of this world; the rational, when it said, 'If thou be the Son of God, cast thyself down' (Matt. 4: 6). In all this it achieved nothing by its wiles, since contrary to its expectations it found no part of him corrupted, as it had vainly imagined. There was no part of Our Lord's soul that gave consent when it was attacked by the enemy's scheming. 'For the prince of this world cometh,' he said, 'and in me he hath not anything'" (John 14: 30).

XVIII. GERMANUS: "There were many errors and illusions which stirred up the desire for our homeland, with empty promises of spiritual gain, as your beatitude has perceived in your attention to our welfare, but one reason in particular has been the greatest, namely that we will never be able to adhere as closely as we would like to solitude and perpetual silence if we are continually being visited by the brethren. The arrival of various brothers would inevitably disrupt our regular pattern of daily self-denial, which we want to preserve unbroken for the sake of constantly mortifying our bodies. Now we are sure that would never happen in our own country, where it is not possible to find anyone who follows this way of life, or at least they are extremely rare."

XIX. ABRAHAM: "If you are never prepared to be visited by other men it indicates that you are unreasonably and inconsiderately strict, or rather it shows your real tepidity. One who is walking but slowly in the way he has undertaken, and still lives in the manner he did before, would not want any one at all to visit him, let alone one of the saints. But you – if you are truly afire with the perfect love of our Lord, and are following God who is all charity with much fervour in your spirit, are bound to find yourselves visited by men, no matter how inaccessible the refuge you seek. The more the fire of divine love brings you closer to God, the greater the multitude of holy brethren that will flock to you. As Our Lord told us, a city built on a mountain-top cannot be hidden; 'For whosoever shall love me, him will I glorify; but they that despise me shall be despised' (I Kings (I Sam.) 2: 30). You should be aware that this is the devil's most subtle deceit, his best hidden trap, and the unwary fall miserably into it; while promising them great things, he takes away from them their necessary daily support. He urges them to seek out the most distant and empty wilderness, giving their hearts a vision of the marvellous advantages to be found there. He shows them pictures of unknown places, which indeed may not exist at all, as if they were well known and accessible, well within our power to find and to possess with no difficulty. He feigns that the men of those parts are docile, and ready to follow the way of salvation, and thus by promising a rich harvest over there, he destroys the gain that was being reaped here. When through this vain hope someone has been separated from the fellowship of the elders who might have saved him, and finds himself without all those things which he had falsely imagined, he wakes as if from a profound sleep, to realise that none of his dreams have come true. The devil never gives him a moment's enjoyment of any of the things he had promised, but burdens him with greater needs and the clinging obligations of the things of this world. He is compelled to receive visits, not occasionally from brethren in the spirit, which he had been trying to avoid, but every day from men of this world, so that the devil never again permits him to have even a moderate amount of peace in the regular life of a hermit.

XX. "To interrupt our observance for a moment of human contact, as often happens when the brethren visit us, is very pleasing, even though you seem to think it dangerous and to be avoided. Listen patiently for a minute: it is beneficial and salutary both for your body and your soul. It can often happen, not just to novices and the unwary, but even to the most perfectly experienced monks, that they fall either into a spiritual torpor or into a dangerous bodily infirmity, if their intense mental effort is not moderated by some remission when occasion demands. For that reason frequent visits by other monks are welcomed with joy, and not just tolerated, by the most perfect and prudent monks. Firstly, because it always incites us to a greater longing for solitude, so that while it may appear to be an interruption to our purpose, it actually keeps us constant in our perseverance. If our purpose were not occasionally held up by some obstacle, our natural perversity would prevent it enduring to the end. Secondly, since such visits make us practice hospitality, and thus attend to the necessary nourishment of our bodies, they bring us a greater benefit through the enjoyment of our physical recreation than we could have acquired by exhausting abstinence. I will tell you a well-known short story of long ago to give you an apt illustration of this point.

XXI. "Once upon a time the holy evangelist John was gently stroking a pet partridge, when he suddenly saw someone coming towards him in search of wisdom, and dressed as a hunter. The latter was astonished to find a man of so great a reputation engaged in such a trivial pastime, and asked, 'Are you really that John whose fame and repute have brought me here with such an eager desire to meet you? Why are you engaged in such a ridiculous pursuit?' Saint John replied, 'What are you carrying in your hand?' 'My bow', he said. 'But why do you not always keep it strung as you carry it about?' He answered, 'It would not do, because if it were always bent and tensed it would slacken and lose its strength, and so become perished. Then if I needed to shoot an arrow effectively at some game, it would be unable to supply enough force, having lost its power through being kept tensed too long.' 'Then do not take offence, young man', said St John, 'at my brief moment of recreation. Unless we relax the rigour of our purpose from time to time by some remission, we will be unable to draw on the power of the spirit when it is needed, since uninterrupted austerity would weaken it.'"

XXII. GERMANUS: "You have cured us of all our delusions, and the Lord has given you a teaching to uncover the snares of the devil which were assailing us – so now, we beg, explain to us in the same way what is said in the Gospel, 'My yoke is sweet and my burden light' (Matt. 11: 30). It seems to contradict the words of the prophet, who said, 'for the sake of the words of thy lips, I have kept hard ways' (Psalm 16/17: 4). Moreover the Apostle tells us, 'all that will live godly in Christ Jesus shall suffer persecution' (II Tim. 3: 12). But something hard, or inviting persecution, cannot be called light or sweet."

XXIII. ABRAHAM: "We can easily show the truth of what our Lord and Saviour said by our own personal experience. If we have undertaken the way of perfection rightly and according to the mind of Christ, mortified all our desires and cut away our evil intentions, we shall not allow anything of the substance of this world to remain in us. It is through that substance that our enemy finds power to harry us and torment us whenever he pleases. More than that, we shall know that we are not even our own masters, for we shall fulfil St Paul's words in reality: 'I live, now not I; but Christ liveth in me' (Gal. 2:20). How indeed could anyone who has taken the yoke of Christ upon him with his whole heart find anything hard or difficult? If he be truly grounded in humility and looks constantly towards the Lord, he would rejoice in all the injuries hurled against him, and say, 'For which cause I please myself in my infirmities, in reproaches, in necessities, in persecutions, in distresses, for Christ. For when I am weak, then I am powerful' (II Cor. 12:10). How, I ask you, could anyone suffer from the loss of property if he has made himself glorious by perfect poverty, and willingly given up all his worldly wealth for the sake of Christ? He considers all his desires to be mere dross, in comparison to the gain which is Christ, and ponders ever on the words of the Gospel as he casts aside in disdain all ambition for material profit, for it is written, 'For what doth it profit a man, if he gain the whole world and suffer the loss of his own soul? Or what exchange shall a man give for his soul?' (Matt. 16:26). What grief could he feel in the loss of any object, if he acknowledges that he has no claim at all on anything which others could take away? With undaunted vigour he proclaims, 'We brought nothing into this world; and certainly we can carry nothing out' (I Tim. 6:7). Could his strength be diminished in any way by lack of anything, if he knows how to live without 'a scrip for his journey, nor money in his purse' (Matt. 10:9–10)? With the Apostle he glories in 'fastings often, in hunger and thirst, in cold and nakedness' (II Cor. 11:27). Is there any labour, any order given by a harsh superior, that could disturb the tranquillity of his heart, if he has no will of his own, and welcomes everything that is commanded him not just with patience but with joy? Following Our Saviour's example, he seeks not his own will, but that of his Father, for Christ prayed thus to his Father: 'Nevertheless, not as I will, but as thou wilt' (Matt. 26:39). Is there any injury, any persecution that can terrify him, any pains that he will not find joyful, if he is like the apostles in rejoicing at his suffering, and longing to be found worthy to endure attack for the name of Christ (cf. Acts 5:41)?

XXIV. "If, on the other hand, we do find the yoke of Christ neither sweet nor light, we must blame our own perversity for that. If we are depressed through lack of faith and trust, it must be because we are contravening the Lord's command, or rather counsel, 'If thou wilt be perfect, go sell (or give away) what thou hast, and come, follow me' (Matt. 19:21). Our struggle would be perverse and futile, if we retained possession of our earthly goods, for the devil uses these as bonds to restrict our lives; all he needs to do if he would deprive us of spiritual joy is to sadden us with the thought of how these goods are diminished or lost. He uses various devices to make the sweetness of Christ's yoke and the lightness of his burden become heavy for us through our vicious desires, and he entangles us with the chains of the wealth and property we had reserved for our solace and repose. He torments us with anxiety over worldly matters, finding within ourselves the means to destroy us. 'He is fast bound with the ropes of his own sins' (Prov. 5:22), as the prophet says, 'Behold all you that kindle a fire, encompassed with flames, walk in the light of your fire and in the flames which you have kindled' (Isaiah 50:11). Solomon also tells us that 'by what things a man sinneth, by the same also he is tormented' (Wisd. 11:17). The very desires we follow become a torment to us, the pleasures and delights of the body recoil murderously on their perpetrator. One who depends on his family fortune and property will neither find real humility of heart nor complete mortification of his evil desires. If we are defended by the virtues, then we shall be able to endure all the difficulties of this life and everything the enemy can hurl at us, not just with patience but with actual joy. But if the desires have free rein, we

XXIV. On Mortification

would become dangerously elated, so that the slightest injury would be able to pierce us with mortal wounds of impatience. The prophet Jeremiah's words would apply to us, 'And now what hast thou to do in the way of Egypt, to drink the troubled water? And what hast thou to do with the way of the Assyrians, to drink the water of the River? Thy own wickedness shall reprove thee, and thy apostasy shall rebuke thee. Know thou, and see that it is an evil and a bitter thing for thee, to have left the Lord thy God, and that my fear is not with thee, saith the Lord' (Jer. 2:18–19).

If the marvellous sweetness of the Lord's yoke appears bitter, it can only mean that the bitterness of our own aversion has tainted it. If the joyous lightness of God's burden has become heavy, it can only mean that we have disdained the one who supported us in our perversity. Scripture itself bears witness to this, saying, 'If they were to walk in good ways, they would find the paths of the just easy' (Prov. 2:20, LXX). It is we ourselves, I tell you, who make rough the ways of the Lord, which were straight and easy, with the harsh rocks of our depraved desires. The imperial road was paved with basalt by the apostles and prophets, and smoothed by the tread of the Lord himself and all his saints, but we have deserted it in our madness, and followed swampy by-paths. Blinded by unlawful and transitory pleasures, we are stumbling along tracks that are difficult to find, and blocked with the brambles of vice. Our legs are scratched, our wedding garment torn, we find ourselves pierced by the sharpest of thorns, and stung by the most poisonous of scorpions and snakes that are hiding there. 'Thorns and snares are in the way of the perverse: but he that feareth the Lord departeth far from them' (Prov. 22:5, LXX). Of such men the Lord speaks through the prophet, 'My people have forgotten me, sacrificing in vain, and stumbling in their ways, in ancient paths, to walk by them in a way not trodden' (Jer. 18:15). 'The ways of the slothful,' as Solomon tells us, 'are as a hedge of thorns: the ways of the just are well trodden' (Prov. 15:19, LXX). If we deviate so far from the imperial road, we will never arrive at the capital city, which should be the goal of our unswerving journey. The Preacher says that clearly enough, 'The labour of fools shall afflict them that know not how to go to the city' (Qo. 10:15). The city, that is, the heavenly 'Jerusalem, which is our mother' (Gal. 4:26).

Anyone who genuinely renounces this world takes upon himself the yoke of Christ, and learns from him through the training he receives every day in accepting injuries, for he is 'meek and humble of heart' (Matt. 11:29). In all his trials he remains unmoved, for 'all things work together unto good' (Rom. 8:28). As the prophet [Obadiah] tells us, 'Are not my words good to him that walketh uprightly?' (in fact Micah 2:7). And again, 'the ways of the Lord are right and the just shall walk in them: but the transgressors shall fall in them' (Hosea 14:10).

XXV. "Our Saviour, in his loving grace towards us, confers a greater reward of praise on us through the trials that grieve us than if he had taken away from us all opportunity for struggle. It is a mark of sublime and exceptional fortitude if we remain steadfast when besieged by passions and trials and endure fearlessly all that rages against us, confident in the protection of God; if we triumph gloriously over adversity during the attacks made on us by men, being armed with the unconquerable harness of virtue, and build up that virtue out of our very weakness, for 'power is made perfect in infirmity' (II Cor. 12:9). 'For behold,' says the Lord, 'I have made thee this day a fortified city and a pillar of iron and a wall of brass, over all the land, to the kings of Juda, to the princes thereof and to the priests and to the people of the land. And they shall fight against thee and shall not prevail: for I am with thee, saith the Lord, to deliver thee' (Jer. 1:18–19). As Our Lord has truly taught us, the imperial road is sweet and light, even if it appears hard and rough. Those who serve him in love and faithfulness, when they take the yoke of the Lord upon themselves, and learn from him who is meek and humble of heart, have already laid down the burden of earthly passions to some extent, and will find that the Lord offers them, not toil but rest for their souls. As he tells us through the prophet Jeremiah, 'Stand ye on the ways, and see, and ask for the old paths, which is the good way, and walk ye in it: and

XXIV. On Mortification

you shall find refreshment for your souls' (Jer. 6:16). Immediately they shall find 'the crooked shall become straight, and the rough ways plain' (Isaiah 40:4). Tasting, they shall see how sweet is the Lord, for they listen to Christ who cries out in the Gospel, 'Come to me, all you that labour and are burdened; and I will refresh you.' Lay down the burden of vice, and understand what follows, 'my yoke is sweet and my burden light' (Matt. 11:28, 30).

The way of the Lord gives refreshment, if we follow it according to his law. It is we ourselves who create grief and suffering for ourselves by our wild behaviour, if we choose to follow the wicked and perverse manners of this world, even at the cost of great difficulty. In this way we can, blasphemously, make the Lord's yoke harsh and heavy, and fret under the yoke itself, complaining that Christ who lays it on us is hard and cruel, as in the text, 'the folly of a man corrupteth his ways; and he fretteth in his mind against God' (Prov. 19:3, LXX). The prophet [Haggai] says, we 'have said, the way of the Lord is not right,' and the Lord rightly replies, 'Is it my way that is not right, and are not rather your ways perverse?' (in fact Ezech. 18:25). In truth, therefore, compare the flowery meads of virginity and the sweet-smelling beauty of chastity with the foul quagmire of vice; compare the carefree peace of the monks with the perils and losses which embroil the men of this world; compare the ease of our poverty with the all-consuming sorrows and ceaseless cares of the wealthy, which wear them away day and night to the great peril of their lives – you will easily see how sweet the yoke of Christ is, how light his burden!

XXVI. "To consider the payment of rewards, Our Lord promised a reward of a hundredfold in this life to those who make their renunciation in full, saying, 'And everyone that hath left house or brethren or sisters or father or mother or wife or children or lands, for my name's sake, shall receive an hundredfold in this present world, and shall possess life everlasting' (Matt. 19:30). This may be taken literally and believed without any wavering in our faith. There have been many who took advantage of this text to attribute it in a crass way to the reward to be made to the saints during the earthly millennium, an era which they say will come in the future after the resurrection, even though they admit it cannot be understood as being 'present'. It is much more credible, and more obvious, that the one who has, at Christ's bidding, renounced all worldly goods or attachments, receives even in this life a hundredfold grace from the brethren and colleagues of his way of life who are attached to him with a spiritual bond. Brief enough, and frail are the relationships which are formed by law or blood between parents and children, cousins, spouses and neighbours. Even good and dutiful children, when they grow up, are often cut off from the homes and property of their parents; the marriage bond also is often severed for perfectly respectable reasons; brothers are sundered by argument and disagreement. Only monks can preserve the unity of their fellowship for ever, and possess all things without division, in that they believe that everything their brethren own is theirs, all that is theirs belongs to the brethren. Then if you compare the grace of our mutual affection to the emotions that join people in earthly unions, you will realise how truly ours is a hundredfold sweeter and more sublime. The pleasure, even, of a chaste marriage is a hundredfold better than that which is given by the conjunction of the sexes. The enjoyment which one might have in the possession of a single farm or house is surpassed a hundredfold by the joy in great riches of the one who has been adopted among the children of God, and therefore possesses everything that belongs to our eternal Father, as his own. In imitation of the true Son he will exclaim in all sincerity, 'All things whatsoever the Father hath are mine' (John 16: 15). No longer has he any anxiety or expense, the punishment of sin, but succeeds to his own in peace and gladness, constantly hearing what St Paul affirms, 'all things are yours . . ., the world . . ., or things present, or things to come' (I Cor. 3: 22). Solomon also says, 'The whole world is the fortune of a man of faith' (Prov. 17: 6, LXX).

There you have the hundredfold reward, realised in the greatness of the prize beyond all comparison. If someone were to give for bronze, iron or any other base metal the equivalent weight in

XXIV. On Mortification

gold, it would be deemed no less than a hundredfold return; in the same way when the reward of spiritual joy and precious delight in charity is given in exchange for the contempt of lust and earthly desires, it is a hundredfold greater and more brilliant, even if numerically the same. As an example to emphasise this yet again, I was once married to a wife, under the emotion of passionate weakness: now I hold her in honour for her holiness and the true love of Christ. She is the same woman, but the merit of our love has increased a hundredfold. If you balance the disturbance wrought by anger and rage against meekness and patience, the anguish of worry and indecision against peaceful confidence, the futile and grievous sadness of this world against the benefit of saving sobriety, the vanity of temporal delight against rich spiritual joy, you will come to see that the reward for making this change in our affections is a hundredfold. If again you compare the merits of the contrary virtues against the brief and guilty pleasure of each vice, the great increase in joy will prove the former to be a hundredfold better. If you transfer the figure one hundred from left to right of the balance sheet, it will appear to be the same figure in terms of digits, but it is vastly greater in terms of real value. We who appear to stand on the left in the form of goats, find ourselves transferred to the right side as true sheep.

Now let us move on to consider the measure of reward which Christ has returned to us in this life for the sake of our contempt of the world: he tells us in the Gospel of St Mark that, 'there is no man who hath left house or brethren or sisters or father or mother or children or lands, for my sake and for the gospel, who shall not receive an hundred times as much now in this time; houses and brethren and sisters and mothers and children and lands, with persecution; and in the world to come life everlasting' (Mark 10: 29–30). Anyone, therefore, who renounces the affection of one father, one mother, one child, for the sake of Christ, receives in return the affection of everyone who loves Christ, and finds brethren and parents a hundredfold. Instead of one he finds so many fathers and brothers who are bound to him by a more fervent and devoted affection. He is enriched by the possession of many houses and estates, if he exchanges one house, renounced for the love of Christ, for the countless monasteries which he will possess as his own, finding himself at home in every part of the world. If he leaves the unreliable and grudging service of ten or twenty slaves, he will find a hundredfold (or even more, if I may be permitted to add to Our Lord's estimate) when he is supported by the assistance of so many distinguished and noble souls. You yourselves can prove this by your own experience: you have left your individual fathers and mothers and homes, but have found uncounted fathers, mothers and brothers in every part of the world you have visited; houses too and lands, faithful servants as well, without any anxiety or difficulty. They welcome you and defer to you as if you were their masters, they cherish you and do you honour by their service. Those who submit themselves with freely given love to serve the brethren will enjoy this attention for the sake of their holy service and faithfulness. As Our Lord tells us, they will receive back freely what they have given to others. If you had not begun by humbly giving this service to your companions, how do you imagine you could bear to receive it from others? You would feel it more burdensome than supportive if you chose to be served by your brethren rather than to serve them. You will, nevertheless, receive all this reward, without losing your peace of mind, or attention to what you are doing, but it will be, as Our Lord said, 'with persecutions', that is to say there will be pressure from this world and great suffering. As the sage assures us, 'he who liveth in sweetness and without pain, will be in want' (Prov. 14: 23, LXX). The Kingdom of Heaven is seized not by the idle, the lazy, the delicate and frail, but by the violent. Who then are these violent ones? Surely those who do violence to their own souls, not those of others. They deprive themselves, in a praiseworthy restraint, of all the lusts of this present world, and in Our Lord's words are called noble plunderers, using this sort of deprivation to invade the kingdom of heaven with violence. For Our Lord told us that 'the kingdom of heaven suffereth violence and the violent bear it away' (Matt. 11: 12). The violent ones that he praises are those who use force against their own perdition. It is written,

XXIV. On Mortification

'Man laboureth for himself in sorrows, and he doeth violence to his own perdition' (Prov. 16: 26, LXX).

Our 'perdition' is delight in this present life, or to speak more clearly, the pursuit of our own desires and lusts. If anyone cuts these off from his soul and mortifies them, he is doing violence to his perdition, with credit and merit. He denies the desires that delight him, which the word of God opposes in many places in the prophets, saying, 'in the day of your fast your own will is found, . . . if thou turn away thy foot from the sabbath, from doing thy own will in my holy day . . . and glorify him, while thou dost not thy own ways and thy own will is not found, to speak a word' (Isaiah 58: 3, 13). The prophet goes on at once to show him how great is the promised bliss, saying, 'then shalt thou be delighted in the Lord and I will lift thee up above the high places of the earth and will feed thee with the inheritance of Jacob thy father. For the mouth of the Lord hath spoken it' (Isaiah 58: 14). Our Lord and Saviour, therefore, taught us the way to cut off our desires: 'I came not to do my own will but the will of him that sent me' (John 6: 38), and, 'not as I will, but as thou wilt' (Matt. 26: 39). This virtue is particularly exercised by those who dwell in monasteries, are governed by their superiors, and do nothing at all on their own initiative, but make their will dependant on that of the abbot.

Finally, to bring this conference to a conclusion, I ask you is it not obvious that those who serve Christ faithfully receive a hundredfold grace in the present, since they are respected by the mightiest princes for the sake of his name? Certainly they have no need of human respect, but they are held in awe by all their judges and those in authority even while they are in the throes of persecution. They were of such lowly condition that even men of mean stature would have despised them for their humble birth or servile condition, had they remained in the world. Yet they are ennobled by their service of Christ, so that no one would dare to despise them because of their class, nor to disdain their obscure origin. The servants of Christ are given a nobler glory through the very reproaches and disdain which would discomfort or debase another. This we can show you very clearly in the case of Abba

John, who lived in the desert near the city of Lycus. He was born from a very humble family, but because of the name of Christ he became the admiration of virtually the whole world. The masters of this present age, who hold imperial sway over the world, and are a terror to all kings and potentates, revered him as their master. They came from afar to consult him, and committed to his prayers and merits the security of their empire, and all their hopes of victory and prosperity in war."

Such was the instruction the blessed Abraham gave us, concerning the origin and cure of our mistake. He uncovered to our understanding the deceitful ideas which the devil had insinuated into our minds, and inspired us to desire true mortification. This we believe will encourage many, however inadequately we have recorded his words. The smouldering ashes of our eloquence may well have obscured the blazing brilliance of the great fathers, but we think that the hearts of many can be warmed if they are willing to search out the fiery meaning hidden under the cold clinker of our words.

To you, my holy brethren, I have not been so rash as to presume to send that fire which the Lord came to set to the earth, and which he longed to see burning, as if I could kindle your all-consuming desire by adding my own heat, but I have written so that your authority over your disciples might increase, in that the teaching of the greatest and most ancient fathers can confirm what you teach already by your living example more than in lifeless words. It only remains for the spiritual breeze of your prayers to waft me, now tossed by the perils of the storm, into the safe harbour of silence.

www.ingramcontent.com/pod-product-compliance
Lightning Source LLC
Chambersburg PA
CBHW021713300426
44114CB00009B/131